Sibylla Palmifera. Reproduced by permission of the Lady Lever Art Gallery, Port Sunlight.

THE
CORRESPONDENCE
OF
Dante Gabriel Rossetti

THE CORRESPONDENCE OF
Dante Gabriel Rossetti

THE CHELSEA YEARS
1863–1872

Prelude to Crisis

VOLUME IV
1868–1870

EDITED BY
WILLIAM E. FREDEMAN

D. S. BREWER

Text and Editorial Matter © Estate of William E. Fredeman 2004

All Rights Reserved. Except as permitted under current legislation
no part of this work may be photocopied, stored in a retrieval system,
published, performed in public, adapted, broadcast,
transmitted, recorded or reproduced in any form or by any means,
without the prior permission of the copyright owner

First published 2004
D. S. Brewer, Cambridge

D. S. Brewer is an imprint of Boydell & Brewer Ltd
PO Box 9, Woodbridge, Suffolk IP12 3DF, UK
and of Boydell & Brewer Inc.
668 Mt Hope Avenue, Rochester, NY 14620, USA
website: www.boydell&brewer.com

ISBN 0 85991 794 0

A CIP catalogue record for this book is available
from the British Library

Library of Congress Cataloging-in-Publication Data

Rossetti, Dante Gabriel, 1828–1882.
 [Correspondence]
 The correspondence of Dante Gabriel Rossetti / edited by William E. Fredeman.
   p. cm.
 Includes bibliographical references and index.
 ISBN 0-85991-528-X (v. 1 : acid-free paper) – ISBN 0-85991-637-5 (v. 2 : acid-free paper)
  1. Rossetti, Dante Gabriel, 1828–1882—Correspondence. 2. Poets, English—19th
century—Correspondence. I. Fredeman, William E. (William Evan), 1928– II. Title.
PR5246 .A4 2002
821'.8—dc21   2002016424

This publication is printed on acid-free paper

Printed and bound in Great Britain by
The Cromwell Press, Trowbridge, Wiltshire

CONTENTS

The Editorial Board, its Contributors and Advisers	VI
William E. Fredeman: Editorial Statement and Principles	IX
List of Illustrations	XVII
Abbreviations	XIX
THE LETTERS, 1868–1870	1

THE EDITORIAL COMMITTEE

EDITORIAL BOARD

Chair: Betty C. Fredeman
Editor: Roger C. Lewis
Editor: Jane Cowan
Editor: Roger W. Peattie
and
Luke Fredeman
Library Liaison: Joan Selby
Allan Life
Page Life

CONTRIBUTORS

David Latham
Carolyn Hares-Stryker
Lorraine Janzen Kooistra
Julian Moore
Andrew Stauffer
David W. Thomas
Christopher Whittick

ADVISERS

Anne Drewery
Betty Elzea
Robin Gibson
Mark Samuels Lasner
Phillip Marcus
Christopher Newall
Virginia Surtees
Angela Thirlwell
Stephen Wildman

The publishers wish to acknowledge the generous support of the
Paul Mellon Centre for Studies in British Art

This volume is printed and published with the aid of the
Modern Humanities Research Association

WILLIAM E. FREDEMAN: EDITORIAL STATEMENT, EDITORIAL PRINCIPLES, DESCRIPTION OF LETTER ENTRIES AND STYLISTIC CONVENTIONS

EDITORIAL STATEMENT

In editing Rossetti's letters, my first priority has been to generate an accurate, clear, uncluttered, and readable text that is totally faithful to the verbal, but not necessarily to every minute calligraphic symbol on the manuscripts. While I am sensitive to the arguments of G. Thomas Tanselle* and other textual critics who argue vigorously for quasi-facsimile typographical or diplomatic transcriptions that reflect with absolute fidelity every mark on the manuscript, I do not agree that verbatim and literatim texts are invariably the best or the only editorial models. The conventions of such editing, derived by analogy from the methods and techniques of textual criticism as these are applied to primary literary texts or from the abecedarian and mathematical formulae of descriptive bibliography, can produce letter-texts that are so complex as to overwhelm the content. The prescription to employ them, however, poses a crucial question about the status of literary letters: namely, whether they are to be regarded as an inherent part of an author's canon or as personal biographical and historical documents. If a writer's letters are construed as literary texts, as in some instances they may well be, then the editor has virtually no flexibility in the standardization and regularization of punctuation, spelling, capitalization, abbreviations, titles, salutations and closes, and even matters of spatial format, such as the placement of addresses, dates, postscripts, endorsements, illustrations, and other

---

* See G. Thomas Tanselle, "Texts of Documents and Texts of Works," in *Textual Criticism and Scholarly Editing* (Charlottesville, VA: Bibliographical Society of the University of Virginia, 1990): 3–23; and "Reproducing Texts of Documents," in *A Rationale of Textual Criticism* (Philadelphia: U Pennsylvania P, 1989), a publication of the A. S. W. Rosenbach Fellowship in Bibliography.

notations on the manuscripts. Whether, even then, the dogma applies equally to all the calligraphic incidentals and accidentals – substantive matters are not in question – is, in my view, open to debate.

In Rossetti's case, his letters are revealing as life documents, characterizing the man, the poet, and the artist, but they cannot, in my opinion, be construed as "creative" in the literary sense, notwithstanding that they do contain dozens of examples of fine writing. As a consequence, in editing them I have striven first for accuracy, readability, clarity, and consistency. Fortunately, Rossetti's hand is in most instances perfectly clear – indeed, one commentator described his calligraphy as the most beautiful among English writers – so there are few transcriptional problems affecting the substantive content of the letters. While Rossetti is normally an impeccable speller, he is thoroughly inconsistent in his handling of titles, both of literary and of artistic works, which may appear in the same letter within quotes, underlined, or unmarked. Similarly, he is often casual, if not careless, in his punctuation, frequently substituting short dashes for periods, colons for commas and semi-colons, placing these inside or outside parentheses. Capitalization is erratic and often indistinguishable from lower-case letters; paragraph delineations are not always certain, even when present; and ampersands and abbreviations abound, often in different forms within the same letter. In fact, the manuscripts of his letters give every indication that his exclusive concern in letter writing – as opposed to his poetry, in which he was almost paranoid about punctuation – was with content. In contrast, his sentences tend to be carefully drafted in balanced and parallel style, virtually free from syntactical and mechanical errors. Meaning is almost never ambiguous.

The *sine qua non* of editing is in every instance transcriptional accuracy in the context of authorial intent, or, in the case of the distinction Tanselle makes between private writings and works written for publication, meaning. But printed letters, however typographically ingenious, tend to be even less faithful to the original manuscript than photocopies; and to achieve even a semblance of verisimilitude necessitates employing an arsenal of intrusive sigla from multiple styles of brackets, over-and-under-lineations, scorings out, and [sics] that are both ugly and distracting. That said, little editorial licence has been exercised in editing Rossetti's letters: transcriptions retain virtually all of Rossetti's punctuation and all his calligraphic eccentricities, such as multiple interrogation or exclamation marks, which sometimes serve as mini-illustrations. Calligraphic slips, however, such as false starts or duplication of words, whether or not crossed out, are recorded only if they are in some way revealing. Extensive cancellations, on the other hand, if legible and relevant, are restored within angled brackets, as are speculative readings in the case of mutilated letters.

EDITORIAL PRINCIPLES

General

1. Texts follow manuscripts wherever possible; when only printed sources are available, the earliest is followed.
2. Transcriptions are in the main literal, but in the interest of consistency some regularization has been imposed, as noted below.
3. Illustrations in the text are reproduced wherever possible in approximately the position they appear in the letter. Those too large for inclusion with the letter text, such as those in letters to Walter Deverell and Christina Rossetti, appear as plates and are signalled in the headnotes.
4. All editorial interpolations are indicated by square brackets; angled brackets are reserved for restored readings, marginal insertions, and a few other instances, and are usually explained in the headnotes.

Specific

Format

1. No attempt has been made either to replicate typographically the spatial arrangement on the manuscript page of headings, salutations, closes, postscripts, and endorsements or to preserve the lineation of the text.
2. Headings: flush right; addresses and dates normally follow the manuscript, but for balance and appearance, it is sometimes necessary to override Rossetti's lineation or to conflate two lines, indicated by a virgule (/). Unless the text is taken from a printed source, addresses are given only when they are appear on the manuscript. After 1862, when the address is taken from Rossetti's embossed, monogrammed stationery, 16 Cheyne Walk is italicized. Other embossed stationery he uses is recorded in the headnotes.
3. Dates: follow Rossetti's practice. Days of the week are not added if not present in the manuscript; hypothesized dates, whether editorial or taken from an endorsement or postmark, are placed in square brackets. Dates derived from a postmark are indicated in the headnote (P/M) and adjusted to the day of the week when it is certain that the envelope and letter are conjugate. The presence of envelopes is noted only when dates are taken from postmarks.
4. Salutations and complimentary closes: salutations are flush left, complimentary closes flush right; both follow as closely as possible DGR's

punctuation and lineation. However, the spacial positioning of some of DGR's closes can be ambiguous, owing in part to the disparity in paper size between the manuscript and the printed page. Because he almost always makes a clear distinction between the text and the close, in those instances where he included a hanging phrase, such as "I remain, dear Sir," in addition to the conventional two-line close (including signature), and when there is no syntactical evidence that the phrase is intended to be run into the body of the text, the close has been extended to three (sometime even four) lines rather than leave the phrase dangling, as a kind of ort, though, admittedly, that would be another option. When it is clear that the close and signature are juxtaposed owing to a paucity of space, they are separated; otherwise, like marginal closes that run horizontally across the length of the entire page, they are printed as a single line. Closes missing from the manuscript are indicated in the headnote, unless the letter is indicated as a fragment of a verse letter; missing signatures are designated as "unsigned" within square brackets.

Transcriptions

1. Abbreviations (including proper names): Rossetti's abbreviations, including single and expanded ampersands (&, &c), are retained as he wrote them, with or without periods, as are those in which he characteristically employs a colon (photo:, vol:, mag:, affect:); superscript abbreviations, however, whether for titles or dates, because Rossetti's use of these is so inconsistent, are printed in regular type on the same line: this is the single calligraphic liberty taken in translating Rossetti's manuscripts to type.
2. Rossetti's signature follows his practice (DGR, D. G. R., DG Rossetti, D. G. Rossetti, D. Gabriel R.), which varies considerably. When Rossetti abbreviates a name, as in Frederic Shields, it is retained, as are names he writes only with initials, whether single or multiple letters (B, FMB). To minimize annotation, initials of other than obvious names, when identifiable, are expanded within square brackets on their first appearance in a letter, but not if they appear again or if, in the first instance, they follow the expanded form of the name. However, his frequent abbreviation of Wm or W. M. for his brother William Michael is not expanded.
3. Punctuation and Capitalization: occasional silent (and light) adjustment in Rossetti's punctuation is made for clarity. His preference for the colon over the period in some abbreviations is respected, as is his use of hyphenation in compound words. Terminal dashes, however, except at the end of a line of poetry, are replaced by full-stops. His erratic use of capitals is normally followed, but if his intention is uncertain, the letter is

made lower-case, except in closes, where the initial "y" in "Your/Yours" is always upper case.

4. Spelling: Rossetti's occasional misspellings and omitted apostrophes in contractions and possessives are silently corrected, but orthographic irregularities that are inconsistent but not inaccurate, such as Shakespere/Shakespeare, are retained. Words which Rossetti spells variously (dare say/daresay, connexion/connection) and other words, such as today, to-morrow, and cooperation, which he writes with and without a hyphen follow his usage. Since Rossetti almost never uses an 's' to form the possessive of a name ending in s, his practice is followed in the transcriptions.

5. Interlineations, deletions, and marginal notes: Interlineations and deletions are indicated only when they are revelatory in some distinctive way; the occasional palimpsests, rejected readings, and false starts that are retained are shown in angled brackets. Marginal notes that clearly belong within the body of the letter but for which Rossetti has not provided a caret are inserted at the appropriate place within angled brackets and indicated in the headnote.

6. Titles of articles and books, poems, and art works: While Rossetti's practice makes for considerable inconsistency, transcriptions follow his practice. However, titles that he underscores are printed in italics.

7. Numerals: Rossetti's practice of mixing cardinal and ordinal numbers and his frequent substitution of ordinal abbreviations (1st, 2ndly, &c) for spelled-out adjectives or adverbs is respected.

8. Postscripts: Postscripts follow the close regardless of their position on the manuscript. Rossetti often omits the abbreviations P.S. or P.P.S. These are not added when they do not appear on the manuscript; however, his occasional manuscript instruction to his reader to "turn over" has been silently deleted.

9. Emphasis: single words or phrases underlined in the text are italicized; double underscorings are indicated by capitalization; triple underscorings are capitalized in bold.

Description of letter entries

General

Arrangement of the letters is chronological and numbering is sequential within each year: 48.5 for letter 5 in 1848. Letters that either surfaced or that were dated or redated after the entire sequence from 1835–82 was officially "closed" are intercalated using subdecimals (48.5.1). Letters to Rossetti are indicated by "A" numbers. After the grouping of early letters, covering the years 1835–47, letters are arranged by year, each commencing with a synopsis of the major literary and artistic works of the year, a brief summary of the contents of the year's letters, and a chronology of Rossetti's activities.

Headnotes and Footnotes

1. Names of recipients in headnotes follow customary form and are not necessarily given in full. Normally, no account is taken of later acquired titles, name changes, or sobriquets, but there are exceptions: Edward Jones is always cited as Burne-Jones, Theodore Watts as Watts-Dunton.
2. Contents: Headnotes contain all textual information about the letters: text source, manuscript or printed; publication history of the letter; non-editorial authorities for dating – postmark (P/M), "unidentified endorsement," or the initials or name of the source, often the recipient ("WMR" for William Michael Rossetti, who endorsed most of the family letters); and any other textual details relevant to a letter, such as the fact that it is a postcard (PC) or a fragment, mutilated, written in another hand, or inscribed on a card, envelope, or another letter.
3. Order: Letter number, name of the recipient, source of the letter (either MS: or Text:); publication history (Published:, Printed:, or Excerpt:); source for dating (Date:); textual and informational notes. Fragments and postcards are noted in parentheses following the MS or Text source.
4. Text Sources: References to manuscript sources are by short title – Yale, UBC, Texas – without indication of special collections, accession or catalogue numbers, or other particulars, except when a collection is totally discrete, as in the case of the Berg Collection in the New York Public Library, or when specially requested by an institution. Printed works are also truncated by name or short title and, like manuscript sources, identified in the List of Abbreviations. The identification of private manuscript sources respects the wishes of the owners.
5. Footnotes: Superscripts in the letter texts indicate the notes immediately following the letter. Cross-references are by letter number and, where applicable, note number. Cross-references to letters within the same year (except for 1835–47) are printed in bold, omitting the year and point; thus in the annotation to letter 61.39n1, **43** refers to 61.43. Notes on Rossetti's diction and the identification of literary sources are usually indicated by an asterisk and precede the footnotes. References to modern editions of letters are by letter number unless otherwise specified.

EDITORIAL PRINCIPLES

Stylistic conventions in footnotes

Abbreviations

MS/MSS   manuscript(s)
PR(s)   Pre-Raphaelite(s)
PRB/PRBs   Pre-Raphaelite Brotherhood/Brothers
PRISM   Pre-Raphaelitism

Proper names of Rossetti's family, friends, associates, and patrons that recur in the letter-texts are compressed into two or three initials and are fully identified in the List of Abbreviations. Other abbreviations used throughout are also listed (see below, pp. XIX–XXXIV).

Months (with year): three letters without periods (Jan, Apr, Dec); months (without year) are spelled out.

Dates: 30 Apr 53, 27 Mar; single years given in full.

Shorthand references

Letters and **Notes**:
DGR:WHD/WHD:DGR means a letter to/from W. H. Deverell; normally followed by a (date) and a verb, the siglum implying "DGR in writing (or in a letter to) WHD"; DGR::WHD = a reciprocal exchange of letters.

MS sources in parentheses (AP) are all unpublished.

Documentation in footnotes and headnotes: standard and recurring works are identified in the List of Abbreviations. Less frequently cited works are listed in the Bibliography. For unabbreviated separate publications, only the year is given in the notes; full documentation is provided for serial entries.

Ampersands are used only in linking conjugate pairs (DGR & FMB) or in series, never to introduce coordinate or subordinate syntactical units.

LIST OF ILLUSTRATIONS

	Letter	Recipient	Source	Description
1.	68.77	JM	BL	Embroidery design
2.	68.87	FLR	UBC	Sideboard
3.	69.72	AB	NLS	Heraldic carving
4.	69.152	JM	BL	Wombats
5.	69.166	Murray Marks	Fitzwilliam	Pot
6.	69.167	AB	NLS	Spell pot
7.	69.167	AB	NLS	Small pot
8.	69.167	AB	NLS	Small pot
9.	69.167	AB	NLS	Pots arrangement
10.	69.183	WMR	UBC	Wormhole in MS
11.	69.225	J.F. McLennan	Columbia	Design for JFM monogram
12.	70.96	ACS	BL	Cover design for *Songs*
13.	70.111	FSE	BL	Cover design for *Poems*
14.	70.231.1	Aglaia Coronio	Princeton	Janey sketch

Frontispiece
Sibylla Palmifera. Reproduced by permission of the Lady Lever Art Gallery, Port Sunlight.

Plates (All plates in this volume reproduced by permission of the Prints & Drawings Department of the British Museum.)
Plate 1 The Bard and Petty Tradesman
Plate 2 The M's at Ems
Plate 3 The German Lesson
Plate 4 Resolution; or the Infant Hercules
Plate 5 Death of a Wombat

ABBREVIATIONS INCLUDING MANUSCRIPT AND MAJOR PRINTED SOURCES OF LETTER TEXTS

RECURRING NAMES, locations, and frequently cited printed works are abbreviated or truncated in the notes and apparatus, except in those instances when their use might prove awkward or misleading. Because the sigla cover the entire edition, many are not employed in the first set of letters.

PROPER NAMES

References to Rossetti himself (DGR) and to his immediate family and more prominent friends, patrons, and fellow artists are always abbreviated by their initials in capital letters.

FAMILY NAMES

CLP	Charlotte Lydia Polidori
CGR	Christina Georgina Rossetti
FLR	Frances Lavinia Rossetti
GR	Gabriele Rossetti (to 1854)
LMR	Lucy Madox Brown Rossetti
MFR	Maria Francesca Rossetti
WMR	William Michael Rossetti
EES	Elizabeth Eleanor Siddal

THE PRE-RAPHAELITE BROTHERHOOD AND AFFILIATES

FMB	Ford Madox Brown
CAC	Charles Alston Collins
JC	James Collinson
WHD	Walter Howell Deverell

ABBREVIATIONS

WHH	William Holman Hunt
JEM	John Everett Millais
FGS	Frederic George Stephens
TW	Thomas Woolner

EARLY FRIENDS AND ASSOCIATES

WA	William Allingham
GPB	George Price Boyce
EBB	Elizabeth Barrett Browning
RB	Robert Browning
EBJ	Edward Burne-Jones
GBJ	Georgiana Burne-Jones
FC	Fanny Cornforth
AG	Alexander/Anne Gilchrist
EH	Ellen Heaton
AH	Arthur Hughes
WJK	Walter J. Knewstub
AMc	Alexander Macmillan
WM	William Morris
AM	Alexander Munro
CEN	Charles Eliot Norton
CP	Coventry Patmore
VCP	Valentine Cameron Prinsep
JR	John Ruskin
WBS	William Bell Scott
JPS	John Pollard Seddon
TS	Thomas Seddon
ACS	Algernon Charles Swinburne
WCT	William Cave Thomas
JLT	John Lucas Tupper

OTHER FRIENDS, ASSOCIATES, AND PATRONS

AB	Alice Boyd
OMB	Oliver Madox Brown
THC	Thomas Hall Caine
LC	Lewis Carroll (Charles Lutwidge Dodgson)
LCD	Lowes Cato Dickinson
HTD	Henry Treffry Dunn
FSE	F. S. Ellis
HBF	H. Buxton Forman
CEF	Clarence E. Fry
FJF	Frederick James Furnivall
EG	Ernest Gambart

ABBREVIATIONS

WG	William Graham
GGH	George G. Hake
TGH	Thomas G. Hake
JAH	John Aldam Heaton
CAH	Charles Augustus Howell
FH	Franz Hueffer
JWI	John William Inchbold
JL	James Leathart
FRL	Frederick Richard Leyland
WJL	William James Linton
AML	Alicia Margaret Losh
FMc	Francis MacCracken
PPM	Peter Paul Marshall
PBM	Philip Bourke Marston
JWM	John Westland Marston
JM	Jane Morris
CFM	Charles Fairfax Murray
TEP	Thomas E. Plint
GR	George Rae
JAR	James Anderson Rose
FS	Frederick Sandys
WS	William Sharp
FJS	Frederic James Shields
JS	James Smetham
WJS	William James Stillman
HVT	Henry Virtue Tebbs
JHT	John Hamilton Trist
LRV	Leonard Rowe Valpy
TWD	Theodore Watts-Dunton
GFW	George Frederic Watts
PSW	Philip Speakman Webb
JMW	James McNeill Whistler

OTHER ABBREVIATIONS

16CW	16 Cheyne Walk, Chelsea
AS	Annual Summaries
AP	Angeli–Dennis Papers, University of British Columbia Library
BFAC	Burlington Fine Arts Club
HC	Hogarth Club
LP	Leathart Papers, University of British Columbia Library
MMF&Co	Morris, Marshall, Faulkner, & Company
MS/MSS	Manuscript(s)
OWCS	Old Water-Colour Society
PP	Penkill Papers, University of British Columbia Library

ABBREVIATIONS

PR(s)	Pre-Raphaelites
PRB/PRBs	Pre-Raphaelite Brotherhood / Brothers
PRISM	Pre-Raphaelitism
RA	Royal Academy
RSA	Royal Scottish Academy
WMC	Working Men's College

JOURNAL ABBREVIATIONS

The following journals and bibliographies have been abbreviated throughout:

AUMLA	*Australian Universities Modern Language Association*
BJRL	*Bulletin of the John Rylands Library; later Bulletin of the John Rylands University Library of Manchester (BJRULM)*
BN&Q	*British Notes and Queries*
BQR	*British Quarterly Review*
ELN	*English Language Notes*
JPRAS	*Journal of Pre-Raphaelite and Aesthetic Studies*
JPRS	*Journal of Pre-Raphaelite Studies*
JWMS	*Journal of the William Morris Society*
MLN	*Modern Language Notes*
N&Q	*Notes and Queries*
NCBEL	*New Cambridge Bibliography of English Literature*
O&CM	*Oxford and Cambridge Magazine*
PBSA	*Papers of the Bibliographical Society of America*
PMLA	*Publications of the Modern Language Association*
PULC	*Princeton University Library Chronicle*
TLS	*Times Literary Supplement*
VP	*Victorian Poetry*

MANUSCRIPT LOCATIONS

Abbreviations are employed for public collections housing three or more letters; other collections are cited in letter headnotes, where privately owned letters are identified either as Private Collection or as specified by the owner.

ABL	Armstrong Browning Library, Baylor University
Arizona	Arizona State University Library
Ashmolean	Ashmolean Museum, Oxford University
Beinecke	Beinecke Library, Yale University
Berg	Berg Collection, New York Public Library
Berkeley	Bancroft Library, University of California, Berkeley
BL	British Library
Bodleian	Bodleian Library, Oxford

ABBREVIATIONS

Boston	Boston College Library
BPL	Boston Public Library
BR	Biblioteca del Risorgimento (Rome)
Brotherton	Brotherton Library, University of Leeds
Bryn Mawr	Bryn Mawr College Library
Buffalo	State University of New York Library, Buffalo
Cambridge	Cambridge University Library
Cape Town	University of Cape Town Library
Chelsea	Kensington/Chelsea Public Libraries, London
Columbia	Columbia University Library
DAM	Delaware Art Museum
Duke	Duke University Library
Durham	Durham University Library
Exeter	Exeter University Library
Fitzwilliam	Fitzwilliam Museum, Cambridge
Folger	Folger Shakespeare Library
Fondation Custodia	Fondation Custodia, Paris, France
Getty	Getty Center for the History of the Arts and Humanities
Glasgow	University of Glasgow Library
Harvard	Houghton Library, Harvard University
Huntington	Henry E. Huntington Library, San Marino, California
IHM	Iowa Historical Museum
Iowa	University of Iowa Library
Kansas	Spencer Library, University of Kansas
Kentucky	W. Hugh Peel Collection, University of Kentucky
LC	Library of Congress
Lilly Library	Lilly Library, University of Indiana
Liverpool	Liverpool Public Libraries
LLAG	Lady Lever Art Gallery, Port Sunlight
Manx	Manx Museum
McGill	McGill University Library
Mitchell Library	Mitchell Library, Sydney, NSW, Australia
Newcastle	Newcastle University Library
NLS	National Library of Scotland, Edinburgh
NYPL	New York Public Library
PHS	Pennsylvania Historical Society
PML	Pierpont Morgan Library, New York City
Princeton	Princeton University Library
Rylands	John Rylands Library of the University of Manchester
SANG	South African National Gallery
Scripps College	Scripps College Library
Somerville	Somerville College Library, Oxford
Syracuse	Syracuse University Library
Texas	Harry Ransom Humanities Research Center, University of Texas, Austin

ABBREVIATIONS

UBC	University of British Columbia Library
UCLA	University of California at Los Angeles Library
Union College	Union College Library
University College	University College Library, London University
V&A	Victoria and Albert Museum, London
Walker	Walker Art Gallery
Washington	University of Washington
Wightwick	Wightwick Manor, Wolverhampton (National Trust)
WMG	William Morris Gallery, Walthamstow
Worcester	Worcester College Library, Oxford
Yale	Yale Center for British Art, Yale University

PRINTED SOURCES

Works most frequently cited, including standard reference works, Rossetti's own publications, and printed books and articles, if cited elsewhere than in letter headnotes, in which three or more of DGR's letters are published, are abbreviated as follows. Works cited only occasionally are listed in the Bibliography.

ROSSETTI'S WORKS

B&S	*Ballads and Sonnets* (London: Ellis, 1881).
EIP	*The Early Italian Poets* (London: Smith, Elder, 1861).
HL	*The House of Life* (Poems 1870, *Ballads and Sonnets*, 1881).
Poems (1–6 eds.)	*Poems* (London: Ellis, 1870–72).
Poems: New	*Poems: A New Edition* (London: Ellis, 1881).
"Scraps"	William Michael Rossetti. "Some Scraps of Verse and Prose by Dante Gabriel Rossetti." *Pall Mall Magazine* 16 (December 1898): 480–96.
Tauchnitz (1/2)	*Poems/Ballads & Sonnets*. With a memoir of the author by Franz Hueffer. Leipzig: Tauchnitz, 1873/1882.
Works	William Michael Rossetti, ed. *The Works of Dante Gabriel Rossetti*. London: Ellis, 1911. Enlarged from the *Collected Works* (*CW*). 2 vols. London: Ellis, 1886.

FREQUENTLY CITED SOURCES

ABDD	Alice Boyd's MS day diaries at UBC.
Adrian	Arthur A. Adrian. "The Browning–Rossetti Friendship: Some Unpublished Letters." *PMLA* 73 (December 1958): 538–44. Eight letters to Browning and one to EBB.
AG	Herbert H. Gilchrist, ed. *Anne Gilchrist: Her Life and Writings*.

	With a prefatory note by W. M. Rossetti. London: Unwin, 1887. 12 letters from DGR.
AJMD	Derek Hudson, ed. *Munby: Man of Two Worlds: The Life and Diaries of Arthur J. Munby 1828–1910*. London: Murray 1972.
ALC	*The Ashley Library: A Catalogue of Printed Books, Manuscripts, and Autograph Letters Collected by Thomas J. Wise*. Reissued with a new preface by Simon Nowell-Smith. 11 vols. London: Dawsons, 1971.
Amor	Anne Clark Amor. *William Holman Hunt: The True Pre-Raphaelite*. London: Constable, 1989.
AN	William Minto, ed. *Autobiographical Notes of the Life of William Bell Scott and Notices of His Artistic and Poetic Circle of Friends*. 2 vols. London: Osgood, 1892.
Annals	Henry Irving. *The Annals of Our Time: A Diurnal of Events, Social and Political, Home and Foreign from the Accession of Queen Victoria June 20, 1837, to the Peace of Versailles, February 28, 1871. A New Edition Carefully Revised*. London: Macmillan 1880. Three supplements (Macmillan, 1881–89) extend the chronology through the Jubilee Year: S1, February 1871– February 1874; S2, March 1874–July 1878; S3 July 1878–June 1887.
Atlay	J. B. Atlay. *Sir Henry Wentworth Acland*. London: Smith, Elder, 1903.
BCR	Philip Kelley & Betty A. Coley, comps. *The Browning Collections: A Reconstruction with Other Memorabilia*. Winfield, KS: Wedgestone Press, 1984. The original 1913 Sotheby catalogue is abbreviated *BC*.
Bennett 64/67/69	Mary Bennett. Successive catalogues of retrospective exhibitions at the Walker Art Gallery of Ford Madox Brown (1964), John Everett Millais (1967), and William Holman Hunt (1969).
Bibliography	William Michael Rossetti. *Bibliography of the Works of Dante Gabriel Rossetti*. London: Ellis, 1905.
Blake	Alexander Gilchrist. *Life of William Blake, "Pictor Ignotus." With Selections from his Poems and Other Writings*. 2 vols. London: Macmillan, 1863.
Blunt	Wilfrid Blunt. *"England's Michelangelo": A Biography of George Frederic Watts, O. M., R. A.* London: Hamish Hamilton, 1975.
Boase	Frederick Boase. *Modern English Biography*. 3 vols. London: Cass, 1965. Reprint of 1st ed., 1892–1921. Contains many persons omitted from the DNB.
Bodichon	Hester Burton. *Barbara Bodichon, 1827–1891*. London: Murray, 1949. Contains three unpublished letters with references to 15 others.
Boyce	Christopher Newall and Judy Egerton. *George Price Boyce*. Catalogue of an exhibition at the Tate Gallery, 1987.
Bryson	John Bryson, ed., in association with J. C. Troxell. *Dante*

	Gabriel Rossetti and Jane Morris: Their Correspondence. Oxford: Clarendon, 1976.
Buchanan	Robert Buchanan. *The Fleshly School of Poetry and Other Phenomena of the Day.* London: Strahan, 1872. Expanded from RB's pseudonymous attack on DGR in the *Contemporary Review* 18 (October 1871): 334–50.
Cabinet	William E. Fredeman. *A Rossetti Cabinet: A Portfolio of Drawings by Dante Gabriel Rossetti Hitherto Unpublished, Unrecorded, or Undocumented Including Paintings, Original Early Drawings, Portraits and Caricatures, Designs and Juvenilia.* Stroud: Ian Hodgkins, 1991. Reprinted from *JPRAS* (1989).
Caine	Hall Caine. *Recollections of Rossetti.* London: Stock, 1882. 79 excerpts and conflations from DGR's 129 letters to THC. An additional letter, in facsimile, is printed in the 1928 edition.
Casteras	Susan P. Casteras. *James Smetham: Artist, Author, Pre-Raphaelite Associate.* Aldershot: Scolar, 1995.
Checklist	Roger Peattie. "William Michael Rossetti's Art Notices in the Periodicals, 1850–1878." *Victorian Periodicals News-letter* 8.2 (June 1975): 79–92. When information is taken from the checklist in Peattie's Ph.D. dissertation (see WMR, below), the citation reads *Checklist* (D).
Clabburn	H. J. Clabburn. "Some Relics of Rossetti." *Pall Mall Budget*, No. 1165 (22 January 1891): 14. Excerpts from DGR's letters to Clabburn, now in the Yale Center for British Art.
ClassLists	William Michael Rossetti. *Dante Gabriel Rossetti: Classified Lists of His Writings with the Dates.* London: privately printed in 100 copies, 1906.
Clayton	Ellen C. Clayton. *English Female Artists.* 2 vols. London: Tinsley, 1876.
C&H	Clara E. Clement and Laurence Hutton. *Artists of the Nineteenth Century and Their Works: A Handbook.* 2 vols in 1. Boston: Houghton, Mifflin, 1889.
C&W	E. T. Cook and A. D. O. Wedderburn, eds. *The Works of John Ruskin: Library Edition.* 39 vols. London: Allen, 1902–12.
CGR	*The Poetical Works of Christina Rossetti, with Memoir and Notes.* Ed. William Michael Rossetti. London: Macmillan, 1904.
Cline	Clarence L. Cline, ed. *The Owl and the Rossettis: Letters of Charles A. Howell and Dante Gabriel, Christina, and William Michael Rossetti.* University Park, PA: Pennsylvania State UP, 1978. Full texts and summaries of 335 letters from DGR to CAH, 15 to Kitty Howell, 83 letters from CAH to DGR, plus other incoming and outgoing letters between the Howells, WMR, and CGR.
Cohen	Morton N. Cohen. *The Letters of Lewis Carroll.* 2 vols. New York: Oxford UP, 1979.
Compton-Rickett	Arthur Compton-Rickett. *Portraits and Personalities.* London:

	Selwyn and Blount, 1937. Nine letters from DGR:ACS reprinted from TLS (16 Oct 1919): 565–66.
CP	Basil Champneys. *Memoirs and Correspondence of Coventry Patmore*. 2 vols. London: Bell, 1900.
CR	Lona Mosk Packer. *Christina Rossetti*. Berkeley, CA: U California P, 1963.
Crump	*The Complete Poems of Christina Rossetti: A Variorum Edition*. Ed. Rebecca Crump. 3 vols. Baton Rouge, LA: Louisiana State UP, 1979–90.
CWS	*16, Cheyne Walk, Chelsea. The Valuable Contents of the Residence of Dante Gabriel Rossetti*. London: T. G. Wharton, Martin, & Co., 5–7 July 1882.
Dalziel	*The Dalziel Brothers: A Record of Fifty Years in Conjunction with Many of the Most Distinguished Artists of the Period 1840–1890*. London: Methuen, 1901.
DGR	*Dante Gabriel Rossetti Painter and Poet*. London & Birmingham: Royal Academy of Arts, City Museum and Art Gallery, 1973. Exhibition catalogue.
DGR:ACS	*Letters from Dante Gabriel Rossetti to Algernon Charles Swinburne Regarding the Attacks Made upon the Latter by Mortimer Collins and upon Both by Robert Buchanan*. London: privately printed for T. J. Wise, 1921.
DGRDW	William Michael Rossetti. *Dante Gabriel Rossetti as Designer and Writer*. London: Cassell, 1889.
DLB	*Dictionary of Literary Biography*. A multi-volumed series containing biographical entries by individual contributors. Ed. Matthew Bruccoli and published by Gale Research. When cited in the notes, full bibliographical information is provided.
DNB	*The Dictionary of National Biography*.
Doughty	Oswald Doughty. *A Victorian Romantic: Dante Gabriel Rossetti*. London: Oxford, 1949. 2nd ed., 1960.
DW	Oswald Doughty and John Robert Wahl, eds. *Letters of Dante Gabriel Rossetti*. 4 vols. Oxford: Clarendon Press, 1965–67.
EBJ	Georgiana Burne-Jones. *Memorials of Edward Burne-Jones*. 2 vols. London: Macmillan, 1904.
Elzea	Rowland Elzea, ed. *The Correspondence Between Samuel Bancroft, Jr. and Charles Fairfax Murray 1892–1916*. Delaware Art Museum Occasional Paper, No. 2. Wilmington, DE: DAM, 1980. Contains many references to the PRs.
Engen 1/2	Rodney Engen. 1) *Dictionary of Victorian Engravers, Print Publishers and their Works*. Cambridge: Chadwyck-Healey, 1979. 2) *Dictionary of Victorian Wood Engravers*. Cambridge: Chadwyck-Healey, 1985.
EES	Jan Marsh. *Elizabeth Siddal 1829–1862: Pre-Raphaelite Artist*. Sheffield: Ruskin Gallery, 1991. Exhibition catalogue.
Faxon	Alicia Faxon. "Dante Gabriel Rossetti and Photography."

	Apollo 140 (July 1994): 23–27. Locates seven letters and prints, three in the Lafayette Butler collection at the Ellen Clarke Bertrand Library, Bucknell University, Lewisburg, PA.
FC	Paull Franklin Baum, ed. *Dante Gabriel Rossetti's Letters to Fanny Cornforth.* Baltimore, MD: Johns Hopkins, 1940.
Fennell	Francis L. Fennell Jr., ed. *The Rossetti–Leyland Letters: The Correspondence of an Artist and his Patron.* Athens, OH: Ohio University Press, 1978. Reciprocal correspondence (141 letters: 107 by DGR, 34 by Leyland) between DGR and Frederick Richard Leyland. See Prinsep, below.
FL/FLM	William Michael Rossetti. *Dante Gabriel Rossetti: His Family Letters with a Memoir.* 2 vols. London: Ellis, 1895. Vol 1: Memoir (*FLM*). Vol 2: Letters (*FL*) prints full and partial texts of 317 letters: 143 to WMR, 107 to FLR, 67 to other relations.
FLCGR	*The Family Letters of Christina Georgina Rossetti*, ed. WMR. London: Brown, Langham, 1908. Five letters from DGR:CGR; 57 CGR:DGR.
FMB	Ford Madox Hueffer. *Ford Madox Brown: A Record of His Life and Work.* London: Longmans, 1896.
FMBD	Virginia Surtees, ed. *The Diary of Ford Madox Brown.* New Haven, CT: published for the Paul Mellon Center for Studies in British Art by Yale UP, 1981. All quotations from this source retain FMB's grotesque spellings.
FMBEx	*Mr. Madox Brown's Exhibition.* 191, Piccadilly. London, 1865. The notes to the pictures are by FMB.
FSE	Oswald Doughty, ed. *The Letters of Dante Gabriel Rossetti to his Publisher, F. S. Ellis.* London: Scholartis, 1928. 92 letters DGR:FSE from MSS in BL.
Gardner	Joseph H. Gardner. "Letters of Dante Gabriel Rossetti in the W. Hugh Peel Collection." *Kentucky Review* 10.3 (Autumn 1990): 67–85. Nine unpublished letters in the Special Collections Department of the University of Kentucky Libraries. Also includes DW 419.
Gazette	William E. Fredeman. *A Pre-Raphaelite Gazette: The Penkill Letters of Arthur Hughes to William Bell Scott and Alice Boyd, 1886–97.* Manchester: Rylands, 1967.
GFW	M. S. Watts. *George Frederic Watts: The Annals of an Artist's Life.* 3 vols. London: Macmillan, 1912.
Gooch & Thatcher	Bryan S. Gooch and David S. Thatcher, eds. *Musical Settings of Early and Mid-Victorian Literature: A Catalogue.* New York: Garland, 1979.
Goodwin	*A Collection of Engraved Portraits (Further Selection) Exhibited by the Late James Anderson Rose at the Opening of the New Library and Museum of the Corporation of London, November, 1872. Accompanied by Biographies and with an Introduction by Gordon Goodwin.* London: Marcus Ward, 1894. See Kashnor, below.

ABBREVIATIONS

GPBD	Virginia Surtees, ed. *The Diaries of George Price Boyce*. London: Real World, 1980. Text reprinted from 19th annual volume of the Old Water-Colour Society's Club, ed. Randall Davies, 1941.
Graves	Algernon Graves. *The Royal Academy of Arts: A Complete Dictionary of Contributors and their Works from its Foundation in 1769 to 1904*. 6 vols. Wakefield & Bath: S. R. Publishers Ltd. & Kingsmead Reprints, 1920. Original edition, 1905.
GRC	*Gabriele Rossetti Carteggi*. Ed. Alfonso Caprio, P. R. Horne, J. R. Woodhouse. 5 vols. Naples: Loffredo, [1992].
Grieve 1/2/3	Alastair L. Grieve. *The Art of Dante Gabriel Rossetti*. Hingham & Norwich, Norfolk: Real World Publications. Nos. 1 & 2, 1976; No. 3, n.d. No. 1: *The Pre-Raphaelite Period 1848–50*. No. 2: 1. *Found*. 2. *The Pre-Raphaelite Modern-Life Subjects*. No. 3: *The Watercolours and Drawings of 1850–55*, n.d.
Grylls	Rosalie Glynn Grylls (Lady Mander). "Rossetti and Browning." In *Essays on the Rossettis*, ed. Robert S. Fraser. Princeton, NJ: Princeton UP, 1972. 11 letters from DGR to Browning in the Troxell Collection. Reprinted from PULC 33 (Spring 1972): 232–50.
Gunnis	Rupert Gunnis. *Dictionary of British Sculptors 1660–1851*. New revised edition. London: Abbey Library, [1951].
Harrison	*The Letters of Christina Rossetti*. Ed. Antony H. Harrison. 3 vols: vol 1: 1843–73. Charlottesville, VA: U Virginia P, 1997. 34 to DGR.
Harrison & Waters	Martin Harrison and Bill Waters. *Burne-Jones*. 2nd ed. London: Barrie & Jenkins, 1989.
Horne	[Herbert P. Horne]. "Rossetti: Some Extracts from His Letters to Mr. Frederic Shields." *Century Guild Hobby Horse*, n.s. 4 (April 1889): 82–96. See Mills, below.
Houfe	Simon Houfe. *The Dictionary of British Book Illustrators and Caricaturists 1800–1914*. London: Antique Collectors' Club, 1981.
HRA	Helen Rossetti Angeli. *Dante Gabriel Rossetti: His Friends and Enemies*. London: Murray, 1949.
Hunt	Violet Hunt. *The Wife of Rossetti: Her Life and Death*. London: John Lane, 1932.
Ingram	John H. Ingram. *Oliver Madox Brown: A Biographical Sketch*. London: Stock, 1883. Prints five letters from DGR to OMB.
JEM	John Guille Millais. *The Life & Letters of Sir John Everett Millais*. 2 vols. London: Methuen, 1900.
JLT	James H. Coombs, et al. *A Pre-Raphaelite Friendship: The Correspondence of William Holman Hunt and John Lucas Tupper*. Nineteenth-Century Studies. Ann Arbor, MI: UMI Research, 1986.
Kashnor	*Whistler & His Circle: Letters and Documents*. London: Kashnor,

	1927. Bookseller's catalogue. Items 144–230 related to DGR: his correspondence with James Anderson Rose, the Plint estate, Morris & Co., &c. (now in Pennell Collection, LC). See Goodwin, above.
Keats	Dante Gabriel Rossetti. *John Keats: Criticism and Comment.* London: printed for private circulation by T. J. Wise, 1919. Five letters to H. Buxton Forman.
Kelvin	Norman Kelvin, ed. *The Collected Letters of William Morris.* 5 vols. 1: 1848–80 (1984); 2 (2 vols): 1881–84, 1885–88 (1987); 3 & 4: 1889–92, 1893–96. Princeton, NJ: Princeton UP, 1984–96.
Lady A	Virginia Surtees. *The Ludovisi Goddess: The Life of Louisa Lady Ashburton.* Wilton: Michael Russell, 1984.
Lang	Cecil Y. Lang, ed. *The Swinburne Letters.* 6 vols. New Haven, CT: Yale UP, 1959–62. Three letters from DGR to ACS; 14 from ACS to DGR; and three others from Lady Jane Henrietta Swinburne (2) and Admiral Charles Henry Swinburne (1) to DGR.
Lewis	Roger Lewis. *Thomas J. Wise and the Trial Book Fallacy.* Aldershot: Scolar Press, 1995.
Lutyens	Mary Lutyens, ed. "Letters from Sir John Everett Millais, Bart, P.R.A. (1829–1896) and William Holman Hunt, O.M. (1827–1910) in the Henry E. Huntington Library, San Marino, California." In *The Forty-fourth Volume of the Walpole Society 1972–74.* Printed for the Walpole Society by Glasgow UP, 1974.
LWA	H. Allingham & E. Baumer Williams, eds. *Letters to William Allingham.* London: Longmans, 1911. A supplement consisting of seven letters from WA to the Brownings was published in 1913, ed. Helen Allingham (*LWAS*).
Maas	Jeremy Maas. *Gambart: Prince of the Victorian Art World.* London: Barrie & Jenkins, 1975.
Mackail	J. W. Mackail. *The Life of William Morris.* 2 vols. London: Longmans, Green, 1899.
Macleod	Dianne Sachko Macleod. *Art and the Victorian Middle Class. Money and the Making of Cultural Identity.* Cambridge: CUP, 1996.
Macmillan	Connie Beth Macmillan. "A Catalogue of the Letters of Dante Gabriel Rossetti at the University of Texas at Austin." Unpublished Ph.D. dissertation: University of Texas, 1975.
Marillier	Henry Currie Marillier. *Dante Gabriel Rossetti: An Illustrated Memorial of His Art and Life.* London: Bell, 1899.
Marks	G. C. Williamson. *Murray Marks and His Friends: A Tribute of Regard.* London: John Lane, 1919. Numerous letters from DGR to CAH and Murray Marks.
Marsh & Nunn	Jan Marsh and Pamela Gerrish Nunn. *Women Artists and the Pre-Raphaelite Movement.* London: Virago Press, 1989.

MFR	Lona Mosk Packer. "Maria Francesca to Dante Gabriel Rossetti: Some Unpublished Letters." *PMLA* 79 (December 1964): 613–19.
Mills	Ernestine Mills. *The Life and Letters of Frederic Shields.* London: Longmans, 1912. Contains 50+ letters from DGR to FJS, many of them conflations of two or more letters; see Horne, above.
Moxten	Alfred Tennyson. *Poems.* London: Moxon, 1857. Illustrated by the PRs and other artists.
MSL	Mark Samuels Lasner. *William Allingham: A Bibliographical Study.* Philadelphia: Holmes Publishing, 1993. A revised reprint of his two-part article in the *Book Collector* (1990).
Murray	Christopher D. Murray. "D. G. Rossetti, A. C. Swinburne and R. W. Buchanan. The Fleshly School Revisited." 2 parts. *BJRULM* 65.1/2 (Autumn 1982/Spring 1983): 206–34; 176–207.
Newman & Watkinson	Teresa Newman and Ray Watkinson. *Ford Madox Brown and the Pre-Raphaelite Circle.* London: Chatto & Windus, 1991.
Nicoll	Allardyce Nicoll. *A History of the English Drama 1600–1900.* Vols 4–5: 19th Century. 2nd ed. Cambridge: CUP, 1959.
OMB	William E. Fredeman. "Pre-Raphaelite Novelist Manqué: Oliver Madox Brown." *BJRL* 51.1 (Autumn 1968): 27–72.
Packer	Lona Mosk Packer, ed. *The Rossetti–Macmillan Letters: Some 133 Unpublished Letters Written to Alexander Macmillan, F.S. Ellis, and Others, by Dante Gabriel, Christina, and William Michael Rossetti, 1861–1889.* Berkeley, CA: U California P, 1963.
Peattie	Roger Peattie, ed. *Selected Letters of William Michael Rossetti.* University Park, PA: Pennsylvania State UP, 1990. 22 letters to DGR.
Pedrick	Gale Pedrick. *Life with Rossetti, or, No Peacocks Allowed.* London: Macdonald, 1964. Includes 124 letters (in V&A) from DGR to Henry Treffry Dunn.
PFB 1/2/3	Paull Franklin Baum, ed. 1) *Dante Gabriel Rossetti: An Analytical List of Manuscripts in the Duke University Library with Hitherto Unpublished Verse and Prose.* Durham, NC: Duke UP, 1931. 2) *The House of Life: A Sonnet Sequence.* Cambridge, MA: Harvard UP, 1928. 3) *The Blessed Damozel: The Unpublished Manuscript Texts and Collation.* Chapel Hill, NC: U North California P, 1937.
Portraits	William Michael Rossetti. "The Portraits of DGR." *Magazine of Art* 12 (1889): 21–26, 57–61, 138–40.
PRBJ	William E. Fredeman. *The P.R.B. Journal: William Michael Rossetti's Diary of the Pre-Raphaelite Brotherhood 1849–1853 together with Other Pre-Raphaelite Documents.* Oxford: Clarendon, 1975.
PRDL	William Michael Rossetti, ed. "Some Early Correspondence of

	Dante Gabriel Rossetti." In *Præraphaelite Diaries and Letters.* London: Hurst and Blackett, 1900. 24 letters from DGR, principally to GR and FMB.
Preface	*The Germ.* Facsimile edition in 4 numbers, with a separate preface by William Michael Rossetti. London: Stock, 1898.
Prelude	William E. Fredeman. *Prelude to the Last Decade: Dante Gabriel Rossetti in the Summer of 1872.* Manchester: Rylands, 1971. Based on 151 unpublished letters in MS and printed sources from various correspondents relating to DGR's breakdown in 1872.
Prinsep	Valentine C. Prinsep. "A Collector's Correspondence." *Art Journal* 54 (August 1892): 249–52. Selections from DGR's letters to FRL. See Fennell, above.
PRISM	William E. Fredeman. *Pre-Raphaelitism: A Bibliocritical Study.* Cambridge, MA: Harvard UP, 1965.
PRP	Leslie Parris, ed. *Pre-Raphaelite Papers.* London: Tate Gallery, 1984. Besides general and specialized essays on Pre-Raphaelitism and the major Pre-Raphaelites, the volume contains valuable studies of JC by Ronald Parkinson, and WHD by Mary Lutyens.
PR Sculpture	Benedict Read and Joanna Barnes, eds. *Pre-Raphaelite Sculpture: Nature and Imagination in British Sculpture 1848–1914.* London: Henry Moore Foundation in association with Lund Humphries, 1991. Includes chapters on Bernhard Smith by Juliet Peers, TW by Benedict Read and Leonée Ormond, AM by Katharine Macdonald, JLT by Joanna Barnes and Alexander Kader, John Hancock by Thomas B. James, and EBJ by John Christian.
PRT	Helen Rossetti Angeli. *Pre-Raphaelite Twilight: The Story of Charles Augustus Howell.* London: Richards, 1954. Besides CAH's letters to DGR and WMR, mostly reprinted in Cline (above), HRA prints four letters from Rosa Corder to DGR.
Purves	John Purves, ed. "Letters of Dante Gabriel Rossetti to Miss Alice Boyd." *Fortnightly Review*, n.s. 123 (May 1928): 577–94. 15 letters in the National Library of Scotland.
Roberts	Leonard Roberts. *Arthur Hughes: His Life and Works. A Catalogue Raisonné.* With a biographical introduction by Stephen Wildman. Woodbridge, Suffolk: Antique Collectors' Club Ltd., 1997. Item numbers cited are given R numbers.
RP	William Michael Rossetti, ed. *Rossetti Papers, 1862–70.* London: Sands, 1903. Besides WMR's invaluable diaries, the volume prints 76 letters from and 59 to DGR.
RRP	W. M. Rossetti, ed. *Ruskin: Rossetti: Pre-Raphaelitism.* London: Allen, 1899. 39 letters from and 56 to DGR.
RW	*The Remaining Works of the Painter and Poet, Dante Gabriel Rossetti.* London: Christie's 12 May 1883. Sale catalogue.

Sandys	Betty Elzea. *Frederick Sandys 1829–1904: A Catalogue Raisonné.* Woodbridge: ACC Ltd., 2001. Item numbers cited are given E numbers.
S/Surtees	Virginia Surtees. *Dante Gabriel Rossetti: A Catalogue Raisonné.* 2 vols. Oxford: Clarendon, 1971. Includes full texts and excerpts of dozens of DGR letters. S with period (S.66) = entry numbers in the catalogue; otherwise Surtees' name is spelled out.
Skelton	[John Skelton]. *The Table Talk of Shirley: Reminiscences of and Letters from Froude, Thackeray, Disraeli, Browning, Rossetti, Kingsley . . . and Others.* London: Blackwood, 1893. Ten letters from DGR to Skelton.
Smetham	Sarah Smetham and William Davies, eds. *Letters of James Smetham, with an Introductory Memoir.* London: Macmillan, 1891. Five letters DGR:JS.
SR	William Michael Rossetti. *Some Reminiscences.* 2 vols. London: Brown Langham, 1906.
S&I	Virginia Surtees, ed. *Sublime & Instructive: Letters from John Ruskin to Louisa, Marchioness of Waterford, Anna Blunden and Ellen Heaton.* London: Michael Joseph, 1972.
Tate	*The Pre-Raphaelites.* London: Tate Gallery/Penguin, 1984. Catalogue of the most extensive Pre-Raphaelite exhibition ever held. Picture titles followed by "T." and a number refer to catalogue entries.
THC	William E. Fredeman. "'Fundamental Brainwork': The Correspondence between Dante Gabriel Rossetti and Thomas Hall Caine." *AUMLA* 52 (Nov 1979): 209–31.
TR	Janet Camp Troxell, ed. *Three Rossettis: Unpublished Letters to and from Dante Gabriel, Christina, William.* Cambridge, MA: Harvard, 1937.
TW	Amy Woolner, ed. *Thomas Woolner: His Life in Letters.* London: Chapman & Hall, 1917. Five letters from DGR:TW.
V&A Morris	Linda Parry, ed. *William Morris.* Centenary exhibition catalogue. London: Wilson in association with the V&A, 1996.
Vincent	E. R. Vincent. *Gabriele Rossetti in England.* Oxford: Clarendon, 1936.
WA/GBH	George Birkbeck Hill, ed. *Letters of Dante Gabriel Rossetti to William Allingham, 1854–1870.* London: Unwin, 1897. Reprinted from *Atlantic Monthly* (May–Aug 1896): 377–93, 744–54, 45–57, 242–45. (Hill was at Oxford during the "Jovial Campaign.")
WAD	*William Allingham's Diary.* Introduction by Geoffrey Grigson. Carbondale, IL: Southern Illinois UP, 1967. A reprint of the 1907 edition.
Walker	"The Life and Work of William Bell Scott, 1811–1890." Unpublished Ph.D. diss., Durham University, 1951.
Waller	R. D. Waller. *The Rossetti Family 1824–1854.* Manchester: Manchester UP, 1932.

ABBREVIATIONS

WBD	*Webster's Biographical Dictionary.* Springfield, MA: Merriam Webster, 1965.
WBS	William E. Fredeman. *The Letters of Pictor Ignotus: William Bell Scott's Correspondence with Alice Boyd, 1859–1884.* Manchester: Rylands, 1976.
WDVP	*The Waterloo Directory of Victorian Periodicals, 1824–1900.* ed. John North, *et al.* Waterloo: Wilfrid Laurier UP, 1976.
Wellesley	*The Wellesley Index to Periodicals 1824–1900.* 5 vols., ed. Walter E. & Esther Rhodes Houghton. Toronto: U of Toronto P, 1966–87.
WHD/WHDT	[Frances Deverell]. "The P.R.B. and Walter Howell Deverell: Letters from Dante Gabriel Rossetti and others with a Narrative and Illustrations." Prefaced by William Michael Rossetti. Manuscript journal of Mrs. Wykeham Deverell in the Huntington Library. Most citations are from the typescript (*WHDT*).
WHH	William Holman Hunt. *Pre-Raphaelitism and the Pre-Raphaelite Brotherhood.* 2nd edition, revised from the Author's Notes by M.E.H.H., 2 vols. London: Chapman & Hall, 1913 (each volume indexed). When the 1st edition is cited, "1905" follows in parentheses.
WMR	Roger Peattie. "Bibliography," in "William Michael Rossetti as Critic and Editor, Together with a Consideration of his Life and Character." Unpublished Ph.D. diss., University College (London), 1966. See Peattie, above.
WMRD	Odette Bornand. *The Diary of William Michael Rossetti 1870–1873.* Oxford: Clarendon, 1977.
WMRUD	William E. Fredeman, ed. "A Shadow of Dante: Rossetti in the Final Years: Extracts from William Michael Rossetti's Unpublished Diaries 1876–1882." In *Centennial Essays on Dante Gabriel Rossetti,* a Special Issue devoted to the works of DGR. *Victorian Poetry* 20.3/4 (Autumn–Winter 1982).
Wood	Christopher Wood. *The Dictionary of Victorian Painters,* 3rd edition, 2 vols. Woodbridge: ACC Ltd., 1995.
"Woodman"	William E. Fredeman. "'Woodman, Spare that Block': The Published, Unpublished, and Projected Illustrations and Book Designs of Dante Gabriel Rossetti." *JPRS* n.s. 5 (Spring 1996): 7–41.
Worth	George Worth. *James Hannay: His Life and Works.* Lawrence, KS: U of Kansas P, 1964.

THE LETTERS
1868–1870

1868

MAJOR WORKS OF THE YEAR

Literary: "Willowwood" sonnets; "Venus Verticordia."

Artistic: *La Pia* (S.207) begun, *Lady Lilith* (S.205) completed, studies for *Mariana* (S.213) and *Pandora* (S.224), *Reverie* (S.206), numerous studies and drawings of Jane Morris, including *Aurea Catena* (S.209).

SUMMARY OF THE YEAR'S LETTERS

Ends relationship with C. P. Matthews; arranges for CAH to act as a broker for chalk drawings, particularly with LRV; buys *Lucrezia Borgia* at auction and later sells it to FRL; EBJs and, later, CAHs move to Fulham; JM models in March and December; recurrence of eye problems and consultations with specialists; visits FRL at Speke Hall; ceases painting for several months; goes on walking trip with HTD; views Leeds exhibition *en route* to spend six weeks at Penkill; uses CAH as go-between for letters to JM; meets AB's cousin AML and accepts loan; resumes painting in December. At about this time in their relationship, HTD concluded that DGR "suffered from illusionary fears with regard to his health. . . . His nervousness over trifling symptoms turned him at times into a veritable *Malade Imaginaire*," and found that comforting words, gossip, and "walks with a definite object, to wit the picking up of blue china and things generally for use in his pictures and the adornment of his house . . . banished all fears" (*Recollections*: 29–30).

CHRONOLOGY

15 Feb
B.G. Windus sale; DGR buys *Lucrezia Borgia* (S.124) for 70 gns.

4 Mar
House-warming at EBJ's new home, The Grange, North End, Fulham; the studio ceiling collapsed shortly after the artists left (see *WBS* 38 & **45n2**).

7 Mar
Visits C. P. Matthews in the country – The Bower House, Havering, Sussex.

13 Mar
Morrises spend c. three weeks at 16CW; work begun on *La Pia* for FRL.

March
Renewal of eye disorder begins, leading (by August) to wide consultation with several specialists (Bader, Gull, Bowman, & Marshall), fear of blindness, even death, and the abandonment of painting from August to December.

9 Apr
William Graham commissions *Dante's Dream* (S.81R.1) for £1500.

9 May
Takes small house for Fanny.

6 Jun–4 Jul
WMR on the continent and robbed in Verona.

3–8 Aug
With CAH at Leyland's house, Speke Hall, where he suffers a minor breakdown.

10–20 Aug
Recurrence of eye disorder.

1–8 Sep
With HTD at Stratford, Warwick, and Kenilworth.

23–24 Sep
To Leeds for exhibition.

25 Sep–3 Nov
At Penkill; renews interest in poetry; controversial loan offered by Alicia Margaret Losh, AB's cousin (see WMR's MS diary).

4 Oct
First reference to wearing of spectacles.

16 Oct
Vague project of renting Penkill for half a year.

6 Nov
Consults with JAR on deed of transfer (now bill of sale) of property to WMR (see 15 Sep).

30 Nov
Morrises visit 16CW for "some days."

7 Dec
Resumes painting; studies of Jane Morris as *Pandora*.

18 Dec
"Willowwood" sonnets written by this date.

LETTERS

68.1 TO JAMES ANDERSON ROSE
MS: Berg. Published: DW 763.

2 January 1868
16 Cheyne Walk
Chelsea

My dear Rose

I have felt rather bewildered about my best course as to the stables which has prevented my writing to you since seeing Lawson.

I should like much to have seen you and talked it over, and am very sorry to hear from more than one source how unwell you have been. I hope it is only the visitation of Christmas sins, & that all will soon be well.

I suppose it is your opinion that *the* thing to do above all is to stop the action, lest it should come to be a serious expense to me before I well know where I am. I cannot help feeling serious dread of this, being so ignorant as I am of such matters. Thus my best plan will be I suppose to make one of two offers. Either to pay £50 almost immediately for surrender of Strong's lease, and to forego rent now due; or else to pay £100 in 2 bills of £50 each at 6 & 7 months respectively, and forego rent; the latter proposition if he declines the former. I feel anxious & mithered* about it, and should be very glad of your serious and friendly advice how to act. A large expense possibly accumulating on account of an action only begun through the solicitors to the estate & of no interest to me, is a bugbear of a very serious kind.[1]

Ever yours
DG Rossetti

---

* See 49.21n*.
[1] DGR got possession of the stables on 16 Aug 69 (see 69.128), when Strong signed the consent order to give up possession on payment of £20 (Kashnor 221).

68.2 TO C. P. MATTHEWS

MS (unsigned draft): UBC. Published: *RP* 290–91; DW 764.

No V

3 Jan/68

Dear Mr. M –

The subject of your letter requiring some consideration is the cause of delay in my reply. I may now say that on the whole I think with you the best course will be to abandon the Medusa subject for which you originally commissioned me and to substitute another. When you wrote me your objections some weeks ago, my own great interest in my design made me sanguine as to satisfying you with my work in the end; but since then I have not been without misgivings that after all, the feeling you express might not be removed by the completed work; and perhaps eventually I myself might even, on this account, have become the proposer of a change of subject. Thus all is well, as you will agree with me that our joint assent was needed to any change in our concluded engagement.

As to the time and trouble already devoted by me to the work in preparation and studies, and your proposal to compensate me for this, I need only say that, as I shall of course continue the Medusa picture sooner or later on my own account, either on the life scale or a smaller one, the studies made will still serve me & will also themselves be saleable. This matter therefore need not be pursued further.

The great question remaining is, what subject can I substitute for your commission in place of the Medusa?[1] And here I must speak like yourself with perfect frankness. I have not any subject in my mind which I specially desire to paint at this moment, which would precisely correspond in its amount of material (2 figures) with the Medusa, and so fall within the same price (1500 guineas). At the same time I cannot afford to forego the commission. It remains for me therefore to propose the only alternative by which I can avoid being a sufferer in the most painful way by the change of plan – that is in having to paint a work which I should not otherwise be doing instead of one which I greatly desire to do.

Among the subjects I most wish to carry out in my lifetime is one of which I already, some time ago, made a small watercolour drawing which I always regarded only as a preparation for a larger work. The subject is *Dante's Dream*, an incident taken from the *Vita Nuova* of the poet, the autobiographical record of his early life and love. This however, being a composition of 5 figures, could not be painted for the same price as the Medusa. My proposal is to paint it for you for 2000 guineas, on a good scale though not life size, the extent of the composition precluding this.[2]

Though this proposal involves an extension of commission, it would be in fact of no pecuniary advantage to me but the reverse, except in the one all-important particular that I should thus be both complying with your wish for a change of design, & at the same time substituting for one subject after my own heart another in which I should take equal delight. Otherwise, the figures being more than twice the number of those in the first subject, I should be taking on myself an amount of labour much more than proportionate to the increase of price. I already explained to you, when we were discussing the Medusa subject, that the size of figures in a picture, whether that of life or less, made no difference in the labour of the work, supposing them to be still on a good scale.

The small watercolour of this subject which I once made I have no longer, but in case of your entertaining the proposal, I would show you very shortly a sketch of the composition, and would put the work in hand (in case of our agreeing upon it) at the outset of this New Year without further delay.

Memorandum –

In afterwards copying the letter I made some alterations and additions, but they were all in the direction of securing to myself a fair equivalent for the abandoned subject.

1 For the original commission of *Aspecta Medusa* (S.183), see 67.103. 67.160 suggests Matthews's reservation about the severed head. The oil was never completed, but some of the pencil & chalk drawings were sold to other collectors (see S.183C-F).
2 The large oil version of *Dante's Dream* (S.81R.1), based on the watercolour done for EH in 1864, was later commissioned by WG (see 71.3); DGR worked on this picture until 1881.

68.3 TO C. P. MATTHEWS

MS (draft): UBC. Published: *RP* 292–94; DW 765.

No.VII

7th January 1868
*16 Cheyne Walk
Chelsea*

Dear Mr. Matthews

I cannot disguise from you that your last letter causes me great disappointment, which I feel sure you will not consider unreasonable on considering the course of events. After much careful preparation, during some months, for a work on which I built the greatest hopes, and the nature of which was so fixed that change seemed out of the question, I nevertheless felt it necessary to admit the force of an unconquerable objection coming thus late from you since if the work failed to please you at last, it could not but leave a painful regret with me. However, the substitution which you now suggest of small & comparatively casual works to the amount of the commission, instead of the one serious work, would destroy all the pleasure and (in the higher sense) all the advantage which I had promised myself from executing your order in its original form. In saying this, I speak without reserve, as you have rightly done, regarding an agreement which your wishes make it necessary we should modify, but in which my own interests are also greatly at stake.

When I proposed the Dante subject in my last letter, I thought that probably, considering what you had said as to compensation for my trouble till now with the work which (though I felt a difficulty in charging for it) has been in many ways very considerable, and most of all as regards the discouragement of the present change, you would not object to an extension of commission. This in fact involved no advantage to me except that of painting a second subject I greatly desire to paint in lieu of the first, rather than having to seek something as a mere substitute: otherwise, as I said, the new plan was less advantageous to me than the old one.

As to the price fixed for the *Medusa*, I perfectly recollect my first saying that if possible I would paint it for 1200 guineas though 1500 was the limit which I thought might be reached; but in answer to this you very liberally said that in that case you should wish the larger sum to be fixed at once between us, that so I might have full scope in carrying out the work. I am not sure whether our friend Halliday was present at this part of our conversation;[1] but I feel confident, without now asking him, that you would find his impression derived either from his being present or from his talk with you on the subject at Havering that evening or shortly afterwards, to be the same as my own.

It has struck me that you may have been led to think it possible, from the months which have elapsed since the commission was given, that the execution of an important work would in my hands be prolonged indefinitely. To this I should reply that many preparations and various studies have been made by me for the *Medusa* since it was first ordered, and that the only reason why I have as yet shown you nothing was my great desire that what you first saw should leave the best possible impression. With the substituted subject, I would now fix a precise longest date for the delivery of the work, if that seemed desirable to you.

I have now to make a fresh offer regarding the Dante design, which you say in itself would you believe thoroughly please you. This is, to paint it on such a reduced scale as to size (which of course should still be not unimportantly small,) and so far as possible with justice to the work reducing the labour throughout, as would enable me to execute it for 1500 guineas. The picture, you may rely, should still be my best, though smaller than I should have wished to make it. This offer may I trust prove satisfactory to you both as to subject scale and price, as it seems now to correspond both with the original commission and with your requirements since. In making it, I accept all the *onus* of the change of plan, in respect of time already spent and of sacrifice in some respects as regards the new work; but this I shall be content to do if I can both satisfy myself with the nature of the work and please you with its result.[2]

One point of difficulty under which I labour, as regards a change, I have not yet mentioned. That is, the degree of discredit for an artist which attaches to the subject of a commission being altered. During the time I have been getting the *Medusa* in hand, my work and the fact of its being commissioned have of course become known to various frequenters of my studio and have been reported pretty widely; and the unavoidable consequence, that when I resume the work I shall have to offer it to some one who will probably know it was originally ordered in another quarter, is not the least inconvenient feature of my position. In spite of this and other difficulties, I assented to your request that our original subject might be withdrawn, and have also used my endeavour to meet your further views. This being so, I feel assured, remembering the spirit in which the commission was first given, you will think with me that my own preferences now in their turn claim consideration.

I regret troubling you again with so long a letter, but could not manage to express myself more briefly. I shall be very glad to receive a visit from you at any time, and remain, dear Mr. Matthews,

yours very truly,
D.G.Rossetti

[1] For Michael Frederick Halliday, see 54.15, 56.16n2, & **Volume II: Index**.
[2] Matthews declined this reduced offer in terms DGR found offensive (see **5**).

68.4 TO ELLEN HEATON

MS: Yale. Excerpt: Surtees 44. The close and signature at the outer edge of the MS have been clipped away, affecting several words on page 3, reconstructed here within angled brackets.

9th January 1868
16 Cheyne Walk
Chelsea

My dear Miss Heaton

Thanks for your kind letter, but I assure you it is absolutely *against* my interests that I should come forward now, after so long abstaining from exhibition, unless with a work of great importance. Indeed my intimate knowledge of art matters in this country has induced me now to believe that only the most serious immediate motive ought to persuade me to exhibit at all. I hold a fortunate position at present, in possessing a market unassailable by incompetence, ill-will, or to put it in its mildest & frequently true form, by mere diversity of taste. You will greatly oblige me therefore by declining to send anything of mine; and indeed I have lately made the stipulation, when parting with works, that they are not to be exhibited without my consent. Mr. Waring knows my views on this subject, as I have corresponde<d> with him and his Sec<retary> about it, and indeed have their undertak<ing> not to make such applications.[1] I mu<st> therefore attribute it <to> some accident tha<t> you have received <it>.

It so happens I w<as> already going to trou<ble> you with a letter wh<en> I got yours. I am now about immediat<ely> to take *Dante's Dream* in hand on a good scale in oi<l>. I remember your kindly lending it to me before when I held a similar intention but did not then carry it out. At present having the photograph, I should only need the drawing as a guide when I come to the *colour* of the picture, and then not for very long. I would therefore trust to your friendly interest in my work to borrow it again for a short time but only at the precise proper moment; & would try further to coax you by the offer of a sketch of some sort which you should choose, for my obligation to you in the matter.

With best . . .

[1] For Waring, see **10n1**.

68.5 TO C. P. MATTHEWS

MS (draft): UBC. Published: *RP* 294–95; DW 766.

No.IX

9th Jan. 1868

Dear Sir

Pray acquit me at once of all intention to "tie you down hand & foot" to any plans whatever. There are points of expression in your present letter which have given me too much pain for me to wish to comment on them at all. I will merely say that, whether or not I could have courage to paint large pictures on speculation, I have too much self respect to have any dealings as an artist except on a footing of mutual confidence. This being the case, I must now decline at once to paint you any picture at all.

I am, dear Sir

yours faithfully
D G R

No X

Jan 10. evening.

Received another letter from M[r]. M[atthews]. which I readdressed to him & returned by post unopened.[1]

[1] See **8** & **11**.

68.6 TO CHARLES AUGUSTUS HOWELL
MS: Dartmouth College.

[9 January 1868]

Dear Howell

Don't forget Sunday at 7, but come much earlier.

Now here's to worry you. I shall be much in need of 20£ on Monday. Do you think you could at all let me have it on acct of the picture?[1] If so, it would be a boon. But this is not a deliberate plan to bore you – only a question. If you can't easily, I'll manage some other way.

That fellow who was to have had the Medusa picture has behaved so badly that I have been obliged to refuse to paint him any picture whatever. What do you think of that to begin the New Year?[2] Pazienza!

Your
DG R

[1] See 67.177 for the drawing DGR was doing for CAH and **8** for Howell's payment on account.
[2] See **2**, **3**, & **5**.

68.7 TO C. P. MATTHEWS

MS (unsigned fragment): UBC. Published: *RP* 295; DW 768. Date: WMR. The MS appears to be a draft.

[13 January 1868]

I have seen Halliday & need only say after all he tells me, that I shall be as happy as ever to see you again at any time or to hear from you. As regards pictures (should you wish to renew that subject) I would carry out either of the proposals made by me, or else the original one. Should I see you, you will agree with me heartily, I know, that we need not talk of past misconceptions.[1]

[1] See 67.103 for Halliday & Matthews. WMR notes that "with this letter the Matthews correspondence came, I think, to a close; but Mr Matthews and Rossetti met at least once afterwards" (*RP* 295).

68.8 TO CHARLES AUGUSTUS HOWELL

MS: Texas. Published: Cline 52.

Monday [13 January 1868]
16 Cheyne Walk
Chelsea

Dear Howell

Thanks for the cheque.[1] I fear it's been a trouble to you – or rather would have been to any less genial Owl.

Valpy's affair is off, so I suppose there's no need to think about showing him drawings just now.[2]

It seems after all Matthews's letter which I sent back was a humble apology, & Halliday has just called on me with the crittur's remorse and desire of reconciliation. I will tell you the circumstances when I see you. I'm going to take old Brown's advice on the matter.

Love to Kate. Come soon. I want to see you. Look in tomorrow or next day.

Your
Gabriel

[1] See **6**.
[2] The question of which pictures LRV bought at this time is vexed. Apparently, he bought *Contemplation* (S.204) in 1867, and CAH had acted as intermediary in offering him a chalk drawing of Alexa Wilding (see 67.94). DGR thought he would prove to be a regular patron both for his own works and those of FMB. Shortly thereafter, he changed his mind, declaring LRV "a bad lot. Just as he was beginning to buy, he has engaged to get married & is

done for" (67.104). The present letter suggests that DGR's hopes for commissions from LRV had risen and fallen again. The explanation may lie in the fact that DGR had struck a deal in mid-Nov to supply "chalk-drawings (female heads, etc.) to the value of £300, £150 each to Leyland and to Valpy (for the latter the drawings remain to be done)" (*RP* 244). Presumably, that is the deal that is "off." Nevertheless, by the time **18** was written, CAH had apparently struck a new deal with LRV for 5 drawings, with DGR to receive £100. See **25** & **45** for evidence of the number & payment.

68.9 TO FRANCES CATHERINE HOWELL

MS: Texas.

14 January/1868
16 Cheyne Walk
Chelsea

My dear Kate

I'm exceedingly vexed at the misunderstanding, – all the more that, on trying to trace this cock-&-bull (or hen-and-cow) story, I now find it denied on all hands & indeed utterly ignored. Whether I *am* or my informant *was* mad, or whether both of us were and are so, I cannot say. Let us put it to the general account of the mysteries of this universe, & only hope that no Pan Anglican Synod will ever declare it indispensable to our salvation that we should know exactly who *did* invent this little narrative. I fear the night of history has already so closed upon its details that we should all have to be condemned on uncircumstantial non-evidence.

Seriously I feel that an apology from myself is owing to you for having repeated to Charley this foolish gossip which turns out as meaningless as one ought to have known it to be.

Pray forget it all, my dear Kate, & believe me,

most sincerely yours
DGabriel R

68.10 TO LORD HOUGHTON [RICHARD MONCKTON MILNES]

MS (fragment): Trinity College, Cambridge. The MS has suffered extensive water damage indicated by ellipses.

16 January 1868

My dear Lord Houghton,

Our friend Miss Heaton of Leeds writes me word that, through Lord Menton or yourself, of a drawing by me in her possession, she has been applied to for the loan of it by the Leeds Committee and has declined at my request. Your intention was of the friendliest nature and deserves my sincere thanks – but it so happens that at present . . . appear in public until such time as I am able to make a collection of my best works arranged by myself with all due care for exhibition together. It is of the greatest professional importance to me that scattered specimens should not be put forward – perhaps in themselves far from being the best I could show, and certainly not sufficient in of themselves to represent favorably one who is quite new to the public . . . have not exhibited, chances of this kind would be of little moment; but placed as I am, they might prove of serious detriment to my position.

I have not a list of the Leeds Committee, but I make no doubt that your name must appear on it. I write with this to Mr. Waring (to whom I have already had an opportunity of expressing my wishes and received his assent to them at the time) begging that he will most kindly attend to the matter which is of great consequence to me, however . . . important to the . . . of the world, and . . . that all work of mine is strictly excluded (as I was assured it should be on the former occasion referred to) from the Leeds exhibition, to which it could not be sent with my sanction. I also trouble you with this letter requesting that you will do me a serious service by keeping this in mind also and acting in concert with Mr. Waring, if opportunity offers it towards what I know to be my interest. In conclusion I should say to you, as to this, that my only motive. . . .[1]

I am, dear Lord Houghton,

Ever truly yours,
D. G. Rossetti

---

[1] The large *National Exhibition of Works of Art at Leeds, 1868* (catalogue dated 1869), which opened in May, gave DGR considerable cause for alarm. The best account of the exhibition is by Hesketh Hubbard in *A Hundred Years of British Painting 1851–1951* (Longmans, Green, 1951): "The Great Exhibition at Leeds was really a charity exhibition organized to raise funds for the new Infirmary, which Gilbert Scott had designed in the Gothic style, and the Prince of Wales had opened in the Victorian manner. The pictures were shown in the hospital wards before the beds were installed. It was a novelty to turn, even temporarily, a piece of Gothic architecture into a picture gallery and an uncommonly bad gallery it must have made. Three of the wards were devoted to the Old Masters, two to British artists, deceased and living, and one ward each to water-colours and the work of foreign artists" (75). Although approached to allow his works to be shown by two patrons, EH & Frederick Craven, and by the General Manager & Chief Commissioner of the exhibition, J. B. Waring, DGR declined (*DGRDW* 62), as he did also an invitation in early January from the Queen's Limner in Scotland, Sir Noel Paton, to show *The Beloved*, belonging to GR, and the still uncompleted *Venus Verticordia*, commissioned by John Mitchell in 1863 or 1864, at the Royal Scottish Academy (see **50**). In the correspondence of this year, DGR further elaborates on his reasons for not exhibiting to EH (**4**), FJS (**38**), & John Miller (**50**). Works by WHH, JEM, FMB, AH, FS, FJS, GPB, Wallis, & Windus were offered for show and sale by their owners. Lord Houghton was not, as DGR assumed, a member of the Exhibition Committee (see Catalogue 1869).

Friday [17 January 1868]

68.11 TO CHARLES AUGUSTUS HOWELL

MS: Texas. Published: Cline 53. Date: CFM.

Friday [17 January 1868]
16 Cheyne Walk
Chelsea

My dear Howell

Wednesday next will suit me well to dine with you.

On looking again at that *Loving Cup* I find something could be made of it if necessary. Its price in that case ought to be 100 gs but I would take 80 from any friend of yours if the 100 could not be got.[1] Or else there is the larger drawing – Dragon business.[2] I merely mention these matters, but dare say nothing is feasible.

Matthews has written a very penitent letter & I am to see him shortly, so probably all will be well. Look up

Your affec:
D G R

P.S. The Christmas Carol is getting towards completion.

---

[1] This version of *The Loving Cup* is probably one of the 3 replicas dated 1867, most likely S.201R.3 (see 74.130).

[2] In 1868, DGR painted in watercolour over one of the ink drawings from his *Story of St. George* series (S.146); however, the dragon does not figure in that picture. He is probably referring to the replica watercolour of *St. George and the Princess* (S.151R.1), dated 1868, which was finally sold to Craven in 1871. Since DGR notes that he has "given her a face" in **15**, it is also possible that he is referring to a version of S.148, a small picture, where the princess's face is barely sketched in. DGR still possessed a dragon picture in 1878 (see 78.53).

68.12 TO FREDERICK RICHARD LEYLAND

MS: LC. Published: Fennell 10.

17th January/1868
16 Cheyne Walk
Chelsea

My dear Leyland

I remember you telling me to ask you when I needed the last 50 gs on the picture in hand. That critical period has arrived and I should be much obliged if you would send me the amount by return of post. There is hardly anything to do to the *Lilith* now except the kitten, & the massacre of the feline innocents not having yet taken place, I have to wait awhile.¹ The other two are substantially finished.

I shall be very glad to see you on the 22nd & all the gladder if I can then return with you. If not absolutely then, it will be soon after I doubt not, & the change will be a benefit to me. But just at this moment I am sunk deep in many miry ways of work & business. Venus has got a face at last however!!!!!!!!!!²

Howell's affair about his cousin has caused him the greatest vexation, but nothing would have relieved it so much as your kindness in the matter. I feel that I myself am not blameless in having helped to introduce him to you, but I see you are so well disposed to a general amnesty that I will not bother you with more apologies. Sad indeed it is to have such a relation in one's family as this one of poor Howell's.³

With kind remembrances

Ever yours
DG Rossetti

---

1. For the kitten, which was never added to *Lilith*, see 67.31.
2. The *Venus* purchased by FRL was a chalk drawing (S.173A).
3. For Murray Howell, see 67.98. CAH informed WMR in 1871 that he had sent Murray to Australia (*PRT* 56). He succeeded his grandfather, Sir John Murray, as baronet of Stanhope and assumed the surname Murray. He married in 1876 and died in 1878 (see 78.156 & 165).

68.13 TO JAMES ANDERSON ROSE

MS: LC. Excerpt: Kashnor, item 197.

17th January/1868
16 Cheyne Walk
Chelsea

My dear Rose

I have been arranging the preliminaries for an insurance on my property & my own pictures in hand with the Sun Office. I enclose you a circular just received from them and a copy of my reply. Can you kindly attend to this for me within the necessary time, or send Lawson. The terms will be explained to you by my rough copy enclosed. Would you find out at what rate they propose to insure me, & tell me if you consider it a fair one. On hearing from you I will immediately pay what is required. Also would you come to an understanding what I should claim in case of *partial* damage to either household effects or my own works.¹

Yours sincerely
DG Rossetti

JA Rose Esq

¹ Three papers related to the insurance are listed in Kashnor (227); see also the following letter.

68.14 TO C. H. BAUMER

MS: LC; UBC (copy in another hand). Excerpt: Kashnor 198. Published: DW 767.

16 Cheyne Walk/Chelsea
17 January 1868

C H Baumer Esq
Sir

I have requested my solicitor, Mr. J.A. Rose, of 11 Salisbury St Strand to call on you for the purpose of completing the insurance.

Its terms are –
£3000 on property of my own in this house – including China, pictures, furniture, &c – and
£2000 on pictures & drawings by myself painted or painting on commission or as yet uncommissioned. Of these I always have a considerable number in hand, but of course some are continually leaving me & others being commenced. The policy would therefore have to be strictly a *floating* one, as I could not at any time undertake to specify individual works in case of fire.

The £100 added to the £5000 in your circular I do not understand. Perhaps you will kindly explain this to Mr. Rose or anyone sent by him.

I am, Sir,

Your obt servt
D. G. Rossetti

68.15 TO CHARLES AUGUSTUS HOWELL

MS: Texas.

Friday [17 January 1868]

My dear Howell

Wednesday (it just now occurs to me for first time) is the 22nd, the day Leyland is coming and on which I wrote him word I should be happy to see him. So I cannot well be going out. Suppose we say Friday or Saturday instead for coming to you – that is if I am to be there as I should like to be.

You see I cannot help myself as to Wedy and Thursday wd very likely be awkward.

I've just altered the Princess in the Dragon picture and given her a face which gives the thing a chance of selling.[1]

Your
Gabriel

[1] For the dragon picture, see **11**.

68.16 TO FREDERICK RICHARD LEYLAND

MS: LC. Published: Fennell 11.

18 January/1868

16 Cheyne Walk
Chelsea

My dear Leyland

Thanks for enclosure £55 completing payment for the 3 pictures I have in hand for you.

My own impression as to the sum due was the same as yours, but not being quite certain I thought it best to be on the safe side. However as we both thought so, I have no doubt so it is.[1]

Ever yours
DG Rossetti

P.S. I hope you'll dine with me Thursday at 7, and I'll get Howell.

[1] See **12**.

68.17 TO GEORGE PRICE BOYCE

MS: University College. Excerpt: Surtees 99.

28 January/1868
16 Cheyne Walk
Chelsea

My dear Boyce

Since last writing to you I have heard repeatedly from various quarters of your improving health, but still feel most unmistakably that it seems an unfriendly thing in me not to have been near you. I should have written before this, were it not that I have been meaning daily to pluck up courage & come to see you. For I must confess at once, my dear fellow, that what has kept me away has been sheer cowardice as regards the possible danger of visiting a house where fever has been. This should not have prevailed with me had you been alone, believe me, but knowing how well you were cared for, I must not deny having succumbed to a perhaps morbid feeling which some years ago would never have entered my mind at all. I suppose the increase of nervousness with years must be allowed to account for it, and then there is the additional feeling that one has heard to be afraid doubles the danger. You will make allowance I know for this weakness which I think it necessary to confess lest it should seem that my mind has not been occupied with friendly anxiety on your account, which, dear Boyce, is far indeed from being the case. Let me have a line from you to say how you are now, and how soon you are likely to be among us again, as I believe you have not yet returned to Blackfriars. Perhaps you do not intend to do so at all, but to seek some other quarters before you move. If so, could I be of any service in arranging anything for you? It would be a satisfaction to me if I could.

I see all your friends from time to time, & they are all well and often wish you well. We were deploring your absence at a dinner given the other day by Howell and hoping it would not be for long.

I fear I have little news. Things in my studio drag terribly, but I have at last erased completely & completely repainted the figure and head in my *Venus*, and this time I really believe satisfactorily. I have made a lot of chalk drawings, studies for various projected works, and hope by the time you are ready to see I may be ready to show. I hope your own appearance at the Watercolour Gallery will not be very seriously affected by your long seclusion from work. I cannot help thinking that that inn-yard must have been the origin of your ailment.

With loving wishes for the New Year, believe me dear Boyce

Yours ever affectionately
DG Rossetti

68.18 TO CHARLES AUGUSTUS HOWELL

MS: Texas. Published: Cline 66. Text within angled brackets is a restored deletion.

[c. January 1868]

Regiostissimo Gufo*

I find the Owl & not the Dog is the friend of man. I write with this to the best of Vampires.¹ <I must treat the drawings in a foggy manner in my letter, as> I do not understand if they are supposed to be all done or not. You will arrange all that.²

See you on Saturday. Love to Kate.

Your
Gabriel

P.S. You said V's letter was left with yours on the table but I only found his envelope addressed to you.

---

* Most (royal) illustrious Owl.
1. Vampire here refers to LRV; elsewhere it is also applied to EG. WMR describes LRV as "something of a sentimentalist, of a nervous and flurried turn: a conscientious gentleman, of high and fidgeting standards in life" (*RP* 267).
2. See **8** for the new arrangement for drawings.

68.19 TO CHARLES AUGUSTUS HOWELL

MS: Texas.

Wednesday [January–February 1868]

Dear Howell

It strikes me Valpy might be game for that head of Christ. So suppose if feasible you mention it to him beforehand. You can call it a circular head of Christ as the True Vine.¹

Like a fool I forgot to ask you what day you would come with Kate. You can tell me tomorrow.

Your
Gabriel

I wrote thanks to Leyland.

---

1. *Head of Christ* (S.109E), originally executed as a watercolour study for *Mary Magdalene at the Door of Simon the Pharisee*. DGR mentioned this head to EG in 67.1, and he must have eventually bought it; Moncure Conway acquired it from the EG sale at Christie's (1 Apr 71).

68.20 TO CHARLES AUGUSTUS HOWELL
MS: Texas.

Saturday [January–February 1868]

Dear Howell

Will you let me have a line about the circular head.[1]

Your affec:
Gabriel

[1] See previous letter.

68.20.1 TO CHARLES AUGUSTUS HOWELL
MS: Texas.

Wednesday [January–February 1868]

16 Cheyne Walk
Chelsea

My dear Gufo[*]

I expected you yesterday but you came not. Suppose you come tomorrow (Thursday), hang the pictures, dine, & go with me to Ned Jones's, whither I go.

Ever yours
D Gabriel R

[*] See **18n***.

68.21 TO FRANCES MARY LAVINIA ROSSETTI
MS: UBC. Published: DW 769. Date: FLR.

Monday [3 February 1868]

16 Cheyne Walk
Chelsea

Good Antique

Here is your funny old portrait. I am coming up this evening. The paper over the picture had better be removed by yourself, as the picture is sticky.[1]

Your affec:
Gabriel

[1] The half-length oil portrait of FLR, dated 1866 but "perhaps not completely finished until the beginning of 1868" (S.450).

68.22 TO CHARLES AUGUSTUS HOWELL

MS: Texas. Published: Cline 54.

Tuesday [4 February 1868]

Dear Owl

Graham will have the 3 Roses & take it with him when he calls before long. I suppose he will then also pay.¹

About our conversation yesterday. I certainly understood you to say that the encouragement of the Lucrezia to Ellis if I did my best with it (as I think I did) would be such that he would be willing for the future always to go and do likewise in case of need. Indeed I had a letter of yours which urged this view while I was working on the Lucrezia, but I dare say it is lost. The difficulty you raised yesterday "What is Ellis to do if he finds he can get it cheaper than the sum named?" is of course nothing to the purpose as regards my interests – the point in question being that it should be bought not below a certain sum. Otherwise it would be much better for me not to direct the attention of a well-disposed man like Ellis to the fact that it is possible for my work to go ill in sale-rooms, and instead to let the thing just take its chance & be heard of as little as may be. I should be happy to give 50 myself in the present case.²

Your affec:
Gabriel

---

1. WG bought the 1867 version of *Rosa Triplex* (S.238A).
2. *Lucrezia Borgia* (S.124) was coming up in the Windus sale; DGR's plan to recover it was recounted in WBS:AB (18 Feb 68): "One by Gabriel . . . would have gone at 25, but he had Howell and someone else to bid [it] up to the price he would charge for such a picture £75, and the public is done!" (PP). See also **27**. The reference to FSE is not clear; it probably relates to the fact that he was the 2nd bidder at the sale, but **52** suggests that he was involved in larger dealings with CAH. DGR also had an outstanding £50 debt with FSE, a bill that he renewed repeatedly, finally paying him £50 on 19 Apr 69 and asking him to draw a new bill for the same amount (see 69.46).

68.23 TO CHARLES AUGUSTUS HOWELL

MS: Texas.

Tuesday night [4 February 1868]

Dear Howell

I forgot this morning to say that I have been doing something to the V[ampire]'s drawings, so now there are 3 for him besides those you have.

Your
Gabriel

68.24 TO JOHN GILBERT

MS: Mills College.

6 February/1868
16 Cheyne Walk
Chelsea

My dear Gilbert

It vexes me much to refuse your kind invitation, as it would have given me real pleasure to come; but tomorrow (Friday) has been bespoken with me for more than a week, to dine at another friend's house. Will you give my friendliest remembrances to Holland & to Christie with whom and with yourself I shall be in the spirit.[1]

Ever yours truly
DG Rossetti

John Gilbert Esq

[1] DGR had known the watercolourist & illustrator John Gilbert since the 1840s (see **Volume II: Index**). James Holland (1799–1870) painted landscapes, first in watercolour and later in oil; "Christie" may be the Scottish painter James Elder Christie (1847–1914).

68.25 TO CHARLES AUGUSTUS HOWELL

MS: Texas. Published: Cline 31.

Monday [10 February 1868]

My dear Howell

I am going to see Boyce this evening & I judge from a letter in which he sends you his love (he had done so also once before) that he is a little hurt at not having seen or heard from you in his illness. If you could dine here today at 6, we would go round together afterwards. He is leaving town on Thursday. His address is

5 Park Place Villas
Maiden Hill West

which is his mother's house. Infection it seems there has never been.

As regards tin, I am only answerable for £100 of the £500 outlay, & the only thing which has prevented the *Carol* reaching you yet is the degree to which I have worked on your *Venus* drawing.[1] This & 3 others – that is 4 out of the 5 – are now ready for delivery, though I may possibly do more to the *Triple Rose* drawing, which nevertheless is finished as it is.[2] I know, my dear

Howell, that you did not for a moment mean to complain of my proceedings, & that being so – let me say frankly that I really think we had better be off the bargain for the 5 drawings and this wholly & solely for your sake. They are not marketable commodities – at least only so by a fluke sometimes, – and if you are bent on keeping any of them they are all the worse as an investment. I shall be all right as I will raise funds elsewhere. My reason for sending to you is wholly the Boyce question.

Your affec
Gabriel

The Carol shall reach you in a very few days – I would say tomorrow or next day, but may be forced to work first at the Dragon drawing on certain accounts. Valpy asking one for Tuesday – tomorrow week!
P.S. If you could not get here by 6 to dinner, 7 would probably be early enough for going to Boyce's.

---

1. The *Carol* referred to here is either the pencil version dated 1867 (S.195A) or the undated crayon version (S.196B) later owned by Aglaia Coronio & Mrs. LRV; FRL had returned his version at DGR's request (see 67.159). For the dragon, see **11**. The *Venus* drawing may be the one that went to FRL (see **89n2**).
2. According to Surtees, LRV acquired only one of the drawings mentioned in this letter, a study (S.238B) for *Rosa Triplex*. However, he also owned several other works done between 1867 & 1870: *Peace* (S.197); a study (S.183F) for *Aspecta Medusa*; *Contemplation* (S.204); *La Pia* (S.207D); *Aurea Catena* (S.209); *The Portrait* (S.212); & *La Donna della Fiamma* (S.216). The last 3 are portraits of JM.

68.26 TO GEORGE PRICE BOYCE

MS: Chelsea. Date: GPB.

Monday [10 February 1868]
16 Cheyne Walk
Chelsea

My dear Boyce

Thanks for your very welcome letter. I had fully made up my mind on receiving it to come this evening, but now I have been detained by accident till 8 o'clock & as I suppose you must be an early bird I had better come tomorrow (Tuesday) evening instead. That I shall certainly do, & hope to bring William with me, as he will probably dine here.

Certainly I seem to have derived quite an exaggerated impression as to the degree of fever you suffered from. One thing was I heard that Mrs. Tebbs had been taken ill after going to see you, but I imagine from what I understand now that her illness was not the same as yours. Still it looked uncomfortable. Not that I have more reason by any means to cherish life for its own sake than yourself, but I am so constantly under the necessity of meeting fixed liabilities that even an illness – not to speak of a fatal one – has become a morbid bugbear to me. Enough however of self & weaknesses.

I fear you may fail in finishing Miss W[ilding]'s head after all, as that young person has gone out of town for some time as I understand – an inconvenience to me. Perhaps however she may be back in time.[1]

I hope for a good chat with you tomorrow evening and am ever

Yours affectionately
DG Rossetti

[1] Alexa Wilding had modelled several times for GPB in 1867 (*GPBD* 47). DGR visited on 14 Feb, when he, Henry Wallis, Gerald Blunt, WBS, & AB were at GPB's for "whist and supper" (*GPBD* 52).

68.27 TO CHARLES AUGUSTUS HOWELL

MS: Texas. Date: CFM.

Monday night [10 February 1868]
2nd letter

Dear Howell

If you *can* come tomorrow (Tuesday) to dinner, I now remember there is something else about which I want particularly to see you, connected with the Windus sale.[1] If you can't come then, will you let me know when you can, & make it as soon as possible.

Gabriel

[1] See **22**.

68.28 TO CHARLES AUGUSTUS HOWELL

MS: Texas. Published: Cline 64.

Wednesday [12 February 1868]

Dear Howell

I can't be bothered with that bad old drawing, but will finish you the full face one of Miss W. if you like for 60£. In that case I'll let you have also the drawing of J[aney]. which I cleaned while you were here on the terms you propose.¹ Only I'm wanting the cash, & will when I get it finish the larger drawing at once.

Ever yrs
D G R

[1] A chalk head of Alexa Wilding, which is not full face (S.534), dated 1868, went to FRL, who also owned S.368 or S.369, both charcoal drawings of JM done in 1865.

68.29 TO GEORGE PRICE BOYCE
MS: Texas.

12 Feb 1868
16 Cheyne Walk
Chelsea

My dear Boyce

It has struck me that while you are away I should be very glad to borrow the *Bocca Baciata* for the purpose of making a replica¹ – most probably in water-colour. I might as well at the same time take the *Belcolore*.² If you have no objection (and I remember I once asked you and you said you would have none) would you send word to Mrs. Birrell that I may have the pictures, which I would then send for.

I hope you may come back thoroughly set up and eager for work. At any rate I am sure one always does one's best after a forced interval of this sort.

Your affec:
D Gabriel R

[1] GPB's picture (S.114) has recently been acquired by Vassar College. Its slightly larger watercolour version, *La Bionda del Balcone* (S.114R.1), was sold to the oculist Bowman for 150 guineas (see **138n2** & *RP* 239). The face was repainted in 1877.
[2] S.160. An enlarged version, also in watercolours (S.160R.1), was painted in 1868 and altered in the 1870s.

68.30 TO FREDERIC JAMES SHIELDS

MS: Bucknell University. Published: Faxon 23–27; *The Rossettis: Brothers & the Brotherhood*: 22.

14th February/1868
16 Cheyne Walk
Chelsea

My dear Shields

I should be delighted to have some news of you if I did not know practically what an agony letter-writing usually is. At present I am spurred to it by a cause in which you will sympathize.

I saw the other day some most remarkable and indeed admirable photographs of pencil drawings (studies of children from nature) which were sent by some friends to my mother. The information accompanying them was that they were the work of a young man who had never any training whatever in art & who was in a very humble position, and also, I regret to say, reported to be hopelessly consumptive. It seems the photographs of his sketches were set on foot by friends to add if possible to his comforts in illness. Much doubt is expressed whether he can still be alive. It appears the drawings were procured from

Warwick Brooks
1 Egerton Grove
Stretford Road
Manchester

but I do not know whether this can be the artist as I am not sure whether the name tallies with the initials on the drawings. There no doubt however all information could be procured and the photos: purchased. I am anxious to have a set, if their purchase would still assist the artist, and to do anything further in that case which might be in my power. I know your sympathies will be roused to make the necessary inquiries at once, as you are so near; and I feel sure of your admiring the drawings as much as I do. Indeed their production by an un-trained hand seems almost incredible. Will you let me know as soon as you have any news about it.[1]

Yours affectionately
D. G. Rossetti

[1] For FJS' reply, see *RP* 345–46 (excerpt: Faxon's article). See also **38**, **39**, & **41**.

68.31 TO MURRAY MARKS

MS: Fitzwilliam. Published: *Marks* 53, 59; DW 770.

14th February/1868
16 Cheyne Walk
Chelsea

My dear Marks

I will take up the Tibullus again at once, and send it you as soon as at all possible – I hope perhaps at the end of next week.[1]

Now do be a good fellow & address me when writing for the future in a more friendly & genial form. Business relations are all right enough, but we have known each other long enough now to be at all times on easy terms. Pardon my saying this. I know your meaning is of the kindest.

Ever yours truly
D G Rossetti

M.Marks Esq

[1] A watercolour version (S.62R.2) of *The Return of Tibullus to Delia* was sent to Marks on 30 Mar; see **62**.

68.32 TO CHARLES AUGUSTUS HOWELL

MS: Texas.

Sunday [16 February 1868]

My dear Howell

I find I have one more Mrs. Morris rather larger than the average ones, which I would put to Valpy's lot,[1] so there are 4 done for him besides the one for you.

Your
D G R

[1] The larger portrait of JM is probably the *Aurea Catena* mentioned in **25n2**.

68.33 TO FREDERICK RICHARD LEYLAND

MS: LC. Published: Fennell 11.

17th Feb 1868
16 Cheyne Walk
Chelsea

My dear Leyland
Here are the dimensions:

	Picture	Frame
Lilith	33 x 38½	48½ x 53½
M[onna].Rosa	28¾ x 21½	33 x 40½
Carol	17½ x 14½	22¾ x 25¾
L[oving].Cup	25 x 17½	34½ x 26½

If you want the 3 last named at once, I will do at once the very little remaining to be done & send them to you. Will you let me know.[1]

I have not yet thanked you for much succulence in the shape of oranges by which I have been profiting for more than a week past. My reason for not writing has been, as you may have guessed, that I wanted at same time to fix a day for coming to you. The demon Worry has so marked me for his own lately that this has as yet proved impracticable, but I live in hope of soon coming yet, & the bright looking days we have had make me often think of you and the country.

I congratulate you on the "blessed change" you have effected in the case of Leighton's picture.[2] Is it to be at Speke or in London? I shall have to paint you some stunning composition – Medusa or other – to be properly represented among these heroes.

I have come into possession of a drawing of mine of which the photo: was always a favorite with you: – Lucrezia Borgia washing her hands. I saw it at Christie's in Windus's sale, & seeing things I should like to alter in it I bought it myself for 70 gs. I shall not show it till altered, but then shd like you to see it. It is quite a small affair.[3]

With kindest remembrances to Mrs. Leyland & Miss Parke.

I am ever yours
DG Rossetti

[1] Except for *Lilith*, the works mentioned were all previous purchases of FRL's returned at DGR's request, presumably to make replicas.
[2] Probably Leighton's *The Syracusan Bride leading Wild Animals in Procession to the Temple of Diana*, 1866. FRL sold the picture at auction in 1874 (see 74.109).
[3] S.124; see **22**.

68.34 TO CHARLES AUGUSTUS HOWELL

MS: Texas. Excerpt: Cline 93.

Monday [17 February 1868]

Dear Owl

Thanks for the address & the frames. I don't know exactly when I shall want to paint any owls again as I have no subject from Der Freischutz in hand, but when I do I'll holloa.[1]

I think as soon as feasible I'll shoot all Leyland's drawings on to you for mounting, as you say you'll do it and the frames when empty are much in demand with me. One thing however – I really don't know who in any way rewards your owlish labours which though probably chiefly nightwork, as is the wont of owls, are laborious all the same. If Leyland has no ideas on the subject we must enter into some arrangement for an artistic guerdon from me, as your labours save me the valuable frames.

Your affec
Gabriel

P.S. I'll have the remounted Mrs. Top when you like, to be photo'd.[2]
Suppose you dine here Wednesday.

[1] *Der Freischütz* (see 53.29n*), in which a monstrous owl figures.
[2] See **28**.

68.35 TO CHARLES AUGUSTUS HOWELL

MS: Texas.

Tuesday [18 February 1868]

My dear Howell

I am very sorry to have missed your visit last night. Tonight I have to go to Valpy's to dinner. Would you write me a word of any news by bearer if you are at home, or perhaps Kate would write. Should you be in tomorrow evening if I were to call? Or could you come here in the day?

Ever yours
Gabriel

68.36 TO MURRAY MARKS

MS: Fitzwilliam. Date: P/M.

Tuesday [18 February 1868]

My dear Marks

A day or two will decide whether the drawing is fit to offer you – that is the only question as to your having it.

Now is the time for that cup if you can borrow it for me. Will you kindly see about it. I want to get on the picture in a hurry if it may be.

Ever yours
DG Rossetti

P.S. Excuse grubby paper – I am at work.

68.37 TO MURRAY MARKS

MS: Fitzwilliam.

20th February/1868
16 Cheyne Walk
Chelsea

My dear Marks

I have now been at work some days on the "Tibullus" since taking it up again, and find that as usual it absorbs time. As I cannot stick to it exclusively, I believe all I can undertake with any degree of confidence will be to deliver it properly finished within a month, – not I fear much earlier but I trust certainly not later.

Yours very truly
DG Rossetti

68.38 TO FREDERIC JAMES SHIELDS

MS: Kansas. Published: Horne 83–85; Mills 117–19; DW 772.

16 Cheyne Walk
21 Feb 1868

My dear Shields

Your letter calls for my thanks in various ways. First about Warwick Brookes, whom I almost guessed to be necessarily more of a regular artist than had been represented to me. I shall be anxious to have a set of his admirable photo'd. drawings and will write to him with this, enclosing the £4. When here, I have little doubt their being seen must lead to further sales. Howell, to whom I spoke on the subject & who saw the photos: at my mother's, at once said he would undertake that Ruskin would wish to have an original drawing. I will speak further to him when my own photos: arrive. It is melancholy to think that any aid & appreciation such as the drawings cannot fail to excite will come only at such a painful time. Is there really no hope of recovery? I cannot understand how such an artist can have failed so long to obtain employment from the dealers in Manchester. His babies are worthy of William Hunt & have never been surpassed. Does he work in colour? In such case I fancy employment in London as a copyist to begin with might easily be obtained. But I suppose the health question now quite negatives this.

Now as to Mr. Johnson & the cartoons – I still have the Vineyard set, and though I have lately been asking more for them shall be happy to sell them at the price named to him. My own impression is I must have said 100 *guineas* not *pounds* (because I always do so.) But if he and you are under the other impression, so be it. The frame will require to be written on, after which I can send the set. Where should it go to? I should have to charge carriage & case to Mr. Johnson. What is his address? One thing more on this point. I have another set of 6 (the Vineyard is 7 including a double sized one) from the Legend of St. George and the Dragon. They are framed to match the vineyard set; and as it would be a relief to me to clear my walls and hang other things, I would part with the 2 sets together for 170 guineas, if Mr. Johnson liked to have both. As I presume he must propose hanging the one set in some hall or such like place, the effect would be greatly enhanced by having the 2 sets, and one is quite equal to the other. If you can conveniently mention this to him, will you do so, otherwise it does not matter, as also regarding the question between pounds & guineas which must not be raised at all if you would have to write or be in any way troubled about it.[1]

What you say of the Tristram drawing is very gratifying to me. As regards the application by the Leeds committee for it, this makes me somewhat anxious, as it is the 3rd application of the kind which has come to my ears. I had some time ago, & have since had renewed, a promise from Mr. Waring the head commissioner, that no works of mine should be applied for or even admitted if offered; but it is quite comprehensible that in such a multitudinous scheme of operations, a slight matter of this kind might get overlooked. I consider the point all-important to me now, as to which you will understand my precise views. Only a thoroughly well-considered & sufficiently important appearance in public, after all these years of partial reputation on grounds chiefly unknown, could do otherwise than greatly damage me; & thus could only be attained by my having myself full control & selection. In short at present nothing would be so discouraging to me as to be forced before the public in a sudden & incomplete way, and I am most anxious to do all I can to prevent it. Mr. Craven & Mr. M'Connel (thanks to you) have now been secured on my side.[2] You know Mr. Tong. Shall you be seeing him, & if so could you see whether he has been applied to & with what result? I would write to him if necessary. Do you know Mr. Mendel who has a picture of mine? I do not. Don't suppose that I mean to worry you about my trumpery thin-skinned interests, but a hint from you, if you possess the means, might enable me to act for myself. Do you know when the Leeds Gallery opens?

Daylight at this distance from town being only available for painting, I have actually as yet never seen the old water colour sketches, though I have meant to do so and may yet. I am glad you will appear in the main exhibition, but you do not tell me much of your doings. I heard from Chapman that the Drummer-boy drawing was exhibited at Manchester. I hope with good result as it certainly ought to have served you well. Chapman is now in town again but I have not yet seen him this time. I hope he may have had some luck in your neighbourhood. Have you continued on the tack of the *Rahab* in subject and treatment, or have you done subjects of the present day?[3] I hope to have a full & satisfactory talk with you on all points of interest to both of us (and we have many in common) when you come again to London, & hope further that that may be soon. Old Brown is as choice an old master as ever, & all friends I think well on the whole.

Your affec:
D. G. Rossetti

P.S. You know I could always lodge you on a run to London.

---

[1] Johnson, a Mancunian, bought the *Vineyard* series (S.133–39) made for The Firm in 1867; he later sold them to T. H. McConnell (*RP* 300).

[2] McConnell bought *Sir Tristram and La Belle Yseult* (S.200) and sold it in 1872 (see **10n1** & **72.30n1**). FJS had been instrumental in the purchase and evidently persuaded McConnell not to send it to the Leeds exhibition.

[3] FJS' 1866 watercolour *Study of a Drummer Boy* is now in the DAM; his *Rahab Awaiting the Coming of Joshua* derives from the story of Rahab the Harlot in Joshua 2: 1–24.

68.39 TO WARWICK BROOKES

MS: Bucknell. Published: Faxon 23–27; *The Rossettis: Brothers & the Brotherhood* 22.

> 16 Cheyne Walk/Chelsea/London
>
> 21 Feb.1868

Dear Sir

I lately saw a set of photographs from some admirable drawings from nature by you, and I understand from our friend Mr. Shields that a set can be obtained from you for £4. Will you therefore allow me to enclose that sum by P.O. order, and to request that they may be kindly sent me at your convenience. I cannot doubt that, when seen they will be widely appreciated in London by all whose judgment is of any value.

I cannot refrain, though a stranger, from saying how deeply I regret to hear of your present state of health, and how sincerely I hope it may still change for the better; and with all best wishes, remain

> yours sincerely,
> D.G. Rossetti

Warwick Brookes Esq

68.40 TO HENRY VIRTUE TEBBS

MS: Texas.

> Monday [c. 24 February 1868]

My dear Tebbs

I have 6 cartoons from the story of St George in one frame which I would sell for 75 guineas. One is the subject you have, & the rest would be interesting as developing the story. Do you like to buy them? I should ask 100 of anyone else.[1]

> Ever yours
> DG Rossetti

---

[1] HVT did not buy the cartoons (S.145–50), which evidently stayed in CAH's hands for many years. The picture he already owned was a watercolour version of *St. George and the Dragon* (S.148R.1).

68.41 TO WARWICK BROOKES

MS: Bucknell. Published: Faxon 23–27; *The Rossettis: Brothers & the Brotherhood* 22.

> 28 Feby 1868
> 16 Cheyne Walk
> Chelsea

My dear Sir

Many thanks for the beautiful portfolio of photographs which I value highly & which are already meeting with equal appreciation from others. The babies in particular seem to me triumphs, every one of them; not that they are better than many of the other figures, but because every artist knows to his cost how difficult it is to attain such success in representing babyhood.

I do not know whether you allow any one to purchase fewer photos: than a complete set; but if you do, my brother is anxious to have about half the number, & in such case would send you word of his favorites among the series.

With kind remembrances to Shields if you should see him,

> I am yours very truly,
> D.G. Rossetti

Warwick Brookes Esq

68.42 TO CHARLES AUGUSTUS HOWELL

MS: Texas. Published: Cline 55. Date: Cline. The letter is misdated 9 Mar 68 by CFM.

> Monday [2 March 1868]

Dear Howell

I've not tackled the Borgia yet & don't know whether I shall be able to show it to Leyland on his coming to town – you don't tell me when. However I will if in a showable state by then, but do not mean to show it till altered, & have much to do on all hands.[1]

I had better not keep you waiting about the parcel to Leyland's, but will write to F. & D.[2] when ready & send off my section by itself. If not to-day, then Wednesday, I hope to get the things ready to go, but there is a little to do to two of them.[3] I should be really glad to talk to you on various points if you could look up tomorrow (Tuesday) (say) at 5, & we'd either dine out together or dine here. Do come.

> Your affec:
> Gabriel

P.S. I'm afraid I can't afford the print. I gave the picture to Rose.

1. The repainted *Lucrezia Borgia* (S.124) was bought by FRL (see **48** & **56**), but it was not completed until 1872 (see 72.128).
2. Foord & Dickinson were artists' colourmen & framers in New Bond Street. See also **44**.
3. The works are those mentioned in **33**, with the exception of *Lilith*, which was not delivered until May 69.

68.43 TO CHARLES AUGUSTUS HOWELL

MS: Texas.

Monday [2 March 1868]. 2nd letter

My dear Howell

I've written to F.&D. to come & pack Leyland's pictures Thursday. If you think they had better then go on to you, let F.&D. know.

Your
Gabriel

68.44 TO FREDERICK RICHARD LEYLAND

MS: LC. Published: Fennell 13.

Monday [2 March 1868]

My dear Leyland

I've written to Foord & Dickinson to bring the case & pack the 3 pictures & the framed sketches of Mrs. Leyland on Thursday – so I trust they'll reach you that night or Friday morning.[1]

In haste

Ever yours
DG Rossetti

1. DGR did send all 3 pictures back, but he apparently asked for the *Loving Cup* again in 1870 (FRL:DGR, 26 Dec 71, Fennell 32), intending to paint a new picture as "a pendant of *Lilith*" (71.217). This plan was not fulfilled, and DGR returned it to FRL on 18 Mar 73 (73.83).

68.45 TO CHARLES AUGUSTUS HOWELL

MS: Texas. Published: Cline 56. Date: CFM.

Thursday [5 March 1868]

Dear Howell

The brandy has just come, and I will pay for it when I see you, as there was nothing in the house but a big note.

Do you think you can secure me £50 if not the 100 for the 5 drawings by

18th of this month, as I then have a bill for that amount coming due,¹ & shd thus be free to work when Janey Morris comes to sit, without thinking of pot-boiling for the moment. She & Top are to be here next Wedy to stay. Would you dine here that day with them. I want to see you, but that must be always the cry of your friends.

What a triumph Ned's party was! Nothing like it ever known in the circle.²

I am getting the Lucrezia really good now I think, & shall finish it straight off, & it certainly ought not to sell for less than 120 gs. Indeed I cannot doubt that may be got for it, & shall advise Leyland to buy it with a good conscience. I wish you'd keep me informed as to that infernal report of further things of mine for sale. Anything done with Carol?³

Your
Gabriel

On Saturday I'm going to Matthews in the country. Could you look in to dinner tomorrow?

---

1. See also **49** & **52**.
2. WBS wrote JL about the party on 8 & 14 Mar. In the first letter he says: "[EBJ] actually invited all the world and had azaleas and orange trees to decorate his studio.... Howell was Major Domo, and the supper was sumptuous. Everybody of course was there, that is every body of the *true creed*." The 2nd letter explains that "after... all had left, a great part of the ceiling of the studio came down, about 4 hundredweight, had we all been there, the new school as Brown said might have been extinguished, – he, Gabriel, Holman Hunt, Morris, Swinburne, Little Simeon, Jones and myself, might have been squashed at one go" (LP).
3. For the *Carol*, see **25n1**.

68.46 TO JANE MORRIS

MS: BL. Published: Bryson 1.

6 March/1868
16 Cheyne Walk
Chelsea

My dear Janey,

Next Wednesday was the day I hoped to see you, but I think perhaps to secure my finishing something I am about beforehand, I had better say Friday – i.e. 2 days later. On Friday next then I will expect your kind visit, and if you can come early enough to sit that day – i.e. about one o'clock, my gratitude will commence at that hour.

All is ready for the picture, as I have already made some studies and know exactly what I have to do as to the action of the figure, which, my dear Janey, is a very easy one, so you shall be punished as little as possible for your kindness. The drawing of your head will take I expect two days, & then straight to the picture.

If you find it more convenient to come only in time for dinner on Friday, & so have a rest after the journey that night before you sit, that plan will of course do perfectly for me; but if I do not hear to the contrary, I will expect you in time to sit on Friday, & Morris at dinner time. It strikes me as probable that you and Bessie might like to come together, as otherwise she would be left very dull at home, unless she thinks it necessary for the safety of the establishment to stay behind.[1] If she can come, it would give me much pleasure, and there will be no difficulty as to an extra bed-room, as there are several in the house.

So on this point perhaps you would in any case write me a line again when you have settled your plans.

Yours affectionately
DG Rossetti

[1] Elizabeth Burden, JM's sister.

68.47 TO CHARLES AUGUSTUS HOWELL
MS: Texas.

Sunday night [8 March 1868]

My dear Howell

You said you were coming in tomorrow (Monday). Do you remember that I asked you to ask Lucas & Alecco to dine here with you tomorrow? I do not know if they are coming, as you have never mentioned the matter since. Perhaps if they do not know of it yet, we will defer the invitation a day or two, & so ask a few more friends. If however they are coming tomorrow, will you manage to be here as early as may be & let me know so, or else send me early word to expect them & yourself to dinner.[1]

Ever yours
Gabriel

[1] The Ionides brothers evidently came; see **49**.

68.48 TO FREDERICK RICHARD LEYLAND

MS: LC. Published: Fennell 15.

> Monday [9 March 1868]
> 16 Cheyne Walk
> Chelsea

My dear Leyland

When are you likely to be in town? I want to give you the first offer of the *Lucrezia Borgia* (size 17 x 10 inches) which I have taken up again, & which is coming very much to my satisfaction. You know I repossessed myself of it at the price of 70 gs for the purpose of making some alterations, & this has resulted (according to my wont) in completely taking out the figure and drapery and repainting it all from nature with a fresh turn of action given. It is now one of my very best things, and on seeing it you will agree with me that though small, it will be one of my cheapest at 120 gs. It will be finished by the end of this week, and will have taken me at least 10 days to alter, so I think I am fairly entitled to the profit on my purchase, especially as I cannot doubt, that, fetching 70 as it was before in the saleroom, it must have fetched double now.

I should like you to have it, as you have nothing better of mine, nor anything so distinctly wrought out as a historical subject; so I write to ask whether you will be able soon to see it, or whether you like me to consider it yours at the price named, before I offer it to anyone else.

With kindest remembrances to all yours,

> I am yours sincerely
> DG Rossetti

68.49 TO CHARLES AUGUSTUS HOWELL

MS: Texas. Published: Cline 57. Date: CFM.

> Wednesday [11 March 1868]

My dear Howell

Don't forget Friday dinner at 6-30 – Top & wife coming.

I wrote to Leyland offering Lucrezia at 120 gs & expected an answer this morning but it has not come yet. The drawing will I expect be finished by Friday.

I'm very unwilling to bother you, but do you think that £100 for the 5 drawings could be managed now – i.e. 50 now & 50 by the day I named before? Funds are exhausted, & I want to be doing Janey's picture which is not potboiling. If the whole thing is a nuisance to you, say so, & I will try to dispose of the drawings at once elsewhere.

Tibullus will soon I hope be in Marks's hands.[1] I suppose B. Foster did not buy the Carol as I did not hear from you to that effect.[2] I meant to have talked of these things the other night, but 2 big Greeks were in the way.

Your affec:
Gabriel

P.S. Of course an answer on Friday when I see you will do as to the money matter.[3]

[1] See **31** & **62**.
[2] Myles Birket Foster, the watercolourist & book illustrator.
[3] CAH evidently paid; see **52** for DGR's request for the second £50.

68.50 TO JOHN MILLER

MS: LLAG. The 16CW monogram has been cut from the MS.

11th March/1868

Dear Mr. Miller

Many thanks for your introduction to Mr. Saunders[1] who seems a capital fellow & whom I was very glad to see as he put my mind quite at rest as to the Leeds Exhibition with whose directors I had already had some correspondence as to offers they had received of my works for exhibition. This I am most desirous to avoid – not because I doubt that the show will be a first-rate one, but because after all these years of non-exhibition, no plan of putting my work before the public could serve my turn or be otherwise than detrimental to me, except one which was entirely under my own control & which included a sufficiency of my work to afford a complete opportunity of judging it to those who have heard of and never seen it. Mr. Saunders most kindly entered into my views & promised me his valuable aid in carrying them out – that is in seeing that no works of mine are accepted at Leeds.

I lately had a most generous & flattering letter from Sir Noel Paton requesting me to exhibit this year at Edinburgh, & couched in such terms that I could not possibly have refused were it not that my recent correspondence with the Leeds Commissioners prevented me from appearing at Edinburgh without showing a marked slight to the Leeds scheme. Thus I was obliged to decline. Paton spoke of his recent ill health. I have not heard from him again but shall be anxious to know that he is better again.

Monday [16 March 1868]

My plan of going to Liverpool was certainly a failure, partly owing to continual pressure of work and general difficulty of getting uprooted under which I labour. Still I hope to come ere long both to Liverpool & to Leyland's new home at Speke Hall. I sent him a couple of small pictures lately but I think you had seen them in London.

What a dose of personal & family ailments poor Marshall has had! However he looks now to be plucking up quite steadily, & I doubt not ere long will be his own man again.

Your friends often speak of you here & wonder when they are to see you in London again. Till then & ever believe me dear Mr. Miller

Yours most sincerely
D G Rossetti

John Miller Esq

[1] R. C. Saunders, Superintendent of the English Galleries at Leeds.

68.51 TO CHARLES AUGUSTUS HOWELL
MS: Texas. Published: Cline 58. Date: CFM.

Monday [16 March 1868]

Dear good Owl

Don't be in a rage. Just today turns up my necessity of one of those wretched drawings you took away. Leyland writes that he is going to call tomorrow with a bloke named Hamilton who collects daubs & wants something of mine.[1] So as I'm going to do the Venus like the drawing[2] & he might order it I ought to have the drawing here. My messenger will take it now & bring it back to you on Wednesday if that will do, as I believe you only want it for Thursday.

Your affec:
Gabriel

[1] George Hamilton, WG's partner, bought the watercolour version of *Venus* (S.173R.2; see *RP* 302–03).
[2] FRL's chalk drawing of *Venus* (S.173A), which DGR kept until August (see **130**).

68.52 TO CHARLES AUGUSTUS HOWELL

MS: Texas. Published: Cline 65.

[18 March 1868]

Dear Owl

Let us gather up the ravelled threads of business. You see I mean to charge Leyland £10 for alteration to Borgia – that will be my sole profit. But I think also (as I have lost much time over it) that this wd be the right moment for me to receive the other £50 for the 5 drawings – i.e. if the transaction for them is Ellis's as well as yours.[1] What do you say? I shall be receiving immediately the tin from Leyland, & would be glad of a line from you on this point.

Ever yours
DG. R

P.S. If *not* Ellis's transaction of course no more about it.

[1] See **22** & **54** for FSE's involvement with CAH.

68.53 TO MURRAY MARKS

MS: Fitzwilliam. Published: *Marks* 59; DW 771. Date: P/M.

Thursday [19 March 1868]

Dear Marks

On taking up the Tibullus, I find it will be impracticable to do anything to any purpose to it till Mrs. Morris's sittings are over which will be before many days. Then it shall be my first job to follow.

Yours
D G Rossetti

68.54 TO CHARLES AUGUSTUS HOWELL

MS: Texas. Published: Cline.

Thursday [19 March 1868]
16 Cheyne Walk
Chelsea

Dear Howell

I'm infinitely sorry not to come tonight, & so is Topsy, but he is prevented coming & I was so late last night that I cannot face Brixton at 3 in the

Thursday [19 March 1868]

morning, & really without humbug know that my own inclination would not let me leave the owl-hutch earlier.

As to the £50 it strikes me it may really not be convenient to you not to hand it over to Ellis as his profit on the Lucrezia in the first instance, after which you could perhaps get it for me again in the course of the week. Otherwise he might be disappointed & the brilliant *coup* of getting him this profit might fail of its effect. I must trouble you for a line again on this point as I shall get the tin tomorrow I expect from Leyland, or look in if you can.

All you say is like the brick you are.

Your affec:
DGabriel R

68.55 TO CHARLES AUGUSTUS HOWELL
MS: Texas.

2nd letter
Thursday [19 March 1868]

Dear Howell

I remember now I had better come to you tomorrow (Friday) evening, as I want to see that piece of furniture,[1] so if you cannot be in, wd you let me know at once.

Your
Gabriel

[1] The "furniture," a chest, also referred to as a cabinet or drawers, was soon presented to DGR by the CAHs (see **58–61.1**). On 25 Apr 82, CAH wrote WMR a letter of condolence in which he asked to buy it, "unless you or Lucy wish to retain it" (AP). In *CWS*, it is described as "*a 3ft. 3in. Italian beautifully inlaid marquetrie chest of 3 long and 2 short drawers and extra shallow drawer in plinth, fitted with glass handles and escutcheons*" (Lot 98).

68.56 TO FREDERICK RICHARD LEYLAND
MS: LC. Published: Fennell 16.

20 March/1868
16 Cheyne Walk
Chelsea

My dear Leyland

Thanks for remittance – £157-10/- – in payment for Lucrezia Borgia & chalk drawing of La Pia.[1] I think you will not think it unreasonable if I charge you a "tenner" when I send *Borgia* home for the alteration you asked me to make; as the drawing is not yet finished & has taken me already longer than I anticipated when last writing you.

I got La Pia on the canvas yesterday & the head will come stunning.

Ever yours
DG Rossetti

[1] Surtees does not record FRL as owner of any of the 3 chalk drawings she identified (S.207A–C), but he certainly had one (see **130**).

68.56.1 TO CHARLES AUGUSTUS HOWELL

MS: Texas.

Friday [20 March 1868]
16 Cheyne Walk
Chelsea

Dear Owl

If quite done with at present & quite convenient you might bring the *Venus* drawing tomorrow (Saturday) when you come to dinner.[1] If not don't mind in the least.

Yours affec:
Gabriel

[1] By 27 Mar, DGR had "altered and partly repainted his Venus picture . . . the same with his Lady with a glass and background of white roses . . . and beautiful studies from Mrs. Morris and Miss Wilding" (*GPBD* 47).

68.57 TO CHARLES AUGUSTUS HOWELL

MS: Texas.

Sunday [c. 22 March 1868]

Dear Howell,

I want those 3 Janeys in your drawing room to be photographed.[1] Will you send them to Parsons, 95 Wigmore Street Portman Square,[2] or will it be more convenient to you if I send Sharp for them & let him take them on? I hope I shall not be inconveniencing you. I suppose they need only be away a day or two.

Your
DGR

[1] CAH had already forwarded them to FRL, who returned them at DGR's request (see **70**).
[2] John R. Parsons, art dealer & photographer, had earlier been a portrait & landscape

painter. DGR had previously used him as a photographer, as evidenced by the famous photographs taken by him of JM in the garden of 16CW in Jun 65.

68.58 TO CHARLES AUGUSTUS HOWELL
MS: Texas.

[before 24 March 1868]

Dear Howell

I thought we were to have the cabinet for £12. As it is, I had better say at once that I yield it to you. Indeed I dare say it would serve you more than myself. So if it suits you to take it, do so as soon as you like.

I am rejoiced to hear of your prospects as a stockbroker, & to look forward to a period when I shall never be in want of £10 nor you of £2-10/-.[1]

Your
Gabriel

P.S. Thanks for Brandy.

[1] A reference to CAH's expanding business interests. CAH was now acting as a broker for DGR & other artists, including FMB, FS, EBJ, & JMW. Moreover, he had also begun dabbling in art objects and was trying to establish himself as an interior designer (see 67.163).

68.59 TO FRANCES CATHERINE HOWELL
MS: Texas. Date: Unidentified endorsement.

Monday [23 March 1868]

16 Cheyne Walk
Chelsea

My dear Kitty

I am so glad you fancy the cabinet & shall be gladder still if you like it in its place.

I enclose what Charley sent for.

Your affectionate
Gabriel

68.60 TO CHARLES AUGUSTUS HOWELL

MS: Texas. Published: Cline 59.

Tuesday [24 March 1868]
16 Cheyne Walk
Chelsea

My dear Howell

Valpy has asked me to meet you Friday next at 7-30 to dinner. As you are going I accept, so take care you do go.

Many & many thanks for yielding me the cabinet which looks splendid. It has displaced an old foe of yours & Janey's – a black chest of drawers in the first floor bedroom.

It has arrived quite perfect except for one half of the ivory scutcheon on the upper keyhole. Surely this was all right when I saw it at your place – was it not? It has been looked for here in vain. Is there a chance that it might be found knocked off on your staircase or elsewhere? If not I must have one made.

Love to Kate whom I must inveigle to fix a sitting soon.

Your affec:
Gabriel

68.61 TO FRANCES CATHERINE HOWELL

MS: Texas. Published: Cline 60.

26 March/1868
16 Cheyne Walk
Chelsea

My dear Kate,

How shall I thank you for such a very delightful present as that lovely old chest? It is even unreasonably treasured by me, if something which is your gift as well as a beauty in itself can possibly be so. I had had, as I think I told you, a pang for some years at not having secured it long ago, and here after all you are the good fairy who enriches my house with it.

Charley promised me that he and you wd dine here next Wedy to meet the Morris's and Jones's. But since seeing him I have fatally remembered that that day was already engaged with me, so I am writing to Ned to fix either Thursday or Friday instead. I hope one of those days (whichever he may fix) may suit you also but if not must try & make a further change, as I want to secure all.

Affectionately yours
DGabriel R

P.S. I shall be seeing Charley tomorrow evening & he can then tell me about it.

68.61.1 TO CHARLES AUGUSTUS HOWELL
MS: Texas.

[26 March 1868]

My dear Owl

This is stunning news about the money that Top tells me.[1] Why didn't you come up to my room & tell me? So many thanks. We can talk about it when I meet you at Valpy's. Would you drop me one line to say if togs will be needed there. His letter gave me some idea it was to be only you & me, in which case we can be happy & dirty.

Top is enraged at my possession of the drawers.[2] You did not see the screen with peacock's eyes which is a triumph.[3]

Your affec:
Gabriel

[1] The reference may be to the money JR gave CAH to move to Fulham near the EBJs (*RP* 320).
[2] See **55n1**.
[3] Used in the background of *Monna Rosa* (S.198).

68.62 TO CHARLES AUGUSTUS HOWELL
MS: Texas. Published: Cline 62.

Sunday [29 March 1868]
16 Cheyne Walk
Chelsea

Dear Good Owl

The Tibullus goes to Marks tomorrow (Monday).

I find there will be 14 at table on Thursday. Suppose you were to come early & superintend arrangements! Of course I am engaging the man cook. I suppose it wd probably be wise to get another waiter besides Emma. What think you? If you come I will confide to you the fruit and flower department (how kind of me!) as with ladies I should like to get a nice little dessert. What do you say to a special bottle of wine or two which you might let me have on tick for drawings?

I hear by the bye that little Swinburne is considering himself neglected, and am almost inclined to ask him (making 15) but am rather afraid of results.[1]

Your affec:
D G R

---

[1] ACS' drunkenness frequently led to disruptive behaviour at social occasions (see 62.87&n3).

68.63 TO CHARLES AUGUSTUS HOWELL

MS: Texas.

Tuesday [31 March 1868]
16 Cheyne Walk
Chelsea

Dear Owl,

Mrs. Morris & I hope that Kate will give us the pleasure of her company during the day on Thursday, as she can so conveniently come down with you. So do not let her say no, as it would be too bad if your devotion cost her a solitary ride from Brixton in the evening, and there are Owls to remind her of you in absence, while you do the major domo. As ladies are coming, I mean to honour the occasion with togs![1]

Of course I will furnish the funds for all expenses beforehand. I forgot to say this necessary detail.

Your affec:
Gabriel

---

[1] GPB lists the guests at DGR's dinner party on 2 Apr: "Burne-Jones and wife, Wm. Morris and wife and her sister, C.A. Howell and wife, Madox Brown and 2 daughters, Charley Faulkner, Wm. Rossetti, Webb" (*GPBD* 47). FMB gave an account to GR on 9 Apr: "A grand dinner was given . . . in honour of the 'Topses', and we were all warned to appear in Togs. At the hour named, however, the host was still in dirty painting-coat . . . but he soon made himself smart. However, Morris, at the last moment, was despatched to Queen Square to forcibly bring back his partner, Faulkner, thirteen at table being otherwise the mishap. But Morris was scarce gone when it turned out that Rossetti had miscalculated, and we were thirteen without Morris, and so had, perforce, to wait till he returned" (*FMB* 238). See also previous letter & **61**.

68.64 TO EMILY TEBBS

MS: Texas. An envelope postmarked 4 Mar 69 is filed at Texas with this letter. JM, however, met Mrs. Tebbs, apparently for the first time, when she attended with DGR a séance at the Tebbs's house on 1 Apr 68. While the letter here is clearly dated "Tuesday," 4 Mar 69 was a Thursday.

Tuesday [31 March 1868]
16 Cheyne Walk
Chelsea

Dear Mrs. Tebbs

May I and another friend of yours take a great liberty and add one more to your séance tomorrow evening? The purposed additional student of necromancy is Mrs. Morris. She and Morris are staying here just now, and as Morris has to be away tomorrow evening, the lady would be glad to accompany me instead of remaining at home by herself. So, as there is hardly time for your answer, she and I will reckon on your kindly receiving us both.[1]

Ever yours truly
D G Rossetti

[1] WMR discussed the séance with DGR the following Monday: "He agrees with me that there was nothing in it which could reasonably be called convincing – unless possibly the mysterious light seen by Mrs. Morris as well as others" (*RP* 304). See also **72**.

68.64.1 TO CHARLES AUGUSTUS HOWELL

MS: Texas.

Wednesday [c. March 1868]
16 Cheyne Walk
Chelsea

Dear Owl

Here come more bulletins. I don't know if those rugs we spoke of were ever chosen, but if so, suppose I were to send for them tomorrow to embellish the crib.

Your
Gabriel

68.65 TO GEORGE PRICE BOYCE

MS: Berg.

Monday [March–April 1868]

My dear Boyce

Fanny has been looking at that house to let in the Kings Road, & thinks it would probably suit you. It has good garden. The landlady seems disposed to do any necessary repairs. Rent seems uncertain to the Lumpses between 115 & 150 but I suppose it is the former, & might be got for less.[1]

Your
D G R

---

[1] In Oct 68 GPB decided instead to build on Cheyne Row; he received the building agreement from PSW in Mar 69, moving into West House on 3 Mar 70 (*GPBD* 48–49, 51).

68.66 TO ALICE BOYD

MS: UBC.

Sunday [early to mid-1868?]

Dear Miss Boyd

Could you and Scotus come up tomorrow (Monday) evening at 8-30 for a "wubber"?* It would be nice if you could. I'll hope to see Mrs. W.B. also if she cares to come, only I know she hates cards.

Ever yours
D G Rossetti

---

* "wubber": rubber of whist.

68.67 TO CHARLES AUGUSTUS HOWELL

MS: Texas.

Friday night [3 April 1868]

Dear Howell

Leyland came after all today & I have spent the evening with him, but as he brought another bloke I have not been able to speak to him on that matter. I will write about it as soon as he sends me the tin for the drawings. He had been down to you again, & was extremely vexed to have missed you both there & here.

Your
Gabriel

68.68 TO CHARLES AUGUSTUS HOWELL

MS: Texas. Published: Cline 61.

Sunday [5 April 1868]

My dear Howell

I made an appointment for yesterday with Graham to show him the Tibullus up to 3-30. He came later & I was gone out with Leyland, but Dunn showed it him & tells me he appeared pleased.[1] He is coming again, – perhaps it may be on Tuesday.

On seeing the drawing again I find it not disgraceful but so inferior to the original (for which I only had 225 gs) that I shd hesitate to ask more than 250 gs for it. Do you like to take this price if Graham is willing? *Let me know at once without fail.* You would thus have a profit of £62-10/-. I would of course gladly ask the 300 to serve you, but am afraid of frightening Graham.[2]

Your
Gabriel

[1] WG's visit to view the picture, despite HTD's showing, did not produce a sale.
[2] The *Tibullus* WG saw was perhaps the "bad copy" DGR refers to in 67.42; he had received £235 for the watercolour replica (S.62R.1) done for Craven in 1867. The original watercolour belonged to FC (S.62), and CFM also had a replica of the 1867 watercolour done in 1868 (S.62R.2). See **62**; Surtees does not mention Marks's version.

68.69 TO CHARLES AUGUSTUS HOWELL

MS: Texas.

Tuesday [c. 7 April 1868]

Dear Howell

I expect to see you tomorrow & have written to Leyland to be here & go round with me to Brixton.

Your
Gabriel

68.70 TO FREDERICK RICHARD LEYLAND

MS: LC. Published: Fennell 17.

11th April 1868
16 Cheyne Walk
Chelsea

My dear Leyland,

I must write you a good piece of news, for does it not come through you in the first instance? Mr. Graham, whom you brought here, has asked me to paint him the "Dante's Dream" subject on a good scale – the design of which you have seen photographed over my mantelpiece.[1] He seems a very fine fellow the more one knows of him, & shows the kindest goodwill towards me & my doings.

By the bye, I am afraid I am going to bore you. I meant, before those chalk drawings went to you, to have had the 3 of Mrs. Morris photographed, and much wish to do so as otherwise I should not have liked to part with them. With many preoccupations, I inadvertently let Howell send them away before this was done. Would you mind letting me have them again for the purpose? I would gladly pay carriage, & you should be no loser, as now the lady is sitting to me, I would retouch the full-face one from her, as it was never quite finished. This whenever convenient to you.

I am trusting to see you again in a fortnight. If then you still fancy to have those rugs you saw here (as I think you seemed rather inclined to do) I have come to the conclusion that it will be wiser in me not to keep *them* but the money instead.

Ever yours
D.G. Rossetti

[1] For *Dante's Dream*, see 73.248, 251, & 256.

68.71 TO CHARLES AUGUSTUS HOWELL

MS: Texas.

Friday [17 April 1868]
16 Cheyne Walk
Chelsea

Dear Owl

More letter writing. Leyland is sending up his Janeys. How about Valpy's.[1] Could we get it that they might all go together to the photographer's?

Ever yours
Gabriel

P.S. Couldn't you persuade Kitty to dine here with you tomorrow? Let me know at once & I'll get nice things.

[1] See **57**. "Valpy's" may have included *Aurea Catena* (S.209).

68.72 TO EMILY TEBBS
MS: Texas.

20th April 1868
16 Cheyne Walk
Chelsea

My dear Mrs. Tebbs

Pray pardon my negligence in not acknowledging your kind note before, but work I suppose is answerable. I shall be very glad to bogify or be bogified again in your good company, as will also Mrs. Morris who is again staying here. Our gravity shall this time be worthy of the grave itself.

With kind remembrances and in the hope that we may be thought "worth a rap" at least on Friday night,[1]

I am yours sincerely
DG Rossetti

---

1 See **64** for the first séance at the HVTs attended by DGR & JM.

68.72.1 TO JOHN MARSHALL
MS: Exeter.

20th April 1868
16 Cheyne Walk
Chelsea

My dear Marshall

Brown told me that you would like an introduction to Leighton which I accordingly enclose. You will find him a very good fellow. However, Howell, to whom I was mentioning the matter last night, says that if you prefer it, he will keep any appointment you may make for the purpose of his accompanying you to Leighton's (with whom he is intimate) and introducing you personally. So if you wish this, will you write him a line.

The other day I remembered & forgot again, all the time you were here, that I wished to ask you about your candidateship. I wish you all luck, or rather I wish the Academy the luck to get you.[1]

Ever yours
D. G. Rossetti

P.S. I never can remember whether people are RA's or A R A's, so have taken the safe course on Leighton's envelope.
P.S. Holland Park Road is up the turning by Phillimore Place which leads to Little Holland House.

---

1 Marshall was finally appointed professor of anatomy at the R.A. in 1873.

68.73 TO JAMES LEATHART

MS: UBC (LP).

> 22 April 1868
> 16 Cheyne Walk
> Chelsea

My dear Leathart,

I believe you will find that my own view as to the sum due from me to you is correct. At least a note made by me in a list of commissions (which note however must have been made some time after the payments) says £250.[1]

Mr. Stevenson has 2 watercolour reductions from late oil pictures of mine. I do not know whether he has any "collection."

As regards Albert Moore, there can be no doubt that he possesses certain gifts of drawing and of design (in its artistic relation) in an admirable degree. I have not seen anything of his done lately.

> Very truly yours
> D G Rossetti

Jas. Leathart Esq

[1] DGR eventually paid the money back, borrowing from WBS to do so (WBS:AB [Nov 69], AP).

68.74 TO WILLIAM MICHAEL ROSSETTI

MS: Brotherton. Published: *FL* 193; DW 773.

> [28 April 1868]
> 16 Cheyne Walk
> Chelsea

Dear W

Will you address & post this at once.[1] Sandys's picture of Medea has been turned out of the RA – a most disgraceful affair. I have written also to Burnell Payne.[2] Can *you* do anything in the way of denunciation?[3]

> Your
> Gabriel

[1] Probably the unlocated letter to FGS mentioned by WMR in **n3**.
[2] John Burnell Payne (1838–69), eldest son of the educator Joseph Payne, brother of Joseph Frank Payne, physician of St. Thomas's Hospital; both brothers frequented the circle of George Eliot & G. H. Lewes. A graduate of University College, London, & Downing

College, Cambridge, he was recommended by a tutor at Cambridge as possessing "great intelligence and an unusual amount of information." For an account of Payne, see Richard Aldrich, *School and Society in Victorian Britain: Joseph Payne and the New World of Education* (New York, Garland, 1995): 81–86. While an assistant master at Wellington College, he was an unsuccessful candidate for the post of Professor of English Literature and History at Owen's College, Manchester in 1866. In Oct 67 he became curate of Christ Church, Marylebone, but by 1869 he had "from scruples of conscience, given up the clerical profession" (G. S. Haight, ed., *The George Eliot Letters* 5 [1955]: 12). During 1866–69 he published articles and reviews in *Macmillan's Magazine, Fortnightly Review*, and other periodicals. WMR mildly disparaged his 2-part article, "Pre-Raphaelite Art and Poetry," in *London Student* (see *PRISM* 76.02, & *Preface* 28), but also praised him as "a writer on art, of keen perception and uncommon promise" (*FL* 193). For DGR's response to his death, see 69.145.

3 WMR entered in his diary on 28 Apr: "Sandys called, wishing to get as much publicity as possible given to the affair of his picture and the R.A. Gabriel is writing to Payne and Stephens: I wrote to Hamerton, and promised to say something in my pamphlet, though I would rather keep it free from any such controversies" (*RP* 306). True to his word, in his notice of FS' head of George Critchett (735) in *Notes on the R.A. Exhibition*, WMR spent the best part of a page reflecting on the RA's hanging policies as indicated by the rejection of *Medea* (25). Betty Elzea suggests that the principal reason for the rejection, though the picture was at first accepted, was "the copulating frogs which would have been an unacceptable image to Victorian spectators" (*Sandys* 186n10). WMR recorded a 2nd visit from FS on 1 May: "He says that several critics have called to see his picture – Tom Taylor, Payne, etc; among them the critic of *The Morning Post*, who asked to be furnished with some details that he could introduce into his review. Sandys, not liking to do this himself, asked my aid; and I wrote off something which may perhaps appear as it stands, or be used as material" (*RP* 307).

68.75 TO JENNY AND MAY MORRIS

MS: BL. Published: Bryson 1–2.

Thursday [30 April 1868]
16 Cheyne Walk
Chelsea

Dear Jenny and May

Here come 2 little dormice to live with you.¹ I know you will take great care of them and always give them everything they are fond of – that is, nuts apples and hard biscuit. If you love them very much I dare say they will get much bigger and fatter and remind you of Papa and me.

Your affectionate
D G Rossetti

1 Two years later DGR sent dormice to Barbara Bodichon with similar instructions (70.83).

68.75.1 TO GEORGE JAMES HOWARD

MS: Castle Howard Archives.

Saturday 2nd May 1868
16 Cheyne Walk
Chelsea

My dear Howard

Gambart tells me that Baron Leys will do me the great honour of coming here with him tomorrow.[1] As he will certainly have seen enough that once of such poor stuff as there is here, I have no hope of seeing him with you on Monday; but should he not after all come before then, I need hardly say that I will then hope to enjoy in your company the long desired pleasure of seeing him, and such advantage as ought to result from the salutary sense of humility his presence will occasion.

Ever yours
D G Rossetti

[1] For Baron Leys, whose works were being shown in EG's gallery, see 69.144n1. For Howard, see 67.55.

68.76 TO CHARLES AUGUSTUS HOWELL

MS: Texas.

Monday [c. 4 May 1868]

Dear Howell

Here you see is another skeleton in the house.

I suppose as Sandys appears too, that the things are probably some of Rose's again, & that mine is most likely the Bogie drawing.[1] In that case I should be very glad to give as much as 60 for it myself & think that you might safely run it up if so inclined on your own acct even to 80. I would do something to it to give more richness to the colour & then it would be a thoroughly good thing. However if you bought it & I worked on it I should (when sold to advantage) have to charge a trifle for my labour, as the fortnight lost on the Lucrezia will be no joke though all my own doing & well worth while for once.

I find my banker's acct running low, so when you *can* quite conveniently pay me for the 3 chalks[2] (£80) you will earn the gratitude of

Your own
Gabriel

[1] The "Bogie drawing" was JAR's copy of *How They Met Themselves* (S.118R.1); however, the

picture on sale was *Fiammetta* (see **84**, **91**, **93**, & **96**), which EG owned by 1870.

2   If these are Valpy's drawings, they are probably *Aurea Catena* (S.209) & 2 studies for *La Pia* (S.207C & D). However, since the £100 deal for 5 pictures for LRV was still not completed, they may be the chalk drawings sent to FRL (see **125**, **126**, **129**, & **130**).

68.77 TO JANE MORRIS

MS: BL. Published: Bryson 3.

5th May 1868
16 Cheyne Walk
Chelsea

My dear Janey

About the blue silk dress it occurs to me to say that I think the sleeves should be as full at the top as is consistent with simplicity of outline, and perhaps would gain by being lined with some soft material, but of this you will be the best judge.¹ The piece of gold embroidery in front might (if you have time to make it) be some-thing like this,

unless as is very possible a better idea strikes you. However it is a great pity that the last portrait (which I fancy is the one you will choose) is in such a position that both this & the embroidery which you propose to put at the back will be hidden. In the other front view portrait these will show to great advantage. Every one seems to like the last picture of you the best, including Leys who was here the other day and recognized it at once. I am most desirous to get to it again, & make no doubt of being quite ready by the time you told me you expect to be in town again, as the *Venus* gets on rapidly and I hope will soon leave me.²

I am very glad little Jenny and May liked the dormice. When I chose them they both seemed all right, and I hope the "downy cove" who sells them did not substitute an invalid. I fancied you had left London before, or should probably have brought them down myself.

What do you think? Yesterday the stray dormouse was caught at last. I had heard a scratching constantly in the room for a day or two, but never guessed what it was or thought of looking in the trap till yesterday afternoon when I found the poor little chap in it almost dead, hardly thicker than his tail and with his eyes nearly shut, but still gnawing at the wires. His bones were almost through his back and his hair had got stuck together in little spikes which made him look like a porcupine. At first he was almost too exhausted to eat, famished as he was, but is now coming round again.

I hope Leyton will agree with you as well as Chelsea and trust to show you some improvements in the garden when you come here again. Meanwhile please give my love to Morris and believe me

Yours affectionately
D Gabriel R

P.S. I hope you will wear the dress to take away the stiffness.

---

[1] JM wore this dress at sittings for several pictures of this period, e.g., S.213 & 372 (see *RP* 327). DGR refers to the dress again in **79**, **103**, & 70.45.1.
[2] Watercolour replica (S.173F) for WG of *Venus Verticordia* (begun in 1864).

68.78 TO GEORGE AUGUSTUS SALA

MS: Princeton.

5th May 1868
16 Cheyne Walk
Chelsea

My dear Sala

Thanks for the "Young Augustus" which is a beautiful thing, and certainly the resemblance you speak of is very striking. Thanks also for the precious promise of the Michael Angelo, of which however I am almost ashamed to rob you, much as I shall value it.[1]

I find that Sandys has to be at Hastings on Friday & Saturday. May I therefore hope to see you to dinner Tuesday next (this day week) at 7? – as it would be a pity not to have him. Come an hour or so earlier if you can and smoke a pipe in the garden. Whistler is coming also.[2]

I am delighted to think that you will yet be able to speak another good word for Sandys' good picture which has been so disgracefully treated. On the whole I never heard of so bad a case of rejection.[3]

Of course "No dress" on Tuesday, – though I fear our cartes de visite would hardly gain by a complete application of the phrase so much as certain ones which have been glorified in your sketch-books.

Ever yours truly
DG Rossetti

George A Sala Esq

---

[1] The work promised has not been identified.

² DGR's party on the 12th was held in a tent set up in the garden of 16CW (see *RP* 308, & **79**).

³ For the rejection of FS' *Medea* by the RA, see **74n3**. In an undated letter in the Rylands, Sala:FS: "If you look at the *Telegraph* of today you will find that I have laid the foundations for some remarks on 'Medea.' It was 6 o'clock when I got away from the private view and midnight [before] I had finished my task and I deem that it would have been cruelly unjust to your picture to despatch it in a few hasty lines when I found that I was tired and fagged out."

68.79 TO JANE MORRIS

MS: BL. Published: Bryson 4.

7th May 1868
16 Cheyne Walk
Chelsea

My dear Janey

The silk is just the thing, and the idea delightful. I re-enclose the pattern in case you should need it. I suppose, in order to be thoroughly useful, it ought to be as much as 20 inches square, in which case it could be slipped over one of my sofa cushions but only one side of the cushion-case need be embroidered. Between this and the dress I shall be giving you an awful lot of work.

On reading your letter I took out the little mouse to report on his condition. He is wonderfully improved & is getting quite plumped out and sleek again – only a place he had worn bare on his nose by gnawing at the trap does not fill up yet.[1]

Will you tell Morris that I have not got any Earthly Paradise whatever at present,[2] though I understand one is being offered to a lethargic world no further from Chelsea than Covent Garden. Meanwhile I have attempted some approach to a private Eden by sticking up a big tent in my garden. Would you also tell the Bard & P.T.[3] (I will not indulge him with his favourite title in full) that I think the little chimney glass and shelf I am to have had better be in ebony if not a monstrous addition to expense.

Affectionately yours
D Gabriel R

[1] See **77**.
[2] Volume 1 of *The Earthly Paradise* was issued in April; WM soon remedied the neglect by sending DGR a large-paper copy (see **100n2**).
[3] DGR's full title for WM, "The Bard and Petty Tradesman," puns on his role as poet & proprietor of The Firm (see **100n4**).

68.80 TO CHARLES AUGUSTUS HOWELL

MS: Texas.

Friday [8 May 1868]
16 Cheyne Walk
Chelsea

My dear Howell

Sala is going to dine here on Tuesday at 7. I wish you would come, and be as much earlier as you can. Sandys & Whistler are coming.

Your affec
Gabriel

68.81 TO JAMES ANDERSON ROSE

MS: LC. Excerpt: Kashnor 200. Date: JAR.

Saturday [9 May 1868]
16 Cheyne Walk
Chelsea

My dear Rose

Here is an agreement for a small house I am taking, *not* for my own use. Would you let me know whether you think it all right, before I sign it. Ought not the clause saying that a delay for 21 days in a quarterly payment involves my expulsion to be objected to? And is there any thing else objectionable? I ought to be sending the agreement in signed on Monday.[1]

Ever yours
DG Rossetti

---

[1] DGR leased a house in Hemus Terrace for FC (Kashnor 200–02); see also **85, 86, 88,** & **109**. He was still preoccupied with whether he should buy a house for her during his 1872 breakdown (see 72.45&n1 & 51), when he told her that she was "the only person whom it is my duty to provide for, and you may be sure I should do my utmost as long as there was a breath in my body or a penny in my purse" (72.62).

Monday [11 May 1868]

68.82 TO GEORGE PRICE BOYCE
MS: University College.

Monday [11 May 1868]
16 Cheyne Walk
Chelsea

My dear Boyce

Is it too late in the day to ask you to dinner tomorrow (Tuesday) at 7. I hope to secure you yet. A few fellows are coming – all known to you I think except perhaps Sala.[1]

Your affec:
D Gabriel R

1 GPB doesn't record his attendance at this party, but he did dine at 16CW with DGR on 1 Jun, with WMR, the WMs, PSW, EBJ, CAH, & WA: "Before and after dinner we lounged in tent in garden" (*GPBD* 48).

68.83 TO FRANCES CATHERINE HOWELL
MS: Texas.

Monday [11 May 1868]
16 Cheyne Walk
Chelsea

My dear Kitty

Many sincere thanks for so kindly remembering me. The frame has arrived safely. No doubt you are now in the full whirl & worry of moving, so it was all the kinder of you to think of me.[1]

Ever affectionately yours
D Gabriel R

1 The CAHs were moving to Northend Grove, Northend, Fulham (see also **61.1**).

68.84 TO CHARLES AUGUSTUS HOWELL
MS: Texas. Date: CFM.

Monday [c. 11 May 1868]

Dear Howell

I forget what day that Fiammetta is to be sold – but I suppose we shd go to £50 for it. Don't fail to come tomorrow as early as you can.

Yrs
Gabriel

68.85 TO JOHN PERRY
MS: UBC.

Monday [11 May 1868]
16 Cheyne Walk
Chelsea

Dear Sir,

My solicitor whose letter I enclose has made some changes (in which I can see no particular real alteration) in your draft. Would you kindly show it to Mrs. Evans in order that if agreeable to her it may be returned to my solicitor as soon as possible & fairly copied by him for signature. You will see that the only clause which raised a doubt in me is untouched by him.[1]

Very truly yours
D G Rossetti

– Perry Esq.

[1] See **81n1** & the following letter.

68.86 TO JAMES ANDERSON ROSE
MS: LC. Excerpt: Kashnor 201.

12 May 1868
16 Cheyne Walk
Chelsea

My dear Rose

I have shown this to the agent who says all right. Will you kindly let me have the copies in the course of tomorrow (Wednesday) as everything is waiting – furniture &c. – & I want to get into the house at once. I am very sorry you could not come to dinner today.

Ever yours
D G Rossetti

P.S. The place is *Hemus* (not Haus) Terrace.

68.87 TO FRANCES MARY LAVINIA ROSSETTI

MS: UBC. Excerpt: *FL* 193–94; Knight, *DGR* 102. Published: DW 775.

12 May 1868
16 Cheyne Walk
Chelsea

My dearest Mother

The reminder of the solemn fact that I am a man of forty now could hardly come agreeably from any one but yourself. But considering that the chief blessing of my forty good and bad years has been that not one of them has taken you from me, it is the best of all things to have the same dear love & good wishes still coming to me today from your dear hand at a distance as they would have done from your dear mouth had we seen each other. This we shall again soon I trust.

I meant to have given you for your last dear birthday a sideboard which I have got, but some doing up which it needed was not finished in time nor indeed is yet quite done. I hope it may be of use to you though rather large, but it is a really beautiful thing. It has a great plate glass back with beautiful carved pillars and some convenient drawers and receptacles. I forget the exact arrangement but this gives some notion of it.

It strikes me the best place for it would be against the folding doors either in the drawing or dining room. The pillars are carved in the "Chippendale" style and are really beautiful.

Will you give my love to Christina. I am writing to Uncle Henry with this. I hope you are benefiting by the change and am ever

Your most affectionate son
D Gabriel R

P.S. I am really ashamed to send you such a tattooed letter.[1] But after elaborately writing all the Postscripts I have now erased, I suddenly remembered that the cabinet-maker's note must refer to a much smaller thing he has in hand for me. Yours however will not be long delayed.

DG. R.

P.P.S. Louisa Parke is in town with Mrs. Leyland. I saw her the other day.

1. A long P.S. on the 4th page and a shorter P.P.S. on the first page have both been crossed out by DGR.

68.88 TO JOHN PERRY
MS: Kansas.

Thursday/14th May/1868
16 Cheyne Walk
Chelsea

Dear Sir,
   I send you the enclosed 2 copies of the agreement which I am quite ready to sign at once – only am not aware whether it may be necessary to do so in your presence as a witness. Will you kindly let me know about this. I also return the original draft.

Yours truly
D G Rossetti

– Perry Esq.
P.S. It is desirable for me to obtain possession, as furniture is waiting to go in as soon as possible.

68.89 TO CHARLES AUGUSTUS HOWELL
MS: Texas.

Friday [15 May 1868]

Dear Howell
   You spoke of tin next week. Would it be *absolutely* convenient to let me have £50 on Tuesday?[1] If not say so frankly as I can ask Leyland then for the tin for the large chalk drawing, only don't want to write if possible till I settle about going down there.
   I'm getting the Venus drawing all right.[2]
   Thanks for the urn sketch.

Your
Gabriel

1. DGR refers to this £50 again in **91** & **93**. See **96** for his receipt of the money.
2. A watercolour version (S.173R.2) of *Venus Verticordia*, which was sold to Hamilton on 17 Mar for £300 (see *RP* 303 & **51**). During this period, DGR was working on both FRL's chalk *Venus* (S.173A; see **125** & **130**) and the original oil commissioned by Mitchell (S.173), which WMR refers to as near completion on 29 May (*RP* 308) but which was not sent to Mitchell until September (Surtees 99). On 17 Mar, he also sold a watercolour replica (S. 173R.2) to Hamilton, also completed in 1868, which Surtees suggests was bought for WG (see **51**).

68.90A GEORGE AUGUSTUS SALA TO DANTE GABRIEL ROSSETTI

MS: LC.

Thursday [14 May 1868]¹

My dear Rossetti

In the hope of finding Sandys at his studio (as I *must* see his Medea² again and my last chance of noticing it fully in the D[*aily*]. T[*elegraph*]. is slipping away) I am going to call at Leicester Square at 5. p.m. on *Saturday*; and, if he has no better engagement will bring him on to Putney. If *you* have no better engagement, come you on to P. at 6.30 for 7. p.m. There will be cold meats and colder drinks, and although I have no tent the shining Thames is below the window, into which we can plunge if the temperature grows intolerable. I don't know Swinburne's address but would you mind asking him to excuse short notice and come on to Putney as afore said. No dress and no ceremony. Let him bring Menken as Mazeppa³ if he will and we will all revert to "first principles" and, joining hands recite "La Soeur de la Reine"⁴ in sounding strophe and antistrophe. Drop me a line – I hope, to say "yes."

G. A. S.

---

1. The date assigned this letter is a midpoint. The twin references to the "tent" and to "Menken as Mazeppa," place the letter after 12 May, when Sala, FS, ACS, JMW, & others dined at 16CW, where WMR records that "a large tent [had] been set up in the garden" (*RP* 308; see also **78**), and before 30 May, Adah Menken's (see **n3**) last performance of her revival of *Mazeppa*, which opened on the 11th, at Astley's Theatre. By mid-Jun, she had left England to return, via Le Havre, to Paris, where she died on 10 Aug. On 28 Jul, ACS sent the letter – a "curious little double autograph" – to George Powell for his collection (Lang 1: 269).
2. Sala's urgent concern to notice *Medea* also argues for a date within the range suggested in **n1**. See also **78**.
3. Adah Isaacs Menken (?1835–1868), American-born actress, infamous for her portrayal of the female Mazeppa in tights – hence the title of Bernard Falk's biography, *The Naked Lady* (Hutchinson, 1934) – her bohemian life style, her staged liaisons with Dumas *Père* & ACS, and her multiple marriages. "The Menken," as she was known, achieved in life after death an almost mythical status. Her relationship with ACS, frozen in 2 photographs, was the subject of widespread gossip in 1868. A persistent legend maintains that DGR & Sir Richard Burton encouraged Menken to seduce ACS as a kind of anodyne for his drunkenness. While ACS encouraged the belief that she was his mistress, that role is contested by Julian Osgood Fields ("Sigma"), who had it from Adah's own testimony that "these camera-caresses were really all that passed between them" (*Things I Shouldn't Tell* [Eveleigh Nash & Grayson, 1924]: 103). The extent of contemporary quidnuncery is humorously suggested in WMR's account of the affair to JLT on 15 Mar: "Swinburne had a liaison with her. I am told by A, who had it from B, who has it from C, who has it from Swinburne's landlady" (Peattie 140). Not all was fabrication, however: on 26 Jan, ACS promised to send George Powell a photograph of "my present possessor – known to Britannia as Miss Menken, to me as Dolores (her real Christian name) – and myself taken

together" (Lang 1: 248). In late March, commencing with a piece in the *Pall Mall Gazette* on the photograph, described as "after Dumas" and "a freer adaptation of a French scandal," the affair became a *cause célèbre* in the literary journals, replete with parodies of "Dolores" (which Menken was mistakenly said to have inspired) and prognostications of future classics such as "Adalanta in California" (Allen Lesser, *Enchanting Rebel* [New York: Beechhurst, 1947]: 229). EBJ, reputedly at the urging of DGR, executed a series of 11 cartoon sketches parodying the affair, which he gave to ACS (now in BL, Ashley 3428) entitled *Ye treue and Pitifulle Histories of ye Poet and ye Ancient Dame*. Number 4, which may accurately epitomize the nature of the relationship, is the only one that has been reproduced: "Ye Poet claspeth ye hand of ye ancient dame, sweareth evermore to regard her as a sister and inviteth her to his abode" (Falk, 230). Nor was all jest: after her death, ACS wrote to George Powell on 26 Aug: "I am sure you were sorry on my account to hear of the death of my poor dear Menken – it was a great shock to me and a real grief – I was ill for some days. She was most lovable as a friend as well as a mistress" (Lang 1: 272).

Poetry, it has often been alleged, was the bond between them, and ACS did apparently make minor revisions to the proofs of some of the poems in her posthumously published *Infelicia* (1868), which, though dedicated to Dickens and adorned with a reproduction of a portmanteau letter from him accepting her dedication and praising her verse, also has an unacknowledged 4-line epigraph from ACS' "Dolores." ACS' public repudiation in 1883 of the authorship of "Dolorida" (Lang 5: 1256) is regarded by both Falk & Lesser as an act of perfidy, unworthy of the affection that had once existed between them. Cecil Lang in his elegantly succinct note on Menken (1: 232n1) regards her poetry as "appalling," and most modern readers of her pastiches of Whitman & Poe will not seriously disagree. DGR, on the other hand, found her book "remarkable" and urged WMR to include her in his volume on American poets in the Moxon's Popular Poets series. He even offered to make the selections and to write a short introductory notice on them (71.86), subsequently begging off when he failed to turn up his copy of the book (71.91). WMR did, however, include 2 of the poems he recommended (see 71.91 & 98n1).

4 ACS' burlesque drama, commenced around 1861, about Queen Victoria's twin sister who, kidnapped at birth as a possible rival for the throne, becomes a common prostitute. When discovered and informed of her claims, she confronts the Queen, who swoons. Caught up in political machinations, she is later denounced as an imposter. In the end, the victim of unrequited love for Lord John Russell, she charcoals herself to death (paraphrase of ACS' own description – see Lang 1: 27). Though never completed – the fragmentary text was first published by Lang in *New Writings by Swinburne* (Syracuse: Syracuse UP, 1964): 103–18) – "La soeur de la Reine" was a favourite among ACS' friends; it figures in several retrospective contemporary accounts summarized by Lang in his commentary (225–31).

68.90 TO ALGERNON CHARLES SWINBURNE

MS: LC. Written at the bottom of **90A**.

[15 May 1868]

Dear Swinburne
    This from Sala. I am sorry I can't go but have to dine at Leyland's.

DGR

68.91 TO CHARLES AUGUSTUS HOWELL

MS: Texas. Published: Cline 72.

16 May [1868]
16 Cheyne Walk
Chelsea

My dear Howell

I was telling you that I have a bill of £50 to pay on Thursday the 21st. Could you let me have that amount by then on acct of the chalk drawings as my tether is almost run out at the bank? If impracticable please let me know *at once*.

Can you tell me what happened about the Fiammetta? I have heard something from Dunn about the result of your enforced sleep walking the other night. I suppose you are beginning to settle.

That Venus has given me more botheration and kept me off your chalk drawings as yet but you shall have them in a day or two now I trust.[1] I can *not* get the frame for Graham's 3 Roses out of Williams. Did you stir him up? If I had it I could send that in.

I shall be painting the Medusa after all if I don't die first, as Leyland has commissioned it for 1500 gs like a brick![2]

Love to Kate and yourself from

Your affec:
Gabriel

[1] See **89**.
[2] *Aspecta Medusa* (S.183). "The commission failed somehow, and the picture was never painted" (*RP* 308).

68.92 TO ALGERNON CHARLES SWINBURNE

MS: BL. Published: DW 774. The 16CW monogram has been cut from the MS.

[18 May 1868]

My dear Swinburne

I have just heard from William that you are describing in your pamphlet my *Lilith* & *Palmifera*. It is jolly beyond measure to be included in what you write if still possible at this date to give reference to my work [of] leading importance in respect of other unexhibited things described. I know your affectionate enthusiasm and the beauty which will be in every word you write; but should like greatly to have had the opportunity of looking at my work with you at this particular moment, since much that is necessary to the scheme of the Palmifera (for instance) is not yet included. There is also the Beata Beatrix (which you have seen) the La Pia, (which I have not yet shown you but which I trust to make my best single figure picture on hand) and the design of "Aspecta Medusa" which I shall shortly commence painting. It would be important to me at this moment that the above 3 should not be left without some mention if possible.[1] Would it be practicable for you to come to dinner today, or indeed at any time in the afternoon after receipt of this?

Your affec:
D Gabriel R

[1] With what justification it is difficult to imagine, ACS devoted the final 3rd of his section in his and WMR's *Notes on the Royal Academy Exhibition, 1868*, Part I. by Wm. Michael Rossetti, Part II. by Algernon C. Swinburne (Hotten, 1868), to a eulogistic discussion of works by DGR, who, of course, never exhibited at the RA, and seldom elsewhere. In addition to the pictures mentioned by DGR, ACS also expounded on *Venus Verticordia* (S.173), then undergoing major revision. DGR's sonnets accompanying *Venus Verticordia*, *Sibylla Palmifera* (S.193), and *Lady Lilith* (S.206) – the last 2 included in *HL* 77–78 as "Soul's Beauty" & "Body's Beauty" – were also first published in ACS' article.

68.93 TO CHARLES AUGUSTUS HOWELL
MS: Texas.

[18 May 1868]

Dear Howell

Couldn't talk business because of the Greeks. What answer as to tin, & as to Fiammetta?

Your
Gabriel

68.94 TO JAMES ANDERSON ROSE
MS: LC. Excerpt: Kashnor 199. Date: JAR.

Tuesday [19 May 1868]
16 Cheyne Walk
Chelsea

My dear Rose

Here is a summons from a rascal who has polished a clock-case very badly for me & done other things & charged exorbitantly. I am willing to pay his claim but want the thing set right first. The upper part has been varnished instead of polished and a circular moulding which is in the centre of the door has been gilded instead of being restored as originally – that is, blacked & polished. Would you kindly give me a reply as to whether the fellow's claim cannot be successfully resisted until this is set right as per agreement.[1] I could *not* attend at the court myself.

Very truly yours
D G Rossetti

N.B. Please kindly let me know at once as you see it draws near.

[1] The clock in question may be the one DGR intended for his mother (see 66.160 & 162).

68.95 TO MURRAY MARKS
MS: Fitzwilliam. Date: P/M.

Tuesday [19 May 1868]
16 Cheyne Walk
Chelsea

My dear Marks
 I wish you would send me that Lanthorn for the tent.

Yours ever
DG Rossetti

P.S. I am much wanting a Chinese gong on stand. Could you get me one at once, or shall I order it of Hewett?

68.96 TO CHARLES AUGUSTUS HOWELL
MS: Texas. Published: Cline 73. Date: CFM.

Tuesday [19 May 1868]
16 Cheyne Walk
Chelsea

My dear Howell
 Thanks for cheque £50.[1]
 As you say nothing of Fiammetta I suppose nothing was done. I am sorry

for this or in case you could not see about it I wish you would have said so as I would then myself have attended to it. It is important at present that my things should not go badly in sale rooms as it wd discourage those from whom I have commissions.²

Your note reaches just as I have finished the Janey drawing (La Pia) & made it such that it certainly ought to be worth 40 or even 50 gs.³ On looking at the Andromeda I really do not see my way to do any more to it as it does not bear a background.⁴ If leaving this as it is leaves our bargain incomplete I will include something else besides. As to the Venus I hardly know what to do to that either on reconsidering it.⁵ It all seems in good tone. If you keep this I suppose there can be no hurry about it, I being just now much pressed.

To put great things after small – poor Taylor is dying. I saw him last night.⁶

Ever yours
D G R

---

1. CAH's cancelled cheque of this date is at Texas (Cline 73n1).
2. *Fiammetta* (S.192) was finished and for sale "cheap," as DGR told GPB, for 80 guineas by 4 Dec 66 (66.183); he had offered it to EG with another work for £140 on 1 Jan 67 (67.1), and EG may have put it up for sale (see **84**).
3. Either S.207A or B.
4. One of the studies for *Aspecta Medusa* (perhaps S.183D). The bargain referred to is presumably the one for the 5 drawings mentioned in several previous letters.
5. *Venus Verticordia* (S.173) was 4 years in the painting; commissioned by John Mitchell of Bradford in 1863–64, it was finally completed and sent to its owner in Sep. One of the chalk versions (S.173A) was sent to FRL at Speke Hall in Aug (see **125**).
6. In August DGR found Warrington Taylor "comparatively speaking and for the time being, well," though in anticipation of his death he had months before ordered his coffin specifying "no nails" (*RP* 325). Beginning in 1865, Taylor was the manager & accountant for The Firm; he died of consumption in early 1870.

68.97 TO CHARLES AUGUSTUS HOWELL

MS: Texas.

Wednesday [20 May 1868]

My dear Howell

About that clock, the lying scoundrel will have it that the wooden balls now at the top are the original ones, whereas I am convinced there were metal ones at the 2 sides, & the middle one being wanting he has made the 3 of wood to save trouble. I wish you wd make me a sketch of the balls at the top of your clock & tell me whether they are made of metal as I believe.[1]

Ever your
D G R

[1] See **94**.

68.98 TO AGLAIA CORONIO[1]

MS: Kansas. Published: DW 776. Date: Unidentified endorsement.

Thursday/ [21 May 1868]
16 Cheyne Walk
Chelsea

Dear Mme Coronio

Many thanks for your very kind invitation which however finds me engaged for Saturday. Howell leads me still to hope for your visit on Monday.

Very sincerely yours
D. G. Rossetti

P.S. Will you tell Alecco how sorry I was he did not come last Sunday evening, and how thankful I am for the lion pot.

[1] Aglaia Ionides Coronio (1834–1906) was the second child in the Ionides family. She modelled for EBJ's *The Mill* (1872–80) with Marie Spartali & Maria Zambaco. Her father's home at 1 Holland Park (later owned by her brother Alecco and redecorated by WM) was a gathering place for artists, and she often served as hostess (Julia Atkins, "William Morris and Aglaia Coronio," *William Morris Society Newsletter* [April 1990]). Her own residence was at 1A Holland Park, her brother Constantine's main home was at 8 Holland Villas Road, and Luke lived at no.16. Later letters suggest there was a regular salon on Wednesday evenings (see **161.1**, **162**, & **165**).

68.99 TO CHARLES AUGUSTUS HOWELL

MS: Texas.

Friday [22 May 1868]

My dear Howell

Two letters enclosed.[1] Please will you see to the *Three Roses* frame *at once.*[2]

Your
Gabriel

1. The letters enclosed may be from JM. W.E. Fredeman suggested that DGR wanted CAH to deliver letters to JM and also to keep letters from her for safekeeping, especially when he was out of town. His request in **132** that CAH not allude to any "private affairs" while he is out of town implies that DGR suspected that FC would open any letters that came. In addition, the reference in **138** to "manag[ing] the enclosed" means forwarding letters to JM, since he thanks CAH in **143** for his "postal delivery the results of which have just appeared in a reply."
2. Possibly the chalk version WG had bought in Feb (see **22**). The other chalk version (S.238B), which Surtees suggests may have gone to LRV, seems too unfinished to call for a frame.

68.100 TO JANE MORRIS

MS: BL. Excerpt: Surtees 212. The accompanying plate is in Prints & Drawings, BM.

Friday [22 May 1868]
16 Cheyne Walk
Chelsea

My dear Janey

I shall keep Wedy the 27th sacred to the Earthly Paradise.[1] Will you tell Top that my soul expands to meet "large paper," but that meanwhile I extend my patronage forthwith to him and Ellis as one of the average public.[2] I was touchingly reminded of his Eden today by the advent of asparagus at dinner. How each fresh article of food as it appears recalls the progress of the Poet's Year! Might not this afford a hint for a second series of Months if such is needed for Part II?[3]

As it is now the fashion for successful men in any walk of literature to start a newspaper at once, I offer overpage a heading on the principle of the "Globe and Traveller." Will you endeavour to make the great original "seriously incline" thereto? Fancy the number of Editorial chairs which would be smashed in the course of a week![4]

Yours affectionately
DGabrielR

1. WA records attending a "full-dress party" at the WMs, at which the FMBs, EBJs, GPB, DGR, & others were in attendance (*WAD* 182; see also Kelvin 56).
2. While acknowledging receipt of one of the 25 large-paper copies, DGR says he will also purchase a copy of the trade edition. See **79**.
3. Following the "Apology," "The Wanderers," which is the prologue to the poem, and "The Author to the Reader," the dozen stories of *The Earthly Paradise* are organized calendrically, 2 for each month, Mar–Aug, in Vol 1.
4. The *Globe* (founded 1802) merged with a trade organ designed for "commercial gents," who distributed it on their circuits, in 1822 as the *Globe and Traveller*. Originally a Liberal

Friday [22 May 1868]

Plate 1: *The Bard and Petty Tradesman.*

paper, it shifted its political stand around 1862 (see Sheila Rosenberg, "Some Further Notes on the History of *The Globe*," *Victorian Periodicals Newsletter* 15 [Mar 1972]: 40–47). *The Bard and Petty Tradesman*, which depicts WM in his twin roles in an Edenic setting, is a double pun on WM (**79n3**) and the title of the journal. The reference in the imprint to Lord Campbell's Act is an allusion to either the acts of copyright (1842) or libel (1843), which were drafted by John Campbell (1779–1861), later Lord Chancellor.

68.101 TO COVENTRY PATMORE

Text: Meyerstein, *TLS* (28 Apr 1950): 268.

> 25 May 1868
> 16 Cheyne Walk
> Chelsea

My dear Patmore

A neither ungrateful nor unappreciative recipient of your *Odes* hopes you will pardon the delay in acknowledging them which has resulted only from continual hurry of other things.

It was a pleasure to find you had not forgotten me, though we have not met for so long, and a great pleasure to see some of your work again.

The last Ode (which I had already recognized as yours in print) is one of the finest of the series: but my own course of life being even more absolutely than ever (if that were possible) confined to my original bias in thoughts and pursuits, which never included politics, I have to seek my prime favorite elsewhere, and I find it unhesitatingly in the Fourth Ode, which is nobly sustained in conception and in music throughout. The Seventh contains much that is also very harmonious with my own feelings; and in all, I need hardly say, I do not fail to value qualities which are specially your own as a poet.

Thanking you very much for including me among those privileged to receive your *Odes*,[1] and with all friendly remembrances, I am

> Very truly yours
> D. G. Rossetti

Coventry Patmore Esq

---

[1] In 1868, CP's *Nine Odes* was privately and anonymously printed in an edition of 250 copies.

68.102 TO ELLEN CONWAY[1]

MS: Princeton.

29 May 1868
16 Cheyne Walk
Chelsea

Dear Mrs. Conway,

I am hardly going out at all at present, owing to some troublesome work which hangs on hand; and this will prevent my accepting your kind invitation, for which pray accept my thanks.

Yours very truly,
D G Rossetti

[1] Ellen Davis Dana (1833–97), wife of Moncure Daniel Conway.

68.103 TO AGLAIA CORONIO

MS: Kansas. Published: DW 778.

16 Cheyne Walk
Thursday/17 June [1868]

Dear Mrs. Coronio,

I asked you lately whether you had or knew of any Indian muslin of a peculiar yellowish tinge & you said no. I have since had to adopt a whiter kind for the purpose, & this is not *so* rare I believe, but I cannot meet with any just now at the shops. Do you know of any to be had by any chance? It is for a dress which Janey Morris is making up for one of the pictures I am doing from her.[1]

With kindest remembrances (and hoping to see you soon)

I am yours ever truly
D G Rossetti

[1] See 77.

68.104 TO WILLIAM MICHAEL ROSSETTI

MS: NYPL. Published: *FL* 194–95; DW 779.

17 June 1868
16 Cheyne Walk
Chelsea

Dear W

I have paid a cheque £30 into the Union bank for you, and they have written today to Blumenthal & Co 3945 Traghetto Sto Benedetto, to pay you that sum.[1] I wanted the Bank here to telegraph to Blumenthal to pay you the money, but they said this was quite against the rules as frauds might be practised. I am much annoyed at this delay & do not even know whether you will get this letter. I telegraphed to you last night in answer to your telegram & sent the message to Blumenthal's, as you gave me no address in yours. I am sending this to Euston Square in case they know your address there, but otherwise can only send it to the Poste Restante in hopes you may call for it. I greatly regret that your trip should have been baulked by this hitherto unexplained accident. I would have sent more money if you had told me – as it is I send 30 instead of 20 – but I presumed from your only naming that sum, that it was all you needed.

In great haste in middle of a sitting

Your
D Gabriel Rossetti

[1] WMR was in Verona en route to Venice when he was "robbed apparently on railway, about 800 fr" (WMR:DGR, 17 Jun [68], AP). Blumenthal was the correspondent of the Union Bank in Venice. An appeal to "good kind old [Seymour] Kirkup" in Florence brought 300 francs on 18 Jun, several days before the money sent by DGR arrived (*RP* 313–14). See the following letter.

68.105 TO WILLIAM MICHAEL ROSSETTI

MS: Brotherton. Published: *FL* 195–96; DW 780.

16 Cheyne Walk
22 June [1868]

Dear William

It is extremely vexatious to think of the inconvenience to which you have been put. However I judge by the telegram received at Euston Square that you got my first telegram sent immediately on receipt of your first; and I suppose another which I sent on seeing the one to Christina has reached you too. I hope today you will have got the money – £30 – which I sent through the Bank to Blumenthal on the morning following your first telegram, and that you will not find it necessary to cut your trip short. I will show your letter to Mamma tonight, but probably she has one too.

I wish I had come with you to Italy but did not see the great desirable-ness of it till just after you started. I suppose from what you say that your pockets or luggage were rifled without your knowing it, & trust you have not lost your watch also.

Of course I hope to hear of your getting the money as this will ease my mind about your position.

Your affec: brother
Gabriel

P.S. I wished of course that the Bank here should telegraph to Blumenthal to pay you the money, but this they would not do, as they said frauds would follow such a practice.

68.106 TO CHARLES AUGUSTUS HOWELL

MS: Texas. Date: CFM.

1st July [1868]
16 Cheyne Walk
Chelsea

My dear Howell

Holland dines here on Friday at 6·30. I hope to see you, & the wine also if practicable.

Ever your
D G R

68.107 TO AGLAIA CORONIO

MS: Kansas. Published: DW 777.

Monday [c. 6 July 1868]
16 Cheyne Walk
Chelsea

Dear Mme Coronio

I find I cannot get at present to the picture of La Pia, so should be keeping your embroidery frame to no purpose,[1] and had better send it back with thanks now & borrow it again if necessary.

The photograph I send with it is hardly worth sending, but as it has just been taken & happens to be lying on the table, it suggests itself to me to beg your acceptance of one.

Very truly yours
DG Rossetti

[1] Surtees suggests that "in 1868 an unfinished piece of embroidery was prominent in the picture" (110n1).

68.108 TO ALICE BOYD[1]

MS: NLS. Published: Purves 578–79; DW 781.

7 July 1868
16 Cheyne Walk
Chelsea

Dear Miss Boyd

I received Scotus's note with your extremely kind codicil. Of course my mind has been racked ever since with the agonies of weak will as to going or staying, but I believe I must come to the conclusion that it is not practicable just now. Go somewhere I must soon, but it will be such a short trip that I must make it a near one. Moreover I should not want at present to be taking up the picture of La Pia before the rest in hand, as it happens to be the only one which has not yet found a destination. I suppose people don't like such tragic subjects, though indeed it seems £2500 has been given by Gambart for Hunt's Isabella, in which the very way the paint is laid on is certainly a tragedy in itself, to say nothing of the mere sentiment.[2] I was there the other day and found our Scotch friend who does the honours in open rebellion to all appearance. He asked aloud (and indeed appealed to me by name most appallingly) whether *that* could be called a work of colour, and gave the public repeatedly the valuable information that no one subscribed to the engraving. One man however was rash enough not to be deterred even by this from asking particulars as to the subscription. Whereupon the man in office waved his hand towards a distant corner and said almost in Gaelic:– "Ye'll find a book there that's got it a' in; there's columns for the pounds and columns for the shillings & columns for the pence. Ye'll find it a' there!" His state of mind appeared to be inexorable. A gentleman making his appearance was introduced to me (instantaneously) as Stanfield's son.[3] He then went up to the picture to examine it with a very pretty lady who was with him, and I asked in a whisper if this was Mrs. Stanfield. The answer in a loud tone was "It strikes me, Mr. Rossetti, that he's far too attentive for it to be a wife!" After this I fled, leaving the punching of his head to whom it might concern. Whether Stanfield did it on the spot, or whether Gambart has done it since, or whether it is left for Hunt to do on his return from the Holy Sepulchre, I cannot say.

You may see that news is not very rife with me by the space I have devoted to this hero. However last Tuesday Brown gave a monster party to 120 friends & foes. It went off very well however, people managing to amuse each other exactly according as they happened to be packed, making the most of the person next to them, like pick-pockets at a hanging, till they got shoved on to some one else. One rather missed the malefactor certainly, particularly as in so big a company every one could no doubt have picked out his favourite performer for the part, – the artists especially.

Pardon this somewhat grisly rubbish, and remember me very kindly to Scotus, and believe me, dear Miss Boyd,

Your still expectant guest in the future
D. G. Rossetti

P.S. William is just back. You heard no doubt of his being robbed of all his money at Verona.

---

1. AB (1825–97) lived in a ménage à trois with WBS' wife, Letitia Norquoy, that lasted until his death in 1890. See **Volume II: Index**, and *WBS*. DGR made extensive visits to Penkill this fall and the following summer, recuperating from his health problems there and rediscovering his enthusiasm for writing verse with the encouragement of the Penkill group, who urged him to live for his poetry (see *AN* 2: 108–18).
2. WHH's *Isabella and the Pot of Basil*, begun in 1866. The sum of £2500 included the sketch. See *WHH* 2: 202, & *RP* 304.
3. Probably the painter George Clarkson Stanfield (1828–78), son of William Clarkson Stanfield, RA (1793–1867).

68.109 TO JOHN PERRY

MS: UBC.

16 Cheyne Walk/Chelsea
7 July 1868

Dear Sir

I enclose cheque £6-5-6 for the rent due at 7 Hemus Terrace. I shall be always most happy to pay on the day the rent is due, only must trouble you to give me notice in time, as I forget.

Yours truly
D G Rossetti

John Perry Esq
P.S. I have already paid 9/- for laying on water. You will probably think this ought to be re-imbursed.

68.110 TO ALICE BOYD

MS: NLS. Published: Purves 579–80; DW 782.

24 July 1868
16 Cheyne Walk
Chelsea

Dear Miss Boyd

Though with nothing to say in particular, I have been intending ever since I got your kind letter to write a line in reply because of the anxiety you express about Swinburne. I felt the same myself of course, when I saw the paragraph one evening in the Pall Mall, & being unable to get so far next morning, I sent to enquire how he was & whether I could see him if I went that evening. The reply was that he was perfectly well, and so in fact I found him. He attributed the "faint," as he called it, to the heat, and said he was perfectly well by the time he reached home.[1]

Certainly the heat since then has been enough to floor anyone. I have not yet got away, & indeed could not have done so to any purpose in that murderous weather, as I could only have lain on my back wherever I was. The sudden change yesterday was a return to life, & one felt more than I ever remember doing before how much serious good or evil may come of weather even without risking oneself on the waves.

If I am able to visit you in Autumn, I shall promise myself, and I doubt not realize, a great deal of pleasure, only I never know more than the plans for the day I wake to.

I have been working at Mrs. Morris's portrait and have nearly finished it. I think it is better perhaps than the run of my doings.

I was greatly pleased with Scotus's poem in the Fortnightly which I had never seen before.[2] It is full of the real thing, only seems to me a little abrupt in its transitions and a little lacking in basic faith. One can't help seeing

Scotus's grin all through Antony's terror. Every one seems to admire the poem greatly, & I hope it may induce its author to resume the pen.

Believe me, dear Miss Boyd,

ever yours sincerely
D G Rossetti

1   On 10 Jul ACS fainted in the Reading Room of the BM, striking his head on a desk as he fell. Some newspapers (the "penny screamers" as ACS called them – see Lang 1: 268) reported this as a "tragic accident," alarming the poet's friends, but he was out and about the next day (see *RP* 318–19).
2   "Anthony; a Poem" appeared in the *Fortnightly Review* (Jul 68, 81–89).

68.111 TO CHARLES AUGUSTUS HOWELL

MS: Texas.

Tuesday [28 July 1868?]

My dear Howell

I am badly wanting some roses to paint in the Sibyl picture.¹ Are there not a lot in Ruskin's garden at Denmark Hill? – & could not I have some? The great big things one gets from the swell florists will not do.

Your affec:
D G R

P.S. If so, I should be wanting them about Saturday or Monday, & would send Dunn for them.

1   See next letter.

68.112 TO CHARLES AUGUSTUS HOWELL

MS: Texas.

Friday [31 July 1868]
16 Cheyne Walk
Chelsea

My dear Howell

I want a few of your dog-roses to put with those which Dunn will fetch for me tomorrow (Saturday) at 10.30 from Denmark Hall. It would be quite out of his way to go also to Northend. Could you send me some? or I would send for them, if not.

Are you seeing about the washstand, table, &c?

Your affec:
D G R

68.113 TO CHARLES AUGUSTUS HOWELL

MS: Texas. Published: Cline 92.

Friday. [31 July 1868]

My dear Howell

I couldn't come today with you, & indeed only got your telegram at 5 o'clock.

Taylor has just been asking me to add to your botherations by a request as to Ruskin, and in his state one can't refuse him, though I don't know what may be possible. He has determined instead of going abroad to set his wife up in a cigar business before he drops off his hook. He has seen a very eligible shop in Fleet St, and feels quite certain of success. All he wants is a loan of £1000! However I really believe the scheme is hopeful, and that the poor woman is not undeserving of interest after all when we consider his conduct to her. She is now behaving very well and his great wish is to see her settled before he dies, in such a way as may prevent his relations from being able to tempt her with a trifle for the reversion of the property she will eventually have by his will.

Ruskin is the only man he can think of capable of lending the money on interest. Would he do so? – the whole if possible – but if not, a part. I really believe that Taylor's great business faculties would be sure to make the business begin to be successful from the very outset, and of course he is deserving of the most cordial interest on the part of every member of the firm which his efforts have kept alive. It is a great question for him, and will I am sure have your best consideration. He ought to have *some* money one day next week to secure the shop.[1]

Ever your
D G R

Try & look in tomorrow or Sunday.
If absolutely necessary I would even write to Ruskin myself.

[1] See **96n6**.

68.114 TO CHARLES AUGUSTUS HOWELL

MS: Texas. Published: Cline 75.

Sunday [July 1868]

Dear Old Boy

The circular head is finished & vastly improved.[1] Is it really worth your

[July 1868]

while to have it for 50 guineas, or shall I send it to Gambart on account of the exchange pending between us? Either plan will suit me, so do not hesitate to suit yourself. I am always in terror of your getting bad bargains.

As I did not see you, I managed the affair we spoke of yesterday. Do let me see you as soon as you can. I want you much, but do not know if there is any chance of ever finding you at home.

Your affec:
Gabriel

Love to Kate.

[1] A version of *La Pia*; see the following 2 letters.

68.115 TO CHARLES AUGUSTUS HOWELL
MS: Texas.

[July 1868]

My dear Howell

I *am very* hard up myself, & it is *absolutely only* your naming *Thursday* that enables me even to send the enclosed. By the end of this week I must *inevitably* pay it away elsewhere, and so rely implicitly on your promise, & will expect you to dinner that day at 7.

Buying the Pia, my dear boy, does not matter in the least, but I am sorry to say that paying this trifle matters a great deal at this moment. You know well that if it were not so I would not give a thought to the matter & must ask your pardon for so much solemnity.

Ever your
D G R

68.116 TO CHARLES AUGUSTUS HOWELL
MS: Texas.

16 Cheyne Walk
Wednesday [July 1868]

Sir

I take the liberty of enclosing my little account, as I have a heavy payment to make up this week, and would be truly grateful for your early kind attention to it.

I have executed your esteemed order respecting the drawing of La Pia, & will deliver it to your messenger when he brings the cheque.

Yours respectfully

DG Rossetti

C.A.Howell Esq
P.S. If you could honour me with a call tomorrow, I should be most grateful on various accounts.

[Enclosure]

July 1868

C.A.Howell Esq
Dt. to D.G. Rossetti

	£	s	d
To one circular head in oil, with frame complete finished & delivered[1]	52	10	0
Total	52	10	0

[1] Chalk drawings related to *La Pia* (S.207C & D) passed through CAH, but there is no record of a circular head in oil.

68.117 TO CHARLES AUGUSTUS HOWELL

MS: Texas.

Thursday night [July 1868]

16 Cheyne Walk
Chelsea

My dear Howell

I'm horrorstruck at this dreadful *fiasco*. Three mistakes of mine have led to it.

1st The idea that you would be sure to come early (my letter having been posted at 4 o'clock yesterday).

2nd The idea that it was later than it really was when Sandys & I started from here for his.

3rd The idea that you would come on there if you *did* come here after all.

Besides these, there is the stupid omission to leave word for you to do so.

Pray pardon what I most sincerely regret, & come & dine with me next Tuesday at 6. But let me see you before then. Saturday would suit me well – any time. And dine here or out with me.

Your affec:
D G R

The Brandy is even as coals of fire on my head & conscience.

68.118 TO CHARLES AUGUSTUS HOWELL
MS: Texas.

[1 August 1868?]

Dear H.

Can't be helped! I'll hope to see you tomorrow morning. I'm excessively sorry to be giving you so much trouble. You *are* a dear.

You did not enclose Ruskin's note, which I mention to account for my not returning it.

Ever your
Gabriel

68.119 TO GEORGE RAE
MS: LLAG.

Speke Hall
6 Aug 1868

My dear Rae,

I am excessively vexed at being unable to get to you. Of course had I expected to be so unwell here, I should not have left London just now. I have had a constant diarrhea and other troublesome symptoms since coming to Speke; nevertheless, as I found I should not see you here today, I started off this morning with Mr. Leyland for Liverpool, but when about getting into the trap felt so giddy and unwell that I was obliged to return to the house. The fact is I have been fagging myself out for some time.[1] As I see no prospect now of seeing you to any purpose (returning to London as I do either tomorrow evening or Saturday morning) I write this word in explanation. I hope your being away from your office is no sign that you also are more or less on the sick list.

Had I not fully expected to see you, I should of course have answered your note about the frame before this. It is of course the frame of *Palmifera*, but why the wiseacre who now rules the destinies of "Green's" should have said it was sent home "the other day" heaven only knows. His ways are of the shifty and mysterious order. I can only suppose that he supposed you would suppose it to be so, you having perhaps in his surmise just purchased the picture. I believe I spoke to you once about the matter, as, I find it necessary to charge the frames for this class of pictures (the completion of which always gets so tantalizingly protracted) as a separate item. However in giving Green's hero a list of frames, the other day (the accounts for which were to go to the owners of the pictures and thus be struck off *my* acct,) I told him that yours was only to be sent in when I let him know that you were expecting it. He seems however to have preferred his own time, and I can only hope you will not think the precise moment of great consequence. The charge is correct, being the same as that for the "Lilith" (which Mr. Leyland has just paid,) and as other frames of the same size & kind. They are expensive, but cannot (I judge by enquiry among others in the trade) be made cheaper.[2]

If, as I hope, I am able to come to their neighbourhood again before long, I shall not then fail to see Liverpool Birkenhead and you. It seems childish indeed to go away from here without visiting your big city, but luck is against me this time. Mr. Miller I hope may dine here today, unless the weather baffles him.

How fine Windus's *Burd Helen* looks here![3] I like it better than ever. Speke is one of the most glorious places in England – familiar I suppose to you.

With kindest remembrances to Mrs. Rae

I am ever yours
D G Rossetti

P.S. I had a visit in London the other day from a young nephew of yours – George Fraser.

---

[1] The major symptom of DGR's physical deterioration in the second half of 1868 was the near total breakdown of his eyesight (see **121n1**). His eye disorders, however, date as far back as 1861. See also **173n3**.

[2] It appears that Green had sent GR a bill for the frame of *Sibylla Palmifera* and perhaps the frame itself. DGR finally finished the painting at the end of 1870 and sent it to GR (see 70.277).

[3] For DGR's high opinion of *Burd Helen*, see 56.35 & 40.

68.120 TO JAMES SMETHAM[1]

MS: V&A.

16 Cheyne Walk/Chelsea\
10 Aug 1868

My dear Smetham

I never answered your former affectionate letter about my versicles quoted by Swinburne, and now you send me a very fine poem of your own, written in good strong English and to noble purpose. I admire it exceedingly, and cannot but conceive that such power of structural execution must have resulted from considerable practice. You really should cultivate this vein if opportunity offers, & bring out a little collection of such poetry.[2]

I am just back from a few days spent at a friend's house in the country & shall probably be going away again immediately. I must tell you that I have been a good deal out of sorts in various ways lately, and still am. Therefore not much in the way of company at present; but still hope we may see each other again at some favourable time for quiet talk.

Affectionately yours\
DG Rossetti

P.S. I enclose copies of 2 sonnets which I need not trouble you to return. I want your opinion as to which is the best of the three versions of the line about Art in the second sonnet. I take a good deal of trouble with these things, and have found it hard to please myself with the line in question.

Newborn Death I

> Today Death seems to me an infant child
>   Which her worn mother Life upon my knee
>   Has set to grow my friend & play with me;
> If haply so my heart might be beguil'd
> To find no terrors in a face so mild;
>   If haply so my weary heart might be
>   Unto the newborn milky eyes of thee,
> O Death, before resentment reconcil'd.
> How long, O Death? and shall thy feet depart
>   Still a young child's with mine, or wilt those stand
> Fullgrown the helpful daughter of my heart,
>   What time with thee indeed I reach the strand
> Of the pale wave which knows thee what thou art,
>   And drink it in the hollow of thy hand?

Newborn Death II

And thou, O Life, the lady of all bliss,
   With whom, when our first heart beat full & fast,
   I wandered till the haunts of men were past,
And in fair places found all bowers amiss
Till only woods & waves might hear our kiss,
   While to the winds all thought of Death we cast: –
   Ah! Life, and must I have from thee at last
No smile to greet me and no babe but this?
Lo! Love, the child once ours; and Song, whose hair
   Blew like a flower & blossomed like a wreath;
And Art, whose eyes were as God's skies laid bare;
   These o'er the book of Nature mixed their breath
With neck-twined arms, as oft we watched them there: –
   And did these die that thou might'st bear me Death?[3]

And Art whose eyes were worlds by God found fair;
   Whose glance met God's & found Him fair.

---

[1] For JS, see 60.6n1.
[2] The poem was probably "The Rotifer," composed at this time, unpublished except for "a few copies . . . printed by a friend" (Smetham 176). JS sent these copies to some of his friends; the poem is printed in full and discussed in Smetham 175–80.
[3] These sonnets were included in *Poems* as XLVIII & XLIX of *HL*.

68.121 TO CHARLES AUGUSTUS HOWELL

MS: Texas. Published: Cline 77. Date: CFM.

16 Cheyne Walk

Monday [10 August 1868]

My dear Howell

I have seen Mr. Bader, who has been here today, & write you word as you will be anxious.

He assures me I need have no fear of losing my sight. He says the affection is cerebral, & he trusts to diminish it. I am to see him again on Friday, & he has given me one or two prescriptions. Of course I told him all about myself in every way. Of course also I am very much relieved in my mind, as I found it impracticable to work since coming to town. I do not know how soon I may get to work again to any purpose, but will hope for the best, and at any rate need I trust have no great fear of the worst now.¹

Your affec:
Gabriel

I think I shall write also to Leyland, as I know he felt uncomfortable.

1. As WMR reports, "towards the end of the summer of 1867 [DGR's] eyesight began to fail. Sunlight or artificial light became increasingly painful to him, producing sensations of giddiness etc. Even the gas-lamps in the streets affected him distressingly. He consulted the famous oculists, Sir William Bowman and Dr. Charles Bader. They both assured him that his eyes were not organically wrong, but that the weakness of sight depended upon general overstrain and nervous upset" (*FLM* 265). WMR also remembers that DGR began experiencing insomnia by the end of 1867: he was beset with concerns regarding the often profitable but at times vexing relationships with patrons; with financial worries; and with the tensions that existed within his friendship with WM and his affair with JM. The fear of losing his eyesight, one never diagnosed as legitimate by any of the doctors consulted, plagued him and he remembered his own father becoming nearly blind at the end of his life. WMR notes the recurrence of DGR's eye complaints in his diary for 11 Aug: "He has consulted a German oculist, Bader, recommended by Howell. . . . B tells him he will not lose his sight; but G[abriel] thinks he is ominously silent about any improvement of it. For the present G is quite unable to paint. However, I am in hopes that general nervousness and anxiety may account for much, and the sight itself be not much harmed for a permanence" (*RP* 322). For Bowman, see 67.140. Charles Bader (1825–99), German-born ophthalmic surgeon at Guy's Hospital from 1861, was a pioneer in research on the iris and continued work on the structure of the eye begun by Bowman.

68.122 TO FREDERICK LOCKER-LAMPSON¹

MS: Harvard. Published: Birrell, *FLL*: 33–34; DW 783.

13 August 1868
16 Cheyne Walk
Chelsea

My dear Sir

Coming for a few days to town, I find your kind present, sent while I was away. Allow me to thank you sincerely for including me among the recipients of so small an edition. Some of the Poems were known to me already in print. I especially remember "My Neighbour Rose," and the curiosity I felt at the F.L. at the end of so accomplished a piece of writing – your name not being so familiar to me then as since. I here find the poem in company with many others well worthy of it; and am thankful to you for admitting me to so pleasant a circle.[2]

Believe me, my dear Sir,

Faithfully yours
D G Rossetti

Frederick Locker Esq

---

[1] Frederick Locker (1821–1895) added his 2nd wife's surname (Lampson) in 1885. Author of elegant lyrics, he was a collector & anthologist specializing in *vers de société*.

[2] Locker-Lampson had sent DGR a copy of his *London Lyrics*, first published by Chapman & Hall in 1857. The volume proved popular, and was reissued by Pickering (1862), Strahan (1870), Ibister (1874), Kegan Paul (1878), etc. However, it was probably the 1868 privately printed edition (by John Wilson) that was sent to DGR. "My Neighbour Rose" (46–49) first appeared in the *Cornhill Magazine* (Sep 61: 319–20), signed only with Locker-Lampson's initials.

68.123 TO WILLIAM BELL SCOTT

MS: Princeton.

16 Cheyne Walk/Chelsea
14 Aug. 1868

My dear Scott

I hear you are again at Penkill. I went duly to Speke Hall in Howell's company, & found it a very glorious old house, full of interest in every way. I was seedy however while there, and did not feel well enough to go to Liverpool.

I found Leyland only knew Peter Stewart by name, but old Mr. Miller, who dined at Speke one day, of course answered my enquiry by saying he knew Peter well.[1] I mentioned your affair to him briefly, and he did not seem to think it very likely Peter would buy. However I have no doubt he would speak to him on the subject if wished; only I did not press the matter with him, having already, as you requested, mentioned it to Howell who is willing to take it up on commission. If you like him to do so, would you drop him a line exactly describing the progress of events hitherto, and the size and subjects of the pictures. He is in the country now again, but a letter addressed to him

Northend Grove
Northend
Fulham
(*to be forwarded*)

Monday [17 August 1868] 68.124

would reach him at once.

I hope you are enjoying yourself at Penkill. I should like to be with you, but the journey is long & I *do hate* railways. Somewhere I shall be going again almost immediately, I believe, but am kept here just at this moment.

With kindest remembrances to Miss Boyd & to Mrs. Scott if with you

I am
yours affectionately
D Gabriel R

[1] Peter Stuart (1814–88), African merchant (see Macleod, 476–77).

68.124 TO CHARLES AUGUSTUS HOWELL
MS: Texas.

16 Cheyne Walk
Monday [17 August 1868]

My dear Howell

Will you send me *at once* your address at Lowestoft.[1] I want to send you something.

In haste

Yours ever
Gabriel

[1] The CAHs were on holiday in Suffolk, visiting the coastal resorts of Lowestoft, Southwold, & Great Yarmouth. Of more significance to DGR was the fact that they were travelling with the WMs, and DGR could use CAH to deliver letters to JM (see **99**).

68.125 TO FREDERICK RICHARD LEYLAND
MS: LC. Published: Fennell 18.

16 Cheyne Walk
Wednesday [19 August 1868]

My dear Leyland

I know your friendly mind must have been alarmed by my seedy state when I was at Speke. Since returning to London, I at once consulted an oculist who assured me that my eyes were in no way diseased and also said he could guarantee that I should not lose my sight. Of course this allayed my anxiety in some degree, but I cannot say that the symptoms from which I suffer have abated as yet. I have been to another medical man about my general health, so that I have done all in my power.

I suppose now I ought to have a change, and indeed the medical men tell me I must go at once to the seaside and try rest and fresh air and walking. You will not I am sure misunderstand me, or think that I underrate your friendship, when I say that I do not feel able to come to Speke again just now, as I am too nervous and worried to hold my own in any circle of friends, and to shut myself up like a bogie would increase my dumps. My brother says he will go away with me for a little while to the seaside, & this I believe will be my best course. I am anxious to start next week if possible.

Since being in town I have not been able to do much, but have finished your *Venus* drawing in chalk,[1] as you told me you would like to get it. Shall I have it framed and send it you to Speke? At the same time I shall be able to send the other chalk heads (Mrs. Morris) and the photos: I have so long intended to give you, as I have at last just received copies of some and am expecting others tomorrow. I will try also to send at same time the La Pia drawing of Miss W[ilding]. if I can get the background done.

I do not think you saw a watercolour of *Bocca Baciata* (which you may remember in oil.)[2] The watercolour can have been hardly in a state to show when you were last in my studio. It is much altered in the head and hair from the original, and every one thinks it superior to that. It is much larger, being 18 x 15 inches. If you felt inclined to have it for 150 gs, it would be convenient to me at this moment, and you would find it quite equal to any small picture you have of mine, as it is decidedly one of my best watercolours. I could not I fear finish it to my satisfaction before I leave town, but I have brought it very forward and it only needs a few days work for completion. I had engaged it to Howell, but it does not seem to be convenient for him to pay just at this moment, and after all I may as well have the full price as he.

It is very possible however that you would rather wait for larger work, and I would not for the world that you had what does not meet your inclination. So I will trust to you to tell me quite frankly.

Will you give Mrs. Leyland and the children my best remembrances, & the same to Miss Parke, and believe me

ever truly yours
D G Rossetti

P.S. I should have written at once after seeing the doctors, only had hoped by a little delay to be able to report improvement.

---

[1] A few days later (**129** & **130**) DGR tells him again that only the frames are yet to be made, though two of the drawings, according to the following letter, were not finished.
[2] FRL did not purchase the watercolour version of *Bocca Baciata* (see **128**).

68.126 TO CHARLES AUGUSTUS HOWELL

MS: Texas. Published: Cline 79. Date: CFM.

Thursday [20 August 1868]

My dear Howell

Thanks for your note. I am afraid I shall not be able to come before you leave where you are, but have to be seeing doctors just now. Very likely next week William & I may go away somewhere. I wish to God I could come to you just now, as I am horribly seedy; but don't tell anyone I am so. I pass such dreadful nights that there is no getting better.

Needing money, I have written to Leyland offering him the water colour Bocca Baciata for 150 gs.[1] I have not his answer yet. You will not mind this.

I have borrowed from Northend the Venus and one of the La Pias to finish Leyland's 2 drawings from that I may let him have them.

By the bye, you have of mine a large roll of green stuff, and an old curtain. Do let me have them when you can. The green stuff I am needing. Also I think you must have a large white-paper-covered solid strainer which belongs to a frame which you returned to me.

Love to Kitty who I hope is benefiting, and to all friends. Will you tell Janey that I hope she will be able to sit to me again very soon, as I want awfully to begin Graham's big picture where she is to sit for Beatrice, and that is the part I want to begin with.[2] I hope she won't think it too bad of me.

Your affec:
Gabriel

[1] See **128** for FRL's reply that he would prefer a larger picture and **138n2** for Bowman's purchase of *Bocca Baciata*.
[2] In 1869, DGR sold a chalk version (S.168R.1) of *Beata Beatrix* to WG. Apparently he did not begin on WG's commission for another oil version (S.168R.3) until 1871.

68.127 TO CHARLES AUGUSTUS HOWELL

MS: Texas. Published: Cline 80.

Friday [21 August 1868]

My dear Howell

I sent you Graham's address yesterday, & now return the letter. I have not yet heard from Leyland about the picture.

I should like extremely to have the dishes you mention & shall be most happy to pay the price.

I wish I could get to Yarmouth – it is barely possible I may, with William, next week which he has at his disposal and will go anywhere with me. I wish you would write me your address as soon as you get there. But I rather incline to Southwold, as a very quiet place, in spite of what you say. It is provoking to get there just as every one is gone, but I have been seeing doctors till now. Yesterday a fearful night caused me to go to Dr. Gull who is a very eminent man. Marshall is away in Germany, or I should before this have seen him. Gull examined me thoroughly, tested my water &c, & declared there was no organic disease of any kind, that the brain was affected through overwork, & that he would set me right very soon.[1] Of course he told me to get away & recommended Harrogate which however I don't seem to fancy. I have begun taking his prescriptions but had a bad night again last night. Whirling flickering & something like approaching apoplexy has become the order of my nights – much worse than when at Speke. I must hope for the best.

Will you let me know what is doing about everything when you write – what lodging would be best at Southwold, &c, & what is the least miserable way of getting there from Darsham. Didn't Topsy have a house to himself? Could this be got? Don't trouble about what I send unless it is convenient. I couldn't think for a moment of giving you a long job over it. Now really don't as there is nothing of importance.

Your affec:
Gabriel

[1] Sir William Withey Gull (1816–1890), physician to Queen Victoria and one of the many suspects named by Jack the Ripper enthusiasts.

68.128 TO CHARLES AUGUSTUS HOWELL

MS: Texas. Published: Cline 81. Date: CFM.

Saturday [22 August 1868]

My dear Howell
   The address is

George Hamilton Esq
W. &. R. Graham & Co
Rumford St
Liverpool.

I saw the oculist Bader again today; & though I had had some further troublesome symptoms since last seeing him, he, on examining my eyes again, assured me I must not fear for my sight in the least, that the adjusting power was the only thing at fault owing to a slight imperfection in the form of one eye which he said he was surprised to find had never caused me inconvenience before. He said that care with spectacles about which he gave me directions, and Gull's prescription for my head (which I am happy to find today seems already beginning to benefit me decidedly) will set me right again.[1]

Last night Brown was advising me decidedly to go (as I am going somewhere) to Bonn and Coblentz. John Marshall is at Bonn just now for a few weeks, and at Coblentz is the famous oculist to whom every one goes. I may really perhaps look you up at Yarmouth, next week, so send me your address there at once. I couldn't go to Germany alone, but might possibly if you would come with me. William now suddenly finds himself prevented from stirring by the absence of some one else at his office.

Today Leyland writes that he would "prefer waiting for larger work" to buying the watercolour. Under these circumstances I am making up my mind, though much against my will, to get an advance from him of £150 on the Medusa commission and another thing he wants me to do.

With love to Kitty

Your affec:
Gabriel

P.S. I just see in your letter that you will be another week at Lowestoft. So I suppose I *may* look you up there but am uncertain. I thought you would be at Yarmouth all alone next week with Kitty.

P.P.S. I don't know if you like still to take the water colour.

---

[1] WMR writes that DGR "began using strong spectacles, often two pairs one over the other; and as the years progressed, he scarcely ever took the spectacles off, persisting in wearing them even when he was merely seated in talk with friends" (*FLM* 266).

68.129 TO FREDERICK RICHARD LEYLAND

MS: LC. Published: Fennell 19. On the basis of **128** to CAH, it would appear that DGR has misdated this letter 21 Aug.

2[2] August/1868
16 Cheyne Walk
Chelsea

My dear Leyland,

Thanks for your most friendly letter. Since I last wrote to you, some most fearful nights of unrest drove me to Dr. Gull, who said I was suffering from overwork and he would soon set me right. He prescribed for me, & I begin already today to feel my head unmistakably clearer & I think perhaps somewhat less distress in the eyes. Decided benefit in the latter respect, however, I do not yet feel, but am assured both by Dr. Gull and the oculist (Bader of Guy's Hospl) whom I have seen again this morning,[1] that there is absolutely no fear for my sight, but that I must rest and get change of air and scene for a time. I have conceived the idea of possibly, after a week at the seaside here, going to Germany and visiting the great oculist at Coblentz. There also I could see my habitual doctor (John Marshall) who happens to be now at Bonn.

Unluckily one of the most requisite things for such movements is wanting to me at the present moment, – to wit, money. I am very loth to trouble you for advances on work not yet fairly commenced; but some progress has been made in designs and studies towards the *Medusa* commission; and I am constrained unwillingly to say that if you could let me have £150 on acct of this or the new picture I am to paint from Mrs. Leyland (whichever gets in hand first) I should be very glad just now, as I have no other way of managing what is necessary, and want to leave London in as few days as possible. If you can oblige me in this, a cheque will do now instead of sending notes.[2]

I really hope to send the Lilith and Lucrezia very soon, and should have been taking them up lately, only that I find the last finishing of work is exactly what I am least able to do in my present state. I will attend to the sending off of the chalk drawings before I leave town, but the frames will of course occasion some delay.

I congratulate you on having got one of Millais' very finest works,[3] & hope that the Herbert was one ingredient in your "Swop."

With kindest remembrances to your family

I am ever yours
D G Rossetti

---

[1] For Bader, see **121n1**; for Gull, see **127n1**.
[2] FRL sent a cheque for £150 on the 24th with a letter inviting DGR to visit Liverpool "either before or after your trip to Germany" (Fennell 14).
[3] Fennell identifies the JEM picture as *The Eve of St. Agnes* (101).

68.130 TO FREDERICK RICHARD LEYLAND

MS: LC. Published: Fennell 21.

25 Aug 1868
16 Cheyne Walk
Chelsea

My dear Leyland

Thanks for cheque £150 on account of my next work for you.

So much benefit accrued from Dr. Gull's prescription that I was in hopes of very rapid recovery. Today however I must say I do not feel so hopeful, but of course one must not expect miracles. I shall start for the seaside (perhaps Yarmouth) immediately and meditate for a few days on the advisability of going to Germany which is an undertaking & will not be necessary if I find myself getting well.

Ever yours
D G Rossetti

P.S. Six drawings will reach you as soon as frames are made: viz:

Venus
La Pia
Andromeda
3 Mrs. M[orris].

68.131 TO WILLIAM ALLINGHAM

MS: PML. Published: *WA/GBH* 281–82; DW 784.

25 August 1868
16 Cheyne Walk

My dear Allingham

I've been very seedy and still am rather so, but doctors have been doing me some good. I'm going to start away somewhere, but fancy seaside. There's a deadly-lively (or very quiet) place called Southwold in Suffolk, where the Morris's, Howells and others have been lately. I think perhaps of going there. I don't know exactly what my moves may be, but would it be in the nature of things for you to take a trip with me anywhere at present? I think we rather used up the walks about Lymington last year, and seaside is desirable, & certainly no impending female photographers or even poets laureate.[1] I merely ask you the question, as a guide in my plans. We might go to several places even – say including a new visit to Stratford-on-Avon & neighbourhood which will bear seeing often.²

Will you kindly answer *at once*, as I ought to start at once.

Your affec:
D Gabriel R

---

¹ A reference to Julia Margaret Cameron, the photographer & neighbour-friend of Tennyson at Freshwater, Isle of Wight; see 66.4.1n2 for DGR's reluctance to be photographed by her.
² Between 1–8 Sep, DGR with HTD visited Stratford, Kenilworth, & Warwick.

68.131.1 TO MICHAEL FREDERICK HALLIDAY

MS: Adrian Harrington Rare Books. The MS is tipped into a copy of DGR's *Poems: Illustrated from his own Pictures and Designs* 1 (1904).

28 August [1868?]
16 Cheyne Walk
Chelsea

Dear Halliday

Many thanks. If at all possible I will look in on Thursday morning before 2 – probably about 1.

Yours ever
D G Rossetti

68.132 TO CHARLES AUGUSTUS HOWELL

MS: Texas. Published: Cline 83.

16 Cheyne Walk
31 Aug [1868]

My dear Howell

I am going away with Dunn to walk about in Warwickshire for a few days, before moving elsewhere. If you write to me, do not allude to any private affairs in your letter, & if you come to London before I am back it will be better not to tackle the chump-wump who has got into a rage somehow.¹ I didn't know what to do better than this trip with Dunn at present. I'm very unsettled as to plans.

I had a sitting the other day & finished Janey M's portrait. Have done little else. I am sending your two chalk drawings back to Northend, and also a large frame of the same kind which has come & which I presume to be for you.

Love to Kate.

Your affec:
Gabriel

P.S. I don't know if convenient to pay me £12 or rather £7-16- allowing for the four dishes. You will remember the matter.

P.S. I got the £150 from Leyland on acct of Medusa, but find much to do with it.

---

1 The "chump-wump" was FC, who was no doubt angry that HTD had taken control of household expenses. HTD later wrote: "I came to the conclusion that there must be great waste and improvidence in the housekeeping, and . . . I broached the subject . . . and besought him to let me look into his accounts. . . . He gladly acquiesced and consequently, though greatly to the opposition and annoyance of the servants, I looked thoroughly into his expenditure" (Dunn, *Recollections of Dante Gabriel Rossetti* 31). In HTD's opinion, DGR also kept too much cash in the house, and he persuaded him to open a bank account.

68.133 TO CHARLES AUGUSTUS HOWELL

MS: Texas. Published: Cline 84. Date: CFM.

Kenilworth
Saturday [5 September 1868]

Dear Howell

I am likely to be back again in London tomorrow (Sunday) or Monday. Would you write a line to Cheyne Walk if you are back when this letter reaches Northend, and I will try and see you.

The disturbance and weakness in my sight gets certainly rather worse than better, and I pass such dreadful nights that to benefit by air or walking is impossible. I am therefore returning to town to settle on what my next step should be. I may possibly go to see the oculist at Coblentz (in which case I wd try & get your company) or else to Scott at Penkill.[1]

With love

Ever yours
D Gabriel R

P.S. One thing I ought to say which I hope won't frighten and bore you. That bill for £50 – 21 Octr! I am happy to find on referring to notes that it is not 100 but 50, & not 1st October but 21st. Now I hope to be able to meet it, but if I were prevented by inability to work meanwhile, do you think it could be renewed? The other 3 *later* ones *are* renewable. I hope there may be no need, but *if* needed do you think it possible. Of course if I am better in time, nothing will be easier than to meet it.

[1] See **136** for DGR's departure for Penkill.

68.134 TO HENRY JAMES HOLIDAY
MS: Private Collection.

9th Septr 1868
16 Cheyne Walk
Chelsea

My dear Holiday

I have just been in the country a little, & may probably be going away almost immediately for longer, but my plans are rather unsettled at present, & I have no intention just now of taking a permanent country residence. I am much obliged for your kindness in writing me particulars of your house which seems a very desirable one, but any thing I said to Madox Brown on the subject of settling out of London must I think have been said some time ago, on ideas I then had but have never carried out.

Many thanks to Mrs. Holiday and yourself for so kind an invitation which I should have had much pleasure in accepting, were it not that my present movements will have, I believe, to be in other directions.[1]

With kind remembrances

I am ever yours
DG Rossetti

[1] Henry Holiday (1839–1927), painter, illustrator, & sculptor, best known as a designer of stained glass, had probably offered DGR a house in the Lake District.

68.135 TO WILLIAM BELL SCOTT
MS: Princeton.

16 Cheyne Walk
16 Septr 1868

My dear Scott

I returned to town on Tuesday of last week, and reckoned on being away again before this. I had some idea of going to Germany to see an eminent oculist, but could not make up my mind, having a dislike to the journey, and so determined to wait for the return of John Marshall (my habitual doctor) who I found was expected back. I also wrote to Burton (who has been under the German oculist), asking his opinion. Both he and Marshall now express an opinion that it is needless to go – the first saying that Bowman (who however is still away) is likely to do anything that can be done – and the latter that, from his own observation & the oculist Bader's opinion, he would advise me to see what can be done with the general health. He has prescribed for me, chiefly with a view to better nights, and I have improved somewhat in this respect the last two nights, but still it is bad, & the eyes decidedly getting worse rather than better. Marshall wishes me to stay in London this week, that he may observe the progress of his treatment. I have a great inclination to come to Penkill rather than elsewhere, if I pluck up and go away at all, but must confess myself in such a state of nervous depression at present that it is doubtful whether I am fit to go any where. I write this letter (which is not merry) to keep you informed. I suppose if I did come, I should leave London about Tuesday next, and would then telegraph according to your directions.

With kindest remembrances & thanks to Miss Boyd

I am ever yours
DGRossetti

68.135.1 TO SIR WILLIAM BOWMAN[1]

MS: King's College School.

20 Sept/1868
16 Cheyne Walk
Chelsea

My dear Sir

Thanks for your note. I hope to see you tomorrow (Monday) at 12-30.

Yours very truly
D G Rossetti

W Bowman Esq

[1] For Bowman, see 67.140.

68.136 TO ALICE BOYD

MS: NLS. Published: DW 785.

> 21 Sept 1868
> 16 *Cheyne Walk*
> *Chelsea*

Dear Miss Boyd

Many thanks for your note. I have at this moment the fullest intention of accepting your offered hospitality and leaving London on Wednesday – day after tomorrow. I need write no more at present, but will telegraph from the station at starting.[1]

> Most truly yours
> DG Rossetti

---

[1] DGR left London on 23 Sep, stopping in Leeds to see the exhibition.

68.137 TO WILLIAM MICHAEL ROSSETTI

MS: Brotherton. Published: *FL* 196; DW 786. Date: WMR.

> Penkill Castle/Girvan/Ayrshire
> Saturday [26 September 1868]

Dear W

Here I am after toils worthy of Æneas.* I shall write before long to the Antique. This is to ask you to send Scott any Notes & Queries that contain articles about the Fairford windows attributed to A. Durer.[1]

I spent a couple of hours in the Exhibition at Leeds where there are a good many things worth seeing. A most glorious Sandro Botticelli (Nativity) a very fine Carpaccio (*called* Landing of Queen Cornaro in Cyprus) and splendid heads by Titian, Moroni, Bellini, & Velasquez.[2]

This is a delightful place, and I slept better last night than I have done for a long time.

Your friends here send regards.

> Your
> D Gabriel R

---

* Æneas's wanderings following his flight from Troy, recounted in Virgil's *Æneid*.
[1] WBS was writing *Albert Dürer: His Life and Works* (Longmans, Green, 1869). Since much of the glass painted for English churches c.1500, when the Church of St. Mary the Virgin, Fairford, Gloucestershire, was under construction, was by Dutch & German glaziers, the suggestion that the 28 Fairford windows could be attributed to Dürer was vigorously

supported and refuted in *N&Q* (Aug–Oct 68). Brian Coe (*Stained Glass in England* [Allen, 1981]: 20) proposes the German Barnard Flower, King's Glazier, 1505–17.

² See **10n1, 138,** & **142**. Except for mentioning FMB's contributions to the exhibition (**142**), DGR does not refer to the collection of English, French, & Dutch pictures, which *The Times* considered "especially rich." The reviewer disparaged the Italian Old Masters as not being equal in number or quality to the Italian pictures shown at the Manchester Art Treasures exhibition in 1857 (20 & 28 May 68).

68.138 TO CHARLES AUGUSTUS HOWELL

MS: Texas. Published: Cline 85.

Penkill Castle/Girvan/Ayrshire

30 Sept [1868]

Dear Howell

You *will* be a darling if you can manage the enclosed.¹

This is a truly heavenly place for beauty of scenery, & all private. *Such* a glen with running stream & lovely woods & such nooks for loving in if there were only the material. "Bits" too which I really should paint if I were all right. However I get comparatively excellent sleep now without – strange to say – other benefit as yet. If you *could* come down, I've no doubt you'd be offered quarters here. Could you? I fancy that I am keeping Miss B. & Scott from London now, & perhaps if a friend offered to come & be with me here, they might consent to go & leave us to ourselves. Not that they are not the dearest & best of friends, for so they are both – but Scott won't walk – by the bye I hear you say – no more wouldn't the Owl if he could fly or be carried instead. The weather seems to be setting in wet I fear just now, but still in these private grounds & this lovely sheltered glen there is much enjoyable in all weathers.

By the bye, about that bill on the 21st Oct (£50) I begin to funk rather, as to getting to work before then, but I suppose if absolutely necessary I can get the tin out of Bowman.²

I spent half a day at Leeds and saw the exhibition (glorious glorious *glorious* Botticelli & splendid Carpaccio!) and whom should I actually turn up at my hotel in the (let us hope ardent) flesh, but Valpy spooning & honeymooning. I was introduced to Mrs. V. who seemed capable & I think contented enough, so we will not doubt that B. Carew³ has adhered to his principles & "done his best to make her so."

Love to Kate & all friends. Do write me a line *at once*.

Your affec:
Gabriel

¹ A letter to JM; see **143**.
² WMR recorded in his diary (22 Sep): "Bowman ... bought for 150 guineas a copy lately

finished of the *Bocca Baciata*" (renamed *La Bionda del Balcone* [S.114R.1]; *RP* 329). See also **141** P.P.S.

3   DGR & CAH's name for LRV, of whom WMR says: "the rumour ... ran ... that [LRV] was the original of the effusive and tearful solicitor Baines Carew, in the *Bab Ballads* of Mr. W. S. Gilbert" (*RP* 268). See **18n1**.

68.139 TO FRANCES MARY LAVINIA ROSSETTI

MS: UBC. Published: *FL* 197; DW 787.

Oct 2/68
Penkill Castle/Girvan/Ayrshire

My dearest Mother

I have been meaning to write to you, but was in hopes of being able to give better news of my eyesight, which I am sorry to say is not the case yet. My sleep has improved extremely.

The glen belonging to the house here is a perfect paradise – one of the most beautiful spots I ever was in, and much of the scenery around is interesting. I take good walks and have a good appetite, and in most respects am perfectly well. The weather is in the main fine, and everything favourable, Miss Boyd's kindness being extreme, and Scotus a good companion, though not over fond of locomotion. Visitors are fortunately most rare, only one party having as yet turned up. Of this party one member was Lady Waterford, who again spoke of the illustrations she had been making, in conjunction with Mrs. Boyle, to Christina's "Maiden Song," and told me that Mr. Gladstone had repeated the poem to them by heart.[1]

I do not yet know how long I may be staying, but I fear I should find work so little possible were I to return to London at present that I have no temptation to do so. However I may perhaps soon find that I am inconveniencing Miss Boyd in her movements by staying here so late in the year, and that may bring me back.

With love to all at home, including Uncle Henry, I am

Your most affectionate Son
Gabriel

---

[1]   Louisa Anne, Marchioness of Waterford (1818–91), painted watercolours and exhibited at the Grosvenor & Dudley galleries. WMR records in his diary on 17 Dec 66: "G[abriel] says that ... Lady Waterford and Mrs. Boyle are doing a set of illustrations to Christina's poems" (*RP* 199). Since "E.V.B." was a prolific book illustrator, it is puzzling that they did not produce an illustrated volume of CGR's poems. For a later volume by "E.V.B.," *A Book of the Heavenly Birthdays* (Elliot Stock, 1893), which includes designs for excerpts from CGR's poems, see Lorraine Janzen Kooistra, *Christina Rossetti and Illustration* (Athens: Ohio UP, 2002): 161–62.

68.140 TO JAMES SMETHAM

MS: V&A. Excerpt: Casteras 54–55.

4th Oct/1868
Penkill Castle/Girvan/Ayrshire

My dear Smetham

Thanks for your poems and for the improved news of your doings which your letter conveys. Scott, Miss Boyd, & I were walking to Girvan (the port town here) & got your letter at the post office ourselves; whereupon we walked on to the sea-beach, seated ourselves on the spar of an old wreck, and I read the poetry aloud with great success. I think my own favourite is perhaps "Immortal Love" which has a strong tinge of Blake's spirit. But all are excellent. I certainly think you ought to do something with your literary powers which I think quite equal to those you possess in art. If any opportunity should arise for me to help you in making market way, I shall be but too glad.[1]

However I must tell you now what you will be very sorry to hear – that I have for more than 2 months now been suffering from a break-down in eyesight, which precludes me almost entirely from painting or drawing at present, & even makes it somewhat inconvenient to read or write. You may suppose that I have some difficulty in keeping up my spirits at all under such circumstances, and I am constrained to view the future with the utmost uncertainty and anxiety. I am obliged now to wear weak spectacles out of doors & in the house, as well as strong ones when my eyes are at all in use. Unfortunately I cannot but admit that the evil has gone on increasing since its sudden commencement. Not only is my sight a good deal weakened, but there is a continual & increasing distress in the sight which results in a tendency to waving and swimming in all I look at. Were it to continue thus, even without getting worse (of which I begin to fear there is little hope) I should have to consider my painting at an end or nearly so. I had begun to suffer in this way when I last wrote to you, but at that early stage was unwilling to mention the matter. I have tried rest and change of air with beneficial effect. My sleep had long been fearfully bad, accompanied at last by such torturing symptoms that I was induced to look up doctors. Under medical treatment my sleep is now greatly improved, and the brain (which I suspect was the original cause of the evil, and so the doctors surmised) is now calmer, but the eyes do not improve – indeed the reverse is the case. Of course I see oculists – 2 eminent ones, Bowman & Bader – but I can see they are very puzzled & uncertain, though they try to speak with confidence of my recovery, and on repeatedly examining my eyes with the ophthalmoscope at intervals, continue to say that there is no disease whatever originating in the eyes themselves. I would give you the whole history of my cheerful symptoms were we tête-à-tête, but it is hardly worth writing out in further detail, & moreover much writing is probably not good for me. I must still hope for the best.

If I could thoroughly enjoy anything just now I should find this place the most enjoyable possible. It is an ancient castle belonging to the Boyd family, & restored from a ruin, which it had long been, by Miss Boyd's late brother.[2] It is on a small eminence and overlooks a glen of its own which is a perfect paradise to wander in – the most lovely spot I think I was ever in. I wish we could take a walk in it together when I finish this letter and drink in its beauties & mysteries, and listen to its rushing stream.

Scott & Miss Boyd both desire to be kindly remembered to you, and I remain ever

Yours affectionately
D Gabriel R

---

[1] For JS' poems, see **150**, Smetham 87–99, *PRISM* 60.2, Casteras chapter 5 & passim, and Davies, "A Critical and Biographical Study of James Smetham" (Ph.D dissertation, King's College, University of London, 1979).

[2] AB's brother, Spencer Boyd, the 13th laird, died in 1865. He was the first in the family to live at Penkill again; it had been uninhabited since the death of Alexander Boyd in 1750 because the estate passed to a nephew living in Virginia. Alice and Spencer Boyd's maternal grandfather, William Losh, paid for the renovations completed in 1857. Their paternal grandfather, also named Spencer Boyd, younger son of the previous heir, had returned from the United States to claim the title in 1792, and married Sarah Wilkinson in Nov 1796 in a double ceremony held at St. Cuthbert, Carlisle, at which his wife's sister Frances married George Losh. See **141n3** for further details of the Boyd-Losh connection.

68.141 TO FRANCES MARY LAVINIA ROSSETTI

MS: UBC. Excerpt: *FL* 198–99; Knight, *DGR*: 103; Surtees 69n5. Published: DW 788. The P.P.S., written on a separate page, is mistakenly printed with 69.131 in DW 855, but it almost certainly belongs, as Cline conjectured (85n3), with this letter. The error misled Surtees (69n5) into a vain attempt to reconcile WMR's diary account (**138n2**) with DGR's to his mother.

Penkill
6th Oct./68.

Good Antique

I'm afraid I didn't write very hopefully to you last time, so I had better enclose you a letter just received from Bader, the oculist of Guy's Hospital, who was the first I consulted.[1] I have not seen him for some little time, but since being here received a note from him & wrote in reply respecting some

6th Oct./68.

additional troublesome symptoms which had supervened since my seeing him. His favourable view seems, as you see, to be unaltered, however, if that is worth much. I thought at any rate you wd like to see the note.

I have just got your dear letter, and one from William. In yours I think I detect a funny old intention of writing large for the benefit of my sight. This would be quite in the Antique spirit.

The kindness of Miss Boyd is unbounded, & I suppose I shall not be returning to London at present. The weather here continues almost entirely fine in the daytime; indeed, more splendid walking weather could not well be imagined.

Will you tell Wm that I am vexed to find his great discovery (which I saw noticed in the Athenæum) is a sell.[2] I have not yet seen the following number; but a difficulty had occurred to me as follows. In the absence of Tiraboschi's Italian, it seemed possible to me that after all the meaning might be that Lelio somebody signed *himself* Loelius. Is this perhaps what turns out to be the difficulty?

It is capital news to hear of such an improvement in Henrietta [Polydore] and I suppose the season is not the most favourable there so the thing seems really hopeful. I wish the news of her father was equally good. Will you give him my love.

I get up very late here, to give myself the utmost benefit of sleep, which continues in a vastly improved condition. I then simmer gradually to walking heat, and walk accordingly. In the evening, after dinner, we read aloud and sometimes play whist. There is an aunt of Miss Boyd's, an old maiden lady named Miss Losh,[3] a year younger than your funny old self, who is staying here, and is a nice cheerful intelligent old thing. I read a vast amount of Christina aloud the other evening which was much enjoyed though everyone knew it already. The 2nd vol.[4] only is here. A passage occurs in "L.E.L." (C's poem) which says, "And rabbit thins his fur." Miss Losh surmised this to refer to the habits of rabbits female which, when they expect a brood pull off some of their own fur to make a soft bed. This indeed I witnessed in one of my own rabbits just before leaving Chelsea. Was this C's intention? In such case *his* should be changed to *its*, as *her* would not come in well.

With love to all

Your most affec: son,
Gabriel

P.S. I did not mention in my last that Scotus's pictures are now quite finished and look very fine.[5] There is a hedgehog together with other beasts in the last one which would delight Christina.

P.P.S. I suppose I told you of my seeing Bowman before I left London, and that instead of taking a guinea fee (which he refused) he proposes to pay me 150 for a little watercolour which is fortunately just upon finished,[6] so that the tin will come in conveniently on my return to town without much additional trouble.

Scott & Miss Boyd both desire to be most kindly remembered to you.

[1] See **121n1**.
[2] WMR never tired of minute textual study & speculation. His interest in Chaucer's *Troilus and Criseyde* in relation to its source, Boccaccio's *Il Filostrato*, led him to publish a 2-part parallel text (Chaucer Society [1873, 1883]). Two cruxes of Chaucer criticism about the poem concerned him in 1868: John Lydgate's lines about Chaucer's "translacioun / Off a book which callid is Trophe," and Chaucer's naming of Lollius as his "auctour" or authority. WMR reasonably suggested that "Trophe" meant "a trophy or victim of love," which was the "arbitrary meaning" given to the word "Filostrato" by Boccaccio. His "great discovery" was that Lollius was Petrarch, whom Chaucer believed to be the author of *Il Filostrato*, but following a conversation with Charles Cayley, he wrote to the *Athenæum* to acknowledge that he had misread a passage in Girolamo Tiraboschi's *Storia della Letteratura Italiana* (1772–95; 26 Sep & 10 Oct 69: 401–02, 465). R. A. Shoaf (ed., *Troilus and Criseyde* [East Lansing, MI: Colleagues Press, 1989]) concludes that "who Lollius was and what he signifies in the Troilus . . . remain uncertain" (xv).
[3] Alicia Margaret Losh (1801/2–72), the fourth of six daughters born to George Losh & Frances Wilkinson, was AB's first cousin once removed. AB's mother Margaret was the younger daughter of William Losh & the third Wilkinson sister, Alice, and she married her cousin, the next Spencer Boyd (d.1827). AML's father was less successful than his brothers and after a venture in Scotland failed in 1815, he transplanted his family to the countryside near Rouen, France. AML was brought up there and among her uncle James's cultured circle at Jesmond Grove, Newcastle. The Losh sisters often visited Paris, and 3 of them were married at the British Embassy Chapel. AML returned to her grandfather's home at Woodside, Brisco, Cumberland, as companion to her cousin Sarah, when the latter's sister, Catherine Isabella, died in 1835 (see also 69.131). Sarah left AML an annuity & Ravenside House in the nearby village of Wreay. As these letters show, for the next 3 years DGR found her a congenial and rewarding correspondent.
[4] *The Prince's Progress and Other Poems*.
[5] WBS' murals, based on James I of Scotland's *The King's Quair*, were painted on the staircase at Penkill between 1865–68.
[6] See **138n2**.

68.142 TO FORD MADOX BROWN

MS: UBC. Excerpt: *RP* 370–71. Published: DW 789. Date: FMB.

Penkill

7th Octr [1868]

My dear Brown

I had better answer your enquiries to Scott myself. I am still very queer in the eyes, in spite of vastly improved sleep. I lately received a note of enquiry from Bader the oculist, & wrote him my latest symptoms some of which I think very nasty ones. However he still writes expressing the most unlimited confidence in my complete recovery. So let us hope for the best.

Miss Boyd says, – won't you come down? Now do. We should be as jolly as is possible in my queer state, and I dare say I should be helped to forget it. There is a splendid studio here, so you could bring any work you pleased with you. Miss Boyd is the most indulgent of hostesses & you would do precisely as you pleased. Scott's pictures are finished and well worth a visit if there were no other attraction. But the scenery here is simply Paradise within the grounds of the Castle – all private and every opportunity of painting landscape if you felt inspired. The glen belonging to the castle is I think the most lovely spot I was ever in. All kinds of joy and mystery in all its corners – immense variety of background material for any conceivable outdoor subject. There is one spot which even I should be moved to set to work on if my eyes were in order. The extreme quiet & beauty of the place could not but prove invaluable to you.

Now do come at once. It ought to be at once, as the trees are beginning – though only just beginning – to thin very materially. The weather here has been splendid, instead of the nuisances I hear you have suffered from in London – and seems likely to remain so at present.

You know you can come on in one day to Carlisle & next day to Girvan which is only 4 miles from this. A fly can be got at the station, or I doubt not Miss B. would send a trap for you if you sent word of the precise time of your arrival.

Perhaps you have seen some of my letters to others, & know that I spent a couple of hours in the Leeds Exhibn in coming out here. For this of course I had to pass the first night at Leeds. The old Masters are intensely interesting in many cases, but the place is now a bear garden of Yorkshire excursionists. It will be open till 26th Octr. Two of yours – Last of England and Jacob – were extremely well hung and looked very fine. The Work is seen to disadvantage and the Cordelia not as it ought to be, but still pretty well.

With love to all

Your affec:
Gabriel

68.143 TO CHARLES AUGUSTUS HOWELL

MS: Texas. Published: Cline 86.

Penkill
9th Oct/1868

Dear Howell

Thanks for your letter and postal delivery the results of which have just appeared in a reply, which however says nothing of the impediment you so happily overcame.[1] In writing again, give me a history of its nature. It was enough to frighten one certainly.

It shall be all right about the £50 bill for 21st. I have had occasion to write a line to Ellis today (on Smetham's acct, who wants a Topsy book sent him to review) and have assured him to that effect. If it happens I am unable to get the picture to Bowman before that date, Scott will lend me the tin till I do so.

It is splendid weather out here, and all well except the standing ailment. I do not know how long I may stay. I fear it would be of no practical use my returning to London at present.

Are you still available as a pillar post (surmounted by a monumental group of Love & Friendship) or is a permanent statue of Prudence to keep the lid fast shut for the future?

Miss Boyd & Scott send best remembrances & I am your & Kate's affectionate

D Gabriel R

P.S. Write some general news for this wild solitude.
P.P.S. As to the Botticelli, it belongs to one Fuller Maitland and is of course I suppose not for sale.[2]
P. P. P. S. No doubt (whether you come or not on Friday or earlier) you will let me hear from you in reply to this by Friday morning. I need to know, because of arrangements with Dunn.

[1] JM's reply to the letter DGR sent through CAH (**138**; see Cline 87n1). DGR continued to use CAH as a "pillar post" (see **146**).
[2] William Fuller Maitland (1813–76), collector of early Italian & English landscape paintings, had lent his Botticelli to the Leeds exhibition. Then entitled *Adoration of the Infant Christ*, the picture is now called *Mystic Nativity* (National Gallery, London).

68.144 TO FORD MADOX BROWN

MS: UBC. Excerpt: *FMB* 242. Published: DW 790.

12 Oct 1868
Penkill

Dear Brown

Your letter is perfectly insane. If a foold [*sic*] won't buy, try a fool. But meanwhile come down here. It won't be the least use waiting for Graham, who will think all the more of you if you are away when he calls & I'm sure he won't be able to call yet. As to Topsy's opinion on my health, it instantly conjured up a drama which I subjoin –

Scene – Queen Square.
Table Laid.

Alarums. Excursions. Morris discovered ringing a bell with violence.

Enter Brown

B. How are you Morris? Have you heard how Gabriel is?
M. (dancing) I wish to God Gabriel – no I mean the cook – was in Hell! Don't you Janey dear? Damn blast &c &c. Oh ah! Don't you know? Gabriel's all right again. Damn blast &c &c. Of course you'll stay to dinner old chap. I don't know though if we're to have any. Janey dear, it's all your fault. Damn blast &c &c.

Dinner brought in.

Janey (carving) Haven't you heard from Gabriel, Mr. Brown?
Morris (nudging her, in a whining tone) Why Janey dear, that's the bit I always have. You know Brown doesn't like it.
Janey. O I'm very sorry, dear. Here it is. Will you have the other too? What were you saying, Mr. Brown?
Brown. I thought Morris might have heard from Gabriel.
Morris (who has been helped.) Oh ah! Gabri-obble obble – Gabri-unch unch – Gabri-obble obble obble obble –

(*Morris eats. Tableau*)

You really *must* come you know. The weather's splendid and we should be as jolly as possible. I would recite to you all the ignominious rhymes I have made on Scotus & I would make some on you too.

Your affec:
Gabriel

P.S. Miss Boyd says you're to come.

68.145 TO HENRY BUXTON FORMAN[1]

MS: LC (inserted into a copy of *EIP* in the Rare Book Room). Written on monogrammed 16CW stationery.

Oct 13/1868
Penkill Castle/Girvan/Ayrshire

Dear Sir

The volume in question was nearly ready for the press when advertised, but shortly afterwards I got into a state of health and spirits which caused me to destroy the MSS.

I regret this of course though chiefly for my own sake; as the poets who have arisen since then make it of less consequence than ever to any one besides myself.

Very truly yours
D G Rossetti

H. B. Forman Esq

[1] This letter appears to be DGR's first contact with HBF (1842–1917), a civil servant at the Post Office, who was also a man of letters: a literary critic, collector, & book forger (in partnership with Thomas J. Wise). HBF had enquired about the volume of DGR's original verse advertised in 1861 at the end of *EIP*. His sympathetic article on DGR's poetry (*Tinsley's Magazine*, Sep 69) was an important stimulus leading the poet to publish his work in 1870.

68.146 TO CHARLES AUGUSTUS HOWELL

MS: Texas. Published: Cline 87.

Thursday [15 October 1868]

Dear Owl

Not having heard from you yet, I can't resist sending another enclosure,[1] which you will manage I know if possible, though not if impossible.

Scott & I have just settled to return to town together on Monday 27th. So you see the enclosed ought to reach at once if it is to secure a result which is my only solace out here.

When in London I shall try if work is at all possible and shape my plans accordingly. The weather here, which has been splendid hitherto, seems just today to threaten breaking up a little.

Old Brown has been asked down. If you were to find he intended coming, I would of course be only too glad to put off my return, and should probably benefit by doing so. But as Scott has to be going back, I shall do so too unless Brown is coming.

I needn't say you are a dear old thing for all you do on my behalf. You know what the service is to me and what my gratitude must be to you.

Love to Kate.

Your
Gabriel

[1] See **143n1**.

68.147 TO CHARLES AUGUSTUS HOWELL
MS: Texas.

Penkill
Friday [16 October 1868]

Dear Howell
I meant to have sent this yesterday to meet bill 21st Oct. Here it is.

Ever yours
D G Rossetti

68.148 TO JAMES SMETHAM
MS: V&A.

Penkill Castle/Girvan/Ayrshire
16th Octr 1868

My dear Smetham
Ellis writes me word that he has sent you Morris's book. Suppose you send me the London Quarterly with your Blake article hither.[1] There is a dearth of

new reading for the evenings. Perhaps though it is not out. If you send it & have only one copy I will scrupulously return same.

I need not say how grateful I am for all you so affectionately expressed in your last.

Ever yours
D G Rossetti

[1] JS' article on AG's *Blake* appeared in the *London Quarterly Review* 31 (1868): 265–311).

68.149 TO JAMES ANDERSON ROSE

MS: Berg. Published: DW 791.

19 Oct/1868
Penkill Castle/Girvan/Ayrshire

My dear Rose

I expect to be back in town on Tuesday evening next in all probability & will then again write you. I am just as anxious as ever to see you. You may perhaps have heard from Sandys or some intimate (of course I do not bruit it abroad) that I am suffering from the most alarming of all ailments – a sudden and persistent deterioration of eyesight. I have seen oculists but do not know what to think of the matter at present. There is no improvement as yet, after about 3 months, which time it has already lasted. Indeed in some respects there are decidedly worse symptoms.

In connection with this it is most necessary that I should see you & consult you respecting arrangements which the future may call for imperatively. It is no use my saying more as to my ideas on the subject till I see you[1] – and meanwhile

am yours sincerely
DG Rossetti

J A Rose Esq

[1] This letter & **151** refer to legal matters pertaining to DGR's proposal to make a deed of gift or a bill of sale to put 16CW in WMR's hands. JAR advised that such action would not protect it from his creditors (*RP* 333).

68.150 TO JAMES SMETHAM

MS: V&A. Excerpt: Smetham 216–17; DW 792.

27 Oct 1868
Penkill

My dear Smetham

The L[ondon]. Q[uarterly]. R[eview]. arrived yesterday, & I read your article aloud, which gave us all a great deal of pleasure.[1] It is full of real stuff in every paragraph (by the bye it is a pity the paragraphing and punctuation are not better – this I suppose is the printer's fault) and is as just in criticism as it is excellent in style and rich in imagery. I was specially delighted with what you say about Dobell's "Keith of Ravelston" – not only because you have so flatteringly lugged in my name in connection with it, but because I have always regarded that poem as being one of the finest of its length by any modern poet, – ranking with Keats's "La Belle Dame sans merci" and the other masterpieces of the condensed & hinted order so dear to imaginative minds. What a pity it is that Dobell generally insists on being so long-winded when he can write like that. There is a snatch of sea-song (about the "Betsy Jane") in *Balder*, which is fifty times as good as anything in Dibdin, who is nevertheless not contemptible. Our circle here, though small, is a highly appreciative one, and I assure you you could not have been in better hands. Our ladies are Miss Boyd and a charming old lady, an aunt of hers, who (as I thought in reading) exactly realizes what you say of old age in your review, and who has a great love of poetry.

The weather begins to break up here now, and I shall be soon returning to town to see what I can do towards work – not very hopeful I am sorry to say.

I got your second batch of poetry, and much like "Macpelah" as well as the Psalm version; but these – dated some time ago – are not I think so terse or quite so independent in style as your later efforts.[2] I shall be curious to see your article on Blake and also what you find to say of Morris. Have you seen his last poem – *The Two Sides of the River* – in the Fortnightly? It is gloriously fine – I really think his chef d'œuvre hitherto.

I shall have a pleasant neighbour at Chelsea now in Boyce, who has come to live in Cheyne Row, I hear, and will be superintending the progress of a house which he means to build for himself from Webb's designs on a plot of ground he has secured nearly behind my house.[3] He has not, as perhaps you know, been very well lately.

Miss Boyd and Scott send you kindest remembrances and are telling me to say what I have however already said of the pleasure your article gave us. However Scott wishes me specially to add that he is "glad your Methodism has not effaced your humour," and as there is no offence in this, I think, I will put it in.

Love to you, my dear fellow, from

Your affec:
D Gabriel R

P.S. I am afraid I have lost your little note telling me where to send the Review – so I will return it to you in due time.

---

1. JS' review of Alexander Smith's *Last Leaves: Sketches and Criticisms*, edited with a memoir by P. P. Alexander (Edinburgh, 1868), was published in the October number and reprinted in Smetham (195–229).
2. See **120** & **140**.
3. For GPB's house, see **65**.

68.151 TO JAMES ANDERSON ROSE

MS: Berg. Published: DW 839.

Wednesday [4 November 1868]
16 Cheyne Walk
Chelsea

My dear Rose

Can you dine with me Friday at 7, as I want to talk over matters to which I alluded in my last. I hear you left word that you would come any day I might name, but in case Friday chances to be inconvenient, will you take pot-luck tomorrow (Thursday) as I suppose Saturday would not do for you.

In case of tomorrow suiting you best, I need not trouble you for an answer as there is hardly time & I will be sure to be at home. I only came back last night.

Ever yours
D G Rossetti

68.152 TO ERNEST CHESNEAU

MS: Musée Calvet, Avignon. Excerpt: Rod, *Études sur le XIXème Siècle* (1888): 72–73; FLM 128–29; DW 793. Published: Maurin, *Victorian Newsletter* 44 (1973): 24–26.

7 Novembre 1868
16 Cheyne Walk,/Chelsea,/Londres.

Cher Monsieur,

J'ai reçu le cadeau très apprécié de votre livre, "Les Nations Rivales dans l'Art"; et, en le lisant, je me sens tout d'abord fortement impressionné de la

7 Novembre 1868   68.152

conscience enthousiaste avec laquelle vous vous êtes appliqué à rendre justice à notre école anglaise ainsi qu'aux autres écoles de l'Europe. J'ai la conviction que jusqu'ici nul critique étranger à l'Angleterre n'a compris et n'a analysé si bien la peinture actuelle anglaise, surtout en ses sections exceptionnelles. Ce n'est point que je partage toutes vos vues sur des individus. Surtout je crois qu'en voyant plus de l'ouvrage de Poole et de Leighton, vous leur rendriez une attention bien plus sérieuse; et je m'étonne de ne pas trouver en tout votre travail ni le nom de Maclise ni celui de Watts. Toutefois je ne sais pas s'ils aient exposé à Paris en 1867, n'ayant pas moi-même visité l'exposition.

Je me sens porté à vous fournir un renseignement à propos de ce que vous dites si justement du noble ouvrage de Paton ("In Memoriam"), touchant le *fiasco* de l'émotion tragique produit par l'introduction des soldats anglais à l'endroit que les cipayes devraient occuper. Quand le tableau a été exposé à l'Académie Royale de Londres (je crois en 1858) les cipayes y étaient à leur véritable place; et ce n'est qu'après les réclames d'un public et d'une presse assez banales que le peintre a été persuadé de changer sa tragédie en mélodrame. J'éprouverais une vraie satisfaction si par hazard votre critique le décidait à rétablir le vrai catastrophe de son terrible sujet.

Je n'ai trouvé (inévitablement) que les noms seuls de deux de nos plus admirables peintres; c'est à dire, de Madox Brown, le plus doué parmi tous les artistes anglais de force et d'émotion dramatiques, et de Burne Jones, qui est à mon avis (quoique ce soit chose grave à dire) le plus grand maître en couleur passionnée et en poésie mystique de tout l'Art moderne.

À la page 49 vous faites mention de certaines compositions décoratives auxquelles le nom de l'artiste n'était pas attaché. Elles sont de William Scott, peintre de grandes pensées et de grand dignité historique, dont les ouvrages de pure histoire sont loin d'être aussi connus qu'ils méritent d'être chez nous.

Maintenant je dois vous remercier de ce que vous êtes si généreusement efforcé de dire sur mon compte d'après des indices si faibles et, malheureusement pour moi, si peu correctes. Le tableau qui vous a été décrit par la bienveillance intelligente de M. Georges Pouchet cst un des plus beaux ouvrage[s] de Holman Hunt, dont le titre est "The Hireling Shepherd." En ce qui concerne la qualification de "chef de l'école préraphaélite" que vous m'attribuez d'après vos renseignemen[t]s, je dois vous assurer le plus chaudement [que] possible qu'elle ne m'est nullement due. La renommée vêtit toujours l'inconnu de quelques qualités mystérieuses; et c'est seulement à ce phénomène si commun que je puis attribuer le bruit sur mon compte que j'ai trouv[é] dans votre ouvrage et ailleurs. Loin d'être "chef de l'école," par priorité ou par mérite, je puis à peine me reconnaître comme y appartenant, si le style du peu que j'ai fait en peinture venait à être comparé avec les ouvrages des autres peintres nommés préraphaélites. Ainsi, quand je trouve un peintre si absolument original que c'est Holman Hunt décrit comme étant mon "disciple," il m'est impossible de ne pas me sentir humilié en face de la vérité, et de ne pas vous assurer du contraire avec le plus grand empressement. Les qualités d[u] réalisme émotionnel mais extrèmement minutieux, qui donnent le cachet au style nommé préraphaélite, se trouvent principalement dans tous les tableaux de Holman Hunt, dans la plupart de ceux de Madox Brown, dans quelques morceaux de Hughes, et dans l'œuvre admirable de la jeunesse de Millais. C'est la camaraderie plus que la collaboration réelle de style, qui a uni mon nom aux leurs dans des jours d'enthousiasme d'il y a vingt ans. Je puis ajouter que la petite exposition privée qui vous a été décrite (p.73) comme consistant de mes tableaux ne contenait que quelques petites choses de moi parmi plusieurs d'autres artistes. Depuis l'age de vingt-deux ans, je puis dire que je n'ai jamais exposé nulle part, pour des motifs qui me sont personnelles et dont le détail ici serait égoïste.

Encore une parole. L'idée que M. Ruskin a fondé par ses écrits l'école préraphaélite est une méprise que j'ai trouvé être presqu'universelle, mais qui n'est pas moins pour celà une méprise absolue. Je crois en vérité que, parmi les peintres fondateurs de l'école, pas un n'avait jusque-là lu un seul des admirables livres de Ruskin, et certainement pas un parmi eux ne lui était personnellement connu. Ce n'est qu'après deux ou trois expositions annuelles de ces tableaux que ce grand écrivain c'est généreusement constitué leur défenseur contre les attaques acharnées de la presse.

Enfin, je dois m'excuser sérieusement auprès de vous, cher Monsieur, de vous avoir occupé si longuement de moi dans un si mauvais français; mais ne sachant pas si l'anglais vous soit familier, j'ai fait de mon mieux avec une langue dans laquelle je suis loin de pouvoir m'exprimer aussi passablement que dans la mienne.[1]

Croyez-moi, cher Monsieur, avec la plus haute considération,

Vôtre dévoué serviteur
D. G. Rossetti

à Monsieur Ernest Chesneau

---

[1] DGR is referring to a section on the PRs in Chesneau's book, *Peinture, sculpture. Les Nations rivales dans l'art* (Paris: Didier, 1868). WMR states that DGR wanted to correct "some of the errors concerning Pre-Raphaelitism, G[abriel]., Ruskin, etc." (*RP* 334). DGR was particularly hostile to the identification of himself as the head of the school and the statement that these painters had been influenced by JR. Noting that he had been a student of WHH, he rejects the statement that WHH was his disciple and adds that the paintings of

WHH and the early work of JEM embody true PRISM more fully than anything he has done. In addition, he identifies WBS as the artist whose decorations Chesneau had praised, expresses surprise that Maclise & Watts were not mentioned, and regretted that more attention had not been paid to FMB, AH, & EBJ. Chesneau adopted most of DGR's corrections in *La Peinture anglaise* (Paris: Quantin, 1882).

68.153 TO ALICE BOYD

MS: NLS. Excerpt: Purves 580–81. Published: DW 794.

9th Nov/1868
16 Cheyne Walk
Chelsea

Dear Miss Boyd,

I have been deferring writing to you since I came home in the intention of telling you some medical or working experiences, but as I have hitherto not plucked up energy enough either to go to any doctors or to set to work, I will not defer writing now, but will write again ere long.

I called on Scotus on Saturday evening and saw the little pictures improved by various last touches. The rainy one looks very fine, & old Brown says it is as fine as any David Cox.[1] I really think it is the best of the three. Mrs. Scott was very racy, & had I been a Saturday reviewer, would have afforded me material for a whole article on the Ritualistic Lady.[2] Talking of parties in Lent, she at first expressed horror of them, but after re-consideration said in her gravest manner that she should not object to attending one or two *as a penance*. Old Brown was here on Friday night & sat up talking till 5 A.M., not forgetting to liquor up freely all the time. It seems he has heard through Miss Spartali some news of the Duchess's little cad who has returned to London with the most fearful accounts of my bearish conduct on the occasion of his visit to Penkill. His name it appears is Graham.[3]

I am looking up the big sketch-book of Sibson's and some photos:[4] which I shall expedite tomorrow to Penkill by passenger train. I suppose I shall find myself permitted to pay for their carriage beforehand, but if this may not be, I shall have to leave it to you and pay when I see you.

Ever yours sincerely
D G Rossetti

P.S. Don't trouble to answer this.

[1] WBS' "little pictures" have not been identified, but WBS:AB on about the same date says:

"My little pictures have been seen by Brown, who is enthusiastic about the rainy day one, – strange to say, it will be the one most thought of." The Cox referred to is landscape painter David Cox, 1783–1859.

2 Ritualism in the Church of England had sparked much commentary in the periodicals of the time. WMR says of Letitia Scott: "she had a knack at pirouetting around religious subjects, and she tried her luck in every doctrinal camp, from secularism to Roman Catholicism. At last she seemed to think herself well based in Anglicanism" (*SR* 1: 132).

3 The "little cad" must have been one of Lady Waterford's party (see **139**).

4 Thomas Sibson (see 54.10n9). WBS told AB on 17 Nov that DGR had sent the sketchbook "by way of showing me up in sketches he says exist there, which are to open your eyes to the dissipated life in the old days. Is he not in a curious state of mind?" (PP). For Sibson and the sketchbook, see *AN* 1: 155.

68.154 TO ALICIA MARGARET LOSH

MS: Princeton. Published: *TR* 81–82; DW 795. The 16CW monogram has been cut from the MS.

9th Novr 1868

Dear Miss Losh,

I am sending some photographs tomorrow to Miss Boyd, and want to beg your acceptance also of some which I shall enclose with hers. Since my return, my eyes are about the same. Everything else has been all right, both as to health and the events of this chequered existence.

I called on Topsy who was howling and threatening to throw a new piano of his wife's out of window. It unfortunately arrived I believe just at dinnertime and the occurrence had poisoned his peace of mind ever since.

I have written to M. Ernest Chesneau, the author of that book on Art, & set him right about myself, Scotus, and others. So I shall now return his book to you (you need not hesitate to keep it, as I find another copy was sent to my brother) and at the same time shall send you a copy of my own Italian Poets, if I can get it in time for the parcel tomorrow. If not, it shall follow.

Calling on Scotus the other day I insisted on seeing that Forbidden Fruit which he snatched in the Eden of Leicester Square. He professed not to know which it was of a set he had, but I recognized it by an extra amount of affectionate rubbing and mending which it had evidently undergone.

When the large sketchbook arrives, I wish Miss Boyd and you to study Scotus in various favorite characters as performed by him in early life. Unfortunately we have no pictorial record of him in a later rapid act at Puttick & Simpson's, but that has doubtless been photographed by the Recording Angel and retained in an important collection which will one day but too surely come to the hammer & be knocked down (together it is to be feared with the originals) at very doubtful rates indeed.[1]

Now don't on any account bother to answer this but believe me

Most truly yours
D G Rossetti

[1] WBS had stolen a print at Puttick & Simpson's auction room to complete a series in his collection. WMR's description of the incident contrasts with DGR's indulgent mockery expressed here and in **157** to AB. "The insatiable greed of the collector raged or raved in him at the sight. He actually stole that missing print and walked off with it. [WBS] was a mature, a moral, a reflective, and a cautious man, and yet he committed this serious offence and veritable act of lunacy. He might have been detected, and then his whole life was wrecked, and his whole collection of engravings a withered leaf in the whirlwind" (*SR* 1: 383–84). The "favourite characters" from Sibson's sketchbook mentioned in the previous letter might refer to such sketches therein as "The Criminal Law Courts" or "Gin Palace," befitting the dubious character of WBS. The sketchbook, with WBS' bookplate, is now in the BL.

68.155 TO GEORGE RAE

MS: LLAG.

11 Nov 1868
16 Cheyne Walk/Chelsea

My dear Rae

I have now written to Green's to forward you another acct as I have mislaid the one you sent on to me.[1]

I returned a few days ago from Scotland where I had been for 6 weeks or so.

I am sorry to say that I have lately been prevented from doing much work by a troublesome state of health. When I do get to it again, I hope to find myself in all the better trim for my rest.

With kind remembrances to Mrs. Rae

I am ever yours
D G Rossetti

George Rae Esq

[1] See **119**.

68.156 TO WILLIAM RALSTON SHEDDEN-RALSTON[1]

MS: Indianapolis Marion County Public Library.

16 Cheyne Walk
17 Nov 1868

My dear Ralston

Thanks for your note. Mr. Dunn thought it unnecessary to trouble you and we have adopted the suggestions you offered.

Ever yours
DG Rossetti

[1] William Ralston Shedden-Ralston (1828–89) was an assistant at the BM.

68.157 TO ALICE BOYD

MS: NLS. Excerpt: Purves 581–82. Published: DW 796.

16 Cheyne Walk
17 Novr 1868

Dear Miss Boyd,

I got your kind letter yesterday, and am very sorry to hear how unwell Miss Losh has been. Depend upon it, she ought to come up with you to London, and get some amusement. We would have some more rubbers and readings, and make ourselves happy with the assistance of the Poll parrot who is at this moment providing a monologue entertainment of the most striking order. Do persuade her to visit London.

I believe I am going to dine with Scotus tomorrow and meet Morley the editor of the Fortnightly.[1] I have just written W.B. a note and mentioned incidentally that Sibson's sketch-book has now afforded you an insight into the intimate memoirs of his early career. By the bye it was unfortunate (was it not?) that another of THE *fraternity* should have met him at the Ayr Station and not have observed in relation to the wine of the country that "honour among" – members of the craft – which the proverb inculcates.[2] I bemoaned my special pocket-pistol soon after leaving. By the bye I forgot to tell you of the reception I met with under the hospitable roof of Scotus a few days after my return to town. The Demon Olaf first greeted me with a selection from some opera of his own – probably "Scotus le Diable" – and when, after an hour or so, he had subsided & appeared at rest, he suddenly sprang up from the hearth and produced an indented pattern in the style of Morris & Co. round the toe of my boot – the different ornaments composing it being varied in the fanciful style of that firm so as to avoid monotony – some mere depressions of the surface and others complete perforations. I directed W.B.'s attention to this instance of Olaf's adding decorative art to his musical studies; and the remark I received in reply (uttered with slow complacency) was "Ah! then he has some teeth yet, you see!" I may mention in conclusion that I am *not* lamed for life, & that is all I can say.³

I met Topsy the other night at a large party of Greeks. He seemed depressed and complained of deafness, but on a large plug of string being taken out of his ear, he revived a good deal and even scratched himself in places apparently inaccessible. When I left, he was being prepared for departure. The whiskey cork had already been got out of his nose, and Janey had nearly succeeded in fishing the paper-knife up from the base of his spine. He was offering to stand on his head that it might drop out, but this was thought unnecessary.

By the bye, Howell assures me that he wrote me a long letter of 3 sheets just after I sent him that cheque of Scott's. I certainly never got any such, but from the things he told me about it, I think I may go so far as to believe him. He says that it was the only occasion on which he put your name as well as mine on the envelope, so it is still more strange that it never reached. It does not really matter now, but in case Robert were going to Girvan, he might perhaps as well enquire at the P.O. whether such a letter might be mislaid and still discoverable. The cheque must I am sure have been sent on or about the 17th Octr, so Howell's letter was probably due at Penkill about the 20th or 21st.

I have somehow got spell-bound as to work by the long interval of idleness, and have not yet set about anything. Nor can I feel sure as to the result of any such attempt, but am daily intending to try it and shall soon. I have seen no Doctors either, but old Mrs. Whistler and others have again been at me to go to Coblentz. On the other hand other people say the man is a quack.

Quacking reminds me of Quasi and his love, who I hope still waddle and gurgle in the dining room on occasion. I wonder has Scotus's peppermint-and-mud tint been applied yet to the wall surrounding the Topsaic tapestries. I saw it standing in tempting profusion ready for use.

I saw Swinburne once since my return. I think he saw me twice, but simultaneously. He was really almost drowned while swimming – poor fellow – at Érétat, having got apparently beyond that semi-sea-trip which is habitual to him.

With kindest remembrances to Miss Losh

I am ever yours sincerely
D G Rossetti

Miss Boyd

P.S. Christina is a good deal better – indeed very well for her.

1. John Morley (1838–1923) edited the *Fortnightly Review* from 1867–82; in Dec 68 the periodical accepted for publication a group of 16 sonnets by DGR, the embryonic form of *HL* (see **173**).
2. Further "chaff" about WBS' membership in a fraternity of thieves with no honour: evidently someone had stolen his whisky flask at the railroad station (see **154n1**).
3. "The Demon Olaf" was WBS' dog. On 9 Nov, WBS wrote to AB: "Olaf made the most tremendous row when [DGR] came, and as he was standing by my studio fire he trod on the beast's tail and Olaf seized him by the foot and fairly bit through his boot. Bye and bye my friends will keep out of my way on account of this dreadful dog, who is after all harmless as a lamb except when trodden on" (PP).

68.158 TO GEORGE PRICE BOYCE

MS: University College.

Tuesday 24 Nov,/68

My dear Boyce

Of course I remember Mr. Hales perfectly, and shd be most happy to see him again, as well as any friend of his. Only, were it proposed to describe my works in any *published* writing, from such specimens as I could show here, I should have to request that this might not be done; since I have no opportunity of giving an idea of my work and, not exhibiting, do not court criticism. In such case it would therefore be no use to give these gentlemen the trouble of coming.

In any case indeed I should have no satisfaction in receiving visitors at present, since there are only two of my pictures which are in a state in which I choose to show them – the *Lilith* & the portrait of *Mrs M*. If these alone are sufficient (small enough) attraction, and if, as I judge, you would prefer bringing your friends now to doing so at some possible better opportunity, and if above all there is no intention to publish, I shall be most happy to see Messrs. Hales & Cornish on Monday next, and all the better pleased if you come with them.

Your affec:
D Gabriel R

P.S. I don't know whether the green serge can now be got at Morris's where I got it. The manufacturer is an intimate friend of mine, and if you like to write direct to him and use my name, he wd be sure to pay every friendly attention. His address is

J.A. Heaton Esq
Woodbank
near Bingley
Yorks.

68.159 TO GEORGE RAE
MS: LLAG.

25 Nov 1868
16 Cheyne Walk

My dear Rae,

I find that the new bill sent you by Green does not refer to what I told him to send you (and what he *did* send you before) – the price of the Palmifera frame; but does refer to other things (as he tells me) still due from you to him on acct of your transactions through me.

The first entries refer to the pictures bought by you from Morris, and the last to the case of the *Beloved*. The Frame mentioned is that of the *Beloved*, – i.e. the second one, which you have, & which I believe was to be your expense, – I think your memory will coincide with mine in this. He has however entered it at £4 over its price, which I have now corrected with his assent. I never told him to send you a bill about these matters, as I fancied they were already settled, & as I had nothing to do with them. I have struck off one incorrect item at the end of the bill (which does not belong to you but me) and have added the correct price of the Palmifera frame (£20).

If you approve of the bill in this form, will you send it back to Green, and they will formally draw it up again; – that is if you think this further step necessary.

You will remember that, after the second frame for the Beloved was made (the sight of which was rather enlarged on the first) you made me a present of the first, which I have since put to use. This first I paid for to Green.

With kind remembrances

Ever yours
D G Rossetti

P.S. Perhaps I should explain exactly why I got Green to send you the bill for Palmifera frame just now. He sent me a long acct including this frame as well as others for Mr. Leyland and Mr. Mitchell, which were chargeable to the owners of the pictures; and I thought that there would probably be no objection to paying these items now (as Messrs. L. & M have since done,); by which means I became absolved from the necessity of paying at this moment my own share of the bill, which delay in my late state of inertia was a convenience to me.[1]

---

[1] See **119** & **155**.

68.160 TO WILLIAM BELL SCOTT

MS: Princeton. Date: WBS.

Thursday [26 November 1868]

Dear Scotus

Will you dine here tomorrow (Friday); William will be here – 7 o'clock. I enjoyed myself mightily last night at your party, and as I couldn't sleep made a sonnet in the rough which you'll find over-page – (in confidence).[1]

Top & Janey are coming here next Monday to stay some days & I am going to see if I can work a little, for without being forced to it I funk beginning. Before then I hope to send in Bowman's picture, & shall not forget you know what when I hear from him in return.[2]

If Miss Boyd is coming as you say on Saturday, I hope you'll bring her to spend an early evening. However I shall know best what evening to try and fix after the Morrises are here. If you are writing (but I suppose hardly again) I wish you would say how I rejoice to hear that Miss Losh is mending.

Ever your affec:
Gabriel

P.S. If you write in reply to this or at any time with any references of a certain kind, please *seal* letter.

---

[1] WMR records that the three dined together on 27 Nov: "Gabriel . . . has been looking up his poems of old days, with some floating idea of offering some of them to *The Fortnightly Review* . . . . the Editor (Morley) is going to make poems of some substantial length a feature of the magazine " (*RP* 336). Guests at WBS' party on the 25th included *Fortnightly* editor Morley, G. H. Lewes, the WMs, & JM's sister Bessie. WBS' description of DGR's behaviour at this event in his letter of the following day to AB is the first recorded mention of the artist's reckless infatuation with JM: "Gabriel sat by *Jeanie* [WBS' name for JM], and I must say acts like a perfect fool if he wants to conceal his attachment, doing nothing but attend to her, sitting sideways towards her, and that sort of thing. Mrs. Linton sat opposite and I shall be surprised if she did not see anything interesting, also Mrs. Morris' sister. However, I have concluded they (G.& J.) will not go further than they have gone. She is certainly the most remarkable looking woman in the world and *in expression* lovely. Of course a woman in such circumstances, before people, is a sealed book, still I think she is cool. As to Gabriel he forgets everyone else. When we went down, although it was my part to take Jeanie, G. got her arm in his, then abandoned her hurriedly for the nearest other lady, Morris looking at him all the time" (PP). Earlier, on 9 Nov, WBS had written to AB: "Gabriel has not tried painting, nor seen any doctor, nor seen the sweet Lucretia Borgia [JM]. I have now come to the conclusion – often when we meet a person in a new place after a few days cessation a new light breaks on one – that the greatest disturbance in his health and temper, and both are extremely different from what they were, is caused by an uncontrollable desire for the possession of the said L.B. Letitia [WBS' wife] went there on Friday to see an Altar Cloth and was the first to inform her of Gabriel's return, he having refrained from going as he understands they are watched. Even Mrs. Street had spoken to Letitia about Gabriel being so fond of Mrs. Top" (PP). In *Prelude* (24–28), Fredeman

explains the epistolary relationship between WBS & AB and why it illuminates the DGR-JM affair: "Neither of these letters [9 & 26 Nov] concerning Rossetti and Jane Morris contains any hint of the sensational; nor are they gossipy in the ordinary sense of the term. It is obvious that Scott is not revealing to Alice a situation with which she is unfamiliar, but that he is giving her a progress report on an occurrence that she has known about for some considerable time" (28).

    The situation changed for the worse in 1871–72: writing to CAH during DGR's major breakdown in the summer of 1872, WMR asks him for specifics of his brother's minor breakdown during their Aug 68 visit to Speke Hall, FRL's residence: "I should very much like to know the condition of his mind when you and he were at Speke. Of course I know that he was madly in love, and can believe anything in the way of hypochondria on that account, and as concerned the state of his eyes. But had he any and what sort of positive hallucinations?" (9 Jul, Cline 136).

2 The "you know what" is probably WBS' cheque sent to CAH from Penkill, which DGR planned to repay when he received Bowman's payment for his version of *Bocca Baciata*.

68.161 TO JAMES ANDERSON ROSE

MS: Berg. Published: DW 797.

30 Nov 1868

16 Cheyne Walk

Chelsea

My dear Rose

    Thanks for your kind inquiries. I have not yet set to work at all, feeling that I am better without it, but during this coming week am about to make an experiment in that direction, & shall then better know how I am.

    I have had a most frightful influenza cold, but am getting over it now.

    Did you write to the stable tenant claiming my arrears of rent?[1] You would really be doing me a friendly service by seeing to that matter just now, as Christmas is coming & with it many bills, & my enforced inertia has left me aground as to means of meeting them.

Ever yours sincerely

D G Rossetti

1 The first reference to DGR's stable tenant Strong since early Jan (1). See also 67.13; and 69.76, 97, & 110. He reports actually achieving possession of the stables in 69.128.

68.161.1 TO AGLAIA CORONIO

MS: Kansas. Published: DW 2336.

Wednesday [November 1868?]

Dear Mrs. Coronio,

    I find after all it will be impracticable for me to come to Holland Park this evening.¹ I am most sorry, but you know I thought this just possible when I last wrote. I shall come and claim your pardon (of which your kindness makes me sure) two or three Wednesdays hence if not earlier.

> Ever yours,
> D. G. Rossetti

¹ For this & the next letter, see **98&n1**.

68.162 TO AGLAIA CORONIO
MS: Bodleian.

> Tuesday [1 December 1868?]
> *16 Cheyne Walk*
> *Chelsea*

Dear Mrs. Coronio

I shall be very sorry not to see you and yours after all tomorrow evening, but a cold which has hung about me for some time has again got worse since I last wrote, & must prevent me from coming out so soon if I mean to get the better of it. Hoping for some other early opportunity,

> I am ever yours,
> D G Rossetti

68.163 TO CHARLES AUGUSTUS HOWELL
MS: Texas.

> Friday [4 December 1868]

Dear Howell

Will you and Kate dine here on Monday at 7 to meet the Morrises who are staying here.¹ Scott, wife, & Miss Boyd are coming, also William. Of course no togs.

> Your
> Gabriel

¹ DGR was working on crayon heads of JM on 7 Dec (*RP* 337). See also **167n1**.

68.164 TO GEORGE PRICE BOYCE

MS: University College. Date: GPB.

Friday [11 December 1868]
16 Cheyne Walk
Chelsea

My dear Boyce

I am going to my mother's this evening, so hardly expect to get to you at all, though I *may* if in time look to see if there is still a light in your window. Morris & Janey have left me.

Ever yours
D G R

68.165 TO CHARLES AUGUSTUS HOWELL

MS: Texas. Published: Cline 88. Date: CFM.

15th [December 1868]

My dear Howell

I most unaccountably forgot last night (for one appointment was made with Brown at your party itself) that he, Scott & Nettleship are to dine with me on Friday.[1] This precludes for me the Christie-Evans scheme. Would you kindly let Constantine Ionides know at once, as he asked me & I don't know his address.

The date of today reminds me that the bill business is drawing near. To pay would be only not quite impossible to me, so extremely inconvenient should I find it. Could I not renew for one month, when I hope a more settled state of work would make it as easy as it is ever likely to be. I'm sorry to trouble you in the matter.

Ever yours
D G Rossetti

P.S. I suppose the Empress has left the Empire Room desolate ere now.

If you can get the bill for renewal, name a day to dine here & bring Ellis if you think it advisable, but not if you think it would look like giving a sop to Cerberus.[2] But do dine here one day – any one you like – in any case, for I never see you & greatly do desire you.

P.P.S. I shall see you tomorrow week at Holland Park.[3] What is the dinner hour?

London.

1   Those named were present at Cheyne Walk on 18 Dec, and while the general impression was that John Trivett Nettleship's "strange Blakeish designs" were not marketable, "the idea was started that the best thing for him to do at once might be to illustrate some congenial book" (*RP* 339) – a suggestion fulfilled with his illustration of Arthur O'Shaughnessy's *Epic of Women*, published in 1870. The Rossettis had met Nettleship (1841–1902) through either John Payne or O'Shaughnessy; and WMR thought that DGR was his "first purchaser" (*SR* 326). Nettleship also wrote the first full-length book on RB – *Essays on Robert Browning's Poetry* (Macmillan, 1868). In his diaries, WMR records many visits to Nettleship's studio to admire and encourage his work. For DGR's intervention with Leighton & G. F. Watts when Nettleship's drawings were rejected by the RA, see 69.103.

Later in the same diary entry, WMR records that "Howell and others are projecting an 'Arts Company Limited' – Marks as businessman. [CA]H asked Gabriel to take a share in it: he will do so to the extent of £250 in the form of works of art supplied" (*RP* 339). This scheme sounds remarkably like the one CAH was already engaged in.

2   See **22**.
3   See **98n1**.

68.166 TO GEORGE PRICE BOYCE

MS: University College. Date: GPB.

[16 December 1868]

Dear Boyce

Can you come in to dinner at 7 & walk with me afterwards to Scott's, there to have a rubber? Or if too late to get you to dine here, could you come afterwards for the walk? Or if not at all to-day, could you do both things tomorrow?

Ever yours,
D G Rossetti

68.167 TO CHARLES AUGUSTUS HOWELL

MS: Princeton. Published: DW 803.

[17 December 1868]

Dear Howell

I couldn't attend to your letter before, being busy. Janey is gone back now.[1] I'm very sorry not to come to you tomorrow night, but have such lots of things to do that it must prevent my making appointments till Monday when I come to you. Besides, I have not been in a theatre for many months, & don't know how the glare of the gas might suit me.

I will reflect further on the poem question & send you the letter if I come to that conclusion. Really I do not know how to thank you for such a mark of friendship.[2]

I enclose the letter for Story. Can you add Mr. Palmer's initial outside?[3]

About Browning, I hope a few days hence – a very few – will do, as I received his poem some days back and have not been able to read it yet. I should therefore have to say something of it if I wrote and will at same time enclose the paper for his signature.[4]

The next bill comes due on the 21st & I will meet it if at all possible, though the fact of its being considered renewable hitherto had set me at rest on the point till now. Still of course there is nothing gained by renewal if I can pay. I must see how matters stand some days hence & let you know again. But can it absolutely *not* be renewed even for a month? – i.e. with fairness to Ellis.[5]

I will see about the drawings as soon as possible. By the bye I must beg you to remember that none of Janey must be parted with till photographed.

Let us set about getting the La Pia's done at once by Parsons. I hope the seated one you last had is not gone from you unphoto'd. If not, let that be done too. I will send for them when you tell me, & send them on to Parsons.

Give my kindest love to Kate & believe me

Your affec:
Gabriel

P.S. You will apologize from me most sincerely to Mme Coronio, but I cannot help myself.

[1] DGR had been in the midst of drawing JM for *Pandora* and for another *La Pia*. See **163**.
[2] The first reference in the letters to the possibility of retrieving the poetic MSS buried with EES.
[3] For William Wetmore Story, see 64.17; Mr. Palmer may have been the painter Samuel Palmer.
[4] RB sent *The Ring and the Book* on 1 Dec, inscribed "Gabriel Dante Rossetti from his affectionately ever RB" (*BCR* C532; now in the Robert Taylor Collection, Princeton). For DGR's delayed acknowledgement, see 69.7.
[5] See **22** & **165**.

68.168 TO EMILY TEBBS
MS: Texas.

20th Decr 1868
16 Cheyne Walk
Chelsea

My dear Mrs. Tebbs

Your husband was asking my brother how he could get a photograph from one of my drawings as a present to you. Will he and you let me deprive him of the opportunity of giving you such a trifle by myself begging your acceptance of it and a few others, accompanied with friendliest Xmas wishes to both of you.

Believe me yours sincerely
D G Rossetti

68.169 TO ALICIA MARGARET LOSH

MS (fragment): Princeton. Published: *TR* 83–84; DW 800. The final paragraph, following the missing close of the letter, which is reprinted in *TR* facing 84, may be part of a separate letter.

16 Cheyne Walk/Chelsea
21st Decr. 1868

My dear Miss Losh,

When you made me the most friendly offer of assistance I ever received in my life, I told you that only the fear of never doing you justice in the matter, through my declining eyesight, prevented me from frankly accepting it in such degree as I could feel sure of repaying. I have now, for some little time past, made the experiment of working; and have no reason, I believe, to fear being prevented from continuing with such regularity (even allowing for necessary caution) as may set my mind at rest with regard to my prospects for the present. Mr. Bowman, the oculist, whom I have again consulted, assures me that he has no apprehension as to my sight, and I have recommenced regular work, with, as you may suppose, great satisfaction. I do not however wish to overdo exertion for some time to come, and so run the risk of a relapse into total inertia; and with this aim in view, I am induced to propose availing myself still further than I have already done of your most kind offer: – that is, to the extent of an additional sum of £400, making in all £500 received. This would assist me more, at the present moment, in one sum, than by instalments at intervals; and I may add that it would be the last time (I trust for certain) that I should be trespassing on you. I could reasonably hope to repay it, if not entirely within the coming year, at any rate with no very great further delay; and it would enable me, with the many present claims on my purse which have resulted from my enforced inaction, to refrain from overworking myself to meet them, and to enter without hurry on a steady resumption of painting. In saying this, at the same time, I feel it is highly possible that the interval which has elapsed since I declined the greater part of what you so generously proposed to lend me, may have caused you to form other plans not compatible with the offer being renewed. Were this to prove the case, I should know equally well how entirely sincere and unreserved was the feeling with which it was made.[1]

I have heard repeatedly, from Miss Boyd and Scott, respecting your health,

Monday [21 December 1868]   68.170

and rejoice extremely to understand that you are now much as usual, after the severe attack of which I was told. I wish you would make up your mind to a New Year's trip to London. We are instituting a habit of whist-playing both here and at Elgin Road, and you would have every opportunity of exercising the powers of scrutiny which you bring to bear on that game. At any rate, if you do not come to this determination, I shall hope to renew our whist parties at Penkill earlier next year, and so get a sight of the beautiful scenery at its richest time.

Some of my bad symptoms have lessened most decidedly since I last wrote to you. . . .

Many and many thanks for your letter received this morning. I note all you say, but trust to make all well long before your melancholy forebodings come true for either of us – and I believe they are just as likely for me as for you. You have done me the greatest service I could have received at this moment; and I confess that my first feeling this morning is one of shame at having availed myself of so much generosity; but my utmost effort will be to avert all risk to you and yours before long.

1   Both WMR & WBS agree that AML proposed to lend DGR £1000 and that he attempted to decline the loan while he was at Penkill. WMR knew of the £100 cheque AML sent, but there is no evidence that either he or WBS knew of the request DGR makes in this letter or of his promises to repay until after her death. WBS' account is carefully worded, but its tone is nonetheless critical (*AN* 2: 110–11); and it is hardly surprising that WMR decided to reveal that the "I.O.U., or some such document . . . found after her death . . . was destroyed (in my brother's interest) by a friendly hand – I will not say whose" (see *FLM* 267–68). AML had an eye operation in London and died suddenly of pneumonia on 20 Mar 72, and her will was proved on 14 Jun, only days after DGR's mental breakdown. WBS kept AB informed of his condition, but he does not mention the debt in any of his letters to her during the summer & fall; neither mentioned it as affecting their relationship with DGR. In a letter to DGR from Penkill, WBS says that Frances Elizabeth Hutchinson Pennell, a niece of AML and 2nd cousin of AB, who was the executrix of her estate, asked AB what to do with DGR's "sundry acknowledgments of money" and AB "advised her to put them in the fire" (PP). WBS went on to ask DGR to keep the information secret: "by no means mention this circumstance, and put this in the fire" (DW 788n5). See also *TR* 80–85.

68.170 TO ALICE BOYD
MS: NLS. Published: DW 819.

Monday [21 December 1868]

Dear Miss Boyd

W. B. was here the other day, & mentioned a kind possibility of your looking me up one day. My reason for writing is that 4 was mentioned as the hour, but that I find I am never really at liberty till 6, which I fear is rather late to propose, but I am obliged to write this line lest by possibility I should be putting your kindness to a fruitless trouble.

You will be glad to hear that I am now very decidedly on the mend, though all things take time.

With love to W. B. & Mrs. Scott,

Your most sincere friend
DGabriel R

68.171 TO ALICE BOYD

MS: NLS. Published: DW 823.

Tuesday [22 December 1868]

My dear Miss Boyd

Would *you* mind kindly writing one line to Burton (whom I have not seen for many years) to say that you find 6 is my earliest hour? But not if troubling you at all. The coincidence is unlucky. Indeed, though getting round, it is not the moment I wd have chosen for seeing fresh people at all. But it can't be helped, & Burton is a brick.[1]

Affectionately yours
DGabriel R

[1] Probably F.W. Burton. See 59.24n2.

68.172 TO CHARLES AUGUSTUS HOWELL

MS: Texas. Published: Cline 90.

Tuesday [22 December 1868]

Dear Old Thing

I've been haunted with the idea that my P.S. about the bill yesterday was a cross one. What a beast I was if it was! When you have done nothing but all sorts of friendship & jolliness & salvation for me! It's much better the bill is paid as I have just written to Ellis. Don't think me a beast for seeming put out. It was all the first moment, and I know of course that you took all sorts of trouble for me, & that with a thousand other things to think of.

I'll see you tomorrow at Holland Park I hope. I've got another d – d engagement for late the same evening which I suppose will force me to afflict the dinner party with togs & to leave earlier than I shd wish.

Your affec:
Gabriel

P.S. About the claret I should certainly like to have what you offer me.

68.173 TO WILLIAM ALLINGHAM

MS: PML. Published: *WA/GBH* 283–84; DW 801.

Wednesday. [23 December 1868]

My dear Allingham

Many are Xmas nuisances and here comes another, accompanied however by all affectionate wishes.

I have been looking up a few old Sonnets & writing a few new ones to make a little bunch in a coming number of the *Fortnightly*, – not till March however, as they are full till then.[1]

Among them are the enclosed two, about which I want an opinion. It seems to me doubtful whether the 2nd adds anything of much value to the first, & whether it (the 2nd) is not in itself rather far-fetched and obscure. I wish you would tell me what you think. I would excise the 2nd if the first is best by itself.[2]

I suppose you heard that I have been queer with my eyes. This has caused inaction and the looking up of ravelled rags of verse. I am now at work again however.[3]

Affectionately yours
DG Rossetti

P.S. Isn't there a chance of you coming up this Xmas? Come & stay with me.
P.P.S. How do you like the "Ring and the Book"? It is full of wonderful work, but it seems to me that whereas other poets are the more liable to get incoherent the more fanciful their starting-point happens to be, the thing that makes Browning drunk is to give him a dram of prosaic reality, and unluckily this time the "gum-tickler" is less like pure Cognac than 7 Dials Gin. Whether the consequent evolutions will be bearable to their proposed extent without the intervening walls of the station-house to tone down their exuberance, may be dubious. This *entre nous*.[4]

---

[1] "Of Life, Love, and Death: Sixteen Sonnets," *Fortnightly Review* 11 (n.s. 5, Mar 69): 266–73 (see also **160**).

2   Probably "Newborn Death," sonnets XV & XVI concluding the *Fortnightly* group. In August, shortly after writing them, he sent them to JS for comment (**120**) – they became 99–100 (*B&S*) in *HL*.

3   DGR's renewed eye disorder began during his visit to FRL's home, Speke Hall, near Liverpool, in August and continued throughout the fall (see **119n1**). Returning from Penkill, where he encamped with WBS & AB for nearly 6 weeks, DGR's resumption of his poetic endeavours led to a 3-day exchange of letters between WBS & WMR. "Don't you think Gabriel's beginning to take an interest in poetry a very good thing?" WBS asked on 30 Nov (*RP* 372), to which WMR responded the next day: "I was much gratified to find Gabriel looking up his poetry: knew nothing of it before that evening. Gabriel, being an artist and a rational creature would, if he loses his eyesight for painting (which heaven forbid, and I by no means reckon for) quietly dispose of himself by a dose of prussic acid, were it not for some extraneous considerations: and, great as would be my sorrow in that event, I could not and never do dissuade him, for I quite agree in the point of view. But, as considering all that militates against that solution, his right resource is most manifestly poetry, and I have frequently urged it upon him" (Peattie 147). WBS replied at once: "the short ending to his ills, in the worst case," though "often spoken of by him," should not be entertained, "even under the dire misfortune." Poetry was the only viable alternative: "He is poet as well as painter, and was a poet before he was a painter; and even in the interval of rest . . . it would be a great thing to get him to be the poet again" (*RP* 373).

4   WA visited RB on 27 Dec and, when asked how he liked *The Ring and the Book*, which he had not yet finished reading, replied with "nothing but praise" (*WAD* 195).

68.174 TO FREDERICK STARTRIDGE ELLIS

MS: Texas.

16 Cheyne Walk

26 Dec 1868

My dear Ellis

After all I find the bill was not paid at the Union Bank on presentation, whereas there were funds of mine to meet it. I must express my regret at the inconvenience you have had, and am writing to the Manager of the Bank for an explanation. Meanwhile you will probably have received through Howell a cheque of mine for the amount, which I gave him for you on hearing from him of the occurrence. Knowing that my account would meet the bill, I had not the least doubt of its having been paid when I last wrote to you.

Very truly yours

D G Rossetti

F.S. Ellis Esq

68.175 TO CHARLES AUGUSTUS HOWELL

MS: Texas.

Sunday [c. late 1868]

My dear Howell

Did I leave my spectacles at your house last night? If so please let me know at once & I will send for them.[1]

Ever yours
DG Rossetti

[1] See **128n1**.

68.176 TO FORD MADOX BROWN

MS: Ashmolean. Published: DW 799. Date: WMR.

[1868?]

Come earlier than 8 if you can – to dinner at 6 suppose. If not I'll expect you at 8 but have to go to Q. Square shortly after that.

D G R

F M Brown Esq

1869

MAJOR WORKS OF THE YEAR

Literary: For this year, *DGRDW* (293) lists "Eden Bower," "Farewell to the Glen," "Troy Town," "The Stream's Secret," and "The Orchard-Pit" (unfinished).

Artistic: Oils: *Lilith* (S.205, apparently dated 1868) and *The Portrait* (S.372); drawings: *Palmifera* (S.193B), *Penelope* (S.210), *La Mandolinata* (S.211), and *Pandora* (S.224A, B & C); portraits: Calliope Coronio (S.311), Frances Catherine Howell (S.339), Frances Graham (S.318), Willie Graham (S.319), and Marie Spartali (S.518).

SUMMARY OF THE YEAR'S LETTERS

Continued concerns with eyesight; stables dispute settled; break with Frederick Sandys over alleged plagiarism of subjects for paintings; WMR's *Shelley* and engagement to do series of popular poets for Moxon; publication of sonnets in *Fortnightly Review*; Jane Morris travels to Bad Ems; second visit to Penkill, begins to have poems set in type; and, especially, the exhumation of his book of MS poems from Lizzie's grave. Writing to tell Swinburne of the event, DGR said, "I hope you will think none the worse of my feeling for the memory of one for whom I know you had a true regard. The truth is, that no one so much as herself would have approved of my doing this. Art was the only thing for which she felt very seriously. Had it been possible to her, I should have found the book on my pillow the night she was buried; and could she have opened the grave, no other hand would have been needed" (**190**).

CHRONOLOGY

12 Jan
DGR summoned for jury duty; excused on certificate from William Bowman and affidavit from JAR.

January
Raffle subscription for J. W. Inchbold. Crisis in EBJ's relationship with Marie Zambaco. Three FMB children exhibit at Dudley Gallery.

16 Feb
Announcement of death of R. B. Martineau.

February
Plans for WMR's edition of Moxon's Popular Poets.

March
DGR's "Sixteen Sonnets" (for *House of Life*) published in *Fortnightly Review*.

22 Mar
WMR and JLT on European tour; JLT nearly dies.

May
DGR breaks with FS over his appropriation of Lucrezia Borgia subject.

1 Jun
Death of M. F. Halliday.

8 Jun–22 Jul
CGR at Penkill.

June
"Shorn Lambs Exhibition" – supplementary exhibition of pictures refused by the R.A., held in Bond Street.

mid-Jul
DGR launches project to have his poems set in type (see separate chronology of *Poems*, **Volume V: Appendix**). Morrises to Bad Ems (return mid-Sep).

16 Aug
Settles with CAH to proceed with exhumation of EES' coffin to recover buried MSS.

17 Aug
To Penkill; spends two nights en route each way with Alicia Margaret Losh at Ravenside, near Carlisle, where he composes part of "Eden Bower"; at Penkill 19 Aug–18 Sep; returns from Penkill in ill health.

September
H. B. Forman's article on DGR in *Tinsley's*; parallel studies of CGR and WMR in August and October issues; Ruskin elected Slade Professor at Oxford; acquires tame wombat, which dies on 6 Nov.

5 Oct
Exhumation of EES' coffin in Highgate Cemetery undertaken by H. V. Tebbs and CAH; recovered MS entrusted to Dr. Llewellyn Williams for disinfecting.

October
First meeting with Dr. Thomas Gordon Hake.

November
Hand and Soul (dropped from collected poems) separately printed for private distribution.

December
Consults with Sir William Jenner, who prescribes early nights and a six-month rest; considers, owing to continued ill health, taking AG's house at Shottermill, near Haslemere, or another isolated country house.

LETTERS

69.1 TO MARY NICHOLSON ["RED LION MARY"][1]
MS: UBC. Published: DW 516.

8th January/1869

My dear Mary

It is little enough that I deny myself for the sake of other people, but what doubt can there be that you ought to keep such trifles as I have been able to give you as long as you want them worse than I do? So let me never hear of the matter again; but if you need it and I am able to help you a little once more, let me know when such is the case.

Very truly yours
D G Rossetti

PS Fanny wishes you not to forget the photographs.

[1] For Red Lion Mary, see 57.49n1. In 1867, she applied to DGR when her family situation had become desperate (67.155&n1).

69.1.1 TO MRS. ADOLF HEIMANN
MS: Princeton.

8th January/1869
16 Cheyne Walk
Chelsea

Dear Mrs. Heimann

Will you accept which hardly deserves the name of a New Year's gift, in the shape of two little dishes that happen to match your centre piece. All three would not be big enough to hold my New Year's wishes to you all, if they were as tangible as they are real.

Ever yours
D Gabriel Rossetti

69.2 TO WILLIAM BOWMAN[1]

MS: Arizona.

16 Cheyne Walk
11 January 1869

Dear Mr. Bowman

I enclose one of a few cards I have got from my friend Madox Brown whose works you probably know something of already.[2] I am sure, if you have time, that you and your family would enjoy seeing the "Elijah," which is a very noble work. There is also an "Entombment" full of grand feeling and a beautiful small subject from Romeo and Juliet.[3]

The drawing from Morris's "Jason" by Madox Brown's son, a lad of 13 or 14, is a very remarkable and interesting first (or nearly first) effort, and promises great things in the future.

With kindest remembrances

Very sincerely yours
DG Rossetti

W Bowman Esq

[1] For Bowman, see 67.140n1.
[2] An entrance card for the watercolour exhibition at the Dudley Gallery to which FMB, Cathy, LMR, & OMB all contributed. For the subjects of Cathy & OMB's paintings, see **28n2**.
[3] FRL purchased FMB's *Entombment* (see **9**), which is now in the Faringdon Collection at Buscot Park. His *Romeo and Juliet* was one of at least 3 watercolour versions, probably the one dated 1868–71.

69.3 TO JAMES ANDERSON ROSE

MS: Berg. Published: DW 804. JAR's affidavit, a draft copy of which is at Berg, indicates that attendance by DGR at the sessions "would have been attended with risk to himself" for reasons of health (see DW 807n1 for the draft's full text).

16 Cheyne Walk
Tuesday [12 January 1869]

My dear Rose

See here!

What is a b – y affidavit? And can't we get one up?

You know I once sat on a Grand Jury. Surely the same person cannot be

Friday [15 January 1869]

liable both for Grand & Petty Juries, can he? Will you let me know what to do.

Ever yours
D G Rossetti

[Enclosure]

Sessions House/Old Bailey
11 Jany. 1869.

Sir

In pursuance of the Statute 25 & 26 Victoria cap 107.s.12. I have to inform you that at the Session of the Central Criminal Court held this day a fine of £5 has been imposed upon you for not attending as a Juror in obedience to a Summons in that behalf, *and I have to require you within six days* after the date of this letter *to forward to me at* this place, *an Affidavit in writing* of the cause (if any) of your non-attendance in order that I may submit the same to the Court for its decision as to remitting the fine.

You are particularly desired to take notice that as the Statute above cited requires an Affidavit, no other communication from you, by letter or in person can receive attention nor can any letter be replied to under any circumstances; and if after this caution you do not send me an affidavit, the fine will be levied although you may have written any explanation by letter to me.

Your obedient Servant
Henry Avory[1]

---

[1] Clerk of the court at the Central Criminal Court, father of the distinguished jurist Sir Horace Edmund Avory (1851–1935).

69.4 TO JAMES ANDERSON ROSE

MS: Berg. Published: DW 805.

Friday [15 January 1869]

My dear Rose

I wish you would oblige me with a line about the Jury paper I sent you. The time is going by.

Ever yours
D G Rossetti

P.S. On second thoughts, I write with this to Bowman for a certificate. Will this do as well as an affidavit?

69.5 TO JAMES ANDERSON ROSE

MS: Berg. Published: DW 806. A draft of JAR's Affidavit, dated "11 Jany 186[9]" is also at Berg.

Monday [18 January 1869]

My dear Rose

Thanks for your note. I send you Bowman's Certificate. Will it do without a "davy"?

Ever yours
D G Rossetti

[Enclosure]

I hereby testify that Mr. D. G. Rossetti suffers from a weakness of the nerves of the eyes, and that his serving on a Jury would be attended with risk.

W. Bowman

5 Clifford St
Jan 16. 1869

69.6 TO JAMES ANDERSON ROSE

MS: Berg. Published: DW 807. Date: JAR.

Tuesday [19 January 1869]

My dear Rose

My habitual doctor is John Marshall

10 Savile Row,

but I thought Bowman's certificate would be the right one as he attends me for my present local complaint. I hope you have it ere this.

Thanks again.

Your
D G Rossetti

69.7 TO ROBERT BROWNING

MS: Princeton. Published: Grylls 246.

19th January/1869
16 Cheyne Walk
Chelsea

My dear Browning

I have had my third reading of "Caponsacchi" and have not yet thanked you![1] Surely this is the very greatest thing you have yet done. The way in which the ideal element is at last infused into the book without sacrificing one tittle of its supreme reality, is a triumph of Art such as no Englishman but yourself could venture to hope for. How the exquisite glimpses of Pompilia make one long for the personal utterance of

> "The snowwhite soul that angels fear to take
> Untenderly!"[2]

No doubt she will open the third volume, and so form with Caponsacchi the pure central heart of the book.

Count Guido is just as great in his own fitting way. You have made him assume so far the impulsive tone of self-belief as really to awaken sympathy for the issues of such a case as he feigns, and so make the mind recoil upon him with double abhorrence when the truth already known recurs to it, and rejoice all the more to follow him by Caponsacchi's guidance to the side of

> "Judas made monstrous by
> much solitude."[3]

This line is a glorious antithesis to the noble isolation of Dante's Virgil,

> "Chi per lungo silengio parea fioco."[4]

But were one to follow in detail all the heartfelt beauties of Caponsacchi's narrative (perhaps most enthralling of all in the disembodied interval of thought – that "immortal nakedness" of the soul – which precedes the flight,) there would be no end to my letter – only to your patience. I can but feel myself more gratefully than

ever yours,
D.G. Rossetti

---

[1] See 68.167n4.
[2] Volume 2, Book 6: "Giuseppe Caponsacchi" (195–96). Pompilia's book (7) opens Volume 3 (1869).

3   Volume 1, Book 6 (1936–37).
4   *Inferno*, Canto 1, l.63: "As if long silence had washed his image out."

69.8 TO WILLIAM MICHAEL ROSSETTI
MS: Brotherton. Published: DW 808. Date: WMR.

Friday [22 January 1869]

My dear W

I suppose you know Inchbold is hard up and has been staying at Ned's.¹ A subscription has been made (without his knowledge) to raffle some drawings of his. I send you the list, which take care of. I have given £5. Can you give anything? I expect to see you in an evening or two.

Gabriel

1   WMR recorded in his diary on 24 Jan 69: "Gabriel called. He says that Inchbold has for some while past had to give up his own lodgings, and had been living at Brett's: B. going abroad, he had transferred himself to Jones, without (it would seem) any definite invitation. Jones however is also now out of town, and Inchbold houses with Howell" (*RP* 380). For JWI's personal & professional misfortunes, see 54.15n4; for WMR's contribution to the subscription raffle of his drawings, see **10**. His hardships continued: on 7 Jul 70 he accepted £10 from WMR, but only "after very deliberate consideration" (JWI:WMR, 7 Jul 70, AP).

69.9 TO FORD MADOX BROWN
MS: UBC. Published: DW 809. Date: WMR.

Saturday [23 January 1869]

My dear Brown

I want to know how soon you expect to be back in London – as I am desirous to get you to meet Anthony & one or two others at dinner.

What is Cave Thomas's address? You have probably ere this got a letter from Leyland who called at yours with me & found you gone.¹ No doubt you will visit him at Speke Hall before returning. What luck with the Manchesterians, and how is dear old Shields, to whom my true love? How often I have meant to write to him! But perhaps he will come with you to London now.

Private. Poor old Ned's affairs have come to a smash altogether, and he and Topsy, after the most dreadful to-do, started for Rome suddenly, leaving the Greek damsel beating up the quarters of all his friends for him and howling like Cassandra. Georgie has stayed behind. I hear today however that

Top and Ned got no further than Dover, Ned being now so dreadfully ill that they will probably have to return to London. Of course the dodge will be not to let a single hint of their movements become known to anybody, or the Greek (whom I believe he is really bent on cutting) will catch him again. She provided herself with laudanum for two at last, & insisted on their winding up matters in Lord Holland's Lane. Ned didn't see it, when she tried to drown herself in the water in front of Browning's house &c – bobbies collaring Ned who was rolling with her on the stones to prevent it, & God knows what else.[2]

Your
Gabriel

[1] FRL's letter was probably about *The Entombment*, which he bought in 1868.
[2] For GBJ's revealing letters to Rosalind Howard about the affair, see Judith Flanders, *A Circle of Sisters* (Viking, 2001): 118–25. Rosalind & her artist husband George James Howard (later Earl of Carlisle) were close friends of the EBJs, and EBJ also confided in George Howard.

69.10 TO CHARLES AUGUSTUS HOWELL

MS: Princeton. Excerpt: *PRT* 82. Published: *TR* 114–15; DW 810.

Monday [25 January 1869]
16 Cheyne Walk
Chelsea

Dear Old Boy

I send back the list – Wm takes 3 shares. When shd he send the tin? Let him know.[1]

Janey gives me very bad news of Ned, who it seems is likely to return to London in a few days. I am most anxious about him, & have asked for the next news at once, as if it is bad, I shall go and see him without delay. I certainly think they ought not to push on.[2]

Your letter about the poems was very kind, but it's a ghastly business.[3]

You know I expect you and Mrs. Coronio with the little gypsy on Thursday at 1 o'clock.[4]

Janey has stopped her sittings by order during foreign service – just as I supposed.[5]

Do let me know any news of Ned and his affairs. Write or better – come.

Your
Gabriel

P.S. You should make Swinburne take some shares. He is an old friend of Inchbold's, and would be only too glad.

How is poor Mary Z?

---

1. See **8&n1**.
2. See previous letter.
3. A reference to CAH's suggestion that DGR retrieve the MSS from the coffin of EES (see 68.167&n2).
4. The "little gypsy" was Calliope Coronio, daughter of Aglaia Coronio.
5. WM accompanied EBJ on a recuperative holiday after the scandalous incident concerning Maria Zambaco and had forbidden JM to sit for DGR during his absence.

69.11 TO ELLEN HEATON

MS: Yale. Published: Surtees 44.

> 16 Cheyne Walk/Chelsea
> 25th Jany 1869

Dear Miss Heaton,

When last I saw you and we spoke of your lending me the drawing of "Dante's Dream,"¹ your principal objection seemed to be connected with the Leeds Exhibition & the visitors you would have while that remained open. As that has now been some time closed, and as the matter is still of importance to me, I write to express a hope that you will now oblige me with the loan of the drawing. I had expected to need it long before this; but, as you perhaps know, I have suffered for some months the necessity of suspending work, owing to a troublesome state of my eyesight induced no doubt by over application. I am now however at work again, & this Dante picture, long delayed, must now be taken up as soon as possible. The original drawing would be of the greatest assistance to me in getting the composition on the canvas, and I hope you will show the same friendliness as of old and not add to my initiatory labors by withholding it. I am ready to begin *now*, and should not keep it long.

With kindest remembrances,

> I am ever truly yours,
> D G Rossetti

---

1. DGR had written EH the previous year about borrowing her *Dante's Dream* at some future time (see 68.4). The oil commissioned by WG (S.81R.1) was not completed until 1871 (see 68.70).

69.12A AUBREY THOMAS DE VERE TO DANTE GABRIEL ROSSETTI

MS: UBC.

25 Jan 1869

Dear Rossetti

Some ladies who are getting up a useful charitable institution for the protection of young women, especially servants out of place, are trying to procure funds for it by the publication of a book, which is to be called "authors of all nations," is to be dedicated to some crowned head, & is expected to have a great circulation, especially among those who frequent the Parisian Exhibition of all nations each year. I have been particularly asked to apply to you for something by way of contribution to this book. I am sure you have some poem, long or short, which you will send us. Pray do so. Perhaps you could also get us something from your sister.[1] Have we any chance of another Vol of those beautiful translations from the early Italian Poets: – & how has the published volume circulated?

Yours very faithfully
Aubrey de Vere

---

[1] Evidently the collection never appeared. For de Vere, a friend of WA & Tennyson, see 56.9&n1. See also **12, 29,** & **74**.

69.12 TO CHRISTINA GEORGINA ROSSETTI

MS: UBC. Written on **12A**.

[c. 25 January 1869]

Dear C –

If you like, send something to me & I'll send it on. Perhaps I may send some trifle.

[unsigned]

69.13 TO CHARICLEA IONIDES[1]

MS: Texas.

Wednesday [27 January 1869]
16 Cheyne Walk
Chelsea

Dear Miss Ionides

I suppose you must have my note now. I posted it the first thing yesterday, to say that Thursday wd be best & then Friday if necessary to ensure finishing before I leave town.

12 better than one if possible, but not to your or Miss C[oronio]'s inconvenience.

Ever yours
D G Rossetti

[1] Youngest sibling of Aglaia Coronio, see 68.98n1.

69.13.1 TO CHARLES AUGUSTUS HOWELL

MS: Texas.

Saturday [30 January 1869]

Dear Howell

I wish you would write me just a line how Ned is. I have been hoping to hear ever since.

Your affec
Gabriel

69.14 TO WILLIAM MICHAEL ROSSETTI

MS: Brotherton. Excerpt: *FL* 199–200. Published: DW 811.

Thursday [4 February 1869]

Dear W

I like the plan you tell me of.[1] If I were you I would certainly try and get Payne to conclude with (or include in the series) a volume of selected minor poets, comprising many good unknown things, such as Ebenezer Jones &c. I would lighten your labours by assisting you in this. I don't understand if old poets are to be put into the series.

As to the etchings, Smetham is an available man certainly, but do you propose having all the vols done by one man? It seems to me after all that

Thursday [4 February 1869]

Scott would not be so ineligible, besides that he seems to me under the circumstances almost unavoidable with pleasantness. However I wd mention it first of all to Brown, as I know he is particularly short of work just now, & it is just possible he might like to do it, perhaps with help from Nolly, or with Nolly's name & his own revision. Shields I think unlikely, as I have a decided impression he told me he wd do no more book illustrations. If you wish to try him, his address is

F.J.S.
Cornbrook House
Cornbrook Park
Manchester.

The only other man I can think of is Nettleship[2] (unless Halliday might be also eligible.) N. wd do well for Shelley or anything of that sort. Of course I shd be very glad if Smetham were selected, & he has the advantage of being quite as good at landscape as figures.

I send you on a note. I got a similar one but do not know Mrs. Blanding in the least, & have some fellows coming to dine here Monday, so I hope you will come *here*.

I shall see you tonight at Scott's, but write in case talk be difficult there.

Gabriel

The Pole is no good. He wouldn't understand his poets.

---

[1] James Bertrand Payne (1833–98), manager & part owner of Edward Moxon & Co., invited WMR to write prefatory memoirs for a series of Moxon's Popular Poets (Peattie 155n7). Shakespeare & Milton were the only poets earlier than the eighteenth century included in the series, and *American Poems* & *Humorous Poems* were the only selections. On 14 Feb Payne proposed employing "known artists" to illustrate the volumes: "If one could get known artists . . . it would, taken with the fact of yr. editorship, give it an excellent character, & render these volumes *facile princeps* in the market" (Payne:WMR [14 Feb 69], AP). He sent a "Rough List of Illustrators" to WMR on 20 Feb, which included DGR, JEM, Noel Paton, Gustave Doré, Birket Foster, & George Cruikshank. Against Payne's accompanying list of authors & titles, WMR pencilled the names of artists: Keats & Coleridge (DGR); Collection of 17th & 18th Century Poetry (JEM); Selections from the Dramatists (FMB); Byron (Simeon Solomon); Shelley (Frederic Leighton or J. T. Nettleship); Collection of Traditional Poetry English & Scotch (WBS); Cowper (JWI); Collection of English & Scotch Songs (JS); Collection of Modern English Poems (EBJ); Wordsworth (FS); Thomson (Birket Foster); Humorous Poems (Cruikshank); and Collection of American Poetry (Doré) (Payne:WMR, 20 Feb 69, AP). FMB, with the assistance of OMB, illustrated Byron, Doré illustrated Hood, and JS "did the delicate little head and tail pieces to the earlier volumes of the series, of landscape-glimpses, foliage, etc." (*FL* 199), but the other illustrators chosen by Payne were mediocre. Neither Payne nor WMR's list contains the name of a Polish illustrator.

[2] See 68.165n1.

69.15 TO JOHN SKELTON[1]

Text: Skelton 85–86. Reprinted: DW 812.

16 Cheyne Walk, Chelsea

7 February 1869

My dear Skelton,

The *Fraser* containing your article on Morris has been sent me – doubtless through the same kind remembrance of me on your part which is apparent in the article itself.

I think all you say of Morris is very completely and excellently said.[2] It indicates, I should say, on the whole, the same estimate of him which I have long entertained, as being – all things considered – the greatest literary identity of our time. I say this chiefly on the ground of that highest quality in a poet – his width of relation to the mass of mankind; for, in inexhaustible splendour of execution, who can stand beside Swinburne? – not to speak of older men.

You know Morris is now only 35, and has done things in decorative art which take as high and exclusive a place in that field as his poetry does in its own. What may he not yet do? The second volume of the *Earthly Paradise* is getting forward, but will not be ready, I should think, till the spring of next year. In some parts of it the poet goes deeper in the treatment of intense personal passion than he has yet done. After this work is finished, I trust his next step will be in dramatic composition, in which I foresee some of his highest triumphs.

What you say of me comes curiously at a moment when a spell of ill health has limited my painting, and thrown me back a little on old poetic ideas. I fear I shall find on examination that there is not much of the MSS. I lost (a biggish volume ready for the press) which can be got together again. There will be some sonnets of mine in the *Fortnightly Review* next month.[3] I shall probably write some new things, and see whether they seem worth anything among such poets as we have now.

Ever yours,

D. G. Rossetti

---

[1] Eneas Sweetland Dallas had introduced Skelton (1831–97, pseud. Shirley) to DGR in 1859, but though they corresponded (chiefly about ACS), they were never close friends (see 64.116, 156, & 161, 65.44 & 66.148).

[2] Skelton's article "William Morris and Matthew Arnold" (*Fraser's Magazine* 69 [Feb 69]: 230–44) referred to DGR as "a great though little known artist" (235), and in the August issue, he named CGR the greatest living poetess (see also 64.116). He recorded that a few weeks after getting this letter, he received from DGR "a parcel of admirable photographs of some of the artist's best known sketches" (Skelton 85). See also 70.13&n1.

[3] See 68.173n1. Later DGR asked Skelton to review *Poems* (see 70.13&n1).

69.16 TO FREDERICK STARTRIDGE ELLIS

MS: Princeton.

16 Cheyne Walk
12 Feb/1869

My dear Ellis

Here we are again with the old story. Would it be practicable to renew for a month the bill for £50 coming due on the 21st inst.?[1]

Yours very truly
D G Rossetti

F.S. Ellis Esq

[1] See 66.62 & 129.

69.16.1 TO AGLAIA CORONIO

MS: Tim McGee.

Saturday [13 February 1869]
16 Cheyne Walk
Chelsea

Dear Mrs. Coronio

A frame for little Ope has been sent here and I send it on to you.[1]

I forgot to thank you for the piece of cashmere you so kindly gave me.

Ever yours
DG Rossetti

P.S. I dare say Howell will bring the other frame or else I will send for it.

[1] The frame was for the chalk portrait of Calliope Coronio (S.311). See the following letter.

69.17 TO CHARLES AUGUSTUS HOWELL

MS: Texas. Published: Cline 96. Date: Cline.

Monday [15 February 1869]

My dear Owl

I sent B. Carew the portrait, but have no cheque as yet, and am in doubt whether he understands that it is to be 50 gs though I suppose he must. He also seems to think that your proposal as to the Palmifera drawing differed from mine. Mine is that it should be substituted for the 2 drawings remaining due on the original bargain and for Janey's head, making three in all. This was what you told him, was it not? I have told him that the Palma drawing is similar to one of Beatrice which I sold for 80 gs. As you are I understand to dine there tomorrow, (I am not asked) would you find out without seeming to suggest any difficulty what his ideas are as to the price of the portrait and as to the exchange question. He however I should think wd probably broach the latter point.[1]

Little Ope's frame was sent to Holland Park on Saturday. Some time when you are coming from there you might bring me back the other. Unless indeed I send for it which I *may* do.

Your
Gabriel

P.S. I saw Whistler last night who said he understood from you that I wd write about the etchings. I wish I could, old chap, but it is of real importance to me, I believe, not to write a word on Art, or it wd be immediately said that I did so anonymously & habitually.[2] You'd better ask William.

I hope dear Kitty is better. My love to her.

[1] For Carew (LRV), see 68.138&n3. The bill referred to is the one to FSE (see **46**), and the *Palmifera* mentioned is probably the red chalk (S.193B) that was listed in Marillier (M.179), but its whereabouts is now unknown.

[2] CAH was also working as an agent for JMW and had encouraged the artist to begin selling etchings of his works. That relationship too, in time, would fall apart, again as the result of the pressures of business transactions perceived as betrayals on CAH's part.

69.18 TO CHARLES AUGUSTUS HOWELL

MS: Texas.

Friday [c. 19 February 1869]

Dear Owl

I hope you haven't forgotten today at 7 dinner.

Your
Gabriel

69.19 TO ROBERT BROWNING

MS: Princeton. Published: Grylls 247.

22 Feb 1869
16 Cheyne Walk
Chelsea

My dear Browning

I have been reading & re-reading "Pompilia," and so has every one I talk with. Not one but thinks it as noble and lovely as Caponsacchi, and what more can be said? Exquisite indeed is every page of it, whether viewed as character or expression. How you have brought one to the right point now! – and how one stands astonished at the gradual revelation of inmost truth, so new everywhere in spite of your having boldly given a complete glimpse of the story and the relation of its personages at the outset! How, above all, one thirsts for the almost incredible moment (to come next I judge) when Guido will actually have to tell the truth! The surprises of the book are infinite, where, by its plan, surprise seemed almost excluded.

Your lawyers are both admirable and astoundingly individual. And how intensely Italian is the humanity of Dominus Hyacinthus! It quite recalls the domestic life of my childhood, passed wholly among Italians though in England. Are the wonderful Latin Scraps (one wonders) really parts of the original *plaidoyer*?[1] But I suppose not. There is much everywhere in the detail of the book which is in fact too right to be real; though the life of the whole, one sees plainly, is sucked from the very heart, as it verily was, of everyone concerned.

And now for Vol IV!

Ever yours affectionately
D Gabriel Rossetti

Robert Browning Esq

---

[1] The counsel for the defence, whose address (*plaidoyer*) RB took from documents in *The Old Yellow Book*.

69.20 TO FRANCES MARY LAVINIA ROSSETTI

MS: UBC. Excerpt: Knight, *DGR* 103. Published: *FL* 200–01; DW 813.

March 1/69
16 Cheyne Walk
Chelsea

Dear Darling

I send you my sonnets, which are such a lively band of bogies that they may join with the skeletons of Christina's various closets, & entertain you by a ballet. Their shanks are rather ghastly, it is true, but they will keep their shrouds down tolerably close, and creak enough themselves to render a piano unnecessary. As their own vacated graves serve them to dance on, there is no danger of their disturbing the lodgers beneath, and, if any one overhead objects, you may say that it amuses them perhaps and will be soon over, and that as their hats were probably not buried with them these will not be sent round at the close of the performance. It is to be feared indeed that they have left a growing family who may be trained to the same line of business; but in the long run the cock crows, or the turnip-head falls off the broomstick, or the price of phosphorus becomes an obstacle, or the police turn up if necessary.[1]

Your
Gabriel

[1] See 68.173n1. Perhaps the overwrought *danse macabre* imagery here reveals DGR's dread of his mother finding out about the projected exhumation (see also **146**&n3, **147**&n2, **157**, & **181**).

69.21 TO FORD MADOX BROWN

MS: UBC. Published: DW 818.

Monday [1 March 1869]

Dear Brown

As Allan is going to my mother's, I send you the enclosed from the remarkable Craven, which I shd like you to see. I really have nothing I can offer him but it struck me that if you had any thing of the blessed size he wants (which is 28¼ x 21½) I might name it to him (of course cursorily & cautiously) when I write an answer.

I have got a Mag: with my sonnets now, so send you the enclosed correct proof, which you can keep or put to best use.

Your affec:
DG R

P.S. I suppose a head would suit best. Couldn't you project one?
P.S. The price of the Beatrice watercolour is 300 gs so the companion shd be same. Of course do not trouble to answer by bearer.

69.22 TO ALICE BOYD

MS: Jeff Pennig. Published: DW 802.

> Friday [5 March 1869]
> 16 Cheyne Walk
> Chelsea

Dear Miss Boyd,

I trust to come to you Monday evening for our constitutional "Wub."* I have wished to come before,[1] but have had Topsy & Janey staying here till tonight and have been full of things to do.

I had a nice letter today from Miss Losh in reply to mine, but I am sorry to say she describes herself as still suffering greatly with her eyes and "unable to hold her pen"; still the letter *is* hers.

I shall see you at the Tebbs's on Tuesday week.

> Ever yours
> DG Rossetti

* "Wub": rubber of whist.
[1] According to ABDD, DGR was at WBS' on 7 Mar. WBS, AB, DGR, & AML played whist in the evenings at Penkill, and in London GPB & parish rector Gerald Blunt sometimes joined them. See also Reginald Blunt, *Memoirs of Gerald Blunt of Chelsea, His Family and Forebears*.

69.23 TO JAMES SMETHAM

MS: V&A.

> Monday [8 March 1869]

My dear Smetham

I want much to see your work but only one evening this week would suit me – i.e. Friday, & this is not one you name. Will you let me know if it would do or whether we shd put it off till next Monday. Brown I believe proposes to come with me, but I fear we shall not get to you till about 10 in any case as the distance is so great.

Now is not this all very Xtian after your infamous libel in effigy on me and my brain-babes? That was "Squaring up to one's self-conceit" and no mistake. Moreover, worst of all, the likeness was pronounced perfect by one's kind good friends!

> Ever yours
> D Gabriel R

P.S. Wm mentioned your name to Moxon & Co – about those illustrated

Poets I spoke of, & Payne (the Co.) proposed to call on you. I don't know if you've seen him.

69.23.1 TO CHARLES AUGUSTUS HOWELL
MS: Texas.

2nd letter
Monday [c. 8 March 1869]

Dear Owl,

Now howl!

In cutting that drawing off to frame it, I've cut it just a shade too small on one side so that it doesn't fit. Had the flat better be cut a little to make it do? Or what? If you look in tomorrow daytime, I shall be at home painting little boy Graham.[1]

Your
Gabriel

[1] Willie Graham, who died at age 16, was at this time modelling for the page in *Mariana* (S.213): this picture should not be confused with DGR's portrait of him (S.319).

69.24 TO FORD MADOX BROWN
MS: UBC. Published: DW 798.

Wednesday [10 March 1869]

Dear Brown

I have fixed Friday for us to go to Smetham if suiting you. I told him we could not get down till 10, but he begs for 9-30. I suppose therefore that this will clear family worship which is my object. I will call for you in a cab as I suppose that would be much in my way.

Ever yours
Gabriel

69.25 TO CHARLES ELIOT NORTON

MS: Berg. Published: DW 814.

10 March/1869
16 Cheyne Walk
Chelsea

My dear Norton

I am thoroughly ashamed of not having returned your call before now but am a shocking bad "caller."

Will you dine with me *Thursday of next week* at 7? I have asked several friends of yours & it would give me great pleasure to see you. No ceremony of course – least of all in dress.[1]

Ever yours
D G Rossetti

C E Norton Esq

[1] CEN, WMR, WBS, & others dined at 16CW on 18 Mar (*RP* 386, & ABDD).

69.26 TO ROBERT BROWNING

MS: Princeton. Published: Grylls 247–48.

13th March 1869
16 Cheyne Walk
Chelsea

My dear Browning

I feel as if we were in communication now even before I put pen to paper: for is not your completed thought now filling me? – in how many ways, at what strange junctures, to recur to me for ever? Such function I have long acknowledged as yours; but now most strongly, by this confirmed and controlling impression of your greatness at a time when judgment should be mature in me.

How you have summed up the whole drama of your book in that supreme master-stroke at the end of the second "Guido"! – where the wretch, in his one terror-stricken flash of truth, winds up his shriek to the Saving Powers with the name of his wife. This leaves her crowned of unrighteousness itself. When you wrote that line, you must have felt that you owed your Muse a votive wreath; as the world, reading it, awards one to you.[1]

The serene splendour of the Pope's Section comes most nobly between the fluctuating contest of the actors and audience and the final consummation.

In itself I suppose it must be admitted as the grandest piece of sustained work in the whole cycle of your writings. The passage from the Friar's Sermon worthily "repeats the colour" in the winding-up.

And highest of all is the fact that it is to the inmost centre of the emotion that the mind reverts on closing the book; and finds itself still gazing with Caponsacchi on the "lady, tall, pale, beautiful, strange & sad," and still thrilling to those all-expressive words of his, –

> "You see we are
> So very pitiable, she and I
> Who had conceivably been otherwise."[2]

I quote from memory, and perhaps not quite correctly, as Vol. 2 is still among the borrowers.

For this great work of yours now let me thank you, as for a fullness which I have lived to see; and believe me ever

Yours in grateful love,
D. G. Rossetti

---

[1] "Pompilia, will you let them murder me?" Volume 4, Book 11 (2425).
[2] Volume 2, Book 6 (399).

69.27 TO ROBERT BROWNING

MS: Mills College.

19 March/1869
16 Cheyne Walk
Chelsea

My dear Browning

I have been asked by Mr. John Morley, editor of the Fortnightly Review, to ask you whether you would give him the great satisfaction of contributing a poem thereto. He said in such case he would do his best (with rather limited funds) to meet your terms, which of course he would expect to be special to yourself.

I told him that I felt sure your answer was very uncertain, but have put the question as he wished me to do so.[1] If it bores you, pray pardon

Yours affectionately
D G Rossetti

Robert Browning Esq

1. RB replied the next day politely declining on the grounds that he had refused others "who had my apologies along with the assurance that I should write for nobody." He also acknowledged DGR's "Sixteen Sonnets," in the *Fortnightly Review* and the "'other precious, precious jewels' that you made me bright with in your letters" (20 Mar, AP). For RB's response to DGR's presentation copy of *Poems*, see 70.92n3.

69.28 TO GEORGE RAE
MS: LLAG.

20 March/1869
16 Cheyne Walk
Chelsea

My dear Rae –

Thanks for your friendly letter. I did make a little progress the other day with "Palmifera" and hope to finish her with a rush before very long.

I dare say we shall be seeing you in London one of these days. I was very sorry to have missed calling on you when so near Liverpool for the first time last year, but may perhaps have another chance.

Old Mr. Miller is indeed a wonderful specimen of age.[1] "May we be like him!" is almost as foolish a thing to say as it is impossible not to wish.

Brown's children have really done themselves great credit at the Dudley. Lucy has been acknowledged too, and most deservedly, as her picture in many important respects would be worthy of any one. The two others, I am told, suffer so dreadfully from bad hanging that they have no chance. The boy's drawing is an ambitious one & full of true poetic feeling and colour – a wonderful work indeed for so mere a lad, and not even needing that consideration. Lucy's has been bought by a Liverpool man – a Mr. King – and I believe he is likely to have the others too.[2]

With kindest remembrances to Mrs. Rae

I am ever yours truly
DGRossetti

George Rae Esq

1. For John Miller, an early PR patron, see 53.15n1.
2. LMR's picture was a "figure of Cathy painting," and OMB's was *Jason and the Centaur* (*RP* 379).

69.29 TO WILLIAM ALLINGHAM

MS: PML. Published: *WA/GBH* 277–78; DW 712. The 16CW monogram has been cut from the MS.

22 March [1869]

My dear Allingham

I enclose an answer to Aïdé,[1] which will tell you my mind, except that I may add to you that £1400 is £1400 to me, or rather to anybody rather than me, as I never see it at all, & that my plan is to rent, not to buy. I have been pot-boiling to an extent lately that does not hold out much hope of estate buying or even renting. Moreover as I haven't been outside my door for months in the daytime, I shouldn't have had much opportunity of enjoying pastures & pleasances.

I have accordingly no news whatever except of my easel which is too mean a slave to small needs to be worth reporting on. I do not see a fellow of any sort really much oftener than you do I imagine. I lately heard from Aubrey de Vere, with a request to my sister & self to contribute something to a verse collection.[2] We looked up scraps, & were promised proofs, but these come not, & I imagine that the result when in type will be the usual incentive to blasphemy. I wonder do you sail in the same boat – or "funny" as it is likely to prove according to my experience.

Yours always
D G Rossetti

---

[1] Charles Hamilton Aïdé (1826–1906), musician, composer, poet, & novelist, lived in Lyndhurst; in 1862 his friend Frederic Leighton had offered to paint a fresco in the new church there. See *WAD* 103.

[2] See **12A, 12,** & **74**.

69.30 TO CHARLES ELIOT NORTON

MS: Harvard. Published: DW 815.

22 March/1869
16 Cheyne Walk
Chelsea

My dear Norton

Thanks for your most friendly note. I was very sorry to miss your expected visit, but I know how right it was of you to stay away in such weather.

I expect to be so extremely busy for 2 or 3 days to come that I think I will write again for another appointment before many days are over, if you will allow me. I should then be most happy to see your ladies with you, and will not forget, you may be sure.

Ever yours sincerely
DG Rossetti

C. E. Norton Esq

69.30.1 TO A. T. SQUAREY
MS: Terry Meyers.

16 Cheyne Walk/Chelsea
22 March 1869

My dear Sir

I must say frankly that I should myself much prefer you declining to exhibit my drawing:[1] – not that the exhibition of so small a work so inconspicuously is in itself of any great importance; but every precedent, however small, increases the great difficulty I often have in avoiding exhibition in such *cases* as do interfere with my settled plans. You will I am sure pardon my answering your inquiry without reserve, and am

ever yours truly
DG Rossetti

A. T. Squarey Esq

[1] *Hamlet and Ophelia* (S.189). Despite DGR's request to the contrary, it appears that Squarey lent the work to an unidentified exhibition after all. See 70.221, which seems to contradict the fact that DGR had received Squarey's petition for consent to lend the watercolour.

69.31 TO JAMES SMETHAM
MS: V&A.

Wednesday [24 March 1869]

My dear Smetham,

I have just seen Hughes who wd be happy to receive our proposed visit in his new house near here on Wednesday or Thursday evening of next week.[1]

Will you let me know which time wd suit you. I can dine you here if you like (7 o'clock) & give you a bed.

Your insolent cartoon of the Pill Box was much enjoyed by Morris & has been presented to Mrs. M. who keeps a book of insults.

Yours always
D G Rossetti

[1] AH's new house was 2 Finborough Road, Fulham Road, on which he signed a 7-year lease.

69.32 TO JAMES SMETHAM
MS: V&A.

Thursday [25 March 1869]

My dear Smetham

Graham is in town for only a day or two & is very anxious to get down to you if he can & see the large Hesper.[1] So I suppose it is just possible he may call tomorrow, but it is also very possible he may not find the time.

In haste

Ever yours
D G Rossetti

[1] A large landscape described as "a poetical composition five feet long" (Smetham 27). Completed in 1871, it was purchased by James S. Budgett (Casteras 156, 225).

69.33 TO JAMES SMETHAM
MS: V&A.

16 Cheyne Walk
29 March [1869]

My dear Smetham

I should think the best thing you could do for our plans wd be to come up to dinner Thursday at 7 & stay Friday & Saturday. I wd try to get Watts & perhaps Leighton either to dine here Friday & meet you or else to come & see the picture by daylight any time they can spare.[1] I will also try for Graham. Will you let me know whether this suits you.

I went this morning to the German oculist who declares like the others that there is no fear whatever of my losing my sight, and says this & that besides of which I can tell you when we meet.

Ever yours
DG Rossetti

P.S. I may possibly have to make the dinner Saturday. I think it wd be well to bring with you the *Hesper* also, & perhaps the sketch of the Little Cloud & the one near it.

[1] Probably the painting considered by JS to be his masterpiece, *The Hymn of the Last Supper*, completed the evening before Good Friday 1869 and also purchased by Budgett (see **32**). At this time it was being exhibited in DGR's studio, "where it was seen amongst others by Mr. Watts, R.A., who said, 'It must be considered a great picture though it is a small one.' The picture was sent to the Royal Academy Exhibition" (Smetham 26–27). Reproduced as Plate 44 (142) in Casteras. See **34** & **37**.

69.34 TO GEORGE FREDERICK WATTS

MS: Princeton.

29 March [1869]
16 Cheyne Walk
Chelsea

My dear Watts

Do you think you could dine with me Friday at 7? I shall then have an old friend – Jas. Smetham – staying with me for a day or two and he will have with him a picture which is going to the R.A. & which I should greatly like you to look at before the general press of the hanging. I suppose this will not be unparliamentary. If you came an hour or so before dinner you might see it by daylight, or if it is too much to ask of your early habits that you should dine here at all, could you possibly look in Friday or Saturday daylight & see Smetham's picture. He is a truly poetic & superior painter, though not yet known at all, being of very retired habits both personally & professionally. If you can come Friday to dinner, I shall ask Ned Jones & Leighton also, so would you kindly let me have a line at once. If Saturday wd suit you better for dinner, be it then.

I am sorry to say I shall have very little to show you of my own after a good deal of enforced inaction.

Yours ever truly
D G Rossetti

G.F. Watts Esq R.A.

69.35 TO JAMES SMETHAM

MS: V&A.

Wednesday night [31 March 1869]

My dear Smetham

Here is something too stupid! I had it somehow in my head that my appointment with you to dine here & meet Mr. Graham was for to-day! and accordingly I wrote him a reminder yesterday, & he, not realizing the blunder, came! When you & Burton (who was to come also) never appeared, I looked up your answer & found out the inconceivable contretemps. Unluckily Graham couldn't come again on Friday, the real day, but will make another appointment as soon as he can, so for the present I can only ask you to accept this apology which I feel to be seriously needed.

Ever yours
D G Rossetti

69.36 TO AGLAIA CORONIO

MS: Kansas. Published: DW 846. While the MS bears an unidentified endorsement of "Aug. 1869," the date of this letter is uncertain. It has been placed here because it closely follows DGR's portrait of Ope Coronio (see 10, 13, 16.1, & 17).

Monday [c. March–April 1869]

Dear Mrs. Coronio

As I judge from your note that the books are still in use, I am very glad my servant failed to find Lamont's house. I would not have troubled you about them on any account, that being the case.

Pray pardon my bothering you in Alecco's absence. The note to him I threw in the fire on getting it again. There was nothing else in it except the usual side-hit at the poor old Owl, who it seems is safe in Holland by this time.

Will you kindly give the enclosed to little Ope from me.

Ever yours sincerely
DG Rossetti

69.37 TO JAMES SMETHAM

MS: V&A. Excerpt: Casteras 143–44, 153.

16 Cheyne Walk
Thursday [1 April 1869]

My dear Smetham

Graham has been here and thought the "Hymn" a very fine work indeed but did not offer to buy. I told him the price was 400 gs. I fancy perhaps his principal reason for not buying was that with his many commissions in hand he does not care to begin with you on so high-priced a picture. He knew something however of you it seems after all & had much curiosity. It seems your name had slipped his memory when I first spoke of you to him. Indeed he possesses a little picture of yours or sketch – Christ showing the sky to the Scribes &c (?) which he brought & showed me. He would have bought the "Hesper" on the spot had it not been sold (I told him no price) and said he hoped you would paint him something of the same kind, – also expressed a wish to have the "Little Cloud" if you wd sell it. He seemed so anxious to know you, and so cordially taken with your work, that I said I would try and get you to meet him here on Monday next at 7 to dinner. Let me know *at once* if you can come, as I have to let him know. I hope so, as I am sure it will lead to business. No swallow-tails of course. If you come on Monday you had better stay the night & next morning here if possible or else come early on Monday, as I want to get you to alter a very few trifling points of tone here & there in the *Hymn* which have struck me on getting familiar with the work & which will not take an hour altogether. Indeed better come earlyish in any case as we ought to settle what prices to ask before you see him.

Ever your
D G Rossetti

If Monday wont suit you, wd Tuesday?

69.37.1 TO FANNY CORNFORTH

MS: DAM. Published: Baum 101.

Saturday [3 April 1969?]

Dear Fan

I find Smetham would like to stay to dinner, so as I am uncertain of your coming in any case, I will not expect you. I hope to see you tomorrow.[1]

Your affec:
R

---

[1] See 67.148 for further evidence that DGR reserved Sunday evenings for FC.

69.38 TO MARY SMITH[1]

MS: Churchill College, Cambridge. Published: DW 1037. The MS is with an unrelated envelope to Mrs. Smith postmarked 25 May 70.

> Tuesday [c. 6 April 1869]
> 16 Cheyne Walk
> Chelsea

Dear Mrs. Smith

Thanks for your invitation. I trust certainly to dine with you on Sunday the 11th.

I have written a sonnet for my picture of Pandora, the drawing for which is yours;[2] & I copy it overpage for you.

> Very truly yours
> DG Rossetti

Mrs. Eustace Smith

[Enclosure]

Pandora
(Sonnet)

What of the end, Pandora? Was it thine,
   The deed that set these fiery pinions free?
   Ah! wherefore did the Olympian Consistory
In its own likeness make thee half divine?
Was it that Juno's brow might stand a sign
   For ever? And the mien of Pallas be
   A deadly thing? and that all men might see
In Venus' eyes the gaze of Proserpine?

What of the end? These beat their wings at will,
   The ill-born things, the good things turned to ill, –
   Powers of the impassioned hours prohibited.
Aye, hug the casket now! Whither they go
Thou may'st not dare to think; nor can'st thou know
   If Hope still pent there be alive or dead.[3]

---

[1] Mary M. Dalrymple, wife of Thomas Eustace Smith, Newcastle shipowner & M.P; the Smiths had 10 children and lived at 52 Prince's Gate, near the FRLs. Both "Eustacia" Smith (as she liked to be called) and her daughter Virginia Crawford had affairs with Sir Charles Dilke (Macleod, pp. 291–94). See also 70.147.1 & 72.134.

² S.224A, lent by T. Eustace Smith to the BFAC exhibition in 1883.
³ Published, with a few variations in punctuation, in *Poems* (274). When it was reprinted in *Poems: New* (271), DGR altered "hug" to "clench" in line 12.

69.39 TO JANE OCTAVIA BROOKFIELD[1]

MS: UBC (Colbeck).

7 April/1869
16 Cheyne Walk
Chelsea

Dear Mrs. Brookfield

Saturday at about 4-30 or 5 would suit me best for the pleasure of your visit, but if earlier that day would be better for you, pray come at your own hour without troubling yourself to write again.

Yours very truly
DG Rossetti

[1] Jane Octavia Elton (1821–96) was the wife of the Rev. William Henry Brookfield (1809–74), a college friend of Thackeray's. In 1851, Thackeray's longstanding and apparently platonic affair with Jane led to a permanent break between the two men. Mrs. Brookfield published several novels between 1868 & 1873 and a collection of her husband's sermons in 1874. She also provided an introduction to *A Collection of Letters of William Makepeace Thackeray, 1847–1855. With portraits and reproductions of letters and drawings* (Smith & Elder, 1887). She was a member the Committee for Promoting the Higher Education of Women, which met from 1869, along with the Rev. Gerald Blunt & his wife, through whom she may have met DGR. She lived in Thurloe Place, South Kensington.

69.40 TO FREDERICK STARTRIDGE ELLIS

MS: Texas.

16 Cheyne Walk
7th April/1869

My dear Ellis

What a shame to be bothering you again! But can't we cut in two the bill due on the 21st inst. – i.e. £50 then & £50 on the 21st May?[1]

Ever yours
D G Rossetti

FS Ellis Esq

[1] See **16**.

69.41 TO CHARLES AUGUSTUS HOWELL
MS: Texas.

Friday [9 April 1869]

My dear Howell

Will you dine here Monday at 7, to meet Graham & Smetham, and also I hope Ned & Top? Smetham has a picture here,[1] which take care & praise, as indeed you will naturally, it being an enormous advance. It is sold, but hope Graham will buy something else from him. Indeed he has told me he will.

About the chalk drawing, I'll really do it as soon as ever I can, & that *shall* be soon.

Your affec:
Gabriel

I hope Kate is doing well. Love to her.

[1] *The Hymn of the Last Supper* was the last picture JS exhibited at the RA. See **43** & **44**.

69.42 TO JAMES SMETHAM
MS: V&A. Excerpt: Casteras 144.

Thursday [15 April 1869]

My dear Smetham

How shall I thank you for the kind present of my dear old friend the sofa,[1] which I found on coming in last night set down in my hall like the flying couches in the Arabian Nights, with no Jinn to help its progress except perhaps inside the caravan. I consider it quite unique and intrinsically most valuable, besides its value to me as a proof of your friendly feeling, and of Mrs. Smetham's also, as it was most kind – too kind – in her to allow it to change hands. I shall set about restoring the few places in which the patterns are rubbed off.

I have just got a note from Leighton in reply to one of mine, in which he says – "I am much interested in your friend Mr. Smetham's picture – it shall be well seen." So you are all right I doubt not. I drop a line with this to the Athenæum Critic.

Affectionately yours
DG Rossetti

Leighton describes the light in the new building as "beautiful but trying."

[1] The sofa was item 174 in *CWS*: "a Sofa or lounge with cane seat, the back artistically

painted in figures and landscapes, the frame of the painted furniture period, squab and 2 pillows, upholstered in stamped green velvet; a very rare and valuable specimen." WMR's handwritten notes add that it was bought by Frederick Locker-Lampson "for someone else." See **124** & **207** for its refurbishment.

69.43 TO FREDERIC GEORGE STEPHENS
MS: Bodleian.

16 Cheyne Walk
Thursday [15 April 1869]

My dear Stephens

I want to be in time with a request to you to look well in the RA at a picture by Smetham (The Hymn of the Last Supper[1]) which I feel pretty sure will enlist your sympathy as I am glad to say it has Watts's & Leighton's, so that there will be no difficulty in seeing it. It is a very remarkable work by a man who will yet do things to be talked about, though hitherto he has worked chiefly on a very small scale & exhibited hardly at all.

If you could make it one of the things mentioned in your preliminary notice it would be of great service to Smetham & I believe you will agree that he deserves it.

Ever yours
DG Rossetti

P.S. A picture of mine is going to be engraved in mezzotint.[2] I want if possible to get it done in the old Sir Joshua way without nasty mechanical scratching underneath. Is this possible now, & if so who is the man? Did you ever hear of one Tomkins?[3] Or if not, who is the best *line* man in your opinion? I hear some one has done a Titian female figure in line very well lately.

[1] See **33**.
[2] See **100** for EG's desire to do an engraving of JM's portrait and **103** for DGR's comments on it to JM.
[3] Probably Charles Algernon Tomkins (1821–c.1903), a prominent engraver, mostly in mezzotint.

69.44 TO FREDERIC GEORGE STEPHENS
MS: Bodleian.

16 Cheyne Walk
17 April/69

My dear Stephens

Thanks for your note. James Smetham *did* paint *The Moorland Eagle* and the title of his present picture is "The Hymn of the Last Supper." You will like it I know.

As for myself I get more shell-fishy as to publicity of *all* kinds.

Ever yours
DG Rossetti

P.S. It strikes me on looking again at your note that perhaps you require some description of the picture in case you are not at private view. It illustrates the passage – "And when they had sung a hymn they went up to the Mount of Olives"[1] – a text of the subject never before taken & which shows the figures standing, a novel yet unmistakable treatment. Judas is the only one who has "gone out in haste," his seat remaining overthrown; and he is shown lingering outside the door in the moonlight listening to the hymn and hardly daring to go on his deadly errand. The lamplight in the picture, and the balance of all its masses are singularly masterly & successful, – more so than the manipulation, which is somewhat small in character, though the whole is so well felt that this only strikes on examination. The sacred sentiment of the work is really beyond praise, and the simplicity of its high emotion reminds one of nothing but the early Italians, though in point of carrying out the painter will doubtless yet gain much.

[1] DGR was thinking of either Matt 26:30 or Mark 14:26: "And when they had sung an hymn, they went out to the Mount of Olives."

69.45 TO CHARLES AUGUSTUS HOWELL
MS: Texas.

16 Cheyne Walk
18 April [1869]

My dear Howell

Whistler & a few more will dine here at 7-30 on Thursday next. I hope you can join us.

I think you have of mine 2 vols of "Ring & Book" – also a black & ivory chain – also a lot of sketches for mounting. Now *pray do*, PRAY DO let me have them.

> Your affec:
> D Gabriel R

I don't know whether that George & Dragon thing is done for yet.[1] It would be better not to let it go under £40. If a loss to you I will make it all right either by money or work as you please forthwith.

[1] See 68.11.

69.46 TO FREDERICK STARTRIDGE ELLIS
MS: Texas.

> 16 Cheyne Walk/Chelsea
> 19 April 1869

My dear Ellis

I enclose cheque £50 and will be glad to accept a new bill for a similar amount payable 21st May if you will kindly draw and send it me.[1] With thanks

> Ever yours
> DG Rossetti

F.S. Ellis Esq

[1] See **40**.

69.47 TO CHARLES ELIOT NORTON
MS: Harvard. Excerpt: *RP* 433; DW 816.

> 16 Cheyne Walk
> 19 April 1869

My dear Norton

You expressed a kind intention of visiting my studio by daylight. Would Wednesday next (day after tomorrow) suit you? The best hour for me wd be from 1 to 2, but later if you prefer, only then there is a possibility just now of other visitors.

I have long wished to make a proposal to you. It would be a great satisfaction to me to possess the drawing you have by my late wife of "Clerk Saunders"[1] to add to those of hers which are now mine, and which every year teaches me to value more & more as works of genius, even apart from their personal interest to me. None would ever have been parted with, of course, had we not then hoped that these little things were but preludes to much greater ones, – a hope which was never to be realized. I would not offer you a profit on the drawing, as you would probably not accept that; but would esteem it a great favour if you would let me have it at its original price – 35 guineas if I recollect; or would, if you preferred it, make a chalk drawing of Mrs. Norton, life size, of the kind for which I am in the habit of charging 60 to 80 guineas. This I should do with the greatest pleasure & consider myself still greatly your debtor.

Ever yours
DG Rossetti

CE Norton Esq

[1] Purchased in 1857; see 57.36n4 & 62.3&n3. CEN did return *Clerk Saunders* (see 70.8).

69.48 TO CHARLES ELIOT NORTON

MS: Harvard. Excerpt: *RP* 436–37; *Art Journal Easter Annual* (1902); DW 817.

16 Cheyne Walk
23 April 1869

My dear Norton

I send you herewith some photos – chiefly from uncoloured drawings. The "Cassandra" subject I hope one day to paint. I mean her to be prophesying the death of Hector before his last battle. He will not be deterred from going, & rushes at last down the steps, giving an order across her noise to the captain in charge of the soldiers who are going round the ramparts on their way to battle. Cassandra tears her garments in rage & despair. Helen is arming Paris in a leisurely way, & he is amused at the gradual rage she is getting into at what Cassandra says of her. Other figures are Andromache with Hector's child, the Nurse, Priam & Hecuba, & one of the brothers who is expostulating with Cassandra. Hector's companions have got down the steps before him & are beckoning him to follow.¹

The "Hamlet & Ophelia" may need a word of comment. I mean him to be ramping about on the stalls of the little oratory turning out of the main hall, to which Ophelia has retired with the devotional book which her father gives her to read. He throws his arms wildly along the sill of the screen and frays the roses to pieces as he talks, hardly knowing what he says. She still holds out to him the letters and jewels which she wishes to return, but has done speaking & lets him rave on. In the woodwork are symbols of rash introspection – the tree of Knowledge – and the man who touched the ark & died. The outer court is full of intricate stairs and passages & leads to the ramparts where the ghost walks at night.²

I have photos. of 2 sketches by my wife, "Pippa" & another which I send you as you will I am sure enjoy their poetic character. Also 2 or 3 of my sketches of her. I have had all her scraps & scrawls in ink photographed.³ After your kind letter about the "Clerk Saunders" I really hardly feel justified in accepting the generous way in which you meet my wish. It seems shameful to be depriving Mrs. Norton & yourself of what is yours & so much enjoyed by you. In any case I should wish to be quite sure that what I gave you in exchange wd satisfy you equally. Shall I do the proposed drawing of Mrs. Norton? Or would you like one of those of Mrs. Morris? I would take care to give you your choice among some good ones. Or is there anything else you would prefer my doing for you? Small work I have given up for the present.

I shall be with you at 7 next Thursday and meanwhile & ever am

am sincerely yours
DG Rossetti

C E Norton Esq
P.S. I could give you perhaps to make up the measure some of many sketches in pencil I have, if worth giving.

---

[1] DGR's description is very close to that quoted by Marillier (108–09) from an unlocated letter to Colonel Gillum (see 61.9n3). Two studies for Hector (S.127A&B) are known. The latter, listed in *CWS*, is lost, but the main one described here closely resembles S.127 itself. In a letter of 1861 George Meredith wrote: "Rossetti is going to illustrate my *Cassandra*, which pome [sic] has taken his heart." (*The Letters of George Meredith*. Edited by C. L. Cline. 3 vols. [Oxford: Clarendon Press, 1970]: 1:121).

[2] This *Hamlet and Ophelia* drawing, which was done in 1858 (S.108), illustrates *Hamlet* III, i. WMR omitted this description when he printed this letter (*RP* 436) "as that passage has been used by my Daughter Helen [Rossetti Angeli] in her *Art-Journal Easter Annual*, 1902, on Dante Rossetti."

[3] EES' *Pippa* is now in Ashmolean, one of a series on glass negatives that DGR had made in November 1866 to preserve his wife's art work.

69.49 TO JAMES SMETHAM

MS: V&A. Excerpt: Roberts 166.

Saturday [c. 24 April 1869]

My dear Smetham

You once borrowed from me a brown Indian dressing gown which I do not think has been returned. It is in a queer state but useful and I am likely soon to need it for something. Could you let me have it by Parcels Company or otherwise.

I am glad to hear that your picture is well seen and looks well.

Mr. Budgett called here one day and asked for Hughes's address. Do you know if he has bought anything?[1]

Ever yours
D G Rossetti

[1] In May 69 W. Henry Budgett, brother of JS' patron James S. Budgett, purchased AH's *The Guarded Bower* (R.72).

69.50 TO WILLIAM SMITH WILLIAMS

MS: NLS.

2nd May 1869

16 Cheyne Walk, Chelsea

My dear Sir,

I find that I have had several copies of my "Early Italian Poets" which I have not yet paid for. Before doing so, I would be very much obliged if you would let me know the exact state at present of the account regarding the publication of that book. I remember that, some time back, you yourself kindly offered to send me such account, which I should now be glad to see, in order that I may know how much of the edition still remains on hand and how I stand in respect of it.[1]

Very truly yours
D G Rossetti

W. S. Williams Esq

[1] See **59** & **60**.

69.51 TO FRANCES MARY LAVINIA ROSSETTI

MS: UBC. Published: DW 824. Date: FLR.

16 Cheyne Walk
Monday [3 May 1869]

Dear Teak

Could you, with M[aria]. & C[hristina]., & either or both Aunts, dine here one day this week, say Thursday or Friday? Fix your own day of these two. And would you, in such case, mind my asking also the Scotts & Miss Boyd? – no one else I think. I know Scott & his ladies would particularly like such an arrangement, & Miss B. who has come back to town this week (and who was so kind to me in Scotland) leaves for good at the end of it. It would give me great pleasure.

Could you let me have a line in answer at once, as I shall see Scott tomorrow night.

Your affec: Son
D Gabriel R.

P.S. I hope William will be back in time; if he is not already.[1] Of course I should expect you and C. to stay the night, & could lodge M. also if she pleased, without inconvenience, even if W. is here. Dinner 7 o'clock.

[1] WMR returned from Italy on 1 May (*RP* 391). WBS & AB joined the family party on 6 May (ABDD).

69.52 TO JAMES ANDERSON ROSE

MS: Berg. Published: DW 825.

16 Cheyne Walk
May 4th 1869

My dear Rose –

Would you let my friend Dunn, who brings you this, know what I am owing for Insurance which you have kindly paid for me from time to time, and he will settle it for me with thanks for your trouble.

I am very anxious now that that blessed stableman[1] should no longer be laughing at me, and also that I should have the rent owing to me. My work is still limited by my health & I want every penny I can get. Would you oblige me by telling Dunn if there is any difficulty in recovering it after this lapse of time; also whether, among your many transactions, I ought to be asking you at all to bother yourself about the matter. If not, would you, as a friend, allow me to put the necessary papers in the hands of some one else who could see about it for me.

> Ever yours
> DG Rossetti

---

[1] The stableman is Charles Strong.

69.53 TO JAMES ANDERSON ROSE
MS: Berg. Published: DW 836.

> Wednesday [c. 5 May 1869]
> *16 Cheyne Walk*
> *Chelsea*

My dear Rose

Mr. Rae, owner of my picture the *Beloved*, is coming up with his family on Saturday & is to be here in the afternoon. I am sorry this prevents my making any other appointment & therefore coming to you. I'll hope to see you tomorrow eveng if possible.

> Ever yrs
> D G Rossetti

69.54 TO FREDERICK RICHARD LEYLAND
MS: LC. Published: Fennell 22.

> [c. 5 May 1869]

My dear Leyland

I am sorry not to have seen you during the past week as Howell led me to expect you, & still sorrier to hear that the cause is some degree of illness, – I hope only a slight one.

I have been taking up the Lilith, which I think you said you hoped to get about the 20th of this month. I trust it may be ready by then, but am obliged for a few days after today to work at something else. I have painted a garland of silver flowers lying in the lap which is a great improvement, but am now anxious before sending you the picture to take out and entirely repaint (in the same colour) the pinkish brown drapery at the bottom of the picture. It has been so much altered as to be spoilt in execution. To do it again may cause a little delay in waiting till one can glaze it, but it is well worth while. You know we talked of having the frame altered so as to dispense with the black outside case, and have the glass within the frame itself. To do this properly would I find cost about £5. Do you care to have it done? I wish you would let me know at once.

Ned Jones's *Circe*[1] is finished & truly glorious. Watts has sent an *Endymion and Diana* to the R.A. which is a masterpiece; Graham has bought it.

With love to all yours

I am ever yours
D G Rossetti

When do you come now?

Poor Jemmy Whistler! He worked awfully hard but failed to get his work done in time.

[1] FRL eventually purchased *The Wine of Circe*. DGR wrote to both JL (**61**) & AML (**85**) about this picture.

69.55 TO FREDERICK SANDYS

MS: Texas. Excerpt: Cline 99n1.

16 Cheyne Walk
10th May 1869

My dear Sandys

I have only just happened to hear of a subject which you propose to paint. It is described to me as Lucrezia Borgia mixing poisons, with her husband & the Pope (or a Cardinal) seen in a mirror behind her. This so nearly resembles a design of my own that you must pardon my writing you a word about it. I should much prefer speaking; but should feel so awkward in doing so that I must confess sheer cowardice in tackling the question causes me to write instead.

I cannot think I do so hastily, as I know I am not alone in having been struck for some time past by the resemblance which 2 other works commenced in your studio bear to designs made long ago by myself. One of these is "Magdalene at the door of Simon" and the other "Helen of Troy" with the flaming background.

Had these subjects ever been completely realized by me, I should feel less at a disadvantage in having them simply repeated; but as the form in which I have produced them is merely in each instance a preparatory one, I should sustain a great injury by their being forestalled, however inadvertently. It is not as if they were in any wise stock subjects; but I am not aware that anything resembling any one of them existed in Art *before* my designs, whereas in yours, made since, the resemblance is evident.

I hold that, between friends, all things should be, as far as possible, in common, except only the ideas needed for the production of work. To lose one's exclusive property in one of these is a source of such discouragement that one ought not to shrink from asserting it, lest friendship itself should suffer.[1]

Ever yours
DG Rossetti

[1] DGR's allegations were to cause a permanent rupture with FS. See **58**, **64**, & **65**.

69.56 TO CHARLES ELIOT NORTON

MS: Harvard. Published: *RP* 439–40; DW 826.

12 May 1869
16 Cheyne Walk
Chelsea

My dear Norton,

I am very sorry to have been baulked of my visit to you last night; but just after dinner, Mason[1] dropped in, who comes from a distance and is very delicate; so I could not send him adrift, and had to spend the evening with him and take my walk in his company.

I wanted to speak to you on a matter which W. B. Scott was mentioning to me. There is a very fine portrait of Emerson, by his late brother David Scott, (one of the few great painters this country has ever produced,) which has been placed in the hands of W. J. Linton the engraver, now in America, with a view to sale.[2] I believe Scott would take 60 or 70 guineas for it, and he asked me whether I thought you might possibly give a hint of any probable purchaser. It is a life-size half-length. If I meet you once again, as I still hope, before your leaving London, you might tell me if anything occurs to you on the point.

Today is my 41st birthday; and with most good things gone, and others that will never come now, it is something to know of old friends still friendly, even though one may seldom see them; and to say with how much true sympathy I am

always yours
DG Rossetti

C E Norton Esq

1 For Mason, see 66.73&n1.
2 David Scott's oil portrait of Emerson is now at the Concord Free Library. WMR says that Scott sent it to "Linton in America" on 6 May (*RP* 397).

69.57 TO ALICE BOYD

Text: DW 821 (attributed to Courtney-Boyd but unlocated).

16 Cheyne Walk
Saturday [15 May 1869]

My dear Miss Boyd,

I have three small pieces of tapestry no use to myself. I wonder if they would fit at Penkill into any of those ingenious Chinese puzzles of arrangement which share with the reproving eyebrow the softer palpitations of W. B. [Scott]'s soul.

They are

No. 1. History of Joseph and Mrs. Potiphar (!!!)

No. 2. Abraham entertaining Angels, to which is added Hagar in the wilderness with an angel directing her attention to a London pump.

No. 3. Christ and Woman of Samaria.

The two first may be called oblong blurs, being of this form: Mrs. P. is bigger than Abraham. No. 3 is of an arched shape.

The two first have been taken down from the top of the drawing room which they overweighted, and I have nowhere else to put them. They are in black beads* with glasses, and No. 3 has a black frame but no glass.

Would you have time to drop in one day and look at them before leaving town?[1]

Ever yours,
D. G. Rossetti

* a bead or beading is a narrow convex moulding semicircular in section.
1 AB picked up the tapestries from 16CW the next day (ABDD).

69.58 TO CHARLES AUGUSTUS HOWELL

MS: Texas. Published: Cline 99.

Saturday [15 May 1869]

My dear Howell

I wrote to Sandys at the beginning of this week after what I heard from you of his subject of Lucretia Borgia.

I have just received from him a letter wherein he cuts me dead (!) and utterly denies the resemblance of the 2 designs.

You told me that his design contained a glass reflecting L. B's husband & the Pope or a Cardinal. Are you certain as to this particular?[1]

Ever yours
D Gabriel R

---

[1] Since CAH acted as an agent for FS, his appraisal of the similarity between the 2 works would have had some merit. But FS' work has not been traced (see E.2.A.108), and DGR's "original figure of Lucrezia disappeared in the repainting of the watercolour" (Surtees 77). See also *RP* 393–94 & 441 for WMR's version of the events, and 66.179&n1 for an earlier instance of plagiarism involving the 2 artists.

69.59 TO WILLIAM SMITH WILLIAMS

MS: NLS.

16 Cheyne Walk/Chelsea
May 24th 1869

My dear Sir

Everything in this world has its precise comparative value; and the only philosophic moral to be deduced from your letter & account of May 4th (for which many thanks) is the decided superiority of £8-11s-4d over nothing at all. Thus I should be obliged if you would kindly send me the cheque for that important sum which you tell me is my due.

Since our "Joseph" correspondence, it has occurred to me whether its author may be lately dead. Is it so? I should regret to hear that yet another man of genius had failed of recognition in his lifetime.[1]

Yours ever truly
D G Rossetti

W S Williams Esq

---

[1] See **50** & **60**. DGR is presumably referring to Charles J. Wells's *Joseph and His Brethren* (see 49.11n4 & 14&n2). Wells did not die until 1879.

27 May 1869   69.60

69.60 TO MESSRS. SMITH & ELDER

MS: Private Collection. Endorsed verso: "D. G. Rossetti 8.11.8 paid May 27, 1869."

27 May 1869
16 Cheyne Walk
Chelsea

Gentlemen

Thanks for cheque £8-11-8 received as due to me on sales of *Early Italian Poets* to 31 December last.

Yours truly
D G Rossetti

Messrs. Smith & Elder & Co.

69.61 TO JAMES LEATHART

MS (copy; fragment): UBC (LP). Excerpt: Roberts 173. The close, signature, and top half of page 7 have been clipped away.

16 Cheyne Walk
28 May 1869

My dear Leathart

Our excellent friend Rae is an enthusiast, and after long taking much too friendly a view of the merit of my works, he now seems, by what you tell me, even to see their number in a multiplied ratio. I had only 2 finished pictures here when he last visited me; and one (which you knew in a forward state, the "Lilith") has left me since. The other is a portrait of Mrs. Morris which I fear I must in common decency send to her and Morris, its owners, before the time you name; but it *may* still be with me. For the rest, *I* shall be most happy to see you and Mrs. Leathart, & can only hope there may be *something* for you to see, but fear it will not be much.

The same cause which makes my studio empty, – i.e. a long spell of troublesome health, which impeded my work altogether for a time & somewhat since – has prevented me from doing my duty as yet in the matter of settling up after our cancelled commission. To an artist, interruption of work is generally curtailment of means; but I hope the delay may not be very much longer.

As to the Academy, I have not yet been there. I suppose from what I hear that the average continues to rise as to equality of merit, but the style of the school is settling down once more into more inveterate slovenliness than ever. Millais' works are doubtless masterpieces, and had Watts sent a most noble picture I saw of his – the Endymion – that alone should have made the year worthy to commence a new century. No doubt the *greatest* work exhibited this year must be Burne Jones's noble "Circe" – I think his grandest picture as yet – which of course is at the Water Colour Gallery.

I am delighted to hear that Scott is well hung, & everyone says that his "Veil of the Temple" looks very fine. A picture . . . It is a work full of the charm of elevated feeling, and admirably composed.

With kindest remembrances to Mrs. Leathart & the "earlier examples" of your family circle – the only ones known. . . .

P.S. Hughes has a very charming picture at the R. A. & I hear great things of Mason. Sandys has a very fine portrait of an old lady, & a most striking "Medea."[1]

---

[1] The other artists DGR mentions were represented by the following works: AH, *A Nursling Donkey* (R.97); George Heming Mason, *Only a Shower* (153), 3 landscape studies (288, 289, & 331), & *Girls Dancing* (438); FS, portrait of Anne Susannah (Mrs. Thomas Erwin) Barstow (E.2.A.109); WBS, *The Rending of the Veil*. See also **75**. For FS' *Medea* (E.2.A.89), see 67.96&n1, 68.74&n3, 78n3, 90An2, & 69.67.1n2.

69.62 TO MURRAY MARKS

Text: *Marks* 60–61. Reprinted: DW 827.

28 May 1869

My dear Marks,

As you are going to Holland could you try and get me two thimble-shaped lids for two little round pots I have which I value, but which are ruined for want of lids? I suppose among all the breakage of good things there are plenty of good lids which must remain widowed. The size I enclose is that of the unglazed space at the top of the pot left to receive the lid. The hole is the neck of the pot which (the neck) is half an inch high. It would be well, would it not, to lay in a stock of good lids.

Ever yours,
[D. G. Rossetti]

69.63 TO WALTER SEVERN
MS: PML.

30 May 1869
16 Cheyne Walk
Chelsea

My dear Severn

Miss Boyd, at whose house you called last autumn in Ayrshire, is sending two small pictures to the Shorn Lambs' Exhibition in Bond St., – she being among those who are left in need of the tempered wind which blows from that quarter. Do you think you could secure her a nook of the fostering fold in question? Her pictures are both really clever. One is the "Wild Huntsman" – the other "The Incantation of Hervor," – a woman bending over a hand and sword which are rising from a tomb.[1]

Mike Halliday told you, I believe, that I coveted your little marble urn or casket which I saw at his place,[2] & led me to believe there was a hope of its falling to my lot in life. I bide your time in prayer and shall hail it with thanksgiving.

Very truly yours
D G Rossetti

Walter Severn Esq

[1] Walter Severn (1830–1904), watercolour artist, was the son of Joseph Severn the painter and friend of Keats. The "Shorn Lambs" Exhibition is presumably the Supplementary Exhibition of pictures refused by the R.A. (see *RP* 396). Severn was evidently successful in placing AB's pictures in this exhibition (see **69, 85,** & **210**).

[2] Severn's note at the bottom of the letter ("The above relates to my sarcophagus with the inscription you partly made out-/W. Severn.") suggests he forwarded it to Halliday on receipt. Halliday died suddenly on 1 Jun. DGR did acquire this urn (see **210**).

69.64 TO FREDERICK SANDYS

MS: Texas. Published: *RP* 442–44; HRA 36–37; DW 828. Discrepancies between the MS and *RP* texts of this letter suggest that WMR must have printed from a copy.

16 Cheyne Walk
1st June 1869

My dear Sandys,

Thanks for the £50.[1] I remember your showing me your memoranda to this amount after our return from the country in the autumn of /66. I myself have kept no accounts at any time. You view this payment as "a severance of a last tie between us"; and any tie of this kind is so unimportant when compared with those which you spontaneously broke through in your former letter, that I had better proceed at once to reply to that, as I should have done before but for the very painful nature of such a correspondence.

First of all, I must say that I did not even dream of such a result being called for by my first letter to you; but of this you are the best judge, according to the scale of importance at which you rate that letter and the nature of our previous unreserved friendship. I myself should have thought it insincere & unworthy not to speak plainly to so intimate a friend when I felt a difficulty arising between us.

As to the Lucrezia design, my claim was founded mainly on the mirror & reflection of figures in the background, as combined with the subject. This point, according to the description given me (and since confirmed on inquiry) was identical in my design and yours. Without that, the design as you describe it is of course absolutely yours and not mine in the least, & I trust you will paint it.

The "Helen"[2] is surely a strong case of resemblance (the position of the figure being the only difference); and as to the "Magdalene," the moment taken by me was taken then for the first time in Art, and constituted entirely the value of my design.

I must now say what perhaps I did not sufficiently dwell upon before, though I know I indicated it, – that is, that I do not for a moment suppose you to have adopted these points of resemblance with clear intention from my work; but I cannot doubt (I must repeat to be sincere) that they dwelt in your mind from that source and there germinated in a new form. The admirable skill with which you carry out all your work is such that these ideas, once adopted by you in the shape of complete pictures, become yours to all the world, and I could never venture again to claim them under pain of ridicule.

That your memory is not infallible (and therefore that unconscious adoption is not impossible) is proved to me by what you say about not having seen my Lucrezia except in the photograph. I remember clearly showing you the watercolour & your looking at it for some time just about a year ago when I repainted the figure in it.

Again – do you remember once drawing my attention of your own accord to the strong resemblance between your first design in the "Cornhill" & Tintoret's St. George & the Dragon? I am not sure whether you told me that this was intentional or only noticed by yourself afterwards as a reminiscence, but I suppose the latter.

You tell me of my having once claimed two subjects which you proposed to paint – "Perdita," & "Merlin & Nimue." I am quite certain I never thought at all of painting either subject. If, as I suppose from what you tell me, I raised any claim, it must have been on points of detail in your description of your projected designs, – not on the subjects themselves which I never thought of certainly. I very dimly recollect anything about it; but can just remember receiving such a letter as you say you wrote me about the "Perdita" and then perceiving the misconception; though, the matter being uncomfortable, I explained no further.

Thus much for rejoinder on the artistic question. You tell me that four or five friends, being consulted, agree with you. I assure you there are many who not only agree with me but have often suggested these questions of resemblance to me of their own accord.

Any other consideration than the artistic one, it is hardly for me to entertain, as you have told me spontaneously that you "resign my friendship." I myself hold that friendship should only be resigned when one friend can prove malice or deception against another. Of the first of these I know I am innocent; of the second I should have been to some extent guilty if I had held my tongue as soon as I felt strongly impelled to speak. I believe perfectly in the singlemindedness of your friendship for me till this time, and even in all you say of your pain at the termination of it which you think necessary. You add that you believe this matters little to me; but why you say so I cannot conceive. It is however some relief to know that the separation which you make between us comes at a moment when, to my joy, great success and many friends await you; and that I can at least on my side remain still

affectionately yours
D G Rossetti

1   WMR's MS. Diary records that FS owed at least another £50.
2   WMR saw FS' *Helena* at Christie's in Mar 71 and noted that it "is not, I see, founded upon Gabriel's treatment of the same subject: it is a very bad picture, about the worst thing Sandys ever produced" (Bornand 52).

69.65 TO FREDERICK SANDYS

Text: *RP* 444. Reprinted (with additional text, in angled brackets below): DW 829 (attributed to AP but not among UBC MSS).

16 Cheyne Walk
5 June 1869

My dear Sandys,

I have made no "attempt at self-justification," for none was needed. I said to you originally what, as an artist, I had a right to say, however its unpleasantness had delayed my saying it; and I did this after proving amply at all times that, as a friend, I was beyond suspicion.

As for giving people's names, the idea is absurd. I asked you for none when you told me that some friends took your view of the matter. The question is purely one of artistic criticism, whoever raises it; and it would be as ridiculous in me as in you to make it personal to others.

The money-matter I hold to be of no importance, as I showed by keeping no accounts. As you send this again, I merely do not send it back. <The only time I ever mentioned it (last autumn) would have remained the only one, and would never have occurred but for anxious ill health.

I wish Marie to know that I intended no neglect whatever in not seeing her, if she was willing to see me. But> I have been unwell; and poor Mike Halliday's sudden death has combined with other things to make me very sad for a while, though now I am getting round. <This in answer to your note which William showed me.>[1]

Yours,
D. G. Rossetti

---

[1] This letter & the previous one were fully annotated by WMR (*RP* 394–96, 441), who also gives details of Halliday's death in his MS Diary entry for June 4. The DGR:FS friendship never recovered from this rift, though FS tried to revive it around 1880. DGR responded cordially but by then was too reclusive to agree to an actual meeting between the old friends. See **55** & **58**.

69.66 TO FRANCES MARY LAVINIA ROSSETTI

MS: UBC. Published: DW 843. Date: WMR.

Sunday [c. 6 June 1869]

Dearest Darling

I have been extremely vexed at being constantly & unexpectedly baulked of coming to see you for so many evenings and shall certainly do so very soon, but almost fear that Tuesday will just be an impossible time, as I have an engagement which I see no means of avoiding. I am much vexed at this as I am sure you will believe, and if I possibly can I shall come but see little chance.

Your affec: Son
Gabriel

I return William's note.

I also send on review from *Pall Mall* which I know the funny old thing will like to see as it contains 2 scraps translated by me. Will you keep it for me till I see you.

69.67 TO FREDERICK RICHARD LEYLAND

MS: LC. Published: Fennell 24.

16 Cheyne Walk
8 June 1869

My dear Leyland

Thanks for £200 on account of the replica of "Palmifera." This you may depend on my taking in hand as soon as possible, & on getting it infinitely sooner than "Lilith." How soon exactly however I may succeed in finishing the original, on which the replica depends, I do not quite know as yet, but it will not I believe be very long. I believe it is likely Mrs. Morris, who will be going shortly into the country, may be able to recommence sitting to me this week, for a short time. In that case I would not take up the Palmifera till afterwards, but meanwhile the replica can be carefully drawn in. Do not forget that you have to let me know the exact size of the Lilith. Or if necessary I can send some one to measure it.

When you made me an offer of 1500 guineas for the Palmifera & Pia jointly, I had an impression that this was a reduction of 200 on my proposal. Contemplation & Cocker have shown me that 100 gs only is thus eliminated, and I accept your offer. Only I shall tell every one that the price of the Pia is 900 gs (thus 1600 in all), and will rely on your not contradicting this little fiction. This being thus, I dare say you will let me have a second £200 cheque on the "Pia," as it is well begun. Thus we shall have (with the £150 I received from you in August last) £550 paid on the two works jointly, – one being well advanced, & the other, as a replica, promising speedy completion.

In selling the Pia I am in an obfuscated state as to the present law of copyright, & must therefore stipulate simply that I reserve all rights respecting it, as to engraving, exhibition, reproduction, &c.[1]

Affectionately yours
DG Rossetti

F.R. Leyland Esq

---

[1] This version of *Sybilla Palmifera* was never completed, and FRL did not receive *La Pia* until 1881.

69.67.1 TO ALFRED BATE RICHARDS[1]

MS: Getty.

16 Cheyne Walk/Chelsea
10th June 1869

My dear Richards

I was extremely sorry to learn afterwards that I had missed another visit of yours. It was true that I was extremely occupied (painting drapery on a living model, – an occupation more ticklish than the building of card houses.) I expect to be so worryingly busy every day with this sort of thing just at present that I will not try to make another appointment just now, but will hope to see you ere long nevertheless.

Thanks beforehand for the "Medea" which will give me another opportunity of writing to you when I shall have read it,[2] – a reading from which, on all report, I anticipate much pleasure.

With kindest remembrances,

Believe me,
Always yours truly,
D G Rossetti

Colonel Richards

---

[1] DGR's connection with the dramatist Richards (1820–76) was not extensive: a single incoming letter regarding the Cruikshank subscription (8 Mar 67, Princeton) is extant. Richards had a remarkable extradramatic career as a journalist, poet, editor, novelist, & political pamphleteer. As the first editor of the *Daily Telegraph* (20 Jun–31 Dec 55), he promoted the formation of the rifle volunteer movement and in 1858 was secretary of the National & Constitutional Defence Association. In 1859, after the War Office sanctioned the formation of a Corps, he served as an officer in the 3rd City of London Rifle Corps until 1869. The Laureate, who published "Riflemen Form!" in *The Times* (9 May 59; see Ricks 2: 469, 603, & 3: 600), wrote congratulating him "on having been able to do so much for your country" (Lang & Shannon, *Letters of Tennyson*, 2: 223–34).

[2] *Medea: A Poem*. With photograph from the painting of *Medea* by FS (Chapman & Hall, 1869). Richards wrote this poetic rhapsody as a direct response to FS' painting exhibited at the RA this year.

69.68 TO FRANCES MARY LAVINIA ROSSETTI

MS: Princeton. Published: *TR* 133–34; DW 844.

Monday [c. 14 June 1869]

Good Teakey,

I was coming up tomorrow (Tuesday) evening, and shall come. I am sorry I cannot manage dinner-time, but at this distance & in these long days it is impossible when one has a model sitting, as I have tomorrow, even were I to ride instead of walking.

I suppose that Teodorico & his wife will be then with you. After tomorrow I shall be so preoccupied for some little time that I fear it would be no use to make any dinner appointment.

Pardon great haste.

Your most affec: Son
Gabriel

69.69 TO ALICE BOYD

MS: NLS. Excerpt: Purves 503. Published: DW 830.

16 June 1869
16 Cheyne Walk
Chelsea

My dear Miss Boyd

I write you some notes anent the Shorn Lamb Show to which you are a contributor. I duly wrote to the wronged Walt-ah (W. B's last hero) and sent him the circular you had received, but did not hear from him again, & feared nothing could be done as the opening was so near. But i[t] seems he is a champion worthy of all distressed

Fräuleins,

for Leathart told me last night that the Wild Huntsman is hung, Owl & all. The "Herva"[1] Leathart did not notice. I should be sorry to mitigate W.B.'s young illusions by finding that a substitution only had taken place; but let us hope both are there in reality, & Walt-ah's nimbus in full-orbed effulgence.

I have been at work & have got the drapery of my Sibyl actually done at last. Hope to get lots done now in a little while, & in due time to turn up at Penkill. Today the weather has taken a sharp turn round a very nasty corner, but perhaps it may improve again. My tent has been up some time & proves pleasurable at intervals.[2]

I was glad to hear at home that Christina[3] is enjoying herself with you, & I inferred a suppressed groan from the creaking joints of Scotus made to walk. I suppose some "small deer" must have turned up to make Christina so happy. Perhaps even a hedgehog may have taught her that all tears are not born of sorrow. She will regret to hear that my fawn has pulled every feather out of my peacock's tail.

With love to all at Penkill (a group which does not I suppose yet include Miss Losh)

> I am ever yours most truly,
> D G Rossetti

[1] DGR may have used "Herva" instead of "Hervor" (and "Walt-ah" instead of "Walter") to indicate what he regarded as an affectation in Severn's manner of speaking. See **63**.
[2] DGR first erected the garden tent in 1868 (see 68.78n2).
[3] CGR went to Penkill with the WBSs on 8 Jun (*RP* 396).

69.70 TO JAMES ANDERSON ROSE

MS: Berg. Published: DW 831. Date: JAR.

> 16 Cheyne Walk
> Saturday night [19 June 1869]

My dear Rose

I have only heard tonight of my having missed your call & your saying you wanted to see me. I am very sorry you should have come all this way for nothing. Can you let me know by letter or shall I call on you, or shall you be this way again?

> Ever yours
> D G Rossetti

69.71 TO JAMES SMETHAM

MS: V&A. Excerpt: Casteras 144.

> Monday [21 June 1869]

My dear Smetham

I send you the Pall Mall notice of your picture on Saturday, in case you have not seen it. I cut out a little passage about Cathy Brown to give to her. This notice on you is only so-so, and very tame after the enthusiasm which the critic expressed here on seeing the work. The *Judas* touch is worthy of the character. The Times which you sent me is a good deal shabbier however. Such is the luck of exhibiting.

However you have been noticed by the 3 principal papers. I know not if by any others – & pretty well on the whole, though certainly not so well as you deserved.

Your landscape here has been immensely admired by a good many people. I think Leyland would have bought it the other day, had it been for sale.

Graham I daresay will still come up to scratch in due time. He has been away in Holland lately, but I shall be seeing more of him again soon.

I think you have met little Mike Halliday here – a fine manly fellow in every point of character, & possessed of most varied talents. He is suddenly dead, which has grieved me very much, as he was an old and very valued friend of mine.

I have been "breaking the neck" of the Sibyl picture which is really getting out of hand. Poor Mrs. Morris has been very ill & unable to sit which throws me out a good deal in my work, besides being a much greater concern to me on her own account.

Ever yours
D G Rossetti

I shall try & get away before very long to Scotland.

69.72 TO ALICE BOYD

MS: NLS. Excerpt: Purves 503–04. Published: DW 832.

16 Cheyne Walk
22 June/1869

Dear Miss Boyd

I am sending you today a complete chaos of rubbish in the shape of wood carvings. On reviewing them I am not sure that they will serve any more dignified purpose than to make a barbaric retreat for W. B. in some inaccessible corner of the glen,[1] where he can meditate at his ease on the current errors in German pronunciation, or any other topic which he finds too abstruse & complicated for the social circle.

I got your kind note, which crossed my own. You may be sure I shall be only too glad to come to Penkill as soon as practicable; but just at this moment I am kept by various things which must be done. I have been really getting on with the Sibyl picture which is now near completion, and have accepted a distasteful but temptingly lucrative offer to make a replica in oil the same size. I think this is the work which I shall probably bring to Penkill[2] – that is the picture which I must finish for the purpose, & the replica traced in to work up there – a very lazy leisurely job which can be done at odd times. I have also sold the La Pia to advantage now,[3] & may possibly think of bringing the canvas for its background; but the truth is I have been so long on the point of visiting Italy, that it seems almost a pity to do this landscape before I am certain I might not actually have an opportunity of sketching the Maremma itself.

My Janey pictures are in abeyance, owing, I deeply grieve to say, to the continued weakness of the original. She & Top stayed here for some days lately, but she was not strong enough to sit. She is better however than some little time back, & I trust all will be well.

I saw the Leatharts last night at Brown's. L. hangs fire as to his proposed commission to B., & having everything offered him, fixes on nothing.

I am greatly concerned at what you tell me of Miss Losh's ill health & isolation. It would be a great disappointment not to see her again in full face as last year & undergo her searching duplicity at the whist table. Will you give her my love when you write & will all accept the same at Penkill from

Yours ever sincerely
DG Rossetti

P.S. My Scotch servant, who comes from the Girvan neighbourhood(!) has just been telling me, while looking up the woodcarvings, of some place about 16 miles from Girvan called Dundrennan Abbey which it seems is a great show place as a ruin & which might perhaps be worth looking up if not too distant.

Among the carvings you will find two pieces, each broken in half, of very good heraldic carving about the time of Henry VII like this with helmets & lions & scroll-work.

They seem to have formed parts of a cabinet – the places for the locks remaining vacant. One is perfect when joined, but unluckily I can nowhere find a little central fragment of the other, though I certainly believe I once had it. If made any use of however, it would not be an hour's work for W.B. to carve out a little piece for the purpose. It should go between the two other pieces of the carving which are there.

P.P.S. I find the things, when packed, make an appallingly huge lump. They are in a deal skeleton case, the interstices stuffed with straw, & I hope will go safely. I am uncertain whether I shall be able to pay carriage here. I hope they will not make a huge charge.

---

[1] DGR loved to visit a glen and cave by the "brown-pooled, birch-banked Penwhapple"

stream, which flowed through the Penkill grounds on its way to Girvan Water; this locale inspired his 1869 poems "The Stream's Secret" & "Farewell to the Glen" (*Works* 659).
2 The only work DGR did while at Penkill this year was on the MSS & proofsheets of *Poems*.
3 See **67**.

69.73 TO JAMES ANDERSON ROSE

MS: Berg. Published: DW 833.

23 June/1869
16 Cheyne Walk
Chelsea

My dear Rose

Before settling with the Stable tenant, ought we not to ascertain from Messrs. Lee, Pemberton, & Reeves, of Lincoln's Inn Fields, that there will be no objection to my turning the stables into a studio? The question of renewal of lease could remain for after consideration.

Ever yours
D G Rossetti

69.74 TO THE EDITOR, CATHOLIC PUBLICATION SOCIETY

MS: The Late Sir Paul Getty, K.B.E., Wormsley Library. Published: DW 834 (as to an unidentified recipient).

25 June 1869
16 Cheyne Walk
Chelsea

My dear Sir,

I understand that you are to publish some literary contributions made some time back to a Roman Catholic Charity. I believe they include two small poems by my sister and myself. If so, will you kindly let me know, as I should wish to furnish you with a revised copy of my own, and would also beg you to be careful and let me see proofs, both of my sister's and mine; as I have found the neglect of this results in very provoking blunders.[1]

Yours very truly
D. G. Rossetti

---

1 The Catholic Publication Society was based in New York, and Aubrey Thomas de Vere published one book at least with them – *Irish Odes and Other Poems* (NY: The Catholic Publications Society, 1869). DGR is probably speaking of the poems requested by de Vere (see **12A** &**12**).

69.75 TO ALICE BOYD

MS: NLS. Published: Purves 584–85; DW 835.

Sunday [27 June 1869]
16 Cheyne Walk
Chelsea

Dear Miss Boyd

I hope the package has reached you ere this; but in case not, had better enclose the receipt I got for it from the station, where as you will see the carriage was paid. *Brass* was the man whom I employed to take it down.[1]

I am extremely sorry to hear of your sudden lameness, but cannot suppose it will prove other than transitory. Still, it is most provoking and I shall be very anxious to hear that you are getting over it.

I went to the R.A. the other day. Scotus's "greased lightning" looks well though perhaps rather American. Millais' pictures are I think most glorious. Then there is Mason's "Girls dancing" which is a truly lovely piece of poetic painting, but rather queer in execution. Watts is not well represented. Walker's is extremely fine in mechanism but wanting in true imagination, though with an artful counterfeit of the same. George Leslie pleased me, as always, and a man named North has some charming watercolours. Sandys's pictures both look very well, and Moore has his great merits with a good deal of silly conceit & woeful shortcoming. As Millais is the best, so is Hunt the very worst. His horrible daub representing apparently a half-crazed charwoman removing the chimney-ornaments before a hard scrub, is appalling to every inner & outer sense. How grimy and sweaty is the poor thing's face, and how she must yearn for her beer. "Pyrrhic Dance" and Norwegian picture of "Jealousy" are wonderfully perfect.[2]

I met Matthew Arnold the other day at dinner. Poor man! What do you think? He admires Scotus as a bard![3]

Love to all from

Yours always
D G Rossetti

P.S. Janey is getting better.

---

[1] Lot Brass, a builder with the firm of William Brass, 47 Old Street & 18 Silver Street, E.C.

[2] WBS' "greased lightning" was his last picture at the RA, a biblical subject from Matthew (xxvii), *The Rending of the Veil* (525). No fewer than 6 works by JEM were on show. *Girls Dancing by the Sea* (438) is the full title of George Heming Mason's work. Frederick Walker's work was *The Old Gate*; George Leslie exhibited *Lady in a Garden*; Albert Moore, *Venus* & *A Garden*; G.F. Watts, *The Return of the Dove*; John William North's four watercolours were *The Orphans, A Sunny Day in the Field, Quantocks,* & *The Wood Gatherers.*

WHH exhibited two canvases at the RA in 1869: *The Birthday* (a portrait of Miss Waugh, who became his second wife Edith; Bennett 69) & *Portrait of a Lady* (Mrs. George Waugh; Bennett 69), but DGR must, nevertheless, be referring to *Isabella and the Pot of Basil* (1867–68) (see 68.108&n2), which was purchased and exhibited all by itself by EG in April 1868 (see Maas 209–10). *The Pyrrhic Dance* & *A Roman Art Lover* were among the first pictures exhibited at the RA by Lawrence Alma-Tadema.

3   On 24 June, DGR attended a dinner at the home of Fanny Du Quaire (Frances Mary Blackett), where he met Matthew Arnold for the first time (Cecil Y. Lang, ed., *The Letters of Matthew Arnold* [Charlottesville & London: UP of Virginia 1998], 3: 353). ACS dined with Frederick Locker-Lampson & Arnold on 18 Nov 67 (Lang 1: 229). After an enthusiastic discussion, they asked ACS if he could obtain copies of WBS' *Year of the World*. ACS wrote WBS 11 Dec 67 (Lang 1: 233) begging copies for two friends and mentioning Arnold by name. For Arnold's admiration of WBS' "Rosabell" (later renamed "Maryanne"), see Arnold:ACS 14 Dec 67, where he thanks ACS for procuring a copy of the book for him and notes that "Emerson once showed" him a poem in it (Lang, *Arnold Letters* 3: 200). Whether WBS also produced a copy for Locker-Lampson (presumably the second friend) is not known: it does not appear in either the catalogue (Quaritch, 1886) or supplement (Chiswick Press, 1900) of the Rowfant Library.

69.76 TO JAMES ANDERSON ROSE

MS: LC.

16 Cheyne Walk
28 June 1869

My dear Rose

Thanks for your fatherly care. I enclose cheque, as of course I should like to secure the place at once at this figure.

Only there is one serious question which has just struck me. Strong has I believe let the stables to some one who actually lives there. It would be necessary before settlement of any kind to ascertain from Strong himself exactly how this matter stands & whether he can secure the immediate evacuation of this other person. Without that the whole plan would be abortive.[1]

I should like much to hear from you as soon as possible about this.

Ever yours
D G Rossetti

JA Rose Esq

1   See 68.1, **90, 97, 110**, & **122**.

69.77 TO JAMES SMETHAM

MS: V&A. Excerpt: Casteras 80. The close and signature have been cut from the MS.

Tuesday [c. 29 June 1869]

Dear Smetham,

A word about poor dear Shields who I fear is far from well. Hughes saw him lately – having gone to stay with him at Manchester – & gave me a bad account of him. It seems he has got to such a pass now that he can only work occasionally, & then stuffs his ears with cotton to shut out the singing of the birds! – i.e. the birds in the trees outside. Hughes & he went to church together, & H. complimenting S. afterwards on his singing, he said: – "Ah! You little know what a difficulty I had all the time to help screaming out at the birds singing outside." This is most melancholy. He seems to keep up a continual state of painful excitement by constant visiting among the sick poor, & some anecdotes Hughes told were certainly enough to harrow up nerves like his. He penetrates among ruffianism & misery to any extent. It certainly seems to me he *must* have a change of scene & habits.

I said the *Judas* touch in Pall Mall *was* a touch of Judas because the critic, to the best of my recollection, was certainly warm in praise of that very part of the picture when here. He has got talked over by some wiseacre.[1] ...

[1] Probably a reference to critical comment on JS' painting *Hymn of the Last Supper*, which had been displayed at 16CW before being exhibited at the R.A. See **33, 34,** & **37**.

69.78 TO CHARLES AUGUSTUS HOWELL

MS: Texas.

Saturday [June–July 1869]
16 Cheyne Walk
Chelsea

Dear Howell

Will you dine with me Thursday at 7? I am asking Ned, Top, Ellis, Legros & one or two others. I don't know L's present address. Wd you send the enclosed on.

Ever yours
DG R

P.S. Is Howard staying with you?[1] Will he come & pardon the ceremony of a double letter?

[1] George James Howard, see **9n2**.

69.79 TO ALPHONSE LEGROS
MS: Harvard.

Vendredi [June–July 1869]
16 Cheyne Walk
Chelsea

Mon cher Legros,

Je dois vous faire des excuses. Je ne vous ai pas vu hier du tout, mais, pensant à autre chose au moment que votre cab a croisé le mien, j'ai su, le moment après, que j'avais vu Alecco, et le soir j'ai appris que vous aviez été tous deux chez moi. Pardon de la bévue. J'espère vous voir tout à l'heure.

Tout à vous
D G Rossetti

69.80 TO FRANCES CATHERINE HOWELL
MS: Texas.

Saturday [c. 10 July 1869]
16 Cheyne Walk
Chelsea

My dear Kate,

I have told a man to call at Northend on Monday probably about 9 or 10 to fetch the wardrobe which Charlie got me from Guildford. Will you kindly let him take it.

Affectionately yours,
D Gabriel R

P.S. Dunn has just told me about a nest of little hedgehogs. Of course I should enjoy one greatly. You might let the man bring him.

69.81 TO CHARLES AUGUSTUS HOWELL
MS: Texas.

[c. 12 July 1869]

My dear Howell

How in the world could you praise this blessed thing? It is all botched & vamped up, & I doubt if it has ever been original at all. I am really sorry to have given you so much trouble in the matter, but I dare say the trouble will not be greatly increased by the bearer taking it back to you. If Howard does not care to have it, and it belongs to me. I will make a present of it to any willing recipient.

Pray pardon & don't be cross with me, but I would not put this with the other things in my room.

Ever yours
D G R.

P.S. The price they have charged you for it is monstrous. Why, I only gave £15 for mine which is a splendid thing!
P.P.S. They have only just given me Kate's note. I shall delight in an infant hedgehog & must really come up one early evening & see them all in the nest.

69.82 TO FRANCES MARY LAVINIA ROSSETTI

MS: UBC. Published: *FL* 201; DW 840.

14 July 1869

Good Antique

I have not been to see you for whole ages and am really most sorry to be so long without your dear company. The last time I came you were gone to bed, & ever since I have had an extraordinary number of engagements. I have taken to going out more than before to dinner parties &c. in the hope of shaking off ennui, and as soon as one begins that sort of thing one gets involved to an extent quite unforeseen. I shall certainly see you in an evening or two, you dear old thing. And if you can come up to my place, the tent & weather together make the garden charming at present. However I may possibly be out one day before the end of this week so will not ask you to come without appointment.

I hope you continue to have good news of Christina.[1] I shall turn up at Penkill myself some time before very long I dare say.

Your most affec: Son
Gabriel

---

[1] WMR recorded on 8 Jun 69: "Christina went off with the Scotts, to spend a month or more at Penkill" (*RP* 396). She was back by 24 Jul, when she described her return journey to AB (Harrison 1: 386).

69.83 TO CHARLES AUGUSTUS HOWELL
MS: Texas.

14 July [1869]

My dear Howell

I forgot to ask what had happened with Knewstub's sketches. I expect a call from Agnew soon,[1] & if you have them still, wd like them again here as he may probably buy. Dunn told me that he saw some of those sketches of mine mounted at your place. I shall be glad to have them when done.

I hope you were not riled at my not liking the cabinet the other day. I thought it best to send it back at once, that its connection with me might be unknown in case Howard liked to have it.

I saw Leyland the other day, & was grieved to find him not yet completely set up again.

Your affec:
Gabriel

Love to Kate. Won't she and you fix to spend a quiet day with me next week? and dine?

---

[1] See 67.95n1. As subsequent letters show, DGR was looking for some alternatives to EG at this time, patrons & dealers alike.

69.84 TO FREDERICK STARTRIDGE ELLIS
MS (fragment): Texas.

[c. 15 July 1869]

I want to get some poetry of mine printed (in slips probably) to keep by me as stock for a possible volume to choose from eventually. As this would be, as I may say, dead stock, I don't wish to go to much expense with it. Could you recommend me a cheap printer?[1]

Ever yours
D G Rossetti

---

[1] For DGR's first letter to FSE's printer, Strangeways, see **116**. For detailed annotation of DGR's many letters of 69–70 referring to *Poems*, see **Volume V: Appendices** on the origins, chronology, & proof states of that collection. For a full bibliographical analysis of *Poems*, with specific textual revisions & variants, see the **Companion**.

69.85 TO ALICIA MARGARET LOSH

MS: Princeton. Published: *TR* 85–87; DW 842.

> 16 July 1869
> *16 Cheyne Walk*
> *Chelsea*

My dear Miss Losh,

Thanks for your most kind note. Had I been on the move just now, you would have heard from me already, as I was far from having forgotten your kind invitation. But I cannot just at present say when it may be possible for me to leave London, though I hope it may be ere very long. I am already beginning to feel a good deal in want of a change. I have been, I suppose I must say, a good deal better for some time now, though perhaps the improvement consists more in having made up my mind to the unavoidable than in anything else. However it is consolatory to find that there is no further absolute deterioration for some time past, and I do not now that I am used to it experience any decided inconvenience in work of the kind I do. In point of success I have nothing to complain of – indeed much to be grateful for. It is encouraging to see by your handwriting that your eyes must have resumed their usual duties. I hope you are benefiting by this warm weather, which I confess I find for the last few days a little too warm.

I have become (for me) quite a diner-out, and have gone among friends and acquaintances more this season than for some seasons past.

You will be grieved to hear that poor Janey Morris is very ill. She and her husband are going to Ems on the Rhine, where she has been told to go and drink the waters and take baths. Topsy goes on working at a prodigious rate at the second vol. of his Earthly Paradise, and is making it so bulky that it will have to come out in 2 divisions, the first of which will appear I suppose about October. One day lately, working from 10 one morning to 4 the morning after (with intervals of meals &c.), he produced 750 lines! – and this of the finest poem he has yet done.

The Royal Academy is a poor one this year in my opinion. Millais however is in splendid strength. The greatest picture of the year in my opinion is Burne Jones's "Circe" at the old watercolour Gallery. At the Academy Scott's watercolour (The rending of the Temple veil) looks very fine & has been much admired. Miss Boyd was, as you probably know, unlucky with a picture which she sent of the Wild Huntsman, and has since sent it to an Exhibition opened in Bond Street.

I have been much thrown out in my work by poor Janey's illness, as I was engaged on several pictures for which she was sitting to me. I have now taken to finishing another one (Sibylla Palmifera) which has been a long while lying by, and am bringing it to a conclusion. When I come to Penkill, I believe I shall take it with me and carry on a duplicate of it at intervals there, as I have been tempted by a handsome offer to undertake the not very pleasant task of reproducing it on the original scale.

I hoped you might have got before this to Penkill while Christina remains there. At any rate I trust you will be there in my time to renew your inexorable supervision of the whist table.[1]

With kindest remembrances

I am ever sincerely yours
D G Rossetti

P.S. I see lying on the table a magazine containing a poem by my brother which may interest you to read, so I send it.[2]

---

[1] DGR visited AML at Ravenside on his way to and from Penkill (see **128**, **131**, **134**, **153**, & **155**). See also 68.141n3.
[2] WMR's poem "Mrs. Holmes Grey" had appeared in the *Broadway* in Jan 68 (*RP* 296). See 49.18n1.

69.86 TO WILLIAM BELL SCOTT

MS (fragment): Princeton.

[c. 18 July 1869]
16 Cheyne Walk
Chelsea

... me to send it you? I am curious to see what use you have managed to make of the lumps of wood? Is it a mantelpiece?

I have heard the news of Christina all along, & hope she will turn up improved. Tell her Howell found a nest of young hedgehogs in his garden, but having been disturbed they seem to have migrated & have to be discovered again.

The Leatharts have been here once or twice & I rather expect them again today, but am threatened with so many other visitors that I suppose it will all be a "mêlée." They have been to Hughes's but I know not with what result; & Leathart has asked both me & Brown about getting a water picture from Whistler, but is evidently afraid of seeming too eager.

My tent is delightful at times but I have not enjoyed it much having been greatly put about.

Your sonnet is excellent. I have not been in much of a poetizing mood lately, and hardly know how many of my doings remain unseen by you. I copy the last. I am about to have all the poetry I can get together of mine printed roughly for my own use in slips, & keep it by me as stock for selection ultimately with a view to a possible vol. This will induce me to write more & to get advice from the few friends one cares to show the things to. I shall only print a few copies.

Love to all at Penkill. It will be delightful to see the beautiful glen again & feel that the world is shut out. Why can one not have a glen out of oneself too? – or at least out of the way of one's ghosts & skeletons?

Ever yours affectionately
D Gabriel R.

Love's Lovers

Some ladies love the jewels in Love's zone,
    And gold-tipped darts he hath for painless play
    In idle scornful hours he flings away;
And some that listen to his lute's soft tone
Do love to deem the silver praise their own;
    Some prize his blindfold sight; and there be they
    Who kissed his wings which brought him yesterday
And thank his wings today that he is flown.

My lady only loves the heart of Love:
    Therefore Love's heart, my lady hath for thee
    His bower of unimagined flower and tree:
There kneels he now, and all-anhungered of
Thine eyes grey-lit in shadowing hair above,
    Seals with thy mouth his immortality.

69.87 TO EDWARD BURNE-JONES

MS: Texas.

Monday night [19 July 1869]

Dear Old Ned

I looked for you till late Saturday night & am sorry to hear that seediness was the cause of your staying away. Perhaps you will be at Holland Park on Wednesday evening. I expect to find my way there, & we can then make an appointment. If not, I shall then write again or look you up.

Your most affec:
Gabriel

P.S. I hear from Calais this evening that they reached on Saturday night. Janey was tired & laid up all yesterday, but they were going on today. They expect to reach Cologne by Saturday.

69.88 TO JAMES LEATHART
MS: UBC (LP).

16 Cheyne Walk
Tuesday [20 July 1869]

My dear Leathart

I did not see you yesterday.

You were asking me about Whistler. I find he has two sea pieces – one of Valparaiso & one done at Trouville – which are both admirable & both unsold. If you like to make an appointment, we will go and see them.[1]

Ever yours
D G Rossetti

[1] JMW's *Nocturne in Blue and Gold: Valparaiso Bay* was bought by FRL and is now in the Smithsonian; a similar picture, *The Morning after the Revolution: Valparaiso*, was presented to the Hunterian Art Gallery by JMW's sister-in-law, Rosalind Birnie Philip. There are also a number of Trouville pictures painted in 1865 when JMW worked there with Courbet. See the following letter.

69.89 TO JAMES LEATHART
MS: UBC (LP).

21 July/1869
16 Cheyne Walk
Chelsea

My dear Leathart

I find Whistler's price for the Valparaiso is 100 gs – for the Trouville 80 gs – or he would take 160 for the 2 together. They are the same size exactly though the present frames differ.

Yours very truly
D G Rossetti

His address is

J.A.W.
2 Lindsey Row
Battersea Bridge
Chelsea

69.90 TO JAMES ANDERSON ROSE

MS: LC. Published: Kashnor 204. Date: JAR.

Wednesday [21 July 1869]

My dear Rose

Am I ever to hear anything of the stables again? Cannot something be ascertained on the point I raised & the question settled? Do have mercy on a poor devil & let me know.[1]

Ever yours
D G Rossetti

[1] See **97**.

69.91 TO JANE MORRIS

MS: BL. Excerpt: Surtees 605. Published: Bryson 5. Date: P/M. For the integral drawing originally enclosed with this letter, see **Plate 2**.

Wednesday [21 July 1869]

Dear Good Janey

I was so glad to hear from you & know that you had had a pretty good passage. From what you say I judge you were not absolutely ill. And it delights me to know that the cloaks prove of service to you, and that you will be always wearing one of them. I hope you are able to get out a little, at the different places you stop at but indeed I suppose that it is necessary for you to husband your strength as long as the journey lasts.

I went on Sunday to Little Holland House to lay Mrs. Prinsep's unquiet spirit.[1] You may imagine the outpourings, but she is really very nice & kind. We dined in the open air in the garden which was very pleasant and I hoped you were as pleasantly situated to enjoy the fine weather. On the whole I am glad that the heat has decreased now, and suppose it is probably the same where you are. I think it is a very good thing you were not deterred from starting.

I think I told you that Nettleship's drawings had been rejected at the R.A. I enquired of Watts & Leighton about this, and found them expressing the greatest astonishment, as they had never seen the drawings at all! nor was Nettleship's name even on the list of candidates. Some blunder has occurred – whether through his not feeing the porters or what I cannot tell yet; but an enquiry will be made, & let us hope he will get in.[2]

Wednesday [21 July 1869]

I did not see Ned on Saturday night, as he never came round, and wrote to me since that he had been too unwell. I shall go round to the Greek's tonight and probably see him there.

My going out more lately has had the result which has always stopped such proceedings with me – that is, an influx of visitors taking up my time. I have not done much work for some days past, but must remedy this and avert your wrath when you return. Graham saw the Pandora yesterday & was so delighted with it that I shall certainly make this one do for his uncle & begin the full length one on my own hook when you can sit again. I want very much to do this full length, as it is a very favorite design of mine.[3] I also want beyond everything to paint another portrait picture of you – a little more severe in arrangement than the first – as I am sure I can do something more worthy of you than I have yet managed. But I shall get ahead with all the other things now, & really get them out of hand I trust, & the big picture begun.

I expect probably to leave for Penkill in about 3 weeks or less now. I shall take some work to do there in the shape probably of a duplicate of the Sibyl which I have promised to do for Leyland.[4] I want much to get the little Beatrice I was doing from you finished, but the hands are in the way, as I think I *must* alter them and all the models have such vile hands. I have an idea I may ask Mary Spartali to sit for them.[5]

The accompanying cartoon will prepare you for the worst – whichever that may be, the 7 tumblers or the 7 volumes. I hope the weather at Ems will not be so severe as the French Doctor anticipated, & shall be anxious to know whether there, as here, the heat has greatly abated.

I have given Ellis's printer a number of scrappy poems and sonnets to print that I may keep them by me in an available form & perhaps be induced to do more. When I get them, I will send you some.

I suppose Bessie and Lucy are enjoying themselves vastly. Love to them, as well as to dear Top and to your dear self. Yesterday Macmillan rushed in with Field the American publisher who seemed put out because he could not see Top again at present as he seemed to wish.[6] He told me that the news of Norton is not very good. He has been less well since leaving England. That the contrary may be signally your case, and that you may return ere long strengthened and happy is the warmest of all wishes on the part of

your affectionate
Gabriel

---

[1] For Sara Pattle Prinsep (1816–1887) and Holland House, see 61.30n2.

Plate 2: *The M's at Ems.*

Plate 3: *The German Lesson.*

² For J. T. Nettleship, see 68.165n1. See also **103** & **123**.
³ *Pandora* (S.224) was finished for John Graham, nephew of WG in 1871; the full-length oil was never done.
⁴ For the oil version, see **67**.
⁵ For Marie Spartali's sittings for the hands and chalk heads, see **96, 103, 123,** & **148**.
⁶ James T. Fields of Ticknor & Fields, founded by William D. Ticknor in 1832, was located at 124 Tremont Street, Boston, at this time. The firm published the *Atlantic Monthly* & the *North American Review* as well as such prominent British authors as Charles Dickens. The company became Houghton, Mifflin in 1880.

69.92 TO FORD MADOX BROWN

MS: UBC. Published: DW 885.

Friday [23 July 1869]

My dear Brown,

Val is dining here Monday at 7.30. Will you meet him? I have also asked Ned & Howell & Webb.¹

If you'll go with me to L[ittle]. Hol[land]. House on Sunday, look me up here. I shall be starting abt 3 I suppose or 4. I think Howell & wife will likely be there.

Ever yours
D G R

¹ Neither FMB nor the CAHs attended DGR's dinner party on 26 Jul (see **98, 99,** & **103**).

69.93 TO JANE OCTAVIA BROOKFIELD¹

MS: Maine Historical Society.

24 July/1869
16 Cheyne Walk
Chelsea

Dear Mrs. Brookfield

Many thanks, but I am sorry that a previous engagement prevents my having the pleasure of dining with you on Tuesday.

Ever yours truly
D G Rossetti

¹ See **39**.

69.94 TO JANE MORRIS

MS: BL. Published: Bryson 6. Date: P/M.

16 Cheyne Walk. Chelsea
Tuesday, 27 July [1869]

My dear Janey

I got a nice letter of yours from Calais on Monday evening of last week, and on Wednesday wrote in answer to Poste Restante, Cologne, as you told me. I now find Ned has heard from Top at Cologne, & as I have no letter from you, I fear it is possible mine may have miscarried. I find on enquiring that the stupid people at the post office here never weighed it and only stuck on a fourpenny stamp. I am afraid this was under single postage, & I believe the letter must have been double, as it contained a splendid cartoon.[1] If you have not got it, you must indeed have thought me a beast for not answering your good kind letter written when you could hardly write.

It is no use making this a long letter; as I do not know if it will ever reach you, since by the time it gets to Ems you will be no doubt at some hotel. It enrages me beyond measure to think that, through a detestable blunder, days may yet pass leaving you under the impression that I did not answer your letter.

I have heard from others of your progress & health since Calais, and await most anxiously the next news of you. As soon as I know that what I write is sure to reach you, I shall write again; and if I hear from you meanwhile & learn that my letter did not miscarry, it will be the greatest relief to me.

With love to Top

Ever your affectionate
Gabriel

[1] See **91**.

69.95 TO FREDERICK RICHARD LEYLAND

MS: LC. Published: Fennell 26.

16 Cheyne Walk
Tuesday [c. 27 July 1869]

My dear Leyland,

I had already heard with some consternation from Miss S[partali]. of her extraordinary decision.[1] However it is not hers but her father's. *She* was delighted beyond measure at your wish to buy, as old Brown (who first reported it to her from my report) told me before she got your letter.

However when she showed this to her father, he said that the compliment on your & my part (considering the fine works you possess and my flattering opinion) was so great that he could not think of any other course but her offering the picture as a present & it was he who caused her to do so much against her own conviction. Indeed she was very uncomfortable afterwards & said she really feared you might consider it in the light almost of an impertinence. I must explain to you that she *does* sell her works & is quite bent on adopting art as a serious profession, and that her father also takes this view most entirely. Only in the present instance (being an impulsive man) he seems to have felt so flattered by the incident as to have been driven on this extraordinary course. My own impression is that your best plan is to write a very serious note to the lady, thanking her duly, but saying that you really feel awkward and uncomfortable at so unexpected a result, and must venture to press her extremely to view the matter as you intended & accept the price of the picture, for which Brown I believe had advised her to ask 40 gs.[2]

My promise (which I will strictly bear in mind) was to make you a *present* of a portrait drawing in the event of a certain purchase. This was to be one of two, if I made two, or a duplicate of the one if only one was made. You may depend on my adhering to this in such event; and I will give you the refusal of any other such drawings with which I intend to part at all; but shall probably keep one at least. Nor have I yet made any but shall I trust, as I am promised sittings.

I will write again about plans in answer to your kind inquiry when I know my chances of leaving.

Ever yours
D G R

The sittings I had went in painting some hands.

[1] Marie Spartali had given one of her paintings to FRL (see **113**).
[2] See the following letter.

69.96 TO FORD MADOX BROWN
MS: Private Collection.

Tuesday [c. 27 July 1869]

Dear Brown

I had a note from Leyland asking my advice in his dilemma. I have advised him to write most seriously to the lady representing his awkward position & begging her to re-establish matters on a business footing in consideration for him. I told him the price at which you had advised that the picture should be rated – viz. 40 gs. This was correct was it not?

Will you give Miss Spartali, when you see her, the enclosed sonnet which I copied for her and forgot. It illustrates a photo: I gave her.

Ever yours
D G Rossetti

P.S. I suppose from what Miss S. said that next Saturday wd not suit her for a sitting. Could you find out without danger of inconveniencing her?

69.97 TO JAMES ANDERSON ROSE

MS: LC. Excerpt: Kashnor 203. Mistakenly dated "27 June" by DGR; receipt date endorsed by JAR as 28 Jul 69.

Tuesday/27 Ju[ly 1869]
16 Cheyne Walk
Chelsea

My dear Rose

Strong called on me last Saturday (sent I suppose by you) and assured me that his tenant would go out of the stables whenever wished. I told him to send me the tenant who turned out to be a cabman & begged to be allowed to stay a fortnight. I said I saw no particular objection to this, so according to this arrangement he will go out on *next Saturday week*. Do you think it necessary to see him yourself? If so I will send him down to you.

Has the payment to Strong & the surrender of lease yet taken place?[1]

Yours very truly
DG Rossetti

J A Rose Esq

P.S. Of course I have answered for nothing except conditionally on your approval.

---

[1] For the removal of the sub-tenant, see **110** & **122**.

69.98 TO CHARLES AUGUSTUS HOWELL
MS: Texas.

Tuesday [27 July 1869]

Sir

What a beast you were not to come yesterday to dinner. Ned, Val, Webb, & Leyland all came, and impossible stories were plentiful from Val, but he did not add the last charm of saying they had happened to himself, so the want of you was deeply felt.

I have been rubbing at the portrait I began of Kate,[1] & believe it will be like after all. Can she & you come on Thursday & sit & stay dinner? Say 2 o'clock as before.

Ever yours
Gabriel

[1] S.339.

69.99 TO CHARLES AUGUSTUS HOWELL
MS: Texas.

[c. 27 July 1869]

My dear Owl

I'm deeply aggrieved to hear that a Blue Nut is the symbol of your present identity – especially as mystery combines with horror in the impression conveyed to me by the mention of such a vegetable.[1]

But most seriously we missed you very much yesterday at dinner, and it was made all the worse by knowing that suffering was the cause of your absence. I hope by this time you are on the mend. There was a sad lack of startling narratives last night, either conscientiousness or incapacity preventing the guests from conferring that kind of enjoyment on each other. The difference was most marked from the occasions when your presence has graced the board.

With love to Kate

Yours affectionately
D G R

[1] The context suggests that CAH had suffered some form of food poisoning – probably from eating mouldy nuts.

69.100 TO CHARLES AUGUSTUS HOWELL

MS: Texas. Published: Cline 91.

Wednesday [c. 28 July 1869]

Dear Howell

Gambart has taken it into his head to engrave Janey's portrait – the one belonging to her.¹ I want to know who is really the best engraver. He recommends some bloke of the name of Stackpole – the plan at present being to do it in mezzotint which seems fittest for the picture. He tells me that Cousins – the best known mezzotint engraver – has retired from the profession.² Could you find out for me through Ruskin or somehow something about engravers? I am determined to have the thing done thoroughly well or not at all.

I shall have your large chalk drawing done soon but am doing a good deal to it. You ought not to part with it if you can help as it will be one of my best & the drawings of Janey will rise greatly in value when the portrait is published. The frame should be sent *here* when done as I always like to revise a drawing after seeing it framed.³

Your affec:
Gabriel

[1] S.372.
[2] Frederick Stacpoole (1813–1907) & Samuel Cousins, RA (1801–87); the latter engraved many of Reynolds' & Lawrence's works and produced JEM's *Order of Release* in 1856. See also **103**.
[3] CAH's Janey drawing is mentioned again in **147**.

69.101 TO HENRY BROWN

MS: Untraced (formerly Maggs Bros., Catalogue 1292).

28 July/1869
16 Cheyne Walk
Chelsea

Dear Sir

I shall be happy to subscribe to your book on Shakspeare's Sonnets & herewith forward P.O. order for the price.¹

Yours truly
D G Rossetti

Henry Brown Esq

[1] Henry Brown, *The Sonnets of Shakespeare Solved, and the Mystery of his Friendship, Love, and Rivalry Revealed* (J.R. Smith, 1870).

69.102 TO FRANCES CATHERINE HOWELL
MS: Texas.

Thursday [29 July 1869]
16 Cheyne Walk
Chelsea

My dear Kate

I wrote on Tuesday to Charlie proposing that you should sit to me at 2 today and dine here with him. In case it is possible my note miscarried I write to ask if I am to expect you today.[1]

Your affec:
D Gabriel R

---

[1] A sitting for S.339. See the following letter.

69.103 TO JANE MORRIS
MS: BL. Excerpt: Surtees 169. Published: Bryson 7.

16 Cheyne Walk
30th July 1869

Dear kind Janey

It is a great consolation to know that you have reached Ems at last, and that at any rate for the present the annoyance of travelling is at an end. All was well with my letter to Cologne which only mattered so far as you might have thought by not receiving it that I was capable of neglect in your regard. No doubt you have got also my fidgetty note to Ems. Pardon my troubling you with it.

I got yours from Ems last night, but delayed writing because I was to receive the proofs of my poems today & thought I might send them. However they are so huddled and blundered that I must wait to send a better copy. Besides they will not be of much interest to you as they are only those you know already.

Kate Howell was sitting to me yesterday for a drawing I am giving her, and I showed her your letter which induced her to write to you.[1] The news of you must be considered hopeful on the whole so far, as you seem by all accounts to have borne the journey pretty well after all. With what hope I await still better news and with what joy I shall receive it, pray believe better than I can say. All that concerns you is the all-absorbing question with me, as dear Top will not mind my telling you at this anxious time. The more he loves you, the more he knows that you are too lovely and noble not to be loved: and, dear

Janey, there are too few things that seem worth expressing as life goes on, for one friend to deny another the poor expression of what is most at his heart. But he is before me in granting this, and there is no need for me to say it. I can never tell you how much I am with you at all times. Absence from your sight is what I have long been used to; and no absence can ever make me so far from you again as your presence did for years. For this long inconceivable change, you know now what my thanks must be.

But I have no right to talk to you in a way that may make you sad on my account when in reality the balance of joy and sorrow is now so much more in my favour than it has been, or could have been hoped to become, for years past. The great question now, before which all else is as nothing, & for which God knows I would sacrifice all else, is that of your dear health. Never mind what I could not help writing, and of course do not say a word of any kind in answer to this foolish part of my letter.

I shall be going soon away for awhile I suppose, – as you may be sure I am most anxious not to be away & miss seeing you improved on your return. I have been receiving all sorts of country invitations & several to Scotland but shall stick to quiet Penkill unless I am obliged to go to Graham's also for a few days. There seems some danger of a short stay at Speke with Leyland becoming inevitable and this will be a sad bore because of his family. He himself is a good friendly fellow.[2]

I hope to give you some decided news of work soon. I have done the drapery of that drawing of you with the head resting on the hand, & think it certainly the best I have done.[3] I shall not let Norton have it of course, but keep it & make him a copy. I must paint it for myself, if you will let me, as soon as you can sit again. Also I *must* do the full-length Pandora as soon as I have finished this one which will do well enough for Graham as he is delighted with it. Mary Spartali has given me one sitting to paint the hands of the Beatrice I did from you,[4] & she is to give me another. I think they will come well enough, though it is provoking to have made a mull of them from you. However this will be one thing got rid of I hope before long.

Poor Nettleship I find is sold after all. It seems the keeper of the Academy (that old fool Charles Landseer) takes on himself to kick out the drawings he doesn't like before they go up to the Council at all; and unfortunately God, when creating evil, appears to have created an evil opinion of Nettleship in the mind of Charles Landseer.[5] This seems a great shame.

I was at Ned's the other evening and saw what he is doing. I was particularly struck with a most beautiful female figure in profile with some smaller figures by a door in the background. This I thought one of the finest things he has done. I don't know what he calls it.[6] Ned, Webb, Val & Leyland dined in the tent with me one day lately. Howell was to have come but didn't. Val supplied his place well so far as the impossibility of his narratives went, but he did not add the final charm of saying that they had all happened to himself, so must be pronounced on the whole inferior.

I believe I may say I have really got my stables now, and that I shall really set to work on the studio in all probability before leaving town.

Val's studio filled me with envy as it always does one day that I called there, & the sight of it will I think expedite my movements. I cannot say that the same mean feeling was awakened by his pictures. He has begun one which he calls the *Lion's Mouth*, and which represents a number of cheap supers acting in the way they do when the "walking of the ghost"* on Saturday night is very uncertain. In the corner a female "dresser" who has apparently taken the leading lady's part at a moment's notice, is doing something to your knocker in Queen Square, which as I told Val, he had better borrow to paint, as thus one character at least in his picture would be something like the real thing. Val has also done a sketch of Mary Spartali which seems like a faint reminiscence of Watts's feeblest portraits of his mother. I said so to the lady, and found her an entire sympathiser as to the nature of Val's art. She said that he was about 4 hours doing it (it looks like 20 minutes' work) and that her maid said afterwards that she supposed that when that gentleman drew heads he liked to have some one sitting "for company's sake like."[7]

I am glad you saw the Van Eyck at Ghent which I have seen 2 or 3 times and always with the greatest delight. It is certainly the noblest picture of that school I know, though when first I went to Belgium I was I believe more attracted by the curious variety and interest of Memling's pictures at Bruges.[8] These I suppose you did not see, nor do I indeed know yet whether you stopped at Bruges at all. If so, I suppose it would be at the Hotel du Commerce (I think it is called) which is a splendid old mansion with a most curious stair-rail in which each upright consists of a duck with a bull-rush in his mouth, all painted in colours.

I have never myself been at Cologne, but no doubt you must have enjoyed the Cathedral as far as fatigue would let you.

I suppose you will have heard of the sad accident to poor P. P. Marshall, involving I fear for certain the loss of the forefinger of his right hand. I hear he is progressing favorably, but only I fear as regards speedy recovery, not the saving of the finger.[9]

I must try after all and see Cousins the engraver about your portrait. Robertson, who knows him, has made enquiries, and finds that he really is at present very much out of sorts and not working, but that he trusts to resume work. I saw the other day his engraving of Millais' *Minuet* which I had not seen before, and which certainly seems to be more satisfactory than other people's work.[10]

Let me hear *something* from you, dearest Janey, but do not on any account weary yourself with writing, or rack your brain for any news except of your health. All love to Topsy

from your loving
Gabriel

---

* "walking of the ghost" = theatrical slang for salaries payable by the week's end.
1. DGR drew 2 portraits of Kate, S.338 & 339.
2. For details of DGR's departure on 17 Aug for Penkill, see **126**.
3. Perhaps *Reverie* (S.206).
4. For Marie Spartali's sittings & the full-length *Pandora*, see **91&n5**.
5. Charles Landseer (1799–1879), elder brother of Sir Edwin Landseer, was Keeper of the RA Schools (1851–73) and a much-criticized instructor in the antique class. DGR may be right as Nettleship first exhibited at the R.A. in 1874 and steadily thereafter. See **91n2**.
6. Probably EBJ's watercolour *Beatrice*, dated 1870, for which the model was Maria Zambaco.
7. For VCP, see 57.48n2. He had married FRL's daughter Florence; they lived in a house designed by PSW and completed in 1866 at 14 Holland Park. At this time he was painting theatrical scenes.
8. Identified in Bryson as *The Adoration of the Lamb in the Cathedral of St. Bavon* (7n11). 49.20, written from Bruges to JC, is a paean to "the miraculous works of Memling & Van Eyck."
9. For PPM, see 62.48n1.
10. JEM's *Minuet* (1866) is a portrait of his 8-year-old daughter Effie (see **100n2**).

69.104 TO GEORGE PRICE BOYCE

MS: University College. Date: Unidentified endorsement.

Monday night [July 1869]

My dear Boyce

On seeing you this evening I meant to say as follows but missed the moment.

There is a drawing of mine – the *Gate of Memory* – going at Foster's – on view tomorrow Tuesday, to be sold on Wednesday.¹ It is likely to go very low I shd think being dim-coloured, but it is one of my best watercolours. If you're at all in the way of buying, you might get it cheap I shd think.

Ever yours
DG Rossetti

---

1. This sale is not mentioned under S.100, nor is it in the priced Foster's catalogues at the V&A; DGR may have arranged for it to be bought (see 75.91n1 & 153, where DGR says he sold it to EG). Its first owner was William Vokins (see 64.9, which wrongly identifies Vokin's purchase as S.100A, one of the small related pencil sketches, which Mark Samuels Lasner donated to the DAM). The watercolour is now in a private collection.

69.105 TO JULIA MARGARET CAMERON

MS: Wellesley College.

[July 1869]
16 Cheyne Walk
Chelsea

Dear Mrs. Cameron

Many thanks for your still further kind present which I feel half ashamed to accept. I think on the whole the Annunciation is the more complete in composition and light and shade. The Four Sisters is full of beauty, but in so large a group the interference in some degree of unlucky natural accidents in the arrangement is quite impossible to be avoided.[1] Among a bevy of beauties one does not know I should say from the photograph that Nellie and Christina bear away the palm; but photography is not always a trustworthy reporter even in your hands as regards facts: – over the beauty of general effect and arrangement you seem somehow to have acquired a degree of control quite your own.

I will give Mary Spartali the "Kiss of Peace" the next time I see her. It is a most lovely thing – perhaps your masterpiece, and I could not think of asking you to print one specially for me.[2]

Pardon haste in mid-work.

Most truly yours
D G Rossetti

---

[1] The Annunciation may be Mrs. Cameron's *The Guardian Angel* (1868), which Gernsheim notes "arouses memories of DGR's 'Angel of the Annunciation'" (*Ecce Ancilla Domini!* [S.44], later retitled *The Annunciation*). The painting of four sisters, entitled *The Rosebud Garden of Girls* (1868) from a line (902) in Tennyson's *Maud,* is a group portrait of Mary (later Mrs. G.F. Watts), Ethel, Nellie, & Christina Fraser-Tytler. It is "probably," Gernsheim speculates (78), "inspired by Rossetti's equally bad picture 'The Beloved' (1866)." Reproduced in Tristram Powell. ed., *Victorian Photographs of Famous Men & Fair Women by Julia Margaret Cameron*, with introduction by Virginia Woolf & Roger Fry (Boston: Godine,1973): Plate 22; originally published by the Hogarth Press in 1926.

[2] Reproduced Gernsheim, *Cameron* 167. Marie Spartali had posed for several of Mrs. Cameron's photographs in Sep 1868.

69.106 TO CHARLES FAIRFAX MURRAY[1]

MS: Texas.

[c. July 1869]

My dear Murray

I think I may have to alter the background a good deal, so the principal thing to get on with will be the figure.[2]

Your
D G R

---

[1] See 66.182n1. For a full-length biography, see David Elliott's *Charles Fairfax Murray: The Unknown Pre-Raphaelite* (New Castle, DE: Oak Knoll Press, 2000).

[2] This letter and the 2 following suggest CFM was working on the outline for the oil version of *Sibylla Palmifera*, later abandoned owing to DGR's problems with the background. See **72** & **149**.

69.107 TO CHARLES FAIRFAX MURRAY

MS: Texas.

Monday [c. July 1869]

My dear Murray

Have you got on with the things in hand for me? I find I shall be needing the oil picture on Thursday to show to some one, but shall be able to let you have it again the same evening or next morning as you like. I think I must trouble you to bring it down (say on Thursday at 12) as I am afraid to trust a messenger. At same time you might if you like bring anything you have done to show me.

Ever yours
D G Rossetti

69.108 TO CHARLES FAIRFAX MURRAY

MS: Texas.

Saturday [c. July 1869]

My dear Murray,

I think I had better keep the Sibyl over next Thursday unless you are short of other work to do, & send it you next Friday morning. When with you again I shd be glad if you cd get on with it as speedily as may be.

Ever yours
D. G Rossetti

69.109 TO CHARLES AUGUSTUS HOWELL

MS (unsigned fragment): Texas.

Monday [c. 2 August 1869]

My dear Howell

The frame has come this morning. I shall be sending some oil pictures & chalk drawings to Parsons to be photo'd on Wednesday or Thursday, & might as well, if you have no decided objection, include this one of yours. He would keep the things about 2 days I believe.[1]

I enclose a letter of Agnew's to which I propose to send no answer. In case it suggested anything to you, I . . .

[1] For Parsons, see 65.87.

69.110 TO JAMES ANDERSON ROSE

MS: LC. Excerpt: Kashnor 205.

16 Cheyne Walk
Monday/2nd August [1869]

My dear Rose

Strong called on me again this morning, & I told him what you said: – and that, accordingly, his business is to get his sub-tenant out at once. I told him that, as soon as this is done & your clerk can come down & see that the premises are really empty, I have no doubt you will think the time has arrived to pay the £20 on his giving up the lease and keys. Thus I fancy he will now set about clearing the place, and you will soon hear to that effect.[1]

Ever yours
D G Rossetti

J A Rose Esq

[1] See **97** & **122**.

69.111 TO CHARLES FAIRFAX MURRAY

MS: Texas.

4th Aug 1869
16 Cheyne Walk
Chelsea

My dear Murray

Thanks about the Maximilian; but though fine, it is a monotonous affair, & I shouldn't care to spend the money. Thanks for the M.S.S.[1]

Ever yours
D G Rossetti

---

[1] CFM, who developed a superb and diverse collection of books, MSS, & works of art, had a number of early and important works relating to the Holy Roman Emperor Maximilian I (see Hugh W. Davies, *Catalogue of a Collection of Early German Books in the Library of C. Fairfax Murray* [privately printed, 1913]). Whether he was offering DGR an early book or an illustration is not certain. The MSS CFM enclosed were copies of DGR's poems, which he also collected. Most of his DGR MSS and proofsheets, including an almost-complete *HL*, were given by him to the Fitzwilliam, though some early ones are at Texas. DGR was rounding up MS copies of his poems so he could have them set up in print (see **84** & **118**).

69.112 TO JANE MORRIS

MS: BL. Excerpt: Surtees 603. Published: Bryson 8. For the integral drawing enclosed with this letter and described in its first paragraph, see **Plate 3**.

4th August 1869

My dear Janey

You see your great idea has not been sown in barren soil but has immediately borne fruit. I fear that the legitimate leglessness of the pictorial and ideal Topsy has somewhat communicated itself to the German maid in the cartoon, and even you have rather a Georgian air. But these are minor defects. The poetry and philosophy of the subject are I hope complete, while you will see that even Scriptural analogy has not been neglected.

What a joyful hearing it is that you have passed two days almost without pain. I must study donkeys that I may be able to make a cartoon of your first expedition.[1] What a good thing you went after all. I have no doubt now that you will return greatly benefited, and what could happen in the world so good as that?

I shall leave London as soon as ever I find possible, and shall not work much while I am away in order that I may profit by it much & be back soon. It would be too bad to miss the first sight of you in your improved condition. I had already been thinking of this, and may probably, if I find you are sure of being back by the time fixed, return then and if necessary go elsewhere afterwards. But I hate going anywhere if I can stay and work. As it is I see no prospect of getting away before the end of next week, but then I think I shall. Of course I shall be writing you again, & I hope hearing again from you before then.

I am thinking of making a drawing of Mary Spartali if she can sit to me one or two days next week. I began one in the fag end of the 2nd sitting for the hands (which I have got done) but it was not satisfactory & I shall begin another if she can sit.[2] She is very difficult, but putting her against the light as you sat for the Pandora, I found the expression and character perhaps the finest, & want to make the drawing in that way. I have been doing one or two other drawings to raise the wind – drawings from models. Brown has begun a second drawing of Mary S. It is much prettier than the first, but somehow does not seem to have the amount of likeness which that had in spite of its want of beauty.

Kate Howell wrote that note here after sitting to me for a drawing I am going to give her. We talked a great deal of you, you may be sure.

I saw Bessie and Lucy since their return. Bessie seemed to me to look very ill. You have no doubt full accounts of their vicissitudes, so I need not tell you.

I hope to have copies of my verses to send you before long. I think I shall have to get the sonnets printed only on one side of the paper, in order that as I write more, I may be able to slip them into their proper places in the series – so far as it can be called a series. I find I have just 50 sonnets which I shall print after rejecting a good many I have by me. I shall reprint those in the Fortnightly.[3]

I see Topsy is prouded upon in Temple Bar in the inevitable company of Matthew Arnold. I have not seen it but hear that the series is all bestial and written by a little ass named Austin who once wrote a stupid satire.[4] Some one has done Christina in "Tinsley" – the same series in which Top appeared – and it seems William & I are to follow. It is weak beyond even the usual mark, and may I suspect turn out cheeky too before it is over. The author I suppose may be one Forman who I believe did Topsy's article, only this seems worse written.[5]

You see I have no news to speak of since last writing. May the news of you be better still! – is what is most in my mind. Good bye, dear Janey. Love to Top.

Your most affectionate
Gabriel

I hear Topsy wrote a lovely poem at Lille.

1 "When she gets better there are splendid mokes and mules here, whereupon she may climb the hills" (WM:PSW, 31 Jul 69, Kelvin 81).
2 See **91n5**.
3 See 68.173n1. The "series" of sonnets became *HL* (*Poems* 187–255).
4 Alfred Austin (1835–1913, Poet Laureate 1896–1913), "The Poetry of the Period – Mr. Matthew Arnold and Mr. Morris," *Temple Bar* 27 (Aug 69: 35–51). In the article Austin accused WM of escapism. He wrote *The Seasons: A Satire* in 1861.
5 "Criticisms on Contemporaries, VI, The Rossettis, Part 1 [CGR]," in *Tinsley's Magazine* (Aug 69: 59–67). HBF was the author as DGR surmised (see 68.145&n1). Part 2 on DGR followed in the September issue (142–51) and Part 3 on WMR in October (276–81). Despite reservations about HBF's style expressed privately to friends and family, DGR recognized that the articles were inspired by the appearance of his sonnets in the Mar 69 issue of the *Fortnightly Review*. On 24 Feb 71, after HBF had given him an advance copy of his enthusiastic review of *Poems* for *Tinsley's*, DGR sent him a warm thank-you note (see 71.27&n1).

69.113 TO FORD MADOX BROWN

MS: UBC. Date: WMR.

Thursday [5 August 1869]

My dear Brown

Leyland is going in for "Progne,"* & is to write to the artist himself.¹ He asked me about price and I said I supposed about 40 or 50 gs. If you are asked advice, I fancy 50 would be safe or indeed he could not well back out of 60 but I suppose you will think 50 the thing.

Ever yours
DG R

The Lady is to sit to me tomorrow (Friday) and Saturday at 12 each day. Suppose you look in one day.

---

* "Progne" = FMB's version of Procne, the wife of Tereus and sister of Philomela who was turned into a swallow in the Greek legend.
1 Marie Spartali was presumably offering her painting *Procne in Search of Philomela* to FRL. See **95**.

69.114 TO ALGERNON CHARLES SWINBURNE

MS: BL. Published: DW 841.

Friday [c. 6 August 1869]

My dear Swinburne
  I find the address is

Mme Hess
64 Rue Neuve des Petits Champs.

There is no shop, but you go up to some private rooms. The can we got cost 100 francs, & I should think you should get as much as this to give it a fair trial. It is frightfully dear. Certainly a hair-wash would be the unkindest cut of all to bring against the Absalom of modern poetry, if only the Saturday Review knew of it.

I am delighted to hear you are at work.

Your affec:
D Gabriel R

P.S. Fanny says the water did her no good, but I knew a case where it did much.[1]

---

[1] ACS was taking the waters at Vichy for a few weeks this summer.

69.115 TO VERNON LUSHINGTON

MS: European Art Gallery, Dallas, Texas. Published: Gaunt, *Pre-Raphaelite Tragedy* (1942): 119; DW 847.

August 7/1869
16 Cheyne Walk
Chelsea

My dear Vernon

Did I, years ago, give you a M.S. copy of a poem of mine called "Jenny"? I want a copy, not having one in a perfect state. To some one I gave it, & have a faint notion it may have been to you.

Write me a line.

Ever yours
DGRossetti

V. Lushington Esq

69.116 TO MESSRS. STRANGEWAYS

Text: DW 849 (attributed to Courtney-Boyd but unlocated).

[7 August 1869]
16 Cheyne Walk
Chelsea

Please print these: "Ave" after the "Burden of Nineveh," the "Sea-Limit" just before the "Honeysuckle."

D. G. Rossetti

Can you let me have some proofs tonight?

69.117 TO MESSRS. STRANGEWAYS

MS: Princeton. Published: DW 848.

16 Cheyne Walk
Saturday [7 August 1869]

Messrs. Strangeways

I forgot to explain just now that the longer poems can be printed on both sides – only each poem must be separate – not with another begun on the back of the last page.

The poems which occupy only a page each must not have another on the back.

Yours
DG Rossetti

[Enclosure]

(Most of these poems were written between 1847 and 1853. They are here printed, if not without revision, yet much in their original state. They are some among a good many then written, the rest of which I cannot print, having now no complete copies. Many of the sonnets and some of short pieces are more recent work.)

D.G.R. 1869.

Sunday [8 August 1869]   69.118

69.118 TO CHARLES FAIRFAX MURRAY

MS: Texas.

Sunday [8 August 1869]

My dear Murray

Do you mind my tearing your M.S. copies to give to the printer if necessary? I'll give you a set of the printed things.

Is "Weariswa" by Morris or Swinburne – or whom?[1]

Ever yours
D G Rossetti

[1] *Wearieswa': A Ballad* by ACS, posthumously published by Thomas J. Wise in 1917 (*A Swinburne Library* [privately printed, 1925]). In the "Bonchurch Edition" of *The Complete Works of Algernon Charles Swinburne,* edited by Edmund Gosse & Thomas James Wise, 20 vols. (Heinemann, 1925–1927), 20: 388, Wise notes that it was composed "about 1862" and that CFM, "to whom Sir Edward Burne-Jones gave it in the early 'sixties," gave it to the Fitwilliam Museum.

69.119 TO WILLIAM MORRIS

MS: BL. Published: Bryson 9. Date: P/M.

Monday night [9 August 1869]

My dear Top.

I confess to a feeling of great discouragement on not seeing Janey's handwriting when I opened your letter this morning. I hope it does not really mean that she is worse than you say. I would not of course for the world have her write when she is too ill to do so easily but her previous letter had led me to hope more perhaps than was reasonable in so short a time. It would reassure me greatly to hear something like better news from her as soon as possible.

I have been feeling extremely used up myself, and shall leave for Scotland I believe either Saturday or Monday next. It would be a relief if I could hear before then. In any case, all letters will be immediately sent on, so I will hope to continue hearing as usual and shall write regularly myself.

You do not say when you expect to return, and I suppose you hardly know as yet. I would make up my mind to one thing if I were you; and that is, to take care now you have made the journey; that the baths have a fair chance, even were the delay a little longer than you intended. The journey back, too, might undo the good done were not full time for rest allowed.

With love to Janey

Yours affectionately
D G Rossetti

69.120 TO CHARLES FAIRFAX MURRAY
MS: Texas.

Monday. [9 August 1869]

My dear Murray

Thanks, though I am ashamed to murder your M.S. I'll return it if it comes back to me, & will give you all those of the things I have printed. As you seem to care for M.S.S. I enclose the 1st drafts of the Staff & Scrip which I find to contain a good deal since excised. Keep it if you care for it. I wrote it about 1851–2.[1]

Ever yours
D G Rossetti

[1] "The Staff and Scrip" appeared in *Poems* (47–57).

69.121 TO FORD MADOX BROWN
MS: Private Collection. Date: WMR.

Tuesday [10 August 1869]
16 Cheyne Walk
Chelsea

Dear Brown

Will you dine here Friday at 7 to meet Nettleship & I hope Ned Jones?

Your affec:
D Gabriel R

69.122 TO JAMES ANDERSON ROSE
MS: LC.

16 Cheyne Walk
Thursday [12 August 1869]

My dear Rose

The sub-tenant is really getting out, and I am assured that if you will send your clerk to see that the premises are actually clear on Saturday morning, the whole affair can be wound up on same afternoon.[1]

I have to start for Scotland either Saturday evening or Monday at latest.

Ever yours
DG Rossetti

[1] See **97** & **110** for the sub-tenant, and 68.1 for the final settlement with Charles Strong.

69.123 TO JANE MORRIS

MS: BL. Excerpt: Surtees 604. Published: Bryson 10. For the integral drawing enclosed with this letter, see **Plate 4**.

Saturday 14 Aug 1869

Dearest Janey

You may be sure that my joy on receipt of your letter last night was proportionate to the extreme discouragement I had felt at the last news of you through Top. Perhaps after all the attack of illness has been beneficial as clearing the way for improvement now you are using the baths again. I wonder impatiently as to every hour's result upon your health. But it is a glorious thing that you can say so decidedly that you are getting free from pain. The weakness must be expected for the present. If you come back, as I now really hope, set up (to the extent of reasonable hope in so short a campaign) I shall bless the name of Ems which does not take up much room in one's thanksgivings. It seems quite a shame to call it Bad Ems on the envelope, and I should write Good instead if I thought the postman had an intuitive soul.

Now that I know you are on the mend, I shall really get off to Scotland on Monday morning. Even if I do not stay long, it is the readiest and best thing to do at once, as I am most sorely in want of a change, having been for some time more thoroughly seedy than I can tell you. As for my head & eyes, they have been far from well, but I do not now experience the absolute inconvenience in work that I did at one time. So I may (I hope) look on the question without great anxiety at present. However I mean to take no work with me to Scotland, as I am sure perfect rest is what I need. Were I to be staying, I could send for some. I am afraid what I tell you of my used-up condition may induce you to look for much work done, but such is far from being the case. I hoped on getting the hands put into your picture from Miss S[partali]. that I might be able to take it up and get it out of hand; but other things have come in the way and it sticks as it was since then, so after all perhaps I might have done the hands again from you, which is a provoking idea. Since she sat for the hands, Miss Spartali has given me two more sittings & I have made 3 chalk heads of her. The last I think is not unsuccessful, though the 2 first were completely so. I find her head about the most difficult I ever drew. It depends not nearly so much on real form as on a subtle charm of life which one cannot re-create. I think it would be hardly possible to make a completely successful picture of her, and feel a great deal humbler now when I look at other people's attempts.[1] During her sittings she was very much amused with the Polly, who became very expansive towards an old Miss Young who accompanied her. This old body seemed to consider Polly her elective

Plate 4: *Resolution; or the Infant Hercules.*

affinity, and many love-passages passed between them, though for some time, on the Polly imploring a kiss, Miss Y. said that it should be granted when they were alone, which she really seemed to look on as a question of propriety. Now and then Polly would launch an expression at her admirer which I suspect she understood well enough and which used to cause me to bury my nose deeper in the drawing with terror till the air was clear again. It was not till the second sitting that Miss S. relieved my mind very much by saying – "Why, Miss Young, she calls you an old *wretch*!"

I have received from America the water-colour by poor Lizzy for which I am to give Norton a drawing of you. It looks very fine though certainly quite quaint enough.[2]

I wish I had any amusing news. The stable business has still been hanging on, but this very day seems perhaps about to conclude. However it is no use my thinking of building till my return from Scotland at any rate.

Nettleship and Brown dined here yesterday. N. showed me his Academy drawings which are remarkably good, so their rejection was disgraceful. He is painting beasts at that gardens and has done a crouching one for which I have commissioned him (!) – also a roaring one in progress, which is splendid as is mine also. He seems to be getting over his difficulties in painting.[3] I asked him if he had got Top's books which I know were meant to be sent, but he had not, so I suppose it was deferred in the hurry of leaving.

I believe I have got in type all the verses I can scrape together at present. They will be finally struck off in a few days & I will cause a copy to be sent you unless time gets too late for it to reach you at Ems. However there is nothing to interest you much as they are all old things you know, but I have improved some. The chaotic copies of other things I have not yet tackled, but may possibly do so before long though with uncertain results. New writing seems to have departed from me, as I have done nothing for ever so long. Perhaps Scotch air & the neighbourhood of Burns may set me piping. I suppose Topsy is roaring and screaming through the Parnassian tunnels and junctions in his usual style now, not without an occasional explosion.[4] Did he remember the couple of blouses he promised me from Lille, or will he remember them on his way back? The one you gave me gets dirty and not having another to wear while it is washed, I become oblivious and discontinue its use.

You have heard I suppose that poor Marshall's forefinger has had to be amputated. He is going on well now, but was only just in time, as a stupid country doctor had dozed over the question, and it was only through Marshall's calling on John M[arshall]. that he was roused to the necessity of having it off at once.[5]

Ned is gone to Crom's Tower for some days, as you probably know.[6] When you are able to answer this, you can do so either straight to

Penkill Castle
Girvan
Ayrshire

or else to Chelsea, as I take care to leave envelopes duly directed which will ensure all letters being sent on at once. But perhaps the best will be to write straight there. You know without my saying it that I am far from wishing you to write when you do not feel in sorts, but you know also how glad I am whenever I can hear from you.

What you tell me seems to infer a fortnight longer at Ems from the date on your letter, Thursday last. Thus with a week on the way home, which I suppose will be fully required, I judge you may be expected in London in all probability about a fortnight from Thursday next. Will you be sure to keep me exactly informed? I suppose the Doctor has not raised the question of your being sent on to the place in Switzerland which you told me was sometimes made a second stage after Ems.

Conceive if your cure were now to proceed so rapidly that there remained a glut of surplus baths, and Topsy were induced to express a thanksgiving frame of mind by that act which is next to godliness! Give him my love, and if he wishes to be revenged for the opposite diaphragmic diagram, let him know that I have bought the works of the poet Banting, that "idle singer of a too full day."[7]

God bless you, dear Janey. Let me know from you, and I will answer from Penkill.

Most affectionately yours
D Gabriel R

[1] See **91**, **103**, & **112**.
[2] *Clerk Saunders* by EES. See **47** & **48**.
[3] For Nettleship & the RA, see 68.165n1, **91**, & **103**.
[4] At Bad Ems WM was working on Volume 2 of *The Earthly Paradise*.
[5] See **103**. For John Marshall, DGR's physician who amputated PPM's forefinger, see 53.55n1.
[6] Broadway Tower, Worcs., home of Cormell Price (1835–1910), Oxford friend of WM & EBJ.
[7] From WM's *The Earthly Paradise*. William Banting, a London undertaker, published *A Letter on Corpulence* in 1863 relating how he dieted to lose 46 pounds. DGR teased WM relentlessly about his weight, often including references to his own expanding girth.

69.124 TO MURRAY MARKS

MS: Fitzwilliam. Date: P/M.

Sunday [15 August 1869]

My dear Marks

It strikes me that it would be necessary for you just to look up Bartlett about that sofa & take care that *too much* is not done to it.[1] The pictures I should say wanted nothing. The black requires doing up & the patterns in gold to be completed here & there where rubbed away. But I do not want the thing made a lighter tone than it is, nor do I want the sort of complete renovation which B. practises by repainting the thing black & doing the patterns all over again from tracings. This wd cost too much & is I think otherwise undesirable.

I am so completely fagged that I really haven't had the energy to do any work this day or two. I must finish your drawing the first thing on my return. I know you will forgive the delay.

Ever yours
DG Rossetti

[1] For the sofa given to DGR by JS, see **42** & **207**.

69.125 TO MESSRS. STRANGEWAYS

Text: DW 850 (attributed to Courtney-Boyd but unlocated).

Monday, 16 August 1869

Please print this and insert it after "Sister Helen."[1] I am not leaving town till Tuesday morning. If you can send me proofs of the things in order by *tonight*, you can send them here. But I suppose this cannot well be done.

D. G. Rossetti
16 Cheyne Walk

[1] In Proof State #2 of *Poems*, "Sister Helen" was followed by "Stratton Water."

69.126 TO CHARLES AUGUSTUS HOWELL

MS: Princeton. Excerpt: *PRT* 82–83. Published: Troxell, *Colophon* 15 (1933); *TR* 115–16; DW 851.

Monday/16 August/1869

My dear Howell

I feel disposed, if practicable by your friendly aid, to go in for the recovery of my poems if possible, as you proposed some time ago. Only I should have to beg *absolute* secrecy to *every one*, as the matter ought really not to be talked about. If you think this feasible, will you let me know what letter from myself is necessary. I am just at this moment leaving for Scotland, so perhaps you will think it best to defer the matter till my return, especially as you are probably on the move yourself. If however you think it can be done now, so much the better. It is a matter on which – having been lately taking up my old M.S.S. – I begin to feel some real anxiety.[1]

Will you write me a line addressed

Penkill Castle
Girvan
Ayrshire.

I am leaving London tomorrow (Tuesday) at 10 A.M. & shall be on the road 2 or 3 days, (as I have to pay a half-way visit)[2] but will answer as soon as I get your note.

I am sorry I could not find time to apply to Kitty for another sitting before leaving; but will not fail to do so almost immediately on my return.

The last news I have of Janey a few days ago, is, I think I may safely say now, encouraging. I suppose they are likely to be back in about 3 weeks. I trust to Heaven she may be better by then in a decided degree. The cure certainly seems promising at present.

With love to Kitty

I am your affectionate
D Gabriel R

P.S. If I recover the book I will give you the swellest drawing conceivable, or if you like paint the portrait of Kitty.

---

[1] This letter indicates that DGR was now ready to act on CAH's suggestion that he retrieve his poems from the coffin of EES. The first step was securing permission from the Home Secretary to exhume the coffin (see **147n1**). Thereafter, CAH made further arrangements, securing the solicitor, HVT, & Dr. Llewellyn Williams, who had the unpleasant task of disinfecting the pages.

[2] To AML at Ravenside.

69.127 TO CHARLES FAIRFAX MURRAY

MS: Texas.

Saturday [before 17 August 1869]

Dear Murray

I suppose you are not likely to be getting on with the proposed copy of the oil picture, are you? In such case, had it not better return to me?[1]

Ever yours
DG Rossetti

[1] See **106–108**.

69.128 TO FORD MADOX BROWN

MS: UBC. Excerpt: *RP* 452–53. Published: DW 852.

Friday [20 August 1869]
Penkill Castle/near Girvan/Ayrshire

Dear Brown

Here I am since yesterday, having spent one day on the road with the old Lady.[1] Everything is as jolly as possible, and everybody wants *You*. So you see you *must* come instantly on receipt of this. You will enjoy yourself greatly and even profit in subject matter for something to a certainty. The train I took is at 10 A.M. from Euston. You would reach Carlisle at 6-10 & could see the town & stop the night, (at the County Hotel which is in the station) coming on next day at 11, changing rapidly at Ayr and reaching Killochan at 4-25 where Scott & I would meet you.

Another way. Start at 9 P.M. from Euston taking ticket to Ayr, – travel all night, – change carriages at Kilmarnock and go on at once to Ayr. Here you wd arrive at 10-50 and wd have to stay there till 3-32 which time you could occupy in grog at the Tam O'Shanter where you would [see] T.O'S's & Sonter Johnny's chairs & drinking-horns. Coming on at 3-32 you would reach Killochan at 4-25 where (as above) Scott & I would meet you.

So you are posted up for the journey. Don't sneak out of it, but write at once that you are coming.

Ever yours
DG Rossetti

P.S. On Monday I actually got possession of the stables and broke down the door separating them from the garden. On soberly considering them I think them most promising.

[1] AML.

69.129 TO ALICIA MARGARET LOSH

MS: Princeton. Published: *TR* 87–88; DW 853. Written on 16CW stationery.

Penkill – Friday [20 August 1869]

Dear Miss Losh

I reached here all right yesterday, and I found every thing looking perfect except your chair in the chimney corner, which had an empty aspect still open to correction. Miss Boyd tells me to tell you how decidedly this is her view of the subject and how soon she hopes it will be remedied by your becoming visible in the reserved seat. There is plenty of room for both you and old Brown who has been written to by me with this as another defaulter. Miss Boyd repudiates the whole charge connected with her night journey, as the family could not possibly have reached her within the time for the proposed greetings, unless by a certainty of incurring colds catarrhs and asthmas, to say nothing of doctor's bills. As for her reaching the family, that was still more impossible in so short & uncomfortable a halt. So you are to bear no malice whatever.

I hope I did not inconvenience Mr. Wm. Losh very much by accepting his kind offer to drive me to the station before he started on his own journey.[1]

I have got my proofs here and am tattooing them in the usual agonized state which such things bring me to. As soon as I get a complete set I will send it to you – no I wont – I will keep it for you till you come here.

With affectionate remembrances

I am most sincerely yours
D G Rossetti

[1] This William Losh is probably William Septimus Losh, youngest son of James Losh & Cecelia Baldwin, first cousin to AML and her sister Sara Spencer Losh as well as Sara's husband. Sara & William lived at Wreay Syke, near AML's Ravenside House in the village of Wreay. William was living with AML and 2 of his brothers at Ravenside at the time of the 1851 census of Carlisle. He married Sara in 1831 and later inherited Woodside, where he was recorded as a justice of the peace in 1881. See also **160**.

Saturday [21 August 1869]

69.130 TO WILLIAM MICHAEL ROSSETTI

MS: BL. Excerpt: *FL* 204. Published: DW 854. Date: WMR.

Saturday [21 August 1869]

Dear William

After much bother with the proofs & constantly finding new blunders I have bethought myself to bother you with them, so send them with this by Book Post. Would you read them through & if you find anything obviously wrong, correct it. In punctuation I have my own ideas which may not be yours, so I will ask you generally to leave this alone; but if anything seems like a printer's error will you notify it to me & I will tell you whether to alter it. Also I should wish much to know of anything you disliked in any poem, as it is still time to alter.[1]

I believe I am likely to cut out *Mary in Summer, The Choice* (3 *Sonnets,*) and the *Bullfinch* (*sonnet*) but am not yet quite certain. I hesitated much to print *Ave*, because of the subject, but thought it well done & so included it. Do you think the foot-note is sufficient as a protest? The question I asked about "wert" & "wast" refers chiefly to a line in the first paragraph of this – "Thou hast been sister &c" which if admissible I should make "Thou once wert sister" &c so if you think this will do, put it.

I think I must include the Sonnet *Placatâ Venere* as it is one of my best, but if you are showing the things *en famille* you had better remove it (it is torn out as you will see) and replace it at the *end* of the first section of Sonnets – *not* as paged. However of this I may perhaps write further. Another sonnet "French Liberation of Italy" I have removed from the 2nd Section & shall not replace.

When you have realized all your ideas on the proofs I wish you would write me *at once*. You need not send them back to me, as I have another set. But I will write you when to send them on to the printer. Love to Christina.

Your D G R

---

[1] WMR's side of the correspondence about *Poems* is summarized in *RP* (453–69), and excerpted by Peattie (161–66). WMR tells the story of the volume from start to finish in *DGRDW* (146–55). See **84n1**.

69.131 TO FRANCES MARY LAVINIA ROSSETTI

MS: UBC. Published: *FL* 202–03; DW 855 (the P.P.S. printed with this letter has been transferred to its rightful position in 68.141; see headnote). Written on 16CW stationery.

Penkill Castle/Girvan/Ayrshire

Saturday/Aug. 21st/1869

Good Antique

Here I am since Thursday afternoon, as I know you will be glad to hear in your maternal solicitude. I left London on Tuesday & spent two nights and a day at old Miss Losh's house near Carlisle, where as you may be sure she made me very comfortable. I saw in the neighbourhood some most remarkable architectural works by a former Miss Losh who was the head of the family about the year 1830.[1] She must have been really a great genius & should be better known. She built a church in the Byzantine style which is full of beauty and imaginative detail though extremely severe & simple. Also a mausoleum to her sister – a curious kind of Egyptian pile of stones with a statue of the lady in the centre, and opposite a Saxon cross – a sort of obelisk, reproduced from an old one but with restorations by the lady herself. Also a Pompeian house for the schoolmaster, a parsonage, and a most interesting cemetery chapel attached to a cemetery which she presented to the parish before such things were instituted by law. The chapel is an exact reproduction of one which was found buried in the sands in Cornwall & excited a good deal of controversy at the time under the name of the "Lost Church." She also built a large addition to the family mansion at Woodside in the Tudor style. All these things are real works of genius, but especially the church at Wreay, a most beautiful thing. She was entirely without systematic study as an architect, but her practical as well as inventive powers were extraordinary. I am sure the whole of this group of her works would interest you extremely, and I should suggest your paying a visit to the neighbourhood on one of your holidays. There is also most lovely scenery and some amiable Loshes besides the Miss Losh you wot of, whose house is called Ravenside, (5 miles from Carlisle) where I am sure she would be delighted to welcome you and yours if she heard you were likely to come her way. I suppose you would not be able to go this year, or it is possible I may be in the neighbourhood again on my way back to London. However, my movements are rather uncertain at present as to time, as I am not sure how long I may be able to remain here from various causes.

Everything here is as pleasant as ever, and Miss Boyd sends you & Maggie her love, as does Scotus also. I have brought no work down as I felt need of rest and was uncertain as to time.

I hope you are benefiting at Folkstone,[2] and shall be delighted to hear so from yourself. What a good piece of news William's promotion was![3]

There is some prospect of Brown coming down here. Miss Losh seems very uncertain.

I am printing some old & new poems – chiefly old – for private circulation – and shall send them you of course when the proofs are complete. Today I am calling in William's valuable aid for revision. My object is to keep them by me as stock to be added to for a possible future volume; but in any case I thought it necessary to print them, as I found blundered transcripts of some of my old things were flying about & would at some time have got into print perhaps, – a thing afflictive to one's bogy.

With love to Maggie

Your most affec: Son
Gabriel

P.S. I should have said that just before I left town I at last got possession of my stables and shall very probably be turning them at once into a fine big studio, but must first see about getting leave to build and an extension of lease.

---

[1] Sarah Losh (1786–1853), daughter of John Losh, sister of AB's maternal grandfather, William Losh; and first cousin of AML. For the fullest account of Sarah and her still extant buildings admired by DGR, see Bullen, "Sara Losh: Architect, Romantic, Mythologist," *Burlington Magazine* (Nov 2001): 676–84. Bullen argues that the "unique" church of St. Mary's, Wreay ("part romanesque, part basilican style") was the product of "Losh's command of technical detail, her observations of ancient work in France and Italy, her study of the contemporary revival of early architectural styles, and her personal interest in religious myth and symbolism." Of DGR's description of the style of the church as "Byzantine," Bullen notes, citing a writer in the *Christian Remembrancer* (1842), that the term "was used generically at the time for 'pre-Gothic' architecture" (679–80). See also M. A. Wood's illustrated article about this church, "A Memorial to Two Sisters," in *Country Life* (4 Nov 1971): 1230–31.

[2] FLR & MFR were spending a month-long "sea holiday" at Folkestone (CGR:Sophia May Eckley, 2 Aug [69], Harrison 1: 388).

[3] WMR:FLR, 30 Jul [69]: "You and I are richer by £200 a year than when we parted yesterday: today I am promoted at Somerset House to be Assistant Secretary, £800 a year" (Peattie 160).

69.132 TO GEORGE RAE

MS: LLAG. Excerpt: *DGRDW* 68–69.

Saturday 21 Aug/1869
Penkill Castle/Girvan/Ayrshire

My dear Rae

I am just come down here to recruit, – to avoid sudden death myself, not to inflict in on the winged creation, nor to wage battle or murder against any species whatever except blue devils.

I am delighted to hear that the *Monna Vanna* bears not only inspection but possession, the most trying of all tests to the inevitable demon of revulsion which is the unsuspected chum of desire in the lodging of the heart of man. May it be long before it claims its share in the Box & Cox arrangement in question.

Meanwhile I would advise the Beloved to bear up. Much more of my love went to the making of her.

As for "Fazio's Mistress" she ought to be re-named. It was always an absurd misnomer in a hurry, & the thing is much too full of queer details to embody the poem quoted which is a 13th century production. Do have the writing on the frame effaced and call it anything else. "Aurelia" would do very well for the golden hair. I don't think it's bad, but it was done at a time when I had a mania for buying bric-à-brac & used to stick it into my pictures.

Mind, I am far from wishing to disgust you with your acquisitions of which I am not ashamed – especially Monna V. who I believe is good though painted rather hap-hazard. I should have been very sorry if I had thought so staunch a friend as yourself had been buying bad things of mine, & should certainly have dropped you a hint. I only hope you haven't paid too much for the small picture.

Will you tell Mrs. Rae that Palmifera is not forgotten, only you know she has to bear the palm & must first deserve it.

I was very glad to see your son lately & show him what was to show.[1]

The proposed arrangement about a chalk drawing for the outstanding £100 will suit me particularly well, as I do not care much about doing small work at present. Thanks & kindest remembrances.

Ever yours
D G Rossetti

P.S. I suppose you heard about poor P.P. Marshall's sad accident – the loss of the right forefinger.

---

[1] Edward Rae, who later married JL's daughter Margaret. WMR explains DGR's references to *Monna Vanna* (S.191) and *Aurelia* (S.164) in *DGRDW* (68–69).

69.133 TO AGLAIA CORONIO

MS: Kansas. Published: DW 856. Written on 16CW stationery.

22 Aug/1869

Penkill Castle/Girvan/Ayrshire

My dear Mrs. Coronio

Your kind letter has followed me. I have fled hither for the purpose of shooting nothing – not even the moon – but have merely myself been shot here as rubbish quite used up.

I am sorry that all I can do from this distance is to say how glad I am to know that Luke is going to be happy, and how often I hope to see him so.[1]

I trust you will all get a pleasant holiday soon, and with love to all

am yours very sincerely
DG Rossetti

P.S. The last news I have from Ems is very favourable. That is just a week ago.

[1] Luke Ionides, brother of Aglaia Coronio and 2nd son of Alexander Ionides, married Elfrida Bird in 1869.

69.134 TO JANE MORRIS

MS: BL. Published: Bryson 11. Date: P/M.

Monday 23rd August [1869]

Penkill Castle/Girvan/Ayrshire

My dear Janey

I have got your letter today, and certainly it is rather tantalizing after the great hopes your former one had raised. But after all we know that there are all kinds of delays and disappointments in the cure of a long standing evil, and we must remember that certainly there does not seem to be any traceable deterioration in your constitution from the first, so that it is reasonable to feel convinced that the local affection is in all probability open to remedy even though time should prove the principal agent in bringing it about. I cannot but think that possibly a return to London at present is not the surest road to health. Brown and I were talking about the matter often before I left London, and he was decidedly of opinion that the invigorating air of Switzerland should be tried after the Ems system. Some of your friends could come out if you were making any stay, & so save Top and you from suffering too much from blue devils. Perhaps the suggestion is impracticable, though of course could its advisability be known as *certain*, nothing should prevent its being carried out. The best of all would be that such an improvement should take place before you leave Ems as to render further probation unnecessary; but you must bear in mind that, if this does not after all prove the case entirely, the trial will still have been such a short one that its complete efficacy within the time would have appeared from the outset to be something like a miracle. And indeed your telling me that you cannot consider yourself worse than at your former writing shows that something has certainly been already effected.

By the bye, let me most humbly apologize, after your grave rebuke, for the too naked truth of my last historical portrait. You see a feeling of denunciatory duty is involved for Taylor & myself in our letters and cartoons; and Ezekiel and other prophets, if you remember, are not too particular as to the mere outward form of the truths which they are bound to convey.

I have been here since last Thursday, having spent a day on the road at old Miss Losh's house near Carlisle. The neighbourhood there is a beautiful one, and there are some really extraordinary architectural works – a church of a byzantine style & other things – erected from her own designs by a lady of Miss Losh's family who has been dead some years and who must certainly have been a true genius. The works are very original & beautiful, very much more so than the things done by the young architects now, and they were done as far back as 1830 without any professional assistance or directed study, though the practical part of them is quite as remarkable as the invention. I was very much interested and should like Webb to see them. The place is called Wreay.

Since I have been here, I occupy myself chiefly in walking, and am I think benefiting much by the change. It is very fine weather, though the last two days were so hot that a walk became very like a warm bath. Scott is making some designs from Burns for etching, and produces one daily with the most sublime calm and satisfaction. Some of them are really the best things he has done in that way. He has been getting through the proofs of his book on Albert Durer, and a most amusing correspondence has gone on between him and William who has been consulted throughout. Pig-head or even pig-lead conveys but a faint symbol of the immoveable conviction of either party on every vexed point. Scott's absolute certainty that he has hit upon a splendid idea in proposing to call Durer's Melancholia *Il Penserosa* as the best means of conveying the artist's thought, and the raging scorn with which William visits both the grammar and the proposition – together with many other similar conflicts – are really so delightful that they should by rights be printed in an appendix. The book however will be a very interesting one – especially as regards a diary by A. D. of his journey to the Low Countries, and some private letters of a laboriously joky order much reminding one of Holman Hunt's style in letter-writing.

While I write, Scott is busy on a Burns Illustration, produced as it seems in watching him, by dint of aimless groans and fragmentary sleep. One rises and looks over his shoulder and finds the mystic subject which has thus rapt his being to be Tam-O'Shanter in a state of roaring intoxication.[1]

Yesterday I got a note sent on from Mrs. Coronio to apprize me that Luke is going to be married next Saturday – also one from Miss Bird asking me to a party at her house on Friday evening! So she means to die game.

My proofs have hung on hand very much with tattooings that I have gone on giving them. I fear I shall hardly have a set in trim before you return, which shows that Scott might not find it hard to retort on me as to the use of sleep as a productive agent. However I hope to get some new work done perhaps, though here Topsy's mountain must indeed view my mouse with scorn even if he finds his way into the world at all.

I wonder whether we shall be able to realize some sittings on your return. They shall be *such* careful judicious and considerate ones! I have been conceiving a great desire to paint you as Fortune and have the design clearly in my head now, having been long knocking it about there. Fortune will be seated full-faced dealing cards on which will be visible the symbols of life, death, &c. Behind her will be her wheel, the spokes wound with festive and fatal growths, and on either side of it will be seated a dove (or a white peacock) and a raven. I also want awfully bad to get about the full-length Pandora & to do the Beatrice in the big picture. The last will be a nice easy sitting.

But a thousand times more than any work do I desire your renewed health, dear Janey, and you know how anxiously I await all tidings on the subject. Pray take my love and give the same to Top, and believe me

Ever affectionately yours
D Gabriel R

P.S. Miss Boyd & Scott desire me to send kindest remembrances.

---

[1] WBS' illustrated Burns edition never appeared (*AN* 2: 166).

69.135 TO CHARLES AUGUSTUS HOWELL

MS: Princeton. Published: Troxell, *Colophon* 15 (1933); *TR* 116–17; DW 857.

Penkill Castle/Girvan/Ayrshire

Thursday/26 Aug. [1869]

Dear Howell

I am extremely grieved to hear from Dunn of Kate's sudden & serious illness which however he tells me is greatly abated. Will you write me word & let me know your anxiety is relieved on the subject.

Also will you write me in answer to what I wrote before leaving town? The matter occupies my mind.[1] I shall be here for at least a fortnight longer. The news from Ems is pretty well, but I could wish it much better. If this were but well, nothing could be very ill.

I have written to congratulate all parties on Luke's approaching marriage.[2] There is no news here, except that a walk is a warm bath, & that Albert Durer can be not only a pleasure but a nuisance also after a lapse of 3 centuries.[3]

Ever your affec:
Gabriel

[1] The details of the forthcoming exhumation clearly weighed on DGR's mind, particularly the possible disturbances in the Rossetti plot; see **157**.
[2] See **133n1**.
[3] Because the weather was exceptionally warm, DGR spent much time indoors listening to WBS' talk about his forthcoming book, *Albert Dürer: His Life and Works* (Macmillan, 1869). See also **156**.

69.136 TO FORD MADOX BROWN

Text: *RP* 457–58. Excerpt: HRA 44. Reprinted (with additional text, in angled brackets below): DW 858 (attributed to AP but not among UBC MSS).

Penkill

26 August 1869

Dear Brown,

Three pleasant people are desiring you, and you really *must* make up your mind to come. All the pleasures of this place, which are old to us, will be new to you, and that will renew them to us also. So here is one of the sympathetic moments of life awaiting you, and you do not hurry to it.

Tin be blowed! The question is not so grave as to be a real delay. If necessary, of course I can send what is wanted till your work gets done, some of which you could very well do here. There is a capital studio. Moreover, you were thinking of a Nativity; and a spot there is here is the very background you want, both in material and lovely simple colour, and even suggests of itself the composition.

I suppose I shall certainly be staying-on a fortnight from today; but whether longer, or how much longer, I cannot tell. <Scott however will not be on the move by then I am pretty sure.>

My news from Ems leads me to suppose that the second Thursday from this may probably bring the travellers back, <but in my last, written the other day in answer to one just then received, I raised the question whether it would not be wise to go on to Switzerland.> Janey writes that she is not worse than at her last writing, when the news was very hopeful; but I can see by the tone of her letter, and indeed by much she says plainly, that she is discouraged at the slow progress made. <If I were you, and if you have the opportunity, I would write Morris a line seriously on the point of their best course. However, you are best judge whether this is advisable.>

I am extremely shocked to hear of poor Craven's dreadful grief, and must write him.[1] <I think I shall also write Shields, as I feel anxious about what you tell me which seems incomprehensible and would like to know details.[2] However I am not in a very brilliant state of spirits to think about other people's ill luck.

I have been further revising my proofs with good results. The only sonnet I have yet written here I subjoin.>

Perhaps William may have shown you the article on me in *Tinsley's Magazine* for September. It is <shadily written but> encouraging. After twenty years, one stranger has learned that one exists. He is so enthusiastic about our old friend *My Sister's Sleep* that I shall have, I suppose, to include it in my present reprint; <not (far from it) that I value this bloke's opinion more than yours – but> because such commencement of publicity would be likely to lead to its getting reprinted somehow some day, and there are things which should be altered in it.[3] <Can you remember if there was a date attached to the MS. copy you had, and if so, what date?> I gather that next month William will be prolouded upon.

Scott is working in his steady though leisurely way. The sketches for his windows at Kensington (I don't know if you've seen them up there) are extremely clever;[4] and he has lately done three or four Burns illustrations which are really most beautiful in invention and high feeling, and altogether I think much the best he has done. His work on Albert Durer is affording us evening readings, and must I think prove a success. People do not know how much in the way of autobiography and letters exists by A. D. <His letters

remind one by their ponderous jokiness of Holman Hunt.>

He and Miss Boyd send united love, and injunctions to come at once. The weather here is splendid – only very hot for walking. <Love to Lucy who I suppose is your only inmate still. Leathart in a letter inquired of Scott his opinion of my *Blue Bower* – Mendel's picture. Do you know if he hears it is for sale?[5] This would be strange after my interview with Mendel.>

Your affectionate
D. Gabriel R.

<[Enclosure]

Parted Love

What shall be said of this embattled day
And armed occupation of this night
By all thy foes beleaguered, – now when sight
Nor sound denotes the loved one far away?
Of thy deserted life what shalt thou say, –
As every sense to which she dealt delight
Now labours lonely o'er the start noon-height
To reach the sunset's desolate disarray?
Stand still, fond fettered wretch! While Memory's art
Parades the Past before thy face, and lures
Thy spirit to her passionate portraitures.
Till the tempestuous tide-gates flung apart
Flood with wild will the hollows of thy heart,
And thy heart rends thee, and thy body endures.>

---

1 Frederick Craven was a loyal patron of both DGR & FMB; WMR had reported that his daughter had been killed in a carriage accident (*RP* 457).
2 See **140, 149, 182, 221,** & 70.207
3 See **112n5**.
4 WBS had been commissioned to replace the windows of the Ceramic Gallery in the South Kensington Museum (*AN* 2: 107–08; *RP* 108).
5 S.178. See 65.66n1.

69.137 TO WILLIAM MICHAEL ROSSETTI

MS: BL. Excerpt: *FL* 205–06. Published: DW 859. Date: WMR.

Thursday [26 August 1869]

Dear W–

Thanks for your valuable letter. I am attending to it & will do so further when I get your concluding admonitions. I have sent the Italian poem to Maggie to see if she makes the same remarks, & should like to show it to Teodorico. You know I think there is no doubt that metre of this kind abounds in the *early* poets.

One thing wanting correction is – to erase the full stop at the end of line 2, page 23. I dare say you have done so. I think I shall omit the *Song & Music*, page 67. There is the word *Tryptich* in *Hand & Soul*. Ought it not to be *triptych*.

I remember I had made additions (now lost) at points which I thought abrupt in *Stratton Water* & *Staff & Scrip*. In S.W. some stanzas were inserted after "The nags were in the stall" (p. 48) to give the gradual impression of his recognizing the girl whom he thought dead. Do you think it is necessary to write something of the sort again?

In *S. & S.* there was something added where the damsel gives her the relics to develop this incident & help the transition? Does this seem necessary? Or is there any other point in any of the poems which seems to want working out? I have added a first stanza to Sister Helen, as Scott said the impression of what was going on was not perfectly distinct.

Would the title of the Sonnet at page [1]93 run better

On the Refusal of Aid to Hungary 1849, To Poland 1861, To Crete 1867?

Or is it better in the simpler form?

The article in Tinsley is gratifying though not too well done. I suppose from your not being recurred to, there will certainly be a third on you. The raking up of *My Sister's Sleep* will I fancy render it necessary for me to include that rather spoony affair in my reprint, as now attention is attracted a little to it, it may go on till the thing gets into print again without the correction it ought to have. What think you? I don't remember it clearly, & would be obliged if you or Christina could take the trouble of copying it from the *Germ* & sending it here by return of post. If Christina would read my things & give any hints that occur to her I would be thankful. Tell her this with my love.

Your
D G R

69.138 FRANCES MARY LAVINIA ROSSETTI

MS: UBC. Excerpt: *FL* 206–07. Published: DW 860.

Penkill
26 Aug 1869

My dearest Mother

I was very glad to hear from you again, & know that you have been enjoying your trip. The weather here is splendid though so warm for walking that I generally change my shirt on coming in! I am doing no work except a little in the way of revising proofs at which William is now affording me his usual most valuable help. He has fallen very foul of a little Italian poem of mine in which he finds various errors of metre & even of grammar. I wd like Maria's opinion & so enclose it without mentioning the weak points found by William. Will she at her leisure give me *her* verdict? Of course it is meant to be a very irregular sort of antiquated Italian, & I am pretty sure quite as bad slips are continual among the earliest poets.

I have seen *Tinsley* which is so far satisfactory that, after 20 years, one stranger has discovered one's existence. The writing is rather shady but the opinions supremely correct for the most part, *as far as they go*!! From what was said in the former article about William, & from the absence of all recurrence to him in this one, I have no doubt he will furnish matter for a third.

I believe I have yet nine years of my lease at Cheyne Walk to run. Thus my plan will be to apply for an extension of lease before building; but if this is refused, or a very considerable immediate increase of rent made the condition of it, I shall then I think build irrespective of contingencies, as nine years is a long time – indeed Time may be no longer for one, for anything one knows.

With love to Maggie

Your most affec: Son
DGabriel R

P.S. It is pleasant to know that poor Henrietta [Polydore] is suffering somewhat less.[1]

I believe the author of the *Tinsley* articles is probably a man named Forman, unknown to me.[2]

---

[1] Henrietta Polydore, DGR's cousin, succumbed to tuberculosis in 1874.
[2] DGR had written to HBF on receiving an enquiry about the volume of poems promised in *EIP* (see 68.145), but he had other enquiries and no doubt forgot this one.

69.139 TO WILLIAM MICHAEL ROSSETTI

MS: BL. Excerpt: *FL* 207–11. Published: DW 861. Text within angled brackets are marginal insertions.

Penkill
Friday 27th Aug/1869

Dear W –

Your 2nd to hand today. I'll now go over some of your ground – neglecting such things as I quite agree in & ignoring others here & there, where they involve corrections I must attend to.

Page 16. Mummies.

This I had thought of already & it troubled me. I can alter it as follows: –
A traveller. Nay, but were not some
Of these even then antiquity?
or "thine own "antiquity"?"
Which is the best? The word *traveller* I do not quite like. I meant no more by *pilgrim*. Do you think the change desirable?

18. "Eldest grown" &c I will probably alter in some way easy enough.

25. I don't like to shorten the last line. It used to stand *Saint M[ary].V[irgin]*. &c Is this better?
There is a point in this poem I am going to change either less or more; thus : –

22.   The sea
Sighed further off eternally
As heavy/human/ancient sorrow sighs in sleep.
or "Like ancient sorrow or sad sleep." <The present simile trivial for the sea.> The first would require to change *eyes* in the next line to *gaze*. However I am not sure whether I do not wish to omit the whole 5 lines beginning "Within" & ending "through," and substitute one comprehensive line of some sort rhyming to *sleep*. What say you?

21. "Thou once wert &c." would it be better "Thou wast a" &c? Would you give me your opinion about the capital H's appropriated to Urizen in this & in Hand & Soul. I find, especially in the latter, that their abolition is apt to produce confusion with the human personages sometimes. In this poem the one difficulty of this kind however can be obviated by saying (p. 24)
"And that one thought in both, the Same" –
But do the big H's seem necessary to the dignity of the subject? <In last page of *Ave* – I remember I had changed *arrayed* into some word more of the same latinized value as *conjoint*, but cannot remember

	what. Can you suggest a word?>
5.	A question I wish to ask on my own hook is whether *trembling* or *tremulous* would be best in the last line in italics. The first is objectionable because of *stepping* above – but does not the second trip awkwardly? "Circlewise." Would this be better "they sit in circle"? I dare say you agree with the removal of *lapse* for "flight" in last stanza but one.
1.	"And her hair lying down her back." Is the sound awkward? Is And her hair laid upon" &c better?
10.	Does the last stanza of this page seem awkwardly interpolated? – and does it seem that a more distinct speech for the spirit is necessary to introduce the next stanza?
8.	Third stanza – last line sounds shortish, but is not. What do you say? Suggest anything.
65.	Hecate wouldn't do as it reminds the general world of Macbeth. I see no objection to Luna but none either to Cynthia except that people know it less as meaning the moon. Dian would answer best of all for the meaning of the passage, but I didn't like the sound so well as Luna. I like the long lines myself.
81.	I see nothing for it but to alter *soul* to *mind* in 1st line of 3rd stanza in which case it must be done also in 2nd of 2nd.
14.	It occurs to me to go back & ask your opinion on a point here. The stanza "On London stones" is combined from what was once 2 stanzas. The change was made when I printed the poem first.

"On London stones _____
_____
_____
_____
_____ the old earth & sea
How much Heaven's thunder – how much else
Man's puny roar? – What cry of shells
Cleft amid leaguered citadels –
How many lordships loud with bells
Heardst thou in secret Nineveh?

O when upon each sculptured court
Where even the wind might not resort –
O'er which Time passed, of like import,
With the wild Arab boys at sport, –
 A living face looked in to see, –

Friday 27th Aug/1869

& seemed it not &c _____

I hardly know why I made the omission except for the great end of condensation. Is there anything lost by it, and does the present form seem at all abrupt? However Scott to whom I have just read what I am writing for *his* opinion, thinks the second half of the first stanza rather extraneous but the first half of the second a great gain. I have some idea that Brown once suggested difficulties about the shells, bells &c – could they be heard under the earth? – were there any to be heard? – &c <If you think 1st half 2nd stanza *very* desirable & the previous omitted lines objectionable, try & suggest some point of idea to fill the gap.>

147. "Care gold & care" can be altered to "Vain gold, vain lore," which meets your views. There is a very vexatious point connected with this sonnet which was *one* reason for my thinking of omitting the three. The idea – "They die not, never having lived," is identical with one at the close of Browning's "In a Gondola." *I* know that I had never then read that poem, & that on first reading it this annoying fact struck me at once; but then this is not known to the world. The point is just what is wanted & not possible to alter. There is a similar case in the "Nocturn" (page 8) – "Lamps of an *auspicious* soul" stood in my last correction (made long ago) "*pellucid*" which is much finer. But lately in the *Ring & Book* I came on *pellucid soul* applied to Caponsacchi, and the inevitable charge of plagiarism struck me at once as impending whenever my poem should be printed. There is also in the *R&B*. "Pale frail wife" which interferes in the same way with the "*pale frail mist*" of my *New Year's Burden,* also of course written long before. But this I left.[1]

157. *Many years &c* is a favourite line of mine! It used to stand *A few years &c* which of course was one of the impossible intonations of that early epoch.

167. I also object to *difficult* rhyming with *occult* of course most absolutely. But the distance from rhyme to rhyme being considerable, & alteration difficult, I have left it. I suppose I did not notice it at the moment of writing the sonnet (in front of the picture in Brit: Inst: many years ago) though I know I did just afterwards.

169. Life touching lips "&c. I remember you expressed a preference once before for the old line which seems to me quite bad. "Solemn poetry" belongs to the class of phrases absolutely forbidden I think *in* poetry. It is intellectually incestuous, – poetry seeking to beget its emotional

offspring on its own identity. Whereas I see nothing too "ideal" in the present line. It gives only the momentary contact with the immortal which results from sensuous culmination and is always a half conscious element of it.

174. *Mayst &c.* By all means.
177. Venus V[erticordi]*a* I knew the passage in Lemprière – *since* writing the sonnet or rather christening the picture. It is awkward. I'll cut the Va out here I think.
202.⎱ S[an] Rocco. Please
207.⎰ suggest a new Saint.

On reflection, I think the best plan will be for you to post your set of proofs to me *at once* on getting this letter, as I have other changes to make in them before sending back to the printer & can more shortly do them myself than explain them to you. Please answer questions here asked as soon as possible. I will probably apply again for Christina's views with the *next* revise.

Your D G R

[1] See 55.51n3.

69.140 TO FREDERIC JAMES SHIELDS

MS: Yale. Excerpt: Mills 127–29; Horne 86–87. Published: DW 862.

Penkill Castle/Girvan/Ayrshire

27 August/1869

My dear Shields

I was going to write you myself on the 2 subjects of your letter. Not that I have really any word to say to such fateful horrors as the one which is now crushing poor Craven's soul. They leave me dumb with their anomalous enormity. But I wished to know exactly how he was; & may probably make up my mind to write him a word, though a stranger like myself naturally doubts his claim to speak at all at such a time. I had already heard something of this terrible circumstance from Brown since coming here where I have now been over a week and am I hope benefiting by the change. I may probably stay 2 or 3 weeks longer. The surroundings of this house are most lovely and soothing – a glen which is quite private & gives pictures at every turn. The inmates are the lady of the house, Miss Boyd, a rarely precious woman, and our friend W. B. Scott, the best of philosophic & poetic natures – a man of the truest genius & one of my oldest companions. So you see I have peace, friendship, & art, all to help me. I wish you were here to share the pleasure and advantage of such sympathetic surroundings. Scott, who read your letter, sends you his love which you seem to have secured though I do not know how often you have met him. You may be sure the dreadful tidings you give have furnished us with some sad thoughts & talk.

I am very much concerned also at what you say about Graham's commission, already reported to me by Brown. I must say at once that I think his conduct very wrong, much as I believe in his possessing many truly good qualities and excellent as his friendly treatment of myself has always been. I am grieved for him, for I am sure he has made a mistake in acting thus. One of the last times I saw him, he spoke of you and the commission, & certainly then raised the question of colour in rather an anxious spirit which I tried to remove. He is capricious & singular, and you know he treated Brown in somewhat the same way, though this is an even stronger case. I have an urgent invitation to come on to his house at Blair Athol, but do not think I shall be able to accept it as time is short & the complete rest of this sojourn not to be lightly foregone. I may have to be writing to him. If, either by interview or letter, a possibility occurs of giving him a hint of my views on your matter (of course within what I think *you* would desire) you may be sure I shall not neglect doing so. I almost think all must yet come right in some way.[1]

At this moment I hear from London that Agnew has called & bought 2 chalk drawings I left to be shown him for 80 gs each. If he will go on, this will furnish some profitable pot-boiling; & I tell you, as you were the first to suggest a connection with him.

Could I be of any service in lending you a little money just now? Do, *do* tell me if I can. I have plenty of good opportunities of earning at present.

I have brought no work here with me, but am occupied lazily with the proofs of the poetry I am printing – mostly old things which I find sometimes going about in blundered transcriptions which might some time get into print to the affliction of one's still thin-skinned ghost. So I am putting them in a permanent shape, though I shall not publish yet, not having complete copies of a sufficient quantity of verse. However I go on writing at times & may soon break out into publicity. Incentives occur now & then. There is an article on me in Tinsley's Magazine for September, following one on my sister last month, and to be followed as I judge by one on my brother next month! I do not know who is the writer – so after 20 years one stranger does seem to have discovered one's existence. However I have no cause to complain, since I have all I need of an essential kind, and have taken little trouble about it – except always in the nature of my work – the poetry especially in which I have done no pot-boiling at any rate. So I am grateful to that art, & nourish against the other that base grudge which we bear those whom we have treated shabbily.

However I am adding you to that class by all this tirade about myself, and though I do not think the grudge will result on my side, I must beware lest it should on yours.

I hope if you have time to write me again, it will be with good news after all the bad. Your health is a most anxious subject, and I cannot but think that the extreme excitement and exertion to which I know you subject yourself in other kinds of work than Art should be remitted for a time as an experiment. Also & above all I am sure that the matrimonial question should be kept in view, though here I know one is far from being master of the situation according to one's pleasure. Thanks for remembering about the Warburg tincture.

In the matter of chalk drawings I don't know what paper you use. The blue-grey is of course the one tending most to deaden redness, but it is apt to resist covering for a long time & leave the drawing cold – besides much increasing outlay of work to remedy this. I have lately adopted a very slightly greenish tint instead, which has great advantages but of course requires caution as to redness. However if you make a good progress with your tints by merely rubbing with the finger before you put white in at all, this difficulty may be combated, as I think the white rubbed into the red is what chiefly reddens it. I have found the piece of grey chalk you brought me useful to deaden little rednesses in finishing, and have therefore got some more from Brodie. One objection to the greenish paper is that it is so light that the white makes at first little effect on it. I think not a bad plan is to make a mixture of black & red powdered chalk, dip a stump in it, rub it almost off the stump again, and then rub the stump *all over* the paper you are going to work on before you begin. The tint thus rubbed should be no stronger than a sky, but is neutral & pleasant with the greenish tint underneath & gives a good ground to work into, as the white tells on it and you can bread out lights. I suppose like myself you hardly use the stump at all in actual work – but always rub with the fingers.

I will send you my privately printed poems when they are revised and finally struck off.

There is some chance I hope of Brown soon joining us here. I know he would enjoy it enormously.

Ever affectionately yours
D Gabriel R

P.S. If you want grey chalk or anything else in London, write a card to H.T. Dunn at my address, & I am sure he will see about it for you

---

[1] See **149**.

69.141 TO EDITOR OF *NOTES AND QUERIES*

Text: *N&Q* (28 Aug 69): 176. Reprinted: DW 845.

[c. 27 August 1869]

"Violet, or the Danseuse."– Can any of your correspondents give any information as to the authorship of that remarkable novel, *Violet, or the Danseuse*? *The Times* of Sept. 3, 1862, says that it was first published "about a quarter of a century back"; and in the above year Messrs. Routledge reprinted it as a shilling railway volume. I have heard vague reports of its having been written by a daughter of Lord Brougham, occasionally with the astounding "tag" of her having been about fifteen years of age when she wrote it! This incredibly precocious genius is said to have died shortly after the publication of her book. There are few modern English novels more calculated to excite the interest of the highest class of readers; and it is well to make this inquiry before the traces of its authorship become fainter and fainter.[1]

D. G. R.

---

[1] Subtitled *A Portraiture of Human Passions and Character*, the novel was published simultaneously in London (Colburn, 2 volumes) & Paris (Tétot Frère, 1 volume), and pirated in Philadelphia (Carey, Lea & Blanchard, 2 volumes) in 1836. It was reissued in Routledge's *Railway Library* in 1857 (Sadleir 3616). An editorial note to DGR's letter (which WMR:DGR [30 Aug 69] summarizes) points out that, though "considerable pains were taken at the time of publication to conceal the name of the author of *Violet* . . . there is no ground for attributing it to Miss Brougham" (Peattie 164). In introducing this letter in *RP*, WMR notes that "the novel is understood to be the work of a lady; some names have been suggested, but not, I think, with any final certainty" (461). Sadleir (1524), however, attributes it to Lady Malet; Halkett & Laing, on evidence of correspondence in *N&Q* to "Beasley," which might, Sadleir suggests, be the maiden name of "Lady Malet," whom he was unable to identify. Wolff (4406) attributes it to Lady Marianne Dora Malet, whom *DNB* identifies as the wife of the diplomatist, Sir Alexander Malet (1800–86), and the stepdaughter of the first Lord Brougham. Ian Jackson kindly called to our attention (in a letter of 7 Jun 1982) that DGR "seems originally to have been drawn to the book by an allusion in *The Times* . . . not long after his wife's death." His discussion of the parallels between the death of EES and the heroine in the novel, which as Sadleir notes, treats "the back scenes of theatrical life," are worth quoting in full for those, who like me, have not read the novel: "It seems scarcely coincidence that [DGR's] enquiry in *Notes & Queries* about the authorship of the novel was made at exactly the time he was arranging for the retrieval of his MS poems from her grave. The heroine of *Violet* commits suicide with laudanum, and the account of the affair (empty vial marked poison, suppressed suicide note, privacy of the inquest, and even the inevitable exaggerations of gossip), while doubtless no different from many such suicides, must have struck Rossetti with particular force." For the exhumation of DGR's poems, see **164**.

69.142 TO ALICIA MARGARET LOSH

MS: Princeton. Published: *TR* 89–90; DW 863. DGR has crossed through the 16CW monogram.

Penkill Castle/Girvan/Ayrshire
28 August/1869

My dear Miss Losh

A magazine has been sent me which I send on to you by book post, as it contains something about me and I know your kind interest in my doings. I do not know who is the writer, but have been led to believe it is a man named Forman, a stranger to me. There was an article in the August number on Christina, and from what was there said I judge there will be one in the October number on William. So you see the writer means to "do" the family thoroughly.

I have been working at my proofs and adding to them. Shall send a set when finished.

But why don't you come? The weather here is lovely, only almost too hot for walking, even in my opinion. As for Scotus, you may imagine the double-distilled drone that *he* becomes in such a state of the atmosphere. Last night for the first time we attempted a rubber, but it had to be done with the pale shadow of Dummy occupying your vacant place, and was accordingly but a sad reminder of better days.

Scotus has read us his book on Albert Durer right through in the evenings. He seems in composing it to have been seized every now and then with his constitutional somnolence but to have gone on writing all the same. Accordingly after waking from a nap he generally found that the leading incident of the portion in hand had been left out, and these have had to be heaped together in an Appendix. The arrangement may be thought peculiar, but of course (seriously speaking) the book is a most excellent and most interesting one.

Two policemen were seen wandering in this neighbourhood lately. Owing to Scotus's want of hair, it could not betray him by standing on end, so the bobbies overlooked what was doubtless the object of their visit.[1]

Miss Boyd, who is very well, sends love, as does Scotus.

Most sincerely yours
DG Rossetti

---

[1] See 68.154n1.

Monday/30 Aug. 1869 69.143

69.143 TO JANE MORRIS

MS: BL. Published: Bryson 12.

Penkill Castle/Girvan/Ayrshire
Monday/30 Aug. 1869

My dear Janey

Your letter must on the whole be pronounced satisfactory. Miracles are not to be expected unless perhaps from bread puddings; and one day with another improvement seems the rule. Moreover the malady itself is of such a capricious nature that it may be expected to benefit quite as much by rest after the baths as by the baths themselves I should think. It is also satisfactory to know that, with apparent good reason, you do not think it necessary to proceed to Switzerland; although I thought it my duty to suggest the possible wisdom of such a course. However I believe you to be quite right in abstaining, after what you say.

I am getting good I think by my stay here, though till yesterday the heat was so excessive, and the swarm of flies so annoying, as to render my daily walks a martyrdom. Now a good wind has sprung up, and I walk in comfort. During the two last of the hot days I only crawled about the sheltered glen. There are many enchanting spots in it, & particularly a little cave in a concealed position on a slope overhanging the bed of the stream – the very place for Topsy to spin endless poetry in, and for you to sit in and listen to the curious urgent whisper of the stream – though perhaps a better approach than the present one would have to be made before you could reach it conveniently; but this is going to be done, so much have I praised the cave and its capabilities. All this you know is perfectly private; and I cannot go about without thinking that this above all places would be the very one in fine weather for you to get about in to some salutary purpose. How nice it would be to see you here, at ease and liberty, and with an air likely to do you good!

I cannot say by the bye that I have yet made much of the poetic properties of the cave in the way of absolute verse. Some scraps have come into my head but not to much purpose as yet. You may be sure I shall send you anything worthy to be sent. I have been working on what may be called the flea-bite principle, however, at my poetry going through the press, and I find that correction, when one suffers from the vain longings of perfectibility, is an endless task – and Topsy will I fear look with utter scorn on this fidgetty fretting over old ground. He is in the right for himself, I know; but I have nothing of his abundance in production; & to attain confidence first in the plan of any work, however small, and afterwards to aim at rendering it faultless by repeated condensation & revision, is the only system that gives me a chance. I have done a very great deal lately to bring these little things into a state which may lead me to hope they deserve an extension of such life as is in them. Thus their getting finally printed off is prolonged from week to week.

A Tinsley's Mag: for Septr was sent me by Dunn containing a good-natured though shadily written article on me. I sent it on to old Miss Losh, but afterwards it struck me you might like to see it, and I wrote to Dunn asking him to get another copy, tear out the article and enclose it to you; so you will probably get it before this. I do not know whether you can see the English mags: where you are. There was a former article on Christina, & I judge that one on Wm is forthcoming. It is very loud about a thing I once wrote called *My Sister's Sleep*, of a fearfully pious and sentimental kind. I had left it out of my present reprint, but may now perhaps be obliged to include it, as any attention gradually attracted to it might otherwise lead to its ultimately getting into print again without the necessary corrections.

My reprint consists (to avoid raising undue expectation in so friendly a reader as yourself) much of the following: – Firstly, some poems, all shortish: viz: The Blessed Damozel; Nocturn; The Burden of Nineveh; The Card-Dealer; The Staff and Scrip; Ave; Sister Helen; Stratton Water; Dennis Shand. The most important of them I fancy you already know, but I have worked at all I think to great advantage up to the present moment as they have been going through the press. Secondly: – a section called "Songs & Sonnets towards a work to be called *The House of Life*." Nearly all these you know. Thirdly: Sonnets on Pictures & other Sonnets. Lastly: a prose piece called *Hand and Soul*, which is much more of the nature of a poem than anything else, and which I have thought well to include and revise, as I should not wish it to be lost. I have got very imperfect copies of some other longer poems in M.S. but I cannot remember many important alterations which I had once made in other copies now lost; and this has deterred me as yet from tackling them. But it is very possible that I may before long set about doing so and re-writing what is necessary. In this case I fancy I should have a vol: of quite 300 or probably 350 pages without reckoning new things which might probably get written meanwhile. In such case I should rush into publication. Ellis has advised me with that view to have the type of these sheets kept up and pay a rent for it. I find from the printer that this would not be very expensive, and shall probably do so.

I forgot I think to tell you that, the day before leaving London, I actually got at last full possession of my stables & broke open the communication with the garden. On soberly considering them, they afford a mass of space of extraordinary capabilities, and as soon as I return to town I must see about building projects with Webb. Before building, I ought to try for an extension of lease; but I have already nine years still to run; so if the people would only extend the lease with the considerable immediate increase of rent, I think I

Tuesday [31 August 1869] 69.144

should be induced to build at once & postpone the question of extending the term till its expiration, if indeed I myself am not the first to expire. In building my studio, I should have an ante-room for people to wait in, and I think also a bed-room for myself, as I feel sure in some weather it might be a great advantage to avoid the necessity of running about between house and studio. Moreover if I did not sleep there myself, it might probably be advisable not to leave the place uninhabited at nights. I should also have a communication by bells between the studio and house. This would make the place completely convenient.

Well, dear Janey, I am going out on my daily tramp now, and only wish you too were capable of such daily constitutionals. I believe that in this retired region you might soon make some way towards them. I assure you my great anxiety about my own health as I walked these roads last year was a less troublesome companion than the impotent longing for your rapid restoration and constant hope of better news which possess me at present. However there is no cause up to this to view the matter in any but a hopeful way. You do not tell me how much work Topsy has accomplished. I suppose doubtless a great deal, & that the first section of his 2nd vol. will really appear in October. Give my love to the dear old thing and bear in mind how much you are loved by

Your affectionate
D Gabriel R

69.144 TO WILLIAM MICHAEL ROSSETTI

MS: BL. Excerpt: *FL* 211–12. Published: DW 864. Date: WMR.

Penkill

Tuesday [31 August 1869]

Dear W

Thanks for your note today. I think I shall most likely omit the Italian poem. At the same time I got Christina's copy of *Sister's Sleep* which I return tattooed to you for consultation. The thing is very distasteful to me as it stands & I have quite determined on all changes made in pen-&-ink. In pencil I indicate a very radical change in the omission of two more stanzas which wd eliminate the religious element altogether. Scott thinks the poem in this most rarified form is simplest & best, & I incline to that view myself. However I feel by no means quite sure, and have annotated the M.S. explaining my conflicting views. Will you give them your best attention & let me know your views on all the points. I should not care to reprint this thing at all, were it not for the likelihood of its reappearing some day otherwise without even the changes absolutely necessary.

In the note on *Ave*, I think of putting "*all* faiths" instead of "*Classic* faiths. Otherwise it looks as if the Christian was meant to be one of the classics. What do you think?

In "Love-Lily" do you like best

"Ah! let not life be still distraught" (as it stands) or Ah! let not *hope* &c? In this poem it crossed my mind to change the title & merely use a proper name, as *Dorothy*. What is the meaning of that name? I forget. But I do not think I shall really do this. What say you? "Whose speech *Truth* knows not" &c is better than *faith* is it not?

But perhaps, as it occurs to me the proofs will probably have left you before you get this, I had better put off further questions till I can send you them again in a revised state.

Your
D G R

I don't think dating throughout wd do.

I had not heard of Leys's death. It is indeed a sad & premature event. He called on me the year before last or beginning of last, looking perfectly well.[1] P.P.S. What do you think of the proposed note to *S. S.* The curse of In Memoriam wd be thus avoided. I remember too there is some *Xmas Eve* business in *I. M.* but what I cannot remember. Of course the note is strictly true. This *I. M* question was one great reason for my burking it.[2]

Will you thank Christina much with my love.

---

[1] Baron Jan Auguste Henri Leys (1815–1869), Belgian historical and genre painter, had died on 26 Aug. WMR remarked: "The inspiration and excellence of his works were such as could not fail to secure my brother's hearty admiration" (*FL* 211).

[2] "burking" = to burke: indirectly suppress, quietly extinguish, stifle. DGR, once again fearing an accusation of plagiarism, had drafted a note that eventually appeared in *Poems* (169), denying that he had appropriated the metre for "My Sister's Sleep" from *In Memoriam*; he also worries here that he may seem to echo Tennyson's Christmas Eve poems in that elegy (XXIX, XXX, LXXVIII, CIV, CV, & CVI).

69.145 TO FORD MADOX BROWN

MS: UBC. Excerpt: *RP* 463. Published: DW 865. Date: WMR.

Penkill
Tuesday night [c. 31 August 1869]

Dear Brown

Your letter is too calmly brutal. However I trust before you get this you will have received our dispatches sent yesterday & been brought to reason. There is no excuse for you if you don't come.

I am very much grieved to hear of poor Payne's death. He was a good fellow, a good friend, & a man of true inclination to good things in art and poetry. It is singular how these rare birds – whether patrons or critics – get picked off one by one – while no man ever heard of the putrid academic sty being prematurely a pig the worse for all the epidemics and cattle-plagues that turn up.[1]

Leys's death is almost as unexpected. However his work is done and well done. When I saw him some year & a half ago, I should never have thought him a likely man for death to tackle.

Do explain yourself *by return of post* about Byron. I know of nothing bearing on the subject, and am most excited to hear. If anything in print that can be sent easily, please send it.[2]

The new sonnet is one of the most in need of further finish I think.[3] This we can talk over when I see you.

Weather has improved here as to coolness & walking is much less arduous. Do come.

My last news from Ems shows very gradual progress, but still some, I suppose. Miracles are evidently not to be expected. I am very glad to hear what you tell me of Emma's improvement. Love to her & all yours.

Your affec:
D G R

P.S. Your letter reached me this afternoon owing to Scott & Miss Boyd going to Girvan & asking for letters. Else it would not have come till tomorrow.

---

[1] For the young clergyman-turned-art critic John Burnell Payne, see 68.74n2.

[2] On 31 Aug WMR noted "the great scandal turning up regarding Byron" and reported that FMB told him: "Mrs. Leigh was probably not in reality any blood-relation to Byron" (*RP* 406). Augusta Leigh was in fact his half-sister and rumours of their incestuous relations went as far back as 1816. The immediate cause of the reappearance of the scandal was an article on Lady Byron by Harriet Beecher Stowe in *Macmillan's Magazine* (Sep 69: 377–96). For a fuller response from DGR, see **156&n3**.

[3] "Parted Love" (see **136**).

69.146 TO WILLIAM MICHAEL ROSSETTI

MS: BL. Excerpt: *FL* 213–14. Published: DW 866. Date: WMR. Text within angled brackets is a marginal insertion.

Penkill
Thursday [2 September 1869]

Dear W

Today I have sent my proofs to the printers & told them to forward you a corrected set as well as one to me. This I suppose will be before many days. I benefited much by your labours as you will see. Your last line to the *Satan* sonnet I adopted with a slight change but am rather uncertain whether I may not change back again. What you said of the foggy opening of *Nocturn* induced me to restore a second stanza which I had cut out in printing it, in case this might make things any clearer. I have also added three new stanzas towards the close of this poem to develop the sudden flight of the bogey on finding another bogey by the girl's bed, which seemed funkyish though of course the right thing if she was already in love. I have also added 3 stanzas at the point I referred to in Stratton Water & made the proposed restoration (with addition) to the *Nineveh*. Also added a further useful stanza in the middle of Sister Helen. I have changed the title of *Placatâ Venere* to *Nuptial Sleep* which I think will help it to stand fire, and have improved some lines in it. However when you see it, I want you to say if you think one can say "their long kiss *severed*" & "their bosoms *sundered*" or whether "*was* severed" & "*were* sundered" are necessary. I should think either would do. I have kept "O Mary Virgin" which I thought necessary, but have put "O May Queen" above which removes the only objection I can see. I suppose you will think with me that the sonnet I enclose *must* be omitted. I have cut out Mary in Summer, Song & Music, and the Italian thing about which I am sorry you should have taken certainly more trouble than it deserved. I await your opinion about *Sister's Sleep*. I have sent to be inserted one new sonnet, two more old ones revised, and an old poem, the *Card-Dealer*, which I have divested of trivialities.

About *Miching Mallecho*,[1] I must say Keightley's explanation seems to me final unless he has really quite made some mull of the language. Have you reason to think so? Certainly the coincidence you have been struck by is very singular &, failing Keightley, well worth following up. <I suppose the name is not Longfellow's invention.>

Scott sends you word that he has heard from the editor of North Brit: Rev: & will write what is wanted for him.[2] Have you heard of the death of poor little Burnell Payne after a few days' illness?

Love from all here.

Your D G R

P.S. What year & month did our aunt Margaret die & where is she buried? Answer this without asking, if you can.³

---

1. WMR detected a similar sound and meaning in Shakespeare's "miching mallecho" ("malicho" in Folio) ("Marry, this is miching malicho. It means mischief"; *Hamlet* III.2.135) and Longfellow's "Mitche Manito" ("Mitche Manito the Mighty, /He the dreadful Spirit of Evil,/ . . . Very crafty, very cunning"; *The Song of Hiawatha* XIV). Thomas Keightley in his edition of *The Plays of William Shakespeare* (1864) declared the phrase "nonsense." Although the phrase has remained a puzzle, it is usually glossed as "sneaking mischief" or "stealthy iniquity" (Jenkins [ed.], *Hamlet* [Arden Shakespeare, [1982]), miching being a common English word meaning skulking, and mallecho an approximation to the Spanish malhecho meaning misdeed. In preparation for writing *Hiawatha*, Longfellow consulted Algonquin legends, which often employ the word Manito to refer to the good (Gitche) or evil (Matche) power of a person or thing. In his note introducing this letter in *FL*, WMR too modestly dismissed his suggestion in *N&Q* (30 Oct 69: 368), that the phrase had "an expressive idiomatic turn, corresponding to . . . 'It is the very devil: it means mischief.'"
2. Thomas Frederick Wetherell (1831–1908), clerk in the War Office, journalist, editor of the short-lived liberal Catholic weekly, *The Chronicle* (1867–68), edited the *North British Review*, Oct 69–Jan 71. For WBS' reviews in the October "Contemporary Literature" section, see *Wellesley* 1: 693.
3. Margaret Polidori, the eldest of FLR's sisters, died on 8 Feb 67: "Our dear Margaret was buried as near as could be to Philip in Highgate Cemetery" (FLR's MS journal, 13 Feb; AP). DGR was worrying about the looming exhumation of EES (see **135, 147,** & **157**), more particularly about the dangers of exhuming the wrong corpse or having his family discover his intentions (see *TR* 120). WMR was not told of the exhumation until after it had occurred (**181**); his other relatives were probably never told.

69.147 TO CHARLES AUGUSTUS HOWELL

MS: Princeton. Excerpt: *PRT* 83. Published: Troxell, *Colophon* 15 (1933); *TR* 117–18; DW 867.

Penkill Castle/Girvan/Ayrshire

3 Sept 1869

My dear Howell

Thanks for your letter. I write with this to Kitty to tell her how very glad I am she is quite well again after so much suffering & anxiety. She must no doubt take great care of herself for the present.

In connection with the other matter, it has suddenly flashed upon me that I believe a man I know pretty well is now Home Secretary. Is it not Henry A. Bruce? Will you look in some list and see. I cannot find any here. If this is so, I had better perhaps write him direct as enclosed, and tell him that (his sanction obtained) an intimate friend has undertaken to manage matters for me. So, as I feel almost sure he is the man, I enclose a letter. If you think any other plan of action better, let me know at once please – or if you do not think the letter the thing. If you do think this the best course on reflection, perhaps you had better post the letter. I do not think necessary to date it from here, but his answer will be sent me from London, if coming before my return. By the bye, I had better leave you to put his address, which will be easily found. He used to live in Chesham Place, but I don't know if he still does.¹

With a thousand thanks

Affectionately yours
D G R

P.S. The grave is at Highgate Cemetery & the exact spot can be found at once by enquiry at the lodge.²

P.S. I have been taking great trouble with my proofs & roused myself to an interest in the subject.

As for the Janey drawing, take it by all means, only I think I will rely on your exercising self denial & letting me have it again at any time that I wanted it for myself, by my giving you something instead. It ought to be photo'd before leaving my studio, but I think on looking last at it I considered the mouth needed a slight alteration, so this shd be made first. Perhaps therefore you had better let it stand over. Have you found the Janey in a chair?³ Do do do find it.

---

1 CAH had already written to Bruce when he received this letter. Bruce's reply to him on 9 Sep 69 is printed in DW (735–36). For Bruce's reply to DGR's personal letter to him, written between 9 & 12 Sep but not extant, see DW 736&n. See also **157**, **158**, & **164**; and *TR* 109–28.
2 WMR recorded the following: "February 17 [1862]. The funeral. Grave 5779, Highgate (the same grave in which my father lay buried – my mother is now there too, and, even since I wrote this very sentence, my dear sister Christina). Gabriel put the book of his MS. poems into the coffin" (*FLM* 224).
3 For mention of CAH's Janey drawing, see **100** & **109**. Surtees identifies the "Janey in a chair" as *Silence* (S.214), though both it and the pencil sketch are dated 1870 as is S. 377 (where JM is "seated to the right in a chair of Rossetti's design" [Surtees 177]). JM is also seated in a chair in *Mariana* (S. 213) and studies were done for it in 1868 & 1869.

69.148 TO FRANCES CATHERINE HOWELL

MS: Texas. Published: Cline 105.

Penkill Castle/Girvan/Ayrshire
3 Sept 1869.

My dear Kitty,

I cannot refrain from writing you a line to say how rejoiced I am at hearing now of your complete recovery from such a painful attack of illness as I learned you had had. However I judge that all is fortunately well now.

I shall be here possibly for a week or two longer – possibly not quite so much. I have been walking pretty regularly & I hope benefiting, but the heat has been such as to make exercise heroism. However there is a private and sheltered glen belonging to this house which is a refuge from everything, almost including oneself – the supreme bogey.

I have been working hard at some proof-sheets of poetry, mostly old things of mine, which I am about to print in a private form. I think I am getting them into a shape I need not be ashamed of, and if good I do not mind so much their being few.

I suppose you were hardly well enough to assist at the grand ceremony on Sunday last, but no doubt it was well attended.

My news of Janey Morris continues pretty good, but I fear the days of miracles are past. However one must hope to find her improved on her return.

I hope on getting back to finish your portrait drawing. I believe it is like, as several people have recognized it spontaneously, though I cannot say it seems to me a *striking* likeness. Miss Spartali, who was sitting to me lately, did not recognize it at first, yet ultimately thought it a successful portrait.[1] I made 3 drawings of her head, the last I believe pretty good, though the first 2 were failures.[2]

As I am writing to Charley with this, I can send my love to each of you personally.

Ever affectionately yours
D Gabriel R

P.S. Kindest remembrances from Miss Boyd & Scott.

[1] S.339.
[2] Only 2 drawings of Marie Spartali's head, S.519 & S.520, are extant. The first is dated 1869 and was owned by the model.

69.149 TO JAMES SMETHAM

MS: V&A. Excerpt: Surtees 112.

7 Sept 1869
Penkill Castle/Girvan/Ayrshire

My dear Smetham

Your genial "ventilator" was sent on to me here where I have been for some 3 weeks & may stay a week or perhaps fortnight longer. So you see its truculent exterior cartoons met with due humiliation in this bracing atmosphere. I am not sure whether you are likely to be still away – or at home by this time, so write to home. The weather has been splendid here till today when it seems perhaps to be breaking up. The heat however has been all along so great as to render a walk something like a warm bath, or else I am weakening for walking, as I remember experiencing no such excessive results even when walking about the country in the supreme heats of last summer & a dozen miles or more at a stretch. I have brought no work here – i.e. painting – but have not been idle. I am printing privately such of my old poems (limited to new ones) as I can get together, and have given my utmost care to their revision for some weeks past. I am determined to leave them available in a form of which I should not be ashamed if they are ever wanted in this universe. I dare say I shall shortly be able to give you a copy, of which however I shall give very few at present, as I intend to keep the present sheets by me merely as stock towards a larger collection when ready, at which time I shd probably publish. This may be, if I go on writing, before very long; but at present, having lost many of my most careful M.S.S. some time ago, I have not sufficient material.

The article in Tinsley came out this month &, though not very perfect writing, is good-natured and well-meant. This & other such hints of notice attracted by my poems render it advisable to put them in such a state as I like, lest they should eventually get huddled into print anyhow.

I have not seen you for an age & therefore must have done a good deal of easel-work of one kind or other since, though much has persisted in hanging fire. Chalk drawings are getting better pot-boilers than ever for me with Agnew's assistance, and I expect that he will shortly send them up so (from the price he is willing to buy at & the profit he must expect) that they will do me good service in the future. There is one thing in which I want your help – the perspective of the Sibyl's background which I find is in a muddle for want of attention in the first instance. I must see you about it when we are both at home. You do not tell me about your picture of the "Maries" but Shields gave me a very promising account of it. I do not know if you have heard from him lately. I fear he is in a very nervous highly-wrought state & not likely to improve in a hurry. I am sorry to say he has had a great disappointment about a commission he expected from Graham for a large water-colour of *Mercy fainting at the gate.* Indeed the commission, as I thought with him, was quite a settled thing, and I must say I think he has much cause to complain, though I still hope an opportunity may occur of getting Graham to see the matter in a different light.

Scott is here and wishes to be warmly remembered to you, in which Miss Boyd also joins. Scott is doing some etchings for an edition of Burns, some of which I think exceedingly good. He has also just finished his book on Albert Durer which will be out immediately, and is going on with a series of windows illustrating Ceramic Art at South Kensington. Four are already up there on the staircases ascending from the Ceramic galleries. I have not yet seen them, but the designs are very full and ingenious. Morris is getting on splendidly as I hear with his Earthly Paradise. He has been for about 2 months at Ems for his wife's health who I am happy to say is improving. The last of his poems I heard was certainly the finest of all – a long Icelandic story of human passion without supernatural machinery. The second vol. will I believe be out in October but there is to be a third now so much has the material grown.

Affectionately yours
D G Rossetti

69.150 TO JANE MORRIS

MS: BL. Published: Bryson 13. Date: P/M.

Penkill
Tuesday [7 September 1869]

My dear Janey

Your former letter had discouraged me more than I cared to say: – so provokingly small did the improvement seem to be after all your efforts. So you may suppose how proportionately happy your present letter makes me. To think of you restored to daily comfort and activity by so simple a means, and to think of it as a resource always in case of fresh attacks, is indeed reassuring. No doubt you will take the precaution on your return to London of having proper arrangements made to enable you to take the baths at home. I quite agree with you in thinking it desirable to return as soon as the improvement has shown itself to be in any degree permanent. I hope this will have been the case by the time of your starting. I suppose by what you say it will be the safest plan for me to write to Ghent. I judge you will reach London about Tuesday or Wednesday of next week if you travel as leisurely as before. Glad indeed shall I be to see you there in safety.

I have been so feverish & unwell here, and have had such bad sleep, that I do not feel confident in a longer stay being the best course to improve me. However I may perhaps think it well to complete the month, which will not be up till Thursday of next week, as I lost one or two days on the road here. Thus it is possible I may not add one to the number of your congratulatory visitors till you are fairly settled at home again. But perhaps I may leave earlier.

I have begun one or two new poems, and one of them will I hope be the best thing I have done. It is called *The Orchard-Pit*, but I have made little way as yet.¹ I have sonneted a little too and added importantly to some of the old things which wanted working up at the joints

Tinsley is as you say laughably shady, but I only look at these things so far as they are likely to do good or harm, and this cannot at any rate do harm.

I am rejoiced to hear of Topsy's mighty doings and shall expect much enjoyment from them on my return. By the bye I have long seen him eyeing that poor young man's ewe-lamb, "The Death of Paris,"² and am delighted to find him so far after God's own heart as to be no better than the royal bard of Israel; only I hope you learned where Bathsheba bathed and kept an eye on her at Ems. I really think the ewe-lamb business suggests a cartoon which should be carried out with myself as Nathan, but today I have no time as I must be gadding about.

News is sadly scarce, and then I hope to be really seeing you so soon now. One sad thing perhaps you have heard – poor Burnell Payne's death after a few days' illness.

A farmer who is a tenant of Miss Boyd's here resembles Topsy in visage, waistcoat-gusset (as I noticed the other day while he was working his corn-cutting machine) and manner no less. He enters his landlady's boudoir suddenly, stands still & glares with his hat held in front of him and his legs apart, and ejaculates "Ah! about those rabbits!"

Work has been going on in the regular pot-boiling line while I have been away under Dunn's auspices, & Agnew has been buying the drawings I did just before I left. So you see the coast will be clear for your sittings when they become possible.

And now good bye for the present, dear Janey. Don't forget to let me have the further news of your health which you promise, or I shall think all is not well.

With love to Top.

Your affectionate
Gabriel

---

1 Unfinished and unpublished until 1886, when WMR included fragmentary stanzas and a prose "argument" in *CW*.
2 The tale for September in WM's *Earthly Paradise*.

69.151 TO JAMES ANDERSON ROSE

MS: LC. Excerpt: Kashnor 206.

9 Septe/1869
Penkill Castle/Girvan/Ayrshire/NB

My dear Rose

I have a necessity for all the papers – lease &c – relating to my house, to show to a friend here in connection with the studio project. Would you kindly send them to me at once by Post. I shall be back in town now before very long.

Ever yours truly
D G Rossetti

JA Rose Esq

69.152 TO JANE MORRIS

MS: BL. Published: Bryson 14. Date: P/M.

Penkill

Saturday. [11 September 1869]

My dear Janey

I got Top's note from Ghent this morning. I hope you found there my letter posted on Tuesday to Hôtel Royal as you told me. It is a comfort to think that this letter will reach you in friendly London and that your wanderings are over.

What Top tells me is most reassuring. Then, thank Heaven! all the labour has not been lost. I rejoice to hear that you are getting the baths ready at home. Do let me have a word from you when you get this – just a word to say how you are after the journey. I long to see for myself how much better you are, but think it will hardly be wise to leave here before the month, so expect most probably to be in town by this day week. So you will have one visitor less to beset you before you are quite rested. I hope and hope that you may be able to come to me soon and preside at a dinner in honour of your restoration. Not of course that I am expecting miracles, but it is evident much has really been done.

What do you think? I have got a Wombat at Chelsea[1], come the other day, whose portraits (by Dunn) I enclose.

Your affectionate
D Gabriel R

Saturday. [11 September 1869]

Plate 5: *Death of a Wombat*

[Enclosures]
P.S.
Oh! how the family affections combat
Within this heart; and each hour flings a bomb at
My burning soul; neither from owl nor from bat
Can peace be gained, until I clasp my Wombat!

When you've read a good many
Of these pages, dear Jenny,
I know you will say
To your dear Sister May: –

"If Papa at our age
  Had had this little book,
How much more respectable
  Now he would look!"

And May will say, "Ah!
Yes indeed, poor Papa!"

---

[1] This burrowing Australian marsupial was a sort of PR mascot. Discovered by CGR on her regular visits to the London Zoological Gardens, the creature quickly became a favourite with DGR. During the Jovial Campaign of 1857, during which the Oxford Union was decorated by DGR and his young acolytes, little wombats appeared among the mediæval frescoes. As this letter shows, he finally acquired one of his own in the fall of 1869 – the canard that his wombat was the original of the dormouse at the Mad Hatter's tea-party is disproved by the fact that *Alice's Adventures in Wonderland* was published 4 years earlier in 1865. Several comic descriptions of the wombat's activities occur in letters of this time (**156, 159, 160**). However, DGR was not a careful or attentive pet owner: like many other animal denizens of 16CW, Top the wombat survived for only a short period, expiring on 6 Nov. DGR commemorated this occasion with *Death of a Wombat*, a funereal drawing (S.606) of himself weeping over his dead pet with an elegiac quatrain (Plate 5). The wombat was stuffed and placed inside the entrance at 16CW.

69.153 TO ALICIA MARGARET LOSH

MS: Princeton. Published: *TR* 90–91; DW 868.

Penkill
Sunday [12 September 1869]

Dear Miss Losh,
  I expect to be leaving here on Thursday next which will complete the

month since I arrived. I have been extremely sorry to hear, through what Mrs. Kemmis[1] wrote to Miss Boyd, of your fresh attack of illness so shortly after I last saw you. As she has not heard again, we do not know whether you are better. I therefore write to Mr. W. Losh's, in case your indisposition should have led to your going there.

If you can be my hostess again on my way to London, I shall be thankful as before, and am anxious to see for myself how you are now. In that case I need not trouble you to let me know, but will turn up in due course. If however you are not at Ravenside, or if you are unfortunately too unwell still to receive a visitor, will you let me know by Wednesday evening. I suppose of course there is time for a letter to reach, even between Wreay & Penkill which form a sort of postal Scylla & Charybdis. If you are not able to say up to the last moment, perhaps you would kindly send me a telegram in time. However I am in hopes of finding you improved again, & with kind remembrances to all yours,

am yours very sincerely
DG Rossetti

PS. Miss Boyd sends love and is very anxious to know how you are. W. B. joins in same.

As far as we can make out Bradshaw it seems I shall reach Carlisle at 7-28 and I suppose it takes another hour to get to your "diggings." So I fear I shall be rather an untimely arrival.

---

[1] Mrs. Kemmis was AML's sister, Mary Alice, who married James Kemmis at the British Embassy in Paris in 1818. Her husband died in 1840.

69.154 TO WILLIAM MICHAEL ROSSETTI

MS: BL. Excerpt: *FL* 214–17. Published: DW 869. Date: WMR.

Penkill
Tuesday [14 September 1869]

My dear W

I suppose ere this you have doubtless got the new proofs of which I received a set yesterday. You will see much that is due to your labours in them. However I have been at work on them still further now and have done various things. I have revised the additional verses to Stratton Water which were rather in the rough and have added one further on about the priest in a funk. In the additional verses to Nocturn I have made the following change in the third, which now runs: –

> So a chief who all night lies
>   Ambushed where no help appears, –
> 'Mid his comrades' unseen eyes
>   Watching for the growth of spears, –
>   Like their ghosts, as morning nears,
>   Sees them rise,
>   Ready without sighs or tears.

I think you will agree with me that this is preferable, as in the first form the plural pronouns applied to "legion" were awkward.

However I have been worrying about what you said of the obscurity of the opening of this poem & have now put it thus: –

> Master of the murmuring courts
>   Where the shapes of sleep convene! –
> Lo! my spirit here exhorts
>   All the powers of thy demesne
>   For their aid to woo my queen?
>   What reports
>   Yield thy jealous courts unseen?
>
> Vaporous, unaccountable,
>   Dreamland lies unknown to light,
> Hollow like a breathing shell.
>   Ah! that from all dreams I might
>   Choose one dream & guide its flight!
>   I know well
>   What her sleep should tell to-night.

Surely this makes all plain, does it not? *Dreamland* is a rather hackneyed phrase I don't like, but it is so valuable for clearing up that I adopted it.

Now there is another question. The first conception of this poem was of a man not yet in love who dreams vaguely of a woman who he thinks must exist for him. This is not very plainly expressed & not I think very valuable, & it might be better to refer the love to a known woman whom he wishes to approach. There is only one stanza I think that stands in the way of this interpretation – the one beginning – "As since man waxed deathly wise"- and I want your opinion as to whether it would not be better to cut this stanza out? It is a good one, but is rather objectionable as resembling in its rhymes the penultimate preceding one. I think it shd go. Another slight point. The fourth stanza used to say: –

Tuesday [14 September 1869] 69.154

>   Youth's warm fancies all are there:
>   There the elf-girls flood with wings
>   Vallies full of plaintive air: &c

This perhaps flows better, & I have just noticed that in the present version there is "whisperings" rhyming with "rings" which is bad. But on the other hand I like the new meaning best. What is your view?

You will have noticed another new stanza in *Sister Helen* – "But he calls for ever on your name" &c. This is valuable for elucidation. However I have improved both this & Stanza 1.

About *Nuptial Sleep*. I enclose the proof before the last to ask you about the M.S. alteration at the bottom, which is now in print. Above & below it I have written a further variation *underlined*. Do you think this or the present printed one best? I incline to the printed one. Then as to "chirped at each other." This is expressive of the lips kissing *at* each other as they lie apart. But is it clear, or if clear is it pleasant? Would it be better "Kissed at each other" or more likely "moaned to each other"? Or does any other phrase occur to you? Or do you like it as it stands?

In *Penumbra* I have altered in last stanza – "*rasp* the sands" to *chafe*. The other seemed violent and inexact.

In Sonnet *A Dark Day* – "sowed hunger *once*" – I believe this used to stand *since*. Which is better?

In "Mary's Girlhood" – *This is* &c. Could one say as well – '*Tis of* that blessed &c? In *Palmifera* sonnet there is *This is that Lady Beauty* & I think the same form is elsewhere.

Venus Sonnet has – She hath the apple in &c. Now *apple* is here placed awkwardly between 2 vowels which makes the prosody dubious. Does any change suggest itself? In the new Sonnet *Parted Love* the last line is declared by Scott to be too violent. Do you think so? It occurs to me to say "And thy feet stir not, and thy body endures." Do you like this better. It conveys the sense of impotent retention which is wanted, but that is already conveyed in line 7.

You will observe that I have now included 2 old sonnets "Autumn Idleness" and "A Match with the Moon." The first as now revised I like well. The second I like too, but do you think it lays itself open to ridicule? The "Card Dealer" you will find improved I doubt not.

I am now sending the printer 7 new Sonnets, of which 4 are for designs of mine – viz: 2 for *Cassandra*, 1 for *Passover* & one for *Magdalene*. I think this may help me in defending the subjects against plagiarists. I think all are very good. I have also begun 2 new poems – one called "The Orchard-Pit" will be my best thing, but I have not yet got much beyond a careful synopsis in prose which I consider a very good plan of action. I shall certainly go on & finish it as soon as may be, as I feel great confidence in it. The other I have done rather more to. I find this place most favourable to writing & should soon get into very regular habits of production. However I had determined to leave here next Thursday, but find so much more benefit within the last few days than before, that I may perhaps stay on till Tuesday next on which day I certainly expect to start homewards but may be detained a day with Miss Losh. I have felt far from well till just now but am now feeling better.

You perhaps know that the Morrises have returned. If you have seen them I wish you would tell me how Janey is, though probably I may hear from her first. Her letters from Ems were not very satisfactory at first but she seems at last to have really benefited considerably.

I was nearly forgetting the Italian poem which I had put pretty well out of my head. I sent it to Teodorico & enclose you his answer & new version which no doubt you will think with me rather modern and loaded. I cannot gather clearly that he objects on grounds of *prosody* other than what may be said to depend on taste. If you see him you might discuss the point. I must answer his letter. Of course if I print the thing it must be as I wrote it or nearly so. Should a version resulting from mine and his occur to you I would be obliged by your sending it me. I am sick of the affair.

With love to all

Your affec: Gabriel

Have you seen the Wombat?
P.S. Scott has done the work for Wetherell.[1]

---

[1] See **146n2**.

69.155 TO ALICIA MARGARET LOSH

MS: Princeton. Published: *TR* 91; DW 870. Date: WMR.

Penkill
Wednesday [15 September 1869]

Dear Miss Losh

I have been led to see the advisability of staying here a few days longer, and do not expect to get away before Monday or Tuesday. All would be most delightful here were it not for the changeable weather we are getting now.

I suppose by not hearing from you that you are better & kindly ready to receive me. So I write to Ravenside. I will again notify to you my precise movements in due course.

All here send their love, and I am

Most sincerely yours
DG Rossetti

69.156 TO WILLIAM MICHAEL ROSSETTI
MS: BL. Excerpt: *FL* 218–19. Published: DW 871. Date: WMR.

Penkill
Wednesday [15 September 1869]

Dear W

I may as well answer one or two points in your letter.

page 24   I fear the sea must remain at Nazareth. You know an old painter would have made no bones if he wanted it for his background. The lines following this I have altered now.

10   The stanza to which my question referred is now the first on page 11, through resetting. "Funeral" *was* the word meant in my other question – (page 8)

12   I don't myself object to the sound of "Its old share" or "love's foe."

I have made a change in the *Hill Summit* (p.141) thus:

> "And now that I have climbed & won this height,
> I must tread downward through the sloping shade
> And travel the bewildered tracks till night.
> Yet for this hour I still may here be stayed" &c

The symbolism being thus more distinct than before, do you not think this sonnet should properly be transferred to the *House of Life* section?

I am in a rather productive mood & have written 2 Sonnets since writing to you yesterday. For one of the *Cassandra* ones, I want to know whether Achilles killed Hector with a sword or a spear. Will you look this up? or perhaps you know.

Scott wanted me to tell you that you were to keep back a certain proof of his where a newly-discovered Durer picture should be described, till he hears whether it is genuine or not.[1]

Will you thank Maggie for her most complete information about the Passover. Also Christina for the shrine in the Italian taste which she has reared for the Wombat.² I fear his habits tend inveterately to drain-architecture. I wrote for directions about his food to Nettleship who is always at the Zoo, and he has sent me some. It appears the Wombat follows people all over the house!

About the Byron business I certainly think I have heard Swinburne allude to the connection with his sister.³ I also thought at first there could be no doubt but am very uncertain now. It seems to me by no means impossible that Lady Byron laboured under a hallucination on this subject; and that even if she did rear an illegitimate child of Byron's, this particular attribution of its birth *may* have been her own inveterate fancy. The question of relationship raised in the Times is well worth considering also. Did you see a letter by a man named Radclyffe in the Telegraph (I think)? He was brought up by Mrs. Leigh, and speaks in the most reverential terms of her, – employing I must say a rather Irish style of phraseology. It has been sent here, & if you have not seen it I can look it up for you. (P.S. I send it.)

Lastly if Byron f – d his sister he f – d her & there an end, – an absolute end, in my opinion as far as the vital interest of his poetry goes, which is all we have to do with.

Your Gabriel

P.S. Scotus agrees, especially with the last sentiment.

I still bear rather a grudge to the three sonnets called "The Choice." Do you feel sure they ought to be in? Also to the two on Ingres's picture, which are merely picturesque, and which stupid people are sure to like better than better things.

P.S. I saw a letter from W. Howitt in one paper about Lady Byron's great obstinacy in fixed ideas.

---

1   While WMR was reading and commenting on the proofs of DGR's poems, he continued to assist WBS with *Albert Dürer: His Life and Works*, answering questions and checking proofs. WBS earlier apologized for the imposition: "You are taking a tremendous deal of trouble for me. I hope it is not too much of a grind even for friendship" (WBS:WMR, 16 Jun [69], Durham). In his "Catalogue of Pictures," WBS called the "newly discovered" Dürer belonging to the Marquis of Lothian – which FMB brought to his attention – "Virgin and Child with Four Angels," but he was mistaken in identifying 4 angels; the Virgin is accompanied by 3 angels & the infant St. John the Baptist. The painting is now called *Madonna with the Goldfinch* or *Madonna with the Siskin* (Berlin).
2   "O Uommibatto" (Crump 3: 336); CGR coined an Italian word for wombat.
3   Harriet Beecher Stowe's claim that the cause of Byron's separation from Lady Byron was her discovery of his incestuous relationship with his half-sister, Augusta Leigh ("The True Story of Lady Byron's Life," *Macmillan's Magazine* 20 [Sep 69]: 377–96), was debated in the press throughout Sep 69 and beyond. Shortly after the article appeared, FMB mentioned

the subject to DGR, who replied asking him to explain "*by return of post.* . . . I know of nothing bearing on the subject, and am most excited to hear" (**145**), and he followed the controversy in *The Times* and elsewhere. His suggestion that Lady Byron "laboured under a hallucination" was argued in *The Times* (7 Sep 69) by Lord Lindsay. "The question of relationship raised in the Times" refers to a letter (31 Aug 69), which advanced reasons for thinking that Byron & Augusta were "right in considering that there was no blood relationship between them." F.P. Delme Radcliffe wrote to the *Daily Telegraph*, 9 Sep 1869, that he had been "nurtured under the shadow of . . . [Mrs. Leigh's] wing," and attacked Mrs Stowe by quoting Emilia's repudiation of Iago's "foul aspersions" on Desdemona: "You told a lie, an odious damned lie! / Upon my soul, a lie, a wicked lie!" (*Othello* V.2.180–81). William Howitt's letter in the *Daily News* (4 Sep 69) recounted 2 occasions, drawn from his personal knowledge of Lady Byron, when she was "absolutely and persistently unjust" (*The Stowe-Byron Controversy: A Complete Résumé of all that has been written and said upon the subject . . . by the editor of "Once a Week* [E.S. Dallas] [Thomas Cooper & Co., 1869]: 75–78). WMR's interest in Mrs. Stowe's claim was "a practical one," since it required him to modify his memoir of Byron for Moxon's Popular Poets (see WMR:DGR, 12 Sep [69], Peattie 165). In his memoir he calls the claim a "gross and ghastly story" not yet verified (*Byron* [1870]: xv). WMR's willingness to reserve judgment set him apart from the overwhelming tendency of the press & public to defend Byron and attack Mrs. Stowe. The Rossettis would have been subjected to ACS' virulent description of Mrs. Stowe as "the hag that libelled Byron's memory . . . Mrs. Bitcher Spewe" (Lang 3: 811, 852).

69.157 TO CHARLES AUGUSTUS HOWELL

MS: Princeton. Published: Troxell, *Colophon* 15 (1933); *TR* 120; DW 872.

Penkill

Sept 16 1869

My dear Howell

I send you Bruce's answer just received, and also a note of introduction to him, in case you think it well to see him, which I should think might facilitate his movements. I write to him with this to say I am sending you such a note. He is an old friend & will I know receive you cordially. I suppose you sent my letter to him to the Home Secretary's office, and would call on him there.[1]

I am returning to town now almost immediately & will write you word on getting there.[2]

Love to Kitty whose kind letter was very welcome & whose recovery is good news of the best. Will you return her the note she sent me. From that quarter also news seems good; thank God!

Very affectionately yours

Gabriel

P.S. If you write, write to Chelsea.
P.P.S. I should mention a slight possible complication. An aunt of mine died two or three years ago & is I find buried in Highgate Cemetery, but whether

in the same family grave or not I do not know, – however I fancy not. You should enquire whether the burial in question (Feb. 1862) is the last in that grave.³ I have not yet told William of the steps we are taking.⁴

The book in question is bound in rough grey calf and has I am almost sure red edges to the leaves. This will distinguish it from the Bible also there as I told you.⁵

---

1   **158** was enclosed with this letter. See also **126n1**.
2   DGR left Penkill on 18 Sep.
3   See **146n3**.
4   DGR finally advised his brother of the exhumation on 13 Oct (see **181**).
5   See **147n2**.

69.158 TO HENRY AUSTIN BRUCE

MS: Princeton. Published: Troxell, *Colophon* 15 (1933); *TR* 121; *PRT* 83; DW 873.

16th Sept. 1869
16 Cheyne Walk/Chelsea

My dear Bruce

I give this note of introduction to my friend Mr. C.A. Howell. Whatever you may say to him will be as if said to me.

Sincerely yours
D G Rossetti

The Right Honble
H.A. Bruce MP

69.159 TO ALICIA MARGARET LOSH

MS: Princeton. Published: *TR* 92–93; DW 874.

Tuesday [21 September 1869]
16 Cheyne Walk/Chelsea

My dear Miss Losh,

I duly reached here last night at 9.30 after a very rapid and punctual journey. I find everything as it should be, and even better. My servants have been exerting themselves wonderfully and have cleaned and even painted the house to a most satisfactory state of polish. My tent however has had to be taken down, as it seems the winds here were at one time something tremendous. I have seen no one as yet except the parrot and the Wombat who are on either side of me as I write – the former letting fall a remark – or shall I say an animadversion? – from time to time – and the latter burrowed deep in the sofa cushions indulging apparently in the more abstruse forms of thought. He is a round furry ball with a head something between a bear and a guinea-pig, no legs, human feet with heels like anybody else, and no tail. Of course I shall call him "Top." His habits are most endearing. He follows one about everywhere and sidles up and down stairs along the wall with the greatest activity. He is but a babe as yet & very rough as to his coat which however is splendidly thick. The Consummate Wombat is quite smooth, and such he will be when adult. He is tremendously strong and heroically good-natured. I know you would pronounce him a perfect darling.

Of course I have no news at present, but thought I would make sure of writing before that dreadful letter of yours reaches me from Penkill. However, you know I have promised to burn it unopened.

I see the Tinsley article on William is out, and is rather severe on *Mrs. Holmes Grey*. They are not quite wrong about its defects, but then they are obtuse to its merits.[1]

I hope to be sending you some proofs in a forward state soon, and with kind remembrances to all at Ravenside and Wreay, am ever

most sincerely yours
DGRossetti

[1] See **160** & **162n1**.

69.160 TO ALICE BOYD

MS: NLS. Excerpt: Sharp, *DGR*: 363; Purves 566. Published: DW 875. Text within angled brackets is a marginal insertion.

Tuesday [21 September 1869]

My dear Miss Boyd

Here I am since 9-30 last night after a very dragging journey. On Saturday there was a stay of an hour and a half at Ayr, and I reached Carlisle about 7-30. Thence made my way to Miss Losh's, after finding that it was impracticable to start for London on Sunday, the trains being diabolical. So Sunday I spent at Ravenside & there wrote some 14 stanzas of my Lilith poem which I think will be a good one. If not falling so easily into shape as *Troy Town*, and turning out necessarily rather longer, I nevertheless found it yielded ample suggestions for a central representative treatment of its splendid subject. I call it "Eden Bower," and will send you a copy if finished soon, as I dare say it will be in a day or two. I suppose I shall put it in print at once.

I enclose Tinsley on William who I regret to see comes in for some partly justifiable & partly obtuse fault-finding in his character of poet. It seems to me that, considering that the writer starts (in the first of the three articles) by describing W. as a critic, he should have had it out with him on this score at the outset of the present article, & not begun it with an attack of such length on *Mrs. Holmes Grey*. I don't suppose Wm will mind though. <Topsy considers *Mrs. H. G.* an extremely fine though peculiar poem, and so do I.>

I have not yet seen anyone but Dunn & the Wombat. The former is meritorious and the latter "a Joy, a triumph, a delight, a madness!" You will love him at first sight. He is a babe at present & rougher in his coat than he will turn out. His habits are of the School of "Contemplative Absorption," so that W. B. might add a passage on him to the *Year of the World*. However his affections are of the sweetest kind & he follows one about like a dog, and if his leader hastens on, so does the Wombat. I am told he gallops round the garden, but have not seen him do so yet.

I will write again before long, but today have various things to see about. Moreover I will look up blue pots. Thanks for Wm's letter sent on no doubt just after I left you.

With love to W. B. I am

Most sincerely yours
D G Rossetti

P.S. I was actually nearly omitting to tell you that I found Miss Losh much better. Wm. Septimus returned at the same moment as myself.[1] I had a narrow escape from a dreadful Mr. Cholmondeley Pennell (a nephew of the Admiral) whose name has been a terror to me for years in flashy advertisements of some base production called "Puck on Pegasus." If I had gone on Friday I should have had the pleasure of meeting him at dinner at Ravenside, & if I had stayed over Monday, I should have incurred him at Wreay.[2]

[1] For William Septimus Losh, see **129n1**.
[2] Henry Cholmondeley Pennell (1837–1915), who later hyphenated his surname, was the nephew of Admiral Follett Walrond Pennell, whose second wife was AML's niece, Frances Elizabeth Losh Hutchinson, daughter of AML's sister Frances, who had married Francis Coleridge Hutchinson in Newcastle in 1820. Pennell had a civil service post from 1853–75, latterly as inspector of sea fisheries. He wrote chiefly on angling, but Tenniel, Leech, "Phiz," & Cruikshank illustrated his *Puck on Pegasus* (1861), which went through several editions. He also owned the Rossetti Mansions in Chelsea and Palace Mansions in Kensington.

69.161 TO ALICE BOYD

MS: NLS.

Tuesday [21 September 1869]

Dear Miss Boyd

I have written once today, & now just find that I have lost the prose version of the "Orchard-Pits" which I scribbled on some note-paper at Penkill. If you happened to find it among the papers I did not bring away, wd you kindly send it.

Ever yours
DG Rossetti

69.162 TO WILLIAM MICHAEL ROSSETTI

MS: BL. Published: *FL* 220; DW 876.

Tuesday [21 September 1869]

Dear W

I came back last night and shall of course be seeing you immediately but write lest you should write again to Penkill. Your last letter has already been sent back to me here. I wrote some more poetry & one Ballad which is my best thing I think – *Troy Town*.

The Wombat is A Joy a Triumph a Delight a Madness.

I have got Tinsley today. They treat you very respectfully but are obtuse about *Mrs. Holmes Grey* which they discuss at great length.[1] Perhaps you will have it.

Your affec:
Gabriel

I have seen no one yet.

---

[1] HBF's October article on WMR (see 68.145 & **112n5**) did not treat him "very respectfully." He regretted the publication of *Mrs. Holmes Grey*, unfavourably compared WMR's literal translation of Dante's *Inferno* with DGR's "bountiful revivification" of *Vita Nuova*, and criticized his occasional "uncouthnesses" of style as a "slight blemish to the series of products of a family who are remarkable . . . for refinement of taste" (279, 281). For DGR's opinion of HBF's style and his failure to appreciate the strengths of *Mrs. Holmes Grey*, see **149** & **159**. Despite HBF's condescending treatment of WMR, their common interest in the text of Shelley's poems led to a longstanding friendship (Peattie 202n4).

69.163 TO GEORGE AUGUSTUS SALA

MS: Princeton.

16 Cheyne Walk
Sunday [26 September 1869?]

My dear Sala

Your letter of yesterday found me pre-engaged for this evening. I am sorry it reached me too late for me to say so by yesterday's post.[1]

From your extraordinary mention of Burne Jones's name, I must suppose that you are not aware of his being one of my closest and dearest friends. I must add that I do not only *think* but *know* him to rank as high in genius as any artist now living. If you think otherwise, you are so absolutely the only person to be pitied in the matter, that there is no call for irritation.

I am sorry if my notice of this point, while answering so kindly a letter from you, enclosing me some of your own sketches (for which, many thanks), should give to my reply any air of unpleasantness. But I think you will perceive that I had to say this.

Swinburne was with me when your note came last night, & expressed an intention of looking in on you this evening, so you may probably have seen him ere this reaches you.

What you say of the photograph is quite a puzzle to me, but seems almost of the nature of a discovery, (unless, – of which I am not aware, – it happens to be among the known facts of photography.)

Ever yours
DG Rossetti

---

[1] Sala tried again on the 19th, inviting DGR with FS to dine on the 22nd: "I have a particular object in view, so pray say 'yes' as soon as you can, that I may instruct our *chef* as to the due conclusion of the sow's teats stewed in *garum*, and the genitals of a Bombay ape *acommodi* with the classic sauce of peacock's brains and swan's marrow" (Texas).

69.164 TO FUNERAL COMPANY, LONDON

MS: Princeton. Published: Troxell, *Colophon* 15 (1933); *TR* 121; DW 877 (where CAH is cited as the recipient).

28th September/1869

In accordance with the order granted by the Right Honorable Henry Austin Bruce, Her Majesty's Secretary for the Home Department, for the exhumation of the body of my late wife Elizabeth Eleanor Rossetti, buried at Highgate Cemetery: I hereby authorize my friend Charles Augustus Howell, of Northend Grove, Northend, Fulham, to act in all matters as he may think fit, for the purpose of opening the coffin and taking charge of the M.S. volume deposited therein.

Dante Gabriel Rossetti.
16 Cheyne Walk
Chelsea

69.165 TO WILLIAM BELL SCOTT
MS: Princeton.

Chelsea
28 Sept 1869

Dearest Scotus

When I last wrote to Miss Boyd I had as yet seen nobody. Since then Top and Janey have spent two or three days here. She is very decidedly better, though she has not ceased to be an invalid. However, the bad – indeed dreadful – passage they had on their way home is enough to deter her improvement, and I have every hope of further encouraging results. At present she is gone to spend a few weeks at Hampstead. I saw Brown last night. His dental experiments are a complete success & he seems wonderfully well. He will be going to Newcastle but is not quite certain when, and in any case seems to see no chance of reaching Penkill, much as he regrets the loss of the chance. I saw no work of importance, but he has written a song, a French version of said song, and a sonnet, all in illustration of a picture by Mary Spartali for which she wanted a motto; and all I think are remarkably good – the English song a charming thing though a little obscure without the picture.[1] I have seen Jones who is well and working well. Also Howell, who is full of marvels and has made some most beautiful additions to his house. His wife seems quite well again. I am to dine there tomorrow, by which time he expects to have brought to a result the affair about which I wrote to Bruce.

I was extremely annoyed to see in the Athenæum the paragraph on Mrs. Heaton's book. No doubt you have seen the precious thing, but I enclose it. However I suppose you may yet be first in the field.[2]

You will be glad to hear I have found the prose version of the *Orchard-Pits*. I could not get again to my writing till Sunday last, when in one good day's work I finished the "Eden Bower" – 49 Stanzas and not a superfluous word. It is the best of all my doings, as Swinburne pronounced of the early stanzas, the rest not being written when I saw him a few days ago. He also greatly liked "Troy Town" & the sonnets. Morris heard & liked what I had then written, and Brown last night was roused to enthusiasm by the *Eden*. It is really too long to copy, but I shall print it immediately & then send it you. Will you make my peace with Miss Boyd as to the promise of M.S. I hope she will kindly wait for Lilith's amiable outpourings in print. I read it at home last night. Maggie ran away at the first line, and Christina evaporated after a few stanzas, finding that the Oblong Blur became more and more smudgy as it proceeded. William radiated. I have written 2 or 3 sonnets besides. I shall now go ahead soon at the *Orchard-Pits*. A day or two after my return I got much better. The feverish state I was in seems to have subsided and I sleep better.[3] I have been to John Marshall and am taking Quinine. I have not yet got to painting. Things to do thicken round me, and much as I should enjoy a second jaunt to Penkill, I fear the distance denies it to me. Moreover I have got a letter from Leyland pressing a promise of mine to go to Speke if possible, & if I go anywhere I suppose I must find my way there for a few days. It is possible Howell may be going. What a sad hearing it is that the beautiful cave is shorn of its roof! I wonder if it could be replaced on a more solid system. I think of Penkill as the abode of peace and poetic opportunities. It is not only delightful to inhabit but it is wonderful what delightful memories one retains of such peaceful and thoughtful hours.

    I shall see about the pots as soon as possible, but it requires some burrowing to realize what exists. I should like to be at their installation, but this may hardly come to pass.

    Swinburne, when I saw him three days ago, looked strong and well-set – improved in every way. He is now gone or just going to his father's. His aspect and behaviour were angelic. He told me of a poem of 150 stanzas (or indeed I think lines only) which he has written on a subject from Boccaccio, lending itself to charming sentiment, and which he thinks a success, as I judged from what he told me. I was very glad to hear of his having done something not in the Liberty-flibberty-gibberty style of which I confess myself weary, though he puts such wonderful work into it.[4]

    I heard 2 of Morris's new poems for the "Paradise": – viz: "The Death of Paris," and "Acontius & Cydippe." The first has a fine quality & fine passages, but is not among his great successes, and is so careless in structure that he has actually never once mentioned Œnone by name or given any clue to her former relation to Paris. I advised him to supply this absolute necessity & I think he will do so; but the grip of the thing will always be a little loose to my mind. The "Acontius" is certainly I think the least good he has done, & contains a vast amount of mere level writing, though the close is fine. It suffers a good deal too by having just at the commencement a song so exquisitely beautiful that what follows seems doubly flat. For my own part I should keep the song & throw the poem away. However, if these are not of his best, the volume will contain the Icelandic story which is his masterpiece. He read me also several very beautiful lyrics he has done.

Thanks for your trouble with my proofs. You know I am not unamenable to suggestions & have profited materially by several of yours; but here I cannot agree in any instance. I saw William last night but had no time to ask his views. I shall do so this evening as he is dining with me. By the bye, I forgot to say that Swinburne seems to be devoured with fervour for the despised & rejected "Mrs. Holmes Grey," and actually talks of removing its ennobling influence from an unworthy nation by translating it himself into French![5]

The proposal as to the *Song of the Bower* had I believe crossed my own mind, but it would be a great loss of melody & wd not do on the equally important ground that of course *sad* it would be & *not* glad. The italics in *Blessed Damozel* I set no great store by, but on the whole they seem to me to elucidate the scheme of the poem. The lines you object to in the "Sea-Limit" are rather favorites with me, though I know them to be a little peculiar. About this I did ask Wm last night, & he said he thought them the chief motive for including these stanzas!

The objection to "ail" in *Dennis Shand* I do not see. Certainly the signification of the word has nothing to do with being "able to complain." It simply means to "sicken" or one might say "waste away." I am sure it might be found applied in much the same sense, if not in old poetry, in such poets as Coleridge, Scott, &c, – perhaps rather as regards waning light than waning shadow; but I confess it appears to me happily expressive of the gradual pining and weakening of shadows as the dawn comes on. Otherwise "fail" might do instead, without resorting to what seems the most astounding suggestion of making my poor damsels "stale"! Really, Scotus, can you not see the universal grin that such a word would communicate to every studious mug that bent over my poetic page?

Your suggestion of "Ann you once adored" is so good and ingenious an one that I should be only too glad to adopt it if I did not happen to put a special value on the passage as it stands. I don't wish the lady to be over-refined at all, though indeed even high-minded dames used to claw their maids' faces in those days I fancy. Besides she afterwards uses this very illness of the unlucky Ann as a screen to new proceedings, which I think one of the best touches in the ballad which after all only aims at being amusing – and perhaps just a little improper. *Dennis Shand* was written at much the same time as the *Blessed Damozel, My Sister's Sleep* &c. & I confess I look back to it as an encouraging landmark of my mental condition in those early days, which I should find otherwise to have been discouragingly angelic.

However I hope to write some better things now, though I would not print one line, old or new, that I did not think worthy to stand by the rest as finished art.

What a jolly grotesque Miss Boyd has made of the toads & their stools, to which she has superadded umbrellas to match. Will you give her my best of love and believe me

Affectionately yours
D. G. Rossetti

P.S. Ruskin called the other day, & seemed to tend towards a grand proposal of banding together for the regeneration of the world. I told him at once that any individual *I* came near was sure to be the worse for it. You should have seen him waving his hand and soul towards his forlorn species, while the Wombat burrowed between his coat and waistcoat.[6]

---

1. FMB wrote a number of sonnets between 1869 & 1871, several of them for Marie Spartali's pictures (see Newman & Watkinson 151–56).
2. Probably Mary Margaret Heaton's *The History of the Life of Albert Dürer* (Macmillan, 1870).
3. "Gabriel returned to Chelsea yesterday, and I saw him this evening. He looks to me well enough; but says he has been very weak, perspiring excessively, losing sleep, and that his health is breaking up" (WMR's MS diary, 21 Sep).
4. Starting in 1858, ACS worked at translating the Decameron into verse, but he published only "The Two Dreams" in *Poems and Ballads* (1866). He also intended to complete a Triameron of stories after Boccaccio, part of which was privately published in 1909 (T. J. Wise, *A Swinburne Library* [privately printed, 1925]: 183–84).
5. ACS also wrote to WMR proposing such a translation (Lang 2: 307), but it was never done.
6. This visit, which WMR dates 25 Sep (*RP* 408), was probably the last time DGR saw JR.

69.166 TO MURRAY MARKS

MS: Fitzwilliam. Date: P/M.

Friday [1 October 1869]

Dear Marks

I want to be sending some pots to Scotland and of course they must be very carefully packed. Could you lend me Robert tomorrow (being Saturday) or else Monday or Tuesday? If daytime was impracticable, could he come in the evening? I suppose even Sunday would suit *me*, only I have a model coming, but this wd probably not interfere. I will buy two of those 4 little upright pots you showed me at £1 each.

If all are not six marked please send 2 that are. If none are, send the 2 best. Robert can bring them. He would have to bring a good sized packing case for which I would either pay you cost or hire as you liked. *Suppose you dine with me Sunday at 7.*

I should be greatly obliged if you would look in at Bartlett and see that he is not doing *too much* to that sofa. All it needs is reviving the black and completing the patterns in gold *where erased*.[1]

Ever yours
DGRossetti

P.S. I suppose you haven't another cover like the one I took which suits exactly. I'd buy a small pot with it if necessary.

---

[1] For the sofa being refurbished, see **42** & **124**.

69.167 TO ALICE BOYD
MS: NLS.

Saturday [2 October 1869]
16 Cheyne Walk
Chelsea

Dear Miss Boyd

I am today sending to Marks the pots which he will pack carefully & forward to Penkill. If he can get them off today he will do so, – if not, they will go on Monday. They are as follows: –

Imprimis

4 large Pots of a bold and rather rough dragon & flower pattern. Of these 2 are perfect with original lids – 1 perfect with a lid not original & which does not quite fit, and the fourth smashed and mended, but plausible on one side, and without lid. I think this set very likely to look extremely fine on the mantelpiece, from its bold style. The odd lid I have sent in case you determined to discard the mended pot, in which case one of the remaining three could form a centre with this lid which differs from the others. But my own opinion is that your best plan would be to get wooden lids made for this pot & the mended one, to the exact form of the 2 original lids, after which the skillful hand of W.B. would paint them up in an hour (with plenty of varnish to match the glaze) so as really to be unnoticeable. The set would then look quite imposing: and in that case I would ask W. B. to bring me back the odd lid which might prove useful.

Item: 2 large spell-pots with dragons & monsters on them. Both of these have been mended all over but will look well framing corners. i.e. this shape

Item: Two small pots this shape

very good & perfect.

Item: Two small pots this shape

very good and perfect, but the lids, though exactly right when looked at from outside, do not quite fit inside – that is, the inner rim is too small & liable to slip about. But they are exactly the right *kind* of lid.

Item: A bottle which is a good one but has had the neck broken short

Saturday [2 October 1869]

& finished at the mouth with some black wax. But it is a good piece for all that.

Item: 3 bowls, one larger than the 2 others.

Item: 12 plates, only one or two of which I think are at all cracked. I sent these as it strikes me they would look very well if it were possible to fix them by a rail or some means in the spaces between pots, as thus: –

but I do not feel sure how far this might prove practicable.

One plate will awake remorse in your bosom, as it represents a poor bunny sitting up on end with an arrow stuck in him and the most comic expression of countenance, while another bunny waddles towards him with a helpful aspect, and two hard-hearted persons on horseback seem lost in astonishment at having hit him. Another plate is very curious as being a sort of Chinese Annunciation.

When you see the pots you will perceive that their nature makes no distressing claim on your gratitude, at the same time that I think few things could have looked more effective with the large forms of the fireplace.

By the bye the china will need some cleaning. I mean merely washing – but as I know the tastes of W. B. & the leisure of Penkill I have left this to his care. I fancy I have sent as many pieces as will fill the space, the largest pot being a good size.

I have no particular news since last writing to Scotus, as I have spent a day or two in cabs with Howell on some matters of business. Thus I have done little or no writing & have not got to my painting yet.

The Wombat[1] joins in affectionate regards and I am

ever yours
D G Rossetti

P.S. I was forgetting to mention a matter of interest. I was telling Topsy that you and I had started in a quite passing way a notion of your joining with Janey's sister in her schemes of taking to embroidery & decorative work as a business. He seemed to think it very feasible if you cared to do so, and declared that he should be delighted to continue his assistance (as to suggestions & touting) to the firm as he does to Bessie; and also thought that a partnership might please her and forward her views. However I have thought it better to say nothing to her until I had again spoken to you and you had considered the matter further.

---

[1] See **152**.

69.168 TO WILLIAM MICHAEL ROSSETTI

MS: BL. Excerpt: *FL* 220. Published: DW 878.

Sunday [3 October 1869]

Dear W

Will you dine here Thursday? I hope so. Nettleship & Brown are coming – also Tebbs who wants to bring some friend of his – so I haven't asked Top & Ned this time to meet Nettleship as I mean to do so soon – I hope you will manage to come.

I suppose you have the proofs. I have improved a good many lines in the Eden since seeing it in print. Also done other things to the proofs.

I think I have hit the mark now in that line of *Nuptial Sleep*: –

Fawned on each other where they lay apart.

Your
Gabriel

69.169 TO ALICE BOYD

MS: NLS.

Sunday [3 October 1869]
16 Cheyne Walk
Chelsea

Dear Miss Boyd

I send the first proof of my *Eden*, on which I have noted a few corrections and alterations. Others that are merely typographical I have not noted. I hope you will like it as well as Lilith *can* be liked, except by the Sarpint. It ought to come first, but it is such an appalling subject that I've put it second. I believe it is my best one yet. Shall be very thankful for any opinions from you and Scotus.

I'm getting under way with my poem on Lancelot & the Sancgrail[1] but preparatory construction always takes up the most of my time, & I have had little to spare this past week.

The complete set of proofs in their last state I do not send, as several things need further correction; but you shall have them in due course. When do you expect to return to London?

Most sincerely yours
D G Rossetti

P.S. It is very annoying that my navvy (did I tell you that I had found a navvy who suited for my calf picture?) has disappointed me today after promising to come.[2] Now I am all aground again, but shall try and go on now, having made up my mind to it.

[1] "God's Graal," an Arthurian verse narrative begun in 1858 and projected as a late addition to *Poems*, remained unfinished (see **220**). A 13–line fragment appeared in *Works* (239).
[2] *Found* (S.64) remained unfinished at DGR's death. "Navvy" (navigator) is slang for "labourer"; the male figure in the painting is a farm worker on his way to market to sell his calf.

69.170 TO CHARLES AUGUSTUS HOWELL
MS: Texas.

Sunday [3 October 1869]

My dear Howell

I'm sorry I shan't be able to bring the proof sheets to Holland Park on Wednesday. They are gone to the printers for final revision, & as this is a vexed process with me, I am sure they will not be back in time, being a biggish squad now.

Give Kitty my biggest love for her little one, in hopes the male measure may thus approach the female.

Your affec:
D Gabriel R

69.171 TO FREDERICK JAMES FURNIVALL
MS: Huntington.

16 Cheyne Walk
4 Oct. [1869]

My dear Furnivall

Many thanks for your information & enclosures and for sending on my note to Ward.

I sent at once for the "Harrowing" but it seems it has long been out of print. I must try & see a copy somehow. Your "Saint Graal" I once possessed, but it has fallen a prey to the borrowers. I must join their tribe, & shall find no difficulty in victimizing some other possessor in our circle.[1]

With thanks

Ever yours
D G Rossetti

---

[1] See 62.6n1, **169**, & **193**.

69.172 TO FREDERICK RICHARD LEYLAND

MS: LC. Published: Fennell 25.

5 Oct. 1869
16 Cheyne Walk
Chelsea

My dear Leyland

I have been back a fortnight from Ayrshire where I was far from well, & whence I had to return rather unexpectedly. Since coming back I have found myself so walled up with things to attend to, that I really could not answer your kind letter with any certainty before this. All that I can say now is that I still think it possible I may manage to reach you before all fine weather vanishes, and that I shall be only too glad if this proves the case; but I am too hampered just at this moment to feel certain about it.

I never got anywhere in Scotland except to my primary bourne at Penkill, and did not seem at the time certainly to be benefiting, but have felt somewhat better since my return.

I heard Jemmy's account of the doings during his stay at Speke, and of Fred's determination to pay that Howell eventually in his own coin, on which I believe the image and superscription (which have puzzled many) are those of Ananias.[*]

If I don't after all see you at Speke, I suppose it will not be very long before London claims a visit from you on one account or another. I was delighted to hear from Whistler how completely set up you now are in health. I wish I could say the same of myself.

With kindest remembrances to all yours

I am yours affectionately
DG Rossetti

---

[*] Ananias was a man who was struck dead for lying (Acts 5: 1–5).

69.173 TO FORD MADOX BROWN

MS: UBC. Published: DW 879. Date: WMR.

Wednesday [6 October 1869]

Dear Brown

Wednesday will suit me well – I suppose 8 o'clock. When I see you tomorrow you can tell me whether togs are to be a feature.

Ever yours
DG Rossetti

69.174 TO J. R. THURSFIELD[1]

MS: Texas.

Wednesday [6 October 1869]
16 Cheyne Walk
Chelsea

My dear Sir

I shall be happy to see you tomorrow (Thursday) between 4 & 5, & am only sorry you should be put to so much trouble.

Yours faithfully
D G Rossetti

J R Thursfield Esq

---

[1] A Fellow of Jesus College, and chairman of a committee appointed to enquire into the matter of the Oxford Union Murals (see Kelvin 95).

69.175 TO THOMAS GORDON HAKE[1]

MS: BL. Published: DW 881.

8th October/1869
16 Cheyne Walk
Chelsea

My dear Sir

Many thanks beforehand for the great pleasure I shall derive now from a consecutive and careful reading of the "Valdarno" trilogy. In looking again at the first and last sentences, I feel again the same spiritual removal and elevation which I remember from of old.

I have read and partly re-read the first 50 pages of the "World's Epitaph" –

i.e. in its original arrangement in the copy for which I have to thank you. It seems to me that the new arrangement indicated in the other copy you have so kindly sent is decidedly a great gain, as the choral poem makes the reader more distinctly feel at once the harmony between the work and its title; while the admirable "Old Souls" appears, as far as I can yet judge, to make a perfect climax.

Of the nature of your poetry I will only say at present that the quality of complete structure in Art is more touching and pathetic to me always than even the emotional appeal of the subject matter; and I cannot express to you the sense of sympathy and unity with which I blend myself with you as I read. Of the final impression of the work as a whole I shall be able to speak, I hope, when I see you on Sunday. Your preface is completely beautiful and expressive.

Before I see you again, let me thank you more clearly than I could do on Tuesday for having permitted me to know one whose personal acquaintance I still strongly desired, and regarding whose work I felt an unaltered interest and curiosity.

I am, my dear Sir,

Most truly yours,
D. G. Rossetti

Dr. Hake

1 DGR first met TGH when he called at 16CW on 5 Oct; however, as he tells WBS in **177**, and TGH confirms in *Memoirs of Eighty Years* ([Bentley,1892]: 206), he had first written to TGH in the early 1850s relative to his *Valdarno*. The pair became fast friends until DGR's break with GGH in 1877. See **185** & *RP* 410 and, for TGH's acknowledgement of this letter with WMR's explanatory headnote, *RP* 470–71.

69.176 TO ALICIA MARGARET LOSH

MS: Princeton. Published: *TR* 93–94; DW 880.

8th Oct. 1869
16 Cheyne Walk Chelsea

My dear Miss Losh

I have got the proofs now in a state to which I shall not be adding for at any rate some weeks to come, & so I send them you with this by book post. You will see that "Eden Bower," which I began at Ravenside, is among them. Should it happen (which is improbable) that any one, not belonging to your immediate family, wished to borrow the poems, I would be obliged if you would refrain from lending them. I am only giving away 3 copies (yours, one to Miss Boyd, and another,¹) and have now so made up my mind to publish a volume next spring, that I shall not, as I at first intended, be having any more copies printed for private circulation. I find that with the things I am going to write now, and those I shall still be able to recover from old rough copies, I shall have a volume of about 400 pages ready in the Spring if all goes well.

I have been in better health since returning to town, and find all friends well. Topsy goes on writing at a furious rate, but the Second Volume of the Earthly Paradise will not I believe appear till December, & there is to be yet another volume after that.

I sent some blue pots to Penkill the other day. Scotus is to construct a shelf projecting all round the sloping hood of the dining room fireplace, & the blue pots are to figure on it. The edge of the shelf will not project further than the furthest projection of the hood, so that people's brainpans will not be more in danger than now.

I hope you go on improving and that all yours are well, and with kindest regards

most sincerely yours
D G Rossetti

[1] JM also received proof copies of *Poems*.

69.177 TO WILLIAM BELL SCOTT
MS: Princeton.

9th Oct./1869
16 Cheyne Walk
Chelsea

My dearest Scotus

The news of Penkill is fragrant in London and I am truly glad you have got your landscape done and well done, and that the dear old cave is all right again. That matter of the noises is more mysterious than ever now that a Holy Father gets mixed up with it. It will soon be worthy of the Mysteries of Udolpho.¹

About Leathart, I quite agree with you, and wish extremely to be all square with him. Graham is away (and possibly in dudgeon about my swindling him of the promised visit) so I don't want to be writing him, i.e. *again*. I did write about the visit. If I really get on with the picture before I see him, all will then go smoothly, but otherwise I may probably be very glad to avail myself of your friendly offer for a short date. You perhaps remember the plan I had of writing to L. (when paid off) offering him the refusal of the picture at the price offered by Graham. You thought this feasible, but Brown, to whom I mentioned it, considered L. might be seriously irritated by it. So I think my best plan will be, before the picture gets finished, to send L. a really handsome picture as a bonus, to represent the "work not of less value than 50 gs" which I proposed to paint him as interest on the money advanced. If I make it obviously worth, at my present prices, 100 or 150 I think he ought not to bear me a grudge. I quite agree with you that he is a collector of a true order, & moreover he is no bad friend.

I shall be extremely curious to see your ballad. If you get it done much before you leave Penkill, and can spare the MS. (as I judge it will be too long to copy) perhaps you will send it me to read.

I am delighted that you both like "Eden Bower," which I think hits the mark as to character. In the line "Pry the *earth's* will" &c. I meant to say pretty much what you wish to have said, but I think this form says it more philosophically & comprehensively than another. To wit: – the Earth (or Powers of the Earth Earthy) having a new creature, finds it necessary to provide him with a mate, and moulds one from a beautiful form already existing but proves unable to provide the bride with a human soul. God is thus induced to substitute a completely human wife. It seems to me this is the best way to put it, particularly as I presume the King-Snake to whom Lilith is speaking may be looked upon as being presumably Old Nick himself.

About "jewelled" I do not quite seize your objection. Do you object to it absolutely as an English word? Or do you think it inapplicable to the radiant snake-beauty? Or do you mean that Lilith could not well draw a comparison from the jewel-decked daughters of earth before they had even worn jewels? On the first count, I confess I could not agree with you, nor on the second. The third would be debatable, and I rejected several good ideas in the imagery of the poem on the same grounds; but here the suggestion seems so vague and remote that I think it admissible. I am glad I have an upholder in Miss Boyd as I like the line. I have cut "gemmed" out of another line since the last proofs to avoid repetition of the epithet.

Ann Hathaway's cottage is a temptation, but I cannot doubt for a moment that the Shakspere people will step in, nor does the writer of the letter seem to know for certain that they have not yet done so. However I shd really like to run down to the neighbourhood and see.

The Howell business is concluded and successful. I have not the thing yet, as it is in someone's hands for necessary arrangements. It, and all with it, was found quite perfect.

Some days ago I had a visit which gave me great satisfaction & I hope may lead to what is rare indeed after 40 – a new valued friendship. I was talking to you lately of some very remarkable romances of a psychological kind which appeared in "Ainsworth's Magazine" (!) and continued for several years between 1850 & 1854. They formed a trilogy: –

I   Valdarno; or the Ordeal of Art-Worship.
II St Veronica; or the Ordeal of Fire.
III Velthinas; or the Ordeal of Sacrifice.

I remember that just about the time I first visited you at Newcastle I wrote a letter to Ainsworth asking for the author's name and received a reply *from* the author who proved to be one Hake residing at Bury St. Edmunds. I had not then completely read the works, and this being deferred caused me to defer answering his letter – indeed I never either finished reading the works (which had to be read in coffee-shops where I took my meals) or answered the letter at all. This I have always regretted, and never heard of him again from that day to this. On Tuesday last a card – Dr. Hake, Roehampton – was brought up to me. This proved to be the man (a retired physician), a tall thin man of sixty, with nothing in the least old about him but his white hair. We fraternized speedily and he said he wished to ask my advice (living as he did out of the literary world) as to the best steps to take in publishing a book of poems, the expenses of which he was willing to meet. I am to dine with him on Sunday and go into the question. Meanwhile he has lent me his romances (cut out of the Magazines) and has given me a privately printed little volume of poetry called the "World's Epitaph," full of fine things, but very moral and even Christian. However it is structurally and artistically admirable, though a little tough; and on looking again at the romances they seem to deserve almost if not perhaps even quite, the name of masterpieces. I shall take the greatest interest in seeing all he has done, & hope to make a friend of him; as he appears to be a man of true dignity and modesty, equal to either fortune, though of course with a quiet confidence in himself. I hope I shall be able to bring you and him together for I believe you would sympathise with him. He seems very moony on recent people and things.
　With love to Miss Boyd

Affectionately yours
D Gabriel R.

P.S. Janey seems better at Hampstead – looks much improved – and she and Top are to dine with me today & stay tomorrow.
P.S. I should mention as to L. that at *this moment* I am stumped up as to tin but trust to be soon all right again.

¹ WBS & AB claimed to have heard DGR's voice reading his poems upstairs at Penkill on the evening following his departure for London; this phenomenon was confirmed by a visiting clergyman (*AN* 2: 117–18). *The Mysteries of Udolpho* (1794) was a Gothic novel by Ann Radcliffe.

69.178 TO HENRY VIRTUE TEBBS

MS: Texas.

9th Oct,/1869

16 *Cheyne Walk*

Chelsea

My dear Tebbs

I have long wished and intended to make a drawing of your wife, who you know is even an older friend of mine than yourself. If she could spare the time at present, I would write again in the course of a week or two to fix a day, and should beg your acceptance of the drawing when finished.¹

Ever yours truly

DG Rossetti

¹ DGR did a crayon portrait of Mrs Tebbs (S.524), dated 1870, as a gift to his old friend HVT, brother-in-law to JPS & TS, for his part in facilitating the legal aspects of the exhumation. See **183**.

69.179 TO FORD MADOX BROWN

MS: Ashmolean. Published: DW 882. Date: WMR.

Sunday [10 October 1869]

Dear Brown

Thanks for the parcel.

Togs or no togs on Wednesday? Give it a name.

Yours

DG R

If I don't hear I won't tog but am as willing as Barkis* if necessary.

* 'Barkis is willin'' is a comic tag repeated by that character in Dickens's *David Copperfield* to signify his eagerness to marry Peggotty.

69.180 TO CHARLES AUGUSTUS HOWELL
MS: Princeton. Published: DW 888.

Tuesday [12 October 1869]

My dear Howell

I sent the cheque today to Dr. Williams.¹ Let me have the receipted bill for the pictures, made out to myself.

Ever yours
D G R

---

[1] The disinterment occurred on 5 Oct; DGR's cheque was for payment to Dr. Llewellyn Williams of Kennington for disinfecting the pages of the retrieved MSS.

69.181 TO WILLIAM MICHAEL ROSSETTI
MS: BL. Excerpt: *FL* 220–21; *PRT* 84. Published: *ALC* 8: 177–78; Troxell, *Colophon* 15 (1933); DW 883.

13 Oct 1869

16 Cheyne Walk

My dear William

I wished last night to speak to you on a subject which however I find it necessary to put in writing. I am very anxious to know your view of it and to remind you beforehand that no mistrust or unbrotherly feeling could possibly have caused my silence till now.

Various friends have long hinted from time to time at the possibility of recovering my lost M.S.S. and when I was in Scotland last year Scott particularly referred to it. Some months ago Howell of his own accord entered on the matter and offered to take all the execution of it on himself. This for some time I still hung back from accepting, but eventually I yielded, and the thing was done, after some obstacles, on Wednesday or Thursday last, I forget which. An order had first to be obtained from the Home Secretary, who strangely enough is an old and rather intimate acquaintance of my own – H.A. Bruce. The principal difficulty arising was the impossibility of mentioning so painful a matter to our mother, the owner of the grave, and so obtaining her authority. But on the other hand this special coffin was of course my sole property; and Bruce, after considering the matter, came to the conclusion that this difficulty could under the circumstances be over-ruled. Had he not thought so, I should have been forced to invent some pretext for changing my wife's place of interment, & so got our mother's authority for opening the grave. But this fortunately did not become necessary, & the thing is done. All in the coffin was found quite perfect, but the book, though not in any way destroyed, is soaked through & through and had to be still further saturated with disinfectants. It is now in the hands of the medical man who was associated with Howell in the disinterment, and who is carefully drying it leaf by leaf.[1] There seems reason to fear that some minor portion is obliterated, but I must hope this may not prove to be the most important part. I shall not I believe be able to see it for at least a week yet.

I trust you will not – but I know you cannot – think that I showed any want of confidence in not breaking this painful matter to you before its issue. It was a service I could not ask you to perform for me, nor do I know anyone except Howell who could well have been entrusted with such a trying task. It was necessary, as we found, that a lawyer should be employed in the matter, to speak to the real nature of the M.S.S., as difficulties were raised to the last by the Cemetery authorities, as to there possibly being papers the removal of which involved a fraud. This service Tebbs rendered me. He therefore is cognizant of the proceedings, and I have told Janey and Scott and Dunn. It has become known to Morris, Jones, and Watts, through Howell – Watts having been spoken to in order to get an introduction to the Home Secretary before I remembered that Bruce now held that office. I have begged Howell to hold his tongue for the future, but if he does not I cannot help it. The only further persons to whom I mean to mention it are Brown & Swinburne.[2] If you see the latter before I do & you care to speak of it, of course I have no objection. To others I shall say at present that I have made the rough copies more available than I hoped; but I suppose the truth must ooze out in time. It is very desirable, as you will think with me, that our family should not know it.[3]

Your affec: brother
D Gabriel R

[1] See **180&n1** & *FLM* 274–75.
[2] See **190** & **191A**: these letters led directly to a close collaboration with ACS on Proof States #12–16 of *Poems*.
[3] WMR's reply is Peattie 169, answered in **183**.

69.182 TO FORD MADOX BROWN

MS: UBC. Excerpt: *RP* 472. Published: DW 884.

Thursday [14 October 1869]

Private

Dear Brown

I have seen Graham today, & I hope I have made it all right about Shields. He had called on S. the other day in Manchester but he was from home. He talked to me about the matter, & the end was that he said he would write at once & fix the commission.¹

I went today to see those M.S.S. at the Doctor's, and I shall be able to have them in a few days. They are in a disappointing state, – the things I have already seem mostly perfect, and there is a great hole right through all the leaves of "Jenny" which was the thing I most wanted. A good deal is lost but I have no doubt the things as they are will enable me with a little re-writing & a good memory & the rough copies I have to re-establish the whole in a perfect state.

Your affec:
Gabriel

¹ See **136** & **140**.

69.183 TO WILLIAM MICHAEL ROSSETTI

MS: UBC. Excerpt: *FL* 221–22; DW 886. Date: WMR.

Friday [15 October 1869]

Dear William

I am glad to hear you are getting better, and very glad you view the matter on which I wrote as I do.

I had not occasion to ask Tebbs's assistance till a late stage of the affair, & he then told me of the conversation he had had with you, or something of it. However, on hearing all the circumstances, he said he had been mistaken in thinking he could have managed things more easily if first applied to. He has behaved in a very friendly way & I mean to do a chalk drawing of his wife.

Yesterday I went out to see the book at the Doctor's house. It will take some days yet to dry, and is in a disappointing but not hopeless state. The poem of "Jenny" which is the one I most wanted, has got a great worm-hole right through every page of it in this proportion,

destroying much but leaving the edges of the lines destroyed; so I think on the whole memory will serve to recover it. Nothing else is quite so bad I think, and some (among which I noted various things I already have of course) quite perfect. I could not examine it much, as the greater part still sticks together. I shall not have it here for some days yet. It has a dreadful smell – partly no doubt the disinfectants – but the doctor says there is nothing dangerous. I do not think it would be any use giving it to an ordinary transcriber, & propose to take the copying in hand myself, probably with Dunn's assistance for the easier parts. I do not know if you wd have time or inclination to assist in so unpleasant a job. If so, you could do some of the more difficult parts while I did others. We could also call in little Murray who I know would come, though he has not yet been told of it. Thus the whole might be done in a day or two & the original burnt. The best wd be to work all together here.

I should have seen you tonight but have promised to dine with Luke Ionides. I almost think the best will be to write Mamma a letter before long on the matter lest it came to her ears otherwise; but I want your opinion.

Your affec: Gabriel

P.S. You know I always meant to dedicate the book to you. This I shall of course still do, failing only one possibility which I suppose must be considered out of the question.

69.184 TO ALICE BOYD
MS: NLS.

Friday/15 Oct/1869
16 Cheyne Walk
Chelsea

Dear Miss Boyd

You will need the sight of some letters of some sort lying ready to greet you on your return to Penkill, so I write, though with little to say, to thank you for so kindly feeding my curiosity about the effect of the pots, with the aid of W. B.'s dashing pencil. The effect is artistic, and I may add Bacchic, in the highest degree. The brackets seem admirably managed, and I cannot but hope that the bunny is mutely ejaculating "Thou art the woman" from one of the plates which are in evidence. I see your eyes seem to hesitate (in the sketch) between that direction and the consolations at hand to stifle the voice of conscience. I judge from the look of the centre big pot that the odd lid has been rejected, which is probably the better plan, and a plate substituted, surmounted by the bottle with the black rim. I am sorry I omitted to send a pretty Chinese carved ebony lid which I believe fits this bottle and improves its appearance. Also I regretted much to notice the other day 2 large square canisters which I could perfectly have spared & which would make better corner pieces, for proportion with the large pots, than the 2 spill-pots which could then hide their scars round the corners. These however I can bring down next autumn. I hope there was no monstrous charge made for carriage. To tell you the truth, I forgot, when consigning the things to Marks for packing, to tell him to defray this if feasible beforehand.[1]

I shall see Scotus then on Monday or Tuesday. You do not say how soon you mean to follow him to town. What a lot of bother you seem to have gone through for the little excursion you have been having! I have seen Leyland and Graham and made my peace with them for swindling them of promised visits.

I have found it impracticable, even up to now, to get seriously to work again through various interruptions, but shall be in the thick of everything soon I suppose and more than ever unable to stir. Scotus said something of perhaps returning with Leathart to Penkill, but I suppose this has been given up.

Friends much as usual. Bruno still smiles at 5-30 A.M. (but with a more puzzling dental effect) & Topsy still strikes the *lyre*, – I do not mean that he has had a fight with Howell, whose habits are also unaltered.

Most truly yours,
D.G Rossetti

I sent the printed sheets to Miss Losh, but have not heard. I hope she is not laid up.

[1] See **166** & **167**.

69.185 TO THOMAS GORDON HAKE

MS: BL. Published: DW 889.

18 Oct 1869

16 Cheyne Walk/Chelsea

My dear Dr. Hake

I have now read "Madeline" through with great care and great pleasure. The form is surprisingly & most gratifyingly perfect throughout, while there are continual passages both of that sudden breathless quality in thought peculiar to your writing, and of the happiest mixture of familiar with delicately expressive phraseology. Thus far for the form which seems to me as faultless as it can well be. Only a few verbal inversions have struck me here & there which I have marked in pencil in case you thought them worth reconsidering.

On the other hand, the matter of the poem appears to me so difficult to follow to the ordinary mind that I fear no very wide acceptance could be hoped for it, though in some special circles the high ideal nature of the work would of course be duly felt and never forgotten. I must confess that even to myself the subject seems most intricate & its scheme singularly brought together. Moreover the pellucid simplicity and unfailing sweetness of the verse itself makes the obstacles presented by the narrative still more puzzling to the reader, as he cannot understand how such complete clearness & flow of structural medium should still leave the thing said difficult to get at. Some of our modern poets – and some great ones – are both jagged outside and tangled inside: but your outside is such a translucent web that one can hardly believe or bear with one's senses which fail to possess themselves clearly at all times of the thing shown through it.

I am sure you would wish me to say exactly what I think in all respects regarding your work, and that you will fully understand with what entire absence of judicial assumption I venture to do so.

It seems to me, then, that the two elaborate ideal introductions, first the Muses and afterwards Petrarch & Laura, leading up to a story of seduction & revenge which has some real elements in it that seem to conflict to a certain extent with the figurative ones, renders the clue to the point of view taken extremely difficult to catch. I speak after a first reading only, though a careful one, and think it perhaps better to do so before re-reading the work throughout, as first impressions are all-important in poetry. I cannot at this moment recall how far the prelude relating to the *Muses* is *necessary* at all to the scheme of the work. It seems to me that at any rate it should be absolutely detached from the rest so as to show itself as a prelude only.

The point of view taken regarding Petrarch & Laura seems to me certainly most baffling to the intelligence. The mixture of real historical personages with events which in ordinary phraseology must be termed magical ones, and the strange and apparently arbitrary adoption of such an identity as Laura's where only a beneficent spirit of some sort was needed – nay the very name Laura which is so purely a human one, and which in this instance was undoubtedly borne by a human lady to whom Petrarch's homage has generally been imputed – seem to me to pile up difficulties unnecessarily as regards any gain to the main theme. Again, the name of Thor, immediately suggesting Norse mythology, is unfortunate, and at its first introduction the bearer is not even called the *Lord of* Thor. Without in the least suggesting the possibility of any change in the scheme of the poem, I may say generally (& chiefly to elucidate my meaning) that it would appear to me that the introduction of some recognized magician of a high order – for instance, Virgil, as invested with this character by mediæval fancy – and a woman-spirit of consolation acting under his beneficent spells – would have afforded a more easily fitting framework to the narrative. Such a personality as Petrarch's seems to need a special reason – one which no other would serve so well – for its adoption.

Madeline must I suppose be looked upon chiefly as working out her revenge by the authority of heavenly justice. Still, the act is spoken of in the poem so frequently as crime, that one feels surprised at the end to find it immediately followed by her unopposed translation to Heaven. This seems to me perhaps worth considering, as regards the removal of any words seeming to cast a stigma upon her uncontrollable impulse. The birth of the child you no doubt mean to treat in a shadowy way, but it would certainly I think be liable to escape the general reader & leave the end difficult of comprehension. Still I am not sure that any alteration seems to me desirable here.

Finally, I little doubt that much of what I say (in this hurried letter) may have already suggested itself to you and appeared to you to be met by counter-arguments which have not occurred to me.

From such consideration and inquiry as I have been able to make, I fear there would not be any great likelihood of a publisher undertaking the Poems on his own responsibility. Macmillan I fancy would be the best man to try first. I know him and he is (mentally) decidedly superior to the run of his brethren. I have been told that Bell & Daldy and Strahan & Co. would also be worth trying. The best plan I should think would be to apply to these in the above order (failing the first or second) with a proposal of joint profits after the publisher has repaid the expenses which he should defray. If such proposal failed in each instance, it would then remain to consider which firm was the most likely to do the work justice if printed at your own expense. Of course there is no doubt that any would take it on these terms.

I have not yet had time to proceed with *Valdarno* which I am very anxious to read through again at once & shall certainly have done so before very long, but have just now been a good deal preoccupied. My own opinion is most decidedly that it is of great importance to your success that this work & the poems should appear simultaneously.

All negotiation with publishers I shall esteem it a privilege to take on myself if you will allow me. I will hope that you will accept in turn an invitation to dine with me almost immediately, as soon as I can propose a convenient day, and we might then look at "Madeline" together if you liked.[1]

With kind remembrances to your sons

I am ever yours truly D. G Rossetti

---

[1] See **175n1**. TGH's *Madeline, with Other Poems and Parables* (Chapman & Hall) was published in 1871 and reviewed by DGR in the *Academy* for 1 Feb (*Works* 621–27). For TGH's response to this letter, see DW, pp. 757–58.

69.186 TO ALICIA MARGARET LOSH

MS: Princeton. Published: *TR* 95–97; DW 890.

> 19 Oct 1869
> 16 Cheyne Walk
> Chelsea

My dear Miss Losh

I feared the cause of my not hearing from you till today – knowing as I do your kind punctuality in writing (though of course in this instance there was no call for an answer at once) – and am most sorry to hear how unwell you have been again. Still, there is the encouragement of finding that your present letter is not invalided either in matter or manner. I really feel guilty in having sent you a means of perhaps trying your eyes prematurely, knowing as I do (and am so glad to do) the interest you take in my verses.

I enclose you a sketch sent me by W.B. of the arrangement of the Blue Pots at Penkill. Miss Boyd gives a glowing account of their effect. You will observe Miss Boyd and easily supply the opposite figure of Scotus in the act of sketching. The wine of the country, as proper to the hour inscribed in the corner, is not forgotten. In the embrasure of the window are the two sacred vessels full of sea-water, one containing a fish of a mystic order caught at Girvan by Miss B. & Christina in a hair-net, and the other a small but portentous crab, a perfect "pieuvre" of voracity, obtained I believe on the same occasion. Considering that I have several hundred pieces of blue still left, you will think with me that these few were not ill bestowed for the embellishment of Penkill, particularly when the triumphant result is apparent. Miss Boyd, as you perhaps know, has been staying for a few days with an aunt at some place with a name something like Ryndeggan(?) but is now I believe back at Penkill. She appears to have had fearful weather in travelling. To-day, as I write, Cheyne Walk might be Black Gang Chine for the riotous winds that possess and belabour it.[1] Ravenside doubtless fares the same.

I should myself have had the Poems bound before sending them to you, were it not that they form only a portion of what will be in print before I hope very long. A good deal will now be added shortly (being old poems recovered from rough copies), and more yet remains to be composed which is brewing in my head and partly sketched out on paper. I hope, but am not certain, that I may be ready with all I wish to include by next spring. Whenever I *am* ready I shall publish immediately, and feel at present just in the mood to sit down & do nothing but write till all is got together and this poetic question disposed of for the present. However, this may not be. I must not neglect my painting and am even now putting in hand two works of more extended subject than the works I have lately done. When I publish poetry, I may very possibly take a fancy to exhibit some pictures about the same time.

I am glad you were not disappointed with the "Eden" poem, of which Ravenside saw the natal hour. The "Nineveh" I reckon on as destined probably to be the most generally popular thing in the book. I do not regard it with indifference myself, but am inclined to give the preference to the more emotional order of subject. The "Blessed Damozel" and a few others will also I think please pretty generally, but I am well aware that the greater proportion of my poetry is suited only to distinctly poetic readers. To this class belong what I think perhaps the most of myself – that is, the Sonnets; and none more than the one you mention, called *A Superscription*. This is decidedly (painful as it is) a favorite of my own. Nothing I ever wrote was more the result of strong feeling, as you may perhaps think traceable in it. There are a good many new Sonnets in these sheets, and some which I hope may please you. The "Farewell to the Glen" towards the end, I wrote the day before I left Penkill. On reading it over at home I thought it very dismal but still it would have been a pity to exclude it.

I believe Scott must have returned to London yesterday, but do not as yet know when Miss Boyd is expected. When are *you* coming? Do not on any account think of answering this or any other question at present (unless to the above you can say *At once*) but pray observe entirely the best means to avoid a fresh attack of illness.

Will you remember me most kindly to all yours, and believe me

Yours affectionately
D G Rossetti

---

[1] Black Gang Chine is a valley in the Isle of Wight.

69.187 TO FREDERIC JAMES SHIELDS

MS: Durham. Published: DW 1012.

Wednesday [20 October 1869]

My dear Shields

You will be glad to know Mr. Sidney Colvin[1] who brings you this – all the more if you already know some of his writings on the art of the day. You will I am sure set him on the scent of whatever he had better see in Manchester, and first of all show him your own work.

Your affecte:
D G Rossetti

---

[1] Sir Sidney Colvin (1845–1927), scholar & critic of the fine arts who held such positions as

Slade Professor of Fine Art at Cambridge, Director of the Fitzwilliam, and Keeper of Prints & Drawings at the BM. He wrote regularly for the *Pall Mall Gazette*, where his review of *Poems* appeared 21 Apr 70. Colvin met DGR through EBJ; he was also on intimate terms with JR and was the mentor and, ultimately, editor of Robert Louis Stevenson. Knighted in 1911, he retired to write a biography of Keats (1917) and a volume of reminiscences, *Memories and Notes* (Arnold, 1921), which contained sections on DGR & EBJ. See also 73.87.1.

69.188 TO WILLIAM MICHAEL ROSSETTI

MS: UBC. Published: *FL* 222; DW 891. Date: WMR.

Wednesday [20 October 1869]

Dear W

Could you dine here Sunday? One or two fellows are coming, & I would esteem it a boon if you could come. I hope you are better. I got the M.S.S. today.

Your
Gabriel

69.189 TO FORD MADOX BROWN

MS (fragment) UBC. Excerpt: *RP* 475; DW 887. The P.S. has been torn away.

Wednesday [20 October 1869]

Dear Brown

Last night before I came out to you, I had left a note here for Dunn (in case he came in) asking him to bring his sketches here by dinner time today. My intention was to ask you to dinner to look at the sketches & consider the question of enlarging the canvas. I thought it doubtful however whether Dunn would happen to come in & get my note at all, & so, finding you with the toothache, never mentioned the matter. He & the sketches *will* be here however, I now find; so if you like, you would oblige me by coming (7-30). But not on any account of course if you really think you ought not.

I got those papers today from the doctor. They are a sad wreck.

Allan waits for your answer.

Ever yours
DG Rossetti

69.190 TO ALGERNON CHARLES SWINBURNE

MS: BL. Published: Wise, *A Romance of Literature*; Compton-Rickett 565; *Portraits and Personalities*: 313; *ALC* 4: 154–55; DW 892.

Chelsea
26 October 1869

My dear Swinburne

I want to tell you something lest you should hear it first from any one else. It is that I have recovered my old book of poems. Friends had long hinted such a possibility to me, but it was only just lately I made up my mind to it. I hope you will think none the worse of my feeling for the memory of one for whom I know you had a true regard. The truth is, that no one so much as herself would have approved of my doing this. Art was the only thing for which she felt very seriously. Had it been possible to her, I should have found the book on my pillow the night she was buried; and could she have opened the grave, no other hand would have been needed.

The thing was done a few weeks ago. Of course I could not have seen to it myself, but Howell (whose pressure on the subject it was that prevailed with me) took the charge of the matter. The book was in a bad state, but I have recovered and copied every word of the poems I wanted. The matter was of a less dreadful nature than might have seemed possible. Indeed, had not I received medical assurance that all in the coffin would probably be perfect (as it proved to be) I should not have had the courage to make the attempt.

You are the only person to whom I have yet told this except my brother, Scott, & Brown. I find Morris & Ned Jones have heard of it through Howell, (else I should have told them too at some moment.) I had rather write you word before I see you. Perhaps after all it was hardly worth while, but the conflicting states of mind one passes through about work are among the things which most need making allowances for.[1]

Your affectionate friend
DG Rossetti

---

[1] See **191A** for ACS' response.

69.190.1 TO FORD MADOX BROWN

MS: Texas.

Wednesday [27 October 1869]

Dear Brown

William, his friend Stillman, & I hope Scott, are to dine here Saturday at 7, and I have asked Inchbold who will come if in town. Will you come too?[1]

Your
Gabriel

P.S. No one else, unless in Inchbold's possible absence an eligible substitute.

---

[1] This dinner was put off until 1 Nov (see **191**), when DGR also invites ACS, not expecting him to attend, and, belatedly, CAH (see **192**).

69.191A ALGERNON CHARLES SWINBURNE TO DANTE GABRIEL ROSSETTI

MS: BL. Published: Wise, *A Romance of Literature*; Lang 2: 317. The words within angled brackets were deleted by ACS.

Holmwood, Henley on Thames

28 October [1869]

My dear Gabriel,[1]

I cannot tell you how rejoiced I am at the news you send me. None could have given me a truer or deeper pleasure. To our nearest friends I would never allow myself to talk on the subject; but none the less I have thought often and bitterly of the loss sustained. I can say to you now, what of course I could never hint before, how often my thoughts have run in the line of yours as to what her own hope and desire in the matter would have been, who loved art so notably and well. Your expression of such a feeling touched a chord in mine which till now had been one only of fruitless and desperate regret. You I know will understand that no strength of words can seem too strong, can even seem adequate, to render my inmost and sincerest sense of the importance of the question whether we are all to be the richer or the poorer by one more treasure of art: of art which always was and is to me the highest, deepest, most precious and serious pleasure to be got out of life. I do think it is matter even more of justice than of humanity to see that men living who feel this, and men to come who will, should not be defrauded of anything of that noble delight which nothing can replace or repurchase. If – which I do not believe – there was ever a great artist who was – not for a time, not in some fit of irritation, disappointment, weariness, or disease, but habitually and positively – reckless or indifferent to the fate and result of his life's work, I regard him in all seriousness as a man who deserved ill of mankind – who was guilty of lèse-humanité. We have a right to the good gifts and growths of nature, to all the light and strength and lasting joy and glory which she gives best in her highest form – art,

> which does <change> mend nature –
> <mend> change it, rather; but
> The art itself is nature.[2]

(This comes of quoting at random, but for once I could not resist; my memory changed Shakespeare certainly without mending!)

You will not be surprised or impelled, I hope, overmuch to chaff if I do rhapsodize to you on this occasion; it is one of too grave delight for me to write otherwise. If there is one additional reason why I think you have done absolutely and admirably right, it is that to which you refer and I alluded above. I am very glad and grateful to you will all my heart for the resolution.

Ever your affectionate,
A. C. Swinburne

---

[1] See **181n2**.
[2] "The Winter's Tale," IV. iv. 95–97.

69.191 TO ALGERNON CHARLES SWINBURNE

MS: BL. Published: *ALC* 7: 15–16; DW 893.

30 Oct 1869
16 Cheyne Walk
Chelsea

My dear Swinburne

Your letter really makes me feel grateful. It is so friendly, and I have undergone so much mental disturbance about this matter.

As your old interest in my poems is an enduring one, I will bother you with a word or two as to my intentions. On looking through the M.S.S. and copying out the 4 poems I needed, viz: – Jenny, A Last Confession, Dante, and the Bride's Chamber, I found that the last would certainly, when finished, be too long for my book, as on its present elaborate scheme it would need to be at least doubled; & I could not have it swamping everything else.

Besides I am working hard at the other three, and could not (with the new work I mean to do) spare time to remodel the crudenesses of the story in this one & bring it to a fit conclusion. So I shall reserve it for careful treatment at another time. In comparing it with the old rough copy I had, I found a good many stanzas omitted from that, most of which I have restored, as they seemed merely cut out for curtailment's sake (which is impossible to any useful extent) and seemed to leave gaps when I saw them again.

I have taken greatly in affection the Last Confession which I really think may be the best of all my doings. I have now added to it about 130 lines, filling up corners, and also a translation of the Italian Song in it. I really do believe in the passion and reality of this poem, now that I see it again as a new thing, for I had no scrap of the old copies in this case. It is the outcome of the Italian part of me, and I am glad it is not lost.

I am also going to work now more or less on "Jenny," and a good deal on "Dante." I want to make all quite perfect if I can. I have also condensed a shady thing called the *Portrait* which you may remember, & made a good short poem of it I think. Several passages & alterations of value turned up also for things I have been putting in print. As to new work, I finished "Eden Bower" a few days after I last saw you, & I think you will like it. Since then I have been working towards, but not yet at, other new things. By the bye, you do not (do you?) possess Halliwell's edition of the "Harrowing of Hell?" I want it.[1]

So much for egotism.

What a glorious poem your "Super flumina" is! – above all perhaps, the part spoken by the angel: and the metre is of the order of great discoveries.[2] I await impatiently the *Intercession*, which I hope to get on Monday.[3] William told me of your splendid motto, and also the inimitable Mastai & God's-gallows epigram. Really you ought to write (but perhaps you have by this) another couplet to introduce this one, Something to the effect "Shall the Republic honour its foes by making martyrs of them in the hour of victory?" The epigram at present seems hardly to explain itself without this.[4]

I shall hope ere long to see something of your late doings, as I suppose you will be returning to town. A few fellows will be dining here on Monday at 7-30, but I suppose there is no chance of your being up then. However I mention it *en cas que*.

Ever yours
D G Rossetti

P.S. The Monday gathering includes William and his friend Stillman, late American consul at Crete, whom you perhaps know or have heard of.[5]

1 *The Harrowing of Hell* is a Miracle Play edited in 1840 by James Orchard Halliwell (see **171** & **193**). DGR wanted to experiment with this subject by treating it "from the point of view of love-passion – as if the redemption wrought by Christ were to be viewed as an elevation of the conception of love from pleasure into passion, hence entailing the redemption from hell of Adam and Eve, David and Bathsheba, etc. etc." (*RP* 417).
2 "Super Flumina Babylonis" was published in *Songs before Sunrise* (1871: 38–44).
3 Four sonnets which eventually appeared in *Songs of Two Nations* (1875).
4 This epigram concludes the sonnet "A Counsel" in the sequence "Dirae, Part III" of *Songs of Two Nations*.
5 For WJS see 62.3n13.

69.192 TO CHARLES AUGUSTUS HOWELL

MS: Texas.

Saturday [30 October 1869]

Dear Howell

While I was asking Scott if he could come to dinner the other day I meant my next word to be asking you, & then something came between & I forgot it. Will you come? I hope so, but must tell you I am in for Inchbold. The others will be Scott Brown Nettleship William & his friend Stillman late American consul at Crete. If Swinburne is in town he may possibly come too but I don't expect him. Will you let me know if you can whether you come.

Ever yours DG R

69.193 TO FREDERICK JAMES FURNIVALL

MS (fragment): Huntington.

[October 1869]

... Many thanks for making up the Harrowing of Hell.¹
Do you know whether the W. Morris to whom the metrical version is attributed has since engaged in petty trade? If so, it is Exeter (not University) College on which the stigma rests.

Yours very truly
DG Rossetti

1 See **171** & **191**.

69.194 TO FORD MADOX BROWN
Relocated to 71.174.1

69.195 TO HENRY AUSTIN BRUCE
MS: Princeton. Published: DW 894.

6th Nov 1869
16 Cheyne Walk
Chelsea

My dear Bruce

May I venture to trouble you on another matter, which however presents no difficulties like the last.

My friend Howell having yesterday lost his mother-in-law, and promised her and his wife to bury her with her late husband (Edwin Henry Howell, now buried at Southsea,) requires an order to exhume the body and have it brought up at once that both may be buried at Brompton Cemetery next Thursday. As they would like to have both ceremonies on the same day, we have hoped you will kindly grant the order at once. I may mention that the grave is the property of Howell & his wife.

I am, my dear Bruce,

Very truly yours,
DG Rossetti

The Right Honble
Henry A Bruce MP

69.196 TO MESSRS. SMITH ELDER & CO.
MS: NLS.

16 Cheyne Walk/Chelsea
8th Nov. 1869

Messrs. Smith Elder &Co
Gentlemen

Would you oblige me by sending 3 copies of my "Early Italian Poets."

Yours faithfully
D G Rossetti

69.197 TO FRANCES CATHERINE HOWELL

MS: Texas.

8th Nov 1869
16 Cheyne Walk
Chelsea

My dear Kate

It is a difficult thing to speak any word whatever to you at such a time as this, when I know that in my own case no loss could be less soothed by the consolations even of best friends, than one such as yours.

I fear to think, as I write to you, how vain all words would then seem to me; and will only remind you (for I am sure you know) how much I feel with you in your sorrow.[1]

Your affectionate friend
D. GRossetti

[1] FCH's mother had died on 5 Nov (see **195** & **202**).

69.197.1 TO WILLIAM VOKINS

MS: Eton. The letter, which was not posted, is endorsed by DGR on the envelope: "forward by H. Caffieri Esq."

9 Nov/1869
16 Cheyne Walk
Chelsea

My dear Sir

May I, on an old and slight acquaintance, ask you to look at some sketches which a young friend of mine, Mr. Caffieri, has done in Scotland? Whether any of them might suit you I do not know, but perhaps in any case you might kindly give him a hint as to his best course in commencing as a London artist.[1]

Faithfully yours
D G Rossetti

W. Vokins Esq

[1] Hector Caffieri, artist (1847–1932).

69.198 TO JAMES LEATHART

MS: UBC (LP).

10 Nov 1869
16 Cheyne Walk
Chelsea

My dear Leathart,

I enclose cheque £125 completing payment of my money debt to you in respect of the picture of *Found*. I regret the delay has been longer than I looked for.

Manet my debt to you of a work of not less than £50 value as a set-off against the interest of your old advance.

I have heard all along from Scott of the state of your health, and am very glad to think that you have so happily surmounted such a severe attack of illness. I trust you are quite yourself again now.

Will you remember me most kindly to Mrs. Leathart, and believe me, again with thanks,

Very truly yours,
D G Rossetti

James Leathart Esq

69.199 TO FORD MADOX BROWN

MS: UBC. Published: DW 895. Date: WMR.

Thursday [11 November 1869]

D[ea]r Brown

I don't know if you would consider Tebbs as an eligible character for Monday. He has been friendly lately & expressed regret at having gone away before I read here that night of the dinner, & a wish that I would give him another chance. Perhaps you might tone him down with Mrs. Tebbs. However this is only a suggestion.

Ever yours D G R

69.200 TO JOSEPH KNIGHT[1]

MS: BL.

15 Nov/1869.
16 Cheyne Walk
Chelsea

My dear Knight

Many thanks for your friendly proceedings. I incline to think it will be better now to give up the idea of Murray, & fancy he may really be right in saying that his being so much out of the way of poetry renders him an undesirable publisher for it. His suggestion of Blackwood impresses me, as it seems advantageous on various grounds. I am obliged to him for his good wishes, especially as he bears in mind my father, who I know was acquainted with his.[2]

I should really like much to read you "Jenny" and that Italian story a second time, as I have been working at them ever since & have I think benefited them vastly. Could you spare me another evening – say dine at 7 Monday next if suiting you. I think you would pronounce "Jenny's Case" a less alarming one now on the whole.

I hope you're feeling better. I'm very queer indeed myself, and my hand shakes woefully as I write this.

Sincerely yours
D G Rossetti

---

[1] (1829–1907), the drama critic for the *Athenæum* from 1869 to the time of his death. He became involved with the DGR circle at this time, and was first mentioned in WMR's MS diary on 26 Mar 67. He was also a literary critic and Editor of *N&Q*, much cultivated by DGR while he was "working the oracle" to ensure enthusiastic reviews of *Poems*. Knight's minor contributions appeared in the *Globe* (20 Apr 70) and in the *Sunday Times* (1 May 70). Eventually Knight became one of DGR's first biographers with his *Life of Rossetti* (Scott, 1887): WMR wrote, "It gratifies me much to learn that Knight is to write the Memoir of my brother" (Peattie 412). WMR also did a biography in Scott's Great Writers series of biographies: his *Life of Keats* appeared in 1887 under the general editorship of Eric Robertson, Editor of the *Magazine of Art*.

[2] DGR, not yet committed to FSE, was shopping around for publishers for *Poems*.

69.201 TO HENRY VIRTUE TEBBS

MS: Texas.

17 Nov/1869
16 Cheyne Walk
Chelsea

My dear Tebbs

Will you dine with me Monday at 7? Knight (whom I know not if you know) is coming, and I will read some of my proof sheets. I hope too we may then make an appointment for the first sitting from Mrs. Tebbs.

Ever yours DGRossetti

P.S. No *togs* of course.

69.201.1 TO MRS. ADOLF HEIMANN

MS: Untraced (formerly Alexander Autographs).

17 Nov/1869
16 Cheyne Walk
Chelsea

Dear Mrs. Heimann

How good of you to remember one so apparently forgetful as myself! Not *really*, however; but crooked and bothered are the ways of the feet for whom comfort you have so kindly provided; and weeks and months pass without my seeing the friends I mean to see or indeed almost any one but the foe who confronts me when I have enough energy to shave.

I hope you and all yours are well, including Charles who will be in danger of finding himself endowed with a pigtail of atmospheric sympathy if he stays away much longer without home antidotes.[1] I trust your news of him is good. I shall try before long to combine an evening here with my mother and family (who have been long unassaulted under my roof) and try and get you to meet them. I have been writing lately instead of painting, and have been very queer & out of sorts, and this is the very first day for many weeks that my hand can hold a pen pretty steadily.

I recognize Christina's regulation design in the slippers, which are very welcome, as winter ones were beginning to run short with me. Will you give my love to the doctor and take it for yourself, and pass it round wherever it is held in better esteem than it deserves, – which has been so much its graceless lot in this world that what supplementary fate the next may have in store for it does not do to think of.

Affectionately yours
D Gabriel Rossetti

[1] On 27 Aug WMR had heard from Dr. Heimann that his son Charles was "now at Hiogo in Japan; near the residence of the Mikado" (*RP* 324).

69.202 TO CHARLES AUGUSTUS HOWELL

MS: Texas.

Wednesday [17 November 1869]

Dear Howell

I hope you're getting over your great trouble – Kitty & you – and feeling more like yourselves again. I must be looking in as soon as possible, and fixing another sitting with Kitty, but have been kept from all painting work up to this time.

F[oord]. & D[ickinson]. have sent those 2 frames for Kitty's portrait & the circular Janey. If you think of calling to see the frames, I should be more at liberty tomorrow than on Friday.

Your affec:
D G R

69.202.1 TO WILLIAM GRAHAM

MS: SANG (copy in Charles Sayle's hand).

Thursday [c. 25 November 1869]

My dear Graham,

I send you the Pandora.[1] It has occurred to me to beg your acceptance of the first sketch of little Willie if sufficiently like to be cared for by yourself or some other of his relatives. Unluckily the position necessary for the picture does not come well in a drawing by itself. It wd look better if mounted close in oak, but I have not a frame to fit it.

Many thanks for your last letter respecting "Found." The utter darkness of the days lately has interfered sadly with my work. I shall be very glad to see you, but will not be showing you just now what I have done hitherto, as it is too merely preparatory. Shortly I hope to make some show.

Ever yours
D. G. Rossetti

[1] S.224B, a chalk drawing, not the oil completed in 1871.

69.203 TO JOSEPH KNIGHT

MS: BL.

Friday [c. 26 November 1869]
16 Cheyne Walk
Chelsea

My dear Knight

I am rejoiced, and quite relieved after seeing you suffer so much, to hear of your present improvement. I should like very much to read you the poem again, but could not easily make an appointment just as yet, & really doubt if it is wise in you to tempt long distances & vile weather at night for such a purpose.

I dare say you have got Morris's new volume and are going to do it justice. I think *Gudrun* is the most glorious thing he has done yet.

Brown & I were very nearly looking you up the other night, but found it getting too late.

Ever yours
DG Rossetti

I will hope to get you down some evening before long.

69.204 TO ALGERNON CHARLES SWINBURNE

Text: *ALC* 4: 130. Excerpt: Compton-Rickett 565; *Portraits and Personalities* 314. Reprinted: DW 896.

Friday [26 November 1869]

My dear Swinburne,

I have just got the proofs so far complete, and send you a set by book post. I am not printing "The Bride's Chamber," as it will have to be altered a good deal, besides finished, and cannot be got ready for this volume.[1] I also enclose a bit of English poetry combined with French domestic economy, which I only found yesterday. I hope you have not been missing it and thinking it lost.

You know how much I shall value any impressions or suggestions of yours when you have time to look at the things with that view. I hope you will not get an unfavourable first impression of the changes I have made here and there. I feel confidence in all of them, having thought the matter over and over; and were you to differ from me I should really fear that a good deal of the favour the poems have hitherto found with you must have resulted from friendship and old associations.

Of course I am giving no copies away besides at present, and know you will not let them get about, which I am desirous they should not till published. When I say "none," I may perhaps be giving two besides yours.

I got the *Fortnightly* to read your Sonnets. Very find and grand – perhaps the grandest points the close of the third and the opening of the fourth.[2] What a remarkable article that is of Pater's on Leonardo![3] Something of *you* perhaps, but a good deal of himself too to good purpose.[4]

Ever yours affectionately,
D. Gabriel R.

[1] "The Bride's Prelude" appeared as an unfinished work in *Poems: New* (188–234).
[2] Four sonnets called "Intercession" appeared in the *Fortnightly Review* for Nov 69, republished in *Songs of Two Nations* (1875). See **191nn3,4**.
[3] Walter Pater's essay on Da Vinci was also included in the Nov 69 *Fortnightly Review*; it was to become the most celebrated essay in his *The Renaissance* (Macmillan, 1873).
[4] GPB visited 16CW on the date of this letter and found DGR "in a morbid and rather depressed state" and noted that "he was much engaged on preparing a collection of the greater number of poems yet written for publication" (*GPBD* 50). Among the pictures GPB saw in progress were *Found* and *The Death of Beatrice* (*Dante's Dream*), both commissioned by WG.

69.205 TO WILLIAM GRAHAM

MS (copy; unsigned fragment): UBC. Published: *RP* 488; DW 897.

Monday/29 Nov 1869

My dear Graham

I waited to answer your kind letter till I could acknowledge the remittance which you proposed to send next day from Glasgow. As I have not yet received this, I write lest by possibility it should have miscarried.

When you first expressed a wish to have the "Found" picture, I named 800 gs as its price, and you agreed thereto. I do not mention this because I hesitate to meet the wish you express in the matter after all your friendly conduct, but merely because I remember mentioning the price in my last as "agreed on." This, you will perceive, is the picture of all others of which I should not, *under ordinary circumstances*, abate the price, as it is of quite an exceptionally popular kind among my works; nor should I indeed have asked less than 1000 gs at this moment of any one but yourself – not even of Agnew. It is now somewhat larger than before – as I have had the canvas increased to give more space. In now engaging it to you for £800, copyright which I retain, will doubtless prove of value one day, and I make no doubt of selling a replica to great advantage. So be it as you wish.

I know how well you deserve the best I can give you at the earliest date, and shall have quite as great pleasure as yourself in seeing that I am fairly represented among your pictures that you love and live with. I hope this may be the case ere long.

I have not been very brilliant in health since seeing you, and think it is possible I may have to be settling for a short time in the country at no great distance from London, but if so, shall take some of your work with me, & combine working . . .[1]

[1] For WG's reply to this letter, see *RP* 489.

69.205.1 TO ELLIS & CO.
MS: UCLA.

[November 1869]

Mr. Rossetti presents his compliments and wishes to be favored with an account of what is due from him to the firm.

69.206 TO WILLIAM MICHAEL ROSSETTI
MS: Brotherton. Excerpt: *FL* 222. Published: DW 898.

Wednesday [1 December 1869]

Dear William

In setting Dunn to work at your binding today I find I need the exact size. If you will send it me by return of post I dare say I shall be able to let you have the thing on Saturday or Monday at latest. The colour could not be better than that apple green roan, but if they won't take the trouble of staining the cloth to this, let the binder send me his patterns and I will choose a grey of some sort. I remember to have seen a sort of dull indigo grey once which is not a bad colour.[1]

Yours
D G R

I enclose cheque £25 with thanks.
I sent your letter on to Swinburne.
I send cheque lest I forget – but if inconvenient let me have it again & I'll get tin instead.

[1] DGR delivered his design for the binding of WMR's 2-volume *Poetical Works of Shelley*

(1870) to him on 3 Dec 69. WMR was disappointed with it, and correctly predicted that J. B. Payne would reject it as "too elaborate to produce." He recorded that "it would look very nice; but is, I suspect, too elaborate for Moxon's purpose, both as regards expense and time." WMR later doubted that the design "was ultimately used for any purpose" (*RP* 416–17).

69.207 TO WILLIAM DAVIES

MS: Brotherton. Published: *RP* 491–92; DW 899.

3 Dec 1869
16 Cheyne Walk
Chelsea

My dear Davies

Many thanks for the 2 Frescobaldi Sonnets – the first very pretty indeed. I know not Matteo – query, a brother of Dino? They seem likely to belong to that time certainly. I am not acquainted with the little Cino book you speak of and should like to see it some day.

I considered the question as to translating Cene della Chitarra's chaff and have a note about it, but it seemed almost impracticable, as his Sonnets are written to the same rhymes as Folgore's, & this could hardly have been preserved. By the bye, if you look again at my book you will find that the large section of "moral injunction" poetry is pretty abundantly represented from Guinicelli and others.[1]

I was interested in the 2 reviews you sent, & return the *Scotsman*. Certainly with such recognition your book[2] ought to have been at least a tolerable commercial success. These two are amusingly contradictory on some points as usual.

I send you with this a little tale written long ago. I had included it among the poems I am printing, as it is really more a sort of poem than anything else; but coming to the conclusion after all that it looked awkward there I have had a few copies struck off to give away.[3] I send one for Smetham too when you see him. Will you tell him that the lovely sofa he gave me has just come home from the restorer's with every pattern made perfect again & the tone of the whole most exquisite. It is a gcm.[4]

Ever yours sincerely
DG Rossetti

[1] DGR was responding to a letter of 2 Dec from Davies which is printed and annotated in DW (767).
[2] *Songs of a Wayfarer* (Longmans Green, 1869).

3   DGR had enclosed a copy of Proof State #10 of *Poems*, a separate printing of his prose story "Hand and Soul," first published in *Germ* (1850). Now that he had augmented old poems and composed new ones, with plans to complete "The Orchard-Pit" and "God's Graal," he no longer needed to bulk up his volume with poetic prose.
4   See **42** & **124**.

69.208   TO ANNE GILCHRIST
MS: PML. Published: DW 900.

4th Dec 1869
Chelsea

Dear Mrs. Gilchrist

Since getting your kind letter I have been meaning to come round but have been and am so preoccupied that I am induced to write again instead. This unlucky contretemps is a most serious disappointment to me, as I feel confidence in the neighbourhood of Haslemere as likely to suit me and am really & woefully in want of trying some such experiment for a broken state of health & nerves. My only plan would be to have a house to myself & take my own servants with me, and your house would of course have been such a thing as is not to be got among the tents of Philistia. I suppose its present tenant wd not be induced to give it up by the offer of a premium – say £20 or something of that sort.

Failing this, I wished to ask if there were any house-agent thereabouts to whom I could apply for suggestions. If so, could you kindly send me his address. I should not wish to be *at* Haslemere, but any place as remote as possible from other habitations, and the higher placed the better, would be my goal. Yours, I know, is in a village, but its advantages would have outweighed this consideration.[1]

I hope to look you up one evening before long, and meanwhile, with kindest remembrances, am

Yours sincerely,
DG Rossetti

P.S. I know you will pardon my giving you so much trouble.

---

1   Sir William Jenner (1815–98) was family physician to both CGR & DGR; at this time he had ordered DGR to abstain from spirits, go to bed before midnight, and retire to a country life without regular professional work for the next 6 months (*RP* 417).

69.209 TO JOSEPH KNIGHT
MS: BL.

Sunday [c. 5 December 1869]

Dear Knight

Can you dine with me Monday the 13th at 7-30? I hope you are getting all right again & that you will still be in town then.¹

Ever yours,
DG Rossetti

¹ See **200** & **203**.

69.210 TO WALTER SEVERN
MS: Private Collection. Excerpt: DW 901.

8 Dec 1869

16 Cheyne Walk
Chelsea

My dear Severn

Many thanks about the urn which I shall be very glad to have & enclose the tin.¹ My own is much less high in relief but has a cover. Yours is the finer thing. Shall I send for it or will you send it me?

I believe I have never yet thanked you on Miss Boyd's behalf, as she asked me to do, for your friendly exertions in the matter of her pictures at Bond St. last Summer.

I am sorry your laudable intention to encourage the poetic art of this country should have to be deferred by the fact that my poems are not coming out yet. I have about 250 pages in print, but shall not publish till other things doing & to do are completed, and this has to await the intervals of painting & pot-boiling.

Very truly yours
DG Rossetti

¹ For the urn, see **63**.

69.211 TO ALGERNON CHARLES SWINBURNE

MS (unsigned fragment): BL. Published: DW 902.

8th Dec 1869

My dear Swinburne

Your letter came to me this morning most welcomely, with much generous praise, at a moment when I am woefully out of sorts in health and nerves. It is a true pleasure to find that the work I have been doing to my poems wins your acceptance to so complete an extent. The consequence you entail on yourself is that I feel disposed to bore you with some last doubts as to whether a few restorations from old copies would be advisable. I suppose from what you say that you probably include in your approval one such revival of a line in an old imperfect copy of "Jenny" (p. 197)

"and those
their purfelled buds that should unclose."

William I found *dis*approved of this, & I was going to remove it again, but I shall not if you like it. As to these M.S. passages in the enclosed pages of *Jenny* I must say I still feel inclined to reject them all, but should like your opinion. The two at pages 197 & 198 are old lines restored, but perhaps better out. The Sunday lines I think good but I fancy I must have cut them out as making too much of Sunday & moreover interrupting too long the sequence of the idea – "a child can tell" &c. The other marginal notes are new, but I fancy after all best left out.

I propose to restore (with adaptation) 3 or perhaps 5 more stanzas in the *Portrait*. One I feel no doubt about, so do not enclose. On the other 4 I should much like your opinion, so enclose them. I incline to put them in – or at least 2 of them.

I am delighted that you like Eden Bower so well, as several subjects I have in my hand are rather in the same vein. A new idea for a poem "The Doom of the Sirens" occurred to me the other day, & I think the story (which is my own invention) would afford fine opportunities and intense situations, but fear I shall not find time to write it at present, nor indeed to be writing at all just now, which is what I should like best.[1] You do not say whether the Dante (at which I have worked with care) pleases you now. I think it complete in its way, but of course do not value it so much as *Jenny* or the *Confession* or *Eden Bower* which on the whole I think my best 3, with the Sonnets & a song or two. I see what you mean with respect to the new verse in the Bower Song, & certainly it is quite true, – nevertheless I think the stanza a gain on the whole to the beauty of the thing.

I was talking with William about your Hotten business, and we almost think that you *must* have received the whole sum in small cheques, and having cashed them at the Club or elsewhere and kept no account, have forgotten about it. If so, the cheques must have got back to Hotten's hands by this time & be producible. If you have *not* received such payments, only one elaborate scheme of rascality occurs as possible, which one does not like to suppose can be the truth, but which would be difficult to combat perhaps if true. This is that H. should have drawn cheques payable to you or to *bearer* (thus not requiring your signature at the back) and then himself sent someone to cash them at his own bankers, and got them returned to him as. . . .[2]

---

[1] This "lyrical tragedy" in 3 acts did not advance beyond a prose abstract which WMR published in *CW* and reprinted in *Works* (610–13).

[2] DGR is answering ACS' letter of 28 Nov (Lang 2: 324) in which he enquired about closing accounts with his publisher John Camden Hotten and transferring his business to FSE, who was publishing both DGR & WM. See also Lang 2: 327 (to WMR), 331, 334 (both to DGR), & 220. *Songs before Sunrise* was brought out by FSE in 1871.

69.212 THOMAS GORDON HAKE

MS: BL. Published: DW 903.

10 Dec 1869
16 Cheyne Walk
Chelsea

My dear Dr. Hake

I have felt, and must have seemed, extremely remiss in not writing to you further before now, but have been very far from well and unexpectedly preoccupied with matters which had to be seen to at once and for which I was obliged to neglect everything. Thus I have made no progress in reading the works you so kindly lent me or considering the best course to be taken with them. I shall now however I trust be somewhat more free again.

Could you give me the pleasure of your company to dinner at 7 o'clock next Wednesday? My brother wishes very much to meet you, and might possibly contribute some hint as to plans of publication. I found since seeing you, to my surprise, that he had actually received some time back anonymously a copy of the "World's Epitaph" and had been much impressed by it. Indeed I can now remember his having shown it to me at the time, and my having at a glance discerned its beauty of execution; but not having your name to it, I omitted in the press of occupations to look into it thoroughly, as I should certainly have done had I known it to be yours.

By the bye, if, as I hope, you can come on Wednesday, do not let me trouble you to "dress" this cold weather.

Sincerely yours
D G Rossetti

Dr. Hake

69.213 TO ALGERNON CHARLES SWINBURNE

MS: BL. Excerpt: Compton-Rickett 565; *Portraits and Personalities* 314–15. Published: DW 904. Text within angled brackets is a marginal insertion.

12 Dec 1869

My dear Swinburne

Your Sonnet is an admirable one & most splendidly introduces and sustains the last couplet. It is full of unobtrusive perfection in the wording & thought – as for instance lines 3 & 4. "Blast their eyes & ears" might perhaps gain by the substitution (if possible) of some other word for "blast" which in that position recalls the more Topsaic forms of the speech of daily life to some extent, though indeed perhaps this is only morbid Bohemian fancy. "Buonaparte" matches "Mastai" better than does "Napoleon" but the form of the climax is so perfect now that I see no means of making the change to advantage.[1] I wonder if Morley will succumb even "unto this last."[2] Line 7 best I think as now, – chiefly because of similar sound to the other at end of lines 8 & 9.

Thanks for your kindly analysis of my bewilderments.

I agree exactly in all your verdicts as to *Jenny*. "Pillowed" makes that couplet just right, & I shall certainly now use it. I have an inclination, now that you suggest it, to restore those old lines in the 1st paragraph, & have slightly recast them as enclosed with that view. I suppose *one* at any rate of my reasons for omitting them must have been that one gets *er* and *are* again as a rhyme just afterwards. Do you think this fatal? *Fair* flower I can't say now, as *Fair* Jenny is just above. I forgot when I last wrote to send another proposed amendment which I now send but which Wm advised me not to adopt. It makes the passage mean what I meant more closely, – that is a "daughter" in the lapse of descent, but Wm thinks an *immediate* daughter more impressive. The only thing is that one cannot easily suppose dramatically that a man would be ignorant (in most cases) of his daughter's destiny during life.

I believe I agree with you mainly about the last stanza in Dante (& certainly

I think about the closing lines of the penultimate one. <I remember thinking *among paths* &c rather cockney as an idiom, meaning as it does *of all the paths* in this passage.>) But I hardly like to leave out the last after restoring it (for it used to exist once instead of the one before which was substituted,) and you yourself liked it at first sight. It is a shame boring you about such mere trifles amid the mass of magnificent work which you do without worrying your friends with the details; but the fact is I never can feel clear on uncertain points till I get your opinion.

What you say of Top's new vol is of course true criticism, but I think so excellent a poet must after all be allowed his own style in forms of poetry where deliberateness and delay are not absolutely inadmissible. More variety in the verse would, I admit, still be possible and desirable. But Gudrun is a wonderful poem – so great that perhaps it is no serious draw-back to say that the critical situations (in general) being so fine as they are, are still as usual perhaps less convincingly perfect than the more level passages of the narrative. What for instance can be better than the relation of Gudrun's two first marriages, the incidents in Norway, or Refna's recital of what the women said in her hearing? I must say that, hearty as is the praise with which the critics are greeting the book from their own point of view (I have only seen Pall Mall & Saturday) I do not think justice is yet being done by them to this most remarkable poem, which can only be justly dealt with by detailed analysis. The fact is Topsy writes too much both for his own sake & for that of his appreciators. The Death of Paris is a very fine poem now I think, having been much improved since its first state. The subject is a glorious one. I wish it had come to my share.[3]

You do not tell me how you get on with Bothwell or other leading work. William was talking to me about your title – *Songs of the Republic* – and really I cannot see how it is to be bettered, though something better seems somehow to float out of reach.[4] But it is a very good title (which sentence reminds one of Dr. Johnson's consolatory verdict on the discountenanced Hodge, – "but he is a fine cat, Sir, a very fine cat.")

By the bye, about your suggestion of 2nd motto from Othello to "Jenny," I have considered much of its value, which is great, but think on the whole that Mrs. Quickly & Othello wd look queer as companion speakers, & I want to put Mrs. Q. (instead of *Merry Wives* &c) at end of the sentence to remind the virtuous reader strongly whose words they are that his own mind is echoing at the moment.

Your affec:
DG R

---

[1] DGR is replying to Lang 2: 331, to which ACS had appended the sonnet "A Counsel," later

published as Section X of "Dirae" in *Songs of Two Nations* (1875); DGR had earlier praised the 2 final lines as an epigram (see **191&n4**):
>But let the worm Napoleon crawl untrod
>Nor grant Mastai the gallows of his God.

ACS was attacking Napoleon III & Pope Pius X (Mastai) as reactionary enemies of the Italian liberation movement.

2   ACS presumably intended to offer this poem, perhaps with others, to the *Fortnightly Review*; DGR wonders if the editor, John Morley, will be as hostile to ACS' revolutionary liberalism as Thackeray, editor of the *Cornhill*, had recently been to the passionate socialism of JR's articles, "Unto This Last."

3   ACS had faulted the latest tales in *The Earthly Paradise* for dragging: "my ear hungers for more force and variety of sound in the verse. It looks as if he purposely avoided all strenuous emotion or strength of music in thought and word" (Lang 2: 331).

4   *Bothwell*, a tragedy, was published in 1874. ACS considered other titles for *Songs before Sunrise*: e.g., *Songs of the Republic*. See **220**.

69.214 TO THOMAS GORDON HAKE

MS: BL. Published: DW 905. Date: Unidentified endorsement.

Monday [13 December 1869]

Dear Dr. Hake .

I am asking a friend – W. B. Scott, excellent painter & poet – to meet you besides my brother. He is anxious to know you – and I shd like you to look at his poems – pubd long ago & never valued at their worth by the critics or public. So I send you the little book by Book Post. I am sure you will value its beauties though the form here and there is less studied than might be.[1] He is an old & excellent friend of mine for whose genius I have the highest regard.

I may be seeing tomorrow evening a friend who notices poetry in the Pall Mall (Sidney Colvin) & shall try to get him too. He wrote the articles on Heine & Morris lately.[2]

Pardon great haste.

Ever yours
D G Rossetti

---

1   Probably *Poems by a Painter* (Smith, Elder, 1854).
2   For Sidney Colvin, see **187n1**, and for WMR's account of this dinner party, see *RP* 418.

69.215 TO I. R. P. KIRBY

MS: PHS.

14 Dec 1869
16 Cheyne Walk
Chelsea

Dear Sir

Considering that I am now 41, and that if you reverse those numerals you will get my age at the time the rubbish in question was printed, you may believe that I have not much clue to it now. It must have been written some couple of years before that date, and got into print owing to the fancy which an indulgent grandfather of ours had for printing our juvenile efforts at a little private press of his. I suppose he must actually have sent it to the Museum, but all trace of it has vanished as far as I am concerned.[1]

Very truly yours
D G Rossetti

I R P Kirby Esq

---

[1] Kirby, a book collector, must have encountered DGR's *Sir Hugh the Heron* at the BM and written enquiring about the volume. While his letter to DGR has not surfaced, DGR's rather curt response should be compared with RB:DGR in response to a similar enquiry about *Pauline* (see 47.3 & 3A).

69.216 TO FORD MADOX BROWN

MS: Ashmolean. Published: DW 906.

Wednesday [15 December 1869]

My dear Brown

Of course it is not in the least necessary to ask J M on the same occasion as yourself. I fancy now the proposed little gathering will have to take place after New Year's Day. But perhaps I might see you here to dinner alone one day before then. What say you? Only it wd perhaps not be feasible to fix a day before Xmas – that is, some day next week.

With all hopes of better fortune next year, I am ever

Your affec:
DGabriel R

69.217 TO FORD MADOX BROWN

MS: UBC. Published: DW 907.

Thursday [16 December 1869]

Dear Brown

Suppose you were to ask that bloke Bourne the engraver to call on me about Janey's portrait.[1] I've no chance of seeing you now for a new doctor – Jenner – has told me to be in bed by 12 & I'm trying to do it.

Ever yours
D G Rossetti

[1] Possibly Herbert Bourne (c. 1820–85), who engraved plates for the *Art Journal* and contributed plates for S. C. Hall's *Royal Gallery of Art* (1858 & 1860).

69.218 TO FREDERICK STARTRIDGE ELLIS

MS: Texas.

Friday [c. 17 December 1869]

My dear Ellis

Thanks about the Plutarch. Another thing I really ought to have is a *good* English Dictionary – the best recent one which can be had without great outlay. Which is it?

I shall not forget the 22nd.

Ever yours
DG Rossetti

Also I think I ought to have a French Dictionary – not a dear one.
P.S. I have almost made up my mind now to publish in the Spring, not waiting for more than can be got done by then. I suppose May would be time enough, would it not? I think also it might be well to republish with you at same time the Italian Poets, of which about 60 copies remained when I last heard from the publishers perhaps a year ago. What should be done about the remainder? And what do you think of republishing it? Don't trouble to write at length on these points as we can speak when I see you.

69.219 TO THOMAS GORDON HAKE

MS: BL. Published: DW 909.

21 Dec 1869
16 Cheyne Walk

My dear Dr. Hake

Thanks most sincerely for your kind letter. I was very sorry to have missed your visit.

I am afraid all the symptoms from which I suffer could not possibly be referred to increasing fat; nor have I increased to any very appreciable extent simultaneously with these symptoms – indeed at this moment I am wearing a waistcoat made some years ago without the least inconvenience. Certainly there *is* a constant gradual increase in this respect, which occasionally becomes evident to me but then seems either to subside or become unperceived. However, some months ago, I commenced following to some extent a diet suggested by reading Banting's pamphlet;[1] but although I was pretty strict (except a *little* milk and toast at breakfast) for a week or perhaps a fortnight, I failed to experience the remarkable change promised even within the first 48 hours. I have continued ever since to restrict myself a good deal in several things and to banish sugar almost entirely – quite so except in the *very* occasional form of pastry. When by myself indeed I never take pastry at all. It is even possible that I may have profited to some extent by this change, but much certainly remains unremedied.

All my plans are quite undecided as yet, and I shall be very glad to recur to the subject with so kind a friend as yourself when I see you again, which will, I trust, be before long. We can then also discuss more cheerful matters. With all the best wishes of the season I am,

dear Dr. Hake,
very sincerely yours,
D G Rossetti

[1] For Banting, see **123n7**.

69.220 TO ALGERNON CHARLES SWINBURNE

MS: BL. Excerpt: Compton-Rickett 565; *Portraits and Personalities* 316–17. Published: DW 910.

21 Dec/1869

My dear Swinburne

Here I come bothering again, this time with all best seasonable wishes.

In re Jenny, the following modification occurs to me, – being founded on your last suggestion, certainly the best form for the idea, but I don't quite like "Smell" – it is so much too true in some cases of the kind: –

>Fresh flower, scarce touched with signs that tell
>Of Love's exuberant hotbed: –
>(or) Of Pleasure's feverish hotbed: –

if Love's name ought not to be taken in vain in such a case, though perhaps it might fairly be viewed here as a conventional term.

Some one whose judgment deserves some consideration suggested the other day that this poem was rather too long than too short, & threw out a notion of omitting the passage from "Behold the lilies" to "the naked stem of thorns" as less explicit than the rest. Also the passage "Each of such curdled lives" to "has lost his soul" as not particularly valuable. Both such omissions wd require adaptation in their neighbourhood. I merely mention them to see if any objection to these passages had struck *you*. I cannot say it had me.

The same person suggested that the reader at present commences *Troy Town* with the idea that Helen must be in Troy at the time, and that it wd be well to indicate her being in Sparta. This I think might have some value, and have struck off a first stanza which I think may perhaps be a gain, though not *very* explicit on the point in question, which I found would involve too much mere prose in a song of this kind.

>Heavenborn Helen, Sparta's queen,
>   (*O Town Troy!*)
>Had two breasts of heavenly (orient) sheen,
>The sun & moon of the heart's desire:
>All Love's lordship lay between.
>   (*O Troy's down,*
>   *Tall Troy's on fire!*)

What think you of this as a prelude to the rest?

About the last stanza of Dante I think I must stand convinced by you. "Of all paths" *was* the reading in the M.S. book but it seemed to me hardly grammatical.

I suppose your "Songs before Sunrise" are yet to be expected before the Spring, are they not? That title was mentioned to me by Wm & is certainly the most beautiful & in nowise deficient as to clearness. I thought I understood from him that you had rejected it owing to its surface resemblance to Whitman's & Mrs. Browning's Songs before *Parting* and before *Congress*. But

I think there is no great validity in such an objection.

Are you really going to publish this book with Ellis? I believe I have resolved to do so with mine, but should feel a good deal relieved if Topsy was not E's only other author, as he is so fearfully prolific that one would feel like the mouse looking up at the mountain with a clear conviction that everyone thought it had given one birth in some way or other. I hear Ruskin projects dealing in the same quarter, & if you and he both did so, the position wd become tenable. However in any case I really couldn't be bothered with overtures to other publishers, & certainly believe that, as far as taking trouble goes, Ellis wd take more than other people.[1]

By the bye I am very glad you take so much my own view of the surpassing merits of Gudrun, and am quite of your opinion on the other hand about Acontius which I told Topsy was below his mark. What struck me about the "Palace &c" was that the first half was a good deal "*brodo lungo,*" but the second part (strong measures from friends having intervened with the bard) seemed to me very much more brisk and vivid.

"The Man who never &c" is also a very fine poem I think of its kind (from hearing it read) but really Topsy's very titles are almost too much for a Gillott's Magnum Bonum. He has got now into a very fastidious stage and has begun 2 or 3 of the other tales for the last vol, every one of which he seems bent on re-writing.

Finally –

> O thou the Laureate that wast once so good,
> Fallen in the practice of this cursed King,
> What shall be said to *thee*?

Answer –

> A tolerable maunderer if you will.

I must say that to have Sir Pelleas turned into a schoolboy deserving and not getting the birch through pages irrigated with irritation to every poetic sense one possesses (in spite of good verbal passages) is rather too much for one furnished with the helpful vocabulary of Ratcliff Highway as an Appendix to Johnson & Webster.

The same may be said of the rest so far as I have read (except The Northern Farmer which is very good). It is hopeful for rising reputations to find the old Morte d'Arthur (now embodied in this volume) reviewed in the Athenæum as something quite new – after all the fuss made about it only a few years ago.[2]

One thing is that I shall proceed with additional zest to my projected poem of "God's Graal" (Lancelot losing the Sancgraël) where in God & Guenevere will be weighed against each other by another table of weights & measures.

Yours affec:
DGR

---

[1] JR published *Notes on some of the Principal Pictures exhibited in . . . the Royal Academy* (1875) & *Bibliotheca Pastorum* (1877) with Ellis & White.

[2] DGR, who was attempting an Arthurian subject with "God's Graal," is belittling Tennyson's latest addition to his Arthurian epic, Idylls of the King; *The Holy Grail and Other Poems* had just appeared. His mocking verses parody *Othello* V. ii. 291–95.

69.221 TO FREDERIC JAMES SHIELDS

MS: Kansas. Excerpt: Mills 137–39; Horne 87–89; DW 911.

24 Dec /69

My dear Shields

I was very glad to see your capital move in respect to Brown's picture at Manchester.[1] I sent on to Colvin at once, & today he writes me word that he has written to the M[anchester]. *Examiner*. I sent on your letter to him in such a hurry (being at work) that I only read it once, and forgot what you said as to your health, but in fact do not think you said much about it. I hope there was nothing bad to say.

Graham's conduct (this part I carefully scored out – so much as the first sheet contained – in sending your letter to C.) seems to me most extraordinary; considering how invariably & excellently well he has behaved to myself, & the personal & artistic esteem I have heard him express for you. He is I believe now permanently in town again with his family. They came here about a week ago. He had been here several times when on flying visits to London from Scotland, and on one occasion he mentioned 2 heads you were doing for him, and I then said "Did you write further about the picture?" He answered, "No, I called when in Manchester, but Shields was out." This I imagined must have been in allusion to the time he called on you *before* our last conversation, but as he was just leaving in a hurry I made no further inquiry. He certainly had said at the end of that conversation that he should write at once to you on getting home that day & renew the commission. The matter is most vexatious, and you may of course rely on my not importuning him, as this would be sacrificing your dignity; but if an opportunity occurs naturally of discussing the point further with him (as I hope it may) I shall be very glad to have the chance of telling him what I think.[2]

I have been in various queer states of health for some time past. My visit to Scotland seemed to do me no good this time. I have just lately been calling on doctors & oculists again, & the latter still say my sight is not really affected, while the former say much the same as to my health, but speak most warningly as to hours, exercise, & abstinence from spirits, for which Heaven knows I have no taste, but had for a year & a half past fallen into the constant habit of resorting to them at night to secure sleep. I have now relinquished them entirely, and take only at night a medicine prescribed by my last doctor (Sir W. Jenner) – not an opiate against which he warned me in all forms – & have certainly not slept worse, but rather better, since doing so. I also, when weather is fine, take day walks in Battersea Park, whereas my habits had long been to walk only at nights except when in the country.

For many months I had done no painting or drawing, but have just lately resumed work of this kind, and am proceeding as best I may, against the stream of models who cannot be got or do not come, pitch-black days &c. with such things as I want to be doing. These are chiefly the large picture of Dante's Dream, which I had not yet taken in hand since getting the commission from Graham, & (!!!) the old picture of "Found" (the calf & bridge subject) which I am actually taking up at last.[3] I have lost lots of time as yet in preliminary studies for both works, but hope to get the man's head done in the "Found" next week, having found a splendid model, and have also made considerable way towards the bridge background. I am also beginning to make studies again for the picture of "Medusa" and hope to get that in hand as soon as the others are fairly under way. Had I a large fine studio, I should now get all my finest subjects squared out from the designs on canvases of the size needed, & take them all up one after the other whenever possible. This plan I shall pursue vigorously more or less now, as life wears short, & do I trust few single figure pictures except when shut out from other work by the chances of the hour. Studio-building I have rather funked hitherto, as the state of my health has induced me to think I might be leaving Chelsea, just after I had got the stables into my possession. I think it most likely however that I shall begin building shortly after Xmas, as the landlord has demanded that failing that, I should put the stables in repair as stables, which wd be simply throwing money in the dirt.

I have been doing a good deal of work in poetry and shall publish a volume in the Spring. I have got 230 pages in print & want perhaps to add about a 100 more. This is hardly necessary, as it is all very close & careful work, but as I dare say it may be some time before I print again, if ever, I shd wish to do so. At any rate so much will be off my mind when the thing comes out, and it is certainly the best work of my life such as that has been.

Have you seen Morris's new vol of the "Paradise"? It contains glorious things, especially the "Lovers of Gudrun." Tennyson's new vol does not enlist my sympathies, except a second *Northern Farmer*, which is wonderful, and of course there is much high-class work throughout.

I have not seen your heads at the W[ater]. C[olour]. nor indeed do I ever go to any picture shows whatever now except once in the year to the R.A.

I saw Craven yesterday, and was glad to find him resigned & like himself again, though he conversed painfully on the dreadful subject.[4] His wife is with him in London as you probably know.

Old Brown is doing a W.C. for him (Don Juan found on the beach by Haydee) which will I think be almost the finest of his works, & certainly by far the most full of beauty. Indeed to my mind all 8 figures are eminently beautiful in face & figure, & the background of rocks & sea is most fascinating.[5]

Ned Jones is doing a crowd of splendid works though he has sent no sketches to the gathering this time. He was one of the hangers.

Affectionately yours
D G Rossetti

[1] FJS had written to a Manchester paper defending FMB's painting *Elijah and the Widow's Son*. See *FMB* 257–58 & Mills 136–39.
[2] For the misunderstanding about a commission between WG & FJS, see **140** & **182**, and Mills 133.
[3] For WG's commission of *Dante's Dream* (S.81) in Apr 68, see *RP* 304.
[4] The accidental death of his daughter: see **136n1**.
[5] FMB's watercolour of *The Finding of Don Juan by Haidee* had been commissioned by Frederick Craven in May 1869.

69.222 TO FREDERICK STARTRIDGE ELLIS

MS: BL. Published: *FSE* 60; DW 1090. Though placed by FSE in the sequence of 1870 letters and retained there by Doughty in *FSE*, this letter clearly belongs to 1869, as does **224**.

Xmas Day [1869]

My dear Ellis

I am going to add two to my list of high-class orders which you have already been favoured with: viz: a Lemprière[1] and a book called Pierre, or the Ambiguities, by Herman Melville, which I believe is not easily met with like others of his, as it has not been republished in England. I think I may add to these the Complete American edition of Poe's Works (I think in 4 vols).

Have you been able to find whether Fields the publisher is still in London, & if so, whereabouts?[2]

Ever yours
DG Rossetti

P.S. I had a note from Swinburne saying that he meant to publish his "Songs before Sunrise" (on which he is now engaged) with you. The Athenæum notice of the E[arthly]. P[aradise]. is no great shakes though available enough – but did you see the base classification of living English poets in the other jumbled article?

---

[1] John Leprière's classical dictionary, *Biblioteca Classica*, was a standard reference work until 1948.
[2] For Fields, see **91n6**.

69.223 TO FORD MADOX BROWN

MS: UBC. Published: DW 699.

Sunday [c. 26 December 1869]

Dear Brown

I have written to Lady A. today (her address is 16 Park Lane) saying that you wd paint her a half size Romeo for 350 gs a whole size for 500 gs[1] but that I advise her strongly to go & see the Haidee[2] – price 500 gs – and that if she does so she had better write you a line before hand, though (I have said) this is not indispensable.

Ever yours
DGR

---

[1] FMB did several pictures based on *Romeo and Juliet*: see **2** for a "beautiful small subject"; in 1867 Craven commissioned a watercolour now in the Whitworth Art Gallery; and there is a watercolour dated 1868–71 in the collection of Sir Colin Anderson.
[2] See **221n5**.

69.224 TO FREDERICK STARTRIDGE ELLIS

MS: BL. Published: *FSE* 1; DW 914.

[28 December 1869]

My dear Ellis

You say Fields is gone to New York – but is he not a *Boston* publisher? If you will tell me this I will write at once. I suppose you don't know his Christian name.

Ever yours
DGRossetti

69.225 TO JOHN FERGUSON McLENNAN[1]

MS: Columbia.

[c. 31 December 1869]

My dear McLennan

I'm going to bring out a Volume of poems in the spring, and need merely say of them that I have done my best to make them as perfect as I can. I am pretty sure, I believe, of good notices from the London press, but should like to ask you in confidence how the poetic land lies in Edinburgh and what chance one might have of getting some *early* notice which might put the book on a footing not easily shaken. I know various people in Edinburgh, but do not know in what direction appreciation lies, nor who are the special writers on poetry. Who criticises such work in Blackwood for instance – can you tell me? And what prospect might I have of a review from your own friendly hand?

I hope you will not think me too business-like in considering these matters beforehand; but I really believe these poems (some old & some new) to be on the whole perhaps the best of the scattered work of my life, though I have given my more constant (not more careful) attention necessarily to another art: and it would be of importance to my present position that the result of their coming before the world should not be *literary* failure. Commercial failure would not matter.

I am already printing and have got nearly 250 pages in type. I mean to bring the volume to about 300 but probably not more.

I suppose you have not been in London for some time, as I cannot imagine you coming & not looking me up. Let me wish you and yours what I know you will wish me & mine – the best luck of next year, & believe me

Ever yours
DG Rossetti

J F McLennan Esq
P.S. It is big, but could be reduced in carrying out, only you should take care they don't alter it at all, as it would soon get hideous.
I have found your monogram specially difficult to manage, considering as I do that clearness is essential. The one unerased above is the best I can manage

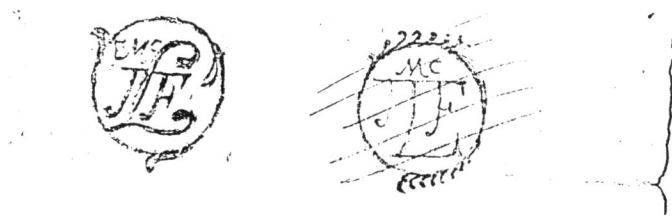

after a good many trials. Combining the lines I found not practicable in this case. It has a hopeful bank-note look which is cheery.

P.P.S. I had a visit from your friend Mr. Fullenton [?] lately, who afterwards sent me some capital lines of his on a picture of Pandora which I showed him.

---

[1] For McLennan see 54.28n2. He was a designated reviewer and co-ordinator of reviewers of *Poems* (see 70.12 & 13, and **Chronology: 1870**).

69.226 TO JANE OCTAVIA BROOKFIELD[1]

MS: Duke.

Wednesday [1869?]

16 Cheyne Walk

Chelsea

Dear Mrs. Brookfield

I am sorry that a previous engagement prevents my accepting your kind invitation for tomorrow evening.

Very truly yours

D G Rossetti

---

[1] See **39**.

1870

MAJOR WORKS OF THE YEAR

Literary: "Circe"; *Poems* (see **Volume V**: *Poems* appendices). DGR's poetry was genuinely admired by those who knew it, especially by ACS, who wrote, while he was waiting to hear whether his review could appear in the May issue of the *Fortnightly Review*, that he wanted to say "early and fully . . . on the advent of the book which I regard now as surely as I did ten years since as the master-book of this generation of English poetry, at once for depth, variety, instinct, and perfection. . . . I should say so if the book had in it but four poems in varying kinds – Jenny, Lilith, Nineveh, Sister Helen" (Lang 2: 343).

Artistic: Oils: *Dante's Dream* (S.81R.2) occupies most of his painting energies after his return from Scalands, *Sibylla Palmifera* (S.193) completed for George Rae who commissioned it in 1866, *Mariana* (S.213, a portrait of JM); drawings (see S.214–23); portraits: Sophy Burgess, Mrs. Coronio (S.310), Mrs. Tebbs (S.524), Maria Zambaco (S.541–43), W. J. Stillman (S.518), and Mrs. George Howard.

SUMMARY OF THE YEAR'S LETTERS

Recovering EES' sketches; "working the oracle" (WBS' term) to designate reviewers of *Poems*; sojourn at Scalands; invitation to visit Nortons in Florence; concerns about ACS' review in *Fortnightly* and about his drunkenness; CGR's publications with FSE; fears for reception of "Jenny"; delays owing to binding error; publication of *Poems*; altercation at Knight's; Deverell Raffle; plans for new studio at 16CW.

1870, WMR said, "was one of the marked years of my brother's life" (*DGRDW* 70). Notwithstanding DGR's concerted work on *Dante's Dream* after his return from Scalands in early May, the year is more singular for the completion of *Poems* than for his artistic work, primarily because it marks the culmination of a resolve made at least as early as 1856 (Vol.III, Recently Located Letters, 56.51.1) and put into action in 1861 when he instructed the printer of *EIP* to insert a slip saying, "*Will shortly be published Poems By D. G. Rossetti*" (61.86). This project, with the working title *Dante at Verona and Other Poems*, was abandoned on the death of EES. Almost seven years passed before he took up this volume again (68.145), building it with painstaking craftsmanship into what is by any standard one of the most noteworthy collections of poetry published during the nineteenth century. In April, still a relatively new acquaintance, Stillman told WMR that he and others "are thinking of entering into a pact . . . to keep up a simple economical style of living. . . . Gabriel (Stillman says) likes the idea . . . and Stillman has advised him to sell off his china etc. . . . and leave the Chelsea house, clear off debts and economise. I told Stillman it would be a waste of faith to suppose Gabriel will ever deny himself any expenditure he feels disposed for" (*WMRD* 3).

CHRONOLOGY

January
Attempts to recover drawings by EES however slight.

26 Jan
After some deliberations with John Murray and rejecting an offer from Blackwood, DGR settles with FSE to publish *Poems*, for which he designs the cover.

31 Jan
DGR begins "working the oracle" by approaching potential reviewers to ensure a favourable reception of *Poems*.

February
DGR encourages CGR to shift publishers from Macmillan to FSE; she contracts for *Sing-Song* on 25 Feb, for *Commonplace* on 29 Mar.

1 Mar
First proofs of *Poems*; copies sent to WMR, Skelton, McLennan (for Alexander), ACS, and WM.

11 Mar
Departs to join W. J. Stillman at Scalands, Robertsbridge.

Mid-March
Composes "Circe" for EBJ's picture, several new sonnets, and "The Stream's Secret"; begins a portrait of Sophy Burgess; introduced to chloral hydrate by Stillman.

late Mar
Alice Boyd commissioned to illustrate CGR's *Sing-Song*.

4–6 Apr
In London, visits Dr. Critchett about his eyes; spends most of the 5th with ACS; requests revisions in ACS' review.

11 Apr
Declines invitation to Florence; then on 18th proposes WMR accompany him; abandons idea on 14 May.

mid-Apr
JM at Robertsbridge, staying at Fir Bank; WM visits periodically; makes studies for JM's portrait as Mariana.

c. 13 Apr
Proposes design for binding of ACS' *Songs before Sunrise*.

14 Apr
Review copies of *Poems* in provisional (plain) bindings issued.

15 Apr
Learns of block-cutter's blunder on binding design, necessitating a gathering of blank leaves to flesh out volume, but there is further delay.

26 Apr
In London at FSE's to sign copies of *Poems*, published on 27th.

April
WMR's edition of *Longfellow*, the first in a 21-volume series of Moxon's Popular Poets spanning the decade 1870–80, published.

Apr–May
Concerns over impropriety of certain poems in ACS' *Songs before Sunrise*.

7 May
CGR's *Commonplace* published.

20 May
2nd edition of *Poems*.

22 May
Receives copies of large paper edition of *Poems*.

25 May
Leases from Benjamin Smith half of Glottenham House, close to Scalands, as an artistic retreat, but never occupies it.

1 Jun
3rd edition of *Poems*; owing to the weak sales performance of *Commonplace* and the unsuitableness of AB's illustrations for *Sing-Song*, CGR releases FSE from his agreement to publish the latter volume.

end Jun
American edition of *Poems* published by Roberts Bros. of Boston, set to DGR's annoyance from the 1st edition; remonstrates with ACS about his drunkenness.

15 Jul
Outbreak of Franco-Prussian War.

end Jul
EBJ resigns from OWCS over reception and withdrawal of *Phyllis and Demophoön*.

mid-Aug
4th edition of *Poems*.

29 Sep–29 Oct
WMR travelling on continent, mainly in Germany.

10–14 Oct
FMB and Emma at Penkill.

25 Nov
WBS moves to Bellevue House, 92 Cheyne Walk.

November
Planning with Philip Webb for a new studio at 16CW.

December
5th edition of *Poems*, dated 1871; DGR finally opens chequing account at the Union Bank.

LETTERS

70.1 TO MRS. ROBERTSON[1]
MS: UBC.

2nd Jan.1870
16 Cheyne Walk
Chelsea

Dear Mrs. Robertson

Many thanks for your kind invitation for the eleventh, which I should have had pleasure in accepting, were it not that I have been lately more peremptorily warned than ever by the doctors not to keep late hours, as well as to do and not to do many things, if I had any preference whether "to be or not to be." There are only one or two things that make me think I have; so at present I will try & obey my doctors.[2]

With all best wishes for the season to you & yours

I am ever yours
DG Rossetti

[1] Possibly DGR's neighbour at 24 Cheyne Walk, the wife of John Ewart Robertson (see also 57.33&n3 & 69.103).
[2] In his Dec 69 letters to TGH & FJS (69.219 & 221), DGR states that he is making efforts to change his nocturnal habits as well as his diet, but his refusal of the invitation may have been prompted by his dislike for engagements outside his immediate circle.

70.2 TO BARBARA LEIGH SMITH BODICHON[1]
MS: PML. Published: DW 912.

11 January/1870
16 Cheyne Walk
Chelsea

Dear Mrs. Bodichon

I shall be very glad to see you next week. I fancy Wednesday or Thursday might suit me best if you also.

I have been for some time past very anxious to get back all such sketches by my late wife – however slight – as were not in my own hands; as I admire her work even more now if possible than I did years ago. I have got most of those which Ruskin had, but find that he has lost sight of, or rather I believe given away, several. Did you happen to be the recipient in any instance? There was particularly a little pen-&-ink design (of a woman kneeling by a fire place with a boy in the background) which I am very sorry to find is lost, as it was done to illustrate a poem of my own.² I mention it with little hope that this or something else which was Ruskin's may chance now to be yours, but thought I would ask you. Were it so, I would gladly give you something of my own in exchange if agreeable to you.

I remember by the bye that you had a pen-&-ink design from *Pippa Passes*,³ but that I do not need, as I have another precisely like it of her doing.

Ever yours
DG Rossetti

---

1 For Mme Bodichon, who was an enthusiastic admirer of EES, see 53.57&n2. DGR's letter to CEN asking if he could purchase or make an exchange for *Clerk Saunders* seems to be the first such request in writing (see 69.47 & 48 & **8**). For his earlier attempts at collecting EES' works, see 66.177.
2 EES made 2 drawings for DGR's "Sister Helen": *EES* 10, an obvious study, is at Wightwick Manor; the finished drawing is known only from a photograph in the Ashmolean.
3 An 1854 pencil version is also in the Ashmolean. CP wrote in his review of the 1857 Russell Place exhibition: "Her drawings display an admiring adoption of all the most startling peculiarities of Mr. Rossetti's style, but they have nevertheless qualities which entitle them to high praise. Her 'Study of a Head' is a very promising attempt, showing great care, considerable technical power, and a high, pure, and independent feeling for that much misunderstood object, the human face divine. *We are Seven* and *Pippa Passes*, by the same lady, deserve more notice than we can stop to give them" ("A Pre-Raphaelite Exhibition," *Saturday Review*, 4 Jul 57: 11–12).

70.3 TO JOSEPH KNIGHT
MS: BL.

11 Jan. 1870

My dear Knight

I think my best plan under the circumstances is to write first to Ellis (with whom I have never entered into any details of arrangement) and ask him what his views are, telling him of my having received some advances from another publisher, but of course without mentioning any names whatever. As soon as I get his answer I will write you again.¹

It is a relief to know you are relieved for the present of so much suffering as you were in when I last saw you. I myself have been decidedly rather better of late.

With all best wishes for the New Year

believe me
ever yours
DG Rossetti

I see I have forgotten to thank you for your kind trouble on my behalf. Believe how sincerely I do so.

1 See 69.200&n1, **7**, **9**, & **20**.

70.4 TO GEORGE PRICE BOYCE

MS: Untraced (formerly Jeremy Maas). Date: GPB.

Wednesday [12 January 1870]

Dear Boyce

You must think me a horrid wretch not to have answered your proposal to go over your house today but I hoped to look in earlyish & was prevented.[1] You don't *really* think, I know, that you are out of mind with me, but the fact is just as I said before – you make long absences and one is apt to forget at times your being available. I shall look you up one evening very soon on chance of a chat.

Thanks for the dress. Mary is already about the copy & I hope to let you have it again in a few days.

Ever yours
D G R

1 See 68.65 for Boyce's new house.

70.5A FROM FLORENCE TAYLOR TO DANTE GABRIEL ROSSETTI

MS: Brotherton (enclosed with the following letter).

No 1 Lower Heathfield Terrace/Turnham Green
[c. 13 January 1870]

My dear Gabriel

You will be sorry to hear poor Warrington is much worse. I thought I would write to you in case you may wish to see him as I do not think he will ever recover from this attack. I suppose you know your brother has kindly consented to be my *Trustee*.[1] Warrington has not expressed a wish to see him but if he could spare the time to come over one evening with you I should like to see him. I do not know that Warrington has any thing to say to him still he might like to see him.

I need not add how pleased I should be to see you.

Yours sincerely,
Florence Taylor

---

[1] WMR recorded in his diary on 29 Jul 68 that Taylor asked him to be "one out of the three trustees for his Wife, on her coming into the reversion of his property" and on 24 Feb 70 that his "functions as executor to Taylor's will, and trustee for his Wife . . . [had] now commenced" (*RP* 320, 499). He attended willingly to the legal issues arising from Mrs. Taylor's remarriage, to Walter Wieland, sometime before 29 Jun 71 (Peattie 193, *WMRD* 73–74).

70.5 TO WILLIAM MICHAEL ROSSETTI

MS: Brotherton. Published: DW 913. Date: WMR.

Friday night [14 January 1870]

Dear W.

Enclosed from Mrs. Taylor. I write to her with this to say I will try & get you to go with me tomorrow (Saturday) after Office hours. In that case I suppose we might get there about 5 if you come straight on here. It is no good I am told going late to see him.

Your
D G R

70.6 TO EMILY TEBBS

MS: Texas.

Tuesday night [c. 18 January 1870]

Dear Mrs. Tebbs

Tomorrow (Wednesday) wd suit me I find for another sitting, if you also. Shall we say 1-30, as I have some visitors coming before that? If not convenient, never mind, as you will not put me out by not coming.[1]

Ever yours
DG Rossetti

---

[1] For DGR's portrait of Emily Tebbs (S.524), see 69.178 & 201.

70.7 TO JOSEPH KNIGHT
MS: BL.

16 Cheyne Walk
22 Jan. 1870

My dear Knight

I have been meaning to call on you, but having repeatedly found it gets too late at this fearful distance, had better perhaps write and enclose Ellis's reply to my note. I suppose after this I had better stick to him, as Blackwood could not probably give better terms than he offers. I see decided advantages (I may say in confidence) in B. as a publisher, but after all he might take fright perhaps at something in the printed sheets when he saw them, & then I had rather not have shown them to him; and you will perceive my position with Ellis, with whom I am on terms of friendly intercourse, is rather an awkward one, though certainly there was no engagement between us at any time. I should like to have your opinion on the situation. I presume you have no notion exactly what terms might be expected from Blackwood, but of course they could be only such as the edition printed rendered possible, and I suppose Ellis goes to the length of that tether.

It is jolly to hear of your continued freedom from pain. Long may it last.

Ever yours
DG Rossetti

70.8 TO CHARLES ELIOT NORTON
MS: Harvard. Published: *RP* 511–13; DW 915.

16 Cheyne Walk, Chelsea
22 January 1870

My dear Norton

I am truly ashamed of the above date and of all my sins of omission – including perhaps some omitted sins, – for these too strike one as mistakes occasionally as life wears on. However at present such is not my remorse, for most certainly it would have been no sin, but a duty, to have written ere now to one who must think he remembers me much better than I do him, – and to whom at any rate I am grateful for past friendliness & even for future instalments of the same, so sure I am of them, whatever my poor deserts may be.

I duly got long ago the drawing of "Clerk Saunders" and was truly pleased to see its face again.[1] It even surprised me by its great merit of feeling and execution, and now takes its place among its fellows on my drawing room walls. I have had the silvered flat gilded, which makes a wonderful improvement in the tone, which the former leaden tint damaged terribly. Silver flats were one of the wilder experiments of our frame-making in those days.

I hope when I see you again you will be pleased with the drawing of Janey Morris destined for you which is now finished. If you like however you know I will send it to you in Florence.[2] But before parting with it I shall have to make a replica for my own keeping, as I like it on the whole the best of the drawings I have made of her, & never mean to let any more go out of my own possession. The chance of such a model is too precious for the ordinary market. You will be grieved to have heard (as you have doubtless done) how very ill she has been since you were in London, nor can I give a good account of her now, though she has been somewhat better just lately.

I have been thinking what there may be to tell you of my work, & am obliged to confess that it does not amount to much. I have been a good deal out of sorts, nor did I benefit much in the autumn by a trip to Scotland. However, poor health has not been the only cause of the little I have got done in painting, as I lost some time preparing a vol: of poems for the press, which I hope to get out in the Spring. I have communicated with Mr. Fields of Boston (whom you doubtless know) as to his undertaking an American reprint; since, when he called on me with Longfellow last summer he expressed a wish to reprint some early poetry of mine he had seen somewhere. I have not as yet received his reply. My proposed publisher, Ellis, had received a request for sheets of the poems from Messrs. Roberts the American publishers, but I thought after what Fields said it was best to write to him.[3]

Of course you know how great a success Morris' new Earthly Paradise is, & no doubt you agree with all the most reliable opinions, that there is some real advance as to strength and human character in this volume even over the former one. The "Gudrun" is surely on the whole one of the finest poems in the English language.

I believe you have been hearing from Ned Jones, so need not convey news of him and his. What a delightful picture – indeed a most precious one – your Giorgione turns out after passing through the hands of a skilful picture cleaner. Why in the world the change in it had ever been made it is difficult to conceive, except indeed that it appears to be part of a larger picture, the rest of which may presumably have been lost and an attempt thus made to give the fragment the look of a whole at the expense of its beauty and real character. It seems, as now cleaned, to be in a quite perfect state, & needed I believe no retouching whatever. The colour is so golden that it gives an idea of being actually painted on a gold ground, though this does not seem on examination to be the case.

We have a very fine specimen of an American over here now in the person of Stillman whom you know. I have known him in a fragmentary way for many years, but am seeing more of him now & like him extremely.[4]

I hope you are all enjoying yourselves in Florence and above all that you have no ill health to interfere with the fitness of things around you. Will you give my very best and truest remembrances to all yours and accept them for yourself, believing me

Your sincere friend
D G Rossetti

[1] For DGR's request to buy back *Clerk Saunders*, see 69.47.
[2] There is no record of CEN receiving this drawing.
[3] Roberts Bros. of Boston published the 1st American edition of *Poems* in 1870. The firm had published WM's *Life and Death of Jason* in 1867 and *The Earthly Paradise* in 1868.
[4] For WJS, see 62.3n13. He accompanied DGR during his stay at Scalands this spring and became engaged to Marie Spartali (see **88**), whom he married, against the wishes of her parents, in 1871 (see **65n3**).

70.9 TO FREDERICK STARTRIDGE ELLIS

MS: BL. Published: *FSE* 2; DW 916.

26 Jan 1870

My dear Ellis

Since receiving your last, I have felt certain that I cannot "better myself" in any way by changing our arrangements. Morris may perhaps have told you this, and I should have written before but for preoccupations. Let me say *en passant* that the delay has not been caused by further inquiry into the views of Blackwood, (the publishers in question) as this was unnecessary – it being certain they could not afford better terms.

I am hoping to get the book really under way now, but have an itching to write one more poem to beat the rest hollow if I can find time, & so don't like to give the hope up & set about advertising yet. I should like to bring it to about 300 pages, & even freer printing wd only make some 250 or 260 as yet.

Ever yours
DG Rossetti

P.S. I hope nothing very dreadful may "happen to Ellis" but if it does he must remember he *would* go in for it. I dare say he won't sell 50 copies.

70.10 TO JOHN ALDAM HEATON[1]

MS: BL. Published: *ALC* 4: 133; DW 917. On page 4 of the MS, DGR has placed 2 watercolour specimens of the desired tints, against which he has indicated the colours used to obtain them: for the first "Indigo, Yellow Ochre, and White"; for the second "Indigo, Raw Umber, and White." The second specimen corresponds closely to the colour of the cloth used for the book.

> 27 Jan.1870
> 16 Cheyne Walk
> Chelsea

My dear Heaton

I am going to publish a volume of poetry in the spring, and have designed a binding for it. As to the material for the binding, you know how disagreeable binders' cloths are – bad colours & most unpleasant texture. Would it be in your way to attempt anything of this kind? I have put overpage one indication of a grey & a sort of apple green which I fancy are the two tints (or approaching them) to which I should most incline. Then as to texture, the desiderata would be to show the thread rather more than in binders' cloths and to avoid the necessity if possible of being so glossy. Do you think you could make any experiments on my behalf in this direction? Probably I should not be the only customer were a success attained.

I hope you are all well at Woodbank. I have not myself been extremely brilliant lately, but rub on somehow. And when are you likely to visit town again?

With kindest remembrances to all yours

> I am ever yours
> DG Rossetti

I suppose any other material than cloth of some kind is out of the question as to cheapness.

P.S. By the bye I am in want of (or likely to want) the address of Mr. John Mitchell who I believe removed from Bradford to Manchester. I know he was not an intimate of yours, but could you find me his present whereabouts?[2]

---

[1] For JAH, see 61.26&n2.
[2] For John Mitchell, see 64.12n1, 57, & 74. JAH must have replied with Mitchell's address since DGR reports having written to him about photographing *Venus Verticordia* (S.173) in **89**.

70.11 TO JANE MORRIS

MS: BL. Published: Bryson 15. Date: P/M.

Sunday [30 January 1870]
16 Cheyne Walk
Chelsea

Dearest Janey

You were so sweet as to ask me to let you know how I got on, so I write to say I am all right again this morning after the mustard last night. The sight of you going down the dark steps to the cab all alone has plagued me ever since – you looked so lonely. I hope you got home safe & well. Now everything will be dark for me till I can see you again. It puts me in a rage to think that I should have been so knocked up all yesterday as to be such dreadfully dull company. Why should it happen just when you were here? I shall look you up on Wednesday evening. Will you see if those spectacles of mine have got into Top's room, as I am quite sure I must have left them at your house. As soon as you are able to sit to me again I will send you that chalk drawing to hang up, and indeed may probably do so before if I find I am not needing it. How nice it would be if I could feel sure I had painted you once for all so as to let the world know what you were; but every new thing I do from you is a disappointment, and it is only at some odd moment when I cannot set about it that I see by a flash the way it ought to be done. Such are all my efforts. If I had had you always with me through life, it would somehow have got accomplished. For the last 2 years I have felt distinctly the clearing away of the chilling numbness that surrounded me in the utter want of you; but since then other obstacles have kept steadily on the increase, and it comes too late.

Your most affectionate Gabriel

70.12 TO JOHN FERGUSON McLENNAN[1]

MS: Columbia.

31 January 1870
16 Cheyne Walk, Chelsea

My dear McLennan

You must have been much surprised at not hearing from me again for a whole month, and indeed, though I have been much preoccupied, I hardly know how it is that I have not answered your very friendly letter before. One cause of delay however is that I have been meaning to send you the sheets of my poems, & as yet have not got the last revisions made in them; thus I delayed writing till I sent them, but had better now write first. It will not be long I dare say before you get them. I hope they may seem likeable to you, but really and seriously am rather flabbergasted at your present view of Tennyson. My own is what it always was – that is, that if he does not possess *all* the qualities of great poetry, that is merely because he is himself only & no other great poet; but to such class he appears to me to belong incontestably, and that is all I want from him.[2] If I were to prove in like manner to have some one point in which I might be said to surpass others as a poet, I should think this ample measure of endowment, & should consider those who expected every one else's gift from me somewhat exorbitant. However, I have no doubt you, for one, are disposed to take a friendly view enough of my doings. I had hoped to have added a good slice more to my book before bringing it out, but am determined to do so this Spring, & am now led to fear that, overdue as I am to my painting again, I shall add little or nothing more. There are some pieces in my book – especially one called "Jenny" – which I suppose will excite a good deal of objection in some quarters – but I am sure it will be evident to all true readers that they (& this one especially) are written in no aggressive or reckless spirit (the results of which in poetry I view as bad art, however good the workmanship) & that accordingly they will find some defenders. Perhaps you have already learnt something about the prospects of your reviewing my book & may be able to tell me what they are. It would be most satisfactory to me if this could be brought about.

I was extremely sorry to hear of your wife's being so continuously an invalid, knowing myself by experience the wearing anxiety & hope deferred which attend such a misfortune. I should be very glad to know that you were relieved to some extent on the subject of her health.

I think I ought tell you quite in confidence that it so happens I have had a kind of offer (through a friend) for my poems from the Messrs. Blackwood lately. I believe however I am too much involved in another quarter (entirely through friendly considerations however) to be able to accept it, which I regret.

Sincerely yours D G Rossetti

P.S. I have been seeing your name (though not the articles) in the Fortnightly advertisements. I must get the papers.

P.P.S. I think I may probably drop a line to Skelton.

---

[1] For McLennan, see 54.28n2, 69.225, **20**, & **25**.
[2] The mature DGR refused for the most part to join his fellow writers in belittling the Laureate, although he was unimpressed by *Idylls of the King*. Many years later he told THC that "all poets are redundant nowadays except Tennyson" (80.340); to William Davies he wrote that Tennyson is a poet whom you can never "open at the wrong page" (81.121).

70.13 TO JOHN SKELTON

Text: Skelton 88–89. Reprinted: DW 918.

16 Cheyne Walk, Chelsea
3 February 1870

My dear Skelton,

I am going to publish some poems, as you have, I think, heard from McLennan, and have been meaning to write you thereanent. After your public *premura** about them, I daresay I may reckon, without too much conceit, on an intention on your part to review them fully in *Fraser*.¹ I am anxious that some influential article or articles by the well-affected should appear *at once* when the book comes out, for certain good reasons. If you thought you could secure the appearance of a notice all the sooner by my sending you proofs of the things as far as printed, and had time to think about it, I could do so very soon. If you then let me know how early you could secure the appearance in *Fraser* I would take this into consideration as to precise date of publishing. I suppose I cannot get out till April. I want to add a thing or two yet, if possible, but am much taken up with painting. Did you see some sonnets of mine in the *Fortnightly* nearly a year ago? I had tried to make them as perfect as in me lay, and have a good number in the volume.

Swinburne wishes to "do" my book in the *Fortnightly*, and Morris elsewhere; and if these and yours, with perhaps another or so, could appear *at once*, certain spite which I judge to be brewing in at least one quarter might find itself at fault.² . . . A model just come in. Farewell in haste.

Yours very truly,
D. G. Rossetti

---

* DGR may have been using "premura" = urgent petition *OED* obs., or he may simply have been using the Italian noun premura (haste, hurry) in a verbal sense: i.e., hurry up.

1. Skelton's "public premura" in the Feb 69 issue of *Fraser's* exhorted DGR to publish his original poems as announced in an advertisement in *EIP*. In "Mainly about Rossetti" in *Table Talk of Shirley*, Skelton quoted from his *Fraser's* piece as follows: "It is said that an accident befell the manuscript [of *Dante at Verona and other Poems*]; but surely from the rough drafts that Mr. Rossetti must possess the poems might even yet be recovered and put together. Even in this prolific age the world can ill afford to lose a volume which would undoubtedly prove a substantial addition to its poetic literature" (Skelton 87). See also 69.15. Skelton's review of *Poems* appeared in *Fraser's*, May 70.

2. DGR was hoping to neutralize hostile reviews expected from Sir Charles Dilke (see **14&n1**) and Robert Buchanan, with whom WMR had been feuding since 1866 (*FLM* 294–95). The strategy seemed to work as the 1870 reviews were nearly all laudatory; but Buchanan finally struck in the *Contemporary Review* for Oct 71, then again in 1872 with his separate pamphlet, *The Fleshly School of Poetry and Other Phenomena of the Day*. See also **22 & 23**.

70.14 TO WILLIAM MICHAEL ROSSETTI

MS: Brotherton. Excerpt: *RP* 518. Published: DW 919. Date: WMR.

Thursday [3 February 1870]

Dear William

I am always forgetting to ask you as follows. Top wants to do a notice of my book – he proposed Fortnightly but there I believe Swinburne proposes to do so, & had long ago started the idea. Do you think the Academy would be available? And if so, could you propose the thing to the editor? Top's name would be useful perhaps to him as well as to my book. If publication & such notices were timed together, Dilke might perhaps be bilked yet.[1]

Your

DGR

Will you dine here tomorrow at 7? I expect Howell, wife, & Boyce. Who could do it for the British Quarterly? I suppose you are shut out though that wd please me better than anything, but then the book is dedicated to you. Do you think Scotus could get the job? It would be the next best? Indeed equal almost.[2]

[1] DGR wrongly suspected that Sir Charles Wentworth Dilke (1843–1911), radical politician & proprietor of the *Athenæum* from 1869, would be antagonistic to *Poems*. However, the *Athenæum* published John Westland Marston's favourable review, and Buchanan brought Dilke into the Fleshly School controversy by denouncing the *Athenæum* as "the leading organ of the Fleshly School . . . as peculiar in its notions of literary decency as Sir Charles himself in his notions of political propriety" (Buchanan 83).

[2] ACS' review of *Poems* appeared in *Fortnightly Review* for May 70; WM's on 14 May 70 in the *Academy*. WBS wrote no signed review of *Poems,* though he is one of those suspected of being the author of the unsigned and unfriendly notice in *Blackwood's Edinburgh Magazine*: see **212&n1**.

70.15 TO JANE MORRIS

MS: BL. Published: Bryson 16. Date: P/M.

Friday [4 February 1870]

16 Cheyne Walk

Chelsea

Funny sweet Janey

A bloke is coming here tomorrow with a frame, so I think I had better take the opportunity of sending you that chalk drawing as said bloke can hang it up. If he should happen not to come tomorrow, then I suppose he will on Monday, & I will send it then.

Dear Janey, I suppose this has come into my head because I feel so badly the want of speaking to you. No one else seems alive at all to me now, and places that are empty of you are empty of all life. And it is so seldom that the dead hours breathe a little and yield your dear voice to me again. I seem to hear it while I write, and to see your eyes speaking as clearly as your voice; and so I would write to you for ever if it were not too bad to keep reminding you of my troubles, who have so many of your own. It is dreadful to me to think constantly of a sudden while my mind longs for you, that perhaps at that moment you are suffering so much as to shut out even the possibility of pleasure if life had it ready for you in every shape. I almost reproach myself with the comfort I feel despite all in the thought of you, when that thought never fails to present me also with the recollection of your pain and suffering. But more than all for me, dear Janey, is the fact that you exist, that I can yet look forward to seeing you and speaking to you again, and know for certain that at that moment I shall forget all my own troubles nor even be able to remember yours. You are the noblest and dearest thing that the world has had to show me; and if no lesser loss than the loss of you could have brought me so much bitterness, I would still rather have had this to endure than have missed the fullness of wonder & worship which nothing else could have made known to me.

When I began this I meant to try and be cheerful, and just see what vague and dismal follies I have been inflicting on you. I hope to look in tomorrow evening and see how you are, even if I only stay half an hour.

Your most affectionate
Gabriel

70.16 TO EDITOR OF *NOTES AND QUERIES*

Text: *N&Q* 4th series, 34 (1870): 154, in reply to a query of 8 Jan. Excerpt: Shepherd, "Studies of Sensation and Event by Ebenezer Jones," in *Forgotten Books Worth Remembering* 1 (Pickering [1878]): 5–7. Reprinted: DW 920.

[5 February 1870]

Ebenezer Jones

I hope Mr. Gledstanes-Waugh may receive from other sources a more complete account than I can give of this remarkable poet, who affords nearly the most striking instance of neglected genius in our modern school of poetry. This is a more important fact about him than his being a Chartist, which however he was, at any rate for a time. I met him only once in my life, I believe in 1848, at which time he was about thirty, and would hardly talk on any subject but Chartism. His poems (the *Studies of Sensation and Event*) had been published some five years before my meeting him, and are full of vivid disorderly power. I was little more than a lad at the time I first chanced on them, but they struck me greatly, though I was not blind to their glaring defects and even to the ludicrous side of their wilful "newness"; attempting, as they do, to deal recklessly with those almost inaccessible combinations in nature and feeling which only intense and oft-renewed effort may perhaps at last approach. For all this, these "Studies" should be, and one day will be, disinterred from the heaps of verse deservedly buried.

Some years after meeting Jones, I was much pleased to hear the great poet Robert Browning speak in warm terms of the merit of his work; and I have understood that Monckton Milnes (Lord Houghton) admired the "Studies" and interested himself on their author's behalf. The only other recognition of this poet which I have observed is the appearance of a short but admirable lyric by him in the collection called *Nightingale Valley*, edited by William Allingham. I believe that some of Jones's unpublished MSS. are still in the possession of his friend Mr. J. Linton, the eminent wood-engraver, now residing in New York, who could no doubt furnish more facts about him than anyone else. It is fully time that attention should be called to this poet's name, which is a noteworthy one. It may not be out of place to mention here a much earlier and still more striking instance of poetic genius which has hitherto failed of due recognition. I allude to Charles J. Wells, the author of the blank verse scriptural drama of *Joseph and his Brethren*, published under the pseudonym of "Howard" in 1824,[1] and of *Stories after Nature* (in prose, but of a highly poetic cast), published anonymously in 1822. This poet was a friend of Keats, who addressed to him one of the sonnets to be found in his works – "On receiving a present of roses." Wells's writings – youthful as they are – deserve to stand beside any poetry, even of that time, for original genius, and, I may add, for native structural power, though in this latter respect they bear marks of haste and neglect. Their time will come yet.

Dante G. Rossetti

---

1 For DGR's interest in C. J. Wells and his poem *Joseph and His Brethren: A Dramatic Poem* (1823–24), see 49.11n4, 14, & 69.51n1.

70.17 TO ALGERNON CHARLES SWINBURNE

MS: BL. Published: DW 921.

[10 February 1870]

My dear Swinburne

The reading of Monna Lisa naturally brings pen to paper to thank you for the pleasure of it, and if this has been deferred some days, the impression of the poem has lost none of its warmth. On your reading it to me I thought it one of your finest pieces of execution and emotion, and the reverberating music of its structure seems perhaps even more striking when it appeals to the eye as well as to the ear on being read to oneself.

I hear from William of the completion of your *Hertha*; and am far from having forgotten the instalment from the prologue to *Tristram & Ysuelt* which your last letter contained, though I have somehow been thus long in acknowledging it. All tends to show that you have got into full swing of productiveness. In the Tristram extract you have made the heroic metre so much your own by characteristic use of it that it does not strike one as having been used at all before, so exceptional is the impression in your hands. Then there was that tantalizing passage which you sent me from what must evidently be the crowning Carol of the era of man's redemption. Surely, surely, this great work cannot be left incomplete. Why is not the rest sent to me, and when am I to see it?[1]

As for myself I have been trying to paint and getting nothing done but generally abortive first steps towards new work. However it will shape itself suddenly into something one day I suppose. As to my poems I think I shall be able after all to add little or nothing as I am so utterly due to my painting, and do not want to delay bringing the vol: out beyond the Spring. I suppose you would agree with me in this.

What words, by the bye, can characterize the hideous & bestial attack on William's Shelley in the Athenæum? It really surprised me, even from that fœtid quarter of the editorial anus.[2]

Let me have a line when you can, and believe me

Affectionately yours
DGabriel R

---

[1] ACS' "The Complaint of Lisa" was printed in the Feb issue of the *Fortnightly Review*; it was included in *Poems and Ballads*, 2nd series, 1878. "Hertha" was published in *Songs before Sunrise* (1871). DGR is answering ACS' letter of 22 Dec 69 (Lang 2: 334), which included 14 lines that ultimately appeared in *Tristram of Lyonesse* (1882). The "carol" is burlesque blasphemy, a genre more appealing to ACS than to DGR.

[2] WMR's edition of Shelley's poems was harshly criticized in an unsigned review of 29 Jan in the *Athenæum*, supposed to have been written by Robert Buchanan. WMR responded in the *Athenæum* of 5 Feb.

70.18 TO WILLIAM MICHAEL ROSSETTI

MS: Brotherton. Published: *RP* 521–22; DW 922. Date: WMR.

[11 February 1870]

Dear W

Top thinks the best plan wd be as you suggest – i.e. for you to tell the editor of Academy that he is willing to write on his own subjects & notify any book he wishes for review. I suppose that plan is likely to suit editor.

Your
D G R

70.19 TO FRANCIS GLEDSTANES WAUGH[1]

MS: Arizona.

12 Feb/1870
16 Cheyne Walk
Chelsea

Dear Sir

I send you my "Ebenezer" [Jones] by book post with this. It is coverless (& meant to get bound) but I dare say you can be temperate with the shorn lambs of Parnassus.* I think on the whole – were E. J. to be republished – he wd have to be left as he is, though modification & even positive improvement wd be easy in many places. But then this ought to have come from himself.

I am surprised not to have yet seen in *N. & Q.* a letter which my friend Mr. W. Bell Scott I know wrote in answer to your query. It contained more biographical matter than my own, as he knew Jones pretty well.

My brother is editing an edition of modern British poets which will include a volume of general selections, & in this he means to include some by E. J.

Keep the book for a month if you like & believe me

Faithfully yours
D G Rossetti

F. Gledstanes Waugh Esq

---

* "shorn lambs of Parnassus" = a fanciful reference to the unbound volume being sent. Mount Parnassus, sacred to Apollo and the Muses in ancient Greece, came to symbolize inspired literary performance.

[1] See **16**. ACS also wrote at least 3 letters to Francis Gledstanes Waugh between 1868 & 1873 (Lang 1: 154 & 2: 470A, & a MS at Beinecke). For Waugh (1846–1902), see Lang 1: 154n1. Chatto & Windus brought out a new edition with an introduction by ACS in 1876.

70.20 TO JOHN FERGUSON McLENNAN

MS: Columbia. The words in angled brackets are reconstructions of those obscured by a postage stamp pasted on the letter.

Saturday [12 February 1870]

Dear McLennan

Your note from Reigate is to hand, and I shall be very glad to see you here. However I expect to be very busy all next week. If you call on Wednesday or Thursday, wd 2 o'clock be a suitable hour? That would suit my engagements <best>, as I should have <about> an hour to spare <at> that time. I hope my being obliged on these particular days to limit the hour will not cause me to miss you, which I should much regret.

I heard from Skelton (to whom I wrote) & also from Alexander.[1] Both seem *on ne peut plus* well-disposed. Thanks for the sonnet. I had it & have printed it, but am I believe about to expunge it after all – not because I do not think it good enough in its way, but it seems too much out of harmony with everything else in the book.[2]

I quite agree with you in regretting that I missed publishing with Blackwood – but I am weak at creating disappointment – & my publisher is a personal friend & would have much regretted being put aside – though indeed I had no *distinct* agreement with him when the other proposition came. I believe I shall be in some respects the loser.

We can talk of things when we meet. I hope your silence as to Mrs. McLennan's health is a sign of lessened anxiety.

Yours sincerely
D G Rossetti

P.S. I am afraid from yr former letter that you hardly think it likely you will be able to "do" one in Blackwood yrself.

---

[1] Patrick Proctor Alexander (1823–1886), literary critic & author. He sent DGR a copy of his *Mill and Carlyle. An examination of J. S. Mill's doctrine of causation in relation to moral freedom. With an occasional discourse on Sauerteig, by Smelfungus* (Edinburgh: Nimmo, 1866) in 1867 (see 67.32). See also Lang 4: 1079.

[2] Probably "On the Site of a Mulberry Tree Planted by William Shakespeare"; DGR did delete this sonnet from his proofs later this month, telling ACS it was "out of harmony" with the rest of *Poems* (**31**).

70.21 TO HENRY VIRTUE TEBBS

MS: Texas.

13 Feb/1870
16 Cheyne Walk
Chelsea

My dear Tebbs

A friend of mine has asked me to ask you what are the steps to be taken in case of marriage by registry – conditions of residence &c. Also respecting licenses about which I once acquired some knowledge but have forgotten. Pardon trouble & believe me

Ever yours
D G Rossetti

70.22 TO ALGERNON CHARLES SWINBURNE

MS: BL. Published: *ALC* 4: 155–56; DW 923.

Monday/14 Feb [1870]
16 Cheyne Walk
Chelsea

Dear Swinburne

Your delightful farrago of blasphemy and indecency has imparted a welcome spiritual "branlement"* to my better nature on this dismal St Valentine's Day.[1] I will not attempt to cope with you on ground so exclusively your own, but will refer merely to those brief, rare, and casual passages which are not aimed against the most sacred associations of early life. Before doing so, however, I must mention that my idea of the Carol having been completed was founded on 2 lines which I have found to be currently attributed to you and to it, saying.–

> "This is what comes of your bloody religion,
> That you have to father your kid on a pigeon,"

which, whether genuine or not, are, you will admit, to be commended. With one word of high appreciation for the supplementary stanza to *Hertha*, let me modestly retire from your special diggings.

The notion of Love's Calendar in your prologue is delightful and the lines given exquisite. I want very greatly to hear all you have been writing. Don't you think of coming up to town before long? If you do, try & give me a day or two's notice, as my evenings have been a good deal occupied lately, and I should greatly regret if I were not free when you came.

There seems good reason to believe that Buchanan was the special atom of the excremental whole from which the scent which took us both unawares emanated in the Athenæum.

What you say about "Holm" disturbs me, though I can't see it myself. Would "Neill" do better? – the *Boyne* seems to make an Irish name desirable, but then would Eastholm & Westholm be Irish enough? I don't think I can revert to Keith. I should be very much obliged for a better suggestion at once, if one occurs to you, as I am going to press now with last corrections. I feel inclined to restore the French motto for which I too have a weakness, but think if so it must be at the head, as I have a great dislike to notes anywhere but just where they are wanted at the moment, and this one especially seems as if it would look quite unaccountable at the end.

I don't see my way to putting back the lines you quote into *Jenny*. I believe I have made up my mind to alter the passage about

A separate man has lost his Soul

which is a sort of statistical blunder as to the balance of first causes in prostitution. This had always struck myself, though the notion is effective perhaps in the place it comes in. I don't know if this was what led to the objection I mentioned as having been made to it.

I have written nothing new to add to the sheets as yet but a sonnet or two; but have serious thoughts of going into retreat for a few weeks almost immediately in the country and trying if I can hammer anything out before the inevitable day of publication is at the doors.

By the bye I expect the B-B-Buchanan to be down upon me of course now in the Athenæum, & am anxious to time my appearance when it seems likely that friends can speak up almost at once and so just catch the obscene organ of his speech at the very moment when it is hitched up for an utterance, and perhaps compel the brain of which it is also the seat to reconsider its views and chances.

You once expressed an intention, much valued by me, of reviewing the book in the Fortnightly. I suppose the book will be ready by 1st May. Do you think the review could be got in then also?

Affectionately yours
D Gabriel R

P.S. There has been a passable review of the Shelley in the Examiner but I have seen no other as yet except a very complimentary but short one in the Standard.

P.S. Did I ever give you the valuable emendation below?

> Who slunk by night to a flash ken,
> And bilked poor Molly Magdalen,
> And got a fresh pox there and then?
> &c &c.

* "branlement" = French for shaking, shuddering, probably used here in the sense of sexual "frisson."
1   This letter responds to ACS' of 12 Feb (Lang 2: 340).

70.23 TO FREDERICK STARTRIDGE ELLIS

MS: BL. Published: *FSE* 3; DW 924.

[14 February 1870]
16 Cheyne Walk
Chelsea

My dear Ellis

I think perhaps my book might be advertised now for once – what say you? – merely

> To appear shortly –
> Poems
> by Dante Gabriel Rossetti
> F. S. Ellis &c

I hope in a few days to get the final alterations & resetting done to the sheets already in type, & have serious thoughts of going into retreat for 2 or 3 weeks in the country to see about adding a sheet or two more. I suppose the close of April will be the right moment to bring it out. A review is promised for the May number of Fraser. I want to appear when I know a few reviews are ready, to keep spite at bay and leave it gaping and goggling without a chance of a good snarl. I fancy Mr. Buchanan probably has his natural organ of speech hitched up for an utterance. It would be nice if he had to make it a silent emanation & get nothing but the smell to enjoy. This might perhaps be managed if a few good men were in the field at the outset. Morris proposes to do the Academy, and I believe Swinburne will come out in the Fortnightly.

Perhaps tomorrow – certainly in a day or two – I'll send you the sketches for the cover & flyleaf. I suppose the latter ought to be cut on wood. If so, I have a draughtsman who can draw it for the purpose.[1]

Of course Strangeways must charge the printing of the prose tale to me.[2]

Ever yours D G Rossetti

P.S. Of course the binding question will be subject to your opinion as to expense.

[1] This letter, **24**, & **30** concern decoration of the cover and endpapers for *Poems*; DGR's design was a woodcut pattern of flowers against "curls," bluish-green for endpapers with gold stamped on dark green for the cover. Some plain-bound copies were issued early; decorated bindings were signed on the bottom left of the back cover by FSE's binding cutter De Lacy (see 72.94).

[2] Proof State No. 10 of *Poems*, a separate printing paginated 1–22 in multiple copies of the story "Hand and Soul," originally published in *Germ*. Some copies had wrappers. See 69.207n3 & Lewis 120–24.

70.24 TO FREDERICK STARTRIDGE ELLIS

MS: BL. Published: *FSE* 4; DW 925.

[c. 15 February 1870]

Dear Ellis

I send you the block. The engraver should facsimile it exactly of course, but take care that he tends rather to thickness than thinness in the lines, as this can be remedied by cutting away if *too* thick, & the other cannot be set right. I think you mentioned some one to whom you thought of giving it: I fancy myself Swain is the best man, & if my name were mentioned as having drawn it, I believe he wd give it his best attention, slight thing as it is. However I dare say the other man wd quite do if more convenient.

Ever yours
DG Rossetti

70.25 TO JOHN FERGUSON McLENNAN

MS: Columbia.

Wednesday [16 February 1870]

Dear McLennan

Thanks, but I find it impossible to join you on Friday, being for some days to come specially preoccupied. I ought to have explained that I never got your card till you were gone, nor heard of your return call till you were gone again, – otherwise I'd have tried to rush out a minute & apologize personally. But the fact is, at such moments a painter is tied hand & foot, and can do nothing but one thing – that is, to abide in his trenches.

I'll hope to see you ere long some other way, & am ever

Yours sincerely
DG Rossetti

70.26 TO MRS. G. H. LEWES (GEORGE ELIOT)

MS: Duke. Published: Baum, *Library Notes* 34 (1959): 18.

18 Feb/1870
16 Cheyne Walk
Chelsea

Dear Mrs. Lewes

I have delayed sending you the photographs of which I wished to beg your acceptance, because I have not a satisfactory impression of the one of Mary Magdalene. I have ordered some, but they do not come, so I send you a bad one which I have, and will send a better when I get it. I enclose 2 sonnets, one on this, and one on the *Pandora*, in case they add anything to the drawings. The single head and little single figure I send because they are from the same model as the Beatrice which interested you. The *Rosa Triplex* is a study of one head in 3 views.

In the Hamlet, I have wished to symbolize the character & situation, as well as to represent the incident. Perhaps after all a simpler treatment might have been better. I fear it results in what a good many even sympathetic spectators might find puzzling and intricate. As regards the dramatic action, I have meant to make Hamlet ramping about and talking wildly, kneeling on one of the little stalls and pulling to pieces the roses planted in a box in the angle – hardly knowing all he says and does, as he throws his arms wildly this way and that along the ledge of the carved screen. Ophelia is tired of talking and listens to him, still holding out the letters & presents she wishes to return.[1]

Most of the things I have got photographed were done some time ago. Perhaps I could do them better now, were I to carry them out in a new form, as I hope to do with the Magdalene at any rate before long. I wish they were better worth offering you, or that, failing this, something else may be so some day.²

With kindest remembrances to Mr. Lewes

I am sincerely yours
D G Rossetti

¹ *Hamlet* III, i.
² For George Eliot's response, acknowledging the photos and discoursing on the possible relationship between anatomical and physiognomical appearances and passion, see Haight, *Selections from George Eliot's Letters* 372. See also the following letter.

70.27 TO BARBARA LEIGH SMITH BODICHON
MS: PML.

18 Feb/1870.
16 Cheyne Walk
Chelsea

Dear Mme Bodichon

I am sorry that I cannot have the pleasure of dining with you next Thursday as I am engaged for the 4 last days of next week.

When I got your note I was just getting a few photographs together, whereof to beg your acceptance. I am also sending some to Mrs. Lewes. I have only one copy of the one of Mary Magdalene, and that a poor impression. This I send to her as she specially honoured it with her approval – but I am expecting others shortly & then shall send good impressions both to you and to her.

The two studies of my wife recall her to me & I hope may do so to you. The head I did shortly before her death. The little figure was done at the very time when we were all together at Hastings. The Triple Rose is meant for one head in 3 views – a sort of exhaustive portraiture which would be interesting were the model a valued one.¹

Of the rather crotchetty construction of the Hamlet I have just been writing to Mrs. Lewes, and in doing so have more than half convinced myself that it seems pretentious when put into writing. So I won't do it again.

Yours most sincerely
DG Rossetti

¹ The drawings of EES are probably the same as those DGR sent to GBJ in 1864 (see 64.144).

70.28 TO JANE MORRIS

MS: BL. Published: Bryson 17. Date: P/M.

[18 February 1870]

Dearest Kindest Janey,

How good of you to write to me so nicely when you are suffering torments in your dear throat. I really feel, seeing you so little, as if I must seem neglectful and careless of all you have to endure. But I hope you believe that it is never absent from my thoughts for a moment and that I never cease to long to be near you and doing whatever might be to distract and amuse you. To be with you and wait on you and read to you is absolutely the only happiness I can find or conceive in this world, dearest Janey; and when this cannot be, I can hardly now exert myself to move hand or foot for anything. If I ever do wish still to do any work, it is that I may not sink into utter unworthiness of you and deserve nothing but your contempt.

I shall come up on Saturday evening and see how you are. But if I *should* be prevented then (or rather to speak plainly if I should resolve that it would be much pleasanter to come when no visitors were at your house) I will then come on Monday.

As for the Academy question, I do not see that I can suggest anything. I suppose all Top has to do is to signify that he wants my book as soon as it appears.[1] If it is necessary it should be advertised to enable him to do so, then Ellis had better advertise at once. I think on the whole I had better write at once to Ellis & tell him he had better do so.

Most affectionately yours
Gabriel

---

[1] WM was a reluctant participant in "working the oracle"; writing to JM on 14 Mar, he said: "I shall set to work about Gabriel's review, wh: I must say rather terrifies me" (Kelvin 107). It appeared in the *Academy* on 14 May.

70.29 TO WILLIAM ALLINGHAM

MS: PML. Published: *WA/GBH* 285–86; DW 927.

21 Feb/1870
16 Cheyne Walk
Chelsea

My dear Allingham

As you expressed a willingness for a little more scratching and sifting at my poetic diggings, I trouble you on a rather abject dilemma regarding a very old piece of work – *Sister Helen* enclosed. The family name used in it was originally "Keith". This I altered because of Dobell's ballad "Keith of Ravelston" which bears also on faithless love & supernaturalism. (I may add however that D's ballad was never published till some years after mine had been originally in print, but still I hate coincidences of this kind.) Thus I have changed it to "Holm" which is objected to, now, from I think a quarter worth considering, as not being a well-sounding territorial name. My reason for asking you about it is that (the Boyne being mentioned in the poem) an Irish name might perhaps do best.[1] Would Neill do? – & would it fit in with Eastholm, Westholm, & Neill of Neill? Would you give me a hint or a suggestion of some better name or system of nomenclature if such occurs to you? The father being "of that ilk" should stand I think, as elucidatory. I write in great hurry, as I am trying to get the things off for a new revise, and should be much obliged therefore if you could answer my question without delay.

I suppose you saw the evidently personal onslaught on William's Shelley in the Athenæum – by Buchanan I believe. I suppose I may expect to fare likewise if nothing interferes.

Ever yours
DG Rossetti

---

[1] See **35** & **38** for a report of WA's answer and DGR's choice of "Weir"; for the poet's return to "Keith," see **40** & **54**.

70.30 TO FREDERICK STARTRIDGE ELLIS

MS: BL. Published: *FSE* 5; DW 926.

Monday [c. 21 February 1870]

Dear Ellis

I think there is one defect in the woodcut which I did not notice to you before because it was too late to remedy it in the natural way, but as it struck Morris too when he saw it, I write now. I said the engraver should be careful to keep all lines rather tending to thicker than thinner to allow of cutting away for alterations. Now he has cut the curls of the diaper forming the background rather too thin. I believe however that by some means – I suppose burnishing them hard, so as to spread them out slightly – this could still be remedied a little & I should think sufficiently. It seems to me that something of the sort has been done for me before by Linton when he has cut blocks for me. Perhaps if you show this note to the engraver he will understand & be able to do something.

Ever yours
D GRossetti

P.S. I should like to have a proof sent me with a very little Raw Umber mixed with the Yellow ochre. Also one printed in dark Blue & another in dark Green – all on white.

70.31 TO ALGERNON CHARLES SWINBURNE

MS: BL. Excerpt: Compton-Rickett 317–18; *ALC* 4: 117–18. Published: DW 928. Text within angled brackets are marginal insertions.

21 Feb/70
16 Cheyne Walk
Chelsea

My dear Swinburne

Thanks truly for your kindest & friendliest of letters. If Morley should prove bent on appending to his name such titular initials as you well know how to bestow, I can bear patiently even the loss of your article (to which I have nevertheless looked forward as the book's best chance,) when I have from you in private such a loyal and generous reiteration of old belief in my old doings. I am well aware how friendship only can account for the point to which you carry the comparison between your friend's work and your own at times; but such friendship is the only thing as well worth having even as poetic pre-eminence.[1] So much for what I really feel on this head, once for all.

It will give me the greatest satisfaction if I can in the least reciprocate your consideration of all my worrying queries by settling in any degree, on perusal of your <or are you printing now? I can never see my own work clearly till in print.[2]> M.S. volume, any of such doubts as are so difficult to settle for oneself. I am very anxious to see it & all the more eager (as one always feels with good work) to read again what I have heard read without setting eyes on it. Moreover there is the Hertha (and others I presume) which I have not seen at all. I must look out, both for you & Hugo in Cassell's Mag.[3] On him, by the bye, as on other publishers, I have lately exercised that power as a rhyming chronicler which has descended to me from purer & earlier times. However the best place to transcribe these efforts would seem to be the flyleaf of that version of Rabelais from which you lately quoted a memorable definition.

I hope you are going to give your new book to Ellis who I think is really a straightforward fellow and deserves to publish for us all.[4] It would be most pleasant to concentrate our forces. My sister is now going to him with a joint edition of her old things (including additions) and also with a book of 101 Nursery Rhymes (illustrated by herself!), which she has lately produced – admirable things, alternating between the merest babyism and a sort of Blakish wisdom & tenderness. I believe no one could have written anything so absolutely right for babies but herself. She will also have a volume of prose tales ready soon. The principal one (modern, of the most matter of fact simplicity) I have not yet seen, but hear at home that it is remarkable. She has resolved to leave Macmillan after a degree of meanness in his proposals which was really laughable. Ellis will pay much better – indeed I believe as well as can be managed.[5]

I hope to be sending you in a few days a further revised set of my proofs, containing a few changes besides 2 or 3 new sonnets. 1st in *Portrait* as you know. 2nd 2 last stanzas of *Penumbra* rewritten. 3. Anecdote about the bones under the table added in *Dante*. 4. 1st stanza to *Troy Town* – but about this I can't make up my mind quite. You objected to

The Sun & moon of the heart's desire

as seeming to infer a difference in the 2 breasts. I confess I like the line, but of course your objection haunts me. Would you give it 5 minutes further consideration (it is on page 1, so important), & tell me if you think it ought really to be changed. I might say

The glowing spheres of the heart's desire,

but I must say I don't like this as well myself.

A good many other changes of a slight kind occur throughout the sheets. I think of omitting altogether Dennis Shand, as rather chargeable with triviality & its objectionableness strengthening those who will rail at the more important *Jenny* and also because the versification is queer, having lines that rhyme in the middle. I have also resolved to leave out the Sonnet about Shakspeare, as out of harmony with all the others. I almost think I shall cut out *My Sister's Sleep* at the last moment – I feel so sure the British fool will greet it with congenial sympathy, & do so hate to please him. Do you think the Italics look a nuisance in The Blessed Damozel? Also there is a line in *Confession* page 187 which I half believe to be silly about

"Tis you shall shriek in Latin."

The passage might run –

"Shall my end be as their end? Some bell rings, &c

Would this be better? Pardon plagues. Even those of Egypt came to an end. Could you give me your verdict on the above slight points by return if possible, as I shall delay sending the sheets to the printer till I hear.

Your affec:
D Gabriel R

Here is a prolonged sonnet of Cecco's which I translated yesterday –

>Never so bare and naked was church-stone
>   As is my clean-stripped doublet in my grasp;
>   Also I wear a shirt without a clasp
>Which is a dismal thing to look upon.
>Ah! had I still but the sweet coins I won
>   That time I sold my nag and staked the pay,
>   I'd not lie hid beneath the roof today
>And eke out sonnets with this moping moan.
>
>Daily a thousand times stark mad am I
>   At my dad's meanness who won't clothe me now,
>For "How about the horse?" is still his cry:
>   Till one thing strikes me as clear anyhow, –
><"No rag I'll get." (which is best?)>
>No clothes he'll stand. The wretch has sworn, I see,
>   Not to invest another doit in me.
>
>And all because of the fine doublet's price
>He gave me when I vowed to throw no dice,
>And for his damned nag's sake! Well, this is nice.[6]

---

1 John Morley, editor of *The Fortnightly Review*, answered ACS at once: "I shall be glad indeed to have your notice on Mr. Rossetti's poems for the May Fortnightly. As for your being a friend of his, that is no reason why you should not both like his poetry and tell us why and how you like it and why the rest of discriminating people should do the same" (Lang 2: 344). ACS' review ("The Poems of Dante Gabriel Rossetti," May 70: 551–79) was less a review than an extensive critical study. He reprinted it in *Essays and Studies* (1875), and it appears in T.J. Wise & Edmund Gosse's *Complete Works of ACS*, Bonchurch Edition ([Heinemann, 1925–27]: 15: 3–49).

² This comment accounts for the profusion of proofsheets, often with MS revisions and additions, with which DGR tormented his printers, and later, his editors.
³ ACS' verse translation of Victor Hugo's poem, "The Children of the Poor," appeared in *Cassell's Magazine* (May 70: 328); the text is included in Lang 2: 341.
⁴ For ACS & FSE, see 69.222. FSE published ACS' *Songs before Sunrise* in 1871.
⁵ CGR published *Commonplace and Other Short Stories* with FSE in 1870. Her *Sing-Song: A Nursery Rhyme Book* was illustrated by AH and published by Routledge in 1872. The Blake allusion refers to his *Songs of Innocence*. For AMc's "meanness" compared with terms offered by FSE, see **38**, Packer 70 & 71&n1, and especially Lorraine Janzen Kooistra, *Christina Rossetti and Illustration* ([Athens: Ohio UP, 2002]: 92–97.)
⁶ This translation of "When His Clothes Were Gone" by Cecco Angiolieri da Siena (1260–1312) was published in DGR's *Dante and His Circle* (Ellis & White, 1874). For ACS' response, see Lang 2: 344.

70.31.1 TO JANE ELIZABETH SENIOR¹

MS: European Art Gallery, Dallas, Texas.

22 Feby/1870
16 Cheyne Walk
Chelsea

Dear Mrs. Senior

Thanks for your very kind invitation. I am sorry that a previous engagement for Thursday prevents my accepting it, and meeting Miss Spartali, to whom please give my kindest remembrances.

Very truly yours
D G Rossetti

¹ Jane Elizabeth Hughes (1828–77), sister of Thomas Hughes, the author of *Tom Brown's Schooldays*, married Nassau John Senior (1822–1891), a barrister, son of the well-known economist, Nassau William Senior. She was the first woman appointed to a salaried government position, Inspector of Workhouses and District Pauper Schools. She and her husband lived at 92 Cheyne Walk.

70.32 TO ALGERNON CHARLES SWINBURNE

MS: BL. Published: *ALC* 4: 109–11; DW 929. Text within angled brackets is a marginal insertion.

23 Feb 1870
16 Cheyne Walk
Chelsea

Dear Swinburne

I rejoice to find I am really to have your invaluable support at starting, & do not care what else happens now. Only do, do, my dear best of fellows, remember that I am your friend not only to the purpose of praising what I do to the utmost (which I know how surely you will fulfil) but also to the purpose of being on your guard against praising me beyond my deserts, which is pretty sure to be your first impulse, I know well. <And do pitch into me when I need it.> Remember that my verses are not yet my Remains or Manes, and do not Sacrifice to them those poets – least of all the living ones – whom I respect and love and with whom I would be but too proud to rank on such footing as the lesser quantity of my work could give me, if only its quality might be found worthy of being classed with theirs. The four I mean above all are Tennyson, Browning, yourself, & Morris.

I am very glad you have taken the embargo off the "Sun & moon" line which was a favorite of mine when I made it. "Father Hilary" I fear I couldn't see *in* without a desire to kick him *out*, so out he had better keep.

This is one of more than 50 short pieces – sonnets, songs &c. (besides translations, unfinished things &c.) which I have found among my reliques and rejected, though in some cases with more doubt than in this. I fear the Shakspeare Sonnet must come out, as among several rejected of a semi-comic sort, the one copied overpage is the best, & I think you will agree it is not good enough.[1] Looking it up I come on what I may call my first poem (after still more childish things) I believe, & enclose it you for a lark. Of course it is on nothing less than Napoleon at Waterloo![2]

The "Cecco" is a real one I feel sure.[3] I found the original somewhere as by "Cecco Nuccoli da Perugia" & therefore omitted it from my book, though with strong suspicions of its being by Angiolieri about which I think now there cannot be a doubt. Nuccoli is either a mistake or an *alias*, & if the latter opens amusing conjectures.

Your affec:
D G R

On certain Elizabethan "Revivals"

O ruff-embastioned vast Elizabeth,
   Bush to these bushel-bellied casks of wine,
   Home-growth, 'tis true, but rank as turpentine, –
What thought'st thou of such skittle-plays at death?
Say, must we watch these brawlers' brandished lathe
   Or to their recking wit our ears incline,
   Because all Castaly flowed crystalline
In gentle Shakspeare's modulated breath?

23 Feb 1870 70.32

What! must our drama with the rat-pit vie,
Nor the scene close while one is left to kill?
   Write thus, & be a poet! Hark, thou man
   Of blood, thou cannabalic Caliban,
What shall be said to thee? – A poet? – Fie!
"An honorable murderer, if you will."

———

The End of It.
(18th June . 1815.)
===

His brows met, and his teeth were set,
   And his mouth seemed in pain,
And madness closed and grappled with him
   As they turned his bridle-rein.
And albeit his eyes went everywhere,
   Yet they saw not anything:
And he drew the bit tightly, for he thought
   That his horse was stumbling.

There was a great shouting about him
   And the weight of a great din.
But what was the battle he had around
   To the battle he had within?
A pond in motion to the stress of the ocean,
   A lamp to a furnace-eye,
Or the wind's wild weeping-fits
   To the voice of Austerlitz
When it shook upon the sky.

Hark, hark, hark! through the spangled dark,
   To the left and to the right,
Hark, hark, hark! how the muskets bark
   Like ban-dogs heard at night:
While the trumpet, all day shrill for blood,
   Laughs with a cruel heave,
Ringing out fame and ringing in shame, –
   A peal for a New Year's Eve.

> He stared right out, and he turned him about,
>   And he knew that It must fall;
> He knew the trodden ground for its bier
>   And the cannon-smoke for its pall.
> Spurring, he gazed not back; but sped
>   As speedeth the speedy wind
> When, bound as far as St. Helena,
>   It leaves Waterloo behind.

===

18th June. 1845.

P.S. I hope to send you before many days a further revised set of sheets.

---

1. The sonnet "On Certain Elizabethan 'Revivals'" displeased ACS (Lang 2: 345). It was not printed in DGR's lifetime, appearing first in Caine (256) and then reprinted in *Works* (208).
2. "The End of It" is not DGR's first poem; the MS is dated 18 Jun 45, but his ballad *Sir Hugh the Heron* was privately printed by his grandfather, Gaetano Polidori, in 1843. The "End of It" was first printed by Thomas J. Wise, who owned the MS, in 1923 (*ALC* 4: 109–10).
3. See **31&n6**.

70.33 TO WILLIAM MICHAEL ROSSETTI

MS: BL. Excerpt: *RP* 524–25. Published: DW 930. Date: WMR.

[23 February 1870]

Dear W

I have sent my proofs for correction & resetting (as I mean now to have only 24 lines in a page instead of 29) and have told them to send a set when done to you at once. I suppose this will not be done for some days but write now lest I forget, as I want to ask whether you could greatly oblige me by reading them carefully through again with a view to punctuation when you receive them – as I am sure stops &c will be sure to drop out in the resetting, and you must have a good habit of spotting these things, besides better eyes than I have.

Swinburne's article will be in the May Fortnightly – one by Skelton in May Fraser, & Top (I trust) in May Academy. So Buchanan may, let us hope, be caught just in the act of hitching up his organ of speech for an utterance & forced after all to restrict himself to scent.

Your
DGR

P.S. By the bye did I or did I not tell you of the leary dodge adopted by Nolly Brown to find out who wrote that thing on you in the Arse-inæum?¹ Lady Hardy (wife of Duffus)² had told Emma Brown that she knew who did it but mustn't peach. So Nolly was coached, and one night said suddenly to old Duffus as he was getting up out of his chair – "By the bye, what a shame it was of Buchanan to write that attack on Wm Rossetti." Old D. turned suddenly, very taken aback, & stuttered – "Ah well! Well! perhaps it was!" So I suppose there can be little doubt that the double or triple B did it.

1   For the *Athenæum* review, see **17**. According to the "Athenæum Contributor Index," compiled from the marked file of the journal, the mark for the review is "Jackson," but there has been no reliable identification. WMR never seriously doubted that Buchanan was the reviewer, declaring in the first draft of *SR*: "so I was informed and so I firmly believe; but I do not know the fact for certain" (Bodleian); in the published version the passage reads: "as I was informed, and indeed I have reason to be pretty sure of it" (380). In *Poems and Ballads: A Criticism* (1866), WMR had ridiculed Buchanan as a "poor and pretentious . . . poetaster" (7); the reviewer echoed this comment in his dismissal of "Mr. Rossetti's somewhat pretentious book [which] is anything but a standard work" and in his contention that he lacked the judgment and taste required of a good biographer and editor.

    The edition, the first since Mary Shelley's of 1839, was widely and favourably reviewed, but the *Athenæum* reviewer sharply pointed out that WMR did not have "the confidence of the Shelley family" and that the "careful reader" would quickly discover that as editor WMR was "anything but a trustworthy interpreter." Both charges were easy to make, since WMR had deliberately not consulted the poet's son, Sir Percy Shelley, and his meddlesome wife, Lady Jane Shelley (Peattie 148n2, 157), and the text of Shelley's poems was riddled with errors that would take 2 or more generations of textual scholars to correct. Although the review was well informed and even commended WMR for the "care and industry" with which he had collated texts and identified obscurities, the animosity that pervades it was not unreasonably interpreted by the Rossetti circle as another move in the series of attacks and counterattacks culminating in The Fleshly School controversy of 1872 that contributed to DGR's breakdown in the summer of that year (see *Prelude*). Certainly Buchanan did abuse WMR's work then, calling it "the worst edition of Shelley which has ever seen the light" in his 1872 *Fleshly School* pamphlet (see **14n1** & *FLM* 295).

2   Sir Thomas Duffus Hardy (1804–78), deputy keeper of the Public Record Office, and his 2nd wife, Mary Anne MacDowell (1824–91), who wrote popular novels, were long-standing friends of FMB.

70.34 TO MRS. WILLIAM GILLUM

MS: Princeton. Published: DW 931.

16 Cheyne Walk

26 Feb. 1870

Dear Mrs. Gillum

  I was a good deal disturbed, as you may suppose, by the news in your note, & wrote at once to Mr. Parsons, the photographer who reproduced the drawings for me, asking for an explanation. I should mention that he is in the same house with Prince, the picture-dealer in question, but not in any way connected with him. I have known Parsons for years & was greatly surprised at the apparent breach of confidence. However I think his answer, which I enclose, seems (as far as I can judge) to explain matters sufficiently, though the details are not quite clear to me; – sufficiently, I mean, when it is taken into consideration that I always believed him to be quite an honorable man & should be much surprised to learn the contrary.[1] So I fancy the matter may be considered at rest, though I certainly should not wish prints to be sold at all without my authority.

Thanks for your inquiries after my health. I have been far from well now for nearly 2 years, & in consequence have been much interrupted in work. However I must still hope for the best, & trust shortly to be making way with things again. Had it not been for this I had hoped to have shown Colonel Gillum before now the picture which I once mentioned to him as possibly (with his assent) calculated to meet my longstanding debt to him.[2] The work is a replica of another which has not yet got done (and thus the replica also remains in statu quo) and is I believe, of all the things I have in hand, the one most likely to please Colonel Gillum and yourself.

With kind remembrances

I am yours sincerely
DG Rossetti

[1] Colonel Gillum's *Cassandra* (S.127), which DGR considerably reworked in 1867, may be the work mentioned here. For Parsons, see 65.87. DGR was evidently satisfied but not clear about Parsons's explanation of the photographs he sold without authority. For further evidence of Parsons selling copies of DGR's photographs, see 74.24 & 31.

[2] Only two of the 11 pencil and pen & ink drawings given by Leonora Georgiana Gillum (d.1915) to the British Museum when Col. Gillum died in 1910 were purchased directly from DGR: a sketch for *Found* (S.64B) and the *Cassandra*. Gillum acquired *Hamlet and Ophelia* at the Plint Sale and the others at CWS.

70.35 TO ALGERNON CHARLES SWINBURNE

MS: BL. Excerpt: Compton-Rickett 318–19. Published: DW 932. Date: Unidentified endorsement.

[26 February 1870]

Dear Swinburne

I am delighted to hear that you are battling with the British dragon on the subject of my "obscurity" in the Sonnets. I opine that I am likely when I read your elucidation to see how much better they might have been made by your light, just as I did with the pictures of mine you described. I trust no

[26 February 1870]

inconvenience will result to your labours by the fact that I am now slightly transposing that section – but only in masses – putting the love-sonnets first – (beginning at *Bridal Birth* & ending at *Stillborn Love*) & the other sonnets following these (*Inclusiveness* to *Superscription* with a new one for a close.) Two other new ones occur in the love-sonnets. The section then winds up with the songs. This is better I think, as the love-sonnets are the preponderant portion.

It is a great relief to me to know that your friendly enthusiasm is not about to "scagliarsi"* against yourself or other bards on my behalf. My humility would have been sincerely humiliated by such a comparison. The variety in my work, of which you in your generosity make so much, depends I suspect, chiefly on there being tentative efforts in different directions. Were I to write as much as yourself, I should doubtless settle down into one course. However, I cannot say how much pleased I am that you should tackle the sonnets seriously, as these I suppose on the whole constitute my most distinctive work, and in that direction, if in no other, I am pretty likely to do something more in spite of other occupations.

I am disturbed by your continued objection to "Stood Confessed" in *Troy Town*. Do you take into consideration that I mean absolutely that Cupid does *see* this arrow there? Thus it ceases to be a mere conventional metaphor. I would alter it if possible on your urgency, but really cannot see my way with the given rhyme which is necessary.

I am sure you would agree with me, were you to see the rejected Squad, that they should all keep out. The one on Wellington is good I think as a piece of writing, but I heartily concur in yr objections, which are of course damning. I wrote it I remember to express the feeling of the nation at the moment without particularly thinking whether it was my own which it certainly was not to any serious extent. So the thing rightly goes rotten.[1]

I hope to be sending you the revised proofs about Thursday next, but fear I shall not get them from the printers before then. On getting your last about Sister Helen it struck me to write to Allingham for an Irish name. He answered however that Boyne being merely Celtic & not exclusively appropriated to one river, Scotch names would do, & suggested several, from which I have chosen *Weir* which I think is not amiss.[2] Neill he said wouldn't do, being merely a patronymic.

Your affec: DG R

---

* "scagliarsi" = to hurl itself; signifying DGR's fear that ACS' expected grandiloquence about the greatness of his poetry might backfire by drawing attacks on *Poems*. DGR is answering ACS' letter of 24 Feb (Lang 2: 345); see also **32** & **137**.

[1] ACS had asked to see again an "elegy on Wellington" (1852), which DGR did not send and

did not print until *Poems: New*, where it appeared as "Wellington's Funeral" (180). Perhaps DGR feared comparison with Tennyson's "Ode," written in the same year on the same occasion.

2   See **29&n1**.

70.36 TO ALGERNON CHARLES SWINBURNE

MS: LC. Text within angled brackets is a marginal insertion.

[26 February 1870]

Dear Swinburne

What do you say (in Troy Town) to

Thence his arrow banished rest.?
(or dart had)

<There is a decided objection in the fact that an earlier stanza rhymes *breast & rest*.>

I don't like it as well as the old one, but might very possibly adopt it if you did.

Overpage I copy the closing sonnet of the H[ouse]. of L[ife]. series in case it served you to see it now.

Your affec:
DGR

70.37 TO ALGERNON CHARLES SWINBURNE

MS: BL. Published: *AL* 4: 126; DW 936.

Sunday [27 February 1870]

Dear Swinburne

I fancy I've hit it –

"Marked his arrow's burning crest."

One line, please, by return, and pardon these babyish bulletins.

Your
DGR

This is better I believe than "Knew his shaft its rankling guest."

70.38 TO WILLIAM ALLINGHAM

MS: PML. Excerpt: *Lady A* 141–42. Published: *WA/GBH* 288–89; DW 933.

28 Feb 1870

Dear Allingham

Thanks for attending so promptly to my bewilderments. I have adopted *Weir* which seems to answer well. *Kerr* has not emphasis enough – runs too much off the tongue – for the poise of the verse.[1]

As for that kind good overwhelming Lady A.[2] – she has written to me from at least 6 different parts of the British Islands during the past year asking me to come down instantly & meet a sympathising circle. But such things are quite impossible to me at the pitch of brutal bogyism at which I have arrived. *You* seem somehow to keep your own man, but I am hardly my own ghost.

I saw Ned the other evening & he seemed well on the whole though rather collywobblyish. I shall get into the country somewhere – where I don't yet know – within a few days & for a few weeks, to try if there is any marrow left in me that can be squeezed out in the form of rhyme before I go finally to press. I mean to be out in April – latter end I suppose – & should like a few more pages – if possible. I want to get near 300 if I can, but have been obliged to give up the idea of finishing several things I had in hand for the purpose, and for all that, have done no work to speak of in painting, with this divided mind. I must cart the things off now, & then get to my easel again.

Ever yours DG Rossetti

Christina has done a book of Nursery Rhymes & is publishing with Ellis who offers her much better terms than Mac does. She will leave Mac altogether.

[1] See **29&n1**.
[2] See 63.37&n1.

70.39 TO ALGERNON CHARLES SWINBURNE

MS: BL. Excerpt: DW 934. A second P.S. accompanying this MS has been placed with 71.199, with which it seems to belong.

Monday [28 February 1870]

Dear Swinburne

Here we are again. I have forgotten hitherto to ask you about 2 points. Viz: –

I had put an explanatory note to Troy Town, which I cut out because the authority (in Pliny) did not quite meet the case, – referring the gift to Minerva, not Venus. Do you think some explanation absolutely necessary to prepare the reader for so outlandish a notion as a cup resembling a bosom. Would the old resource of a French motto do?[2] – (or I mean is it *desirable?*) as thus: –

> "Cette coupe que Vénus
> Eût des mains d'Hélène belle,
> (?) *Ressemblable* au sein d'icelle."
> (*Calendrier de l'Amour*, 1480)

I'd rather do without it if possible, but do you think it needed? And is "ressemblable" possible?[1]

The other question is about *Lilith*. It rather troubles me that the first verse is readable in an inflexion not intended & may set the reader on a false tack of sound – i.e. if he does not at once emphasize the first *It*. Do you think this a decided defect? I *might* make it run thus or somehow: –

> "Twas so with Lilith the wife of Adam
> (&c)
> That not a drop of her blood was human," &c.

But this weakens it in value. Give me your opinion, and don't damn me.

Your affec:
DG R

P.S. About *John of Tours* I can't persuade myself not to like it best as it stands in respect of "It's" or "It is." Not on account of the smoothness but the colloquialism. Nor was it ever otherwise I believe.

---

[1] James Thursfield had written to DGR on 26 Oct 69 that he had sent "to our common friend Tebbs a note on the subject of Helen's Cup, about which you were seeking information. . . . I am sorry the note is not more complete; but I cannot trace the story beyond Pliny, nor can I find any mention of the subject in Greek authors" (*RP* 478). See also 63.11

[2] DGR was thinking of following the practice of ACS & other writers, such as Sir Walter Scott, of inventing fake mediæval sources for epigraphs, mottoes, & quotes to create a patina of antiquity.

70.39.1 TO FREDERIC JAMES SHIELDS

MS: Yale. Published: DW 935.

Monday [February–March 1870]

My dear Shields

I fancy a day's painting here wd do you more good than harm on Wedy. I think you cd get on quite well now with the head without nature, as reinforcing wd probably best be done by yourself, – & then the hands wd follow suit & need no model. I have a notion as to how you shd proceed.

Ever yrs
DGR

70.40 TO JOHN FERGUSON MCLENNAN

MS: Columbia.

[c. 1 March 1870]

My dear McLennan

I am telling the printers to send you a set of the proofs for Alexander as you wished. I have lost his address or wd write to him also direct. I do not know that it is now desirable to hurry any proposed article, as I rather think the spite I anticipated in a certain quarter has been happily crammed down the throat or up some other articulate orifice of the bugbear in question by a new turn of events.

Of course you and Alexander will both think with me that the sheets should not be shown at all till the book is finally published. All at present is confidential, confederate, & conspiratic.

In haste

Ever yours
D G Rossetti

I shall appear in April, & if I should still add anything to the book will send you such additions beforehand.

By the bye very likely Alexander may be struck by the coincidence between the name *Keith* in one of my poems (*Sister Helen*) & the same name in Dobell's also supernatural ballad of which we lately spoke in correspondence. I hate such coincidences but am not to blame. My ballad, which is a very old thing of mine, was not only written but printed in a sort of German annual some years before the appearance of Dobell's.[1]

I thought of altering the name but could not hit on another so well sounding.

---

[1] "Sister Helen" was first printed in 1854 in *The Dusseldorf Artists' Album* (see 53.54n6); the

private printing of 1857, regarded as authentic by WMR, was a Wise-Forman forgery (see Carter & Pollard, *An Enquiry into the Nature of Certain Nineteenth Century Pamphlets* [Constable, 1934]: 215–17).

70.41 TO JANE MORRIS

MS: BL. Excerpt: Surtees 202. Published: Bryson 18. Date: P/M.

Friday night [4 March 1870]

Dearest Janey

I hear from the Greeks that you are going to make one at a party to Evans's on Monday night. I hope it is safe for you to do so, and in that case should stay & go too. I shall see you on Sunday or perhaps tomorrow (Saturday) evening. I am sending a copy of the proof for Top, & shall bring one for you when I come.

I have received an invitation again from Mme Bodichon to go down to her cottage near Hastings, and really incline to think it will be the best thing to do. Only now unluckily it has been lent to Stillman & he has been asked to try & still get me to accompany him. I wish I had taken it when first offered & had it to myself. There is one rather uncomfortable point. Chariclea Ionides told me today that when she was lately at Hastings she found the sea air aggravated the bother in her eyes very much, & who knows but I might find the same? To be sure this cottage is a goodish way from the seaside.

I think I have made a good portrait of Mary Zambaco, & Ned is greatly delighted with it. Indeed I enclose a note from that poor old dear which I have just got, as it shows how nice he is. I like her very much & am sure that her love is all in all to her. I never had an opportunity of understanding her before.[1] Today I have been doing Alecco's flame who is a cousin of Mary's & no great matter to look at, but seems niceish.[2] The party at Evans's will it seems be a large one including her, Mary, Ned, &c. I like Mary because she said the sweet one was far more beautiful than anyone else in the world. And she is really extremely beautiful herself when one gets to study her face. I think she has got much more so within the last year with all her love & trouble. But rainy walks & constant lowness are I fear beginning to break up her health.

Your most affectionate
Gabriel

[1] There are 3 portraits dated 1870 (S.541–43); exactly which this refers to is uncertain. For EBJ's affair with Marie Zambaco, see 69.9&n2.
[2] Alecco's "flame" is presumably his future wife, Zambelou Sechiari (1853–1913). No portrait of her is found in Surtees.

70.42 TO BARBARA LEIGH SMITH BODICHON

MS: PML. Published: DW 937.

[c. 5 March 1870]
16 Cheyne Walk
Chelsea

Dear Mme Bodichon

I am extremely sorry to be prevented from coming to you again, but if in town on Monday, have an engagement I must keep for that evening. I suppose I shall be here then, as I cannot yet settle where to go. Your offer is most tempting,[1] and I must make up my mind immediately now about it & write again, but write this wad now in great haste with a dinner party to go to. Your letter came to me at a most busy moment & I am sorry the answer has got delayed. I will write again almost at once.

Ever yours
DG Rossetti

---

[1] WMR's diary for 2 Mar states: "Mrs. Bodichon offers through Stillman to place her house at Robert's Bridge, Sussex, with studio, at Gabriel's disposal for a while.... This seems a very eligible offer; as G. wants to get out of town a little, with a view to health, and to quiet in writing poetry" (*RP* 499).

70.43 TO JOHN SKELTON

MS: Untraced (formerly John Hart Rare Books). Published: Skelton 89–90; DW 938. Date: Skelton. The MS is tipped into Skelton's Proof Copy of *Poems*.

[5 March 1870]
16 Cheyne Walk

My dear Skelton

I'm sending you the proofs at last today – couldn't get them before.[1] If too late, it will have to be put off to the June number, as I know the calls on your time must be many, & now the thing *does* come out should be specially sorry if you were forced to hurry your notice.

Ever yours
DG Rossetti

I'm going into the country for 3 weeks & may perhaps add a little more. I publish in April.

---

[1] For Skelton, see 69.15 & **13&n1**. His set of proofs lacks the sheets for 145–208 & 257–82.

70.44 TO MR. TUCKER

MS: UBC (Colbeck).

5 March 1870

My dear Tucker

I have just found your last note among some which have remained unanswered through unsettled preoccupation. I am now going into the country within a day or two & shall remain away for some 3 weeks. On my return I will hope to make an appointment, as your friends kindly wish to see the very little I have at present by me to show, but as I said my work (at painting) has been very intermittent lately. If you do not hear from me again, perhaps you will bear with my forgetfulness & give me another reminder in about a month's time.

Thanks for *the* Cardinal's portrait. I have had relacys[?] of him bestowed on me as long as I can remember anything, till he brings times & places back to me when I look him once again in the face. Who he was I have not the faintest idea, but now that I am fat, people begin to say there is a strong family resemblance.

Yours very truly
DG Rossetti

70.44.1 TO JANE OCTAVIA BROOKFIELD[1]

MS: King's College School.

7 March [1870]
16 Cheyne Walk
Chelsea

Dear Mrs. Brookfield

Thanks for your kind invitation which however I shall not be able to accept as I am just now going into the country for about 3 weeks. If anything brings me back earlier than I expect, I shall be very glad to come, but see little chance of this. With kind remembrances,

Very truly yours
DG Rossetti

---

[1] For Jane Brookfield, see 69.39n1.

70.45 TO ALGERNON CHARLES SWINBURNE

MS: BL. Published: *Letters Addressed to ACS*; DW 939. Date: Unidentified endorsement. The second P.S. is written at the head of the letter.

[7 March 1870]

Dear Swinburne

I sent you this morning the new proofs. I believe I have signified before most of the few changes existing. You may be surprised to find "New Year's Burden" & "Even So" removed from the *House of Life*. They seemed to jar with the other love songs & to make a false climax, so I stuck them elsewhere. I rather doubt whether *Even So* is worth including at all, but believe you gave your verdict in favour of it. I have stuck *Keith* back in despair, though Hearne, Lyle, & Carr occurred to me, which I believe would have been free from objection, but the sound seemed inferior. I wonder if the note at the beginning (back of Dedication) seems cheeky at its end. I don't mean to be so, "immature" being measurable by the limit of one's own powers.

I am going away to Sussex in a few days for 2 or 3 weeks to try to do a little more work for the book if it may be at the 11th hour.

The extract from the "Bogshire Banner" is simply sublime. I read it to Ned and others who almost died, especially the former. The simplicity of alteration in 2 of the old English games, – b – my neighbour & p – in the corner – is really a touch of genius that takes one's breath away. The parodies are also of priceless value. Do you know you ought certainly to make Thompson or some one produce a fair copy of all this class of your work that can be got at. Every man wd contribute such effusions as you happen to have sent him; & much you must have by you in some form or other, or could dictate, – thus affording a fine companion picture to Milton & his daughters.[1]

Affectionately yours
D Gabriel R

I converted a select circle to you last night by reading from "Poems & Ballads."

You will notice the things are now printed wider so as to make more pages.

---

[1] ACS' last letter (Lang 2: 348) was for the most part a farrago of Rabelaisian humour which sought a response in kind rather than the restrained snicker which DGR offers here.

70.45.1 TO JANE MORRIS

MS: BL. Published: Bryson 19. Date: Bryson. The date of this letter is dubious since, for instance, the WMs attended a party at their friends the Evanses on 7 Mar; but a better date has not been found.

Monday [7 March 1870]
16 Cheyne Walk
Chelsea

My dear Janey

I have bethought me that you wore the blue dress at your party & may possibly want it for tomorrow evening.

Your affec: Gabriel

70.46 TO CHARLES FAIRFAX MURRAY

MS: Texas.

Tuesday [8 March 1870]

Dear Murray

I am going out of town on Thursday, probably for 3 weeks. Would you let me know what progress you have made with the 2 pictures for me. I was sorry to hear from Morris that you had not been very well. I shall be at home tomorrow (Wedy) about ½ past 12 if you like to look in.

Ever yours D G R

If anything is done you might perhaps bring it.

70.47 TO ALGERNON CHARLES SWINBURNE

MS: BL. Excerpt: Compton-Rickett 319–20. Published: *ALC* 4: 119–20; DW 941.

9 March/1870

Dear Swinburne

It is most annoying to find after all that you are to be in town just after I leave it – you being of all men the one I most want to see at this moment, and indeed so does everyone. All friends are yearning for you after your long absence & hoping that it is not illness which has prolonged it. They are much reassured when I read them your letters which have certainly no flabbiness about them. But the truth is, if I were to delay going now beyond tomorrow, the main object of my going – i.e. to try whether another poem can be screwed out of me – would be, as you know by the necessities of time, entirely made vain. So go I must, and shall hope, when you are once here you will stay long enough for me to find you on my return in about 3 weeks, if indeed you don't mean to stay in London for good now. I am going to a cottage in Sussex belonging to Mdme Bodichon, whom I am not sure if you have met, but who is a very old & good friend of mine, & has lent the cottage to myself & Stillman (Wm's Yankee friend) who is an entirely unobstructive man & will leave me quite to myself. The poem I shall do (if any) will be I believe "God's Graal" – i.e. the loss of the Sancgraal by Lancelot – a theme chosen to emphasize the marked superiority of Guenevere over God. I may also perhaps finish one called "The Stream's Secret" of which I think I read you the beginning.

I am rejoiced you like the new passage in *Jenny* & the new Sonnets. I meant to have marked the few changes in the proofs I sent you to save you trouble but forgot at last moment.

Besides what you mention they are chiefly these. New lines in *Dante* – page 98, & omission of last stanza in same by your advice. Additions to *Portrait*. Removal of Aspecta Medusa (which seemed best as an inscription which it really was) to page 165. Change of title – *Moonstar* to *Plighted Promise* which is more explanatory & clearer. Change of 2 last verses of *Penumbra*, now continuing the parenthesis throughout, as the omission of this was slovenly. There are various slight changes throughout – notably I have tried to make less emphatic the passage at end of *Confession* about the whore laughing, as I found some one to whom I read it actually thought the heroine herself was the whore! Not that this *ought* to have been thought by anyone, but I think the slight change has bettered the passage.

I went to see the French Lancelot at Molini's & found it a most desirable & nice looking 3 volume book – date 1533.[1] I looked up the passage about the first kiss which is very good & full of detail. Lancelot has been doing some wonderful deeds of arms as an unknown knight, & Guenevere calls him to her to ask him of his adventures, & discovers that he can be no one but Lancelot. L. is accompanied by his friend Galahalt who does not know who he is. L. then tells her that all his deeds have been done for her & that he loved her when he first saw her at the time he was knighted, when she said to him, "Adieu mon beau doux ami." She then says that many knights say to ladies what they do not mean in their hearts. On this he nearly faints & Galahalt comes forward & pleads his cause; & when the Queen seems well inclined, he begs that she will kiss Lancelot in his presence. About this she makes difficulties though saying she wd like it, but is afraid of her ladies who are in the room. However Galahalt suggests that they should go into a corner together as if taking counsel; this they do, & Lancelot still being in a blue funk, the Queen takes him by the chin & kisses him, saying nice things to him. Galahalt then begs her to do him (G.) a favour, which is that she will make her knight his companion in arms; and this she does, telling him at the same time that it is Lancelot. The funniest part is the wind-up of the incident, which is, not that the Queen & Lancelot go to bed together, but that he & Galahalt do so! What this may mean I do not pretend to fathom, but must commend it to the correspondents of the provincial paper from which I have to thank you for further inimitable extracts.[2] The provincial form of All Souls could only have been discovered by a Bulgarian Columbus.

Your affec: D G R

---

[1] In a letter of 22 Dec 69 (Lang 2: 334), ACS had expressed interest in a mediæval French version of the Arthurian story but complained that the bookseller Molini was asking too much for it.

[2] *The Bogshire Banner*, see ACS:DGR 1 Mar (Lang 2: 348).

70.48 TO BARBARA LEIGH SMITH BODICHON

MS: PML. Published: DW 942.

Thursday [10 March 1870]

Dear Mme Bodichon

Tomorrow at last I am really starting for Scalands. Stillman went down today & took my man-servant with him, as well as the provisions suggested by your timely warning. I make no doubt we shall be jolly enough & will write again when we get settled.

Most truly yours
DG Rossetti

70.49 TO FREDERICK STARTRIDGE ELLIS

MS: BL. Published: *FSE* 7; DW 943.

[c. 10 March 1870]

Dear Ellis

Perhaps I may as well send you my address in the country: –

D.G. R.
at Mme Bodichon's,
Scalands Gate
Robertsbridge
Hurst Green
Sussex.

Would you send me the proofs of the fly-leaf & binding as soon as you get them. Also please let me know if Forman seems frightened at Jenny or anything else.[1]

Yrs
D G Rossetti

Also you might send me Peter Schlemihl if you get it.[2]

---

[1] For HBF, see 68.145&n1.
[2] An 1813 tale by German writer Adelbert von Chamisso about a man who sold his shadow to the Devil.

70.50 TO FRANCES MARY LAVINIA ROSSETTI
MS: UBC. Published: DW 945. Date: FLR.

[11 March 1870]

Dear good Teak,

I am writing to Bartram (living close to you at 3 Grafton Place) to fetch the pagoda cabinet tomorrow (Saturday) & take it to you. I am sending 3 blue pots with it, as they are necessary to the effect. I dare say if I ever wanted them back *very bad* to fill some place in my collection, you would let me have them, but at present they were lying idle.

Of course G. Catchpole will know that the cabinet is valuable & must be treated very carefully.[1] If you want it taken on to him somewhere else, your best plan will be to let Bartram proceed thither with it at once & only leave the china with you for the present.

I leave town today at 4.

Your affec: Son
Gabriel

I think you wd do well to ask Bartram what he thinks the best plan for mending & steadying the legs of the stand.
P.P.S. I have told Bartram to call on you before he starts hither to ask whether you will want the cabinet taken on elsewhere.
P.P.P.S. Will Christina let Miss Boyd know when she hears finally from Ellis about Murray.[2]

---

[1] George Catchpole was the son of Sarah Catchpole, servant of the Polidori family for 40 years. At this date he was handyman for the combined Rossetti-Polidori households; WMR

noted in his diary on 1 Jan 72 that he was "continually in and out" of 56 Euston Square (*WMRD* 143).

2 CGR wrote to FSE on 25 Feb 70 acquiescing in his suggestion that CFM should illustrate *Sing-Song*, but on 7 Mar, at the urging of DGR, she proposed AB instead, and quoted DGR's opinion that "she would really probably do them with more fun and zest than Murray though perhaps not so artistically – Her ideas of beast drawing are good as you know." FSE was reluctant to involve only AB and replied on 19 Mar that "Mr. Murray has brought me back the Ms. & consents to give up the illustration to Miss Boyd, but says he should like to do four or five which I dare say you will not object to" (Harrison 1: 407, 410, 413). According to WMR's diary, by 9 Feb 71 FSE had decided against publishing the volume, "because he can't see his way to getting illustrations suitable to his position as connected with the best artists. . . . It has been a tiresome affair and I think not well managed on Ellis's part." Routledge published *Sing-Song* in 1872, with illustrations by AH, whom WMR "strongly recommended" to the Dalziels on 15 May 72 (*WMRD* 43, 61).

70.51 TO MRS. JOHN POLLARD SEDDON

MS: Rylands.

Hastings. Saturday [12 March 1870]

My dear Mrs. Seddon

I am sorry I have only just had your kind invitation sent on to me, which has caused this delay in my saying how happy I should have been to come had I been in London instead of here.

Yours sincerely DG Rossetti

70.52 TO EDWARD BURNE-JONES

MS: Princeton. Text within angled brackets is a marginal insertion.

Scalands Gate/Robertsbridge

Sunday [13 March 1870]

Dear Ned

I got your nice good note this morning. Yesterday I did the *Circe* sonnet & copy it overpage. I hope you will only put it on the frame if you think it really expressive of the picture. Else I will put it only in my book. I have tried in the first 4 lines to give something of the picture's colour, & in the last 2 of its *moral* (!). Which is the best form of these last? Unless you are in a hurry to send the picture away, you might defer having it copied on, as I may perhaps do something to it yet.

Today we have suddenly got completely snowed up here – 6 inches deep;

so perhaps I may be forced on doing some work; but am so far from well that I do not feel sure of any result.

I will attend to what you say about the frame.

Your affec:
D G R

Any suggestions as to sonnet will be welcome from the "master."
P.S. If you write a line, say if you have seen Swinburne & how he is, & give him my love. He is to come to town tomorrow – Monday.

> Why sink those black drops in that golden wine,
>   Shed from thy hand, O dusk-haired gold-robed dame,
>   Where o'er the spread feast gleams the fragrant flame
> And the dark-hearted golden sunflowers shine?
> Doth Helios here with Hecate combine,
>   O Circe, thou their votaress! to proclaim
>   For these thy guests all rapture in thy name,
> Till pitiless Night give Day the countersign?
>
> Lords of their hour, they come. And by thy knee
>   Those cowering beasts, their equals heretofore,
> Wait; who with them in new equality
>   To-night shall echo back the far-flung roar
>   Which past thy window sounds from the strown shore
>   <or Which sounds where all spent things bestrew the shore
>   And the &c &c>
> Where the dishevelled seaweed hates the sea.

70.53 TO BARBARA LEIGH SMITH BODICHON

MS: PML. Published: Burton, *BB* 201–03; DW 946.

Scalands
Tuesday [15 March 1870]

Dear Mdme Bodichon

I have not yet written to thank you for a much more independent & promising pied-à-terre than I could have found in the tents of the stranger. To-day things look sunny again – the snow is beginning to vanish – and I no longer feel so sure that my bones are tubes after all and that the devil is turning them to use as wind-instruments. I am getting a little to work steadily & may perhaps do something or may not, but at any rate cannot but benefit by the change in one way or another. Good quiet Stillman is the best of accommodating companions (surely his name must indicate the hereditary character of race,) and walks with me, talks with me, and avoids me with the truest tact in the world. His grave dark face on the snowy roads would make any perceptive person turn round and feel an interest and curiosity about him. He has fallen to work a little on painting, but has some preoccupations of a kind which are apt to interfere with art.

By the bye he tells me, from your information, that there is a British beauty at hand in the shape of a gamekeeper's daughter.[1] Do you think one could ask her to sit for her portrait in chalks? I dare say I could knock off 50 guineas worth of her at a sitting or two, and would give her a sketch of herself besides. But ought one to ask?

I remember the Bayeux Tapestry here of old, and have an impression that, of the 3 sketches over the fireplace, the 2 side ones are yours & the middle one by A. M. Howitt ("as was.")[2] The oriental and Italian pottery is delightful, and there are some splendid indented tiles (I suppose ancient) lying in a heap on the shelves on the landing. I will keep you informed of all the more stirring order of adventurous accidents by flood & field (which should not be lacking to such a Don Quixote as Stillman & such a Sancho as myself,) and meanwhile

am ever yours sincerely
DG Rossetti

P.S. I copy on the spare leaf a sonnet I have just written on Burne Jones's "Circe," which I know you saw at the Water Colour Gallery. I wanted to have some record of his work in my book. I have tried in the first lines to give some notion of the colour, and in the last some impression of the scope of the work, – taking the transformed beasts as images of ruined passion – the torn seaweed of the sea of pleasure. You will remember that in the picture the window shows a view of the sea and the galleys which bear the new lovers and victims of the enchantress.

I heard from Allingham this morning. He has had a press appointment offered him & thinks of trying London again.[3] Absit Omen!*

The Wine of Circe. (Sonnet.)

Why sink those black drops in that golden wine,
   Shed from thy hand, O dusk-haired gold-robed dame,

[c. 15 March 1870]   70.54

    Where o'er the spread feast gleams the fragrant flame
    And the dark-hearted golden sunflowers shine?
    Doth Helios here with Hecate combine,
     O Circe, thou their votaress! to proclaim
     For these thy guests all rapture in thy name;
    Till pitiless Night give Day the countersign?

    Lords of their hour, they come. And by thy knee
     Those cowering beasts, their equals heretofore,
    Wait; who with them in new equality
     To-night shall echo back the unchanging roar
     Which sounds for ever from the tide-strewn shore
    Where the dishevelled seaweed hates the sea.

* "Absit Omen" = may no harm result.
1 Sophy Burgess; for the sale of her portrait, see **101**.
2 For Anna Mary Howitt, now Mrs. Howitt-Watts, see **Volume II: Index**.
3 WA "had been offered by Messrs. Longmans the post of sub-editor of *Fraser's Magazine* with Mr. Froude; and in April he finally gave up the Customs [in Lymington] and came to live in London" (*WAD* 202).

70.54 TO WILLIAM ALLINGHAM

MS: PML. Excerpt: *WA/GBH* 290–92. Published: DW 949. Date: GBH (as postmarked 7 Mar 70, but no envelope is with the letter). Text within angled brackets is a marginal insertion.

[c. 15 March 1870]
Scalands/Robertsbridge/Hawkhurst/Kent

Dear Allingham

 You will be surprised at my address which is Barbara's cottage not far from Hastings (but in Kent as I find, or at least the above seems the proper form). I have been here a few days in company with Stillman, Wm's American friend; <P.S. I think of staying 2 or 3 weeks.> having come for the purpose of recruiting & "working off" my book with the conscientious decency of Mr. Dennis the hangman. I shall have it out before the end of April. Stillman and I have this house to ourselves & he is an utterly unobstructive man. Had your letter reached me in town, I might probably have come down to you at once & discussed the plan you propose which seems promising – only I don't know whether such near seaside is likely to suit my eyes to which I believe sea air is not suitable. However I must take the matter into consideration, & suppose I might even, if convenient to you, close at once with the proposal of joining you in rent for half a year, as it seems this wd only involve me in an expense of £15. So be it so if you like. I shd reckon on probable advantage in a summary move to Lymington at some moment before that time is out, but if this should by possibility not come to pass, must stipulate beforehand that there be no question as to my being liable for my share, as I can only undertake it on those terms.[1]

There is really no news I know of since last writing you. Barbara does not indulge in bell-pulls, hardly in servants to summon thereby – so I have brought my own. What she does affect is any amount of thorough draught, – a library bearing the stern stamp of "Bodichon," and a kettle-holder with the uncompromising initials B. B. She is the best of women, but I fear, from what I last saw of her, that her health is failing like my own.

Ever yours
DG Rossetti

By the bye, I fell back of "Keith" after all, in that ballad. I couldn't quite please myself otherwise.

If I get an extra copy of proof-sheets I may be sending them to you.

[1] WA annotated this statement on the letter as follows: "Means that he will pay, come or not come" (*WA*/GBH 291).

70.55 TO JOSEPH KNIGHT
MS: BL.

[c. 15 March 1870]
Scalands/Robertsbridge/Hawkhurst/Kent

Dear Knight

Thanks for your note. I hope the sheets have reached you by this time & may find favour with you on a quiet reading. I judge from what you say that Marston is not likely to feel specially moved in their direction as to a critical notice (indeed I should wonder if he were after his late domestic sorrows) and need hardly say that I would wish the question on no account to be urged on him. Perhaps after all the things may justify their upholders in the long run, and it is pleasant to know already that some friends are well disposed to them at starting. I am out here recruiting, & may if the spirit moves me add a few pages yet, but have rigidly to be before the public before the end of April.[1]

I thought Dixon seemed friendly to me the other night at your house, but believe he is no longer editor of the Athenæum, is he? I have still a feeling however that every one at your house must have taken me for a most uncomfortable brawler, which I feel sure I never am by any choice of my own. A moment's reflection would have enabled me to settle the matter by quiet chaff, but I have not the coolest of heads.²

Ever yours
D G Rossetti

I suppose Swinburne is in London by this.

1   Knight "noticed" *Poems* in the *Globe* on 20 Apr, and in *The Sunday Times* on 1 May.
2   DGR's teasing of the dramatist Frank A. Marshall, a fellow-guest at one of Knight's dinner parties held just before DGR left London for Scalands, had provoked an angry scene: see **131, 136&n1, & 144**.

70.56 TO CHARLES FAIRFAX MURRAY

MS: Texas.

Wednesday [16 March 1870]
Scalands/Robertsbridge/Hawkhurst

Dear Murray

Please write me a line *here* as to how my work gets on.

Ever yours
D G Rossetti

70.57 TO FREDERICK STARTRIDGE ELLIS

MS: BL. Published: *FSE* 8; DW 950.

Scalands/Robertsbridge
Thursday [17 March 1870]

Dear Ellis

Thanks for the proofs. They seem all right now, so they can be worked off. How about the binding & flyleaf?

I have got to work & am reaching the end of a poem which will take some ten pages, & have done something to another (probably longer) besides some sonnets. But I am getting into that mistrustful state which 11th hour work is sure to engender, & perhaps may not use what I write after all. However be sure I will give you due & timely warning in either case.

Ever yours
DG Rossetti

70.58 TO FREDERICK STARTRIDGE ELLIS

MS: BL. Published: *FSE* 9; DW 952.

[c. 18 March 1870]

Dear Ellis

Now you *will* swear. I have all of a sudden been very strongly advised, I think from a specially trustworthy quarter, that my book wd begin very much better & please a much larger class of readers at the outset if it opened with the Blessed Damozel & not with Troy Town, which latter is supposed (and I think rightly) to be likely to please a smaller class. Now my own wish in the case shd be to put *Troy Town* on to follow the *Burden of Nineveh*, & so secure 3 sentimental or moral things at the outset. All I want you to do is just to tell me what it would cost to cancel & reprint these 2 sheets. I would stand the whole expense if I decided on having it done. Would you let me know at once?

Ever yours
D G R

Of course I suppose the types are still up.

70.59 TO JOHN SKELTON

Text: Skelton 90. Reprinted: DW 954. Date: Skelton. The words in square brackets read in Skelton's and DW's texts as "last finish," which does not make sense in the context; the reconstruction below has therefore been proposed.

Scalands/Robertsbridge/Hawkhurst
Friday [18 March 1870]

My dear Skelton

Your note has only just come to me here. The picture you ask about must be a Venus (now at Manchester).[1] There is a sonnet written for it in the book; but I did not get the roses and honeysuckle into the sonnet.

I am glad you like my book as well as any of its size. This point of size is just the thing that I think [I was least] concerned in rigorously limiting. Thus a good deal has been excluded altogether from my volume, and among other things included, some had originally been written to twice their present length.

I judge that your article is to deal with my book *alone*, which I shall much prefer if so, as studied work, where unity is specially kept in view, suffers I think by the associated plan of criticism, and the comparative treatment seems to me never quite a sound one.

Very truly yours
DG Rossetti

I have added a sheet more to the book, and shall send you this soon – before fitting the things into their places as a whole. I am now shifting the first poem (Troy Town) further on, and opening with the Blessed Damozel. I shall be out for certain by end of April.

[1] John Mitchell's *Venus Verticordia* (S.173). See also **89, 103, 181,** & **207**.

70.60 TO JOSEPH KNIGHT

MS: BL. Opposite the address, DGR has written "right address" and drawn a pointing hand.

Scalands/Robertsbridge/Hawkhurst/Kent
Saturday [March 19 1870]

Dear Knight

Your letter is a refreshment in these lonely latitudes, & now lies side by side on my table with a tumbler brimful of primroses, speaking jointly of the charms & countercharms of town and country.

I am glad my poems are found by you to bear well the transfer from ear to eye acquaintance, and specially glad that the "Nocturn" pleases you, as I am now engaged on a love-poem somewhat akin to it as a combination of structure & sentiment (though the metre is a different one, also my own), and which may perhaps be my last addition (with a few more Sonnets) to the volume, unless indeed I still do at the very cockcrow of publication another thing that simmers in my head just now. I rejoice to hear I am to have your support in the Globe, & from knowledge of your well-enduring zeal, may I dare say reckon on it too in the Sunday Times.

I write chiefly to send you the enclosed Prefatory Note for your opinion as to insertion or non-insertion. I cannot quite make my mind up. Several friends who have seen it – among them Swinburne & Morris – are dead against it, saying that the matter will right itself without my speaking. What think you? I suppose on the whole I am inclined to leave it out.

Coming here I bought a Cornhill Mag: at the station & read young Marston's poem of which you had read me 2 stanzas. I thought the penultimate 2 even superior to those in delicate and closely-expressed feeling. The article on the Iron Mask is of the conclusive order I shd say, but I hear fresh doubts have since this hypothesis been thrown on the identity. Kirkpatrick Sharpe must have been a "rum 'un" worth recording. Did you read about him there?[1]

Ever yours DG Rossetti

No need to return enclosure as I have copied it.

[1] PBM published "After Many Days" in the *Cornhill Magazine* (1870: 343), and Marius Topin's "The Man in the Iron Mask" appeared in the same issue (333). Topin identified the original of Dumas's character as Count Ercolo Antonio Matthioli, a private agent of Ferdinand Charles, Duke of Mantua. He published another article on the subject in the same magazine (1870: 588–590), as well as a book-length study, *L'Homme au Masque de Fer* (Paris: Didier, 1870). Charles Kirkpatrick Sharpe (1781–1851) was a reclusive antiquary, etcher, & authority on Scottish ballad literature, referred to in the *Burns Encyclopaedia* (Hutchinson, 1959) as an "ill-natured gossiper."

70.61 TO FREDERICK STARTRIDGE ELLIS

MS: BL. Published: *FSE* 10; DW 955.

[c. 20 March 1870]

Scalands/Robertsbridge/Hawkhurst

Dear Ellis

I have been thinking of what you said about absolutely *red gold* for the binding. Could you send me a specimen of the kind of gold meant? I think it possible the novelty might be a good one but have no idea what is meant. But would it cost more?

I think you said something once about large paper copies. If there are any such, I shd like to have 2 bound in vellum with the design like the ordinary copies, & with the inner woodcut printed in gold on choice paper.

Ever yours
DG Rossetti

70.62 TO FREDERICK STARTRIDGE ELLIS

Text: DW 968 (typescript attributed to BL but unlocated).

[c. 20 March 1870]

Scalands

Dear Ellis

Many thanks about the money. The bill was accepted some time back and is I believe payable at my banker's – Union Bank of London, Chancery Lane.

So if you would pay it in there just by 1st May – no need before – all will be well.

I note all you say of the book and will attend to all and let you hear further ere long. The printers can if they like work off now at once definitively all the sheets as far as K inclusive, but not further.

Ever yours
DG Rossetti

P.S. By the bye, one word has to be altered, which I forgot at page 131: as thus: –

"Those glades where then she walked with me."

for "then" put "once." Also a slight change in the setting of the pages in Jenny, thus: – the top line at page 110 must be transferred to the bottom of the preceding page, which will involve the same change on every page I suppose. This will make it necessary I fear for me to see another proof of that poem before finally working it off, as the printers have such a pernicious habit of blundering the setting and dropping stops out whenever this sort of change is made. So I must just get you to make them do this and send me the necessary proof at once. I will return it immediately, and all to sheet K can then be worked off as I said. Please make them see to this at once. I suppose your telling Strangeways to work off will do, will it not? The last proofs sent are quite right. I told them to send two sets, one to Knight and one to a friend in Edinburgh.

70.63 TO ALICE BOYD

MS: NLS. Published: Purves 587; DW 947.

[22 March 1870]
Scalands/Robertsbridge/Hawkhurst.

Dear Miss Boyd

I should have written you before this, but wanted to give a pretty good account of myself – but could not – & cannot. So much for that. However surroundings are at any rate pleasant now, though the snow made them rather dreary just at first & the rain seems a little threatening today. Stillman is a most excellent & even loveable companion, & as he strides moodily to & fro reminds me sometimes of the Scotus of earlier days – indeed considerably in various respects. He is a complete Don Quixote in every way, & with such a Sancho as myself to back him, we ought not to lack for adventures. None however have turned up as yet, except the meeting with a tolerably pretty model from whom I have begun a chalk drawing to pay expenses with. However I find myself not much in trim for work of this kind. Poetry suits me better, & I have done just a sheet to add to my book since coming here. It consists chiefly of the "Stream's Secret" which I began at Penkill last Autumn, sitting on that dear little slope of steps by the bed of the stream before the cave became an institution. This now makes about a dozen pages, & a few sonnets complete the new sheet.[1] There are besides 3 new Sonnets in the last set of proofs which I think you haven't seen and accordingly enclose. The new things are now at the printer's. I fancy the Stream's Secret is one of my best. Perhaps I may yet do the proposed Lancelot & Guenevere poem, but time runs short as I *must* be out before end of April. The binding is in hand, & the woodcut flyleaf – which is all I have seen of it yet – looks very pretty.

I am delighted to hear today from Christina that you are to do most of the woodcuts for her. I am sure the book will be the gainer in its bestial features especially.[2] She has sent me a prose tale, which with others already done will make a volume very shortly I believe. It seems by a mere first glance very good I think. It is called "Commonplace," & is the most everyday affair possible.[3]

Love to Scotus & Scota,[*] the latter of whom is I hope all right again. Is the Roman picture gone to Bond St.?

Affectionately yours
D G Rossetti

I hope you have pretty good news of Miss Losh. Send her my love if you write.

---

[*] "Scota" = Letitia Scott.
[1] See **66**. The title of this poem became one of WBS' grievances; speaking of the glen at Penkill frequented by DGR in the autumn of 1869, he wrote: "Here I used to find him face to the wall lying in a shallow cave that went by the name of a seventeenth-century Covenanter, Bennan's Cave, working out with much elaboration and little inspiration, *The Stream's Secret*. After it was done he did not know what to call this poem, till reading over my series of sonnets called *The Old Scotch House*, and finding one called 'The Stream's Secret', he simply appropriated that name for his own performance. Nothing would restrain him: 'No name in the world would suit me but that, it expresses what I want!' No doubt it did, but it also expressed what I wanted to say in my sonnet. . . . A deadly quarrel I could not bear, so here, as always, he had his way" (*AN* 2: 114–16). In fact, the poem was scarcely begun at Penkill: most of it was not written until the Scalands sojourn (see **64** & *FLM* 271).
[2] AB did a number of drawings intended for CGR's "Nursery Songs" (published as *Sing-Song* in 1872). In June DGR objected to a number of the large figure drawings (*WMRD* 11n4);

the illustrations eventually used were by AH. In 71.172, DGR tells AML that the change of publisher from FSE to Routledge was responsible. See **50n2** & 71.120, 125, 189.1, & 199.
3   CGR's *Commonplace* was published by FSE in May. See also **65, 66, 68, 147, 164**, & **173**.

70.64 TO ALGERNON CHARLES SWINBURNE

MS: BL. Published: *ALC* 4: 128–29 (misdated 2 Mar); DW 956.

[22 March 1870]

Scalands/Robertsbridge/Hawkhurst

Dear Swinburne

I have been very vexed all along at being away just when you are in town after so long an absence, and all the more now that I hear what splendid things you have been reading to our friends in London – the *Tristram and Iseult* and a poem which is no doubt the "Hertha"[1] – to say nothing of your arduous and affectionate labours on my behalf, of which I also hear great things. However you are not much more locomotive than myself – so where you are now you may probably be still when I am in town again which will be in a fortnight if not earlier. Stillman is my companion here – an excellent one – and the cottage we are staying at belongs to an old friend of mine – Mme. Bodichon – the surroundings being among my early associations.

I have been here just over a week now and have written just a sheet of new matter for my book, which is gone to the printer and shall reach you as soon as I have a revise. It consists chiefly of "The Stream's Secret" a poem the first stanzas of which I wrote at Penkill last autumn, and which I have developed to about a dozen pages. I hope you will like it. It might be ranked in some degree with the "Nocturn" and so perhaps might be disposed of in your article without giving much trouble. However while that has perhaps more play of metre and fancy, this is I hope a more passionate and weightier thing, and I trust therefore it will not seem to you to suffer in the comparison. I shall be anxious to know your opinion of it. Then there are a few new sonnets too – one on Ned's *Circe*, which you may possibly have seen in his hands. If I do anything else it will be "God's Graal" – (the Lancelot Poem) but this baffled me rather on taking it up, owing to the limitations of the burden I had adopted; however I may tackle it yet, but time runs short.[2]

Good bye, dear old fellow, and believe me

Affectionately yours
DGRossetti

P.S. I think it would be very desirable to put what poetry I have by me into temporary print, and strike off a few copies only to prevent its getting lost by some mishap.³

1   "Prelude. Tristram and Iseult" (Wise & Gosse 4: 25–32) was published in J. H. Friswell's *Pleasure: A Holiday Book of Verse and Prose* (King & Co., 1871), and reprinted in *Tristram of Lyonesse and Other Poems* (1882); "Hertha" appeared in *Songs before Sunrise* (1871).
2   This poem was stillborn: in 1911 WMR printed 19 lines which "come in a notebook in connexion with several pages of prose detail abstracted from the *Mort Arthur*" (*Works* 672).
3   Wise misdated, misquoted, and misapplied this statement in order to pass off proofs of *Poems* he had acquired as Trial Books (see Lewis 112, 127). Here DGR refers to MSS that will not be included in *Poems*. Although in 1869 he had struck off a few copies of his prose story "Hand and Soul" when he dropped it from *Poems*, there is no evidence that he ever carried out this intention of a "temporary" printing of his unpublished poetry.

70.65 TO FRANCES MARY LAVINIA ROSSETTI

MS: UBC. Excerpt: *FL* 223. Published: DW 957. Date: FLR.

Tuesday [22 March 1870]

My dear Mother

Will you thank Christina for the arrival this morning of "Commonplace" which I already like the looks of.¹ Also thanks to yourself for the Pall Mall article which I will return shortly.² It is of course the best I have yet seen. Among the fault-findings as to points of expression at the end, I rather agree with some but not with others – notably not with that about the closing sentence of the memoir to which I see no objection though it certainly belongs in *legitimate* measure to the class of expression which the Yankees have vulgarized by hyperbole.

I should, as you may suppose, have written before this in answer to yours, if I had been able to give any very favourable account of myself, but I am not very brilliant. I suppose I may perhaps stay a fortnight longer. Stillman is a very pleasant & kindly companion, never obtrusive & always helpful. His own affairs with Marie are I believe going all right though passing through a critical moment just now. His little boy is I fear not for this world.³

I have written just a sheet of additions to my book since I came here, & it is now printing: – to wit, a poem called "The Stream's Secret" of which I had a few opening stanzas already done; and a few additional sonnets. I shall certainly get the book out before the end of April, as 3 or 4 friendly hands are already at work on it for the May periodicals. Swinburne is to do it in the Fortnightly, Morris in the Academy, Colvin in the Pall Mall & perhaps in the Quarterly, – a bloke name Skelton in Fraser, Knight in the Globe, & others elsewhere. However, all this is quiet preparation not to be widely known beforehand. The binding is in progress & will I hope be a success.

I was most glad to learn from Christina that your dear ears are somewhat relieved. God bless you, dear old darling, is the heartfelt prayer of your most

affectionate Son
Gabriel

1. See **68**.
2. A review of WMR's *Poetical Works of Shelley* (*Pall Mall Gazette*, 14 Mar 70: 6). Although the reviewer, who was probably HBF, praised WMR's "great industry, enthusiasm, and exactness," he complained, in language that recalls HBF's article on WMR in *Tinsley's Magazine*, of "certain inelegant usages of speech . . . which one would be inclined to call Yankee and slangy"; he especially objected to the concluding description of Shelley as "one of the ultimate glories of our race and planet."
3. See 62.3n13, where the date of WJS' marriage to Marie Spartali should be corrected to 1871. WJS, his first wife, Laura Mack, and their children, Lisa, Bella, and John Ruskin (Russie), remained in Crete during the insurrection against Turkish rule, 1866–68. In Sep 68 they moved to Athens, where his wife, "who had stood up courageously under the awful demands of siege conditions, collapsed into insanity and committed suicide in 1869" (*Catalogue of the William James Stillman Collection* [Schenectady, NY: Friends of the Union College Library, 1974]: xvii). Russie's always precarious health deteriorated following the family's return to England, and he died in 1875 at the age of 13. WMR's diary for 1871–72 charts Marie Stillman's estrangement from her father, Michael Spartali, subsequent to her marriage, from his refusal to recognize her, noted on 29 Aug 71, to their reconciliation following the birth of a daughter, Euphrosyne, in 1872. For Michael Spartali's letter to DGR asking him to intervene against the marriage, see 71.4n1. On 10 Mar 72, WMR "saw [Marie and her father] together – myself the only third party – and there seemed to be no strain nor distance between them. Stillman tells me he is not as yet on any confidential footing with Spartali: but they meet on terms of mutual tolerance and concession" (*WMRD* 113, 176).

70.66 TO ALICE BOYD

MS: NLS. Published: Purves 587–88; DW 948.

Wednesday [23 March 1870]

Dear Miss Boyd

I meant to have asked you in my note yesterday whether you could bring to mind any feature or incident particularly characteristic of the Penkill glen at nightfall.[1] In my poem I have made the speaker towards the close suddenly perceive that the night is coming on, & have had to give a descriptive touch or two.

I expect a first proof in all probability tomorrow morning (Thursday) so if

I get a hint of any kind from you by next day (Friday), it would be in time to insert before I send back the proof with revisions & possible additions.

Ever yours
DG Rossetti

I yesterday read a prose tale Christina has been writing called "Commonplace," rather in the Miss Austen vein I judge & quite worthy of its title, but very good & far from uninteresting.

1 See **63&n1**.

70.67 TO FREDERICK STARTRIDGE ELLIS
MS: BL. Published: *FSE* 11; DW 958.

Wednesday [23 March 1870]

Dear Ellis

The yellow on white pleases me best decidedly. If this is not used, I fancy mere black on white like the book would do best. Have you got Morris's views about it? But if the yellow on white, then the book ought certainly for harmony to be bound in white & gold (stretched on pure white board) like the first edition of Swinburne's Atalanta. People must keep it clean or not as they like. They will *get* it clean from us. Nothing could look as well as this among such colours as are manufactured at present.

I rejoice to hear that Swinburne's book is to the fore,[1] only I expect it will squash mine with the critics.

Now I want you to tell me: –

1st When will the binding be ready for use?

2nd What is the very last day at which the printers must absolutely have finished their work & delivered it to the binders?

Since coming here I have just written *one sheet* which is now at the printers. I am having it struck off as a separate proof to send to the reviewers, before the things are fitted into their places in the mass. If I judge by your answer to my second query that there is time to finish another thing I have in hand, that may make another sheet. Otherwise I will look upon the book as complete in its materials.

I suppose the volume ought if possible to be sent to the reviews for which articles are being written, about the time that the articles are sent in.

I have just read the leading tale of Christina's volume the entire M.S. of which will I believe be offered to you almost immediately. I think it very good (in the Miss Austen vein rather) and sure I should fancy of a good success.

Ever yours
DG Rossetti

1   *Songs before Sunrise.*

70.68 TO CHRISTINA GEORGINA ROSSETTI

MS: UBC. Excerpt: HRA 26. Published: *FL* 224; Packer 81; DW 959.

Wednesday [23 March 1870]

Dear Christina

I have read Commonplace¹ (which I return by Book Post) & like it very much. It certainly is not dangerously exciting to the nervous system, but is far from being dull for all that, and I should think it likely to take. Stillman & I noted one or two trifles on the opposite blank pages for your consideration. Mere trifles. He likes it much also. I return the M.S. by book post. No doubt Ellis will be very glad to have it as soon as you can let him. I am glad Miss Boyd is to do the woodcuts.²

Your affec:
Gabriel

P.S. Of course I think your proper business is to write poetry & not Commonplaces.
P.P.S. You will be sorry to learn that I hear from Boulogne today that old Maenza is dead just as he was thinking of making a move towards Italy. His poor old wife is of course in a sad state.³ If any of you would like to write condolences the address is

19 Rue Simoneau
Boulogne-sur-mer.

She did not write to me herself, but a certain Neapolitan music-master named Siesto, whom I remember there centuries ago – and whose feelings are expressed in 3 notes of admiration at a time.

1   For *Commonplace*, see **31**.
2   For CGR's *Sing-Song* (1872). For a complete discussion of the various illustrators for the book, see Janzen Kooistra, *CGR* 92–97. See also **63&n2**.
3   For the Maenzas, see 43.4. DGR had been sending them an annual allowance since 1868 (*RP* 322).

70.69 TO EMILY TEBBS

MS: Texas. Date: P/M.

[23 March 1870]
Scalands/Robertsbridge/Hawkhurst

Dear Mrs. Tebbs

I fear I am hardly likely to be in town on the 30th though if I am I shall be but too glad to join you. I need all the benefits I can get – if any *is* to be got – by change of air & scene.

I had hoped before now to have had you safely transferred to chalk & paper, but shall be effecting that yet ere very long I trust.[1] With kindest remembrances to your husband and all mutual friends

I am ever yours
D G Rossetti

[1] See **6**.

70.70 TO ALICE BOYD

MS: NLS. Excerpt: Purves 588–89. Published: DW 953.

Friday [25 March 1870]
Scalands/Robertsbridge/Hawkhurst

Dear Miss Boyd

Thanks for reminding me of the glen's leading characteristic which I ought to have remembered. I have remodelled from it the only descriptive stanza which I find this part of the poem will bear; & find it greatly the gainer.[1]

Now let me declare that I view the Scotian view of my sonnets as rather a random one. The "Life-in-Love" refers to an actual love with a reminiscence of a former one; the "Day of Love" to a meeting between lovers who have much to remember, & the "One Hope" to the longing for accomplishment of individual desire after death. Surely there is nothing in any one of these subjects so limitedly personal as to present an obstacle to any reader who cares for writing that has an abstract side at all.

No doubt Graham wd feel much more pleased & flattered than any thing else by an invitation to see Eve.[2] His address is

W. G. Esq. M P.
44 Grosvenor Place.

Friday [25 March 1870]

I feel sure he wd like it & wd come if not quite prevented.

It is most provoking that I shall not have Scotus as my reviewer in the North British. I wonder who it is to be. Is Simcox a contributor?³

I saw a poor dear little mole lying dead by the roadside yesterday, & was so touched by his appearance (I actually never saw one before) that I am trying to get a man here to find me a pair for my garden.

I should like to have joined you at Burges's who is always funny & amusing.⁴ What dreadful people these Martins must be. I know them not.

I shall probably see you again after next week – i.e. as much of you as I see of anything now. I am much worried & must consult Bowman again. With love to all

Your affec: D Gabriel R

I enclose you a bad unfavourable proof of the woodcut for my inner fly-leaf – i.e. inside the binding and opposite – 4 times repeated in all. It is to be yellow on white however.

¹ See **66**. The "characteristic" seems to be the mist that accompanies nightfall in the glen, described in stanza 35 (*Poems* 164).
² The reference is probably to WBS' *Eve of the Deluge*, painted in 1865. In Oct 70, it was at Elgin Road and he was working on the smaller version presented to the Tate by AB in 1891.
³ George Augustus Simcox (1841–1905), poet, critic, & scholar who specialized in classical literature. He was on DGR's list to receive copies of *Poems* (see **92**) but does not seem to have reviewed it; the piece in *North British Review* (Jul 70: 598–99) was unsigned (see **200**).
⁴ For Burges, see 58.30n1.

70.71 TO WILLIAM MICHAEL ROSSETTI

MS: BL. Published: *RP* 527; DW 960. Date: WMR.

Friday [25 March 1870]

Dear W

Do you know if Simcox is on the North British? It seems some one secured my book there before Scott asked for it, but I don't know who it was. Or is there anyone else likely? Do you know the names?

I've been rather worried by your discovery about the resemblance to Petrarch's 1st Sonnet which I verily believe I never read.¹ Wd you mind copying it for me?

I have written just a sheet of new matter which is in print now, and shall do no more but a sonnet or two perhaps. I'm not in trim & time wears too short.

Your
Gabriel

I finished the "Stream's Secret" (begun at Penkill) which makes 12 pages. The rest are Sonnets.

[1] The 6th line of Petrarch's 1st sonnet is:
"Fra la vana speranza e il van dolore."
The first line of Sonnet L of *HL*, "The One Hope" (*Poems* 238) is
"When vain desire at last and vain regret."
Before the month was out, DGR had changed the two "vain"s to "all"s, then changed back to the original reading (77). However, the latest change restoring the original reading did not reach FSE in time to appear in the 1st edition; this was put right in the 2nd edition. See 113&nn & **Companion: Textual Variants in** *Poems*.

70.72 TO FREDERICK STARTRIDGE ELLIS

MS: BL. Published: *FSE* 12; DW 961.

Saturday [26 March 1870]

Scalands/Robertsbridge/Hawkhurst

Dear Ellis

You will be glad to hear that I have just wound up my book with 2 more sonnets to the House of Life (making 50 now) and shall add no more. I am sending all to the printers but must have one revise of the last sheets before they work them off.

Will you see by the bye that the 2 transposed sheets at the beginning do not get stops or letters dropped out. It seems to me that no one at the office sees to these obvious matters at all. I have had to attend to everything of the kind all along myself.

I expect Morris & Mrs. M. here to dinner today from Hastings, & think they may possibly stay a day or two, after which I shall very likely return to town. I am sorry to say Mrs. Morris is far from well now though she seemed to benefit greatly at first.

Ever yours
DGR

Have you my sister's stories & how do you like them?

70.73 TO WILLIAM ALLINGHAM

MS: Huntington. Published: *WA/GBH* 293; DW 962. The accompanying envelope, postmarked 7 Mar, does not appear to be in DGR's hand. GBH accepts this date, but the letter must be later.

[27 March 1870]
Scalands/Robertsbridge/Hawkhurst

Dear Allingham

I now just hear casually that my book has been applied for to the Athenæum by one of its critics, I believe with friendly intentions.[1] So I ought to let you know after my suggestion. Of course I should be very sorry if I had missed you.

Ever yours
DG Rossetti

[1] JWM's sympathetic review appeared in *Athenæum* (1 May 70: 573–74). Having been introduced to DGR's poems by Joseph Knight, JWM "admired them much, and proposes to review them in *The Athenæum*" (*RP* 504). See next letter.

70.74 TO FREDERICK STARTRIDGE ELLIS

MS: BL. Published: *FSE* 13; DW 963.

Sunday [27 March 1870]
Scalands/Robertsbridge/Hawkhurst

Dear Ellis

I'm sending the remaining sheets not yet worked off to the printers today with final insertions & corrections. Will you keep them up to the mark? I shall need a revise of these sheets now, & then all is over. Surely thus the thing might be got out, bound and all, by the *beginning* of the last week in April. This is desirable as the reviews on 1st May will thus look a little less like conspiracy than if they appeared the day the book comes out. It seems necessary to prod the die-cutter about the binding.

Marston has asked for the book for the Athenæum & I suppose will get it, in which case the review will be friendly.

I shall be very glad if you will do the Contents. Perhaps I had better just see a proof. Thanks. There is now some further transposition & new pieces in the last sheets. All *my* work is now done.

Ever yours
D G Rossetti

P.S. Top & Janey are here today – the former insolently solid – the latter better than when I last saw her at Hastings.¹

---

¹ JM also visited Scalands at Barbara Bodichon's invitation; she stayed almost a month, although not in the same house as DGR. He drew her reclining on a sofa (S.376). WM visited briefly between the middle of the month and 1 Apr, when he returned to London.

70.74.1 TO FREDERICK STARTRIDGE ELLIS

MS: Torquay Museum.

[c. 29 March 1870]

Dear Ellis

There are 2 stanzas in Love's Nocturn (page 19 of the set I have beginning with Troy Town) which I have which I have always meant to transpose & always forgotten. That is, the one beginning "Like a vapour" &c which now stands first should be made to follow the one beginning "How should love's &c" which now stands second. As this sheet is cancelled & to be transposed before again working off, would you kindly get this point attended to if not too late. If too late, of course it does not matter, but I should like it done if possible.

Ever yours
DG Rossetti

70.75 TO FREDERICK STARTRIDGE ELLIS

MS: BL. Published: *FSE* 14; DW 964.

Wednesday [30 March 1870]
Scalands/Robertsbridge

Dear Ellis –

I send you the proof sheets in last stage and will trust to your seeing that all corrections are properly made, after which they can be finally worked off without returning again to me. I omit sending only one sheet – sheet **N**. which I shall have to retain for a day or two. The first page of this sheet – "Aspecta Medusa" – can be transferred to the last page of sheet M. instead of the Cancelled Scrap. I shall then insert at beginning of sheet N. a translation of Dante's *Francesca da Rimini* which I write for today to London.¹ This will occupy 2 pages but will not cause inconvenience, as there is a page to spare at present at the end of the 1st section of the book before the "House of Life." So the paging will not be thrown out.

Thus if you will see to the corrections being properly made, all the sheets I now send can be finally worked off, and sheet N. shall reach you I doubt not on Saturday morning.

In the *Contents* you will have to consider various insertions – "The Stream's Secret" & some Sonnets, & various changes of title & rearrangements. The title "Francesca da Rimini" to be inserted after "Aspecta Medusa."

Will you, the moment the sheets are all struck off & before binding, send a set to each of the persons named on the next page, as they are all concerned in reviewing & might quote incorrectly something that has been altered, besides the necessity of their seeing the new things inserted. Proofs – not copies – wd do for this purpose I suppose.

One thing I should like (as indicated at end) is to put the printer's name there on blank page, as the book looks to end with unpleasant abruptness otherwise.

Ever yours
D G Rossetti

Please do not delay a moment in sending copies as overpage.

W. Morris
26 Queen Square

A. C. Swinburne
22A Dorset Street
Baker Street

J. Knight
27 Camden Square

H. B. Forman
(query address?)

John Skelton
Hermitage of Braid
Edinburgh

J. F. McLennan
81 Princes Street
Edinburgh.

---

[1] DGR did not insert this translation; it was not completed until 1878 (*Works* xxxv).

70.76 TO FRANCES MARY LAVINIA ROSSETTI

MS: Ashmolean. Published: DW 991.

Wednesday [c. 30 March 1870]

Dear Mamma

I send by Book Post the missing sheets for your copy, & a copy for William. They are both only provisory, as the book is not complete.

Your affec: Son
DG R

70.77 TO FREDERICK STARTRIDGE ELLIS

MS: BL. Published: *FSE* 15; DW 965.

[30 March 1870]

Dear Ellis

I forgot to mention one last change – which is in fact a change back again – to make if not too late.

Page 288 line one.
      vain   vain
When ~~all~~ desire at last & ~~all~~ regret

Alter as above. If too late, no matter.
  (Ellis loq: G – d d – n!)

Your
D G Rossetti

70.78 TO FREDERICK STARTRIDGE ELLIS

MS: BL. Published: *FSE* 16; DW 970. The enclosure is not with the MS.

Scalands
Friday [1 April 1870]

Dear Ellis

Now don't be in a rage.

If it is still time to make the enclosed addition, please do so, and I will trust to you to see that it is correctly printed & that no accidents occur.

If it *is* too late, it does not matter at all.

Ever your
D G Rossetti

70.79 TO FORD MADOX BROWN

MS: UBC. Published: DW 969.

Friday [1 April 1870]

Scalands/Robertsbridge/Hawkhurst

Dear Brown

I have been meaning to write all along, but partly taken up by other things & partly discouraged from doing so by having no good news. However, as tomorrow is your last evening, I write now to say how sorry I am to have missed several of them by no choice of my own: – pleasant gatherings which recall pleasant things that will not last for ever.[1]

It is barely possible that I may be coming up to town tomorrow & in that case shall turn up at your house after all; but this is so very doubtful that I write notwithstanding. I am at the last gasp of my work for the book (very little new, but a good deal of difficulty & hurry in last getting together.) This may either keep me here tomorrow or carry me to London – *which* the morning's post will determine; & in the latter case I hope to see you. In the former I am, as always,

Your affec:
D G Rossetti

[1] DGR is referring to the fortnightly gatherings held at the FMBs' Fitzroy Square home between 1866–74 (see also 66.180). This was not the final gathering for 1870: WMR's 4 Jul diary entry records that he "went to Brown's soiree – the last for the present year" (*WMRD* 17).

70.80 TO ALGERNON CHARLES SWINBURNE

MS: BL. Excerpt: Compton-Rickett 320. Published: *ALC* 4: 130; DW 966.

[3 April 1870]

Scalands/Robertsbridge/Hawkhurst/Kent

Dear Swinburne

I send you herewith such new matters as I have added. I hope "The Stream's Secret" will find favour with you.

I am inserting the translation of Dante's "Francesca"[1] which you once mentioned, to fill a small gap, having omitted the trifle "Seed of David." There are other slight changes and alterations of arrangement and titles, and I am telling Ellis to send you a set the moment they are struck off, without waiting for the binding, that you may see there is no alteration made in anything you may have quoted. I fear all this is rather trying your patience.

I was in London yesterday for a few hours on an unwilling visit to the doctor's, but was not able to get to see anyone. It is very jolly to see the three of us, you, Top and self, figuring at last together in one advertisement.[2]

Your affectionate
D Gabriel R

Do let me know how you like my additions. All is not at an end. I hear great things indeed of your article, and must needs confess (as that is too obvious) that I long to see it.

---

[1] See **75&n1**.

[2] On the 4 pages of adverts preceding the 8 blank leaves in *Poems*, FSE advertises WM's *The Earthly Paradise* (1), *The Life and Death of Jason* (2), *The Story of Grettir the Strong*, & *The Story of the Volsungs and Niblungs* as well as ACS' *Songs before Sunrise* (3). An advert for CGR's *Commonplace* also appears (4).

70.81 TO FREDERICK STARTRIDGE ELLIS

MS: Princeton. Published: *TR* 66; DW 971.

Sunday [3 April 1870]
(right address. No Mme B. needed)
Scalands/Robertsbridge/Hawkhurst/Kent

Dear Ellis

Fly-leaf quite charming – I see no amendment needed. I should say the colours to try would be dark brown (almost black) on indigo grey, – Indigo grey on warm white, – and perhaps Yellow Ochre or Raw Umber on the ordinary white of the book.

I suppose there's no need of my returning the proof as no change is required.

Ever yours D GRossetti

What a lark about Dante in the Yankee advertisement.[1]

---

[1] Presumably Roberts Bros. of Boston, DGR's American publisher, had committed a blunder in announcing as forthcoming *Dante and his Circle*, FSE's re-issue of *EIP* which appeared in 1874. This book was not advertised in the Roberts Bros. edition of *Poems*.

Monday [4 April 1870] 70.82

70.82 TO FREDERICK STARTRIDGE ELLIS
MS: BL. Published: *FSE* 17; DW 972.

Chelsea
Monday [4 April 1870]

Dear Ellis

All my part in the book is now done. I have been up for a day in town, & with this return the last proof to the printers (sheet N.) You will see I have not adopted the Francesca after all to fill the gap, but have done another bit from Villon.

And *now* – how about the binders. They really *must* get on. I was being warned by a good authority the other day that if the reviews appear only the same day as the book, it may incense the rest of the press & they may ignore the thing. However of course they might be d – d – but it would be well not to fall into this rather ridiculous crisis.

The blue printing of the fly-sheet looks very well but a little cold. Indigo should be the colour used. The blue cloth is just the one I meant & I think it quite satisfactory. I suppose the bulk of the edition had better be blue – but perhaps it wd be nice to have some white & gold copies.

How about the Yankees? I heard no more from you on that head. Will you answer me to Scalands, as I go back tomorrow for a week longer I think. I shall have to send you a list of people to whom copies will have to be sent on my account – mostly expedient as possibly of use to the book. I hope you are seeing to the critics' copies I mentioned. And the Contents.

Ever yours D G Rossetti

70.83 TO BARBARA LEIGH SMITH BODICHON
MS: PML. Published: DW 1041.

Wednesday [6 April 1870?]
16 Cheyne Walk
Chelsea

Dear Mme Bodichon

I hope you will let me be the donor of the dormice which no doubt have reached Blandford Square ere this. They eat apples, nuts, corn, &c – and require no drink – indeed ought not to have water as a rule, but may be allowed a little milksop which they like. Their bed should rather be of hay than of wool. Will you give the young lady my love with them.

Ever yours
D G Rossetti

70.84 TO ALICE BOYD

MS: NLS. Published: Purves 589; DW 967.

[c. 7 April 1870]
Scalands/Robertsbridge/Hawkhurst

Dear Miss Boyd

I send you up the new matter for my book, which will be the last. All is now finally going through the press & will be out on 21st April. The things as I send them are still rather in the rough & not yet inserted in their places.

In haste (this being one of several letters to write)

Yours affectionately
D G Rossetti

70.85 TO FREDERICK STARTRIDGE ELLIS

MS: BL. Published: *FSE* 18; DW 973.

[7 April 1870]

Dear Ellis

I find on inquiry that I owe you £20 of the account sent & that Howell remains owing you the first £10.

Now that H. explains about the drawing & I know which it is, I remember I did tell him he was not to sell it at all. I do not mind your having it & no doubt you can arrange with H.

Swinburne's review of me is to appear in May Fortnightly (this *entre nous* as regards the general world) & one in May Fraser. I hope one is not to be bilked of Morris's but he has not yet heard from the Academy.[1] Strangeways has the sheets now for final changes.

Ever yours
DG Rossetti

---

[1] WM had agreed early on to review *Poems*, but he had trouble writing the review (Kelvin 107) and dealing with the Editor of the *Academy*, where his sympathetic comments finally appeared 14 May (Kelvin 105n1). On 9 May he wrote to WMR: "the reception of Gabriel's book is satisfactory so far isn't it: I suppose we will have to wait to see what the enemies say of what the friends say" (Kelvin 113).

70.86 TO ALGERNON CHARLES SWINBURNE

MS: BL. Published: DW 951.

Friday [8 April 1870]

Scalands/Robertsbridge/Hawkhurst

My dear Swinburne

I have been trying hard to worry you no more with my humilities or inverted self-sufficiencies, but find myself so worried by that one enthusiastic word of yours to which I in all sincerity strongly demurred, that I must even yet expend a prayer and a postage-stamp in imploring you, as you are my true friend (which I know how truly you are) to cancel it for my sake. Do, pray, do this, and let me have quite unmixed pleasure and pride in your generous encouragement. The glorious poetry of your own which I heard that day made me meek indeed, & I feel all the less able to sustain this one last straw of praise, feeling so near donkeydom as I did in *that* comparison, and so all the more desirous to rely on uncompared qualifications, whatever those may prove to be.

Most affectionately yours
D Gabriel R

I forgot to mention, (in case desirable) that 2 titles of sonnets are changed – "Flammifera" to "Love's Redemption" & "Run & Won" to "The Vase of Life."

70.87 TO FREDERICK STARTRIDGE ELLIS

MS: BL. Published: *FSE* 19; DW 974. Item *c* of the four separate sheets enclosed with *FSE* 20 is almost certainly the list of those "likely to 'do' the book," and so it has been inserted here.

Monday [11 April 1870]

Scalands

Dear Ellis

I believe the tenor of my letter yesterday was towards a notion that the outside journals (the unattached, as Athenæum, Saturday &c) had better get their copies on the 14th. But on reflection I think it is undesirable perhaps to let them have these till a week later. However, you are the better judge on this point, & I am willing to leave it entirely in your hands. Whatever you do will be for the best without need of further correspondence.

I find I have a most formidable list of copies I shall have to send myself. I will forward this to you. Meanwhile I send the names of those who I think wd be likely to "do" the book somewhere & might be worth while to send to on that account as I said before. Those marked X are doing it already.

Ever yours D G Rossetti

P.S. Papers for which the thing is being done are

Pall Mall (Colvin)
Globe (Knight)
Edinburgh Courant (Alexander)
Fraser (Skelton)
Fortnightly (Swinburne)
Academy (Morris)
Quarterly (Colvin)

but this last is a spec. I believe.[1]
I hear you heard the Topsaic article.

[Enclosure (*FSE* 20c)]

X Sidney Colvin
14 Arlington Street
Piccadilly.

J.F. McLennan
81 Princes St
Edinburgh

X J. Skelton
Hermitage of Braid
Edinburgh

X J Knight
27 Camden Square

J. Westland Marston
(ask Morris the address)

X W. J. Stillman
(care of self)

G. A. Simcox
Queen's Coll. Oxford

X P. P. Alexander
at Mrs. Irving's
21 Pitt Street
Edinburgh

James Hannay
British Consulate
Barcelona

[1] Only the final item in this list is inaccurate: Colvin's comments appeared in *Pall Mall Gazette* (21 Apr 70: 7) and *Westminster Review* (Jan 71: 55–92); the article in the *Quarterly Review* (Jan 72: 59–84) was by W. J. Courthope. For a complete list of reviews of *Poems*, see **Volume V: Appendix 5**.

70.88 TO CHARLES ELIOT NORTON

MS: Harvard. Excerpt: *RP* 528–29; HRA 171, 258; DW 976.

Scalands/Robertsbridge/Sussex

11th April [1870]

My dear Norton

What very very kind letters from yourself & Mrs. Norton! May I mass the answers I owe into one? It seems natural, when the unity of kindness is so complete in both.

I have been here for a month or rather more now, having left London in very poor health, & not having much to boast of at this writing. There is everything to tempt me in your invitation, I need hardly say; but the weakness I have long been experiencing in my eyes forbids sight-seeing, & to enter Florence under such a prohibition for the first time would be I fear too tantalizing.[1] Better dullness & commonplace at home than such a change so circumscribed. Besides, if work may be, work I must for many reasons, & the day has arrived to try again. So I fear there is little likelihood (though not perhaps quite none) of my seeing you in Florence. Meanwhile I may say truly that no distant place or persons seem to me so pleasantly inviting, but for dismal drawbacks.

I hope you will soon get my volume of poems. It shall reach you as soon as it is out, which will I believe be for certain before the end of this month. Some friendly hands are already at work on reviews of it: Morris for the

"Academy" – Swinburne for the "Fortnightly" – Stillman for an American paper,[2] & others.

Stillman is my companion in these solitudes, and a very good helpful friendly companion he is, as you will judge from your knowledge of him. The house (which has a good studio in it) has been lent us by an old friend, Mme Bodichon, an excellent landscape-painter herself, as you perhaps know. I think you have heard from Stillman that he has actually come in for *the* slice of luck still attainable in our circle – i.e. for Marie Spartali to whom he has got himself engaged by a national rapid act of annexation which has astonished all beholders. He has gone up to town to-day to see her, and I am left to lonely letter-writing. She is a noble girl – in beauty, in sweetness, and in artistic gifts; and the sky should seem very warm and calm above, and the road in front bright & clear, and all ill things left behind for ever, to him who starts anew on his life-journey, foot to foot & hand in hand with her.

However, there is a good deal of opposition at present on the part of her parents, who are rich people and had projected quite a different kind of match for their daughter. But her heart is entirely bent on it, and all *must* go well for him & her in the end. I warmly hope that happiness is in store for them both. She is a pearl among women, and there are points in Stillman's character of the manliest and truest I know. His prospects are at present however very uncertain; and it would be most painful to see Marie dragged down, by her generous attachment, to petty difficulties in life, which she may be and is bravely prepared to face but of which she as yet knows nothing. It would be a great relief to all her friends to know that some opportunity was opening to the man she loves which should put her out of reach of such a danger as this.

I hope that when you get my book you will agree with me as to the justness of my including all it contains. I say this because there are a few things – and notably a poem called "Jenny" – which will raise objections in some quarters. I only know that they have been written neither recklessly nor aggressively (moods which I think sure to result in the ruin of Art,) but from a true impulse to deal with subjects which seem to me capable of being brought rightly within Art's province. Of my own position I feel sure, & so wait the final result without apprehension.

Our friends are all well, with the exception, I most deeply grieve to say, of Mrs. Morris who is still in a very delicate state. She and Morris have been in this neighbourhood lately, and are coming again, and I trust the change may prove eventually of some decided benefit to her, as signs of this have already become apparent.

Good bye, my dear Norton. I am going for my walk now in a pleasing but not very sympathetic entourage of leafless woods and English associations which I have grown old in but am never perhaps quite at home with. I envy you your Italian ones, and shall be very glad to hear more of the study you propose to undertake of Michael Angelo's unpublished letters. I hope the fit of queer health which baulked you at the outset is over now, and that you and yours are all well. To all of you my best love and the assurance that I am ever

Yours & theirs,
D G Rossetti

1   CEN had invited DGR to join him in Florence.
2   WJS wrote a review of both *Poems* and DGR's work as a painter in *Putnam's New Monthly Magazine* (Jul 70: 95–101); for his marriage to Marie Spartali, see **8** & **65n3**.

70.89 TO FREDERIC JAMES SHIELDS

MS: NLS. Published: Mills 139–40; Horne 89–90; DW 975.

Scalands/Robertsbridge/Sussex
11 April 1870

My dear Shields

Some time back I wrote to a Mr. Mitchell of Manchester who possesses that Venus of mine with the roses & honeysuckles, to ask if he wd object to its being photographed; & I ventured to name you as a friend who I thought wd be willing, out of consideration for me, to superintend its removal, photographing, & return to its owner. I proposed to save you such trouble by having the loan of it in London, but to this you will see by the letter I enclose he objects. So if you will kindly undertake this for me, I will be much obliged. Any convenient moment to yourself wd of course do. You will see I am writing from the country, & having none of my photos: by me, cannot give you a precise idea of the size I want it to be done. But you have seen some of them and know the sort of size – fairly large & of course deep tone. Your friend of the Lancashire Committee photo: wd I shd think be the very man to make a fine thing of it if worth his while to take the trouble. Of course it is at my expense, not Mr. Mitchell's.[1] One difficulty occurs to me; & that is, that there is a gold nimbus round the head. I wonder if some white powder of some sort could be rubbed over this, or whether there is nothing for it but to let it come black.

I hope you will get my vol. of Poems towards the end of this month, as I have given your name to the publisher. I shall like to know how it pleases you. There is one piece called "Jenny" which gave Smetham a shock when I read it him; but I was sincerely surprised on the whole at its doing so in his case, though I know many people will think it unbearable. I myself have included it (as I wrote it) after mature consideration & could not alter my own impression of the justness of my doing so; knowing as I do how far from aggressive was the spirit in which I produced it, as I should think the poem itself ought to show.

I saw your newspaper controversy about Brown some time ago & thought your part in it excellent.[2] You seem to have a large share of this sort of power which has grown to be almost a national instinct.

I will not write more, as I am not given much to letter writing at present. I need hardly say that my health brought me here; & that means that there is not much to boast of. I hope you can give a better account of yourself.

Your affec: D. G. Rossetti

[1] *Venus Verticordia* (S.173); see **10**. At first Mitchell agreed, but later he changed his mind; DGR apologized for the trouble it had caused FJS (**103**, **181**, & **207**).
[2] See 69.221n1.

70.90 TO JOSEPH KNIGHT
MS: BL.

Tuesday [12 April 1870]

Scalands/Robertsbridge/Hawkhurst/Sussex

My dear Knight,

I want to ask you a question *in confidence,* and shd be glad for a particular reason to get your answer by *return of post.*

Is Marston sure to be able to do that review for the Athenæum? I met Purnell at Brown's last Monday but one, (he having been brought there by Swinburne.) He was very civil indeed to me & most agreeable; but I heard afterwards that before I came he had been complaining loudly of a "conspiracy" between you & Marston to do my book for the Athenæum, of which it seems he is established poetical critic; & he seemed rather bent on making an example of the work in consequence – raving a little about immorality, Jenny, &c. However as I say he was nothing but pleasant to me & I only heard of all this later. It seems that on hearing of Marston's intention, he wrote at once to the Athenæum demanding that the book shd be sent to him the moment it appeared.[1]

Could you (without troubling Marston) let me know by return if you know aught of this state of things. The book will be definitively out on the 23rd till which day it is inevitably postponed on account of the delay with the binding (a design of my own.) But I believe it will be possible, if desirable, to send copies earlier to the reviews, with a notification that they can be exchanged if wished for fully bound copies.

Pardon my troubling you again about my own affairs & believe me

Ever yours
D G Rossetti

1 Thomas Purnell (1835–89), a literary journalist who was a long-time friend of ACS and contributor to the *Athenæum*, was suspected at this time by DGR of animosity towards *Poems* (see **91–95, & 99**).

70.91 TO FORD MADOX BROWN
MS: UBC. Published: DW 977.

[12 April 1870]
Scalands/Robertsbridge/Hawkhurst

My dear Brown

I suppose you have no further news bearing on the Purnell business. I have written *in strict Confidence* to Knight on the subject, & asked for his answer by *return* as to whether he knows anything. Ellis proposes to send copies to the reviews on Thursday next, though the book cannot be definitively issued to the public till the 23rd. Before he does this however I want to know as far as may be if we shall thus be giving the first start to possible spite, which wd be a pity after all the care taken already. If you *do* know anything further, perhaps you will write me a line by *return*. But of course it wd be unwise to take any steps through Swinburne or I suppose any other channel.

Ever yours
DG Rossetti

I have told Knight not to trouble Marston with questions but answer anything he knows himself.

70.92 TO FREDERICK STARTRIDGE ELLIS
MS: BL. Excerpt: DW 978. Published: *FSE* 20.

Scalands
Tuesday [12 April 1870]

Dear Ellis

I send you the list of recipients, & have marked those with a cross who ought to receive first, if there be an insufficiency of copies. However I suppose you had better let me know when the copies are really ready to be sent out, as I ought to come up to your place one day & write the inscriptions in the given copies. I wd come up to town on purpose for this.

I still incline, after getting your note this morning, to the opinion that it may be better to send the general review copies a few days later than Thursday. At any rate if you will defer doing so you shall hear from me again on Thursday morning or Saturday at latest; but I wish to write a note of inquiry in one quarter before settling. The truth is I have lately had reason again to anticipate some spite brewing, and shd take a pleasure in outwitting this (or at any rate preventing its getting the first start) if practicable. Of course if sufficient copies *with* the binding cd be got for the reviewers it wd be better, but I suppose this is not possible till 23rd inst.

As soon as ever the brass block for the binding can be printed, will you send me a proof on the blue cloth & one on white, or if necessary to prevent delay I will come up & see them if you will notify me *when*.

Please take care of the list sent, as I have no other copy.

Ever yours
D G Rossetti

[Enclosures]

Sydney Dobell Esqr
Noke Place
Gloucester

Mrs. Gilchrist
20 The Terrace
Gunter Green
Brompton

Dr. Hake Alton Lodge
Roehampton

A Munro
Villa Tourelle
Cannes
France

Mrs. Howitt
The Orchard
Esher

Tuesday [12 April 1870]

Seymour Kirkup
ask W. M Rossetti

Theo. Martin Esqr
27 Abingdon St
S.W.

G. Rae. Devonshire Rd Birkenhead

Henry Taylor
(query address?)

X Mrs. G.H. Lewes. The Priory
North Bank (or South Bank?)

G.F. Watts R.A. Little Holland House
Kensington

G.P. Boyce, Upper Cheyne Row, Chelsea

A. Hughes[1]
2 Finborough Road
West Brompton

John Ruskin, Denmark Hill. S.

W. Allingham, Lymington, Hants

Miss Spartali, The Shrubbery
Clapham Common

Mrs. Coronio 1A Holland Park
Notting Hill

T. Keightley. Lessness Heath
SE

H.V. Tebbs. 5 Aubrey Road
Holland Park, Notting Hill

H. F. Polydore, 3 Oxford Street
Gloucester

Colonel Richards,
Windham Club.

Bryan W. Procter,[2] 32 Weymouth St.
W

George Meredith, Garrick Club

F. J. Shields, Cornbrook House
Cornbrook Park
Manchester

J.L. Tupper, Rugby School

John Marshall, 10 Savile Row

Mrs. Howitt.

Madame Bodichon
5 Blandford Square

J.T. Nettleship
22 Newman St.
W

X F.M. Brown 37 Fitzroy Square

X W. B. Scott 33 Elgin Road, Notting Hill

X W. Morris 26 Queen Square

X E B Jones The Grange, Northend
Fulham

X Philip Webb. 1 Raymond Buildings
Gray's Inn

Tuesday [12 April 1870]

X C.A. Howell. Northend Grove
Northend, Fulham

X W. M. Rossetti 56 Euston Square
X Mrs. Rossetti Do

Miss Boyd 33 Elgin Road
Notting Hill

Miss Losh – Ravenside
near Carlisle

X Alfred Tennyson, Farringford
Freshwater, I. of Wight

X Robert Browning,[3] 19 Warwick Crescent
Harrow Road

X A. C. Swinburne 22a Dorset Street

Coventry Patmore, Buxted Park,
Buxted, near Uckfield, Sussex.

W. Bowman 5 Clifford St. W

X Rt Honble Henry A. Bruce MP
H.M. Secretary Home Department

X F. R. Leyland, 23 Queen's Gate

X W. Graham, M.P. 44 Grosvenor
Place

---

[1] AH's copy, in a design binding, is inscribed: "To Arthur Hughes/from his friend DGRossetti/April 1870" (private collection).

[2] See Procter ("Barry Cornwall"):DGR (28 Apr, Texas), thanking him for his gift: "I will read the book, and try to value it, as you might desire. But I am almost 83 years of age and have little (even of judgment or appreciation) left."

[3] RB's copy, also in a design binding, is inscribed "To Robert Browning with old and grateful regard. D. G. Rossetti. 1870" (UBC). While no letter of transmission is extant, RB acknowledged the gift on 16 May: "Really I am too much interested in your being a good poet to

congratulate myself that you prove a great one." While not abdicating his critical faculty – he admitted that the personifications of "Love as a youth, encircling you with his arms and wings, gives me a turn" and that the "archaisms in sentiment and expression please me less than they probably do others" – he found the book in the main "masterly and conclusive, with whosoever shall need it, of your right to all the honors in poetry and in painting, 'double-lived in regions new'" (quoted HRA 168–69). RB reiterated these strictures, but in a markedly different tone, in a letter to Isa Blagden (19 Jun 70), in which he described DGR's poems as "*scented* with poetry . . . like trifles of various sorts you take out of a cedar or sandal-wood box: you know I hate the effeminacy of the school, – the men that dress up like women, – that use obsolete forms, too, and archaic accentuations to seem soft. . . . Then, how I hate 'Love,' as a lubberly naked young man putting his arms here & his wings there, about a pair of lovers, – a fellow they would kick away, in the reality" (Edward C. McAleer, ed., *Dearest Isa: Browning's Letters to Isa Blagden* [Austin: UTP, 1951]: 336–37).

70.93 TO JOSEPH KNIGHT

MS: BL.

Scalands
Wednesday [13 April 1870]

My dear Knight

You will think me an endless letter-writer. Since my writing yesterday, it happens I have got a note from Purnell, of so friendly a nature that I cannot doubt all is well in that quarter. So I just send you word of it.

Ever yours
D G Rossetti

70.94 TO THOMAS PURNELL

MS: Princeton.

Scalands/Robertsbridge/Hawkhurst
13 April 1870.

My dear Purnell,

I came back here, where I am sojourning at present, the same day I last saw you. Thus your note has only reached me now.

Many thanks for the newspaper cutting, which is but too friendly & flattering. As for what is said of Swinburne & Morris, I know that the volume & élan of their genius would always leave me far behind; and if I, as a rather older man, had any influence on them in early years, I feel in my turn that their work has duly reacted upon what I have done since.

The very serious consideration you allude to respecting our friend

Swinburne has occupied my mind also since that morning. To see him, as I did, for the rest of that day – how much he was himself of old, and through what a simple act of abstinence, – made one quite yearn to know him always in that mood. (By the bye, what glorious new poems of his own he read me!) The only thing that deters me in the least from making the proposal in question to him is, I feel, the painfulness of so strongly directing his attention to the danger in which he stands, & of which I verily believe him (strange as it may appear) to be half unconscious. But this is cowardice, and I hope to make the effort, with whatever result. You are, I am quite sure, right in your certainty that he would strictly keep such an engagement if once made.[1]

Good Friday (with the week's laziness in which it seems the British Workman then indulges) causes a delay we had not reckoned on with my book; but it will be definitively published on the 23rd; and I trust, from what Ellis tells me, that it may be possible to send copies to the reviews before that date.

The seal of your letter got almost torn off in the post, so I cannot judge of the impression. I remember that, in the 5 minutes after I first met you, your opinion induced me to abstain from buying some dubious gem specimens.

Very truly yours D G Rossetti

---

[1] DGR had seen Purnell and ACS at FMB's on 4 Apr (**90**), but he also spent most of the day with a sober ACS "recently back from Holmwood" on 5 Apr (*RP* 504), doubtless "that day" mentioned in this letter. Like most of the bibulous poet's friends, DGR hoped to persuade ACS to give up drinking.

70.95 TO FORD MADOX BROWN
MS: UBC. Published: DW 980.

Scalands
Wednesday [13 April 1870]

Dear Brown

After what I wrote yesterday, I ought to keep you informed of my having received a very friendly note from Purnell this morning, inclosing a country newspaper cutting with a puff of myself & forthcoming book, I suppose by himself. So I trust he is all right.

Ever yours
D G Rossetti

70.96 TO ALGERNON CHARLES SWINBURNE

MS: BL. Published: DW 979.

Tuesday [c. 13 April 1870]
Scalands/Robertsbridge/Hawkhurst

My dear Swinburne

I find my book will certainly be issued to the public on 23rd inst. The binding delays it till then, but I believe the reviews will receive copies provisorily bound before that date.

I write you word of this that you may reassure Morley, when you send your notice in, of the certainty of the book being out before it appears.

Your affec:
D Gabriel R

P.S. I have been thinking that some designs of mine for stars, moon, & rising sun, wd. work in nicely for your binding[1] on the same plan as Atalanta.

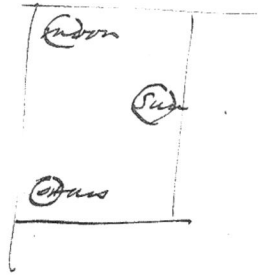

[1] For *Songs before Sunrise* (1871).

70.97 TO FREDERICK STARTRIDGE ELLIS

MS: BL. Published: *FSE* 24; DW 990.

Scalands
Wednesday [13 April 1870]

Dear Ellis

It strikes me that if any special copies of my book are got ready (& I shd like 2 myself) they had better perhaps not be larger-sized, as the harmony of the binding is [of] more consequence than the size, & as you say, this wd be put all wrong by extra size. Let them be on special paper if you like.

The woodcut looks raw on the white paper. If a 2nd edition is ever wanted, this shd be on a light – very light – greenish paper, of the tint I do my chalk drawings on. I think the woodcut had better have been left out of the plain-bound copies, as it looks quaint & provoking without the binding.

Will you look out for the Pall Mall review & send it me forthwith. Or any other.

It occurred to me that a proof of *one* side of the binding might well have been sent me, to see if the lines were right in thickness or if anything shd be cut away. But I suppose it is too late now to do this without delaying matters which must not be.

When are you advertising? I look in the Athenæum & find nothing.

Ever yours
D G Rossetti

70.98 TO JOSEPH KNIGHT
MS: BL.

Thursday [14 April 1870]
Scalands/Robertsbridge/Hawkhurst

My dear Knight

Here I am again. Thanks for your letter. I think it well to let you know that copies are being sent this day to all the principal reviews. I *believe* this day, but perhaps Saturday. Thanks many & sincere for your proposed promptness with your own notices. The copies sent now will have to be bound provisionally as the real binding cannot be ready till 23rd but Ellis will exchange them after that date if wished & inserts a notice to that effect.

I have been reading the poems of Dobell's you gave me (for which I have never thanked you yet) with great admiration. For pure rush of singing power – or what Swinburne is fond of calling "clang" – he has no equal living except the Supreme Swinburne himself: – i.e. always when at his best. But there is such a provoking and endless excess of iteration – a sort of pumping up which gives the idea of a man lashing himself into productiveness by the sound of his own voice – that one continually feels disposed to throw the book down in a rage. The secret of such defects is apparent when one comes now & then upon some naïveté of reminiscence from another poet such as could never occur to a man who overlooked or reconsidered his work in the least; and this reckless neglect is no doubt equally the cause of the insufferable redundance. Besides, most of the finest things in the book have nothing whatever to do with "England in Time of War" but have evidently been shot in because he had them by him & are sometimes degraded & half spoilt by a catchpenny title stuck on to give a *faux air* of their really belonging to the subject in hand. However the upshot of my abusiveness is that I must really send my book to a man who is so great a master of song for all his faults.[1]

Ever yours D G Rossetti

---

[1] Sydney Thompson Dobell (1824–74), a member of the Spasmodic School of Poetry, published *England in Time of War* (the Crimean War) in 1856; DGR especially admired "A Nuptial Eve."

70.99 TO FORD MADOX BROWN

MS: UBC. Excerpt: *RP* 257; *FMB* 258–59. Published: DW 982.

Scalands

Thursday [14 April 1870]

Dear Brown

I write to Dunn with this abt the studies.[1] I should be much obliged to you to look in again. I do not think you or any one understands the extent to which my eyesight now interferes with work. Every moment is an effort. The chalks are a little less painful, so I am apt to do them. I have fortunately several commissions for chalk-portraits which I may get done on reaching London unless my eyes become worse.

No matter about the trifle of tin. There will be moments more convenient for you & more desperate for me yet.

I am sorry about Stillman, but you may easily suppose that his somewhat improvised sorrows seem rather shadowy to me.[2]

I find from Barbara that she is likely to need this house after the 7th May. I suppose I ought to stay till then if possible.

Purnell's address is 90 Camden Road. I hear from Knight today who seems quite confident. Ellis sends out copies to the principal reviews today in provisional bindings, with a notice that copies fully bound can be had in exchange after the 23rd. So the reviews will not have to complain of no chance of speaking first.

The weather here is glorious now – even more than during your visit.

I shall have to come up next Monday week if not before, in order to write inscriptions in the gift copies at Ellis's.

Of course if you could look in at Marston's without seeming to be on my affairs, I should be glad to hear how the ground lay, but don't want to worry him at all.

Your
D G R

No Stillman here as yet.

¹ HTD was working at 16CW on the large oil version of *Dante's Dream* commissioned by WG (S.81R.1); it was completed in 1871 but later returned and replaced by a smaller oil with 2 predellas (S.81R.2).

² WJS, who considered DGR his invited guest at Scalands since Mme. Bodichon had offered the house to him first, left abruptly in protest at the expenses incurred by prolonged and festive visits from the WMs, FMBs, & others, expenses he was expected to share equally with DGR. His account of these matters was set down in Chapter 24 of his *Autobiography of a Journalist* (Boston: Houghton-Miflin, 1901), in which he also gives a rather self-serving account of how he introduced DGR to chloral hydrate, an insomnia medication used by WJS to which the poet-painter became disastrously addicted.

70.100 TO FREDERICK STARTRIDGE ELLIS

MS: BL. Published: *FSE* 21; DW 983.

Thursday [14 April 1870]

Dear Ellis

I telegraphed to you on getting yours this morning, saying the copies had better be sent to the reviews today. Will you send one at once to the Sunday Times – Knight's paper. He is also doing it in the Globe which was down in my former list. I hope to get the pattern bindings tomorrow & will write at once about them to you.

Before I see you on Monday week, do you think you could get me the addresses of Marston, Henry Taylor, & Sidney Dobell? The last could I shd think be got from Macmillan's partner if you see him.

Ever yours
DG Rossetti

70.101 TO BARBARA LEIGH SMITH BODICHON

MS: PML. Excerpt: Burton, *BB* 203–04. Published: DW 981. Text within angled brackets is a marginal insertion.

[14 April 1870]

Dear Mme Bodichon

Thanks for your note the other day. I may perhaps avail myself of the full extent of your kind permission as regards my stay here. I feel now great benefit in the glorious weather, and have for some time past lost the pains which troubled me in the eyes and head. I have got steadily to work with attention to very moderate hours as yet, and am taking great delight in my drawing after the late break in regular work. I am working down stairs however, as the studio light is stronger than I am used to and does not suit me. I find that I can work very well with the blind down in the sitting room, & should like to know what stuff it is made of, as I wd be glad to put up similar ones in my studio at Chelsea. It is not brown holland but a softer, thinner & rather coarser grained material. Is it English?

I finished the drawing of Sophy Burgess & I think made a pretty good thing of it. Have also begun one of Stillman & am now doing one of Mrs. Morris which I think about the best portrait I have made of her.[1] The leisure & pleasure of work in the country is something new to me – no interruptions, no invitations, no anything which is the bane of studious enjoyment. I feel almost tempted to set up my tent in the country altogether & have serious thoughts of beating up this neighbourhood for quarters. I made enquiries about a house between this & Fir Bank, called I think Darvall Bank. It is a most jolly old place, but I doubt the healthiness of the situation <I mean that particular spot which is shut in & low comparatively & must I think be rather damp>; & the rent (£130) and farm responsibilities involving further expense put it out of the question.

Mrs. Morris sends you her kind remembrances. She is benefiting to a really surprising extent, and walks about like anybody else.

I hope you will get my book now in about a week's time, as I have told my publisher to send you one.

Ever yours sincerely D G Rossetti

P.S. I hear you have got into pretty regular intercourse at 33 Elgin Road.[2] I know you *must* like Miss Boyd.

---

[1] The model Sophy Burgess is mentioned in **53, 63, & 118**; this chalk portrait was sold to WG (see **105 & 133**). The portrait of WJS (S.518) is now in the Museum of Fine Arts, Boston. The 2 drawings of JM done at Scalands (S.376 & S.377) remained in the hands of JM & DGR respectively. See *DGRDW* 73.
[2] The London home of the WBSs & AB.

70.102 TO FREDERICK STARTRIDGE ELLIS
MS: BL. Published: *FSE* 22; DW 984.

Scalands
Friday [15 April 1870]

Dear Ellis

I enclose a note from Colvin. You see he was *against* sending the copies, but that is done. I send the letter to you in case there is anything about his article in Pall Mall you wd wish to see.

I suppose you were not aware of this cursed blunder of the block-cutter's (I wd like a cut at his head-block) when you issued the review copies, as after this it would have been better to withhold them at present. How it can be possible to get a book out on the Saturday (23rd), the block for binding which is only cut on the previous Thursday, I do not understand! Of course there must be no delay made now in order to send me proofs of the binding, but the thing must be shovelled out somehow.[1] I have told Colvin he had better get his article in print on the Friday or Saturday, to balance what may appear elsewhere of a hostile kind. I confess to a passion for managing my own affairs, and thought I had done so in this case. So I grudge donkeydom the chance of the first innings after all. But of course this was sure to be.

As for the M.S.S. they are lying – what remains of them – somewhere in waste baskets. I have some idea of having promised them to some one, but can't remember to whom; but I'll see about it if they survive still.

Ever yours
D G Rossetti

[1] The first issue of *Poems* was delayed by several problems with the binding. The original date of publication, April 21, had to be changed to April 23 because the brass block with DGR's design for the binding was not ready in time (**92**). When the poet finally saw a proof of the binding on April 15, he demanded changes that further delayed publication from the 23rd to the 26th. One of the block-cutter's blunders was to make some of the letters on the spine too large (**111**). Recutting the corrected binding then increased the width of the spine, necessitating the addition of 8 blank leaves. The back was recut and the blank leaves removed in the 2nd edition (**120 & 121**). For details of these and other variants in the binding & endpapers, see **Volume V: Appendix 4, *Poems*: Bibliographical Summary**.

70.103 TO FREDERIC JAMES SHIELDS

MS: Yale. Published: Mills 141; DW 985.

Scalands/Robertsbridge/Hawkhurst
Saturday [16 April 1870]

Dear Shields

I shall be delighted for you to work at Cheyne Walk, but am not returning just now. However I shall be on a flying visit for an hour or two or a day or two (I don't know which) about Saty 23rd. I write with this to Dunn to expect you. He is doing some big work for me which may possibly be taking up the whole space in the studio but in that case I dare say the little studio upstairs would serve you. However probably the larger one will be at your service. I don't think the Venus photo: shd be bigger than abt the size of this sheet spread out at biggest.

I see you're frightened of poor "Jenny" (my poem) but I assure you I was surprised at Smetham's galvanic alarm & shall be sincerely so if you share it.

The poem was written in a far different spirit from any which should produce such results in thinking men I believe.

Pardon haste but I am very busy today.

Ever yours
D G Rossetti

70.104A JOSEPH KNIGHT TO FREDERICK STARTRIDGE ELLIS

Text: *FSE* 23n (39–40).

27 Camden Square, N.W.
16 April 1870

Dear Sir,

It is a pity to defer sending the books out. Easter is so good a time for the "dailies." When Parliament reassembles you will not get half the notices. If you reconsider your determination which I think would be wise, drop me another line. I have spoken to the Editor of the *Standard*, and he promises a long review. Send the book directed to him. "Captain Hamber" [sic], Standard Newspaper Office, and he will personally look after it.

I write to the *Telegraph* to-day. They however will scarcely give a long notice unless it reaches them soon. I shall be glad to know of any change as I have another review to write for *The Graphic*. Not easy to write three, is it? Suppose you got home safely.

Yours sincerely,
J. Knight

To F. S. Ellis Esq.
  Marston's address is 9 Northumberland Terrace, Regent's Park Road.
  Dobell's I will send you.

70.104 TO FREDERICK STARTRIDGE ELLIS

MS: BL. Published *FSE* 23; DW 986.

Sunday [17 April 1870]

Dear Ellis

I believe you have heard from Knight, & so have I today. I suppose you have sent the press copies he indicates – Standard (straight to editor, Captn. Hamber) & Graphic. He seems to have some notions of the Telegraph too.

His opinion as to sending the general review copies seems to coincide with yours. So act just as you think best in the matter.

Another friend – Dr. Hake – has got leave to do it in the New Monthly. I have sent him a set of the sheets from here, and I suppose you shd send a copy to the Magazine.¹

Ever yours
DG Rossetti

---

1. The *Standard* (26 May 70: 3) was, DGR later discovered, by Alfred Austin (see **171**); one of 3 reviews by Knight appeared in the *Graphic* (14 May 70: 567); the *Telegraph* for 9 May 70 printed an unsigned notice (5); and TGH discussed both *Poems* and *EIP* in *New Monthly Magazine* (Jun 70: 681–700).

70.105 TO FANNY CORNFORTH

MS: DAM. Published: Baum 28–29; DW 987.

Sunday [17 April 1870]

My dear Fan,

I write to you chiefly because Dunn seems (by a letter of his I receive today,) to have derived from Brown the idea that I am much worse; and I am afraid this may make you anxious. I am certainly no better, and am drawing very little, but there is no decided change for the worse.

Will you tell Dunn, as regards the cartoon, that it should not be made larger, by any alterations, than the canvas will admit of. This is the only point to be considered, as to making it a little larger or smaller; but the figure of Dante should be in the same proportion as the photograph.¹

I wrote to Graham at least a week ago, offering him the studies for the Dante picture (which he once asked me to keep for him) and also a drawing I have made here – 150 gs together. But I have not heard from him since. I think this may perhaps be caused by illness in his family, but yesterday I wrote to him again.

I feel that I ought to stay on here as long as possible, but if money runs quite out, I shall have to come up. Mme Bodichon has other friends coming here after the 7th of May I believe. I expect if I do not come up before the end of next week, I shall have to do so then, as that is the day my poems are coming out, and I shall have to come up for a day probably; even if I return here afterwards.

With love
Ever yours
R

---

1. DGR used FC as a conduit to HTD, who, when not at 16CW, occupied lodgings at St. Leonard's Terrace, just round the corner from FC's residence at 36 Royal Avenue. See 69.37.1n1.

70.106 TO THOMAS GORDON HAKE

MS: BL. Published: DW 988.

Sunday [17 April 1870]
Scalands/Robertsbridge/Hawkhurst

Dear Dr. Hake

Many thanks for your good intentions; and that the paving commissioners below* may gain nothing by them, I hasten to forward a set of the sheets which I have here. I meant & mean to send you a copy of the book duly bound when issued, which will be in another week at latest.

I have been here for the last 5 weeks trying to recruit, after a bad attack in my eyes & general health. Success moderate as yet. I was offered this house by a friend, & as I think the air must be good, & it contains a studio, I accepted it, though hardly working at all just now. I may yet accept your own kind invitation one of these days, I dare say; as I must evidently not look any more for the unbroken course of work I kept till 2 years ago: if indeed working power is to endure at all.

I have been reading as little as possible, and thus still have your Romances by me at home. What are your views now as to publication? It will give me very great pleasure indeed to have a review from your pen.[1] Two or three other friends are already doing likewise.

With kindest remembrances,

Ever yours sincerely
D G Rossetti

---

* "paving commissioners below": i.e., "the road to Hell is paved with good intentions."
[1] DGR wrote to FSE about publishing TGH's work (**171**), but FSE declined (**230**). Later, DGR suggested a subtitle which TGH adopted (**261**). See also **266**. TGH published *Madeline, with Other Poems and Parables* (Chapman & Hall, 1871) and *Parables and Tales* (Chapman & Hall, 1872); both volumes were reviewed by DGR (*Works* 621–27 & 630–35; see also 73.7 & 73.53). DGR designed a cover for *Parables and Tales*, warning TGH that his name should not be advertised in connection with it (72.84).

70.107 TO FRANCES MARY LAVINIA ROSSETTI

MS: UBC. Published: *FL* 225–26; DW 989. Date: FLR.

Monday [18 April 1870]
Scalands/Robertsbridge/Hawkhurst

My dearest Mother

I have not written to you for an age, but have been meaning to do so, only things did not look promising enough to be worth talking about. However for the last few days this glorious weather seems to be doing me good in some ways at any rate. It is impossible not to feel a different being when such a change is going on all round one. But indeed I have improved for some time past in one essential respect, – i.e. that the pains I had constantly in the eyes and head have almost entirely left me, – quite so indeed but for a very slight and occasional twinge. I have been drawing regularly, though not many hours, for several days, and am beginning to feel more cheerful. The air is delicious – the weather very hot just now while the sun lasts – but exquisitely cool in the evenings. I send you specimens of the wild flowers which are all out in immense profusion everywhere, – as to the primroses, the country is already smothered in them. The white violets came in a swarm and are now almost gone. The blue ones are everywhere now, & the wood anemones, of which I send a few, are most delightful as well as the wild daffodils. Lambs have tails and begin to prance a little. They and their mothers make various toy noises, only the mothers' are penny noises and the lambs' halfpenny ones.

I find Mme B. will need this place after the 7th but I may possibly stay on till nearly that time if I can manage it. My book is to be out by the end of next week, and perhaps I shall have to come up then for a day.

Things are not quite idle with me in London, as regards work; since Dunn is grouping the studies for my large picture together, so that it will be ready for me to begin on the moment I return.[1]

Janey Morris is here, and benefiting greatly. Top comes from time to time. I have an invitation to go to Florence to the Nortons, & fancy I might be wise to accept it, but time is an anxious matter. Would William go if I did?[2] With love to all,

Your most affec: son
Gabriel

[1] *Dante's Dream* (S.81R.1).
[2] Neither DGR nor WMR travelled to Florence in 1870.

70.108 TO WILLIAM BELL SCOTT

MS: Princeton.

Scalands
Tuesday [19 April 1870]

Dearest Scotus

Thanks for your note. The weather here is now most glorious, & one cannot help, for all one's doleful dumps, drinking in delight hourly from the mere air. I am accordingly feeling decided benefit now in general health. Moreover the pains in my eyes & head have almost ceased for some time past; only like all crisises hitherto, they have left the eyes decidedly weaker. However I am drawing 2 or 3 hours daily with great enjoyment, and must look on matters as not quite desperate yet. Mdme Bodichon can spare me this house till the 7th May, & it is possible I may stay till then. By the bye, I shd think she & Miss Boyd must exactly suit each other. Janey Morris has been here (in another house lent by Barbara's brother[1]) for a week now, & is very much better, walking almost like anybody else. Topsy is to come down tomorrow afternoon for a day or two. I am making the best drawing of Janey I have ever made, & have done one of a local beauty[2] & begun one of Stillman.

About my book, it will really be out (after some more vicissitudes) next Saturday. I am not in the least afraid of Mr. Palgrave. His malice or obtuseness (if he have either) will hardly get first start now, & cannot matter after what will be said by better men (Swinburne in Fortnightly – Morris in Academy.) By the bye, can *he* be the British Quarterly reviewer who cut you out?[3] As for Colvin, I do not know that I ever expressed the admiration of him which you seem to think I entertain, though I certainly do think him one of the most cultivated & competent scribes on the press. I have not seen his Durer article, but have often thought what he writes open to the objections you indicate. However he has been very friendly & zealous in this matter with me, & if over enthusiastic & so provoking to my ill-wishers, it is a fault for which I can bear him no grudge, though a dangerous one I admit.

I have not been to Hollington yet, but trust still to try & see it. I have made a move or two towards enquiries after a permanent pied-à-terre in this neighbourhood, as I cannot but think I must benefit by leaving London for some time to come, were it to prove possible. If I could find a suitable place, I might perhaps let my London house. By the bye, wd *you* take it? You have said nothing about the house at Chelsea I mentioned to you.

I hope I may not be so unfortunate as to miss Miss Boyd before she leaves London, and do trust I may make my way to your diggings if (as is probable but not certain) I come up next Monday for a day.

I suppose I told you of my having seen a new oculist – Critchett – the last time I was in London, & of his taking as favorable a view of my case as the others.[4] He said I shd no more go blind than he wd & that if I did I might call them all donkies. Time will show. I have some faint idea of going to Italy, having an invitation to Florence from Norton. If Wm were prepared to go too, that wd be an additional incentive. Only the question of work becomes most urgent, & I fear will decide all other questions & plans in the negative.

I was thinking when last I saw Swinburne in London (sober all one day on my instigation & reading me the most glorious poetry.) what a splendid thing it wd be if one could get him to sign a personal undertaking to oneself on his word of honour to abstain from drink (with very moderate provisos) for a year to come. It really might break him of the habit, as I firmly believe he wd keep the promise if he could be got to make it. There are 2 poems in his new vol ("The Litany of the Nations" & "Hertha") which are splendid masterpieces, and perhaps the richest & most overpowering thing I ever heard of his is the introduction to his Tristram & Iseult. But perhaps you too have heard them by this.

With respect to my coming to Penkill, – what could please me better? – but if I spend two months here, I fear it is very doubtful if further moves will be possible. The best I could do would be to settle in the country within reach of London for a year, & paint with the advantage of getting out in good air whenever I was not at work. However, I am loth to think that I shall really not hear the Penwhapple again this year, nor roll lazily towards the cave or the steps leading to the bed of the stream, as idle whim suggests.

With love to all at Elgin Row

Ever your affec: D. Gabriel R.

P.S. I remember no such picture by Hunt.

1   Fir Bank, near Scalands.
2   See **53**.
3   The review of *Poems* in *Saturday Review* (14 May 70: 651–52) may be by Francis Turner Palgrave (1824–97), the poet & critic who compiled *The Golden Treasury*.
4   Sir Anderson Critchett (1849–1925) was pictured as "The King's Oculist" in *Spy* (May 1905).

70.109 TO FORD MADOX BROWN
MS: UBC.

Scalands

Wednesday [20 April 1870]

Dear Brown

I write to you today in much better spirits. I have had a week of real life and enjoyment, and those pains seem to have left me entirely for the present.

Janey has been here for a week, & is wonderfully better. She walks 3 miles a day easily. I believe if she stayed a month, she would be set up better than by all the mineral baths of Germany. This evening Top comes down to stay a day or two, but I hope she may remain longer, as it is most important she shd do so. I have begun a drawing of her which I am sure is the best thing I ever did; and have enjoyed returning to work a little immensely.

Many thanks for your kind attention to Dunn's proceedings. I feel so much more alive that I am surprised at my capacity for gratitude as elicited by your efforts.

You know as to the Dante picture, it *must* be drawn in of a size to fit the canvas I got recently. It is a pity to make it too small for that, & of course it cannot be too large. Not only is this the case, but I have made careful studies of the heads of a certain size which shd be adhered to in order to trace them which is the only way of sure work in painting I find. I am surprised you found the different nude studies I made did not tally in scale, as I certainly thought they did. The one of Dante is, as no doubt you saw, of Dunn's handiwork. If *absolutely* necessary, the head studies could be photo'd on a smaller scale & so still traced from the photos: but I don't wish to do this, as I should think it a pity to paint them any smaller. I write to Dunn with this, asking him to call on you & talk it over.

With love to all yours

Your affec:
Gabriel

70.110 TO THOMAS GORDON HAKE
MS: BL. Published: DW 992.

21 April/1870

Scalands/Robertsbridge/Hawkhurst

Dear Dr. Hake –

How much pleasure it gives me to know that the poems please you so well. My own belief is that I am a poet (within the limit of my powers) primarily, and that it is my poetic tendencies that chiefly give value to my pictures: only painting being – what poetry is not – a livelihood – I have put my poetry chiefly in that form. On the other hand, the bread - & - cheese question has led to a good deal of my painting being pot-boiling & no more – whereas my verse, being unprofitable, has remained (as much as I have found time for) unprostituted.

You ask me about Lilith – I suppose referring to the picture-sonnet. The picture is called *Lady* Lilith by rights (only I thought this wd present a difficulty in print without paint to explain it,) and represents a *modern* Lilith combing out her abundant golden hair & gazing on herself in the glass with that self-absorption by whose strange fascination such natures draw others within their own circle. The idea which you indicate (viz: of the perilous principle in the world being female from the first) is about the most essential notion of the sonnet. I am glad you like Eden Bower.[1] I think that poem, Jenny, A Last Confession, & The House of Life, are the things I wd wish to be known by. I should particularly hope it might be thought (if so it be) that my poems are in no way the result of painters' tendencies – and indeed I believe no poetry could be freer than mine from the trick of what is called "word-painting." As with re-created forms in painting, so I should wish to deal in poetry chiefly with personified emotions; and in carrying out my scheme of "The House of Life" (if ever I do so) shall try to put in action a complete dramatis personae of the soul.[2]

I could not – much as I feel eagerness to see your article in print – read it before then without a sense of gratified vanity which one does not wish to indulge; and can surely rely on you, if on anyone, to say more good things of me than I could ever expect. I hope one thing most sincerely: – and that is, that you will not in the least hesitate to dwell on the weak side of my work, as well on such strength as it may possess. Also if you could in some way refer to the book of Translations also, it might remind people of what I hope ere long to republish & perhaps get better remembered for the future.[3]

Here is a flood of egotism! However, you know well how much your own work interests me, and how pleased I am to hear of Valdarno's new prospects.[4] I shall hope to have some evenings with you ere long for the purpose of our looking over that work together, and for you to read me passages (or the whole by instalments if not bothering you too much) which wd I think be our best plan of action. However within the last week I feel stronger in every way, even a little so in my eyesight, & perhaps reading may soon be to some extent resumed. I did not tell you that I have lately seen not only Bowman again (in whom I have of course the utmost confidence) but also another very rising oculist – Critchett – and that both give very favourable opinions on my case; & laugh at my fears of the worst.

If you will tell me when your letter to the Athenæum is going in, I might perhaps be able to say a word about it to one or two people connected with that paper, in case you are sending it without invitation, which is always a rather risky proceeding among many claimants for space and with an editorial judgment perhaps after all not infallible.

Most truly yours D G Rossetti

P.S. "Excuse this scrawl" is almost as threadbare as "unaccustomed as I am &c."; but vile paper & pens force the appeal on me today.

By the bye, I am glad your article will be in the June – not the May – magazine – as it will thus carry on the war which I hope will be well commenced in May by articles on my book from Swinburne in the Fortnightly & Morris in the Academy. This *entre nous*.

---

1. The "picture sonnet" is "Lilith (For a Picture)" in *Poems* (269); in the final 1881 version of *HL* it was Sonnet 78, "Body's Beauty." The painting of *Lady Lilith* is S.205. W. E. Fredeman possessed a pen & ink sketch of a snake-like Lilith (not in Surtees), much like the description of her in "Eden Bower" (ll. 9–16).
2. This is one of the most important among the few letters containing critical statements by DGR about his painting and poetry and the relations between them. It should be borne in mind when assessing conventional wisdom such as the oft-repeated "DGR should have painted his poems and written his pictures."
3. See **104&n1**.
4. DGR was at first attracted to TGH's work by his *Vates: or the Philosophy of Madness* (Southgate, 1840), now to be republished as "Valdarno: or, The Ordeal of Art Worship" in *Ainsworth's Magazine*.

70.111 TO FREDERICK STARTRIDGE ELLIS

MS: BL. Published: *FSE* 25; DW 993.

[21 April 1870]

Dear Ellis

Your diagram of the binding appals me, as the *back* is all wrongly arranged, but I hope it may be only your memory that is at fault. Thus it is rightly:

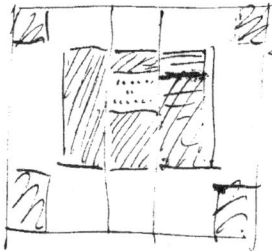

I suppose the inscription at the back of the rough-bound copy sent is from the real block. If so, I don't like it. The O of Poems is monstrously big & makes all crooked. The O of Rossetti too big also. The gold seems a good colour.

Yours in haste
D G R

If necessary at any moment I will come up to see about things.

70.112 TO FREDERICK STARTRIDGE ELLIS

MS: BL. Published: *FSE* 26; DW 994.

Scalands
Friday [22 April 1870]

Dear Ellis

I think my best plan will be to come up to London by the early express on Monday in which case I shall reach your place by about 11, & be able then & there to inscribe copies. This becomes more necessary now that the notices have appeared prematurely, though on the whole the accident is hardly to be regretted.¹ I should then return here by the 4 o'clock express. If the gift copies are deferred now it will excite wonder as the book has got into the reviews. So will you have the copies ready for me by 11 on Monday.

I telegraph to you today to send me a bound copy that I may get it tomorrow.² But perhaps they will not be done till tomorrow. In that case it would reach me Sunday morning. I am curious to see the result of the binding. The notices are doubtless calculated to be of material service. Of course all the publishing details you refer to are entirely under your own control.

Ever yours
D G Rossetti

1. DGR actually went up to London to inscribe presentation copies on Tuesday, 26 Apr (**119**). Notices by Colvin & Knight had appeared on 20 & 21 Apr respectively.
2. See **114.1**.

70.113 TO SIDNEY COLVIN

MS: Scripps College.

Scalands
22 April 1870

My dear Colvin

Your notice has been sent on to me today, and I must not let a post pass without telling you how sincerely I am obliged to you for the care and kindliness with which it is written.¹ For the praise itself I will not thank you; since – how full soever I may feel the measure of it to be – I know you love art too well to make this dependent merely on friendly relations, and you would equally have spoken your mind had I been the merest stranger.

I ought to have directed your attention to the changes made at the last moment in the last sonnet of the House of Life which you quote.² I suppose they escaped you (since no doubt Ellis sent you a complete copy), though indeed I shd not be much surprised in your seeing no improvement in them, as this was not the reason of their being made. They consist in the first line which now stands

"When *all* desire at last & *all* regret"

and in line 12 which I have altered to

"Ah! let none other written spell soe'er."

The first was changed because my brother drew my attention to a certain likeness between its original form & a line in Petrarch's first sonnet –

"Fra la vana speranza e il van dolore,"

though I am sure this was not in my head, nor indeed could have been; for I was never a great reader of Petrarch & had no memory of the sonnet.[3]

Line 12 I altered because of its likeness to line 11 of the Sonnet preceding it (also quoted by you.)[4] This change I think necessary; but rather regret the other, & shall probably restore it if a second edition should be the result of such favorable views of the book as you are taking.

Sincerely yours
D G Rossetti

[1] *Pall Mall Gazette* (Apr 70): 7.
[2] *HL* Sonnet L, "The One Hope." See **71&n1**.
[3] For Petrarch's sonnet, see **71&n1**.
[4] *HL* Sonnet 99, "Newborn Death II," line 11 of which was "And Art, whose eyes were worlds by God found fair"; the earlier reading of line 12 in "The One Hope" was: "Let no such joys as other souls count fair." For line 11 of "Newborn Death II," see 68.120.

70.114 TO JOSEPH KNIGHT
MS: BL.

Scalands
22 April 1870

Dear Knight

To thank you, as a friendly matter, for the praise in your notice of my book wd be a poor compliment; but I may & must thank you for the friendly manner of it. I was glad to find "Sister Helen" raising to your eyes so clear a

[22 April 1870]

picture of its situation, since one or two who have heard it have made the objection that the incident is not easy to unravel, which I could never perceive to be the case myself. I think the early appearance of your notice is an advantage though an accidental one; & so Ellis thinks too.

I may say now how very glad I am to hear that Marston is to review me in the Athenæum. I would not say much before, lest I should seem to be pressing for troublesome exertion; but it is a very great point gained.

I think I shall hardly be coming up for some little time, unless possibly for a few hours one day; so must put off the chat I hope to have with you yet.

Very sincerely yours
DG Rossetti

P.S. By the bye, there is only one point which I know you will forgive my wishing away in your notice. And that is the allusion to Swinburne & Morris, both of whom can show a grand body of splendid work which quite leaves me nowhere. Any influence moreover, which I might possibly have had with them in early days has been more than compensated by their re-action on myself. Nor am I really conscious of *any* relation between myself and the painters named.

70.114.1 TO FREDERICK STARTRIDGE ELLIS

MS (telegram): Princeton. Date: Telegraph stamp.

[22 April 1870]
Robertsbridge

Mr. Ellis
   Post me a full bound copy if ready today.

70.115 TO JOHN FERGUSON McLENNAN

MS: Columbia.

23 April/1870
Scalands/Robertsbridge/Hawkhurst

My dear McLennan

I rather think I *may* be in town for a few hours only on Wednesday next (or possibly Tuesday, but most likely Wedy) to inscribe copies of my book for friends; but shall not be going to Chelsea – only to the publisher's. I will in such case call at Cecil Street, as it is close by, & leave you a book if I don't find you at home, though I shd regret missing a chat with you. I suppose my time for calling wd be about 2.

There is unluckily a hitch with the binding at the last moment which delays the book unexpectedly: and this after one or two reviews have already appeared – the reviewers having been supplied with advance plain-bound copies a week or so ago. I expect it will really be issued on Wednesday.

Ever yours
DG Rossetti

70.116 TO FREDERICK STARTRIDGE ELLIS

MS: BL. Published: *FSE* 27; DW 995.

Scalands
Saturday [23 April 1870]

Dear Ellis

This delay is most infernal, & renders the promptness of friendly critics a nuisance instead of a benefit. It will most certainly put up the backs of the unfriendly ones, & that with no chance of their backsides coming to the level of our boot-toes for a rejoinder.

I see now that you are "letting me down easy," and that whatever day I proposed to come up I shd receive a notification at the last moment that it must be one day later.

Now I say *Wednesday* – looking of course for the due result. However if Tuesday will do, let me know in time: though of course I know it won't. *Now* I hope you're swearing in *your* turn.

I see the advt in Pall Mall with a rather long line abt the binding. It seems to me that "bound from the author's design" wd be shorter & better.

Ever yours
DG R

70.117 TO FRANCES MARY LAVINIA ROSSETTI

MS: UBC. Published: DW 996.

Scalands
Saturday¹ [23 April 1870]

Dear good Teak

Thanks for enclosure. I will answer Wm's letter soon. I suppose you saw the Pall Mall on my book on Thursday. There was one in the Globe too. The book is unluckily delayed at the last moment by a hitch with the binding, but will I fancy get really issued next Wednesday.

Your most affec:
Gabriel

1   The long tail of the "y" flows downward to form the upright of the "T" in "Teak."

70.118 TO BARBARA LEIGH SMITH BODICHON
MS: PML. Excerpt: HRA 258. Published: Burton, *BB* 204–05.

24 April [1870]
Scalands

Dear Mdme Bodichon

I am still enjoying the glorious weather here, but am beginning to have an uncomfortable conviction that I ought to be at home and at work, & do not know how soon it may force me to obey it. However I am not quite idle or unbusinesslike, as I am making a very careful drawing of Mrs. Morris which will be worth money if I choose to sell it, only I like to keep my best studies. Sophy Burgess's head I have sold already for 50 guineas, so trade has not been quite at a standstill. I think when I finish Stillman I shall give him a nimbus & call him his Redeemer by which title he too may be made to pay. This sounds base, I perceive on reading it over.

In answer to your enquiry, I was just going to say I was sorry I do not know (only perceive on reflection that I hope I never may) what is to be got in Norway or further North, – always besides the rheumatism & habit of swearing which I feel confident *must* be acquired there. You see I am an inveterate southerner though I fear no particular patriot.

I told my man to tell your people that you wanted owls in the dovecote; but he says cats climb up there constantly & wd slay them.

My joys here have been overshadowed at intervals by the sight of darling little moles lying murdered. I mean to get two and keep them in a large glass case with a lot of carth, so as to see them sometimes.

Ever yours
D G Rossetti

70.119 TO FREDERICK STARTRIDGE ELLIS

MS: BL. Published: *FSE* 28; DW 998.

Sunday [24 April 1870]

Dear Ellis

I'll be with you on Tuesday at 11. You need not tell anyone (except Morris) that you expect me, as I don't want people to be dropping on me at your place, & shall only stay in town till the 4 o'clock express, without going to Chelsea at all.

I forget if I told you that Marston *is* to do the book for the Athenæum, so that is well.

If you are thinking at all of the special copies (but of course I suppose not yet) these must be delayed till I get a photograph from one of my pictures done for the frontispiece.

Ever yours
D G R

70.120 TO FREDERICK STARTRIDGE ELLIS

MS: BL. Published: *FSE* 29; DW 999.

Scalands
27 April [1870]

My dear Ellis

On looking at the book it seems a 1000 pities the ridiculous blank paper shd be left in the next issue, & it strikes me we ought to set about re-cutting the back only *at once*. No doubt this can be re-cut without the rest, & I will gladly stand the expense myself. So I write to Dunn with this,[1] asking him to call on you & see about it. All it wants is to make it one row of diaper less on each side; & this might just be cut off were it not that the protruding flowers would thus be crippled also. So the only thing is to do it again. I will myself send a pattern for the lettering at once.

I remembered afterwards that among many inscriptions I had forgotten one to *yourself*!

Will you give Dunn a copy for himself when you see him. Also show him this letter.

Ever yours
D G Rossetti

---

[1] DGR:HTD (27 Apr 70) is untraced.

70.121 TO FREDERICK STARTRIDGE ELLIS

MS: BL. Published: *FSE* 30; DW 1001.

Scalands
27 April [1870]

Dear Ellis

The enclosed is the best form for the lettering which will thus come into the reduced space. Do you think that the British Fool, with the heaven-sent help of this stupendous diagram, aided by a few Michael-Angelesque "throes of Composition" (in the style of Solomon Hart's great picture) will be able to conceive of an **O** as something other than a balloon, and of a **T** as not being necessarily a gallows? Do you think he can be brought to observe the precise fittings of the letters – for instance the mighty intellect by which the **P** is made to fill the space pretty well? and the letters curved a little into each other – & the precise thicknesses of the letters? In short, will he copy this, or has he a soul above it? Ask him & let me know.

Did you find Dallas's whereabouts?

> Poor old Dallas!
> All along of his phallus,
>
> Must he come to the gallows?[1]

And did you send the book to Sir Noel Paton?[2] – who I learned after leaving you is yearning to review it somewhere and should be duly encouraged.

Ever yours
DG Rossetti

---

[1] For the critic Eneas Sweetland Dallas, see 55.32&n2 & 56.35. DGR completes his limerick in **125**. He was hoping to get Dallas to review *Poems* in *The Times* (**127**).

[2] For Joseph Noel Paton (1821–1901), see *PRISM* Section 53.

70.122 TO CHARLES AUGUSTUS HOWELL

MS: Princeton. Published: *TR* 123; DW 1000.

Wednesday [27 April 1870]

Dear Howell

I am very sorry not to have seen you to-day, especially after what Dunn told me of your conversation. I should like to see you particularly, in case any good result might ensue by our talking together of the matters on which you wished to speak to me.

At present however I am leaving town for at least a week longer.

I am extremely sorry if you find yourself in any troublesome position & should be much relieved if I could help in suggesting any course of action to meet it. To say nothing of our long-standing friendly relations, you rendered me a very essential service some months back, and one which you may be sure I have not forgotten.

Your affec:
D G Rossetti

If you wish to write me in the country my address is

Scalands
Robertsbridge
– Hawkhurst

You can come & see me there possibly if you like, but I am not quite sure of this yet.

70.123 TO WILLIAM SMITH WILLIAMS

MS: Untraced (formerly Kenneth Lohf). The MS is tipped into a copy of *EIP*; also pasted to one of the book's endpapers is the note (in DGR's c. 1861 hand) quoted below. Unlike many letters accompanying printed volumes which have no relationship whatever to the book, this one is directly relevant to the recipient. Whether or not the volume is also a presentation copy from DGR to Williams, there is no question that it must be Williams's copy.

Scalands/Robertsbridge/Hawkhurst
28 April 1870

Dear Mr. Williams

Might I trouble you for Mr. C. J. Wells's present address? I want to send him a volume of Poems I have just published.[1] Is it "St Pol de Léon" as of yore?

I shd also like much to know what number of copies of my *Early Italian Poets* now still remains on hand since my last notice from Messrs. Smith Elder & Co. If not sold out shortly I shd wish to withdraw these copies from circulation, as I suppose there wd be no objection to my doing so, and I project another edition ere long.

Very truly yours
DG Rossetti

W. S. Williams Esq
P.S. Please write to me addressed as above.

[Enclosure – a separate sheet of paper. On the top in a different hand is written: Dante Gabriel Rossetti artist and author (Original Draft of Title Page). DGR's cross hatching at the bottom is not reproduced.]

The Early Italian Poets
from Ciullo d'Alcamo to Dante Alighieri
(12–1300)
including the Vita Nuova of Dante
translated in the original metres
<u>by D.G. Rossetti</u>

[1] For Wells, see 69.59 & **16**.

70.124 TO THOMAS GORDON HAKE

MS: BL. Published: DW 1003.

28 April/1870
Scalands/Robertsbridge/Hawkhurst

Dear Dr. Hake

I was in town for a few hours only on Tuesday last, in order to inscribe copies of my book to friends – among the rest, one to yourself which I hope has reached you.

One thing in your last letter gratified me particularly. The 3 poems to which you give the preference – viz: Eden Bower, Troy Town, & The Stream's Secret – are the only 3 new ones in the first section though much has been done quite lately to several others and something to nearly all. Much the greater proportion of the Sonnets in the House of Life are also written lately.

If leisure serves from painting – of which I fear there is only too much prospect on account of my health – I may perhaps be in the thick of another poetic venture before very long, as I have several subjects in my head.

I dare say you will agree with me that it is not desirable to mention in print what I say above of the dates of composition. I have thought it better to omit dates in the book. I hope you will like my binding. Unluckily the width of the back has been miscalculated in my design, compelling the ridiculous introduction of some blank paper to fill up. If there is another issue of the book, I shall have the back recut and the lettering, which is horrid, redone. Also the fly-leaves should be printed on a slightly greenish paper. At present they look raw. So much for "I."

Ever yours
D G Rossetti

70.125 TO FREDERICK STARTRIDGE ELLIS

MS: BL. Published: *FSE* 31; DW 1002.

Thursday [28 April 1870]

Dear Ellis

I forgot a bloke who must have the book

> F. W. Burton,
> 43 Argyll Road,
> Kensington.

Please send it him.

Take care to send me notices *at once*. Athenæum (if containing it) cd be sent tomorrow evening. I expect Spectator & Saturday to be nasty, & will take a bet to that effect if you like – especially Spectator. An old foe of mine will I know have his fling somewhere, & I think it will be in one of the two.[1]

If necessary to bring out the next issue before the back is re-cut, surely you cd spread out your list of publications to fill the sheet of blank paper. As thus: Page 1. F.S.E.'s pubs page 2 blank at back of page 1. page 3 Earthly Paradise. Page 4. notices of ditto. Page 5. Jason with notices. Page 6. Grettir. Page 7 Niblungs. Page 8 Me. Page 9. Swinburne. Page 10. Commonplace. Page 11. Nursery Rhymes. Page 12. Maundeville. Page 13. Topsy's Guenevere. Page 14. Advertisement (which I wd furnish) of 2nd edition of my Translations. Page 15. Notices of 1st edition of same.

Thus only 5 pages (including your present list) would remain to let, & these cd probably be easily filled. One might contain notices of me by that time – Jason & notices might be separated &c.[2]

Yesterday's momentary inspiration has developed.

> There is a poor devil named Dallas
> Who tends, as I'm told, to the gallows.
> Yet if not so well hung,
> He might never have swung,
> For it's mostly along of his phallus.

Tell it not in Gath!

Yours D G R

---

[1] R. H. Hutton contributed an unenthusiastic review of *Poems* to *Spectator* (11 Jun 70: 115–18).

[2] FSE did act on DGR's advice. Of the first 1000 copies printed, 250 went to Roberts Bros. of Boston (see **133**). Two leaves advertising FSE's publications were inserted before the blank gathering necessitated by the block-cutter's blunder (**102&n1, 111, 120–21**). The 2nd

thousand (comprising the 2nd, 3rd, & 4th editions) has a recut binding, no blank gathering, different advertisements inserted at the back and a new one at the front, endpapers of a different colour, and corrections by the poet (see **97**, **129**, **132–33**, **138**, **141**, **145**, **147**, **152**, & **160**). An important fact about the blue-on-white floral endpapers of the 1st edition is pointed out by WMR in a note he added at the end of the Troxell Collection's 2nd (partial) copy of Proof State No. 3: "The flowered paper used in the binding appears to have been brought by my father in 1824 from Malta – perhaps from Naples." The endpapers thus encode (semi-privately) an important personal feature of the book, and are further evidence of the kind of deliberate attitude DGR took in marrying the physique of the book to its conceptual and linguistic materials. In this case, the endpapers connect directly to the important poems in the volume that deal with DGR's father.

70.126 TO F. S. ELLIS & CO

MS: Untraced.

[29 April 1870]

Dear Sir

If Mr. Ellis is not back by post time tomorrow, please send me the *Fortnightly Review* (which will be out tomorrow 30th I suppose) and also any notices which may appear in the Saturday papers.

Yours truly
D. G. Rossetti

P.S. Also *Fraser* if containing a notice.

70.127 TO JOSEPH KNIGHT

MS: BL.

Friday [29 April 1870]

Scalands/Robertsbridge/Hawkhurst

Dear Knight

When you mentioned the Times the other day I meant to have asked you whether Dallas was in question. He is an old & intimate acquaintance of mine, & I should not hesitate to write to him & propose sending him advance sheets of the book if he could do a review. But do you know if he is still connected with the paper or whether he is to the fore at all? It is long since I heard of him.

Pardon my troubling you with the question. I suppose I shall now be back in town in a week's time.

Ever yours
D G Rossetti

70.128 TO FREDERIC JAMES SHIELDS

MS: Texas. Published: DW 1006. Date: DW.

Scalands
Friday [29 April 1870]

Dear Shields

A word to say that your copy of my book has been sent by mistake to Manchester – the list of names & addresses having been with the publisher before you came to town.

I am glad to find that you have 2 such important works exhibiting, & must have a look at them. I hope you may still be in London on my return in about a week.

Ever yours D G R

70.129 TO FREDERICK STARTRIDGE ELLIS

MS: BL. Published: *FSE* 33; DW 1007.

Scalands
30 April [1870]

My dear Ellis

Thanks for the papers. The Athenæum is a good deal the better of the two. As for Fraser, the best thing in it is that the Italian book is mentioned which may remind people of it as I think we ought to set about reissuing it. I have written to Smith & Elder about the remainder copies. I think it had better be called this time

Dante & his Circle
with the Italian Poets before Dante

and probably be put in 2 vols., the first containing the Dantesque matter only.[1]

As for Fraser, between you & me nothing could be more inane. Fancy my songs being "arch & lively." But such a gift-horse (even if admitted of market value) does not tempt one to minute analysis either of its mouth or other self-asserting orifice. However one ought no doubt to be duly grateful. Be it for foes to bring one to a sense of every friend's value. They'll do it yet I dare say. Meanwhile it is wonderful to hear of an approaching 2nd edition – or will it be 3rd on your 500 principle? I'll send you the revisions either this evening or tomorrow.[2]

I write with this to Dunn to see about Swinburne's binding, for which I have available sketches. He'll look you up if necessary.[3]

Stillman wishes me to say that he will call some time next week on you about his photographs in Greece which you heard of from Morris, to whom love. I suppose he'll be here in a day or two.⁴

Ever yours
DG Rossetti

---

1   The 2nd edition of *EIP* issued by Ellis & White in 1874 was not in 2 volumes; except for the reorganization of some material and the new title, it is essentially a reissue of the 1st edition of 1861. Texts of poems are almost identical: DGR added one new *Canzone* by Dante.
2   See **125n2**. DGR refers here to the 2nd 1000 printed, comprising the 2nd, 3rd, & 4th editions. Only the 5th & 6th editions, the 3rd 1000, conformed to FSE's "500 principle." A resetting with DGR's corrections, the 5th edition was dated 1871, and the 6th, dated 1872, remained in print until 1879. Revisions by the poet (see **132**) appeared in the 2nd edition; that is why he was angry that Roberts Bros. set up the American issue of *Poems* from the 1st edition (see **190&n1**). For details, see **Volume V: Appendix 4, Poems: Bibliographical Summary**.
3   DGR did a sun-moon-and-stars design for the binding of ACS' *Songs before Sunrise* (1871).
4   FSE published WJS' *The Acropolis of Athens, illustrated picturesquely and architecturally in photography,* later this year.

70.130 TO FREDERICK STARTRIDGE ELLIS
MS: BL. Published: *FSE* 34; DW 1008.

Scalands
Saturday [30 April 1870]

Dear Ellis

One or two points occur to me.

I think if you are getting the *large* paper copies bound, the side blocks would look very well left just as they are. The increased outer margin to the pattern wd not matter; and this must be better than an ordinary binding.

I have been thinking of what you said about the 2 queer sonnets which Swinburne proposes to print. I believe you did not hear the report of them first from me; but shd be most loth to seem to have made mischief in the least about them; & think it wd be greatly to be regretted if the little group of authors were broken up by his secession. So I wd recommend *con*ciliation (not in the style of Hood's butcher) as far as possible. I shd think he might be brought to leave them out. Besides of course you mean to see them in print before you object.¹

I suppose you are kindly attending to the money matter (£125 bill) you promised to meet for me, which will I believe be presented at my bankers (the Union Bk of London, Chancery Lane), on 3rd May. So the tin shd be sent there.

Sunday [1 May 1870]

I got Swinburne's article today – a dear piece of friendliness, but an avalanche of praise which I hope will not overwhelm me altogether.

I hear from Smith & Elder that only 8 copies of my Translations remain. So we might begin to think of the thing if you like. One or two articles are I know writing on it jointly with the new book, so it might have a new chance & become some sort of a property. Would you write me word of any plan you think feasible about it on business grounds.

Ever yours
D G Rossetti

P.S. Would you look in a Directory & see if you can find a Captn Thompson living at Hampstead & if so tell me the address.

---

¹ See **135**. DGR is referring to "A Butcher" by Thomas Hood (1799–1845). In the poem, the Butcher's vice is identified as "the dotage of self-love."

70.131 TO JOSEPH KNIGHT

MS: BL.

Scalands
1 May 1870

My dear Knight

I am quite uncomfortable about you after your last bad news of yourself. Still I trust the 2nd operation may be the end of your troubles.

I was half – or more than half – disposed to enclose a note in this for Dr. Marston, saying how much I feel the kindly tone and valuable promptitude of his excellent notice of my book in the Athenæum; but it finally seemed to me that this, on the strength of so slight a personal acquaintance as I have with him, might seem intrusive respecting an article not signed. I none the less, as you may be sure, feel sincerely gratified by his praise.

The book seems, on my publisher's report, to be doing extremely well as to sale, & will soon I believe have to go to press again.

I had an intensely – overwhelmingly – apologetic & enthusiastic letter from young Marshall, which I have not yet answered but must do so I suppose. After accepting his apology on the spot, I have of course nothing further to say on that head, but think he ought to be made to understand the monstrous & impossible nature of such conduct for all that.

Ever yours DG Rossetti

P.S. Sunday Times not yet to hand. Perhaps not out yet?

70.132 TO FREDERICK STARTRIDGE ELLIS

MS: PML.

Monday [c. 2 May 1870]

Dear Ellis

I send you the corrections. I have cut the passages out of old proof-sheets & marked the pages according to the edition. One scrap has corrections on both sides. Two passages of which I had no proof I have noted in M.S. Furthermore, in the Contents, the title *Willowwood* should have no hyphen in the middle but be all one word. I don't know what you mean to do about my sister's binding. I will make a sketch if you are inclined & there is time left to cut it.

Ever yours
D G Rossetti

P.S. Perhaps I had better see a proof of the corrections.

Tuesday [c. 3 May 1870]

I have no intention to put new matter in, as the buyers of the first edition would seem to be swindled.

I have the design for Swinburne's binding, & it shall reach you in a few days.

As to "2nd edition," it seems almost a pity this has not been started on your usual plan, for why should I be less "Successful" than my fellows. And I suppose there is no means of selling one's book like persuading people that it does sell. But this is your exclusive province.

Thanks much about the tin. I suppose the arrangement about the 50 large copies makes some difference in our accts as they wd otherwise have stood – i.e. if I had had to pay for those I gave away. Wd you tell me how they stand.

70.133 TO FORD MADOX BROWN

MS: UBC. Excerpt: Knight, *DGR*: 138; *FMB* 259; DW 1009. A sketch of a hand points to the letter's address beside the words "Full address."

3 May 1870

Scalands/Robertsbridge/Hawkhurst

Dear Brown

I'm your debtor I believe for a letter but have no very special news. I sold to Graham the 4 small head studies for the large picture & the one I was making from the country girl when you were here – in all 150 gs – & got the tin.¹ Ellis tells me that he has sold out my first 1000 all but 200, and is going to press again at once; so the 2 editions (at one quarter value of 12/– book) will bring me 300£ in a few weeks – not so bad for poetry after all, even if the public find themselves glutted after the 2nd thousand.² The first 1000 ought to have been called 2 editions as with Topsy &c – but 250 having been sent to America the remaining 750 had to be put into one edition – at least Ellis thought it best to do so – though I think it abates one's crow to an unsatisfactory extent.

I suppose you have seen Swinburne's wonderful article. He has modified the passage at the end about the other poets. It is dearly friendly, & full of splendid things of course but much too much in all reason. The Athenæum is a very nice article – and Fraser liable to be useful I suppose though seedy enough as writing – in fact bestial. Now for my foes with a clear course. I expect the Saturday or Spectator, or both, to tune up on that tack.

There is a splendid old mansion here belonging to the Smiths & now let as a farmhouse, which I saw the other day, and of which the farmer wd let me half if I liked, so that I could bring my own servants & be quite to myself. I am seriously thinking about it. There are fine big rooms & windows & a good east light to paint in, & the house is perfectly noble. I am sorry you missed seeing it. It is about a mile or less beyond Fir Bank.

However of course I shall be coming to town first even if I return here, and hope to turn up at most if not all (except the first) of your new gatherings of which I am glad to hear. I dare say if I were fixed here I should see as much of friends in London as ever to any purpose.

I am flooded with letters about my book – a rather shabby one I must say from Tennyson, & none from Browning as yet.³ I find on enquiry that my Italian Poets is just sold out – so shall reprint it immediately with Ellis if he thinks well to do so.

I am very much better on the whole – in fact quite another being from what I was on first coming here – and draw certainly with much more ease. Indeed, though I must admit my eyes to be further weakened lately, the crisis seems again to have subsided. With love to all (including Shields)

Ever yours
D G R

I was extremely sorry to hear of Catty's mishap at RA. Are Lucy & Nolly finally in? Tell me anything about the show there.
P.S. Janey wonderfully better.

---

¹ See **105**.

² News of the "2nd thousand" occurs in several subsequent letters. Commenting on the announcement of the 2nd edition, the *Athenæum* observed on 21 May: "The sale of the first edition in about ten days shows pretty clearly that the reading public has no aversion to poetry when it is really poetry" (678).

³ As the Laureate's letter does not appear in Lang's edition, it must not survive; for RB's, see **92n3**.

70.134 TO ALGERNON CHARLES SWINBURNE

MS: BL. Published: *ALC* 6: 110; DW 1010.

3 May [1870]
Scalands/Robertsbridge/Hawkhurst

My dear Swinburne

After reading your more than brotherly review of my book, what can I say adequate to so good a gift? You know already how much my love must feel the love, and my pride the praise, of so great a poet; and *I* knew already how much your generosity would outrun my deservings. Your words abound, as they always do, in a beauty which any artist but yourself would have had to reserve for his own poetry instead of lavishing it on another's.

I am not least grateful to you for having altered to my wishes the only sentence of the review which I had heard in M.S.

I have made the design for your binding, and Ellis will get it in a day or two.

Affectionately yours
D Gabriel R

70.135 TO FREDERICK STARTRIDGE ELLIS

MS: BL. Published: *FSE* 32; DW 1004.

Tuesday night [3 May 1870]

Dear Ellis

I meant to have answered before but have been interrupted a great deal.

I think the "Crucifix" on the whole less objectionable perhaps than the sonnets, though its last stanzas are startling. Still on the whole it is more the impression of the phrases used than the real drift of the poem that is the awkward part, & this may even be said of the sonnets also. The "Christ" anathematised in the "Crucifix" is the priests' corrupted and falsified God – not the true one. But still this might not appear clearly to everyone to whom the phraseology wd give a shock.

The only thing which wd. induce me in yr place (all this considered) to object to publish wd be any serious apprehension of legal results. I suppose myself that this wd probably be a delusive bugbear. I don't know whether it wd be worth while asking a lawyer's opinion. I really hardly know what to say and am far indeed from wishing to suggest such danger if it does not exist, as I suppose most likely it does not, but am no judge of the question.[1]

I think I'd better send you back 4 copies of my book last sent (which in fact were sent by mistake.) I dare say you can place them; & I had rather have the 2nd edition if I want any more.

Ever yours
D G Rossetti

---

[1] FSE annotated this letter at its head: "respecting the publication of certain sonnets in *Songs before Sunrise*. I declined to publish the book unless they were withdrawn & they were accordingly left out." Both FSE & DGR regarded these poems as blasphemous. "Before a Crucifix" remained in the collection but 2 sonnets lampooning French Emperor Napoleon III as "The Saviour of Society" were omitted; one of them described his birth as an immaculate misconception. After Napoleon III's death on 19 Jan 73, ACS published them in the May issue of the *Examiner*. Despite the *Spectator*'s expression of "horror and disgust" at these "revolting" sonnets, ACS included them as part of "Diræ" in *Songs of Two Nations* (1875). He felt his satire to be justified, as he told the *Spectator* in a letter defending the sonnets, because French admirers of Louis Bonaparte had addressed him as "Saviour" and "Messiah" (see Henderson, *Swinburne* [New York: Macmillan, 1974]: 180–81). See **153** for DGR's direct appeal to ACS not to print 4 of the "Diræ" sonnets intended for *Songs before Sunrise*. Ironically, DGR himself was soon to be attacked as a blasphemer by Buchanan for his metaphorical identification of the sacrament of Holy Communion with sexual intercourse in *HL* sonnet II, "Love's Redemption" (Buchanan 59). By 1881, DGR had retitled this sonnet "Love's Testament" and removed any trace of the Eucharist metaphor from the octave.

70.136 TO FORD MADOX BROWN

MS: UBC. Published: DW 1011.

Wednesday [4 May 1870]

Dear Brown

I meant yesterday to have sent you the enclosed letter from mad Marshall.[1] Wd. you let me have it again by return & just say if you think I had better answer it or not.

Ever yours
DG R

I have received the kindest letter from Marston in answer to my poems which I sent him.

1 Francis Albert Marshall (1840–89) wrote and acted in a number of dramas, operas, and farces. At a recent dinner party given by Joseph Knight (**55n2**), he had quarrelled with DGR. H. Sutherland Edwards (see 53.26nn2,3) gives a secondhand account of the incident in his *Personal Recollections* (Cassell, 1900). DGR, he says, "had fine spirits, an abundance of humour, and even a disposition to 'chaff' his friends when they laid themselves open to it." After dinner, Marshall complained at length that he had put a thousand pounds into a theatre that had nevertheless withdrawn a farce of his "after a single performance.... 'After all,' said Rossetti, when Marshall had begun to tire the company with his lamentations, 'you got some amusement for your money. There are plenty of pretty girls at that theatre; you had an opportunity of making their acquaintance, and doubtless had some very interesting flirtations with them.'" At this perceived slur on his moral character Marshall became so enraged and used such "opprobrious language" that Knight asked him to leave the house. The party then became "somewhat depressed. Knight was vexed for Rossetti's sake; Rossetti was sorry to have provoked, however unwittingly, so disagreeable a scene.... [Eventually] a knock was heard at the street door. Then a servant came into the room, saying, 'Please, sir, Mr. Marshall wishes me to tell you that his brougham is ordered for eleven, and, as it is now only half-past ten, he would be glad if you would let him have a chair outside on the pavement.' ... The picture of the ejected guest, sitting on a chair outside the house from which he had been asked to remove himself, was irresistibly droll. Rossetti, always amiable, begged that he might be called in. It seemed a pity to be seriously angry with such a man, and amid general hilarity Frank Marshall returned" (153–54).

70.137 TO WILLIAM BELL SCOTT

MS: Princeton.

Scalands/Robertsbridge/Sussex

4th May 1870

Dearest Scotus

At the time of sending you the book I did come to town for a few hours only to inscribe copies at the publisher's but returned by the 4 o'clock express – having left at 9 a.m. So I did not even go to Chelsea.

You will be glad to hear that the book is selling so well that Ellis is now going to press with the 2nd thousand. Thus it will have brought me £300 in a month or so, even if the public will stand no more of it afterwards. I mean to republish the Translations now, and see if the 2 can be made anything like a property. I hear from Smith & Elder that the Translations are just sold out.

The papers have spoken up well as yet – Pall Mall (good on the whole I think & none the worse for not being *too* wild.) – Fraser (well-meant but horribly-vilely written.) Athenæum (good & I hear by Marston) Globe (by Knight) & lastly Swinburne's wonderful pæan which is a darling bit of friendly enthusiasm but simply appals me (to speak truth) for the probable result of reaction from its excessive & supernatural laudation. Was such a tocsin ever sounded before in the world? I expect Palgrave will be lurking somewhere – Saturday or Spectator I judge. Morris will be in the Academy on the 12th.

I am a wonderful deal better, and my eyes seem fit for work again. I expect now to return to town in a few days & get on my big picture; but when well started have a notion that I may bring it out here & take some rooms, very available for painting, which are to be had in a lovely old mansion near here. I know if I spent a continuous working & walking summer in the country I *must* be all the better for it, whereas I cannot but forebode an almost certain relapse in London.

Janey is wonderfully better also & walks well daily. Top is coming down again today.

After all this selfish matter I must say one word as to how deeply vexed I shall be if your works are not in the R. A. exhibition – though as a mere matter of self-opinion on any artist's part, no one need feel that lessened in such case when seeing what *is* there annually & doubtless will be there again this year. I think myself the best plan is to give them the go-by on one's own hook and ignore their existence.

I was surprised & delighted to hear what progress Miss Boyd had made with Christina's "pigs in wigs" &c. Will you tell her that the fearful propriety of the inscription in her book was simply owing to the fact that ladies were last on my list & so last reached in the labour of inscription, & that thus after writing some 60 or 70 such scrawls the last came to shorten themselves. This must have been it though I shd have done otherwise had the fact of difference occurred to me.

I had a nice note from Miss Losh written in a hand which seemed to indicate her being better as I thought.

I trust to look in at Elgin Road yet before the 10th probably though it will not be much before.

Affectionately yours
D G Rossetti

P.S. Did you see Forman's sublime glorification of Woolner in Tinsley?[1]

---

[1] HBF's article on TW appeared in *Tinsley's Magazine* (1870: 257).

70.138 TO FRANCES MARY LAVINIA ROSSETTI

MS: UBC. Published: *FL* 226–27; DW 1014.

May 4/1870
Scalands/Robertsbridge/Hawkhurst

Dear Old Darling of 70,

I ought to have put in the book I sent you that it was a birthday present. I did not forget the dear day (27 April), only forgot the inscription. I hope you liked the binding which I think very successful, only the back of the pattern has been made too wide which renders a ridiculous padding of blank paper necessary inside. This will be remedied in the 2nd edition by having the back part re-cut. Also the fly-leaves will be printed on a greenish paper. At present they look raw. You will be glad to hear that the first edition is almost exhausted, & that Ellis is going to press with the 2nd thousand copies. There are going to be a few special copies printed on large paper, of which I shall get one for you. I was in town for a few hours only last Tuesday week in order to inscribe copies at the publisher's, but returned here in the afternoon. I expect probably to come back for good, or at any rate for the present, early next week. But I believe nothing would do me so much good, if I could make it convenient, as to bring work down & spend the summer in this neighbourhood, so as to get out in good air whenever I pleased. There is a lovely old mansion near here in which I could rent a set of rooms which would do well to paint in, and I have serious thoughts of it; but in any case I should have to return to London at present to start fair with my painting & see what I should be going on with.

I dare say you have seen the reviews of my book in Pall Mall, Fraser, Athenæum &c, & been duly thunderstruck at Swinburne's miraculous article.

I am wonderfully better within the last month – specially last fortnight, and have no doubt I am really benefited in every way, but London might bring on a relapse for all that.

Janey Morris is much better. Top is coming down again today & we shall make some more excursions probably as there are various things worth seeing.

My book will have brought me 300£ in less than a month, which is not so bad for poetry, particularly if it goes on. Love to all.

Your most affec: Gabriel

70.139 TO CHARLES FAIRFAX MURRAY

MS: Texas.

Scalands/Robertsbridge/Hawkhurst

4 May/1870

Dear Murray

Many thanks for keeping me informed of your movements.

I am quite annoyed to have omitted sending you my book when I sent out copies. It simply flew out of my head, though I had meant to do so. When I see you, you must let me reimburse you for the copy & write your name and mine in it.

I am very much better within the last month & hope to get back to my painting to some purpose now almost immediately. I am sorry for your mishap at the R. A. but you have time before you & I fully believe the certainty of an early fame yet.[1]

Ever yours

DG Rossetti

P.S. Do you need a remittance?

[1] CFM's *Head of a Young Man* was exhibited at the RA in 1871.

70.140 TO JOHN SKELTON

Text: Skelton 91. Reprinted: DW 1016.

4 May 1870

Scalands/Robertsbridge/Sussex

My dear Skelton

Let me thank you for being so early in the field with your friendly article on my poems. You will be glad to hear that the result of a few such timely notices has been that my publisher is already going to press with the second thousand.

I have been out here for two months now, recruiting after a spell of queer health, and have benefited greatly. I shall return to town almost immediately, and get to my painting again; but it is possible that, after making a good start with a picture I am beginning, I may bring it to this neighbourhood, and go in for a summer's working and walking together, of which I still stand in much need.

Very truly yours

DG Rossetti

70.141 TO FREDERICK STARTRIDGE ELLIS

MS: BL. Published: *FSE* 35; DW 1013.

[c. 4 May 1870]

Dear Ellis

I forward you an advertisement of my Translations which may as well be printed at the end of the 2nd Edn of the Poems. Would it not be well also to print it and the Advt of the Poems together on a good scale now in the Athenæum, Times, & Pall Mall or Academy? Perhaps this might be done after appearance of the Academy, so that Top's review might be quoted. I expect to see you next week. I rather anticipate that the note I have affixed to the advt of the Translations will be calculated to rouse attention among those who take an interest in such things more than has yet been done.

Will you send me Sunday Times which I hear contains Knight's notice.

Ever yours
D G Rossetti

P.S. I should tell you that 2 reviews of the Translations (jointly with the poems) will appear soon – by Colvin in one of the Quarterlies, & by Hake in the New Monthly.

[Enclosure]

New and re-arranged edition of Mr. D.G. Rossetti's
"Early Italian Poets."
In the Press, 2 vols, crown 8vo.
Dante and his Circle;
with the Italian Poets before Dante.
Translated & edited by
Dante Gabriel Rossetti.

In this work, the "Vita Nuova" (the autobiography of Dante's early life and love,) together with the many among his own lyrics and among those of contemporary poets which elucidate their intimate personal relations, are gathered together & brought into clear connection for the first time. No similar exhaustive treatment has yet been bestowed on these most interesting materials by the Italian or even by the German editors.[1]

---

[1] This advertisement appears verbatim as a preliminary insert in the 2nd, 3rd, & 4th editions of *Poems*.

70.142 TO BARBARA LEIGH SMITH BODICHON

MS: PML. Published: DW 1015.

Scalands
Wednesday [4 May 1870]

Dear Mdme Bodichon

Many thanks for your kind & thoughtful note. I certainly had understood that you wd be absolutely needing the house next Saturday, and was taking my measures accordingly. As it is, I shall not make up my mind at once about Glottenham, but stay here at any rate to the end of the week. After that I think it most probable I shall have to come to London & start work again in good earnest; but whether, when once started, I may not bring it to Glottenham & go on with it there, I am as yet uncertain. I feel sure I shd greatly benefit by a continuance of country air, & indeed that London is sure after a time to reproduce its baneful reaction. Glottenham affords excellent painting quarters (being as I judge an east light) & wd I think be altogether a most desirable sojourn, but for the possibility of farm noises interfering with my night's rest. Thus I shd wish to take it for a week at first on trial, & may perhaps even do so before leaving this neighbourhood for the present. I had no clear recollection of the extreme beauty of the old mansion. It is as fine in character as any I know, and how your brother can refrain from living there & making of it what it might be internally, I cannot conceive.

I have now to thank you sincerely for the timely loan of this house, which has had within the last month much more beneficial results than I had ventured to hope. I am quite another man in general strength from what I was on leaving London, & the sudden crisis of my eyes seems completely at an end though I cannot say they are strong; but work no longer presents unusual difficulty. I will keep you informed of my leaving & am

Ever yours
D. G Rossetti

70.143 TO JAMES SMETHAM

MS: V&A.

May 7/1870
Scalands/Robertsbridge/Sussex

My dear Smetham,

I dare say you have heard ere this of my being in the country. I have now been here for rather more than 2 months, and have benefited immensely. At the time of my leaving London I had another crisis with my eyes, & very troublesome symptoms. I went again to 2 oculists – Bowman & a new one, Critchett – both of whom said as always that there was absolutely no danger of the worst kind, but advised rest though not entire abstinence from work. I now return to Town on Monday or Tuesday I believe – certainly much fitter for painting than when I left, & I hope as completely so as I can look to be now.

I trust my silence for some time before leaving London did not produce an unfriendly impression, but I was much bothered. I very much regret not having got to see your work, and was extremely pained to hear the other day in a letter from Brown that both your pictures are among the many good ones of whose rejection at the R.A. I hear on all hands. However it is some consolation that I understand both are sold.[1]

You wd have got my book before now (in spite of your grim resolves against *Jenny*) only on the day I went for a few hours to town to inscribe copies at the publishers I found before reaching the end of my list that the first supply from the binders ran short for my purpose (as the general public could not be left in the lurch) and I was obliged to defer some of my numerous liberalities. I have not since told Ellis to send you one, as I should be sorry not to write your name in it, but will do so at once on getting to London.

The book has been a decided success & they are now going to press with the 2nd thousand.

I have some thought of returning here from time to time this year, & taking permanent quarters for that purpose.

I'll hope to see you soon in town, &

am ever yours D G Rossetti

---

[1] JS was working on *Hesper* & *The Women of the Crucifixion*, both sold to James S. Budgett before they were completed in 1871 (see 69.32n1 & Smetham 20–21, 27).

70.144 TO FRANCIS ALBERT MARSHALL

MS: Yale.

Scalands/Robertsbridge/Hawkhurst

May 7. 1870

Dear Marshall

I should have answered your letter before, but for various preoccupations.

As regards the first part of it, this was not needed, as I had accepted your apology on the spot. However, I am not sorry to receive a renewal of it, – not on my own account, but as showing your permanent regret for so ugly & unworthy a scene. For myself, I had merely to dismiss the matter from my mind at once, as something which everyone present saw to be forced on me, & with which I was not really concerned at all.

I need hardly say that it gratifies me to find my poetry producing on you such impressions as I could desire every one to receive from it. I should not however wish to give any sanction of my own to its being publicly read.

There must be some mistake about Miss Herbert's having asked me to dinner, as I never received any such invitation. I left London just after that evening at Knight's, & have been here ever since, but all letters have been sent on to me.

Yours faithfully
D G Rossetti

70.145 TO THOMAS GORDON HAKE

MS: BL. Published: DW 1018.

7 May 1870
Scalands/Robertsbridge/Hawkhurst

Dear Dr. Hake

I have not yet thanked you for your last letter & all your kind good wishes. I need not say with how much interest I await the sight of your review. I also hope to see you soon & hear from you your ideas (to which you refer) as to the kind of poetic work I ought now to take in hand.

Since my last writing, the book it seems has sold unexpectedly well, & my publisher has now gone to press with the 2nd thousand. In this reissue I have introduced a few further fidgetty changes of a minute kind. As some proofs of these changes have been sent me, I may as well enclose some of them to you while they lie about useless. I have altered a phrase or two in the Stream's Secret which were pointed out to me by friends as obscure. This poem went in at the last moment & had not the advantage of consultation with friends before it was printed.

I am also going to press at once now with a second edition of the Translations, to see if it can be made to benefit by the present good luck of the Poems. This time I shall put it in 2 vols, & call it

Dante & His Circle;
With the Italian Poets before Dante.

This title will I think direct the reader's attention more immediately to the chief literary claim of the book. The Dantesque series will form the first vol.

& the others the second. Among the reviews of the Poems which have appeared, one (in Fraser) includes the Translations. The Athenæum had a very good & kindly notice, & Swinburne in the Fortnightly is but too overpoweringly flattering, not for friendship but for critical moderation. However I dare say my non-lovers will have their word yet – perhaps somewhere this present Saturday.

I believe I shall return to town – Monday or Tuesday – at any rate for the present. I am in every way immensely improved from my condition at first coming here.

Ever yours truly
D G Rossetti

I hope your philological letter will be in the Athenæum before long.

70.146 TO BARBARA LEIGH SMITH BODICHON
MS: PML. Published: DW 1017.

Scalands
Saturday [7 May 1870]

Dear Mdme Bodichon

I believe I shall return to London on Monday, so write you word in case it should be at all necessary for you to know at once. The workmen are to come in, I am told, on that day.

I think it most likely that I shall take the rooms (the whole of one side of the house) at Glottenham – probably for 6 months. I am to write to the farmer settling this question on my return to town. His rent for the rooms is £2 a week, and he tells me General Ludlow paid £2-10/. The expense will be well bestowed if the easy opportunity induces me to spend even 2 or 3 months in the country this summer & autumn.[1] The light is south east, & seems suitable enough for painting, and I judged on further enquiry that the farm operations wd not cause excessive disturbance. The Morrises return to town on Monday also.

Again with thanks & kind remembrances

I am sincerely yours
D G Rossetti

---

[1] WMR noted that DGR rented this old mansion adjacent to Scalands but never lived there (*WMRD* 9n3).

70.147 TO FREDERICK STARTRIDGE ELLIS

MS: BL. Published: *FSE* 36; DW 1019. In the MS DGR has deleted the letter's 6th paragraph (not just "sentence") and also his originally written date of "Friday."

Saturday [7 May 1870]

Dear Ellis

Sunday Times *not* come.

I have only made one further change (enclosed) in the new proof pages. Please see it rightly done, & all can then go to press.

I send you the revised sketch for the back, which I hope is right now. You have the lettering already you know. I have some idea of adding some little sprigs over the plain part of the binding for the large copies. These could be cut separately & stamped.

The gold fly-leaf wd look better I think on very slightly glazed paper like that of the greenish specimen you sent me. I hope by the bye this last greenish paper is being adopted for the second edition.

Dear old Top is here – not very well. His binding for the Volsungs is most lovely – quite perfect.

[I wish you'd send me here by return of post 2 Copies of Commonplace as Top tells me it is out. Do not write here *after* tomorrow, but to Chelsea if at all, as I shall be back there any day now – I don't quite know which.]

I have erased the last sentence, as I remember now it is Saturday – not Friday – to-day. So wld you send the 2 Commonplaces to Chelsea.

It might be well perhaps to insert something from Fraser in the advts as well meaning people should be kept in good humour I suppose. I see a sentence in the last paragraph – ("Mr. R. has proved" to "insight") – which might do.

Ever yours
D G Rossetti

P.S. I hear of a notice in Daily News.[1] Try & send it me.

---

[1] No review of *Poems* appeared in this periodical.

70.147.1 TO MARY SMITH

MS: Untraced (formerly Private Collection).

May 8/1870

Scalands/Robertsbridge/Hawkhurst

My dear Mrs. Smith

Many thanks for your kind note. I shall return to town in a day or two now (after a couple of months' stay here) & shall be very glad to dine with you on Sunday the 22nd.[1]

Very truly yours
DG Rossetti

[1] See 69.38 Headnote for an envelope postmarked 25 May 70, which may have enclosed a thank-you note for the dinner.

70.148 TO WILLIAM MICHAEL ROSSETTI

MS: Brotherton. Published: DW 1020.

Scalands

Sunday [8 May 1870]

Dear Wm

I have not written before about Florence for the simple reason that I have not been able quite to make up my mind.[1] I shall do so more easily when back in town, which will be tomorrow or Tuesday I think. I will then see & talk to you at once.

Ever yours D G R

[1] See **107n2**.

70.149 TO ALICE BOYD

MS: UBC.

Scalands/Robertsbridge

Sunday [8 May 1870]

Dear Miss Boyd

I expect almost for certain to return to town some time tomorrow (Monday) & in that case shall look up same evening at Elgin Road as my last chance of seeing you. I shall come as early as I can. Meanwhile love to all there.

Ever yours
DG Rossetti

P.S. If you would be away, please write a line to Chelsea on getting this.

70.150 TO FREDERICK STARTRIDGE ELLIS
MS: BL. Published: *FSE* 37; DW 1021. The enclosure is not present with the MS.

[9 May 1870]

Dear Ellis,
   Will you give bearer 4 copies of my book, & 2 of my sister's if not already sent.
   Read the enclosed anent *Times* notice coming.[1]

Yrs
DG Rossetti

[1] The enclosure may have been from Knight (see **121** & **127**). No review was printed in *The Times*, by E. S. Dallas or anyone else.

70.151 TO BARBARA LEIGH SMITH BODICHON
MS: PML. Published: DW 1022.

16 Cheyne Walk
Tuesday [10 May 1870]

Dear Mdme Bodichon
   Thanks for your note but the plates cannot evidently be the same as those you showed me. I should not so much mind the price but shd be provoked to get inferior things for it. So I had better wait till you get the *poterie commende* & see if that is it: after which it will be easy for me to order more by same means. I yearn towards the bears but those I judge you have annexed absorbed & monopolized as in duty bound.
   I left Scalands taking care of itself all right, with the workmen just coming in yesterday. I suppose you are on the point of leaving for France & wish you

a pleasant journey & sojourn if I do not see you before. The Morrises returned with me.

Of course I am only too delighted you shd have the photos. I have got a Mary Magdalene one here for you now & will bring or send it one day.

Ever yours,
DG Rossetti

70.152 TO THOMAS GORDON HAKE

MS: BL. Published: DW 1023.

16 Cheyne Walk
10 May 1870

Dear Dr. Hake

Many thanks for all your kind counter-suggestions, but (bard-like) I remain unconvinced!!

All the alterations have been adopted on very mature reflection; – that in the *Confession* for reasons of emotional balance in the rhythm which I still think paramount; & those in the S[tream]'s S[ecret]. generally or always to increase clearness, which I think they effect. The "love's lips" & "amulet" I myself prefer on some accounts; but I certainly think the former phrase creates some confusion, & the latter is only half appropriate in its place.

I cannot see that the syllables "passion of peace" make the line unmetrical; – on the contrary I think such varieties of modulation absolutely a law in passionate lyrical poetry. And they have exactly the same metrical value as the original phrase.

"Deathlier" I beat about before I settled on, but could find nothing so clearly introducing the idea of a *spiritual* locality differing from the *actual* stream-side, the want of which I found left one intelligent reader in the lurch. These are all things which I am sure I shd have done to the poem before it went to press at all, had it not gone in at the last moment. I myself prefer the original line in Sonnet 50, but it is too like a line towards the end of Sonnet 49.[1] That was my reason for the change; as, especially at the close of the series, the monotony had to be avoided.

I am rather scattered in occupations at this first return to town; but I think I would try to propose an evening visit ere long if you thought you could stay the night here.

Very sincerely yours D G Rossetti

P.S. The two "*vains*" in line 1 of sonnet 50 instead of "*all*," I have now restored. I turned them out originally because of resemblance pointed out to a line in 1st Sonnet of Petrarch.[2]

P.S. If you looked up one evening, I hope you'd bring Valdarno for discussion.[3]

---

[1] See **113n4**.
[2] See **71n1**.
[3] TGH & WA joined DGR & WMR at 16CW on 26 May; TGH was "looking up Valdarno etc. and revising that set of tales with a view to republication" (*WMRD* 9). See **162**.

70.153 TO ALGERNON CHARLES SWINBURNE

MS: BL. Excerpt: HRA 106. Published: *ALC* 7: 5–6; DW 1025.

Thursday 12th May/1870

Dear Swinburne

I have just happened to see the proof-sheet of your Sonnets – "The Saviour of Society," – glorious pieces of poetic diction, as none knows better than I. But they resolve me to risk even your displeasure by one earnest remonstrance as to their publication. I cannot but think absolutely that a poet like yourself belongs of right to a larger circle of readers than this treatment of universal feelings can include. You know how free I am myself from any dogmatic belief; but I can most sincerely say that (except as a joke admitted & necessarily restricted to such hearers as will know it to be a joke only) I do myself feel that the supreme nobility of Christ's character should exempt it from being used – not as a symbolic parallel to other noble things and persons in relation with which dogmatists might object to its use – but certainly in contact of this kind with anything so utterly ignoble as this. I should myself feel to breathe more freely in the splendid atmosphere of your genius if this little cloud were cleared away from it; & feeling so, a friend should say so.

You have no right to imperil your Sacred relation to the minds of many men worthy to profit by your mind, by using one form of metaphor rather than another when its use involves such disproportionately grave issues. If you withdraw these consummately written Sonnets from your volume and print them separately for private gift, they can still be made available in all quarters where no misconception is possible; and you will not involve yourself (or, I may add, your publisher, to whom I think you owe some consideration) in an obloquy which I do not myself think (after most serious reflection on a point so serious) that just poetic canons can altogether repel. Do, do, my dear Swinburne, withdraw these 4 Sonnets.[1]

I returned to town on Monday & should be delighted if you happened to be coming my way in the day time on Saturday or Sunday. This is my birthday, by the bye. Do make me the birthday gift I ask of you.

Affectionately yours
D G Rossetti

P.S. I am to dine at Ld Houghton's on Sunday – so dare say I shall see you.

---

[1] See **135&n1** & **154**; ACS had complained the previous day to WMR about DGR's having spoken to FSE on these matters (*WMRD* 9–10). Wise: "This letter marks the beginning of the differences which arose between the two poets, and which ended two years later in a complete severance of their friendship. Rossetti was evidently unaware of the origin of the title" (*ALC* 7: 6). However, friendly correspondence continued between the two through late 1871. DGR sent ACS new poems written at Kelmscott and the latter kept the distressed poet informed on the subject of Buchanan's malicious attack on him, encouraging him to write the rebuttal which was published as "The Stealthy School of Criticism" in the *Athenæum* (16 Dec 71; Lang 2: 410). According to Lang, the end of both contact and correspondence between them is marked by a letter from ACS, dated 5 Jul 72 (Lang 2: 421& n1), responding to WMR's request that he not try to meet DGR again; ACS protested, "no man can love his friend more than I love Gabriel," but agreed to be "debarred." Although social intercourse between them was never resumed, DGR in later years often sent friendly and even jocular greetings through WMR & TWD to "The Bard" in Putney. ACS attended DGR's funeral at WMR's invitation (*FLM* 402).

70.154 TO FREDERICK STARTRIDGE ELLIS

MS: BL. Published: *FSE* 38; DW 1024.

Thursday [12 May 1870]

Dear Ellis

I may as well show you what I have written to Swinburne. Please close & post it. The supposition might be that I had happened to take up the proof at your place, & no more than that need be said.

After all, what is to be done when (to enlarge the old saying) "Poeta nascitur non fit for publication"?*

Ever yours D G R

---

* DGR is punning on Horace's *Poeta nascitur non fit*, meaning "The poet is born not made."

70.155 TO FORD MADOX BROWN

MS: Princeton. Date: WMR.

Thursday [12 May 1870]

Dear Brown

All right – Monday be it, only unluckily I've asked 2 men since whom I must now write to – Allingham & Murray.

Could you look in tomorrow Friday daytime do you think without too much inconvenience, for a last consultation as to the cartoon before it's traced off. I meant to talk to you on Saturday, but Monday is still further off.

Your D G R

70.156 TO FREDERICK STARTRIDGE ELLIS

MS: BL. Published: *FSE* 39; DW 1027.

Saturday [14 May 1870]

Dear Ellis

I'm glad you're not bent in any case on giving up Swinburne's book. It would be a pity – a great pity – to break up the little knot of congenial writers at last got together.

I fancy my 2nd Edition ought to come out as soon as possible; and I, for my part, shd not object to some portion of it being issued with the old back if that would hasten matters. However you are best judge.

The *Saturday* article today is a bestial one – almost confessedly incompetent, but not hurtful, which one soon learns, in the sty of British criticism, to think the only point worth considering.

Morris's article is direct & complete – an honour and a profit to the book.

Ever yours
DG Rossetti

Would it be worth while looking up some of the best reviews of the 1st edn of my Translations to print in the advts? I remember good ones in Spectator & (I think) Westminster or some Quarterly.[1]

---

[1] Reviews of *EIP* appeared in *Spectator* (18 Jan 62): 75–76 (see 62.12); *Westminster Review* (Apr 62): 588 et seq.; and *British Quarterly Review* (Apr 62): 500; see also *PRISM* 29. 1–3. See the following letter & DW 1027n5.

70.157 TO FREDERICK STARTRIDGE ELLIS

MS: BL. Published: *FSE* 40; DW 1028.

2nd note

[14 May 1870]

Dear Ellis

I just remember there was also the British Quarterly (I think) that you sent me, with a short notice. I fancy the best wd be, if feasible to make up an advt with these 4 Quarterlies only.

Ever yours
D G R

70.158 TO WILLIAM MICHAEL ROSSETTI

MS: BL. Published: DW 1029.

Monday [16 May 1870]

Dear W

I think it wd be well for Furnivall to announce in the Gossip that the first edition of a thousand copies of my book has been exhausted in little more than a week. This might do good & would at any rate put certain people in a rage. I don't like to write to him myself but I wish you'd drop him a line to do so, as I think you could without any awkwardness. It should be in the *above terms*, as a thousand copies are generally split into 2 editions, & I believe 250 editions have not been unknown among our purest & highest order of poets.[1]

I expect you to dinner today.

Your
Gabriel

[1] See 62.6&nn. The "Gossip" column of the *Athenæum* duly made such an announcement (21 May 70: 678). See **164**.

70.159 TO JOSEPH KNIGHT

MS: BL.

16 Cheyne Walk

Wednesday [18 May 1870]

Dear Knight

I have been in town now for a week, but received your last note yesterday. I fear you must have thought me forgetful as to the photos: I now send, but it is only lately that copies of some have come in.

Let me thank you once again for your triple service to my book, the success whereof (beyond the limited literary circle in which I thought it would probably find some favour) astonishes no one more than myself. I believe the 2nd edition will be out on Friday, but the sudden sale has caught us napping.

I really feel curious to know who writes the "Book Market" in the Telegraph.[1] Who is it? I thought I was thin-skinned enough, but to *this* telegraph my galvanic wires refused to quiver. So it really procured me a satisfaction.

I hope to Heaven you are not getting into a long plague of queer health again. You do not tell me exactly.

I had the kindest letter from Dr. Marston, & hope to make one at his weekly gathering the Sunday after next. The past & next Sundays I found myself engaged. His article delighted not only myself but my friends, who in exigence on this point beat me hollow.

Ever yours
DG Rossetti

---

[1] An unsympathetic, unsigned notice of *Poems* appeared in the *Daily Telegraph* (9 May 70: 5). See **161**.

70.160 TO FREDERICK STARTRIDGE ELLIS

MS: University of Delaware.

Wedy [c. 18 May 1870]

Dear Ellis

I have just been led to observe that on page 270 of my book the word "In" which should begin the last line, has fallen out. This falling out is a perfect curse. Another instance is at page 210, where a full-stop now stands at the end of line 7. This should be a comma, & was so in the 1st edition. There are other instances but I can't lay my hand on them now. Really the first I have named is so ruinous that either a cancel or a printed slip for the *erratum* seems necessary in next Edition.

Ever yours
D G Rossetti

P.S. I wish you'd get me a Lemprière, please.[1] Don't forget.

---

[1] See 69.222n1.

70.160.1 TO JAMES ANDERSON ROSE

Text (fragment): Knight, *DGR* (1887): 139.

19 May 1870

... Its success has surprised me.¹ A second thousand called for in less than ten days! Poetry is likely to prove no such bad trade in England before long. ...

¹ See **133**.

70.161 TO WILLIAM BELL SCOTT

Text: DW 1033 (attributed to Courtney-Boyd but unlocated). In the second paragraph, it seems probable that DW read "Wm" for "Wr," thus mistaking a reference to JMW for one to WMR. Both DGR and WMR sometimes abbreviated JMW's name to "Wr." See n1 below.

[c. 20 May 1870]

Dear Scotus

If you happen to ask your friend Mr. McD (which it isn't worth while doing) whether he wrote that in the *Daily Telegraph* – I ought to have said – don't of course mention my name, as it would be doing him much too great an honour on my part to recognize his existence at all. By the bye, if you wish (as I should think you must) for a pretext to cut him, here is a good one.

I felt awkward about Whistler and Leyland yesterday. The coolness of Whistler after neglecting to answer Leyland's invitation for three days and forcing him to personal enquiries, was sublime.¹

Old Hake has sent me the proof (unsolicited) of a very good article he has written on me for the *New Monthly*. It is a sell that your good intentions to review me were frustrated. I am much disappointed at not counting you among my reviewers.

I went to the R.A. yesterday, and might really have counted (and more than counted) on my fingers the things I liked at all heartily. Mason's little landscape I really think is the best, together with Watts's portrait of Ned Jones. Then Millais's *Lady Huntly* is very complete I think and his *Raleigh* the best of the others – very fine indeed in colour but empty and unimaginative. Walker I thought unquestionably fine, and yet somehow betraying a want of true imagination taking refuge in an imposing "style." But its vigour and colour are splendid. There is a picture by Houghton of an eastern king in meditation which has more real affinity to high design than anything in the place perhaps; but its painter is a provoking creature – sometimes absolutely vulgar, as last year. Maclise I didn't think quite one of his successes.[2]

Did you see the *Saturday Review* on me. I suppose this is Palgrave – forced to be grudgingly civil.

Your affec:
D Gabriel R

---

[1] At this time JMW was working on *Arrangement in Black: Portrait of F. R. Leyland* both at FRL's home, Speke Hall, and in London (*WMRD*).

[2] WMR visited the RA exhibition on 5 May & 13 Jul (*WMRD* 6, 18), expressing admiration only for Maclise's final painting, *The Earls of Desmond and Ormond* (197), and JEM's *A Flood* (91, now at Manchester) and *A Widow's Mite* (928, Birmingham). The painting by George Heming Mason was *Landscape: Derbyshire* (184); it was lent 3 years later to his BFAC memorial exhibition (30; see 66.73n1) by Ernst L. S. Benzon. GFW's portrait of EBJ (107) is now also at Birmingham. JEM's portrait of Amy Cunliffe-Brooks (989), who married the 11th Marquis of Huntly in 1869, was sold at Sotheby's in 2001 for £600,000 (29 Nov, Lot 22); his *Boyhood of Raleigh* (334) is in the Tate. Fred Walker's *The Plough* (440) is reproduced in J.G. Marks, *Life and Letters of Frederick Walker, A.R.A* ([Macmillan, 1896]: facing 206). The Houghton picture (316) was exhibited without title but bore 8 lines from Isa Craig's "Sheik Hamil" (see Paul Hogarth, *Arthur Boyd Houghton* [V&A, 1975]: 27).

70.162 TO THOMAS GORDON HAKE

MS: BL. Published: DW 1030.

16 Cheyne Walk
20 May 1870

Dear Dr. Hake

How am I to thank you enough for so clearly admirable an article on my book? Of its verdicts it is not for me to judge: but I need not hesitate to endorse many things keenly and excellently said on matters of principle and feeling, as none but a poet could say them. All the passage on "Jenny" is specially grateful to me, and embodies with absolute exactness the view I would wish to be taken of that poem in relation to my other work. And how complete a résumé you have given of the "Last Confession"! Among the many sentences striking for their own sake, I may instance that in which you liken the growths of spiritual art to perennials, "which have always been, but are recognized only when they bloom." This is like the best things in "Valdarno."

I have reached an age now when one must gather up, whether one wills it or no, many of the ravelled threads of life; and in bringing these poems at last together, it is pleasant to find them still knit with many personal memories and art-sympathies from of old which they serve to perpetuate. Thus it is as pleasing to me as it was till of late unexpected, that the book should count among its reviewers a poet whose work elicited my eager interest and curiosity even from the days when, as a boy, I first met with "Vates." Let me thank you warmly for the true additional gratification which you have enabled my own work to procure for me.

Could you dine with me next Thursday? Seven o'clock. And could you bring with you "Valdarno" for joint consideration? I can give you a bed, you know. I am much interested in your steps respecting this work and your poems, and want greatly to have another talk with you after all this time.

Ever yours
DG Rossetti

70.163 TO FREDERICK STARTRIDGE ELLIS

MS: BL. Published: *FSE* 41; DW 1031.

Friday [20 May 1870]

Dear Ellis

I forgot to say at Brown's that I wish you'd kindly send a copy (inscribed inside "from the Author") to an old acquaintance of mine who has written to ask for one to review in the *Inverness Courier* of which he is editor. I don't know that it's worth much, but he asks me & I can't well refuse.

address –
Walter Carruthers Esq
Inverness.[1]

Would you let me have here 3 copies of the new edition.

By the bye, idleness has made me frightfully hard up. Now the new lot is out, we might square accounts as soon as you liked.

Ever yours
DG Rossetti

---

[1] Evidently no review of *Poems* appeared in the *Inverness Courier*. Walter Carruthers was the son of Robert, previous editor of this journal, and brother of Mary, who had married AM in 1861 (see 61.63n1).

70.164 TO FREDERICK STARTRIDGE ELLIS

MS: BL. Published: *FSE* 42; DW 1032.

22 May/1870
16 Cheyne Walk
Chelsea

My dear Ellis

Thanks for cheque squaring our accounts for the 2nd thousand. Also for the large copies kindly sent. The new cutting of the back is exactly right.

If you're writing again on any matter, let me know how *Commonplace* goes off. Colvin has it in hand for the Pall Mall.[1]

What *is* to be done indeed about this dreadful bloke and his book? I suppose you'd better just write "with the Author's compliments" in one, send it and charge it to me.

Ever yours
D G Rossetti

P.S. I have forgotten all along to say that the extract from Fortnightly in the advts should be made to run thus: –

"There are no poems of the class (the Sonnets and Songs) in English" &c.

Else what refers to a special section seems to refer to the whole book & is inappropriate.

Did you see announcement of 2nd edn in Athenæum Gossip? I notice the words "2nd edn" do not appear in the Pall Mall advt. yesterday.[2]

---

[1] Colvin reviewed CGR's *Commonplace* in the *Pall Mall Gazette* (7 Jun 70). According to Emma Parker, the critics "lambasted" *Commonplace* ("A Room of One's Own: Christina Rossetti, Literary Success and Love," *Women's Writing* [1998]: 312). Writing to FSE on 1 Jun, regretting poor sales, CGR hoped that "favorable reviews may rescue *Commonplace* from oblivion; but am sorry to say I know not of any such definite prospect, beyond a rumour that the *Pall Mall* means to treat me well. However, I trust it is not yet too late for hope" (Packer 84&n1, Harrison 1: 427).

[2] See **133n2** & **158**. The *Pall Mall Gazette* carried advertisements of the 2nd edition on 24 May and the 3rd edition on 28 May.

70.165 TO CHARLOTTE LYDIA POLIDORI

MS: UBC. Published: *FL* 227–28; DW 1034.

24 May 1870
16 Cheyne Walk/Chelsea

My dear Aunt

I just hear from Mamma, with a pang of remorse, that you have ordered a copy of my poems. You may be sure I did not fail to think of you when I inscribed copies to friends & relatives; but to speak frankly, I was deterred from sending it to you by the fact of the book including one poem ("Jenny") of which I felt uncertain whether you would be pleased with it. I am not ashamed of having written it (indeed I assure you that I would never have written it if I thought it unfit to be read with good result,) but I feared it might startle you somewhat & so put off sending you the book. I now do so by this post, and hope that some if not all of the pieces may be quite to your taste. Indeed I hope that even "Jenny" may be so, for my mother likes it on the whole the best in the volume, after some consideration. I dare say you have heard from that only too partial quarter of the commercial success of the book. The first thousand sold in little more than a week is not amiss for poetry. The 2nd edition is now out, and I have already received £300 for my share of the profits. Of course it will not go on like this for ever, but perhaps a quiet steady sale may be hoped to go on. I am now about to republish my book of the "Early Italian Poets" as perhaps a new edition may profit by the luck of the other book.

I hope you are well & that it may not be long before we meet.

Your affectionate nephew
D G Rossetti

70.166 TO FREDERICK STARTRIDGE ELLIS

MS: BL. Published: *FSE* 43; DW 1035.

[24 May 1870]

My dear Ellis,

The cry is still "Give, Give" as regards my book, & I must ask you to send me 3 more copies for people I cannot well refuse.

I enclose something sent me today (from Daily News leaders),[1] & a cutting from Athenæum, which caught my eye!!! The blank leaf business is a lark.

How does the sale of 2nd ed. go on? Don't you mean to make this thousand do double duty after the approved fashion & be imposing?

Your
DG R

---

1 "Critics have pointed out the originality of Mr. Dante Rossetti as a poet, but one characteristic of his volume does not seem as yet to have been much noticed. At the end of it will be found about a dozen pages of clean paper, all ready for the notes and illustrations of a reader. An author must have considerable confidence in himself to venture on appending to his work such a claim on the attention of his readers; but Mr. Rossetti doubtless is right in thinking that he has not a few admirers who will be glad of these pages of writing paper on which to record their impressions of his work. The publishers of classical works, let us add, might confer on many of us a boon by taking a hint from Mr. Rossetti" (*Daily News*, 24 May 70). Initially DGR took these wisecracks about the blank gathering as a "lark," but before the day was out he wrote gravely to FSE (**167**) that the newspaper had to be set right on the matter – the poet's thin skin is showing, a premonitory hint of more serious attacks and consequences to come.

70.167 TO FREDERICK STARTRIDGE ELLIS

MS: BL. Published: *FSE* 44; DW 1036.

Tuesday night [24 May 1870]

Dear Ellis

My brother thinks it might be well to set the Daily News right about those blank leaves, and I think the matter would come best from you. So would you mind copying the note overpage & sending it to the office of the paper.

Ever yours
D G Rossetti

[Enclosure]

25 May 1870
33 King St. Covent Garden

To the Editor of the Daily News
Sir.

Will you allow me, as the publisher of Mr. Rossetti's poems, to explain the sole reason for the blank leaves at the end of the first edition, to which I see a reference in your paper of yesterday. The block for the pattern at the back of the binding was cut too wide, and the error having been only perceived at the last moment, the padding had to be introduced to fill the book out. The block has been re-cut for the second edition, and the blank leaves are gone.

Yours &c
F. S. Ellis[1]

[1] DGR's note, with minor changes by FSE, was printed above the publisher's signature in the next day's *Daily News* as a Letter to the Editor.

70.168 TO BARBARA LEIGH SMITH BODICHON
MS: PML. Published: DW 1038.

16 Cheyne Walk
25 May 1870

Dear Mme Bodichon

I have never yet written to thank your brother, through you, for the most kind offer of the loan of Fir Bank for awhile. I was already, however, half pledged to renting the rooms at Glottenham, & have thought it better on the whole to carry out this plan, as my movements are so very uncertain that it is possible the moment of my going into the country might just coincide with Mr. Benjn Smith's own need of his house. I have therefore written now to engage the rooms at Glottenham. I shall probably continue to keep them all the summer & autumn, so as to be able to avail myself of them at a moment's notice whenever I please. My first use of them will not be at once however, as I must make a good start now with some work in London before stirring again.

I hope you are enjoying yourself & benefiting thoroughly by sea air. I send this to Blandford Square whence no doubt it will reach you; and with kindest remembrances

am ever yours
D G Rossetti

70.169 TO FORD MADOX BROWN
MS: UBC. Published: DW 1211. Date: WMR.

Tuesday [31 May 1870]

Dear Brown

Inchbold was here today, very anxious to get his works recommended in any promising quarter. I know it wd be of no use with Leyland or Graham as I've tried both. Do you think you cd. mention his watercolours to Craven with any prospect of success? He seems very desperate. Craven had been in here an hour before Inchbold, or I wd have named it myself, but I don't know C's address in London, & suppose you will be seeing him. I shd be very anxious to be of use if possible but fear it's not very hopeful. I'm writing to Rae. I may probably look in on you tonight but write in case not.

Your D G R

70.170 TO JOSEPH KNIGHT
MS: BL.

16 Cheyne Walk
Wednesday [1 June 1870]

Dear Knight

I've been meaning to call since hearing on Sunday at Marston's[1] how ill you had been, but something always comes in the way at this huge distance, & I only reach your end of the world about 11 at night. So today I will not delay any longer sending to know how you are, & only hope I may get a favourable report. I judged from what Marston said that a crisis had taken place but was over by then.

We had a most pleasant evening there, & I shall certainly try for another on some early Sunday when I hope you may make one at the gathering. I'm going to get a few friends together myself in a few days, but hardly yet know *what* day, & shall hope you may then be well enough to come. I will notify you again on the point.

Ever yours
D G Rossetti

[1] Evidently the first time DGR attended one of JWM's Sunday evening *soirées* (see also **213** & **255**).

70.171 TO FREDERICK STARTRIDGE ELLIS
MS: BL. Published: *FSE* 45; DW 1042.

Wednesday [1 June 1870]

My dear Ellis

I see you've got into the 3rd Edition! How many have you sold of it? I suppose it is bound as usual, but that is not mentioned in the Times advts. I allude to this because some one told me a friend of theirs had got a plain-bound copy, but this must be some mistake I suppose. I ought to tell you that I find stops dropped out repeatedly in the 2nd edn – and in one instance – page 222 – a full-stop at the end of line 12, where the 1st ed. rightly has a comma! How can such a vile blunder as this take place? Before the 3rd thousand is issued (whenever that may be,) these things will have to be set right.¹

Did you see the charming Standard? It is, I find, the notorious Marsyas flayed* lately in the *Pall Mall* – to wit, Alfred Austin.²

About the white-&-gold copies which are to have the photograph? Has anything been done towards these?³ I must see immediately about the photo.

Now for another matter. My friend Dr. Hake (who by the bye has written a good review of me in the New Monthly which you may have seen, & which I shd like to have quoted in advertisements with others) has a volume of poems on the stocks & wants you to publish for him. He is prepared to undertake the expenses himself. I should on the whole be glad if you were willing to publish, as I have a real regard for him. I would not propose it if I had no opinion of the work, but it has real and even high merits in several ways & specially in one very rare direction – that of studied and artistic versification; and though I do not suppose popularity can be expected for it, I believe it must attract some attention. I myself shall write a notice of it if opportunity offers.

Ever yours
D G Rossetti

I wd ask him to meet you at dinner if you like, with a few more friends.
Times don't come out. I have reason to believe it is by Dallas.

---

* "Marsyas flayed" = the satyr Marsyas challenged Apollo, the Greek god of song, to a flute-playing contest; he lost, and the god punished his impudence by cutting off his skin. See 64.161&n2.

1 The 3rd edition of *Poems* was advertised in *The Times* on 1 Jun (8). See also **125n2** & **129n2**. The blunder in the *HL* Sonnet "Barren Spring" was corrected in the 5th edition.

2 For Austin, see 69.112n4 and **104**. His review of *Poems* appeared in the *Standard* (26 May 70: 3). A hostile review of Austin's *Poetry of the Period* was printed in the *Pall Mall Gazette* (28 Apr 70). His 1869 articles in *Temple Bar* disparaging RB, ACS, & Tennyson (see 69.112n4) had probably irritated DGR.

3 Some fine paper copies of the 1st edition (WMR says 12) were printed on Small Whatman's handmade paper, bound in white cloth with gold lettering & decoration; these had orange-on-white decorated endpapers (see **82** & *Bibliography* 18). One of these copies was inscribed by DGR to ACS.

70.172 TO JOHN WILLIAM INCHBOLD
MS: UCLA.

Thursday [c. 2 June 1870]

Dear Inchbold

I saw Craven just now, who will call on you BEFORE 10 tomorrow (Friday) morning. He seemed not to know your work except the picture at the R. A. I posted him up in you as well as I could. He is a shy but excellent man, and really a *good* judge in his reticent way. His great admiration in landscape is for David Cox, of whose works he possesses a leading collection.

I told him I thought you might perhaps have no watercolours by you except portfolio drawings, & he said if he felt inclined to buy he might probably commission such a work as he would wish. He asked me particularly whether you were a man to whom it was possible to express opinions frankly without offence; and I told him you *are* (!!!) so there is a character for you to act up to. I think you may really make something of him probably if you humour him, and I do not think you will find him difficult to deal with, as he is a really good & thoroughly reliable fellow – in fact a genuine buyer in every way, as far as his means permit. He *never beats down*, so name lowest prices.

I wrote to Rae the day I saw you, but have not yet heard from him.

Craven may possibly call at the Hotel today on the chance of finding you, but if not will be sure to come tomorrow.[1]

Ever yours D G Rossetti

---

[1] JWI was often hard up; the Rossetti brothers tirelessly promoted his work. WMR recorded on 1 Jun that LMR informed him that Michael Spartali "has expressed some sort of intention to buy some view painted by Inchbold in the Isle of Wight" (*WMRD* 12). See 69.8n1.

70.173 TO FREDERICK STARTRIDGE ELLIS
MS: BL. Published: *FSE* 46; DW 1043.

Sunday [5 June 1870]

Dear Ellis

Can you dine with me tomorrow week (i.e. Monday after next) at 7-30? I shall be asking a few more friends.

I should remind you (in case an insatiable public should be demanding another "go" of me,) that there are some changes to make with which I must furnish you.

Another thing, – do make them print the flyleaf deeper & richer. Every copy I have seen lately is a beastly faint impression.

At last there is a slipshod but quotable notice of *Commonplace* in Athenæum.¹ I hear the Times one of me is done by Dallas (whenever it may appear²) so our virtue in sending him a copy may perhaps find its reward.

Ever yours
D G Rossetti

I must renew the Hake question when I see you.

¹ CGR's book was noticed here on 4 Jun 70.
² No review was printed in *The Times*.

70.174 TO FRANCIS HUEFFER

MS: Brotherton. Published: DW 1044.

16 Cheyne Walk/Chelsea
7 June 1870

My dear Sir

Will you give me the pleasure of dining here on Monday next at 7-30, when you will meet several of your friends.

Faithfully yours
D G Rossetti

70.175 TO WILLIAM MICHAEL ROSSETTI

MS: Brotherton. Published: DW 1053. Date: WMR.

[10 June 1870]

Dear W

You're quite right abt its being better not to talk about the point referred to, but I cannot but say in writing how annoyed I am to have annoyed you by so stupid a phrase. I can only just remember using it & don't know at all to what it could have referred.

By the bye I've not forgotten that I owe you £30 which I dare say you'll need when you are on the move this year.

I trust to send it you very soon.¹

Ever yours
D Gabriel R

¹ Unlike DGR's loans from WMR, which he sometimes repaid, his derogatory banter about his brother is not easily documented.

70.176 TO EDITOR OF *NOTES AND QUERIES*

Text: *N&Q* (18 Jun 70). Reprinted: DW 1055.

[c. 15 June 1870]

"*By this shore a plot of ground,*" &c.

The noble lyric in which these lines occur is called "The Ruined Chapel," and is by an excellent living poet, William Allingham, whose writings I should have supposed to be more universally known than such a query seems to imply.[1]

Dante G. Rossetti

[1] DGR was responding to a query in *N&Q* (see *N&Q* 4 Jun 70: 534) about authorship of 5 lines from WA's *Music Master* (1855), which had been quoted as an epigraph for 492 in the RA catalogue for 1870:

> By the shore, a plot of ground
> Clips a ruin'd chapel round,
> Buttress'd with a grassy mound,
> Where day and night and day go by
> And bring no touch of human sound.

70.177 TO FREDERICK STARTRIDGE ELLIS

MS: BL. Published: *FSE* 47; DW 1054.

17 June 1870

My dear Ellis

Some one told me yesterday that he was enquiring of one of the large cheap booksellers about the sale of my book, which was asserted to have been excellent in this particular quarter, but that "if pubd at 7/6 it would have gone off nearly as well as Tennyson." What do you think of making the next edition a cheap one when needed – say even 6/–? Would it not be likely to get a new class of buyers, whereas the first class is already supplied?[1]

Ever yours
DG Rossetti

[1] FSE never followed this suggestion.

70.178 TO JOHN BATES BEDFORD[1]

MS: Roger Peattie.

18 June 1870
16 Cheyne Walk
Chelsea

My dear Bedford,

As you wish your friends to state in writing how well they know your abilities as an artist and teacher of art, let me add my voice to those of others.

The importance of obtaining artists like yourself, and not mere mechanical drawing-masters, to impart instruction in our schools and colleges, is now getting better understood than formerly; and I cannot doubt that your candidateship for such a post will meet with due success.

Sincerely yours
Dante G. Rossetti

J. B. Bedford Esq

[1] John Bates Bedford (born 1823 in Yorkshire). London painter of literary, religious, portraits, flowers, and historical subjects. His works were shown at the Royal Academy and other London exhibitions between 1848 & 1886. The titles of his exhibited works show an affinity for the kinds of Arthurian and biblical subjects associated with the PRs.

70.179 TO EMILIE BARRINGTON[1]

MS: UBC.

20 June/1870
16 Cheyne Walk
Chelsea

Dear Mrs. Barrington

I am sorry I cannot come to your kind invitation for Wednesday, the more so that I should have had much pleasure in meeting Mr. Hutton.[2] But I have been for some time in a tug & tussle of impeded work, & shall not be fit to see or be seen now until I can say that my dragon is under me. So I must needs deny myself your pleasant dinner table; remaining

ever truly yours
D G Rossetti

[1] Born Emilie Isabel Wilson (c. 1844–1933), she was the daughter of James Wilson, founder of *The Economist*. Her early interest in drawing and painting was fostered by Watts &

Leighton. She later published books about both of them, several novels, & a collected edition of the works of her brother-in-law, Walter Bagehot.
2   R. H. Hutton (see 62.22n1) had reviewed *Poems* in the *Spectator* (11 Jun 70: 724–25).

70.180 TO MRS. GERALD BLUNT[1]

MS: Yale.

23 June/1870
16 *Cheyne Walk*
Chelsea

Dear Mrs. Blunt

I should have been very pleased to dine with you next Tuesday, but it is probable I may have visitors staying here that day & Wednesday. I am not yet sure of this, but in the uncertainty I cannot make an appointment for either day, so have no choice but to decline your kind invitation, as I could not leave the question open with any convenience to you.

Ever truly yours
D G Rossetti

[1] Frances Mary Forsteen (b.1820), daughter of Col. William Henry Forsteen and Eliza Fitzherbert. See also 69.22.

70.180.1 TO CHARLES AUGUSTUS HOWELL

MS: Texas.

Friday [24 June 1870]

Dear Howell

As you're always bobbing about town, wd you do me the favour to get me a *first-rate* box for Don Giovanni next *Thursday* at the Cov: Gard: Opera. I enclose cheque. Janey & Top & Bessie will go, – will you come? I suppose Kitty won't, but should rejoice if she could be persuaded – always if box big enough for all – like the last.

Your affec: Gabriel

P.S. Better send the box to *Janey*. I wish you'd buy a book of the Opera & send at same time to her.

70.181 TO FREDERIC JAMES SHIELDS

MS: NLS. Published: Mills 141; DW 1056.

25 June 1870

Dear Shields

Have you been able to do anything about the photo of the picture of Venus?

Your affec:
D G Rossetti

Do you know if the brothers Agnew have really got to hear of that blessed rhyme? I might wish to be writing them, but shouldn't if I thought they were riled.[1]

---

[1] Probably a reference to DGR's limerick on the art dealers Thomas and William Agnew:

> There are dealers in pictures named Agnew
> Whose soft soap would make an old rag new:
>   The Father of Lies
>   With his tail to his eyes
> Cries – "Go it, Tom Agnew, Bill Agnew!" (*RP* 496).

70.182 TO CHARLES AUGUSTUS HOWELL

MS: Texas. Published: Cline 5.

Sunday [26 June 1870]

Dear Howell

Can you, who are "Townier" in your habits than I, do me the good turn of getting an opera box as heretofore for Friday? Will you thank Kitty for letting me know that Don Giovanni is played that night. The best box available of course, as before. If at same time you would post to Janey, 26 Q. Square, a book of the opera, you would still further oblige her & me.

Your affec:
DG R

The box had also better be posted to her.

Kitty's portrait is done now, & improved since you saw it. It has no back board to the frame, but only a strainer which is not needed.

70.183 TO FRANCES CATHERINE HOWELL
MS: Texas.

[c. 30 June 1870]

Dear Kitty

I have heard nothing from Charley about the box. Can you write me a line by bearer on the subject.

Your affec:
Gabriel

70.184 TO FRANCES CATHERINE HOWELL
MS: Texas. Date: CFM.

Thursday night [30 June 1870]

Dear Kitty

If you can come to the Opera tomorrow (Friday) evening, Janey will be very glad. So in that case will you dine with us all at Cheyne Walk at 6.

Ever yours
Gabriel

70.185 TO JAMES SMETHAM
MS: V&A.

30 June 1870

Dear Smetham,

I was very glad to hear from you, & to learn what I hardly reckoned on – to wit that you were preparing good offices for my book. I trust you may find an easy "placement" for your article, & if you do not readily meet with this I wd ask my publisher if perhaps he could command a place for it somewhere. I feel confident it will class with the other articles I have seen of yours, as the best work of the kind I know at all nowadays. I am not sure whether you know what a real and quite unusual gift you have for this kind of writing.[1]

I do not generally court articles on my pictures, because as I do not exhibit, the evident complicity of such a thing is apt to look pretentious & necessarily displays its friendly origin. But in your hands I am glad the work should be done just in your own way.

The book continues to sell, & has now been reprinted in America, whence I have received various notices, generally enthusiastic but not without disparagement in some instances. My own impression is that the book will remain for those that like it, and that some here and there may perhaps always do so; but that its present decided success is destined to subside shortly. However I hope to run other ventures yet, in painting & possibly in poetry too, though about the latter I'm not very sure to any serious extent. I'm getting steadily forward with my big Dante picture, though it won't show anything for some time yet. I have put aside all other work till the back of that is broken.

I am sorry Graham & I did not reach you. It was talked of several times, but the evenings did not suit him, & one day when he proposed to go at short notice it was impracticable to me. However I dare say we shall find some other time to turn up in your quarter. I hope you're getting other work under way to your satisfaction. I got Davies's little pamphlet & have been meaning to write & thank him for it. I saw an extraneous notice of you at the end, & also of Mr. Somebody Else unknown to me, but who wore to me an American aspect.

I am able to work regularly now without any inconvenience, & hope this state of things may last. I really think regular work, such as sets the mind at rest, will help health & eyesight with me a good deal, when once I get thoroughly into the rut again which I am only beginning now to do since my first break down. However I must take care not to overdo exertion; but certainly at present am in every way vastly better.

I must try & get you down for a feed and a chat as soon as I am a little more certain of my footing with work; & meanwhile & ever am

affectionately yours
D G Rossetti

[1] JS was proposing to write an article on *Poems* but never did so (Smetham 262). See **205**.

70.186 TO FORD MADOX BROWN

MS: UBC.

Wednesday [June–July 1870]

My dear Brown

Have you got any draperies of mine? I am in want of some of those old mediæval ones – white velvet chiefly – & find an entry of having lent some to you, but do not know if they were returned. If you have any, Allan can take them.

I am going now to make the drapery studies for my picture, & suppose I ought at once to get your views about the lighting of it. Would it be possible for you to come down tomorrow daylight & see about this? It wd be doing me a great service.

Ever yours
D G Rossetti

I want particularly a dress slit at the sides – côte-hardie.[1]

---

[1] See the following letter.

70.187 TO CHARLES FAIRFAX MURRAY
MS: Texas.

Friday [June–July 1870]

My dear Murray

Morris tells me he gave you a lot of costumes. Now I am wanting some for that Dante picture – to wit – a cote-hardie & under kirtle for a woman – an angel's long dress for Love – a dress for Dante &c. I'm rather preoccupied these two days, but if I sent for them, wd you leave out for my messenger such things as you thought most likely to suit. It is possible that I may come myself on Monday instead, but if I sent then – or before, wd be much obliged for the loan if you can spare them.

Ever yours
DGRossetti

70.188 TO FORD MADOX BROWN
MS: UBC. Published: DW 1062.

Friday. [June–July 1870]

My dear Brown

I remember when I last saw you, you gave me a wrinkle or two about Benzine painting which I have entirely forgotten. I have got on to the big picture now, & shd be much obliged if you could kindly write me any details on the subject by *return of post* if possible – else Sunday is lost, & I am rather mithered* with the system.

Ever your D G Rossetti

* See 49.21n*.

70.189 TO CHARLES AUGUSTUS HOWELL

MS: Texas. Date: Unidentified endorsement.

[June–July? 1870]
16 Cheyne Walk
Chelsea

Dear Howell

I don't know what possessed me to suppose I could be doing Miss Story's likeness at present.[1] I shall have to stick to my picture simply till it is well forward or it will never get done at all. I hope this pentimento causes no inconvenience.

Ever yours
DG Rossetti

[1] Apparently the daughter of William Wetmore Story. See 64.17.

70.190 TO FREDERICK STARTRIDGE ELLIS

MS: BL. Published: *FSE* 56; DW 1072.

Friday [1 July 1870]

Dear Ellis

Thanks for the Yankee Book. Why did they print from the first edn – not the 2nd? You might direct their attention to this.[1]

I hear of a review I never saw in the Illustrated News. Could you find the no: and send it me?[2]

Ever yours
D G Rossetti

[1] FSE had sent DGR *Poems* as published by Roberts Bros. The 2nd edition would have made a better copy-text than the 1st since it contained the poet's corrections (see **129n2**).
[2] The *Illustrated London News* carried no review of *Poems*.

70.191 TO FREDERICK STARTRIDGE ELLIS

MS: BL. Published: *FSE* 48; DW 1057.

5 July 1870

Dear Ellis

The numerals remain dark to me, but we can talk when I see you. I'll send you in a few days the last corrections, but whether they *are* the last when stereotyping comes in question, I must consider. Morris seems very doubtful as to the advisability of a cheap edition at all – quoting Tennyson's non-adoption of any such plan; & I should think it might possibly be a mistake after all. But this we can see about. He will perhaps have mentioned to you a sort of proposal to reprint him & me from a German publisher, who is going to call here today.¹ I shall give no answer till I have talked it over with you.

I *very much* want Lewis Filmore's translation of *Faust*, which is much the best I ever saw, though no one seemed to think so. It was published some twenty years ago or more in a series (printed I think both in large 8vo double columns & in a smaller shape also) called something like "Smith's Classical Library." Whether it was the firm now known as Smith & Elder I don't know. I fancy the translation was also republished later in an independent form. I should be *very* glad if you could get me a copy as *soon as possible.* I should think it possible something might be heard of it through Williams and Norgate, or Nutt.²

Ever yours
D G Rossetti

¹ Dunkel (see the following letter). DGR eventually published with Tauchnitz: *Poems* appeared in 1873 and *B&S* in 1882, both volumes edited and introduced by Franz Hueffer (1845–89), a music critic, Wagnerian scholar, & literary man who married FMB's daughter Cathy in 1872.
² Published by W. Smith in 1841 in "Smith's Standard Library." Williams & Norgate specialized in scientific books. The Nutt family firm (printers, booksellers, & publishers) was established in the 17th century and directed by, first, Elizabeth, then David and Alfred Nutt.

70.192 TO FREDERICK STARTRIDGE ELLIS

MS: BL. Published: *FSE* 49; DW 1058.

Wednesday [6 July 1870]

Dear Ellis

Please send me 2 copies of my d – d book. The cry is still "Give, give." Also, pending the discovery of Filmore's Faust (which however I want) please send me Theodore Martin's at once. Pubd by Blackwood, cheap ed. 3/6.

The German Publisher (named Dunkel I think) came yesterday, but managed to come just when the room was crowded & went away without saying any thing, as it was not practicable. Dr. Hüffer (who introduced me to him) tells me he (Dunkel) is projecting an English series on the Tauchnitz plan. Wd you write me a line *at once* whether you see any objection to Morris's books & mine being included, & if not, what you think ought to be paid for mine. The great Top had better settle for himself. I have promised to write

Hüffer a line on the subject *before Saturday* on which day he leaves England. Of course I suppose much cannot be got. Dr. Hüffer's address is 11 (I think) Charlotte St. Portland Place, in case you wished to see him, but I suppose you will not care to do so. I suppose on the whole it wd be advantageous (wd it not?) to get the things pubd in Germany, as a sort of advt – & no doubt they wd not come into England & interfere with our sale.

Ever yours
D G Rossetti

Should you think of calling on Hüffer you wd find him a nice fellow. He is writing an article for a German Quarterly on Morris & self, as well as Tennyson &c., with translations.

70.193 TO GEORGE RAE

MS: LLAG. Date: Unidentified endorsement.

Friday [8 July 1870]

My dear Rae

I am sorry not to see Mrs. Rae and yourself, but every moment of my daylight is due to models just now. Besides, the studio is so entirely blocked up with a big picture just beginning & with nothing to show for itself as yet, that I am obliged to defer all proposed visits in the impossibility of looking at anything under such circumstances.

With kindest remembrances

Very truly yours
D G Rossetti

70.194 TO GEORGE RAE

MS (unsigned fragment): LLAG.

16 July 1870

My dear Rae

The last I heard from you about the chalk drawing (in a letter I must still have) was, as you will remember, that you could not decide till Mrs. Rae saw it & did not wish me to refrain from placing it else-where meanwhile. Accordingly I engaged it to some one else after due delay, but it is not yet finished & therefore still with me. . . .[1]

---

[1] See 69.132.

70.195 TO HORACE M. MOULE[1]

MS: McGill.

21 July 1870
16 Cheyne Walk
Chelsea

My dear Sir

Lord Herbert of Cherbury is the writer whom I most readily call to mind at this moment as having used the metre in question: I think Donne is another, and I am confident I have met with it elsewhere also.

As for that little piece of my own, I should have preferred omitting it, but for some bye-reasons; only if it *was* to be re-printed, the note seemed unavoidable at this date.[2]

Yours faithfully
D G Rossetti

Horace M. Moule Esq

[1] (1832–1873) classicist & teacher; friend of Thomas Hardy whom he knew from the 1850s. He committed suicide in Sep 73.
[2] DGR seems to be answering a query about "My Sister's Sleep." A note below the first 3 stanzas (*Poems* 169) reads: "This little poem, written in 1847, was printed in a periodical at the outset of 1850. The metre, which is used by several old English writers, became celebrated a month or two later on the publication of *In Memoriam*." The periodical was the *Germ*. DGR worried that he would be perceived as borrowing what quickly became known as "the *In Memoriam* stanza" (see 69.144&n2).

70.196 TO FREDERICK STARTRIDGE ELLIS

MS: BL. Published: *FSE* 50; DW 1059.

23 July 1870

My dear Ellis

I have been very busy, or shd have sent before the corrections I now enclose. I suppose they are in time still, or you wd have written again for them. If you will look carefully to the changes being correctly made, I need not see a proof. But will you look *very* carefully.[1] The 3rd 1000 is doubtless not yet printed off – still less in circulation. But it wd be convenient to me at this moment if you could let me have my £150 on it – that is if not inconvenient to yourself. If you can, will you kindly pay it in to my account at the Union Bank of London, Chancery Lane.

Ever yours
D G Rossetti

[Enclosure]

Page 3 line 3
For sp*a*ke *read* sp*o*ke. ["The Blessed Damozel"]

Page 7 line 11
Put full stop after *ceased.* ["The Blessed Damozel"]

Page 68 line 21
For *darkness* read *dimness.* ["A Last Confession"]

Page 142 line 4
Erase the 2 words "*Nay, flame* & put instead the one word *Fire* ["Sister Helen"]

Page 167 line 11
Restore *st* fallen out at end of the line. ["The Card-Dealer"]

Page 222 line 5
for *now,* read *here,* ["Barren Spring"]

Do line 12
Put *comma* instead of *full stop* at end of line. ["Barren Spring"]

Page 224 line 7
For *the* read *this* ["The Choice II"]

Page 264
make lines 12 & 13 read thus:

To-night shall echo back the sea's dull roar
With a vain wail from passion's tide-strown shore ["The Wine of Circe"].

---

1 On the enclosure DGR corrected the 4th edition for the 5th, in which these changes all appear (see **129&n2**).

70.197 TO JOHN ABRAHAM HERAUD[1]

MS: PML. Published: DW 1060.

16 Cheyne Walk/Chelsea
23 July 1870

Dear Sir

I have to thank you for your very kind gift of the "In-Gathering." Among the poems it contains, my own attention is particularly attracted to the Sonnets, in which I see you allow yourself the wide range of treatment which seems to me unavoidable if an unfettered scope of ideas is to be dealt with. There is one license which I confess I should be disposed to question, – that of commencing a Sonnet with a rhymed couplet; and accordingly it appears to me rather unfortunate that the first of the series should afford an instance of this. But to bring much various thought within such rigid structural limits is an effort of precisely the kind which must ever be most tempting to the practised artist.

Again thanking you for your gift, I am, my dear Sir,

Yours faithfully
D. G. Rossetti

John A. Heraud Esq

---

[1] (1799–1887), a reformer & editor of the *New Monthly Magazine*, had sent DGR his *The In-Gathering. Cimon and Pero: A Chain of Sonnets: Sebastopol etc.* (Simpkin, Marshall, 1870).

70.198 TO GEORGE PRICE BOYCE

MS: University College.

Tuesday [26 July 1870]

Dear Boyce

Can you come in to dinner tomorrow (Wednesday) at 7, or else after dinner at 9. There is to be a mesmeric adept here and we are to have some experiments on some girls he will bring. A former evening of the kind here afforded some interesting results.[1]

Ever yours
D G Rossetti

---

[1] GPB described this "mesmeric phenomenon" in his diary. It was attended by Boehm, Chapman, Dannreuther, Luke Ionides, FRL, WMR, HVT, & the Whistler brothers (*GPBD* 11). WMR also recorded the event in his diary for 27 Jul, noting that DGR had held a

similar séance "a short while back" (*WMRD* 19–20). HTD describes the earlier gathering in his *Recollections* (1984): 48–49. Invited guests were HTD, CAH, FRL, Alexander, Lord Lindsay, WMR, & G.A. Sala. Lord Lindsay & Sala were both members of the Spiritualism Committee of the London Dialectical Society along with Bergheim (see **200n9** & **Volume V: Appendix 7** on DGR's interest in spiritualism).

70.199 TO FREDERICK STARTRIDGE ELLIS

MS: BL. Published: *FSE* 51; DW 1061.

16 Cheyne Walk

29 July 1870

Dear Ellis

Never mind about the tin, if, as I judge may be the case from your note, it is more convenient to you to defer the matter. Thanks for writing me word again about it. I suppose all poetry will be as dead as ditch water now with this blessed war.[1] I send another correction overpage.

Ever yours

D G Rossetti

Page 54 lines 3 & 4
Read –

> "Thy conquering guest returns to-night,
>   And yet &c.

I think also I omitted to notify a semicolon which is wanting at the end of line 6 page 159.[2]

---

[1] The war was the Franco-Prussian War, which had started on 19 Jul 70.
[2] Further corrections for the 5th edition of *Poems* (see **196**).

70.200 TO WILLIAM BELL SCOTT

MS: Princeton.

10 Aug 1870

16 Cheyne Walk
Chelsea

Dear Scotus

I have often thought of the Penkill conclave as something in which I had a vested interest, though I have not written yet. I wish I saw any prospect of reaching those quarters this year. How lovely it must all be just now, and how much I should enjoy a few days with you if they could be had more readily &

London reached again without so much labour. But I have got quite immersed in my work for the present, and am only too glad to see it getting forward after so long an interim of struggling with impediments. I have got 3 of my figures nearly finished on the canvas now – viz: Love, Beatrice, & the Lady at B's head. In 3 weeks more I expect to have all the figures done except final glazings which I leave for the general completion of the picture. After these 3 weeks I may perhaps make my way to the farmhouse in Sussex for a month, taking some other work with me, and then back to London to finish the big picture I hope well within the year. It takes me, as I anticipated, wonderfully little time to do when once the drapery studies are so thoroughly made beforehand as to secure no mulls on the canvas. I am beginning to believe now that serious work is setting in for me, and that I shall get a good number of my long cherished & deferred subjects really painted within a few years. Whether sales may go on however with this blessed war and all that may yet come of it (and whether consequently one will be let to work at all) Heaven only knows. Poetry is at a discount already no doubt, and it is as well not to think much about that. Did you see the smash up of me in Blackwood (article "New Books.")? I don't know who did it, but I thought all along it might happen, as you know Blackwood & Co. wanted to publish the book, only I stuck to Ellis.[1] Now it is not to be supposed that if they *had* been the publishers the article wd ever have come out. It really has bored me not at all, neither have several Yankee attacks (notably one in the *Nation*, written I suspect by poetaster Lowell) which have been sent me.[2] Whether the book will suffer here or there as to sale I cannot tell. The 2nd thousand is not yet sold out, and the Times article (though long ago as I heard in type) will not appear now I shd judge, when a whole page of the Times is taken up every day with a map. The *North British* had a beneficent short notice of me – by whom I don't know.[3]

Give me some news of Penkill. There news *is* news: here it is so plentiful that one has to give up collecting or conveying it. What are you up to, and Miss Boyd? Mrs. Scott is now I judge with you. To both my love. Is Miss Losh coming?

Swinburne, after many vicissitudes, is safe at his father's. He should risk everything now to bring his book out, as it is the only thing that would sell at this moment, and even if Hotten's threats are more than mere Fustian, the profits would cover law costs and all.[4]

Miss Deverell (eldest sister of poor Walter) has been at me again just now about those pictures I have here, & I wrote offering the two (*Hamlet* & *Irish Beggars*) together to Leathart for £40. But he won't buy. Do you think a word from you as to their merits wd do anything? They are dirt cheap of course at the money, and she'd really take 30 I believe. She is in a melancholy position and most anxious to get a housekeeper's or useful companion's place anywhere. She is over 40 and has very good health – is perfectly willing to drop the "lady" if she can only be independent in a humble way. £20 or 30 a year wd content her well. She is very nice and likeable. Do you think there wd be a chance in any quarter you know? I have written to Ruskin (and heard vaguely in reply), to Leathart (vague also) and to the Howards (no reply as yet) detailing the case.[5]

Brown got his Romeo picture off to Leathart without showing it to a soul. His Byron designs have been woefully mauled by the steel-engraver, but the book is nevertheless a wonderful three-&-sixpenny one.[6] William goes on steadily with his editorship of the series, reading & correcting the proofs of all the whole squad of British Parnassus as if they were a handful of police reports in the Times. All his memoirs are now I think written.[7]

Jones has given up the Old Water Colour. They asked him to reconsider his resolution but he sticks to it & is painting entirely in oil at present.[8]

I had 2 mesmeric séances here which were tremendous larks and very surprising. They came off in the tent. The operator was one Bergheim who is a "wunner" at it, and the patients 2 girls brought by him who certainly afforded fine sport. However all who witnessed it were astounded and impressed.[9]

Topsy will get his last vol. of Earthly Paradise out at Xmas, & after that means to drop poetry & paint pictures.

Now good bye, dearest Scotus. I am going out after a hard day's painting (Miss Spartali's head in my picture) for my solitary night-walk as far as Maiden Lane, where I shall meet Allingham at Rule's oyster shop & have a feed with him. It is a nice old fashioned nook, which ought to be, & perhaps is, known to you.

Your affec: D.Gabriel R.

---

[1] An unsigned review of *Poems* appeared in *Blackwood's Edinburgh Magazine* (Aug 70: 178–83).W. E. Fredeman tentatively identified the author as Mrs. Margaret Oliphant, a regular contributor to the periodical. However, in *Pre-Raphaelitism in the Nineteenth-Century Press: A Bibliography* (Victoria, B.C.: English Library Studies, 2002): 77, Thomas J. Tobin's suggests WBS as the author. See Spector, "The Unattributed *Blackwood's* Review of D.G. Rossetti's *Poems*, 1870" (*N&Q* 23 [1976]: 398). The review contains the following passage: "There is something in the character and temper of a painter so contemptuous of common public opinion that he refuses to exhibit his pictures – and of a poet who keeps his productions for some twenty years in the dark before he condescends to unfold them to the common eye – which in the first place attracts the imagination. Such a man walks serene at a height inaccessible to the common din, the comments and criticisms of lower earth. Such a man is too far removed from us to desire to be understood upon our level; he addresses himself to the choice souls – the world within a world – the select of humanity. In none of these poems, however, is there the least indication of a new poet arisen to bless us."

2   The American poet, essayist, & diplomat James Russell Lowell (1819–91) was probably the author of a review of *Poems* in a New York periodical (*Nation* 263 [14 Jul 70]: 29–30).
3   *The North British Review* printed an unsigned review of *Poems* (13 [Jul 70]: 598–99). See **70**.
4   ACS stayed with DGR for several days in late June following his resignation from his club, where his drunkenness had been the cause of another disturbance. From 16CW he wrote WMR that "Gabriel and Fanny have nursed me up again" (Lang 2: 357), and shortly he returned to his Dorset Street lodgings. He did not manage to stay sober, and in early July suffered an attack of "delirium tremens" (*WMRD* 17), necessitating his removal by his father to the family home at Holmwood, Henley-on-Thames. His former publisher John Camden Hotten was claiming that ACS was under contract to him for all his future books, threatening legal action if the poet brought out *Songs before Sunrise* with FSE. WMR & CAH were representing ACS' interests in this matter (see Lang 2: 357–59 & 361–64). Later he hired TWD to deal with his ongoing problems with Hotten, which did not cease with that publisher's death in Jun 73; for a full account of ACS' subsequent problems with publishers, whom he treated with aristocratic disdain, see Henderson, *Swinburne* 178–80.
5   For the postmortem negotiations for the disposition of WHD's unsold and unfinished works, see **224**.
6   FMB's watercolour *Romeo and Juliet* and his series *Byron's Dream* are now in the Whitworth Art Gallery, Manchester.
7   WMR was writing Prefaces for Moxon's Popular Poets; these "memoirs" were later revised and collected as *Lives of Famous Poets* (Moxon, 1878).
8   A committee of the OWCS had objected to the chief work EBJ sent for exhibition that year, *Phyllis and Demophoön*, because the male figure was naked. At the President's request, he removed his picture from the gallery without objection; but after the exhibition closed, he resigned from the Society, stating: "I accept your desertion of me this year merely as the result of so complete a want of sympathy between us in matters of Art, that it is useless for my name to be enrolled amongst yours any longer" (*EBJ* 2: 11–12). The picture was bought by FRL.
9   WMR mentions EBB's interest in 1860, and his own beliefs (*SR* 1: 241) – he also attended séances in Nov 65, one with WBS (*RP* 154–161). See **198&n1** & **Volume V: Appendix 7** on DGR's interest in spiritualism.

70.201 TO GEORGE RAE

MS: LLAG.

Tuesday [mid-August 1870]
16 Cheyne Walk
Chelsea

My dear Rae

I'm still in the same plight as to a blockaded studio and nothing to show.¹ But I mustn't say no again to your proposed visit. Will you dine with me on Friday then at 7, in order that there may be something to discuss instead of works of fine art. Say yes by return & I'll try & get Brown to meet you.

Ever yours
D G Rossetti

1   See **193**.

70.202 TO WILLIAM ALLINGHAM

MS: Huntington. Excerpt: *WA/GBH* 294. Published: DW 1063.

Tuesday [16 August 1870]

Dear Allingham

I'm sorry to have missed you yesterday. Surely my letter went out to you before 5. Could you come tomorrow (Wedy) instead? 7 o'clock dinner, till near which hour I shall not be free of work.

Have you seen the last Blackwood? If you have not, & need a relish before dinner, try it instead of Gin & bitters. What Brother Bard but must find an added zest in the meal dispensed by the hand of detected mediocrity?

Ever yours
D G Rossetti

70.203 TO FREDERICK STARTRIDGE ELLIS

MS: BL. Published: *FSE* 52; DW 1064.

16 Cheyne Walk
19 Aug.1870

Dear Ellis

Overpage 2 more emendations for next edition.[1]

"Blackwood" & the "Nation" have come too late to smash me, as no doubt the war has been beforehand with them as regards poetry in general. I suspect the "Nation" is by Poetaster Lowell. The other genius I can't guess at. The number of editions seems to stick in his gizzard. You won't have forgotten Blackwood & Co. having wanted to publish the book themselves. "Illæ lacrymæ" (sive pedita)* may perhaps be thus partly traceable.

How about the Translations? Are you disposed to publish them on same terms as the Poems?[2] If so my ardour will be stimulated in getting to work on them for Xmas, when I suppose they ought to come out. I want to do so, but am most frightfully busy with a big picture which I am resolved the year shall see completed.

Ever yours
D G Rossetti

P.S. I think it wd be time to quote something new as well as the old when advertising, to make head against the foe. The Westminster & North British have been civil, though short. So also I think was The Contemporary, – but that I have not by me. Perhaps you have. Also I wd not always quote Topsy first, as it seems rather like a joint stock Company, though of course he well deserves the place. I shd rather like to quote Blackwood (I remember Swinburne once doing the like) but it would be taking too much notice of him perhaps. I enclose the Westr & Nth British marked for extract. In the last Athenæum advt there is a fault of print which I enclose corrected. I think it wd be as well to carry on the war by putting a new advt (in the Athenæum perhaps best) at once with the new notices. If any old must be omitted I think the Academy & Fortnightly shd be this once, as being friends in the camp.

What a pity Swinburne doesn't bring out his book now. It wd pay law costs and all, if these are not a mere bugbear as I believe.

If you've got Contemporary Review, I'd try & make an extract from that also if worth it which I forget now.

[Enclosure]

Page 51
After stanza ending "He kissed her face" insert following stanza.

> Born of the day that died, that eve
> Now dying sank to rest;
> And he, in likewise taking leave,
> Once with a heaving breast
> Looked to the west.

Page 143 line 18
read –

> "But he and I are sadder still,"

N.B. Will you look carefully to the proofs, and see specially that they don't put "sunk" for "sank" in the stanza above, as they nearly always do.

---

* ' "Illae lacrymae" (Sive pedita)' = In Terence's *Andria* I i l.126; *Hinc illae lacrymae* means "hence those tears." The phrase added by DGR means "or, rather, farts." The final word in the much-echoed Latin tag is today spelled "lacrimae" but DGR's spelling was typical for that time.
1   See **196&n1**.
2   FSE's generous plan with *Poems* was to pay the author's royalty as soon as an edition was in type; he agreed to follow it again with *Dante and His Circle*.

70.204 TO CHARLES AUGUSTUS HOWELL

MS: Texas. Published: Cline 111. Date: CAH.

Friday [19 August 1870]

Dear Howell

Wd it suit you to take your pick of the drawings we were looking over the other day – the studies for my picture & the other odd ones (including the Miss W[ilding]. I did that day) – and buy 20 at 10£ apiece – £200 in all. I am wanting tin *at once*, & for that reason wd part with them in that way if it could be had *now*. You could take most of the drawings *at once*, though I might need to keep one or two for use.

Ever yours D. G. R.

I shall be very busy tomorrow & Sunday. If you want to see me could you look in Monday about 5?

70.205 TO JAMES SMETHAM

MS: V&A.

19 Aug. 1870

Dear Smetham

I remember you told me you were beneficently reviewing me at some length – poems & pictures together. Have you gone on with it and have you found a "placement?" If not, I think I might possibly suggest one. The foe has reared his head in Blackwood & it is time to organize defences. Not that I am in much of a funk for I suppose in any case the book will go on selling if vital & would have stopped in any case if not. The war too I fear is a worse extinguisher than Blackwood. The fun is that B. wanted to publish the book himself, & wd probably then, (one may venture to surmise) have fired his artillery from quite another position. However I'm not much thinking of poetry now, as I'm much stronger & have been getting to work finally on my big picture. In another 3 weeks or so I expect to have all the figures in on the canvas. I shall then recruit for a while in the country, & back at it again, finishing I hope before the year is out. A big picture is glorious elbow-room for one's efforts. In another week or so I trust to try & get you down to spend an evening & dine in the tent. What are you up to? But perhaps indeed you are away.

In haste

Affectionately yours
D G Rossetti

70.205.1 TO CHARLES AUGUSTUS HOWELL

MS: Texas. Written on WG:DGR (19 Aug).

[c. 20 August 1870]

Dr Owl

This from Graham. You had better read it where marked. You see he has given the 50 for *Taylor's* panel.[1]

D.G.R

Address

Urrard House
Blair Athole
Perthshire

[1] The relevant passages in WG's letter read: "I enclose a cheque for the price of the panel for which of course I could not think of making any lower offer under the circumstances you mention. . . . Maybe[?] some day if you have the chance if you would ask Mr Howell whether he ever got a letter I wrote him three weeks ago & have never had a reply to."

70.206 TO FORD MADOX BROWN

MS: UBC. Excerpt: *FMB* 259–60; DW 1066. Date: WMR.

Friday [26 August 1870]

My dear Brown –

My soul is vexed with the following point: – The women in my picture being 62 inches high, will it do for the man to be 65 inches, that is 3 inches more, or shd he be taller? I've got him traced on the canvas & fancy he looks all right, but am rather nervous about beginning to paint him lest he shd possibly need heightening. The women's faces are 5½ inches long. Do you think ½ an inch more is enough for *his* face – i.e. 6 inches? Proportions always bother me more than anything else.

I've been meaning to get up to you in the evenings, but unable. May probably come Sunday.

The soul of Nolly will be sad to hear that yesterday morning the poor little mole was found dead after being all right overnight & eating worms like fun. I had gone to the expense of a magnificent glazed mansion for him which was picked up at a broker's shop – the glazier having declared it wd not cost more than putting glass into Nolly's box, & be stronger. Both boxes are now at Nolly's service if of any use to him in his menageristic manœuvres.

Your affec:
D G R

70.207 TO FREDERIC JAMES SHIELDS

MS: Kansas. Excerpt: Horne 90–92; Mills 142–44. Published: DW 1065.

28 Aug. 1870
16 Cheyne Walk/Chelsea

Dear Shields

I cannot easily thank you enough for so much friendliness under such very troublesome circumstances. I now regret extremely that I did not write on receipt of your former letter, as I meant to do, to beg you to take no further trouble in a matter which presented such unexpected obstacles. But I delayed doing so through excessive preoccupation at the moment, & then thought that it was no use writing as further steps were probably already being taken. I can now only say that I could never have conceived from Mr. Mitchell's very straightforward conduct on former occasions, that he was capable of so much changeableness and disregard of his word. I do not like to make a cause of quarrel with him (after very agreeable relations hitherto) out of a matter which, in itself, is of no importance to me; but am excessively irritated at having been led on by him into causing you so much disturbance, and on that account write him with this to express my surprise at his conduct. As far as myself am concerned, it is well the matter is no more important than it is; but I feel how much apology I owe you for this unpleasantness which I could not have foreseen.[1]

I wish I could say something to any good purpose on what gives me great anxiety – the infinitely more important matter of your own affairs to which you make some allusion, & which I assure you, already often occurred to my mind. It is most disappointing to me that the various conversations I have had with Mr. Graham at intervals about his negotiations with you should have had no better result. Here again is a man, usually most honorable in my experiences of him, behaving with unaccountable disregard of obligations really incurred by himself. Nothing could give me greater pleasure than being able, should such opportunity occur, to be of any service to yourself who have so often served me so warmly and at the cost of so much personal exertion. Is there any way suggesting itself to your own mind by which I could be of the least use in forwarding any object you have in view? If there were, the very friendliest thing you could do would be to let me know.[2] Of your health you do not specially speak, nor do I gather clearly whether what you say of your "suffering" from this truly atrocious and insufferable war relates simply to what all must feel or to more direct influence of a baneful kind on your own immediate prospects. Such would doubtless be a possible result for any of us, as there is no knowing the moment at which retrenchment may be forced upon the wealthy classes of this country by the state of affairs abroad or even at home, and naturally art goes first to the wall.

You allude in the kindest way to my poetry, and say also that you would like to write me something about "Jenny." Pray believe that anything coming from you could only be what I should sincerely desire to hear, whatever its point of view; only I really think there must be too many affairs of your own to attend to, for it to be worth your while to dwell on my verses except by word of mouth when we meet again which it would please me much to hope might be soon. The book has prospered quite beyond any expectations of mine, though just lately signs of depreciation have been apparent in the press ("Blackwood" to wit,) I am only surprised that nothing of a decided kind in the way of opposition shd have appeared before. However I have also been surprised (and pleasantly) to find such things producing a much more transient & momentary impression of unpleasantness than I should have expected – indeed I might almost say none at all; particularly as I cannot help in this instance putting against the Blackwood article the fact that B. & Co. wished to publish the book & I went elsewhere. But above all, these things probably do not touch me much for the reason that my mind is now quite occupied with my painting, and has been for some time past. I am making very rapid progress with my large picture of "Dante's Dream", about 10 or 11 feet by 7. A big picture is glorious work, really rousing to every faculty one has or ever thought one might have, and I hope I am doing better in this than hitherto. In another fortnight or so I shall have all the figures painted on the canvas and only the glazing of the draperies left to do. The background is as yet untouched & before I resume the picture after bringing it to the completion of the figures as above I intend to go for a month or so into the country to recruit. However, though I have been working decidedly hard, I find that it chiefly seems to have the effect of consolidating & steadying the beneficial results which my spring trip to the country had already had on my health. I am not at present sensible of any inconvenience with my eyes, though working good hours daily, and have not been for months past.

I have often spoken with Brown about you, and need not tell you what a constant interest he takes in all that concerns you. He himself is, I am glad to think, doing well at present, and is just thinking of an excursion to Newcastle & perhaps to the Highlands in company with his wife. He lately finished his large oil picture of *Romeo & Juliet*, but I did not see it, as he would not show it while in progress, & most stealthily and surreptitiously spirited it away at the last moment to Leathart who is its possessor. I believe however it is one of his best works. His children are all at work & making great progress. You probably know of Burne Jones's having left the O. W. C. Society, but probably will be surprised to hear that Burton has now done so also. I believe B. finds it necessary to take to larger work, & thinks such scale better suited to oil; but his warm feeling on Jones's behalf in the differences occurring between him & the Society has doubtless led to his taking the step at this particular moment.

I will give your kind remembrances to Dunn, whom I saw yesterday again for the first time since a month's stay he has been making in Cornwall on the occasion of his father's sudden death. He has been doing some really very good work of his own in oil lately, and is undoubtedly making great advances. Indeed, if he goes on like this, he must make his mark.

Let me again beg of you, before I conclude, that you will tell me without the slightest reserve of any way that may occur to you in which I could serve you at all. To know that you were happier would be a real encouragement to me.

Believe me as ever, my dear Shields,

Affectionately yours,
D. G. Rossetti

[1] See **89&n1**.
[2] For business troubles between FJS & WG concerning commissions, see 69.136, 140, 182, & 221.

70.208 TO BARBARA LEIGH SMITH BODICHON

MS: PML. Published: DW 1067.

29 August 1870
16 Cheyne Walk

Dear Mdme Bodichon

I am afraid you must have been surprised at not hearing from me before this in answer to a letter of yours some considerable time ago. The fact is I lost that letter & delayed answering in the hopes that it might turn up for the consultation of its contents in answering. Every now and then I attacked hopeless heaps of paper in corners of my studio, but never found it, and the matter lapsed through preoccupation. I remember you asked me whether I had brought away a book – I forget what – from Scalands – but I am quite sure I brought none. Also there was a question about a little Dante left there by me, which I will ask you either to send or keep till I see you.

Another matter has been much too long delayed which I hope will fulfil itself just before or after your receipt of this letter. I allude to my duty towards your cellar. Some wine is now on its way to Scalands to replace my share of the ravages. Stillman was always to have talked over this subject with me but never did up to the time of his leaving, and I myself continually forgot it when I saw him. Perhaps you heard from him as to his share in the matter. I believe he had kept some notes, but in the absence of these, I have been obliged to mass my obligations to various vintages into 3 simplified classes of sherry claret & champagne.[1]

I have heard of you more than once from Allingham, & certainly expected to have seen you before now & put to use the rooms at Glottenham which I suppose are still in my nominal occupation. I think however my best plan will now be to pay up & take my chance of getting them again when I really want them; as the luxury of working after so much enforced idleness has been so great to me that I know I shall not be able to leave off till pulled up short again by a break down of some sort. I am really getting on fast now with my big picture, and expect to have all the figures nearly done by a fortnight hence. I have been a wonderful deal better ever since my visit to Sussex which I certainly think must have been the direct cause of the improvement, while steady work has since consolidated the benefit instead of impairing it as I feared possible. I feel no inconvenience with my eyes now, though working good hours & never missing a day.

I duly got the Service of Bears &c from Switzerland, but the packing was so shockingly bad – amounting indeed to no packing at all – that a great proportion of them were smashed to atoms before their arrival. However a quantity of capital things remain, & I would even be glad to go in for another similar lot – or one differing in detail but of the same class. I wonder wd there be no means of protesting in the proper quarter against the infamous packing. I expect the people who sell them there think they can only be wanted in England for use in madhouses, to prevent the patients from throwing prettier things at each other's heads. Did you have a package at the same time I wonder, or did Miss Edwards? & were they all in the same condition?

No doubt Scalands and the neighbourhood must have been looking most lovely all this time, while I have seen no daylight hardly except on the surface of my canvas. I suppose you have heard from Stillman & know that he contrived, poor fellow, to have another accident on board ship before he got to America – breaking one of his ribs. I fear he has not been very well ever since.

With kindest remembrances, believe me, dear Mdme Bodichon,

Ever truly yours,
D. G. Rossetti

[1] See **99n2**.

70.209 TO LUCY MADOX BROWN[1]

MS: UBC. Published: DW 1503. Date: WMR. DW mistakenly date this letter "[? summer 1874]" and identify the addressee as "Mrs. WMR." However, it was in the spring and early summer of 1870 (11 Mar–9 May), when DGR and WJS shared Barbara Bodichon's house Scalands, that DGR rented temporarily, and considered taking on a short lease, half of a nearby house at Glottenham. Thus, the letter was clearly written after DGR's return from Scalands.

Thursday [early Summer 1870]

Dear Lucy

I ought to tell you (with apology) that I have lent my rooms at Glottenham now to Janey Morris who is so ill again that she *must* get away as soon as possible. I know you will pardon this under the circumstances, though I had hoped you might avail yourself of my proposal. And perhaps this may yet be, as I suppose her stay will be short, & my own use of the rooms is sure to be very intermittent.[2]

Ever yours
DG Rossetti

Don't let your Papa forget Monday.

[1] (1843–1894), eldest daughter of FMB, later Mrs. William Michael Rossetti.
[2] DGR's proposal to LMR is uncertain but must have involved the possibility of her staying in the house.

70.209.1 TO CHARLES FAIRFAX MURRAY

MS: Texas.

[August–September 1870?]

Dear Murray

I believe what I send are yours, & are all I can lay my hands on at this moment, besides one or two I am still using & which I venture to keep as the things are only wanted for Topsaic uses.

Ever yours
DGR

70.210 TO JOHN POLLARD SEDDON

MS: Texas.

Thursday. [c. 1 September 1870]

My dear Seddon

I possess no pictures of Blake's, & could certainly give no information about him beyond what exists in print. Moreover, my studio is at present blocked up completely by a large picture with which I am very busy, & which I shall not show to any one till finished – thus rendering it difficult for me to receive friends & forcing me in many cases lately to postpone proposed visits to me. Will you pardon me if I do so in this case, hoping to see you here instead at some better opportunity.

With kind remembrances

Ever yours
D G Rossetti

70.211 TO VERNON LUSHINGTON[1]

MS: European Art Gallery, Dallas, Texas. Published: DW 1068.

4 Sept 1870
16 Cheyne Walk
Chelsea

My dear Vernon

I'm very sorry to say No; but just now I'm a slave to a big picture which blocks up all my studio. It is not yet in a state to show, (nor do I mean to show it till done which will be about the end of the year,) and everything else has had to be turned into holes and corners out of the studio where there is no light to see anything. So I am obliged to put off all visits for the present.

Pray pardon & believe me

Ever yours
D G Rossetti

---

[1] See entries for Lushington in **Index, Volume II**.

70.212A THEODORE MARTIN TO DANTE GABRIEL ROSSETTI

MS: BL. Enclosed with the following letter.

31 Onslow Square
28th April 1870

My dear Rossetti,

I was on the point of writing to express my personal thanks to you for the admirable additions you have made to our poetical literature, – for I got your book as soon as it was out – when a copy of it with your inscription reached me. I will not say, how highly I value this act of remembrance, & how doubly welcome it has made your book. Now I can have a copy both here & in my country home, when I want to read something that speaks to the inner nature, which the trivialities of daily life do so much to overlay. I am an old lover of your writings. Well do I remember the intense delight I had when I first came in the Exhibition Catalogue on your sonnet, "This is that blessed Mary." It stamped itself on my memory as indelibly as the picture it accompanied, & I can even now repeat it word for word, as, if I had the limner's hand, I am sure I could repeat the lines of the picture. You may judge from this, how much pleasure you have given me by so rich & varied an addition to the picture gallery of my mind.

Mrs. Martin[1] has not yet been able to find time to get at your book, but she knows something of it from me – and I anticipate you will have her among your most sympathetic readers. Again thanking you

Believe me
my dear Rossetti
Most truly yours
Theodore Martin

[1] Helena Saville Faucit (1817–1898) continued her acting career for twenty years after she married Martin in 1851 in Brighton.

70.212 TO JOSEPH KNIGHT

MS: BL.

Tuesday [6 September 1870]
16 Cheyne Walk
Chelsea

Dear Knight

Will you read the enclosed which on receipt of your letter I took the trouble to hunt up from a heap of letters & was lucky enough to find still extant. Having read it please *return it me at once*, for if what you say is really the case I cannot deny myself a lark of some sort with the providentially preserved epistle. But surely, *surely*, there *must* be some mistake. You're not *quite* sure about it, are you? The written expressions have since been warmly repeated to me by word of mouth, and really the thing would be too good altogether. Seriously, I find it impossible to believe.

The article in Blackwood touched me up on the raw a little no doubt, but circumstances you well remember which preceded the publication of the book seemed enough partly to account for it in these highminded days. By the time it appeared I was already in the thick of a big picture & poetry had begun to seem shadowy to me again.[1]

Your poetry is worthy of at least *one* of the greatest of living poets. Need I name him?

Thanks about the N.Y. *Herald* which I haven't seen I think. One in the *Tribune*[2] of a flattering kind was sent me from several quarters & many other American ones – some enthusiastic – some much the reverse – notably a real good bit of ill-nature in the *Nation*.

Ever yours
D G Rossetti

---

[1] Knight had evidently informed DGR that the offending *Blackwood's* review of *Poems* had been written by one of his earliest and most ardent admirers, Sir Theodore Martin. See entries for Martin in **Volume II, Index**, and also **200n1, 212A, 213–16,** & **222**.

[2] An unsigned review, "New Publications: Rossetti's Poems" appeared in the *New York Daily Tribune* (8 Jul 1870: 6).

70.213 TO JOSEPH KNIGHT

MS: BL.

Thursday/8 Sept 1870.

My dear Knight

I'm afraid I can't get to Marston's next Sunday evening, but shall try to do so with Brown the one after that, and if we can fit the time so as to accept your invitation & dine with you beforehand I'll let you know in time. My big picture drives me into corners as to time and is beginning to make my back ache as it never did in my life before. I must be very weak & ought to get into the country. I am very glad you have had such an unwonted & most desirable amount of change of air this year. It must have quite set you up.

I have had sent me, I suppose by young Marston, the new Cornhill containing a new poem of his – "Out of Eden." It seems to me to show as much feeling and finish as any I have seen of his – being very superior by the bye, to the one you lent me, called "Between Sleeps" & which I did not think up to his mark as to structure & coherence. Who could suppose that one situated as he is had written that line in the new poem, conveying an image of summer drought –

"Its kiss with over love has charred the green."

It shows a singular degree of some intuitive mental vision.[1]

I felt forced to write to Martin enclosing the cutting from your first note & asking him to say "No," of course in the friendliest way. I did so on Monday morning but have not yet heard in reply. However most likely he wd be out of town, so it is not late yet for an answer. The thing worried me, though in itself as you say of no importance, but I have known Martin well & on pleasant terms for many years, & cannot & do not believe this possible. I used no names, but it ought to be cleared up.

Ever yours
D G Rossetti

[1] DGR became, over the next dozen years, a mentor to and advocate of the blind poet Philip Bourke Marston, son of JWM. WMR tells us that his brother considered the young man to have a natural gift "and his attainment in the poetic art, considering his mournful privation, a matter for fervent praise, and even astonishment" (*FLM* 292).

70.214 TO WILLIAM BELL SCOTT

MS: Princeton. Text within angled brackets is a marginal insertion.

Chelsea
8 Sept 1870

Dearest Scotus

You must have thought me a dreadful laggard all this time in not answering your letter which I cannot lay my hand on now I want to answer it, but I do not think I shall miss answering anything of moment.

Of course I have felt rejoiced at the Prussian successes – not that I love Prussia but that I do not love France if I do not absolutely hate her. Her attitude at the outset of the war I hated as much as you could. Altogether one has to hate her & hers less now, has one not? Down she is & likely to remain so. I suppose after all she will make peace when the Prussians are at the door. It is a pitiful thing to see even from afar off.

I hardly know when I am likely to get away, but I know well I am beginning to feel the want of it. My back has taken to aching & forces me to lie down for half an hour at a time several times in the day's work. I get on steadily with my picture, but each week a little less fast than I looked for; however I am breaking the back of it if it is breaking mine. I must be very weak & ought to get away for a change now, but am always sticking on to get to some stage I want to reach in my work.

That was bad news you gave me about your money matters – I hope things get no worse since.

I cannot send you that blessed Blackwood, for I had lent it already & don't get it back, nor do I feel game to buy a 2nd for you. Something funny has occurred – I have received assurance ("as a secret") from some one who I find has what seem good grounds for the idea, that the article is written by an old acquaintance or I might say friend of mine who was especially enthusiastic to me about the book both by letter & word of mouth. I shan't mention names yet, as I really *can't* think it true; but I've written to ask him to say No, & if he doesn't (he has had my letter now several days, but may be out of town,) I shall know what to think & mean to have a lark. However I can't & won't believe it till quite proved which I hope it won't be at all.

I heard a rumour that you were about to return to London before long, but if so, you will be making a shorter stay than usual at Penkill. However perhaps the house business requires your attention. Will you give my best love to Miss Boyd, whose hooping cough (!) is I hope quite well now. I haven't seen Mrs. Scott but heard her report about Alma Tadema & Miss Epps. I like A. T. & am glad of it.[1] Another reported engagement was quite new to me & quite contrary to the last (recent) reports I had heard before from headquarters in Fitzroy Square.

Brown, as you possibly know has been to Newcastle & Edinburgh the last week or so on a hurried trip. He must now be just back or nearly so. You doubtless heard of Ned Jones having left the O. W. C. Society, but perhaps it will be new to you to learn that Burton has followed suit on the strength of Jones's quarrel. However I think this has only decided him, as I know he told me some time back he must do larger work & try oil.

Morris wrote a long poem about Aristomenes & the revolution of the Messenians against Sparta, but it got longer & longer till at last he couldn't get it into the Earthly Paradise at all & had to give it up. He had already made a mull after much work (or he thought it one) of the Orpheus Story; & now in despair has written a rather short one about Hercules to fill the last empty classical gap. I haven't heard the Hercules yet. The Aristomenes was very fine especially in the fighting parts.[2]

But book publishing is a hopeless job at present. Everything has stopped selling, & the only book the time would have helped – Swinburne's "Songs" – doesn't come out. He seems to have got into a chronic state of helplessness about it, but otherwise is I hope better after perhaps his worst time of all, but his father's carrying him off was just not too late.

I seem to have exhausted both news & energy, so with love to Penkill & Penkillites, believe me

Your affectionate
D Gabriel R

I remember you asked all about the editions of my book. The 2000 were pubd in four 500s <or something like that; but it is confusing.> & the 4th isn't yet sold out.[3]

---

[1] Laura Epps (1852–1909), painter & illustrator, studied at the British Museum under WBS & WCT. In 1870 she became a pupil of Lawrence Alma-Tadema (1836–1912), whom she married in 1871.

[2] These drafts were written in the spring & summer of 1870. The "short one about Hercules" became "The Golden Apples," the December tale in *The Earthly Paradise* Part IV of Hercules and Nereus who sail to an island where a serpent guards Hesperus's three daughters: Hercules kills the serpent and takes the apples. "The Story of Aristomenes" is the longest unpublished tale of *EP*. "The First Foray of Aristomenes" is lines 225–380 of the 2302 lines WM wrote of this tale; it was published in the *Athenæum* (15 May 1876: 663–64) and later included in the Wise-Forman forgery of Mar 90, *The Two Sides of the River* (Barker and Collins, *A Sequel to an Enquiry* [Scolar Press, 1983]: 210–12). See also David Latham, "Paradise Lost: Morris's Re-Writing of *The Earthly Paradise* (*JPRAS* [Fall 1987]: 67–76).

[3] See **129n2**.

70.215 TO FREDERICK STARTRIDGE ELLIS

MS: BL. Published: *FSE* 53; DW 1069.

9 Sept 1870

My dear Ellis

As I am profoundly convinced that the 5th Edition will be the last, I should I think like the cancels to be made in *Staff & Scrip* & in *Sister Helen*, as indicated in my last, especially as I notice another change needed on the back of the same page in the first-named poem. For this, see last page of this note.

I suppose there is plenty of time to make the cancels carefully, as the edition will lie fallow doubtless for a long while yet.[1]

What do you think of the Blackwood article being written by an intimate of mine? Perhaps Morris told you. It isn't certified yet, but looks suspicious. I've written to ask him if he did it.

Ever yours D G R

P.S. About the Translations I mean to set about the job soon now – as soon as

I get into the country which will be before long. I suppose if ready for the printers by end of October, that wd be time enough, to be out by end of year.

Page 51 last stanza.
Make the first line read –

> And there the sunset skies unseal'd,

Page 52
Transpose stanzas 2 & 3, putting 3 before 2.

P.S. If it can be done without inconvenience I shd like a large paper copy of the book with last revisions as a present.

---

[1] The last FSE edition of *Poems* was the 6th, but DGR probably means that the 3rd 1000 copies would be the last printing, which it was. No doubt FSE had warned him that any further corrections would have to be made as cancels, for the resetting of the text was now complete. However, these changes were made without resorting to cancel leaves. See **196n1** & **203**.

70.216 TO JOSEPH KNIGHT

MS: BL.

Monday [12 September 1870]

My dear Knight

I have just got the enclosed reply from Martin to my *second* note posted last Saturday. I must hasten to let you see it, as no doubt you will view it as I do – i.e. as a complete proof that he *did not* write the article. I have written in reply to him today enclosing in explanation a fresh copy from a rough draft I had kept of my first letter. Will you return me his.

Ever yours D G Rossetti

Your name has of course not been mentioned. The post must have miscarried in the first instance as the devil would have it.

70.217 TO FREDERICK STARTRIDGE ELLIS

MS: BL. Published: *FSE* 54; DW 1070.

Thursday [15 September 1870]

Dear Ellis

I need hardly say there's no hurry about the account question. I shd have explained that my only reason for asking was, – that if practicable the money paid by you at my bankers lately had better go to the book score than remain chiefly as an advance payment for the portrait drawing of Morris.[1] This can then be settled when done, which will be a more ship-shape transaction on my part.

Ever yours
D G R

I shd like an answer as to 2nd edn of Translations.
P.S. There is an account also, as I am aware, in which I am your debtor for purchase of certain books & for that affair of Howell's.[2]

[1] Surtees does not record a portrait of WM.
[2] See **85**.

70.218 TO FORD MADOX BROWN

MS: Texas.

Thursday night [15 September 1870]

Dear Brown

I was very sorry I couldn't meet Tadéma & Hüffer tonight, but was engaged up to a late hour. I wd have come even then had it not been that I was so late in bed the night before, & I have to be a little careful about hours.

Don't forget Monday next here – 7 o'clock. I've written to Knight to expect us on Sunday, & will call for you at ½ past 6 or so.

Ever yours
DGR

70.219 TO FREDERICK STARTRIDGE ELLIS

MS: BL. Published: *FSE* 55; DW 1071. The enclosure, a cutting from *The Times* of 16 Sep 70, is pasted at the top of the letter; on the back of the MS is a pencilled note in FSE's hand: "The extract is from Morris's review in the Academy."

[c. 16 September 1870]

Dear Ellis

It would appear that the world, or at any rate the *Times* is beginning to credit you personally with the dulcet tones of Topsy and to sign them with your name, so unalterable an affection do you evince for them. They deserve it well from you and from me but suppose we give something else a chance next time.

Ever yours
D G R

[Enclosure]

Fourth edition of
Mr. Rossetti's Poems. Price 12s., in an ornamental binding designed by the author. "I think these lyrics the most complete of their time; nor do I know what lyrics of any time are to be called great if we are to deny that title to these."

F.S. Ellis, 33 King-street, Covent-garden.[1]

---

[1] The corrected advertisement appeared in *The Times* for 19 Sep.

70.220 TO JOSEPH KNIGHT
MS: BL.

Friday [16 September 1870]
16 Cheyne Walk
Chelsea

Dear Knight

I find Brown (who is just back from Scotland) could not come to you Sunday next. So I'll take your goodwill for granted when I see him this evening & propose the following Sunday – may I? If it wouldn't suit you, you can let me know & I will then tell him, but if I don't hear from you I'll write you his answer.

Ever yours D G Rossetti

Swinburne's ode is of course very grand, but I think it's rather a pity he has opened with one of the metres of Shelley's Prometheus. Moreover I can't say that this compulsory French patriotism inspires me with the same ardour as it seems to produce in him.[1]

---

[1] ACS' *Ode on the Proclamation of the French Republic, September 4, 1870* was published by

FSE 12 Sep and reprinted in *Songs of Two Nations* (1875). After the French defeat at Sedan on 1 Sep by the Prussian Army, Napoleon III's Empire collapsed and the Third Republic was proclaimed. ACS was ecstatic, writing on 7 Sep to WMR: "An Ode literally burst out of me, which I have sent to Ellis today to print as a loose sheet or pamphlet" (Lang 2: 366). As DGR remarks, the Ode is very Shelleyan.

70.221 TO GEORGE RAE

MS: LLAG. Date: Unidentified endorsement.

Tuesday [20 September 1870]

My dear Rae

Of course I am a good deal annoyed at this result; but all the more I should wish not to give it the look of a "demonstration" on my part, & therefore shall be glad to prevent any further contributions. It seems as far as I can see that the show is only to be open for 2 days to the public. I think Mr. Hamilton (who is the possessor of the "Beatrice" & "Venus" – the latter a watercolour for I suppose it is not the oil one,) must have known of my great objection to exhibiting casually, and shd have been seriously obliged to him if he wd have applied to me first. The same as to Mr. Squarey.[1]

I have no intention of getting pictures together *next* year, but may the one after, if, as I trust will certainly be the case, I have by that time 2 important pictures finished. One is already more than half done & will be completed by the close of this year I doubt not. It is "Dante's Dream," 10 ft by 7. My absorption in this work must be my excuse for not having yet got onto the "Palmifera" again. I trust yet to do so shortly, & shall then infallibly finish her out of hand. As for the drawing of "Margaret," I believe that must be considered as engaged elsewhere, as far as I am able to say, but have not seen about it yet.

Pardon a busy and bothered creature, & believe me (with kindest remembrances to Mrs. Rae)

Ever yours
D G Rossetti

---

[1] George Hamilton, WG's partner, owned a watercolour of *Venus Verticordia* and a chalk drawing, *Beatrice* (probably S.168R.1), which he had evidently contributed to an exhibition; DGR is discouraging GR from doing likewise. A. T. Squarey bought a watercolour of *Hamlet and Ophelia* (S.189) in 1866. See 69.30.1n1.

70.222 TO JOSEPH KNIGHT
MS: BL.

28 Sept/1870
16 Cheyne Walk
Chelsea

My dear Knight

I must not omit to send you Martin's most satisfactory ultimatum. I am sure you will pardon him under the circumstances, poor fellow, if he tends to adopting a view of my "unknown Correspondent" somewhat akin to the definition in Ash's Dictionary.

I haven't seen O'Shaughnessy's Poems, but feel a curiosity about them. I know him and he is a clever cultivated fellow.[1]

Ever yours
D G. Rossetti

P.S. It suddenly occurs to me that the close of my first paragraph may be (to you) a fresh instalment of our chapter of mysteries. The anecdote is a good one if you don't know it. In Johnson's dictionary the word "Curmudgeon" has this derivation thus appended.

CURMUDGEON. derived from "coeur" & "mechant" (An Unknown Correspondent.)

Ash when he compiled *his* dictionary (not being a French scholar, poor man!) gave this version of it.

CURMUDGEON. derived from "coeur" (unknown) & "mechant" (a correspondent.)

---

[1] O'Shaughnessy's *An Epic of Women and Other Poems* (Hotten, 1870). This contemporary (1844–81) of DGR drew detailed critical comment from him on this and subsequent presentation copies of his poems, *Lays of France* (1872) & *Music and Moonlight* (1874). See **233–35, 246**, PRISM Section 51, & DW 1077n4.

70.223 TO JOSEPH KNIGHT

MS: BL.

[September 1870]

My dear Knight

I think the conception of your poem when read by the light of your note, is excellent, & much of its execution charming – witness stanza 8 especially; but I must say I think the reader is a little thrown off the true scent by your associating the idea with that of the antique Sirens who are certainly not connected in our minds with any notion of sentiment or yearning unresponded to. This seems to me a serious difficulty. An allusion is certainly made at last to "bones of many lovers," but does not this rather put a stopper on all sympathy?

Curiously enough I have a siren subject myself that I have for some time been meaning to work out as a Tragedy of the lyrical kind. I may tackle it some day.[1]

Ever yours
D G R

---

[1] "The Doom of the Sirens (A Lyrical Tragedy)" exists as a prose sketch for an opera libretto in 3 acts (see 69.211n1). WMR tells us that DGR & Franz Hueffer talked of a collaboration (*Works* 610–13&n).

70.224 TO MISS DEVERELL

MS: Huntington. Published: DW 1026.

[September–October 1870]

16 Cheyne Walk
Chelsea

Dear Miss Deverell

I give this note of introduction to you to my intimate friend Mr. C. A. Howell, who has very kindly undertaken to interest himself in getting on foot the proposed raffle for Walter's two pictures.[1] As I have not heard from you in reply to my letter on the subject, I fear you may be unwell, & being so busy myself have begged Mr. Howell, who lives close by you, to call & save you the trouble of a letter by asking your opinion personally. If you approve of the plan, it will be set afoot at once.

With kindest remembrances,

I am yours sincerely
DG Rossetti

---

[1] The prospectus for the raffle of WHD's *Irish Vagrants* & *The Banishment of Hamlet* is printed in *RP* (506). See **200&n5**.

70.225 TO FREDERICK STARTRIDGE ELLIS

MS: BL. Published: *FSE* 59; DW 1084. Mistakenly dated "Nov" by DGR.

2nd [October] 1870

Dear Ellis

Are things any brisker with my book now? If so, & you [are] nearing the end of the 4th Ed. I'd be glad now if you could oblige me with my share on the 5th & 6th already printed. Can you do so without inconvenience?

Ever yours
D G Rossetti

70.226 TO FREDERICK STARTRIDGE ELLIS

MS: BL. Published: *FSE* 57; DW 1073.

3 Oct 1870

Dear Ellis

Thanks for cheque £150, closing our accounts for the 5th & 6th editions of my Poems (being jointly the 3rd thousand) now in print.

I shall be very glad to talk over the points you mention when we meet. I shall try & get you to meet a few friends here at dinner ere long.

Ever yours
D G Rossetti

70.227 TO ALICE BOYD

MS: NLS.

16 C. W.

3rd Oct 1870

Dear Miss Boyd

Many thanks for your note & sketch. Our letters must have crossed. As regards the colour of the dress, I don't think it matters much, as I can paint it what colour I please in the picture – but I think it ought not to be very light. Scotus was talking to me about it and saying that the things were generally cotton prints. This of course is a material which could not be adopted for mediæval purposes though one could of course render it somehow. If they are also made in stuffs or cloths of any sort, that would suit better & without pattern if possible. But the shape is the principal thing, & another very important matter is that trouble should not be given to you beyond the minimum possible. I should think the long sleeve were the most desirable, as it can be tacked up if needed, and I think on the whole the collar with frill *won't* do as not mediæval. In short, *no* collar I think. My own impression on the whole is that if I do adopt this costume I shall have to use the skirt & not the jacket, in which case I should show the chemise as one sees the girls about. But I should like to hem the jacket *in case* of this or other use, and also if no trouble you might get me one of the chemises with the dress.

I am extremely sorry to hear of your persistent colds, but really fear that your Penkill out-door habits are not sufficiently guarded to avoid such casualties. The weather here is getting cold & foggy.

At the same time with your letter I have just got one from Ellis saying that the 4th ed. of my book is nearly exhausted & enclosing me a cheque for £150 (the 3rd such) on account of the next 1000 copies already printed off.

Ever yours affectionately
D Gabriel R

70.228 TO FREDERICK STARTRIDGE ELLIS

MS: BL. Published: *FSE* 58; DW 1074.

Friday [7 October 1870]
16 Cheyne Walk

Dear Ellis

Can you dine with me tomorrow (Saturday) at 7? I have several things I want to talk about. Or if this is impracticable could you look up in daytime? Not however to your inconvenience. In that case I will myself manage to come to King St. if you telegraph to that effect.

Ever yrs
D G R

70.229 TO AGLAIA CORONIO

MS: Princeton. Published: DW 1075. Date: Unidentified endorsement.

Friday [7 October 1870]

Dear Mrs. Coronio

I am so beset at present with evening work as well as day work that I fear I must defer yet a while the pleasure of seeing you. So many thanks for remembering me. I shall hope to see you here as soon as I have any work to show, but my big picture has got to that advanced stage at which work always seems all the more impossible to get done, & I haven't shown it as yet to any one, thinking it best to keep it to myself till finished.

I wish I could send you the flower pattern, but the copyright of it belongs to Janey who expressed an intention of embroidering it herself, and I still hope she means to do so. Should she have changed her mind I am sure she will transfer it to you.

With kindest remembrances to all yours

I am ever yours sincerely
D G Rossetti

70.230 TO THOMAS GORDON HAKE
MS: BL. Published: DW 1076.

13 Oct 1870
16 Cheyne Walk
Chelsea

Dear Dr. Hake

I have been long meaning to give you some sign of my hitherto continued existence, but have been so absorbed in a big picture I am engaged on that this with many other matters has got neglected. I have never got into the country again since the spring, – an unwise course perhaps, but one which will at any rate show you that I have been well enough not to have wisdom forced upon me – a rather dubious advantage.

I received thankfully your kind recollection of me in the sending of the Athenæum papers which however I had already read. I must confess to an even unusual indifference as to first causes of all phenomena whatsoever, and am therefore but a poor judge of the actual basis on which your theory rests. That it is singular and no doubt fascinating to the pursuer I can perceive. It is also valuable in relation to the Epitaph which I always believed to be Milton's.[1]

In the important matter of your poems, I spoke to Ellis shortly after last seeing you, but he then deferred his answer for further experience of his very limited publishing enterprises. I fear such would not now incline him to new ventures, as I believe the war has made poetry a drug in the market for the present. This has made me sluggish as to the new edition I projected of my translations, as I find terms wd not be tempting just now. However I may perhaps pluck up and do it when I find time.

I wish I could at this moment hit upon any new suggestion as to a publisher, in mental search for whom I have paused between this sentence & the last. Macmillan, whom I know, wd not I fancy care much for my recommendation as I do not publish with him & my sister has lately left him; & I stand in the same relation to Smith & Elder. I must really speak to Ellis again, as it seems a pity he should not do it.

I am so much occupied with my picture, & have got so nervous about it, that I hardly see any one & do not show my work at all till finished which will be I hope by the end of this year, if, as I suppose, I may now consider myself settled down for the winter. I have not forgotten your kind invitation, & believe I should still accept it rather than another if suiting you at any time when I may be forced to make a move. I gave up some time back the pied-à-terre I had taken in the country, finding that months passed without my using it or seeming likely to use it.

Believe me, dear Dr. Hake, with kindest remembrances,

Sincerely yours
D G Rossetti

1   TGH sent 2 long letters to the *Athenæum* under the title "The Unpublished Epitaph Attributed to Milton"; they appeared 10 & 17 Sep 70. Arguing for a "scientific" approach to literary criticism, they are discussed in some detail in DW 1076n1.

70.231 TO WILLIAM BELL SCOTT

MS: Princeton.

[13 October 1870]

Dear Scotus

I will duly deliver your book to William. It has afforded me a very pleasant evening's reading, and is thoroughly well done – full of true taste & tact without the least bias or forcing. I didn't know you could transform yourself into the popular-penman so successfully.[1]

Your affec:
DG R

It is a pity you did not have a specimen of Delacroix, but of course I judge the selection was done before they came to you, & as the photos are from engravings it might have been difficult to get one from D. who has not been much engraved I think. One or two slight oversights I noticed but did not note & fancy there were a few more than I can recall. In one place you call Courbet a landscape painter – he is chiefly a figure painter. In another you speak of Vernet's daughter marrying Delacroix – surely it was Delaroche. Courbet you know is a fine fellow & should not be snubbed. I must say I think you over-rate Gleyre. His picture with all its imposing aspect & striking technical merit of arrangement, always seemed to me to be essentially the very essence of the French artificial.

Another thing – you say Delaroche's Marie Antoinette was done abt same time as his Jane Grey. I believe on the contrary it was almost his last work. I don't like his religious sentiment pictures half or a quarter as well as you do.

P.S. You say in your Essay that any picture aiming to be a poem must prove a failure. I don't think this at all, but I do think Gleyre has that aim & does fail in it. For my own part I don't care much for any picture *not* a poem.

---

1   *Gems of French Art.* Photographs with an Essay by William Bell Scott (Routledge, 1870).

70.231.1 TO AGLAIA CORONIO

MS: Princeton. Published: DW 2320.

Friday [14 October 1870]

Dear Mrs. Coronio

Here I come bothering you again. I am painting that picture of Janey Morris for which you have a large chalk drawing and find I need it to look at.

Would you most kindly let the bearer bring it me & it shall be returned without fail either tomorrow or Monday – tomorrow I make little doubt.[1]

Ever yours
DG Rossetti

---

1   Mrs. Coronio had a chalk drawing (S.213A) dated 1868 which closely resembles *Mariana* (S.213), on which the painter was working at this time.

70.232 TO FREDERIC GEORGE STEPHENS

MS: Bodleian.

Friday [c. 14 October 1870]

Dear Stephens

You and Mrs. Stephens are better judges than I can be whether any little sum for poor P[atmore]'s benefit had better be handed to him or used otherwise for the advantage of his family during his illness.[1] So I leave it to you two in my own case, & will only ask you not to mention my name, as it wd cause an awkward feeling if I were to meet him at any time. I wish I could in the least see my way to finding him employment – I suppose of the press kind. If I knew exactly what he was fit for I wd of course seize any chance that *did* occur, though you know how rare these are. The kindliest circle I know is connected with the Athenæum and therefore with yourself – including Marston, Knight, &c. Knight is a good-hearted fellow, and might possibly know of something.

My present work is of a whacking big kind & won't be showable for some time yet. Thanks for your goodwill in the matter. Also about Miss D[everell] – I will of course send you the circulars & remember you as a subscriber. The housekeeping scheme did not come to my ears till Boyce was suited, but in any case I fear it wd have been too painful to him to be employing the sister of an old friend in such a capacity.[2]

Ever yours
D G Rossetti

P.S. On 2nd thoughts I write to Knight with this on the subject.

---

[1] This is the first of more than a dozen letters to FGS, Joseph Knight, WMR, & others that discuss financial assistance for Gurney Eugene Patmore (1826–83), younger brother of CP, who had suffered a stroke (see **243**). Described by Alfred Fryer as CP's "nice good-natured brother" (Basil Champneys, *Memoirs and Correspondence of Coventry Patmore*, 2 vols. [Bell, 1901]: 1: 100), he was never a close associate of DGR. Following the financial ruin of their father, literary journalist Peter George Patmore (1786–1855), from speculation in railway shares in the mid-1840s and his departure from England, the 2 brothers lived together and subsisted on journalism & translation (Champneys 1: 61); for a time Gurney was literary editor of the *Derby Mercury* (Ian Anstruther, *Coventry Patmore Angel. A Study of Coventry Patmore, His Wife Emily and The Angel in the House* [Haggerston, 1992]: 84). Grylls (Lady Mander) recounts an earlier occasion when DGR, WMR, & TW came to Gurney's aid, DGR sending money (*Portrait of Rossetti* [Macdonald, 1964]: 105).

[2] See **200**.

70.233 TO ARTHUR WILLIAM EDGAR O'SHAUGHNESSY

MS: Duke. Published: DW 1077.

16 Cheyne Walk/Chelsea
15 Oct. 1870

My dear Sir

I have to thank you very much for the gift of your volume. I mean to read some parts more carefully than I have yet been able to do, but have already made good acquaintance with it and must not defer my acknowledgments. Your book is a fresh evidence among others lately apparent that the contemporary English school of poetry is becoming far more organized than heretofore in respect of artistic style, which seems now at last to be taking its place as a settled and technical quality – a gauge of craftsmanship without which admission to the guild cannot be granted. Such a pervading element exists throughout Elizabethan literature and makes it a parallel to the true Schools of painting and sculpture, from which poetry should not at all differ in this respect.

Coming to details in your volume, it seems to me that "Bisclavaret" dominates the whole series as regards sustained dignity of execution so decidedly that I should judge it to be perhaps the last, or at any rate among the last, written. I say this in spite of the fact, which I must confess – that after 2 careful readings it still remains obscure to me, much as it impresses the mind and stimulates conjecture. Nettleship's drawing for this poem is a masterpiece.[1]

The others marked in my copy on this first comparatively hasty reading (my marks chiefly referring to what seems to me superiority in *executive* merit) are the Sonnet 1867, Death, The Fountain of Tears, Galanterie, The Heart's Questions, The Slave of Apollo, & the Three Flowers of Modern Greece.

Among the poems forming the "Epic of Women," the one which struck me most in conception was The Daughter of Herodias, which is particularly striking at the point where the metre changes; but you will perhaps think that I am rather testing your work by a personal hobby when I say that this poem particularly & some others seem to me as if they would have greatly gained by being cast in a much more concentrated form. Bisclavaret seems to me, as I have said, a complete success in terseness and deliberate value of diction. Vague it may be but wordy it is not.

Ever yours D G Rossetti
16 Oct

P.S. Having read Bisclavaret a 3rd time, I find my former impressions of it strengthened both as to its beauty & apparent purpose. It seems that the reprobate element in man is represented as pervading space personally & exerting both terror & fascination over every soul. Is this a summary of its meaning at all? If so, I do not think the poem is absolutely inscrutable, but speakers & situations seem unnecessarily complicated & mixed up in it. It would be well worthy of some further work for its disentanglement.

I can only half make out the meaning & not at all the application of its motto & title. Of the others, the Fountain of Tears establishes itself as decidedly my next favorite, being clearly though symbolically representative of a distinct phase of emotion. I think the Slave of Apollo perhaps stands third in value to my mind.

---

[1] The *Epic of Women* was illustrated by J. T. Nettleship (see 68.165n1).

70.234 TO ARTHUR WILLIAM EDGAR O'SHAUGHNESSY
MS: Duke. Published: DW 1078.

18 Oct 1870
16 Cheyne Walk
Chelsea

My dear O'Shaughnessy

I have now read Bisclavaret again, and of course after your word of enlightenment, light it is. But I must confess to have been unacquainted hitherto with the Werewolf nomenclature. The two names in the title & motto I judged to be names of a place or state of some sort, and the motto itself, I fear you will find, is not of a philological character adapted to make it serve the turn of the poem as an illumination of fifteen hundred lamps. When one understands it clearly, the poem is, of course, all the finer for it, but I think it is a pity you did not somehow introduce the word Werewolf somewhere to help the reader. The two opening stanzas in italics seem too to indicate at the outset an abstract theme.

However, obscurity is a little byword which we modern bards have a habit of passing round to each other as we used to do with slips of paper in schooltime. Each of us in turn gets caught as the holder of it by our Schoolmaster the British Critic & duly rapped on the knuckles. However, he is but a poor trembling drudge himself, and there is a council which meets further on in term and has a habit of calling him to account & perhaps sending him forth to advertise afresh for a bogey's livelihood, While his old victims grow up for better or worse without him.

I haven't heard of Nettleship's return yet, but shall try & get you to meet him here one evening when I do.

Ever yours D G Rossetti

70.235 TO JOSEPH KNIGHT

MS: BL.

> Wednesday [19 October 1870]
> 16 Cheyne Walk
> Chelsea

Dear Knight

I send you Stephens's answer to mine enclosing him your letter. I send you this that you may see how urgent the case is and how much your good offices are needed. I write in great haste, expecting a model every minute.

> Ever yours
> D G Rossetti

P.S. I have got O'Shaughnessy's Poems. One poem is I think decidedly a success, both in impressiveness & execution. This is "Bisclavaret," only it needs the explanation that the speaker is a Werewolf! Nettleship's drawing to this poem is grand & original to a degree – albeit odd beyond all degree. Of the other poems I think I like best the "Fountain of Tears." Try & say a good word for the bard if you can. What strikes me most in this and some other recent poetry is the real comprehension of artistic style evinced, so much beyond the untutored average of the Gerald Massey period.[1]

P.S. I forgot that I never wrote between yours & this & have still to express my sense of your extremely kind promptitude.

---

[1] Massey (1828–97) was a poet & critic who had lectured on PRISM in 1858; see 54.63&n11 & PRISM 66.6.

70.236 TO CHARLES AUGUSTUS HOWELL

MS: Texas.

> 16 Cheyne Walk
> 22 Oct 1870

Dear Howell

Your statement is quite correct. Twenty guineas is the price which you paid me for my chalk drawing from Mrs. Morris which I saw at Howard's & which he has since returned to me.

Love to Kitty.

> Your affec:
> D G Rossetti

70.237 TO CHARLES AUGUSTUS HOWELL
MS: Texas. Date: CFM.

[22 October 1870]

Dear Howell

Will the enclosed do? I hardly know how to make any appointment just now, but if you wish it will appoint a day & ask you to dine with me, (as readiest way of meeting) only in such case the probability will be that I shall have to go out after dinner.

Ever yours
D G R

70.238 TO GEORGE PRICE BOYCE
MS: University College.

24 Oct 1870
16 C.W.

Dear Boyce

I ought to have answered before about Warren's affair, but your letter reached me just as Rae & Tebbs were dining here. The former it struck me might buy, so I showed it to him, & the latter took charge of it meaning to write you. Whether anything has yet come of it I know not. However the letter being gone I lost your address (inadvertently forgetting to take it down) and now send this to Tebbs to post. I hope the drawing may get bought by Rae. I don't know any one else at hand to whom to offer it, but perhaps Leathart might buy if Warren wrote him a line. His address is

Jas: Leathart Esq
Lead Works
Gallowgate
Newcastle on Tyne.

All other buyers of mine buy only larger things.

I'm glad you're on the mend at last & hope we may be seeing you again here soon. I've never got away all this time at all – rashly I fear, – & suppose it is now too late to think of a move. You may judge by this that I have been absorbed in my big picture, which is very forward indeed now.

Ever yours
D G Rossetti

70.239 TO FREDERIC GEORGE STEPHENS
MS: Bodleian.

16 C W

Monday [c. 24 October 1870]

Dear Stephens

Read the enclosed. What *can* be the meaning of the passage I have marked? You see Knight is exerting himself in the fullest & kindest way & deserves some assistance & enlightenment if any can be given, but I hardly know how to act. Had I better write him word that the man who won't give his name shd be asked at any rate to specify his charge privately, after which some enquiry might or might not, as you thought best, be made of G[urney]. P[atmore].?

Ever yours

D G R

Let me have a line in reply. Has G. P. any Australian testimonials?

70.240 TO JOSEPH KNIGHT
MS: BL.

16 C.W.

25 Oct 1870

My dear Knight

I suppose my best plan is to keep you *au courant* about poor G[urney]. P[atmore]. & trouble you with the letters I now enclose, for your attention *at leisure*. I did not write at once in reply to what you told me, because I thought it better to learn whether Stephens had ever heard any hint of the kind, which you will see he never did. It is a mystery to me, as I have known G. P. (and *of* him) for some 20 years or nearly that, and always as the most worthy & innocuous of men. My own impression about Cov: P. was like that of others you allude to, that he is rich enough to do all, but Stephens seems on consideration to think otherwise (at any rate you know the money he enjoys comes from his *wife*,) and in any case the question is I think in all such cases – Seeing that others do *not* do all, shall we do what we can? It is plain that you act on this principle, as I try to do myself.

One thing I think. Surely if your informant on the Australian question will not allow his name to be used, he should at least specify his charge. Enquiry would then be possible. Do you not agree with me in this?

I want to be seeing you here soon & to get a few fellows together but some are still out of town. I saw Chapman last night who told me you had written an excellent Sonnet. Do send it me. About O'Shaughnessy, I like him better & better the more I look at him, & hope he won't come in for snubbing & nothing else. If you prolude on him in the S[unday]. T[imes]. or elsewhere, I wish you'd send me the paper. I'll get you to meet him.

Ever yours
D G Rossetti

70.241 TO FREDERICK RICHARD LEYLAND
MS: LC. Published: Fennell 27.

16 Cheyne Walk
25 Oct 1870

My dear Leyland

I had been expecting you in all likelihood to turn up in London for a flying visit, but I begin now to believe that the society of the great Jemmy makes you sluggish as regards pleasures far afield. I should otherwise have written you before to tell you that I finished the last drawing of you – putting a background and otherwise improving the tone of it, and that I am now very much better pleased with it, though it will be far from able to compete with the vast labours to which Jemmy has doubtless been addicting himself to the like result.[1]

This week I determined that as I did not see you the drawing had better be sent off, and to that end was about to place it in the frame of the old one when lo! it (the frame) was not large enough. So I have had to order a new one which will be ready in about a week. Will you tell me whether you wish it sent to Speke or to Queen's Gate.

I have worked chiefly on my big picture since seeing you, & have it so forward that I hope now soon to tackle the Medusa also. I have got absorbed in the work & never gone away for any autumn change after all. I suppose it is now too late to be worth while stirring.

Will you remember me most kindly to all at Speke, including Jemmy, & believe me

ever yours
D G Rossetti

[1] JMW was painting FRL's portrait at this time. See **161&n1**.

70.242 TO JOSEPH KNIGHT
MS: BL.

Sunday [30 October 1870]

Dear Knight

Will you come at 6 on Sunday & stay dinner at 7. We can have a quiet talk over the matter & I'll get my brother (if he's able to come) who is just back from Germany & knew G. P. better than I did I think.

Ever yours
D G Rossetti

I'll ask Brown & Stephens also. Do come.

70.243 TO WILLIAM MICHAEL ROSSETTI
MS: Brotherton. Published: DW 1079. Date: WMR.

[30 October 1870]

Dear W

I forgot to tell you some sad news I heard through Stephens about poor Gurney Patmore who has been (or perhaps still is) in the Nth London Hospital with paralysis – he & his wife & 6 kids being in utter destitution.[1] I did what I could & mentioned the case to Knight who has been trying to get others to help too. Knight is dining here on Tuesday, when I propose asking Brown & Stephens also. Will you come?

Your
D G R

[1] See **232&n1**.

70.244 TO FORD MADOX BROWN
MS: UBC. Published: DW 1080.

Sunday [30 October 1870]

Dear Brown

I'm asking Knight, Stephens, & William to dine here Tuesday at 7. Will you come? No one else. I didn't tell you that I heard through Stephens of poor Gurney Patmore – Coventry's brother whom you may remember –

being in the hospital with paralysis & his family utterly destitute. Knight has been exerting himself in the matter, & I want him & Stephens to talk it over. Do come.

Ever yours
D G Rossetti

70.245 TO WILLIAM MICHAEL ROSSETTI

MS (postcard): Brotherton. Published: DW 1081. Date: WMR.

Monday [31 October 1870]

Dear W

I find men can't come, so am dropping my plan for tomorrow.¹ But you'd better come & see the marmot all the same.

Your
D G R

¹ See 243.

70.246 TO JOSEPH KNIGHT

MS: BL.

Monday [31 October 1870]

Dear Knight

This is to say that of course my invitation for tomorrow is "off" now, as you are dining elsewhere. I shall be glad if you meet Stephens. I have heard nothing as to the *Daily News* but certainly it seems a thing to be tried.

I must appoint another day for dinner here almost immediately, & shall try to get O'Shaughnessy & his friend Payne to meet you.¹ I think I understood from them that they did not know you yet. I do wish you'd send me your article of which O'S. spoke on his book. It interests me also increasingly. "Galanterie" is one which I noticed too. I certainly think the "Epic" less in the author's true vein as a whole than the rest. There is something like an affectation of cynicism (or perhaps rather an undue indulgence of such morbid mood) which doesn't please me. And these poems are less concentrated & genuine in form than others. Payne seems a very nice & extremely well read fellow, but I don't think his book half so personal or promising as his friend's. I was sorry not to meet you at Brown's, & so were the 2 rising bards. I've been deferring asking them here because I want to have Nettleship with them, & he's away now but I believe not for long.

I think you are much too critical on yourself as regards the Sonnets. They are full of charming and true feeling. I certainly prefer the second as to special value of expression, and the last 3 lines are unmistakably excellent.

I begin to weary a little for my lyre or hurdy-gurdy again, having lots of new subjects filling my head & no time to tackle them, as I cannot manage painting & writing together. I think poetic craftsmanship is growing in me.

Ever yours
D G R

---

[1] Information on John Payne (1842–1916), lawyer, poet, & translator, is contained in *PRISM* Section 54. However, he is more highly regarded as a translator than that section suggests. His first published translation was *The Poems of Master Francis Villon of Paris, now first done into English verse, in the original forms* (Villon Society,1878), which first came out in an edition of 127 copies, but he is best known for *The Book of the Thousand Nights and One Night: now first completely done into English prose and verse, from the original Arabic* (Villon Society, 1882–84), which contains the best literary translation of many narratives in the work. In 1885, Sir Richard Burton dedicated the 2nd vol. of his better-known and more complete translation to Payne. See also **248** & **254**.

70.246.1 TO CHARLES AUGUSTUS HOWELL

MS: Texas. Date: CFM.

Friday night [October 1870]

Dear Howell

I shall be extremely busy the whole of tomorrow. Am very sorry I missed you today. Would it suit you to dine with me on Sunday instead, at 7 o'clock, & we could then talk over any thing you like.

Sunday day time I expect to be busy too, as generally now, with my work.

Ever yours
D G Rossetti

If it is *quite necessary* for you to see me tomorrow, all right.

70.246.2 TO CHARLES AUGUSTUS HOWELL

MS: Texas. Date: CFM.

Saturday [October 1870]

Dear Howell

Can you dine with me tomorrow (Sunday) at 7? We can then talk over whatever you please.

Ever yours
D G R

70.247 TO JOSEPH KNIGHT

MS: BL.

Friday [October–November 1870]

Dear Knight
Here is another letter from Stephens to await your leisure.

Ever yours
D G Rossetti

70.248 TO ALICE BOYD

MS: NLS. Published: Purves 589–91; DW 1082. Date: AB.

16 Cheyne Walk
Tuesday [1 November 1870]

Dear Miss Boyd
I suppose you must be actually on the backward move to London now again & all this year since the Spring I have not only failed in getting to Penkill but anywhere else either. Every year of my life I promise myself that the best season shall not pass again without my enjoying it in the best way – every year indeed I quite smile at myself for long neglect to do so as I look out of my bedroom window at the spring leaves beginning to tell against the black London tree-bark; & every year the result is the same, – here I stay either till the leaves are getting brown or till they are gone altogether, as is now pretty well the case here. However I had lost the greater part of 2 years with illnesses before this summer, so perhaps this one might be put aside for work as out of the ordinary pale, & I may still hope to put the next to more summery use! I suppose I certainly shall not get away at all now, as the season becomes less & less tempting, & my picture more and more captivating now that I approach the final enjoyment of working up the effect all together. I have not shown it to anyone as yet, and so it has all the more hold on me. No one has had the chance of breaking to me delicately as a painful necessity all the needs I most meant to supply in it, or of smiling when I tell them so & still saying with an incredulous air – "Ah yes, that *must* be done." However I'm quite willing to admit that a picture often gains by being shown in progress, only one loves it so much better as long as one keeps it to oneself, & is so much likelier to go straight on with it than when A. has patronized it, B. stood silent before it, & C. fancied you *must* have got so much further forward. I hope it is rather better than my other doings hitherto, & that is really all I do hope, for to suppose one is producing a masterpiece as the next work following what one perceives to have been so far otherwise, is a thing

one does not do after 40. However I cannot at all get rid of my absorbing interest in what I do as mere occupation. I believe this wd outlast even a final conviction of its hopeless nonentity.

I got Penkill news from Brown some time ago, who was no less charmed I believe than myself – charmed and astonished indeed with its beauty. He told me you had painted an excellent picture which no doubt I shall see. I have seen less of Scotus than I could have wished since his return, but now that he is so soon to be a near neighbour one feels lazy as to seeking him in the deserts of stucco which he still inhabits, particularly at present when there is no chance of a rubber. His book on French pictures is excellent. I went with him over Bellevue House which is really a most splendid old place – only much bigger than his needs.[1] He has already begun his nefarious career there by selling a marble mantelpiece as you may have heard – at least I do not see why he should not have told you so mild a fact, after the never-to-be-forgotten revelations made to us one dinner-time at Penkill.[2]

I believe you must ere this have heard from W. B. of a piece of trouble I propose giving you – that is to procure me a Scotch lassie's equipment for a picture I am proposing to paint to be called "Michael Scott's Wooing"[3] – need I say with the laudable view of displaying the characteristic habits of a mutual friend's worthy ancestry? However I only wish to give you this trouble if it gives you no trouble at all, – for I don't exactly know whether the things would quite suit my purpose if I did get them! Only I should much like to have them if not putting you to inconvenience.

William is here this evening & joins in kindest regards. He is just back from Germany – chiefly Nuremberg & Munich – where he has seen a good many enjoyable things. He called on Kaulbach & found him a kindly old fellow with a sly touch of satire about him.[4] Having heard from William that his former pupil Miss Howitt had married & was not blessed with a family, he sent her by W.'s hands the appropriate present of a photograph from his picture of the Happy Mother![5]

I have seen unusually little of friends lately, having been much at work & even improved my hours of bed time & rising to some appreciable extent. My picture got on incredibly fast for some time at first; but as such things happen, it began to hang fire just as I thought everything was getting secured & has dragged on slower ever since. However it does still progress for all that, & if I go on steadily at it I can't well fail to get it pretty nearly done within the year.

New bards are rife. Nine of them – reckoning old Brown & Nolly[6] as two – supped together at Fitzroy Square the other night as you may have heard from W. B. *He* viewed his rising brethren from afar with a sardonic eye, but might perhaps have softened its ray if he had heard their reverential views on his poetry as I walked home in their company. The youths in question are two – O'Shaughnessy and Payne – both clever artistic poets, the former especially, & showing a decided advance in the practice of the art as an art in our day – that is I mean they *contribute* to the result which I think is becoming apparent in poetic craftsmanship.

I suppose you have not had Miss Losh at Penkill, and am anxious to know how she is. I presume she must have uncomfortable news (if any) of her Paris circle of friends. I must write her shortly & send her a batch of my reviews which have been preserved by my mother & other true believers – that is all but the abusive ones.

I was rejoiced to hear that you were none the worse for past casual ailments, though hooping cough sounded portentous! I am pretty well and

affectionately yours D G Rossetti

1 WBS was moving from Elgin Road to Bellevue House in Chelsea near 16CW. DGR is looking forward to more frequent games of whist with the WBS ménage.
2 See 68.154n1.
3 DGR was fascinated by this supernatural subject from a tale, *Mary Burnet*, by the Ettrick Shepherd, James Hogg. WMR tells us he made 2 or 3 drawings towards a large picture, never executed (see S.56 & 222), wrote one stanza of an illustrative poem and a one-page prose summary of the tale; the stanza and prose sketch were first published in *Works* (214, 616&n.)
4 Wilhelm von Kaulbach (1805–74), German artist admired by the PRs. A student of Peter von Cornelius, he painted murals and monumental subjects, and eventually became director of the Bavarian Academy of Painting in Munich.
5 For Anna Mary Howitt, see **Volume II: Index**.
6 For FMB's son OMB (1855–74), see *PRISM* Section 47.

70.249 TO JOSEPH KNIGHT
MS: BL.

[1 November 1870]
16 Cheyne Walk
Chelsea

Dear Knight

I have written the enclosed to Mr. Dixon. Will you post it if you think it suitable. I am sorry to say I do not know any of the gentlemen whose names you give.

Thanks for promise to send me Globe and Sunday Times.

I hope you may be meeting Stephens today. I hope you understand how much I feel that I have shifted the difficulties of this case on to your shoulders (which I would not have done had I not felt sure that you moved more than I in the necessary circle) and how sensible I am of your efforts in the matter.¹

Ever yours
D G Rossetti

---

1   See 232&n1 and the following letter. For William Hepworth Dixon, who had recently retired as editor of the *Athenæum*, see **Volume II: Index**.

70.250 TO WILLIAM HEPWORTH DIXON

MS: Royal Literary Fund.

1st Nov 1870
16 Cheyne Walk
Chelsea

Dear Mr. Dixon

May I ask your assistance in bringing before the Literary Fund the case of Mr. Gurney Patmore, for many years a journalist in London and the provinces and at one time also in Australia. He was some years ago sub-editor of the Daily News, and from that quarter and all those with which he has been connected he has excellent testimonials. At present, owing to persistent attacks of ill health, he has fallen out of employment, and is now in the North London Hospital, recovering from a stroke of paralysis. His family (wife & six children) are wholly dependent on him, and are at present in a most melancholy position, aggravated by the absence of hope in the future, as medical opinions forbid Mr. Patmore's attempting work – even if he could obtain it – for some time to come.

I feel sure of your sympathy with this painful case, and if possible of your assistance for the object above named and remain

Very truly yours
D. G. Rossetti

W. Hepworth Dixon Esq

70.251 TO MARGARET HUNT[1]

MS: Brotherton. Published: DW 1083. Date: P/M.

[2 November 1870]

My dear Mrs. Hunt

I'm afraid I must admit complete abrogation of all my duties as a social being of the festive order, & so can only thank you for your kindness in asking me.

Ever yours truly
D G Rossetti

[1] Née Raine (pseud. Averil Beaumont; 1831–1912), author of *Magdalen Wynyard; or, the Provocations of a Pre-Raphaelite* 2 vols (Chapman & Hall, 1872). In 1861 she married Alfred William Hunt (1830–96), the Liverpool-born landscape watercolourist. They were the parents of Violet Hunt (1862–1942), who wrote more than 20 books, among them the sensational (and unreliable) *The Wife of Rossetti* (New York: Dutton, 1932).

70.251.1 TO MARGARET HUNT

MS: Untraced (formerly Maggs Bros.). The date of this letter is unknown; it is placed here for convenience, due to its similarity to the previous letter.

Tuesday [c. late 1870?]

16 Cheyne Walk
Chelsea

Dear Mrs. Hunt

Will you pardon my delay in answering your kind invitation. I am at present so busy that in these short days I find evening work necessary pretty often if I am not to lose half the following day in preparations. This prevents my making any evening appointments just now, so I can only thank you for so kindly remembering me.

Will you give my best regards to Mr. Hunt & believe me

Ever yours truly
D G Rossetti

70.252 TO OCTAVIAN BLEWITT

MS: Royal Literary Fund.

4th Nov. 1870
16 Cheyne Walk
Chelsea

Dear Sir

Let me thank you for your communication just received, and hereby vouch formally to the Committee for the correctness of the statements made in my letter to Mr. Hepworth Dixon relating to Mr. Gurney Patmore's case. I will do my utmost to meet the requirements necessary to the application by Monday next.

One thing I should mention. Mr. Patmore has been all his life a contributor to the newspaper press and actively engaged in the various functions of editorship, but I am not yet aware that he has produced any literary works which could be laid before the Committee. I trust this would not (should it so prove on enquiry) be considered as excluding from the bounty of the Society one who belongs to so important a section of the literary class.

I am, dear Sir
Yours faithfully
Dante G. Rossetti

Octavian Blewitt Esq.

70.252.1 TO ARTHUR WILLIAM EDGAR O'SHAUGHNESSY

MS: Kentucky.

Friday [4 November 1870]

Dear O'Shaughnessy.

(Do let's drop Misters!)

Will you look in Monday at 3 (not later but rather earlier) & bring Nettleship – as I see you write from his place. I'll show you both my big picture – indeed I was going to write N. about it. Then I hope you'll both stay dinner & you can read me a poem after & I've got a new one to read you. If a dark day however it's no use coming before 6 to dinner, as I can't show picture in the dark.

Ever yours D G R

Love to N. Ask him to bring any new designs that are portable. If both can't come Monday will fix new day.

70.253 TO GEORGE PRICE BOYCE

MS: University College. Date: GPB.

Sunday [6 November 1870]

My dear Boyce

I only just hear this instant that you are expected perhaps to dinner to-day & an hour ago I unluckily engaged myself to dine out. This is most provoking, & my only alternative is to ask you to come another day instead – say Tuesday at 7. Will you?

Ever yours
D G Rossetti

70.254 TO JOHN PAYNE

Text (typescript): Huntington. Excerpt: Wright, *JP* 34–35; DW 1085. Published: Stauffer 183–84.

16 Cheyne Walk,
7 Nov. 1870

My dear Payne

(You see I've scratched out *Sir* which I hope you will let drop between us).

Will you dine with me on Wednesday at 7? I've asked O'Shaughnessy & Knight. Nettleship I suppose must be given up for the present.

When I last met you I had hardly any knowledge of your volume, which I had only just succeeded in borrowing from Madox Brown. I now have to thank you for the copy so kindly sent, & need not say my acquaintance with it is largely increased, though I have not yet read the last poem. Of the three I have read, I think on the whole the Building of the Dream is my favorite, though the metre of the Masque seems to be much better suited to a poem of any length. On the other hand the Rhyme of Redemption has incomparably the finest ground work of the three as regards its subject, but I do not myself think that the modernized ballad stanza in which it is written can possibly be made agreeably available for anything (at most) but quite a short piece. In the "B. of D." the description of the fairy lady is worthy of the finest examples of this kind of romance & the Incidental song is exquisite in structure. This (as indeed the others are too) is full of imaginative picture work to quite a remarkable degree & conveys most notably that sense of the poet's self-enjoyment which is indispensable to the enjoyment of the reader – much more in this direction I might say which must have been said to you by others & of which you must have been aware yourself before anyone said it. But I am sure you will be best pleased by my giving my whole opinion on your work. I think then that the pouring forth of poetical material is the greatest danger against which an affluent imagination has to contend, and in my own view it needs not only a concrete form of some kind but immense concentration brought to bear on that also, before material can be said to have become absolutely anything else.[1] If this is neglected the time is apt to come soon when the poet finds that he has written as much as any one can ever read, the work being in fact what ought on another plan of production, to have occupied his lifetime. Self-repetition is certainly the quality which must be absolutely eradicated from work before it can be looked upon as finally dealt with, & nothing but the most complete attention will ever eradicate this. I hope I do not seem presumptuous in undertaking to indicate – solely on the grounds of study – not of personal pretension on my own part – what seems to me to be perhaps your rock ahead. It is a danger heaven knows, which everyone does not incur, but it is none the less a real one. I should be very much interested to see the Ballads & Poems, you announce, as well as the Sonnets, since I judge these must belong more to the order of work on which I should expect you finally to rely for successes. Will you bring something with you on Wednesday (if, as I hope you can come then) and read it to us?

Ever yours,
D. G. Rossetti.

[1] For Payne see **246&n1**. He had sent DGR an inscribed copy of his new poems, *The Masque of Shadows and Other Poems* (Pickering, 1870). This passage anticipates DGR's famous "fundamental brainwork" letter written a decade later to THC (81.104). Payne did not like DGR's advice: see DW 1085n2.

70.255 TO JOSEPH KNIGHT

MS: BL.

Tuesday [8 November 1870]

Dear Knight

No appointment ever seems to come right with me now. It seems both the bards are pre-engaged; so the affair must be put off. I haven't heard yet from you, so perhaps you couldn't have come either. I shall probably see you on Sunday at Marston's.

Ever yours
D G Rossetti

70.255.1 TO ARTHUR WILLIAM EDGAR O'SHAUGHNESSY

MS (postcard): Takuji Oda. Date: P/M.

16 Cheyne Walk
Monday [14 November 1870]

Dear O'S –

Can you dine with me Thursday? I'm asking Payne. When I know you can both come, I'll ask Knight.

Ever yours
D G R

70.256 TO MRS. WILLIAM COWPER-TEMPLE[1]

MS: PML.

16 Nov 1870
16 Cheyne Walk
Chelsea

Dear Mrs. Cowper

Many thanks for so kindly remembering me. I have never got away from town since last Spring, having been so very busy with my large picture. I hoped to be now approaching completion with it, but such is hardly the case as yet though it is very well advanced, and I suppose I shall be quite unable now to leave town with any comfort to myself till I have really put it out of hand. So I hardly see any likelihood of accepting your invitation, much as I should like the change. In any case however I believe the solitude which you anticipate when winter is more advanced would be the most tempting state of things to myself who am but poor company where many are together. But I fancy my easel & I will have to be each other's cronies all this winter under pain of getting nothing done. I must be a very bad manager, for other people seem to work and enjoy themselves too, which is more than I find myself able to contrive.

With very kind remembrances to Mr. Cowper as well as to yourself

I am ever yours truly
D G Rossetti

---

[1] They met in 1865: see **Volume II: Index**, and 65.121 & 129&n1.

70.257 TO CHARLES AUGUSTUS HOWELL

MS: Texas. Date: CFM.

Friday [November 1870]

My dear Howell

I needn't say how sorry I am for poor Jessie[1] and also for the addition to Kitty's & your anxieties & griefs. The other matter of course is not of the least importance at such a moment. Give my love to Kitty & believe me.

Ever yours
DG R

[1] Jessica Ann Stewart Homan (1833–70) was the daughter of the Howells' aunt Louisa Ann Howell and Walter William Homan.

70.258 TO WILLIAM ALLINGHAM

MS: PML. Published: *WA/GBH* 296; DW 1086. Date: GBH.

[November 1870]

Dear Allingham

I can put your books on my basement floor – (stone-paved servants' hall) – where they will not be in the damp I believe & can stand clear of the floor if thought necessary. Or if you think it absolutely needed, I can clear space in a lumber room up stairs.

Ever yours
D G Rossetti

70.259 TO WILLIAM ALLINGHAM

MS: PML. Published: *WA/GBH* 296; DW 1087. Date: GBH.

16 Cheyne Walk
Friday [November 1870]

Dear Allingham

I'm very sorry to tell you that the high tide yesterday got into my basement floor, & that 3 of your boxes were a foot or more deep in water for some time. It is most vexatious to think what may have happened to the books. Will you look in today at dusk & stay to dinner at 6. I am only sorry that I have to go out about 7.

Ever yours D G Rossetti

70.260 TO FREDERICK GEORGE STEPHENS
MS: Bodleian.

5 Dec 1870

Dear Stephens

Thanks for notification about G. P.[1] I meant to have written before to tell you that I lately saw Bateman whom you may remember many years ago as going with Woolner to Australia. He has only just returned thence & I questioned him about G. P.'s career there, as I know P. took letters of introduction to him. He was cognizant of P's doings as long as he remained at Melbourne & never heard a word to his discredit. He seemed to have an impression that the wife was not of the wisest or most provident order.[2]

I was extremely sorry to hear from Wm that you are in anxiety about your beautiful little boy whose praises I have heard on all hands. I trust he is getting better.

Ever yours
D G Rossetti

[1] See **232**.
[2] For Edward Latrobe Bateman, see **Volume II: Index**. Gurney Patmore was "connected with the Melbourne Argus" before he returned to England in 1868 (Boase 2: col. 1382).

70.261 TO THOMAS GORDON HAKE
MS: BL. Published: DW 1088.

Friday [before 9 December 1870]

Dear Dr. Hake,

Madeline,

with other Poems & Parables.

This has just occurred to me as the proper title for your book, since it includes "Madeline" as in some sense a Parable, which might be a help to the reader. Do insist on this being adopted. I assure you no one has better business instincts than I have in matters of this kind. Cancels be blowed! I would make 50 if needed. And do put *Parables* instead of *Tales*. This is all very "cheeky" on my part, but I speak from conviction![1]

In haste
Ever yours
D G Rossetti

I'm all over red chalk, & so my paper gets so too. Pray pardon.

1   TGH followed this suggestion. See **106n1**.

70.262 TO JOSEPH KNIGHT
MS: BL.

Friday [9 December 1870]

Dear Knight
   Patmore's case *is* coming on again I understand.
   I didn't know the new Earthly Paradise was actually out. I suppose yours is an early copy. I have heard the greater part of it – glorious work as usual.

Ever yours
D G Rossetti

I trust your besetting evil is not virulent now.

70.263 TO FREDERIC GEORGE STEPHENS
MS (fragment): Bodleian.

[c. 10 December 1870]

. . . . I should think could not much tax the brain, but whether the legs might be taxed too much by it I cannot say.
   I think it best to keep you informed of anything relating to this matter. I should also mention that in thus reviving my correspondence with P[atmore]. I have felt constrained to tell him that I gave in the first instance, through your hands, such personal aid as I could offer; this I felt at last forced to say by the awkwardness of always seeming otherwise to exert myself only through third persons.
   I hope all is well with you and yours now

& am ever yours
D G Rossetti

70.264 TO JAMES HEDDERLY[1]

MS: Mitchell Library. Published: Dingley & Lawson, "Three New Rossetti Letters," *N&Q* 236 (Sep 1991): 321–22. Curiously, despite the endorsement, the authors are unable to identify the recipient of this letter.

16 Cheyne Walk, Chelsea

12 Dec 1870

Dear Sir

Thanks for letting me know of the Society. This is the first I hear of it. I enclose cheque which please apply to its purposes, deducting first my debt to you for the glass case.

I had no idea that you also were among the bards. Your verses show clearly that you were no beginner, nor are they beset by our modern sin of obscurity, except indeed the mention of one name which may prove a puzzler to your audience.

Yours very truly
D G Rossetti

Mr. J. Hedderly

[1] (c. 1815–85), active as a photographer in Chelsea from the mid-1860s to the 1870s; his favourite subjects were the Chelsea Embankment and river frontage. A small collection of his work is held by the Chelsea Reference Library (see *Local Historian* 18 [1988]: 142–44).

70.265 TO THOMAS PURNELL[1]

MS: Princeton. The 16CW monogram has been cut from the MS.

14 Dec 1870

My dear Purnell

I'm sorry that on due consideration I cannot do as you ask me and as on some accounts I should like to do. The reasons I mentioned before are against it, and besides that, I am so extremely busy just now as not really to have time to write anything at all.

I suppose Morris's book is out, having been announced for last Monday, but he is out of town and it has not yet been sent to me. Swinburne's Songs are, as you probably know, to appear immediately.

Ever yours
D G Rossetti

[1] See **90n1**.

70.266 TO THOMAS GORDON HAKE

MS: BL. Published: DW 1089.

> 14 Dec 1870
> 16 Cheyne Walk
> Chelsea

Dear Dr. Hake

Your letter was a surprise to me as regards the imminence of publication it announces. It is too late no doubt to propose looking at proof-sheets, which I should have done with much pleasure. I presume "Madeline" and the "Epitaph" in part or whole are to form the volume which I shall look into eagerly when it arrives. I shall certainly try for some opportunity of noticing it if practicable in any quarter worth doing it in.

I forgot in my last to answer what you said about the "Old Souls" and my brother's proposed volume of Selections.[1] I am sorry to say that all extracts from living writers in such volume will have, on the publisher's reconsidered plan, to be omitted, on account of the fact that copyrights interfere with the possibility of extracting from the most popular contemporary ones.

Thanks for all you say so kindly of my possible visit to you one day, which may come off yet. I have been horribly busy for months past and hardly seeing any one, but shall trust to try & tempt you here one day ere long to see something of what I have done. I have been finishing the Beatrice which found favour with you for one thing, and all the other old ones on hand, but my principal work has been on the large picture of *Dante's Dream*. This I have not yet shown to a mortal, feeling more en rapport with it by keeping it to myself till finished, which I hope it may be about the end of February if all goes well.

> Ever yours
> D G Rossetti

[1] No doubt a reference to the work WMR was doing for the Moxon's Popular Poets series.

70.267 TO FREDERIC GEORGE STEPHENS

MS: Bodleian.

> 16 Dec 1870

Dear Stephens

I am extremely sorry to hear just now from G[urney]. P[atmore]. of his failure at the L[iterary].F[und]. – on what grounds I know not. I should be very anxious to assist in any further steps to his benefit if it is possible. I begin to fear however that he must be quite exceptionally shiftless & mismanaging. His handwriting is something monstrous in carelessness, and I have received 2 post-cards from him, both so filthy as even to excite remark from the servants & to suggest a previous use only negatived by the thickness of the tissue. Surely there can be no reason that his post-cards shd be dirtier than other people's. Do you think he is really willing to work when possible – that is, to seize as his best privilege the first chance of work, whatever it be, that health & opportunity allows. If a man will not do this at our age, the help of friends can only retard his ruin to no purpose. I should like, if you thought any good would come of it, to get him to meet you, William & Knight here for consultation as to his prospects. Is it your opinion that he ought now to be able to work if work were found?

Ever yours
D G Rossetti

Answer only at your leisure.

70.268 TO JOSEPH KNIGHT
MS: BL.

Sunday [18 December 1870]

Dear Knight

I am uncertain whether you ever met Dr. Hake at my house. He is about to bring out a volume of poetry possessing remarkable artistic qualities but perhaps less of the popular element than anything ever seen in these latter days. I am anxious it should fare as well as may be with the critics, & want you to tell me in confidence whether you think there would be any chance of my getting leave to review it for the Athenæum. I want to get your answer privately, as to your idea of probabilities, before the thing is mentioned to anyone else. The book will I believe be out almost immediately. Dr. Hake lately published in the Athenæum a couple of letters on metre connected with Henry Morley's Miltonic Epitaph, which you probably saw there.[1]

I heard nothing from John Morley about you & O'Shaughnessy. Have you heard from him?

I was sorry to hear from poor P. that his case caved in at the Lit. Fund meeting. Martin was away. I want to get him to meet you & Stephens here before long, to see what his prospects of being able to work may be. But I begin to think he must be sadly shiftless. His handwriting is monstrously careless & his post-cards as filthy as the *carte* of a Justine-ian banquet.

Ever yours
D G Rossetti

1   See **230&n1**. DGR reviewed TGH's *Madeline, with Other Poems and Parables* in the *Academy* (1 Feb 71: 105–07), reprinted in *Works* (621–27).

70.269 TO FREDERIC GEORGE STEPHENS
MS: Bodleian.

Monday [19 December 1870]

Dear Stephens

After receipt of your letter I think I shall defer any attempt to get up a consultation on P.'s behalf until I have reason to think he will avail himself of work found for him. I am so busy both evening as well as day time that I should have to give time I could ill spare, & it is no use if he could or would not avail himself of a chance. I confess those filthy post-cards (as you must feel too if you have received such) are a sickener to me of the man and all his belongings. Not but that I would try anything for him that seemed really possible.

I rejoice to hear of your little boy being all right again, & with kind remembrances to Mrs. Stephens

am ever yours
D G R

70.270 TO GEORGE RAE
MS: LLAG. The signature has been cut from the MS.

16 Cheyne Walk/Chelsea
20 Dec 1870

Dear Rae

Thanks for cheque concluding transaction for "Palmifera." Cheques are quite convenient to me now.

I rejoice to hear that you are getting all right again. I will send the picture as soon as ever it is possible.[1]

Ever yours

1   See **277**.

70.271 TO JOSEPH KNIGHT
MS: BL.

Wednesday [28 December 1870]

Dear Knight

All sorts of jollity to you for the New Year. I ought to have answered your former note before. I should be very glad to write notice of Dr. Hake's Poems for the *Post*, and am also writing to him to send you an early copy, as to a *homo bonae voluntatis*.* I wish your capital notice of Morris in the S[unday].T[imes]. had been in the Athenæum. Now wasn't the latter our friend Buchanan, & didn't he do a certain Shelley article also? Echo answers *Rather*. The usual critic *didn't* do it as doubtless you know.¹

I know you'll see a great deal to like in old Hake's work, but he is a man who has let his best time go by in other pursuits. Still his claim is the artistic one, which I know appeals to you.

Ever your
D G Rossetti

---

* "*homo bonae voluntatis*" = man of good will.
1. WM's *Earthly Paradise* (Part IV) was reviewed anonymously in the *Athenæum* (17 Dec 70: 795–97), and by Knight in the *Sunday Times*.

70.272 TO THOMAS GORDON HAKE
MS: BL. Published: DW 1091.

16 Cheyne Walk
28 Dec 1870

Dear Dr. Hake

I've been meaning to write & wish you all pleasant things of the season, but I hope you are getting them in spite of my silence. May I make a suggestion about your Poems? It is that you should let me have 3 copies at once if possible – 1 for self & brother, & 2 for 2 homines bonae voluntatis (or who I trust may prove so) in the critical world. No doubt you know how well it is to be in good time in these cases.

Is there any chance of your being this way by daylight tomorrow (Thursday.)? If so, would you be able to look in some time in afternoon & stay dinner at 6? We might then look over the Poems together if you could put the sheets in your pocket, and I could show you the Beatrice finished.

If tomorrow won't suit you, I fear I must put off trying for you for a few days longer, as my engagements are uncertain this week.

With best regards to your sons

I am ever yours
D G Rossetti

70.273 TO THOMAS GORDON HAKE

MS: BL. Published: DW 1094.

16 Cheyne Walk
Thursday [29 December 1870]

Dear Dr. Hake,

Thanks for your notes, & a hearty rejoinder to your good wishes for the New Year.

I am very glad the title of your book is to be amplified. I trust the word *Tales* in the body of the book, will be either substituted (as *Parables*) or removed, which latter wd be a much better plan than the slip of Erratum proposed by the publisher – an impracticable thing altogether to my mind.

In reading *Madeline* again, I have still to confess, when I endeavour to incarnate myself as the general reader, that it is not suited to any wide circle, and I am all the more glad that the book is to put forward also in some way its other claims on its title-page. I must say frankly, even in my own person, that it seems to me Madeline must have been conceived in a mood more susceptible to certain structural aims than to the passion of its story as a piece of human nature, which it has to be in order to interest the world, however superhuman its machinery. The introduction of the passages in heroic verse is an advantageous variation & tends in some degree to clearness, but I must confess that the alternation of Valclusa (a vague unexplained personification, & all the vaguer now Petrarch is gone) and the Chorus as speakers throughout seems to me likely to put a grave additional stumbling-block in the way of many readers. I suppose it would not be possible at this 11th hour to introduce before the opening just a page (perhaps in italics) of rhymed argument – say in short couplet metre – in which the whole scheme of the thing might be compendiously embodied. The best thing, as it still seems to me, would have been a running marginal argument alongside of the whole poem. The rest of the book will I think assert strong claims in some fit quarters; & be even to ordinary minds clearer by its evident metaphysical side than Madeline's somewhat complicated warp & woof.

Thursday [29 December 1870] 70.273

The lines from Madeline to which you allude certainly afford a curiously close parallel to the general notion of my "Michael Scott" design. I have not yet received the copies of your poems, but I suppose there is no great hurry as yet, since I do not yet see the book advertised. In reading the 4 central poems, I notice great improvements on the old text, particularly in the "Deadly Nightshade." I almost think it a pity that these 4 did not come first in the book, with *Old Souls* at their head, as this is the piece of yours undoubtedly which appeals to the largest circle.

I am the slowest of snails at reading, and accordingly it is only within the last few days that I have made acquaintance with your novel "Her Winning Ways," the numbers of which you kindly lent me so long ago. I am quite surprised at it.[1] It is certainly the very last kind of thing which I should have thought you likely – even adapted – to deal with; and accordingly I think it very valuable to a general estimate of your powers. Its movement and variety are so unflagging that I should think it must amuse everyone who reads it, though in reality it is made up of quaint peculiarities in character & incident which need an exceptional man to notice & record them. Still there is no doubt at all that here you move on *terra firma* & prove yourself quite capable to meet the common world on its own ground. I do not know what estimate you entertain of this work, nor whether it is quite a late one or not, but I should judge it to be so, as, in spite of a slight degree of dryness & stiffness in mere style at times (as of a new kind of undertaking), the easy terms on which it takes the world at its own value seem to me, in a mind like yours, a sign of maturity which is perhaps just what is wanting in your earlier & more important prose writings. I judge that this novel must have been produced with perfect fluency, and in such case should certainly in your place make another effort in the same direction, as I believe something must come of it. "Her Winning Ways" ought surely to be republished with your name. I have not yet read all that is by me of it, but it amuses me thoroughly, and I have been reading it aloud to an appreciative hearer with great success.

Here is a long letter to no great purpose. Pray pardon whatever may be outspoken in it and attribute this to the sincere interest which I have, as you know, always felt in your writings, and to the wish I cannot but feel that their highest beauties were always within reach of a wider circle of readers.

With kindest remembrances,

Ever yours
D G Rossetti

P.S. Is the novel finished yet? I must be borrowing the further Nos of you. And are you aware whether it has attracted any decided attention? Many things never do, as long as they appear in magazines, & yet do in the long run.

P.P.S. Have you seen the Daily Telegraph of yesterday, where the world, among other news, is informed that *Jenny* is "maudlin maundering." I thought I was shaky & galvanic enough, heaven knows! but am astounded to find that my wires cannot quite be set in motion by the Telegraph, for all that!

---

[1] TGH's novel appeared irregularly in the *New Monthly Magazine* between Sep 68 & Dec 71. It was never published separately.

70.274 TO ALEXANDER MACMILLAN

MS: BL. Published: Packer 91–92; Macmillan, *Letters of Macmillan*: 97–99.

16 Cheyne Walk
30 Dec 1870

Dear Macmillan

As there are so many Goblin Markets, will you kindly send me one.[1] My messenger must have spoken to someone who didn't know, as he was certainly told that both books were out of print & reprinting. He is much too unimaginative to have conceived the idea.

I shall be very glad to see yourself, son, and all friends, some time in March, but till then shall be completely boxed up with a big picture I am doing. It & I have now been tugging against each other for some months, but I mean to get it under by then.

By the bye, my dear Macmillan, it is all very well talking about "Fame in the next generation," but why does your magazine resolutely ignore the best things going? It's no business & no meaning of mine to speak for myself – let anyone do that who pleases – but why in the world has Morris been left in the lurch till now? I don't know who your present editor is, but I may assure him that it is of no use sulking over good work. There is some credit in acknowledging it at first, and it has to be acknowledged at last without any credit at all. So far my New Year's gift of plain speech to your publication.

To yourself & to yours come all good & seasonable wishes from

Yours always
D G Rossetti

---

[1] AMc had published CGR's *Goblin Market* in 1862.

70.275 TO FREDERICK STARTRIDGE ELLIS

MS (postcard): BL. Published: *FSE* 61; DW 1092. Date: P/M.

Friday [30 December 1870]

Dear Ellis

I hope you can dine with me Friday of next week at 7 when I expect a few friends. I trust your home anxieties proved unnecessary.

Ever yours D G Rossetti

70.276 TO AGLAIA CORONIO

MS: Kansas. Published: DW 1093.

Saturday [31 December 1870]

Dear Mrs. Coronio

Many thanks for your kind note. I need not trouble you further, as I have borrowed a similar frame from Queen Square. I feel horribly guilty towards you and all my friends, but can only hope that I shall seem to have shut myself up to some purpose in the long run. I'm finishing several other long-standing daubs now as well as the big one, and am in such a muddle with so many things in hand that I must defer showing any of them till *something* at least is finished. I know you will bear with me & believe me

Ever yours sincerely
D G Rossetti

70.277 TO GEORGE RAE

MS: LLAG.

Saturday [c. 31 December 1870]

My dear Rae

I trust the picture will leave me on Monday by Passenger Train.[1] I have not been able to get at the writer to do the inscription on the frame, but this can be done when I borrow the picture again from you.

Ever yours D G Rossetti

---

[1] Commissioned in 1866 by GR, *Sibylla Palmifera* (S.193; see **Frontispiece** to this Volume) was now finally completed. The promised inscription of the illustrative sonnet (*HL* 77) on the frame was never carried out (see 73.330). See also **221** & **270**.

70.278 TO BARBARA LEIGH SMITH BODICHON
MS: PML.

Monday [c. 1870]
16 Cheyne Walk
Chelsea

Dear Mme Bodichon

Thanks for your very kind invitation, but, seldom as I go anywhere, it happens I am engaged tomorrow evening.

With kind remembrances

I am yours vy truly
D G Rossetti